MW00779901

FOUR APPROACHES TO THE BOOK OF PSALMS

SUNY Series in Judaica: Hermeneutics, Mysticism, and Religion

Michael Fishbane, Robert Goldenberg, and Arthur Green, Editors

FOUR APPROACHES TO THE BOOK OF PSALMS

From Saadiah Gaon to Abraham Ibn Ezra

Uriel Simon

Translated from the Hebrew by Lenn J. Schramm

State University of New York Press

Uriel Simon
Four Approaches to the Book of Psalms
From Saadiah Gaon to Abraham Ibn Ezra

© 1991 English Edition by State University of New York Press

© 1982 Hebrew original and other languages by Bar-Ilan University, Ramat-Gan, Israel

Published by
State University of New York Press, Albany

All rights reserved

Printed in the United States of America

No part of this book may be used or reproduced
in any manner whatsoever without written permission
except in the case of brief quotations embodied in
critical articles and reviews.

For information, address the State University of New York Press,
State University Plaza, Albany, NY 12246

Library of Congress Cataloging-in-Publication Data

Simon, Uriel.
[Arbaᶜ gishot le-Sefer Tehilim. English]
Four approaches to the Book of Psalms: from Saadiah Gaon to Abraham Ibn Ezra / Uriel Simon; translated from the Hebrew by Lenn J. Schramm.
p. cm. — (SUNY series in Judaica)
Translation of: Arbaᶜ gishot le-Sefer Tehilim.
Bibliography: p.
Includes indexes.
ISBN 0–7914–0241–X. — ISBN 0–7914–0242–8 (pbk.)
1. Bible. O.T. Psalms—Criticism, interpretation, etc., Jewish.
2. Saᶜadia ben Joseph, 882–942—Contributions in Biblical criticism.
3. Karaites—Controversial literature—History and criticism.
4. Ibn Ezra, Abraham ben Meir, 1089–1164. Contributions in Biblical criticism. I. Title. II. Series.
BS1430.2.S4913 1991
223′.206′09021—dc20 89–11451
CIP

10 9 8 7 6 5 4 3 2

Cover design adapted from the miniature "David playing the harp", from the *British Library Miscellany.* Add. 11639, France, Troyes, c. 1280.

CONTENTS

PREFACE

This book was spawned by a fortunate discovery. During the process of cataloguing all the manuscripts of Abraham Ibn Ezra's extant commentaries on the Five Scrolls, a photocopy of MS Verona Municipal Library 204 (82.4), which contains his commentary on Esther, was found to also contain a fragmentary commentary on Psalms that is quite different from the familiar published ("standard") commentary. Although the fragment is short (four 34-line pages), containing only the introduction—three times longer than the introduction to the standard commentary—followed by the commentary to almost all of Psalm 1, its importance cannot be overstated.

This discovery led to another. Several months after the publication of the Hebrew edition of this book, Mr. Benjamin Richler, assistant director of the Institute of Microfilms of Hebrew Manuscripts at the Jewish National and University Library in Jerusalem, stumbled across the continuation of the first fragment in a photocopy of MS Leipzig, the University Library 40 (B.H. 2°14). This second fragment comprises a mere twelve lines: the last few words of the commentary on Psalm 1 and the commentary on Psalm 2:1–5. A critical edition of the Hebrew text of both fragments, accompanied by an English translation, will be found at the end of the present volume; the book itself is a reaction to the challenge posed by these two discoveries.

Ibn Ezra, more than any other Hebrew classical Bible exegete, was in the habit of writing two commentaries on the same scriptural book. Of these parallel commentaries to the "standard" ones, only five were known to be extant: the fragmentary commentary on Genesis; the short commentary on Exodus; the "second recensions" on Song of Songs and Esther; and the short commentary on Daniel. To these we can now add the fragmentary commentary on Psalms and a commentary on the Minor Prophets, which I have recently published alongside a critical and annotated edition of the standard commentary. The author's colophon at the end of the standard commentary on Psalms attests that it was written in Normandy in the year 1156. The fragmentary commentary seems to have been composed some fifteen years earlier, in Rome or Lucca, shortly after Ibn Ezra's arrival in Italy from Spain (1140).

A comparison of Ibn Ezra's parallel commentaries on a single scriptural book not only helps us understand some of his more obscure statements; it also allows us a glimpse into his workroom. In his two introductions to the Pentateuch, Ibn Ezra defines and describes his exegetical method via his rejection of the "four paths" followed by his predecessors. In a similar vein, his two Psalms introductions present his own ideas about the literary nature and prophetic status of the Psalms via a critical discussion of two basic conceptions offered by his predecessors. In the introduction to the standard commentary Ibn Ezra made only anonymous references to the disputants who had championed the two positions. Nevertheless, we can easily identify the advocate of the position that "the entire book is by David, who was a prophet," since this is the position expounded by Saadiah Gaon in his long introduction to his Arabic translation *cum* commentary on Psalms. On the other hand, it was impossible to be certain who had held "that this book contains no future-oriented prophecies" and therefore " 'by the rivers of Babylon' was written by a poet [who lived] in Babylonia." The fragmentary commentary provides the identification, since it explicitly attributes this opinion to R. Moses ha-Kohen Ibn Giqatilah. This Spanish scholar—who lived a century before Ibn Ezra and was referred to by the latter, in his Hebrew grammer *Sefer Moznayyim,* as "one of the great commentators" and "the greatest grammarian"—wrote, inter alia, a comprehensive Arabic commentary on Psalms. Most of this commentary has survived in the Firkovich collection in Leningrad, but we have been unable to examine the manuscript or a photocopy thereof. Consequently we are forced to rely chiefly on Ibn Ezra's citations from it, whose number has been significantly increased by the newly discovered introduction.

Just as Ibn Ezra's two introductions shed light on the methods of his predecessors, so too their commentaries enable us to arrive at a better understanding of his own commentaries. In fact, it is impossible to properly grasp Ibn Ezra's exegetical method and correctly evaluate the literary nature of his introductions to Psalms without some familiarity with his precursors' approaches (as they themselves phrased them, if possible) and without inquiring into the form and structure of their own introductions to Psalms. The principal sources for this attempt to write the history of the evolution of the fundamental approach towards the Book of Psalms during the more than two centuries from Saadiah to Ibn Ezra are Saadiah's two introductions, the introductions by the Karaite exegetes Salmon ben Yeruḥam and Yefet ben ᶜAli, and Ibn Ezra's two introductions.

Saadiah totally ignores the Talmudic assertion that the psalms were composed by David along with "ten elders," and firmly holds that the individuals mentioned in the headings of the various psalms were not poet-authors but merely musician-singers; consequently he can attribute all 150 psalms to David's exclusive authorship. Moreover, while the Sages viewed the psalms as prayers inspired by the Holy Spirit, Saadiah vigorously rejects this idea and endeavors to prove that their psalmic form is merely a rhetorical husk: correctly understood, the entire book consists of God's word to David. As Moshe Zucker has shown, this revolutionary view of the Book of Psalms as a sort of second Pentateuch given to David the prophet was intended to pull the rug out from under the Karaite belief that Psalms constitutes the immutable prayerbook of the Jewish people. Just as they asserted that the Mishnah was no Oral Torah, so too they asserted that Rabbanite prayer was not of prophetic but of human origin. And just as Saadiah countered that the brevity of the Written Law is prima facie evidence that it cannot be observed without the Oral Law, so too he demonstrates from the paucity of scriptural prayers that the obligation of prayer cannot be fulfilled without reliance on the extra-scriptural prayer incorporated in the rabbinic *siddur*.

This sweeping denial of the liturgical nature of the psalms may have been of some passing help in the defense against the Karaite schism. It is clear, however, that it did not appeal to other Rabbanite scholars and exegetes; certainly the Karaite commentators Salmon ben Yeruḥam and Yefet ben ᶜAli (who wrote their Arabic commentaries on Psalms in Jerusalem during the tenth century) had no trouble refuting it and proving from the text and style of the psalms that they were indeed prayers. Ironically, their conception of the psalms as prophetic prayers brought these rejectors of the Oral Law close to the view of the Talmudic sages. Nevertheless, the Karaite view of Psalms as the Jews' mandatory prayerbook for all time encouraged them to interpret it as alluding to current events, thus applying the prophetic psalms not only to the details of the Exile but even to the Karaite struggle against the Rabbanites and their anticipated glorious victory at the advent of the Messiah.

Whereas Saadiah had detached the Psalms from their literary form, and the Karaites pried them loose from their historical setting, Moses Ibn Giqatilah sought to restore their literary and historical dimensions. In his view the inclusion of the Psalms in the Hagiographa and the literary terms used in their headings prove that they were not prophecies, but rather "poems and psalms and actual prayers." Since, moreover, non-prophetic prayer cannot use the present tense to describe a future situation, each psalm ought to be dated in accordance with its historical background. For this reason Ibn Giqatilah postponed to the Babylonian exile the composition not only of many anonymous psalms, but also of all those ascribed to Asaph and the Koraḥides, holding that these names refer not to contemporaries of David but rather to their descendants who lived in Babylonia.

Abraham Ibn Ezra did not invalidate this view on theological grounds and frequently cited it as a legitimate exegetical option in the body of his standard Psalms commentary. At the same time, however, he himself tended to accept the opinion of the Sages and demurred from the late-dating of some psalms for exegetical rather than doctrinal reasons. He infers from the prayers of Jonah and Habakkuk that prophetic prayer, like prophecy itself, is not necessarily anchored in the circumstances of the prophet's life, but can refer to the distant future, and even speak on behalf of the members of that latter-day generation (such as the Levites of Psalm 137). Midway between Saadiah and Ibn Giqatilah, he believes that the psalms were composed by David and other prophetically inspired and for the most part contemporary poets; in this his stance is identical to that of the Karaite exegetes. But in utter contrast to their marked tendency to find detailed descriptions of future events in the scriptural text, Ibn Ezra reduced the prophetic element of the psalms to an irreducible minimum, while giving maximum weight to their fundamentally liturgical nature.

To sum up: Saadiah had no qualms about totally ignoring the Sages' view in order to answer the pressing needs of the hour. The Karaites' vigorous demand that prayer be based essentially on the Book of Psalms rested on a fundamental concept of the book that was close to the Talmudic view. Ibn Giqatilah allowed himself to rely on the plain meaning of the text, even where this meant deviating from the Sages' conception. Finally, Ibn Ezra's approach—when considered in the light of the previous history of psalmic exegesis—is not so innovative and radical as has been supposed, but is rather a moderate synthesis.

In the four chapters of this book, the conceptual elucidation of each of the four approaches is accompanied by close attention to the line of argument presented in each of the introductions and analysis of the nature of the proofs offered to support the argument. I have endeavored to leave nothing in these six introductions without explication; consequently the reader is offered a sort of thematic and methodological commentary on each of them. In addition, Ibn Ezra's newly discovered introduction and commentary (on Psalm 1 and 2:1–5), critically edited and annotated, are included in the appendix, along with an English translation. To assist the reader in locating the many references to Ibn Ezra's introduction to the standard commentary, it too is included in the appendix, based on the *editio princeps* (Venice 1525), with punctuation and citation of sources, but no textual apparatus (the critical edition of Ibn Ezra's commentary on Psalms 1–41 being prepared by Emanuel Silver will include the introduction).

My description and analysis of the four approaches is based not only on explicit statements found in the introductions, but also on how they are applied within the body of the respective commentaries. To this end I have examined how and to what extent each of the five exegetes implemented in his commentary the fundamental approach and concrete positions expounded in his introduction, especially with regard to the headings of the psalms, which furnish most of the information about the psalmists, the biographical and historical setting of the psalms, and their literary genre and musical performance. The indexes are intended to help the reader locate the many discussions of various topics that required clarification and have implications for various issues relating to medieval Jewish biblical exegesis.

This book was written at the Institute for the History of Jewish Bible Research, affiliated with the Department of Biblical Studies at Bar-Ilan University. Thus I was able to take advantage of the many research aids found there and the gracious assistance of its staff. First and foremost I stand in debt to my friend and colleague Dr. Maaravi Perez, who translated the Arabic texts for me and was always quick to provide generous help whenever I required his advice. May he soon merit to see publication of the critical edition and Hebrew translation of the commentaries of Judah Ibn Balaam upon which he has been working with Prof. M. Goshen-Gottstein. I would also like to thank Mrs. Herzlia Wagner, a graduate student and research assistant at the Institute, for her skillful assistance in all stages of my work—from research through publication. It was she who discovered the fragment and called my attention to its significance. Warm thanks also are owed to Mrs. Esther Cohen, secretary of the Institute, who met all my requests with fidelity, care, and understanding. Beyond the practical assistance, the devoted and heartfelt cooperation of these three was emotionally satisfying as well. I am also grateful to my friend Emanuel Silver, who placed at my disposal the first draft of his edition of Ibn Ezra's commentary on Psalms 1–41. Variant readings for this portion of the commentary are generally taken from his apparatus. I would also like to express my gratitude to the authorities of the Verona Municipal Library and of the Karl-Marx University Library, Leipzig, for permission to publish herein the only surviving fragments of the "First Recension" of Ibn Ezra's Psalms commentary. I had access to the many manuscripts cited in the book thanks to the good offices of the Institute of Microfilms of Hebrew Manuscripts of the Jewish National and University Library, Jerusalem. My thanks to its staff for their assistance and generosity. I would also like to thank Prof. Michael Schwartz of Tel-Aviv University for his important criticisms of the Hebrew edition of the book, Mrs. Zippora Brody, who provided a first draft of the translation of chapters one and two, and especially Mr. Lenn Schramm, for his accurate and fluent English translation of the entire book.

The revision of the Hebrew text upon which the translation is based was done while I was a Fellow in the Institute for Advanced Studies at the

Hebrew University of Jerusalem. The translation itself was made possible by the endowment for the Herman Merkin Chair for the Study of the Commentaries of R. Abraham Ibn Ezra and his Contemporaries at Bar-Ilan University (of which I have the honor to be the incumbent). I am most grateful to its donor, Mr. Herman Merkin.

Nine hundred years have passed since Ibn Ezra's birth (Tudela 1089). It is a great privilege to add another link to the long chain of the study of his contribution to biblical exegesis and Jewish culture.

Uriel Simon

Jerusalem
Spring 1989

1

Saadiah Gaon: The Book of Psalms as a Second Pentateuch

I. The Rhetorical Thesis: Commandment and admonition phrased as prayer and petition

Although Saadiah Gaon was not the first commentator on the Book of Psalms, all subsequent Jewish exegetes of that book are in a sense his descendants.[1] His view that the 150 psalms comprise a sort of second Pentateuch, revealed to David, was not based on rabbinic sources, nor was it accepted by later commentators; nevertheless, its echoes continue to resound in their writings. Abraham Ibn Ezra, for example, in his two introductions to Psalms, disputes at length several of the Gaon's original ideas about the nature of the Book of Psalms, without, however, explicitly attributing them to him.[2] A thorough study of Saadiah's view is thus important not only for its own sake, but also in order to appreciate the reasons for its total rejection by his successors.

We have two introductions by Saadiah to the Book of Psalms.[3] One is extremely short (pp. 51–53 in the Kafiḥ edition), the other some eleven times as long (ibid., pp. 17–50). Both present the same basic conception of the Book of Psalms; but the long introduction develops the argument and proofs in much greater detail and appends a translation of the first four psalms, accompanied by a full-fledged commentary on each of them as an example of the exegetical method derived from that conception (see Saadiah's statement of purpose: ibid., p. 50). In my opinion, the short introduction is probably Saadiah's preface to the *Tafsir* on Psalms, while the longer one belongs with the long commentary he wrote later (this chronological order is suggested by the fact that the long commentary often refers to the *Tafsir* and has no independent existence apart from it). I find this assumption persuasive, even though the rather confused picture offered by the manuscripts fails to support it. Only two manuscripts of the long commentary are extant. Both introductions are found in the Munich MS (Hebrew #122 = Arabic #236); it is the short one, however, that is prefaced to the body of the commentary, preceded by the long introduction, in the handwriting of another scribe.[4] Nor can the Yemenite MS designated Q in the Kafiḥ edition demonstrate any link between the long introduction and the long commentary, since it contains only the short introduction. Neither introduction is found in MS Oxford-Bodleian 2484 and the two Yemenite manuscripts designated M and V in Kafih's edition, which include only the *Tafsir.*[5] In any case, the short introduction apparently antedates the long one, and Saadiah's astonishing conception of the Book of Psalms is clearly and forthrightly expressed in both.

Saadiah begins his short introduction by stating his basic thesis, which expands and develops the rabbinic principle that "the Torah speaks in human terms" (BT Berakot 31b): Since ethical literature requires many and varied means of expression, the Lord in his wisdom saw to it that the prophetic literature, which was also intended to guide and edify man, is phrased in a variety of styles and idioms. To illustrate his thesis Saadiah enumerates ten rhetorical devices normally employed by human speakers to persuade others to follow the just path. Some of these devices are specific and direct: commandment and prohibition, encouragement and threat, parables and tales (about exemplary heroes and villains, and their respective reward and punishment). Others are general turns of style recommended by their indirect appeal and subtlety: a phrasing appropriate to overt guidance—the direct address of master to servant—may be supplemented with the sophisticated distancing achieved by referring to the readers or audience in the third person or by transforming the master's authoritative pronouncements into the humble entreaty of the servant. Since these devices are so widespread, Saadiah sees no need to give examples of them from daily usage and proceeds immediately to cite from the Book of Psalms two or three instances of each. Only after presenting this mass of examples does he explain his purpose:

> . . . to keep the reader of this book from discriminating among its contents and understanding what is placed in the mouth of the servant as his own speech and not that of his master; that is, the reader should not think that 'have mercy upon me,' 'succor me,' 'save me,' and the like are the words of the servant rather than part of the prophet's vision from the Lord; nor should he think that 'they will praise' and 'they will sing' are really in the third person instead of direct address; nor anything that might be construed opposite to the Lord's intention. We must realize that all of these were phrased by the Lord in the various forms of speech employed by his creatures. (Saadiah, *Psalms*, p. 53)

Thus the rhetorical analysis is intended to ground his view of Psalms as a prophetic work of religious guidance on a firm theoretical foundation by preventing two prevalent errors: (1) seeing the multiplicity of verbal and grammatical forms as evidence of multiple topics and speakers; (2) understanding indirect forms of address literally. Only a simplistic rhetorical theory considers form and content to be necessarily identical, so that a psalm worded as a man's address to his Maker must be interpreted as a request or as praise, or that third-person speech is inappropriate in the Lord's direct injunction to his creatures that they obey him. For Saadiah, Moses' song in Deut. 32:1–42 is incontrovertible proof that variation of form and changes of speaker do not negate the unity of a work. Although the song is explicitly described as the words of the Lord—"in order that this poem may be My witness against the people of Israel" (Deut. 31:19)—we find, alongside the Lord's direct address to his people ("see, then, that I, I am He" [Deut. 32:39]), that "it is stated partly in the voice of his prophet, as if he [Moses] were speaking to his people in the name of his master" (e.g., "For the name of the Lord I proclaim, Give glory to our God" [v. 3]). This song also intersperses direct address (vv. 7 and 18) with the third person (vv. 21 and 36). Consequently Saadiah can take this as the model for his far-reaching exegetical approach to the Book of Psalms:

> We must understand the prophet's words in this book, such as 'have mercy upon me,' as [spoken by] the Lord—'I will have mercy upon my servant'—and [understand] 'heed my prayer' as 'I will hear your prayer,' . . . and similarly everything in this book. All is the word of the Lord and nothing is human discourse, as the faithful transmitters of our tradition have attested. (Saadiah, *Psalms,* p. 53)

Since the multiplicity of rhetorical forms can be interpreted either literally (as reflecting a multiplicity of topics and speakers) or as a stylistic device (indirect and variegated expressions of a single subject by a single speaker), some sort of external evidence is needed to permit a choice between the two options. For Moses' song in Deuteronomy Saadiah could bring the explicit testimony of the text itself, found in the narrative framework in which the poem is set (Deut. 31:19). In the absence of any explicit internal proof of the topical and rhetorical unity of the Book of Psalms, Saadiah must depend on the faithful testimony of the "transmitters of our tradition"—without, however, specifying the rabbinic statement to which he is alluding. It is all but impossible to penetrate the veil of indefiniteness that envelops this statement; many rabbinic statements deal with the issue of the authorship of Psalms (most attribute the book to "ten elders,")[6] but there seems to be no direct Talmudic support for his assertion of the rhetorical unity of the book ("All is the word of the Lord").[7] The long introduction is of no assistance on this point, since there Saadiah follows a different line of argument, as we shall see (pp. 13 ff.). In my opinion, Saadiah is not referring to some explicit rabbinic passage that could be quoted to prove his contention, but to the common Talmudic practice of introducing prooftexts from anywhere in Psalms with "as it is said" and "as it is written," ignoring the specific context and making no distinction among speakers and styles.

We have traced Saadiah's argument in the short introduction in some detail and quoted him extensively both because this is the only way to come to an understanding of his unique approach and the unusual method it requires and because on at least one major issue the short introduction is clearer and more comprehensible than the long introduction. This enables us now to be relatively brief in our exposition of the long introduction, concentrating primarily upon whatever was added to or modified from its predecessor. The first part of this introduction (Saadiah, *Psalms,* pp. 17–24) is again devoted to examining the rhetorical modes employed in Psalms, but in much greater detail than the parallel passage in the short introduction. Akin to the richness and variety of persuasive devices found in human language, the divine language of Scripture relies on five basic forms of speech: direct address, interrogation (in divine speech only rhetorical or ostensible questions are possible!), narrative, commandment and admonition, and prayer and petition (these too cannot be taken literally when spoken by God!). These five elementary forms yield eighteen rhetorical modes (as opposed to the ten enumerated in the short introduction); a scriptural occurrence of each is demonstrated by a quotation from the Pentateuch (for most) and from Psalms (almost always). These eighteen modes constitute "the totality of edification" (p. 22), since the frequent variation and changes of speaker guarantee that the "reader will be edified by all of them and not become impatient" (p. 23). What is the aim of edification served by the Book of Psalms? Saadiah answers by means of an analogy to Scripture as a whole: "Since the declared purpose of all of Scripture is commandment and admonition, and the other sixteen modes of speech are merely ancillary to them, so too this book, which is part of Scripture, also has no purpose other than commandment and admonition, and requires the other sixteen modes only to strengthen and reinforce them" (ibid.). Saadiah then attempts to prove that this basic principle, which posits a very narrow common basis for all the biblical books, is tenable from the rhetorical point of view. In order to do this he shows how narrative, direct address, and prayer (for some reason he omits interrogation) are actually used to persuade people to obey divine commandments and warnings. Given the frequency and importance of prayer in the Book of Psalms, what Saadiah says here about prayer would seem to be the essential point; the discussion of the other rhetorical forms is included chiefly to provide analogies that will buttress the legitimacy of this transformation: "Thus [the Lord] found it necessary to set down for them supplications and prayers and entreaties, in order to remind them of their frailty and powerlessness and of their dependence upon him, so that they would submit and abase themselves before him and accept his commandments and admonitions" (p. 24).

II. The Polemical Motive: An attack on the Karaite order of prayer and support for the Rabbanite prayerbook

The purpose of Saadiah's disquisition on rhetorical devices is to ground his firm denial that the Book of Psalms has any literary uniqueness within the biblical canon. He is somewhat more forthcoming in presenting his motivation for this denial in the long introduction. Since the correct interpretation of the passage in question remains a subject of controversy, the Arabic original of the major cruxes is given below:

> What has brought me to include these matters in the introduction to this book and explain that all of them aim at commandment and prohibition is that I have seen a few of our nation who imagine *(jatawahhamun)* that this book was uttered by David the prophet on his own *(min tilḳa nafsihi)*. It seems to me that the cause of this delusion *(ʾelmuwahhim)* is that they find many prayers in it. This has caused them not to attribute it to the Lord, since it is the speech of men *(kalamu ʾn-nas);* in particular they came to do so because they use it in their prayers. Therefore I have seen fit to reveal the entire meaning of this book: I say that it is divine speech, what the master says to his servant, commanding him and warning him and encouraging him and threatening him and describing to him his exalted glory, and reminding him that he is weak before him and dependent upon him. (p. 24)

According to Rivlin ("Prefaces," pp. 384–85) the thrust of this passage is that Saadiah wanted to "uproot the idea that the Book of Psalms is not of divine origin." Rivlin does not identify those "few of our nation" who believed this; evidently he assumes it refers to the various heretical Jewish sects that proliferated during Saadiah's time.[8] Kafiḥ (note 92) apparently believes that Saadiah had the Sages in mind, since his note to the phrase "uttered by David the prophet on his own" refers the reader to BT Baba Baṯra 14a–15b. Rivlin's tacit attribution must be challenged, because, in Saadiah's summary of the opposing view, David is explicitly called "the prophet." Kafiḥ's view is also hard to accept, since it would require us to understand the words "I have seen a few of our nation" as referring to the Talmudic Sages; even harder to accept would be the estrangement from them implied by "because they use [psalms] in *their* prayers," which Kafih admittedly notes is unclear (note 93). Zucker ("Notes," p. 225) asserts that the text here is corrupt, since *ʾelfiʿlu ʾilaihi* is a "nonexistent expression"; he suggests the reading *ʾelmajlu ʾilaihi,* i.e., "and that is what caused them to address him [with it] in their prayers." This fits in well with Zucker's novel explanation of the entire passage:

> The Gaon transferred the Book of Psalms from the sphere of prayer to that of commandments and admonitions, which entangled him in various problems and difficulties. He even disagrees with the rabbinic view (Zucker's note: since according to the Sages the Book of Psalms was written by ten elders, . . . whereas Saadiah, following his approach, proves [later in the introduction] that the entire Book of Psalms was written by David) and derives a *halakhah* concerning the Levites' chanting of psalms in the Temple that has no known source in the rabbinic literature (in a note Zucker explains that Saadiah's assertion that only the singers named in the superscription of a given psalm were allowed to chant it in the Temple has no basis in rabbinic law). He did all this in order to refute the Karaite view that the Book of Psalms is Israel's prayerbook and there is no need for the prayers ordained by the Sages. (p. 225)

Accordingly, the "few of our nation" to whom Saadiah refers are the Karaites,[9] whose failure[10] to comprehend the true literary nature of the Psalms "caused them to address him (with it) in their prayers," that is to say, to make the Book of Psalms the keystone of their prayerbook. Zucker substantiates this explanation of Saadiah's concerted attempt to prove that the Book of Psalms is not a book of prayers with two quotations from Saadiah's other works that repeat the same arguments about the distance between the words of the servant and those of the master and about how prayer and entreaty are really commandment and admonition. The first is the sharply polemical passage on prayer in his anti-Karaite work *ʾEśśa Mešali,* epitomized in: "[See] how the servant returns to his Maker / the words of commandment that come from his Lord."[11] The second is Saadiah's statement in the introduction to his *Siddur:* "Even those places in the Bible that sound like prayer cannot (truly) be prayer, since they are juxtaposed with commandments, admonitions, promises, and threats."[12]

Zucker does not explain the logical connection between the dispute with the Karaites over how the obligation to pray should be fulfilled—through the prayers composed by David or the non-biblical liturgy of the Rabbanite prayerbook—and whether the Book of Psalms "was uttered by David the prophet on his own," or was "Divine speech—what the Master says to His servant." Shunari (who accepts both Zucker's emendations and his theory of Saadiah's anti-Karaite motive) consequently returns to Rivlin's idea that in his introduction Saadiah is also combatting the notion that the Book of Psalms is not a prophetic work (*Methods*, pp. 18–19). It is hardly plausible, however, to ascribe an attack on the holiness of the book to the Karaites. First, there is no direct evidence of such a Karaite position, and the Karaite commentaries on Psalms adopt precisely the contrary.[13] Second, it is only reasonable that those who see the psalms as prayers incumbent on all generations would insist more forcefully on the prophetic nature of these biblical prayers! One must conclude that Saadiah and the Karaites saw eye to eye about the prophetic status of the psalms; the disagreement was about their *literary* nature and the *halakhic* implications thereof: are they truly prayers (in which case no text is more apt for use in our liturgy), or are they rather commandments and admonition mainly expressed in the rhetorical guise of prayer (and therefore must not be misused for worship)? Indeed, everything by Saadiah that has come down to us on the subject (in his two introductions to Psalms, in *ʾEšša Mešali,* and in his two introductions to the *Siddur*) focuses on the rhetorical contrast between "the words of the Master" (i.e., commandment and admonition) and "the words of the servant" (i.e., prayer and supplication), and not on that between the word of the Lord (i.e., prophecy) and human discourse (not inspired by revelation). An exception to this is the passage from the long introduction cited above, at whose core are the words *haḏ ʾl-kitab Daudu ʾn-nabiyu ḳalahu min tilḳa nafsihi,* rendered by Kafih as: "This book was uttered by David the prophet on his own."

At first sight these words could be translated literally: "This book was said by David the prophet concerning himself." This would have them refer to the rhetorical plane, and fit in well with Saadiah's other pronouncements on the subject. However, as Ben-Shammai has shown ("Review," p. 402), the idiomatic use of *min tilḳa nafsihi* both in the Koran (10:15) and in Saadiah's own works (*Beliefs,* 3:4, p. 150 [Kafih ed., p. 126, lines 25–26]; 5:8, p. 232 [ibid., p. 191, lines 8–9]) supports Kafih's rendering, "on his own," rather than inspired by divine revelation. (To this we should add Saadiah's translation of "not of my own devising" [Num. 16:28] in the *Tafsir: walajsa min tilḳa nafsi,* quoted by Razhabi, *Dictionary,* p. 25.) How, though, can Saadiah attribute to the Karaites a view that derogates the psalms from prophetic utterance to human speech? Ben-Shammai (ibid., pp. 402–403) suggests that Saadiah, faithful to his position that the Book of Psalms is a complete prophecy revealed to David word for word, was taking issue with a hypothetical Karaite view that the psalms were created merely under the influence of "the holy spirit," in the sense of "an inspiration under whose influence a person seems to speak of his own accord."

The difficulty with this answer is that the available evidence indicates that Karaite views of "the holy spirit" are close to those of the Sages and rather remote from what Saadiah attributes to them (for Salmon ben Yeruḥam see below, p. 63; and for Yefet ben ʿAli, pp. 80–82). Perhaps we should assume that Saadiah projected on the Karaites a view of his own, not held by their scholars, namely, that prayer is not authentic unless the worshipper utters it *min tilḳa nafsihi* (of his own initiative), as Hosea said (14:3): "Provide yourself with words and return to the Lord . . ." (see note 12 above). Saadiah accordingly differentiates between the ostensible prayers of Moses and David, which are in fact pure prophecies, and Rabbanite prayer, which is indeed human speech that truly expresses the worshipper's standing before his heavenly Master (although not an individual supplication, since it is couched in terms set by the elders and prophets, as explained below, pp. 10–11). Thus from the fact that the Karaites use the psalms in their worship he concludes not only that they are guilty of a rhetorical error (failing to understand that these are really "the words of the Master"), but also that they ignore the prophetic nature of the psalms in order to render them fit for utterance by a worshipper.[14] The truth is that the Karaites had no trouble bridging the gap between the liturgical nature of the psalms and their prophetic status because they had adopted the Rabbanite conception of the dual nature of prophetic prayer: the prophet addresses the Lord, even while it is the Holy Spirit that shapes his words.[15]

We will find it difficult to understand why Saadiah had to resort to such a radical argument about the nature of the Book of Psalms if we fail to comprehend the full effect of Karaite polemics on the subject of prayer. Let us begin with a Genizah fragment from the Hebrew commentary on Leviticus by the Karaite Daniel al-Kumissi, who lived in Jerusalem at the end of the ninth and beginning of the tenth century. In his commentary on 16:31 he asks pointedly why the Lord does not respond to the prayers and fasts of his people Israel and save the sons of his beloved Jacob, given that they no longer worship idols. He answers:

> This is due to the perversion of the commandments given us and to the wicked laws taught by the misleading shepherds. . . . Worse than all of this is that even when Israel gathers on fast days and on the Day of Atonement they have placed in their mouths many words, liturgies in which there is no delight, instead of songs from Psalms, or "I will recount the kind acts of the Lord," and "O Lord, You are my God and I will extol You. I will praise Your name," from Isaiah (63:7, 25:1); Daniel's prayer, "O Lord, great and awesome God" (9:4); and Nehemiah's "Bless the Lord your God who is from eternity to eternity" (9:5–6). [The Rabbanites] say none of this.[16]

This "perversion of the commandments," which delays the redemption of Israel, manifests itself in the realm of prayer by the Rabbanites' abandonment of the mandated biblical prayers[17] and their replacement by non-prophetic *piyyuṭim*[18] in which God takes no delight. This grave indictment evidently impugns not only *piyyuṭim* in the narrow sense, but also the entire prescribed rite of the Rabbanite prayerbook. As Jacob al-Kirkisani, Saadiah's Karaite contemporary and main polemical adversary, wrote in his Arabic *Book of the Luminaries and Watchtowers:*

> One [of the rabbis' mistakes] is that they stopped praying from the Book of Psalms and made [their prayers] from what they themselves composed. This contradicts Scripture: "To give praise to the Lord as David had ordained" (Ezra 3:10). Moreover, they themselves say, at the beginning of their prayers: "who chose David His servant and found pleasure in his holy songs."[19]

Elsewhere in his book Kirkisani supplements these scriptural texts and the conclusion of the *baruk̲ še-ʾamar* benediction of the Rabbanite *siddur* (in the Palestinian rite, as shown by Genizah fragments published by Scheiber and Asaph)[20] with rational, historical, and psychological arguments:

> That prayer [ought to consist of] the Psalms and the words of David, would be almost a logical imperative, even were there no [scriptural] proofs thereof. None of our people disputes this, except for the rabbis. But they, after admitting its necessity, reneged and denied it. It is known that they admitted because, as mentioned at the beginning of our book, they say, at the beginning of their prayers, "who chose David His servant and found pleasure in his holy songs," etc. Similarly, they begin their prayer called *šᵉmoneh ʿeśreh* with David's words, "Lord, open my lips" (Ps. 51:17) and conclude with his words, "May the words of my mouth find favor" (Ps. 19:15). Their denial seems to be caused by their hatred and disdain for those who pray in this way, carried to the point, it has been said, that once upon a time they considered removing the Book of Psalms from the canon.[21]

In this fashion Kirkisani attempted to reinforce the historical *ʾiǵmaʿ* (i.e., the general consensus of the faithful, which was considered a most reliable proof)[22] by means of the exaggerated suspicion that the Rabbanite prayerbook owed its very existence exclusively to the vehement hatred of its authors for the Karaites. This wild accusation seems not to have ruffled any feathers among the Rabbanites, who probably did not even deign to respond to or refute it. They could not display similar equanimity in the face of the claim that non-scriptural prayer is illegitimate, which parallels the Karaite attack upon the status of the Oral Law. In fact, several lines after the passage quoted above Kirkisani considers at some length six scriptural proofs offered by a Rabbanite author to confute the Karaite belief that the Book of Psalms satisfies every need for prayer for every generation:[23]

> One of the Rabbanite polemicists has expressed his view on this issue and answered those who claim that prayer must be drawn [exclusively] from the Book of Psalms by citing the verse: "So that they may offer pleasing sacrifices to the God of heaven and pray for the lives of the king and his sons" (Ezra 6:10). What prayer, he asked, can be drawn from Psalms concerning King Darius and his sons? He adduced another proof from the verse: "any prayer or supplication which shall be offered by any man" (1 Kings 8:38); if prayer is to be taken only from the Psalms, what is the meaning of "by any man"? True enough, "shall be" is in the future and not in the past tense. Another proof is that the text reads "by any man" [and not][24]—"by any of the children of Israel": although the Jews know the Book of Psalms and can pray from it, he demanded, how can other people, to whom "by any man" refers, do so? And those that came from a distant land to pray in the Temple, how did they know the Psalms to pray from them? He said: Another proof derives from the words of David—"Who can tell the mighty acts of the Lord, proclaim all His praises?" (Ps. 106:2), while elsewhere [David] said, "I will add to all the praises of You" (Ps. 71:14): if it is impossible to proclaim all the praises of the Lord, how can one add to them? What is meant by this is: I will add to the praise by which the righteous men of yore praised you, like Adam, Enoch, Noah, Shem, Abraham, Isaac, Jacob, Moses, Aaron, and all the righteous men. This is the meaning of "I will add to all the praises of You." He said: Another proof from Scripture is, "in assemblies bless God, the Lord, from the fountain of Israel" (Ps. 68:27[26]). By this he meant the sages of Israel who composed and disseminated many praises and glorifications of the Lord, like [the *payṭanim*] Yannai and Eleazar and Phineas and their like. He said: this is the meaning of the verse, "this nation I formed for Myself, that they might declare My praise" (Isa. 43:21), i.e., from the wisdom of your hearts!

We have quoted this passage at length not only because of its intrinsic importance, but also because it is generally assumed that the Rabbanite polemicist in question is Saadiah. This was surmised by Harkavy (the first to publish the passage);[25] Poznanski agreed with him that the arguments were evidently taken from Saadiah's lost polemic against Anan.[26]

This endeavor to bring scriptural proofs that the Book of Psalms is inadequate to fulfill all facets of the obligation of prayer and also that liturgical composition began before David and will continue after him seems to parallel Saadiah's well-known assertion that the terseness of Scripture proves that it was complemented *ab initio* by the Oral Law.[27] The truth, however, is that Saadiah was much more radical than this adversary of the Karaites. He was not interested simply in finding justifications for supplementing biblical prayer with liturgical poetry, an issue on which the Karaites eventually agreed with him, just as they recognized that their own ''oral tradition,'' the *sevel ha-y^e^ruššah,* as complementing the Pentateuch.[28] Rather, Saadiah staged a frontal assault against the very charge of perversion, according to which Rabbanite prayer had usurped the place of scriptural prayer. To this indictment he had a clear answer: the psalms were never intended to serve as a prayerbook for Israel, while the liturgy handed down by the Sages (meaning primarily the *ʿAmidah*) is not only of ancient origin, but was even ordained by the prophets! This unyielding position is clearly expressed in the introduction to his *Siddur:*

> Since the Jews' prayers and benedictions to the Lord are not formulated in Scripture, just as many of the laws and commandments are not explicated therein, He Who ordained them made us dependent upon the tradition enunciated by His prophets. Those passages in Scripture that sound like prayer cannot be prayer (in truth), since they are juxtaposed with commandments, admonitions, promises, and threats in every chapter, and reason dictates that none of these can be incorporated into prayer, as we have explained in the *Proof for Prayer.*[29] In both prayers and benedictions they depended on the tradition handed down by the prophets of the Lord. They had two rituals, one for the era of the monarchy and the other for the Exile.[30] (*Siddur,* p. 10)

In this way Saadiah enveloped the perversion argument on both flanks: the prayers we recite are not our own innovation, since, like the Oral Law, they have been handed down to us in a reliable tradition going back to the prophets;[31] by contrast, the psalms, which the Karaites employ in their prayer, were never intended to be used in that way, as their style makes clear. Hence Saadiah, who viewed the Book of Psalms as God's word to man, could never have entered into a dispute about the exclusive liturgical status of the psalms; nor could he have accepted the proofs of Kirkisani's adversary, namely, that from three verses in the Book of Psalms one could deduce that David added to the prayers of the ancients and anticipated that others in the future would write new *piyyuṭim* to be recited along with his poems.[32]

III. The Ritual Thesis: The five-fold condition

The radical claim that, since the psalms are not truly prayers, the Book of Psalms is actually a manual of theological and moral guidance required both a rhetorical theory of extreme complexity, to explain the frequency with which the servant addresses his master in a book said to comprise only the master's words to his servant, as well as an innovative theory of ritual, which could explain away the personal references and musical instructions in the headings of many psalms. For what do biographical notes, such as "when he fled from Absalom his son" (3:1), and performance instructions, such as "for the leader; on the *š^{e}miniṯ*" (12:1) have to do with a "book of guidance"? Although Saadiah ignores these problems in the short introduction, most of the long introduction is devoted to developing two theories intended to resolve them.

If the Book of Psalms is not an anthology of prayers composed by David and other prophetic poets, the question arises as to why it was given to Israel precisely under his reign. Saadiah attempts to give a reasonable explanation for the date of its revelation while stressing the excellence of Psalms, by virtue of its similarity to the Pentateuch. Just as the Torah was not given until "*mankind* attained its most perfect number, which His wisdom ordained should be maintained forever" (p. 25), "so too the Lord did not give this complete and perfect book until the *nation* attained its most perfect number, its breadth of knowledge, wealth, heroes, and the like" (p. 26). He proves the first part of the equation (Earth's population reached its optimal level during Moses' time) through the assertion that the longevity of the first generations was intended to allow the rapid proliferation of mankind; the institution since Moses' time of an upper limit of 120 years indicates that this process of proliferation was completed then. That the Israelite population achieved "its most perfect number" in David's time he finds in the results of David's census: "All Israel comprised 1,100,000 ready to draw the sword" (1 Chron. 21:5).[33] From the multiplicity of prophetic bands during Samuel's judgeship he deduces that scientific knowledge flourished in that age: "In every corner you would find them learning and contemplating" (p. 26). Saadiah adduces two proofs of David's impressive military success: the large numbers of those who surrendered to Israel, on the one hand, and the long lists of Israelite heroes, on the other. The multi-faceted perfection of this period culminated in Solomon's construction of the Temple, where the psalms assumed a dual role: the Levites encouraged the laborers by serenading them with the psalms that begin *lam^{e}naṣṣeaḥ* (as proven by the use of the verb *l^{e}-naṣṣeaḥ* in 1 Chron. 23:4 and in Ezra 3:8, which allude to the Levites' role in the construction of the First and Second Temples); and when the Temple was completed, the Levitical watches sang day and night the special psalms assigned to them (as related by 1 Chron. 9:33).

The appropriateness of the timing is augmented by the stature of the prophet who received the book: "It was given to the most excellent of kings, David the prophet, may he rest in peace, who was chosen, as it is written of him: 'I have found David, my servant; [with my holy oil I anointed him]' (Ps. 89:21[20])'' (p. 27). The spirit of the Lord rested upon him from the day he was anointed (proven by 1 Sam. 16:13); he received the psalms in installments starting then. The biographical and geographical information found in the headings of some psalms should not astonish us, for they resemble ''the journeys of the Children of Israel, which the Lord recorded in the Pentateuch for their sake, as it is said: 'these were the marches' (Num. 33:1), as well as the incidents that occurred at each encampment'' (p. 27). This analogy may not convince, but it is nonetheless an impressive attempt. Moreover, it reinforces the similarity between the Psalms of David and the Torah of Moses.

Are all the psalms by David, though? The concept of the Book of Psalms as a ''book of guidance'' can, perhaps, be reconciled *a posteriori* with its attribution to several (prophetic) authors; but it is clear that allowing multiple authorship weakens such a monolithic conception, since it permits questioning the literary unity of the book. Thus Saadiah could have taken a minimalist approach and merely demonstrated that the ''ten elders'' named in the headings were all prophets.[34] As was his wont, however, he preferred to go all the way and prove that ''the whole book is prophecy uttered by David'' (p. 28). His first argument is that on this matter an *ʾiǵmaʿ* (consensus) exists: ''The entire nation is unanimous in calling [Psalms] 'the Songs of David' '' (ibid.). The appellation ''Songs of David'' (given in Hebrew even in Saadiah's Arabic text) derives, of course, from the second part of the *baruk̲ še-ʾamar* benediction, which in Saadiah's *siddur* (p. 32), as in our own, introduces the group of psalms included at the beginning of the morning service. This liturgical reference to the ''Songs of David'' had such weight for Saadiah that he quite ignored, here and throughout his two introductions, the Talmudic statement that ten elders wrote the psalms collected by David in the Book of Psalms—a statement that seems to contradict his claim of a consensus regarding the authorship issue.[35]

The second proof supplements the first: Scripture itself attributes the psalms, generally and with no comment (according to his interpretation, of course) to David (see Neh. 12:24; 2 Chron. 7:6 and 8:14). The third proof is more complex: while the internal evidence might lead one to infer that the book includes prophecies by several persons (such as Asaph, Heman, and Moses), another datum entails the conclusion that ''there is nothing that is not by David'' (p. 28)—namely, that the superscriptions of several psalms mention two names, like ''*la-mᵉnaṣṣeaḥ* to Jeduthun, a psalm of David'' (39:1). Since ''the Lord does not usually send two prophets on one mission, even though the Torah says, 'the Lord spoke unto Moses and Aaron, saying' (Lev. 11:1 and nine other loci), the clear truth [or, reading with Zucker, the accepted truth] is that Moses alone was entrusted with this commandment, and Aaron merely heard [it] from him'' (ibid.). Saadiah holds that we cannot understand this verse and others like it literally, since according to scripture only Moses' prophecy was direct revelation, in contrast to the indirect revelation received by all other prophets, including Aaron (Exod. 33:11; Num. 12:1–8). Consequently they must be interpreted via the technique of *taʿwil:* The Lord spoke to Moses, and he transmitted the message to Aaron.[36] Moses' prophecy was of such high degree that Aaron, who heard it from him, was himself accounted a prophet; since, however, ''David was spoken to through an angelic intermediary, one who heard [the prophecy] from [David] was inferior to a prophet, with regard to what he heard, and was like all the masses'' (p. 29). The implication is that when the superscription of a psalm mentions a second name alongside David's, that other person must be a musician; even when David is not mentioned at all, the two names in a heading (e.g., Jeduthun and Asaph in Ps. 77:1) both indicate performers; and, to carry the implication yet further, even when David is not mentioned and some other name appears, it too denotes the performer of the psalm in question. Saadiah adheres so firmly to this method that he even manages to demonstrate that ''A prayer of Moses, the man of God'' (90:1) is a prophecy by David and no one else: in Scripture we find that the later descendants are designated by the name of an important ancestor (e.g., ''but Aaron and his sons made offerings'' [1 Chron. 6:34(49)] clearly refers to priests serving in David's time); here too the ''Prayer of Moses'' ''is a song presented to Moses' descendants who were contemporary with David to sing'' (ibid.).[37] Since Solomon, unlike Moses and his descendants, was not a Levite, he could not be a singer in the Temple; Saadiah was thus compelled to deal with the two psalms whose superscriptions mention him (72 and 127) in a different way: the prefix *lamed* in *li-šᵉlomoh* means neither ''by'' nor ''for,'' but rather ''about'': Solomon is not the author of the psalms, nor their performer, but their subject—''a prophecy concerning Solomon and what will happen to him. That is why the verse 'End of the prayers of David son of Jesse' (72:20) was appended to this psalm[38]—to tell us that this is a prophecy of David's'' (p. 30).

The feebleness of the third proof is so conspicuous that we must assume that Saadiah did not view it as a freestanding argument, but merely as an explanation of the apparent contradiction between the headings and the external testimony that all the psalms are ''the songs of David.'' The general principle that two prophets are not entrusted with the same mission is certainly insufficient proof that the anonymous psalms are David's; it is, however, possible to assert that, just as a name mentioned alongside David's designates the performer rather than the poet, so too the other names that appear in the headings (except for David and Solomon) are those of Levite choristers. Anyone who accepts the validity of the two first proofs must find this conclusion not only possible but in fact unavoidable; the only remaining question is why David gave his prophecies to singers. Saadiah answers that in addition to being chapters in a "book of guidance" to be read and studied, the psalms had an important function in the Temple service. This was not, as is mistakenly believed, *liturgical*—an impossibility, since they express God's words to man rather than being man's appeal to his God—but *ritual*. For Saadiah, the use of the psalms as sacred poetry, limited by their very nature to the Temple, is conclusively demonstrated by the ritual instructions given in the superscriptions, which have no meaning for prayer in general. Thus he draws a sharp distinction between two aspects of the Book of Psalms, and, correspondingly, between *reading* the psalms and *chanting* them. As a "book of guidance" "it is read everywhere, at all times, by all people and of every age" (p. 27); as sacred poetry, however, "we have called it *kitabu ʾt-tasbiḥ* [the Book of Praise] since it is a special song, for particular individuals, in a particular place, with particular instruments, and particular melodies" (ibid.).[39]

Saadiah now launches a detailed demonstration that these five conditions (the personal, musical, instrumental, temporal, and local), which in his view strictly regulated the performance of the psalms in the Temple, is anchored in both Scripture and logic. Before considering the proofs we should mention that this argument later convinced even the critical mind of Abraham Ibn Ezra, who, while totally rejecting all of Saadiah's other hypotheses about the Book of Psalms, adopted these five conditions and presented them in a more moderate form in the introduction to the First Recension of his commentary.

The first condition—the *personal*—asserts that "every psalm that is designated to [specific] Levites, they are obligated to recite it; all others are forbidden to recite it except for reading" (p. 30). Saadiah brings passages from 1 Chronicles to prove that all those named in the heading were Levites and that the assignment of certain psalms to them was on a familial rather than an individual basis, encompassing their brothers (e.g., "Asaph and his brothers"—1 Chron. 16:7), and descendants (e.g., "the sons of Jeduthun"—1 Chron. 25:3). Not only is he able to identify the descendants of Moses—to whom, in his opinion, Psalm 90 was entrusted—with the family of Rehaviah son of Eliezer son of Moses (1 Chron. 23:15–17); he goes further and glosses even common nouns with a preceding definite article—*la-ben* (Ps. 9:1) and *ha-gittiṯ* (8:1; 81:1; 84:1)—as the names of two Levites mentioned in 1 Chron. 15:18: Ben and Obed-Edom the Gittite.[40] These identifications are the underpinning for his fundamental assertion that these familial assignments are strictly exclusive, i.e., "that

Obed-Edom is forbidden to recite Asaph's text, and Heman to say that of Ben'' (p. 31). Saadiah derives this restriction, of which I have found no echo in the halakhic literature,[41] by means of an impressive juxtaposition of similar scriptural texts. The Torah states about the Levites' tasks: ''Each one was given responsibility for his service and porterage [*at the command of the Lord through Moses*]'' (Num. 4:49); in 2 Chronicles, concerning their singing, we read: ''The Asaphite singers were at their stations, [*by command of David*]'' (35:15); and also: ''[*Following the prescription of his father David,* he set up the divisions of the priests for their duties,] and the Levites for their watches, to praise . . .'' (8:14).[42]

In the Munich MS the second half of the second condition—the *melodic* one—and the beginning of the third are missing. Fortunately, most of the lacuna can be supplied from a Genizah fragment published by H. Avenary,[43] so that Saadiah's discussion of the melodic condition has reached us almost intact. It enumerates the six performance instructions he identified in the headings (excluding the instrumental instructions, discussed separately under the third condition) and explains them in terms of contemporary Arabic musical theory. Avenary, as a musicologist, dealt almost exclusively with the instrumental aspects, so I am compelled to tread in a realm where I have no expertise in order to understand Saadiah's arguments about the second condition.

It was clear to Saadiah that the six instructions do not refer to a single aspect of musical performance, and that only two can be explicated simply as the names of melodies (or modes). Consequently, he could not maintain his claim that the singing of the psalms in the Temple was restricted to ''particular melodies/modes *(ʾalḥan)*'' (p. 27) unless he could categorize the musical instructions and demonstrate that they all serve as designations of melodies/modes. To this end he divides them into three pairs, relating to three different aspects: a single *laḥn* or a medley of several; high or low pitch; and the names of two of the *ʾalḥan*. Musicologists who have discussed the section on music at the end of the tenth treatise of *Beliefs and Opinions* conclude that Saadiah used the Arabic term *laḥn*—whose usual meaning is a melody or melodic mode—to designate a rhythmic mode (Arabic *ʾiḳaʿ*; in later Arabic music *maḳām;* Indian *raga*).[44] While the consensus is that the discussion in *Beliefs and Opinions* refers to rhythmic modes, it is rather difficult to know how we should render *laḥn* as used here in the exposition of the second condition. For now we shall circumvent the problem by not translating *laḥn,* keeping in mind its dual meaning.

The discussion of the melodic condition starts by explaining *ʿal nᵉginaṯ* (Ps. 61:1) as an instruction that the psalm be sung ''*entirely* in one *laḥn,* which should not be changed'' (p. 31). The plural directive *bi-nᵉginoṯ* (ibid. 4:1; 6:1; 54:1; 55:1; 67:1; 76:1) he explains as having the contrary meaning:

"it is to be said with many different *ʾalḥan*" (ibid.).[45] I have emphasized the word "entirely," since I believe it shows that Saadiah's meaning was that in any given performance of the psalm one *laḥn* must be used from beginning to end, not that every performance had to use the same *laḥn*. Accordingly, the meaning of the opposite instruction *bi-nᵉginot̲* is that the Levites should change the *laḥn* in the middle of the performance.[46] Such a change is conceivable with regard to both the melody and the rhythmic mode; however, according to Prof. Amnon Shiloach (oral communication), there is no historical evidence for the former possibility, while Saadiah himself praises the blending of various rhythmic modes as the quintessence of musical excellence (*Beliefs*, 10:18; p. 402). Moreover, in *The Epistle on Music of the Ih̲wan al-Safaʾ*, an entire chapter is devoted to "mutations," i.e., the artistic transition from one rhythmic mode to another.[47]

The next two performance instructions are also presented as a pair of contraries, referring to the relative pitch of the notes, a topic also anchored in Arabic musical theory (see *Epistle*, p. 23). Saadiah explains *šir ha-maʿalot̲* (Pss. 120–134) as designating a "high-pitched *laḥn*" (relying on the use of the root *ʿlh* in the sense of raising the voice in 1 Sam. 5:12; Jer. 14:2, and of the noun *maśśaʾ* (literally: something raised) in 1 Chron. 15:22 to describe Chenaniahu's high-pitched singing). *ʿAl ʿalamot̲* (Ps. 46:1) is explained as the opposite of the former, i.e., an instruction to sing "in a small quiet voice." The philological connection of *ʿalamot̲* with lowering the voice, missing from the Munich MS as well as the Genizah fragment, is preserved in the body of the commentary (on Ps. 9:1): "One of the eight *ʾalḥan* was called *ʿalamot̲;* since it is thin and quiet, derived from *neʿelam* (hidden)."[48] Note that in this case Saadiah is not content with explicating the term as an instruction for musical performance (as he did concerning *nᵉginat̲/nᵉginot̲*); he rather asserts that this characteristic is so essential to the *laḥn* that it is actually named *ʿalamot̲* after it. This apparently applies to its opposite *maʿalot̲* as well. In this way he managed to identify two of the *ʾalḥan* used in the Temple. His assertion is not so far-fetched if we recall that the eight Arabic modes have names like "light" *(ḥafif)* and "heavy" *(t̲aḳil)*[49] and that Saadiah was convinced that sacred poetry was based on just eight *ʾalḥan*. This he deduced from the third pair of performance instructions, discussed in the beginning of the Genizah fragment.

The beginning of the first sentence in the Genizah fragment, which discusses the designation *šušan/šošannim* (Ps. 45:1; 60:1; 69:1; 80:1), is missing. We can fill in the gap, however, from the *Tafsir* on the four headings in which it appears: "*bilaḥn julaḳḳab baʾs-sausan*" (in the *laḥn* called *šušan*). Evidently Saadiah could not adduce a direct proof that in biblical times it was customary to call *ʾalḥan* by such picturesque names, for the passage opens with a problematic analogy from the plastic arts: the carvings in the Temple were called *peraḥ šošan* and *maᶜaseh šušan* (1 Kings 7:19, 22, 26). Unlike the first two pairs, this instruction is matched, not by its opposite, but by its parallel: *ᶜal ha-šᵉminit* (Ps. 6:1; 12:1), which indicates that the psalm should be sung in the eighth *laḥn*. Saadiah expands on this in his remark on the reading of Ps. 6: "*ᶜAl ha-šᵉminit* teaches us that the Levites in the Temple had eight *ʾalḥan*, one assigned to each group of them" (p. 61). Here no scriptural proof that *šᵉminit* denotes a *laḥn* (rather than an instrument)[50] is offered; later in the introduction, though, in his discussion of the third condition, he infers this from 1 Chron. 15:21. There is no doubt, however, that for Saadiah the real proof was the astonishing correspondence between the number eight, found in the headings of the psalms, and the eight basic rhythmic modes of Arab musical theory,[51] which he accepted as true in all places and times: "There are altogether eight distinct [rhythmic] modes (*Beliefs*, 10:18; p. 402).[52]

It is only in light of this concordance between revealed truth and the music theory of his age that Saadiah's unequivocal assertion that no more than eight *ʾalḥan* were used in the Temple can be understood. We can see it as strengthening the assumption that in the "second condition" he is referring to the eight rhythmic modes (which he also describes in *Beliefs*) and not to melodies. It may also help us understand Saadiah's motive for trying to discover in the biblical text more families of Temple singers: without Ben and Obed-Edom the Gittite the headings name only six Levite families (Asaph, Ethan, Heman, Jeduthun, the sons of Koraḥ, and [the sons] of Moses); with them, however, there are exactly eight! Although Saadiah did not emphasize this number in his discussion of the "first condition," it seems to be the basis for the strange sentence quoted above from his commentary on Ps. 6:1: "The Levites in the Temple had eight *ʾalḥan*, one assigned to each group of them." Still, it is hard to understand this sentence in its maximum application—as if each family sang only one *laḥn*—since this is explicitly contradicted by the text: two *ʾalḥan (šošannim* and *ᶜalamot)* are assigned to one family (the Koraḥides—45:1 and 46:1), while one *laḥn (ᶜalamot)* is given to two families (Ben [9:1] and the Koraḥides [46:1]). I can only assume that Saadiah was impressed by the agreement between the number of *ʾalḥan* and the number of families, but did not follow through to the ultimate conclusion, since he nowhere asserts that each family was permitted to sing only the *laḥn* assigned to it.

Whatever the case, the Genizah fragment continues in a minimalist vein: the fact that specific terms for *ʾalḥan* are mentioned in the headings proves "that the nation had *ʾalḥan* which they used in the Temple." There is no gap in the passage where the word "eight" could be inserted, as proposed by the editors in their translation[53] (apparently because of the vagueness of the sentence). Thus it seems to me that Saadiah means no more than that it has been shown that there were specific and defined *ʾalḥan* in the Temple. They are clearly compulsory as well, as he goes on to explain: "It is clear to us [that] a psalm designated by one *laḥn* [should not be said] in different [i.e., numerous] *ʾalḥan;*[54] what is [to be said] in a raised voice [should not be said in a lower voice and the low] ered should not be said in a raised voice; thus too the other [*ʾalḥan* shall not be] changed. If someone does change them he has sinned, [as] emerges from the verse 'For the ordinance was by the Lord through His prophets' (2 Chron. 29:25). This shows that they [the *ʾalḥan*] are fixed thus as commanded." As in the first condition, Saadiah has no clear proof that changing the modes is a sin, and must content himself with an analogy, since the above-mentioned verse which he cites refers in fact to musical instruments: "He [Hezekiah] stationed the Levites in the House of the Lord with cymbals and harps and lyres, as David and Gad the king's seer and Nathan the prophet had ordained, for the ordinance was by the Lord through his prophets." Only someone who is already convinced that the melodic condition goes hand in hand with the instrumental condition can see this verse as a proof that the *ʾalḥan* are "fixed as commanded."

The first sentence of the third condition—the *instrumental*—is badly preserved in the Genizah fragment, and roughly six lines are missing from there to the continuation in MS Munich. Saadiah begins the discussion by listing the instruments "with which these psalms are said." According to the reasonable reconstruction of the editors, he first listed the Hebrew names of the instruments, followed by their Arabic translations. Of all this only four Arabic names remain: "*ʿud*, *ṭunbur*, *daff*, and *ṭabl*" (which apparently correspond to *nevel*, *kinnor*, *tof*, and *maḥol*). The Munich MS, resuming after the lacuna, completes the sentence, with a mention of the salutary influence of music upon the prophet Elisha. We cannot be certain, but evidently Saadiah cites this incident in order to infer, from the precise words of the text—"Now then, get me a musician, and as the musician played . . ." (2 Kings 3:15)—that Elisha's request was quite specific: "He requested a player of one[55] of the modes and of one of the instruments" (p. 31). This seems to be the theoretical background for the instrumental condition. He attempts to demonstrate from Scripture the obligatory nature of this condition for the chanting of the psalms in the Temple. This is no simple task, since, according to Saadiah, in the entire Book of Psalms only one heading contains an instrumental designation—ʿal maḥalaṯ (which he renders, in Ps. 53:1, as *biṭubul* "with two-headed drums," and in Ps. 88:1 as *ʾelmuṭabbilin* "drummers on two-headed drums").[56] He must rely, therefore, on the direct and indirect testimony of 1 Chronicles about the relationship between the various Levite families and certain instruments.

He again divides the evidence into three categories; here, though, the classification is by method of inference rather than by the nature of the evidence in the headings. The first category comprises those psalms whose superscription mentions only the name of a Levite, while the instrument is identified by the clear link found in Chronicles between it and the Levite family. Accordingly, cymbals should accompany the singing of all the psalms listed under the names of Asaph (50; 73–83), Ethan (89), and Heman (88), since 1 Chronicles clearly states: "And Asaph sounding cymbals (16:5)"; "the singers Heman, Asaph and Ethan to sound the bronze cymbals" (15:19).

The second category consists of those psalms that require no supplementary information, since the instrument is named in the heading. As mentioned above, this is true only of the two psalms bearing the designation *ʿal maḥalat̠* (53, 88), which Saadiah derives from *maḥol* and identifies that instrument, as accepted in his day, with the *ṭabl,* a large two-headed drum. Why, though, does he not infer from the assignment of one of these psalms (88) to the sons of Koraḥ that the many other psalms associated with this family (42; 44–49; 84; 87; 88) were accompanied by the *maḥol* drum? His silence on this point evidently stems from the ambiguity of the evidence about the Koraḥides, to be noted below.

The third category includes those psalms whose headings provide the name of a Levite family or *laḥn,* while the instrument is identified by its association with the *laḥn* in 1 Chronicles. From the juxtaposition of *nᵉvalim* and *ʿal ʿalamot̠* (15:20) Saadiah deduces that Psalm 9 (whose superscription has *ʿalmut̠ la-ben*) and Psalm 46 ("for the Koraḥides *ʿal ʿalamot̠*") should be accompanied by the *nevel* (which he identifies with the *ʿud*, the short-necked lute). He thus associates the Levite Ben with the *nevel,* and the mode *ʿalamot̠* with the *nevel;* but once again he is silent about the instrument played by the Koraḥides. As we have already seen, they sang certain psalms to the accompaniment of the *maḥol* drum and others to the *nevel,* so that it is impossible to arrive at a clear-cut rule about them.

From the tripartite association of the Levite Obed-Edom, the instrument *kinnorot̠,* and the mode *šᵉminit̠* (1 Chron. 15:21) Saadiah next deduces that psalms whose headings specify the *laḥn šᵉminit̠* (6, 12) or the family designation *ha-gittit̠* (which he interprets as referring to Obed-Edom the Gittite) should be accompanied by the *kinnor* (which he identifies with the *ṭunbur*, the long-necked lute). We can readily understand why he refrained from inferring from the association of Asaph with the mode *šošannim* in Ps. 80:1 that the two other psalms whose headings mention only *šošannim* (60 and 69) should be played by the sons of Asaph on the cymbals: Psalm 45, also "on *šošannim,*" is assigned to the Koraḥides. But I cannot fathom why, given the juxtaposition of Asaph with *nᵉginot̠* (76:1), he did not conclude that the other three psalms in this *laḥn* (54, 55, and 67) should also be played by Asaph on the cymbals. He does not mention 1 Chron. 25:3—"*Jeduthun* on the *kinnor,*" probably because verse 6 reports that Asaph, Jeduthun, and Heman played the *m^eṣiltayyim* (cymbals), *nevel*, and *kinnor.* But if the sons of Asaph and Heman played only the cymbals, as he asserts, then what instruments were used by the sons of Jeduthun to accompany the psalms assigned to them—the *kinnor* or the *nevel?*

We have presented all this in order to show how many constraints limited Saadiah in his attempt to conclude that "what was [ordained to be accompanied] with the *nevel* was not said with the *kinnor,* and what was [ordained to be accompanied] with the *maḥol* was not permitted to be said with the *m^eṣiltayyim*" (p. 32). The indirect testimony from Chronicles permitted him to increase the number of psalms with an identified accompanying instrument from two to twenty,[57] but this is still too narrow a base on which to ground the instrumental condition. The information regarding the musical condition is more substantial and more reliable: twenty-nine explicit designations, and three more inferred. Of both conditions he remarks: "It is possible that for brevity's sake they omitted mention of other instruments and other *ʾalḥan*" (p. 32). In other words, omission does not prove nonexistence, since it is quite likely that Scripture's customary brevity, relying on the Oral Tradition to fill in the gaps, is at work here too (although the tradition on this subject has not reached us). Saadiah concludes his exposition of the third condition by emphasizing its implication, namely, that musical performance of the psalms outside the Temple is strictly forbidden: "In the proper way, it is forbidden to chant [the psalm] with anything [i.e., with any instrument and *laḥn* whatsoever]; only reading and reciting [are permissible]" (p. 32).[58]

The available information about the *temporal* condition is even scantier, since only one heading includes a clear temporal condition: "A song for the Sabbath day" (92:1). To this Saadiah adds the "Psalm of thanksgiving" (100), which he assigns to festivals on the basis of the verse: "With glad shouts and songs of thanksgiving, a multitude keeping festival" (Ps. 42:5[4]). A mere two psalms are insufficient to ground the temporal condition, however, so Saadiah begins his argument with an attempt to prove that "some psalms were said with the daily morning burnt-offering and some were said with the daily evening burnt-offering" (p. 32). He relies on the description of the inaugural ceremony when David placed the Ark of the Convenant in the tent he erected for it after bringing it to Jerusalem (1 Chron. 16). The text there includes a long psalm sung on that occasion, as the verse preceding it testifies: "Then, on that day, David first appointed that thanksgiving be sung to the Lord by Asaph and his kinsmen" (v. 7). The fact that David "divided this psalm in this book [Psalms] into two parts, after making it a single recitation in Chronicles, teaches us that they are [assigned] to two different times'': Psalm 105:1–15 (= 1 Chron. 16:8–22) is to be chanted with the morning sacrifice, while Psalm 96, plus the three verses 136:1 and 106:47–48 (= 1 Chron. 16:23–36a) is to be chanted with the evening sacrifice. Since the end of 1 Chron. 16 notes that Zadok and his sons continued to offer the daily morning and evening burnt-offerings in *Gibeon* (vv. 39–40), Saadiah explains that the Levites in Jerusalem sang at the hour of the daily burnt-offering [*ḳorban tamid*] in Gibeon, as he inferred from the verse: ''[David] left Asaph and his kinsmen there before the Ark of the Convenant of the Lord to minister before the Ark regularly [*tamid*] as each day required'' (v. 37). This proof is found in essence (as pointed out by Zucker, ''Notes,'' p. 228), in *Seder ʿOlam Rabba*, chapter 14; but Saadiah ignores the additional information given there, namely, ''thus they kept saying for forty-three years before the Ark in Zion, until Solomon brought it [the sacrificial altar] to the Temple.'' This explanation is intended to harmonize the information inferred from Scripture about the recitation of Psalms 105 and 96 with the clear testimony of Mishnah Tamid (7,3–4 and see also BT Rosh Hashanah 31a) that while the daily sacrifice was being offered the Levites would chant the psalm for that day. It is most strange that Saadiah supported his theory with a forced proof based on David's temporary arrangement (ignoring the fact that it had nothing whatsoever to do with the singing of the psalms in Solomon's Temple) yet ignored the best proof for the temporal condition—the six psalms of the day chanted in the Temple by the Levites, as enumerated in the Mishnah. The reason is probably rooted in the anti-Karaite nature of the introduction: Saadiah endeavored to bring proofs exclusively from Scripture, to which his adversaries were also committed.[59] Thus he could prove to them as well that the king-prophet who instituted the sacred poetry also ordained the temporal condition even before the Temple was built. But when he winds up the discussion with a sort of apology for the paucity of data—''perhaps there were other times to which particular psalms were assigned, but they were not specified'' (p. 33)—he relies on the Rabbanite reader to complete his sentence: they were not specified in Scripture, but have been handed down by the oral tradition.[60]

The fifth condition—the *local*—specifies that some psalms were limited to specific places: ''it should be said in that place and no other, even though it is also in the Temple'' (p. 33). Saadiah cannot claim support for this in even one psalm heading, and must have recourse to a somewhat remote topic: the description of the distribution by lot of the Levite watches to the four sides of the Temple (1 Chron. 26:14–16). He fails to mention that the passage clearly refers to gatekeepers rather than singers, so that his ''proof'' is at best an analogy. He continues: ''Afterwards [David] stationed the twenty-four divisions of the Levites in each of the four directions, as is said explicitly . . .'' (ibid.),[61] and quotes (with omissions) verses 17–18, where the four directions are again mentioned, in association with the twenty-four divisions of Levites. It is true that in BT Tamid 27a the Amoraʾim suggested that these two verses are the scriptural basis of Mishnah Middoṯ 1,1, concerning the arrangement of the watches in the Temple: ''The Priests guard the Temple in three locations, and the Levites in twenty-one locations.'' It is possible, though, that Saadiah means that according to the plain meaning of the scriptural text another division is described here, related to more than guard duty, since it encompasses all the Levites, both singers and gatekeepers.

Saadiah had no other proof with which to substantiate his original theory that certain psalms were sung in specified places within the Temple. Consequently he passes to a demonstration of a more moderate version of the local condition, which, however, applies to all the psalms: ''The entire book may not be *sung* except in the Temple. [Elsewhere] it can only be *read,* for its use for musical supervision [or encouragement of the service] is restricted to the Temple, as it is said: '[They appointed the Levites from the age of twenty and upward] to supervise (*le-naṣṣeaḥ*) the work of the house of the Lord' (Ezra 3:8)'' (p. 33). Just as the psalms were sung to encourage the builders of the Temple alone, so we must infer from Hezekiah's vow upon his recovery—''we will offer up music (*neginotai*) all the days of our lives at the House of the Lord'' (Isa. 38:20)—that ''the music (*neginot*) is restricted to the Temple'' (p. 33). These two proofs demonstrate that the psalms were sung to encourage the builders of the Temple, and were sung with instrumental accompaniment in the Temple; but they hardly prove that it is forbidden to do so elsewhere. This objection does not apply, though, to Saadiah's next proof: ''Thus all singing is reserved for the Holy Land, since we know that the Babylonians asked the ancestors to sing according to the proper order in exile and they refused'' (ibid.). In the first two proofs Saadiah used the term *ʾl-ḳuds*; Kafih correctly rendered this in its narrowest sense, ''in the Temple,'' since the two quotations from Ezra and Isaiah read ''the house of the Lord.''[62] In the third proof, however, we find instead *bibaladi ʾl-ḳuds* (which Kafih translates ''in the Holy Land''), represented as the opposite of ''alien soil'' (Ps. 137:4). This change in terminology is somewhat perplexing; it seems preferable to translate the term as ''in the Holy City'' (as suggested by Ben-Shammai, ''Review,'' p. 406, based on Saadiah's use of *balad* for ''city'' in the *Tafsir* on Ps. 107:4, 7, 36), in order to eliminate an outright contradiction between two versions of the restriction on singing the psalms—to the Temple or to the entire land of Israel.[63] It could be argued that for Saadiah Psalm 137 does not refer to ''the song of the Lord'' collected in the Book of Psalms, but to other "songs of Zion" whose singing was not restricted so drastically. This is not the case, however, since in his commentary on Ps. 137:4. Saadiah explains: "Because singing to the Lord is not completely forbidden outside the Holy City (*fi baladi ʾl-ḳuds*), in the gloss (*fi ʾt-tafsir*) I added 'the special' and rendered [the verse]: how can we sing the special song of the Lord" (p. 272). In the *Tafsir* on the verse, "on the poplars there we hung up our lyres," he supplied another explanatory phrase—"in a manner of cessation," in order to make it clear that this act was intended to demonstrate that it is forbidden to play the sacred instruments on alien soil, just as it is forbidden to sing the psalms there.

The distinction we have discerned in the fifth condition between all the psalms, whose singing is permitted throughout the Temple, and those few that must be sung in certain parts of it agrees with Saadiah's statement at the beginning of his discussion of the conditions: "With regard to singing there are five conditions; some are applicable to all [the psalms] and others only to some" (pp. 27–28; and see there note 29). Nevertheless, Saadiah attempted to expand the application of the conditions to as many psalms as possible, by inference from explicit to implicit and by pointing out the reasonable possibility that certain conditions applied to additional psalms, but this information was transmitted by oral tradition alone. His endeavor does not pretend to endow the five-fold condition with general validity. For him, even what he does manage to prove is sufficient to provide a firm grounding for his view of the Book of Psalms. The rigorousness of the five conditions was not meant to glorify and exalt the psalms (as claimed by Shunari, *Methods,* p. 16), but to erect the highest possible wall between the two aspects of the Book of Psalms—between its prophetic-didactic and its ritual-hymnal aspects, between the "book of guidance" read everywhere and the "book of praises" sung in the Temple alone. Since the conspicuous ritual aspect of the book could not be gainsaid, he chose to augment its importance and emphasize its authority, thereby unequivocally restricting its use to the Temple service: what we are *commanded* to do only there we are *forbidden* to do anywhere else!

Saadiah returned to this issue in his commentary on Psalm 150; somewhat to our surprise, there he mentions only three conditions: "We say that listening to [the psalms] is permitted under three conditions: particular instruments—those mentioned; particular persons—the Levites; and a particular place—the Temple (*ʾl-ḳuds*). If any one of these three conditions is missing it is forbidden [to listen to the psalms]" (pp. 287–88). What seems to be a narrowing of the conditions is really an expansion thereof; for the omission of the melodic and temporal conditions does not mean that they do not apply to those psalms for which their validity has been proven. Rather, in order to assert a clear definition of a contemporary prohibition on listening to the musical performance of the psalms (and ipso facto performing them) he must set up the minimum basic principles that apply in equal measure to all the psalms. In his introduction Saadiah wanted to prove that the personal condition was valid and exclusive (a psalm assigned to one Levite family could not be sung by another), whereas here he derives from this the more fundamental principle that no psalm could be sung by a non-Levite. This applies to the local and instrumental conditions as well: no psalm may be sung outside the Temple precincts or to the accompaniment of any instrument not mentioned in the body or headings of the psalms.[64] In other words, even if it is impossible to know how, when, and where those psalms whose conditions of performance are not explicitly stated by Scripture were sung, it is clear that sacred poetry may be sung only by consecrated individuals, in the sacred place, and with sacred instruments.

Saadiah's vigorous battle against the Karaite prayer service is clearly reflected in the fact that the concluding words of his Psalms commentary, quoted above, are not phrased as an exegetical-historical pronouncement but as a currently valid prohibition that applies to every Jew. His unequivocal assertion that "if any one of these three conditions is missing it is forbidden [to listen to the psalms]" is meant to make it plain that, as long as the musical performance of the psalms is forbidden, so too are singing and listening to them. This conflation of the three conditions into a single indivisible unit leads to the conclusion that while the Temple lies in ruins any ritual use of the psalms is absolutely forbidden. I have found no basis for this three-fold prohibition in rabbinic texts; it seems to rest entirely upon Saadiah's theory of the special conditions that apply to the "special song." It was mentioned above (note 63) that the karaite Salmon ben Yeruḥam had no trouble agreeing with Saadiah that from Psalm 137 we learn that it is forbidden to sing the psalms to the accompaniment of the sacred instruments outside the Temple; but he did not expand this prohibition to cover singing them without such accompaniment. On the contrary, he cites prooftexts from Psalms itself for the obligation to worship the Lord by singing psalms, in every place ("Sing to the Lord all the earth"—96:1) and in every age ("I shall praise the name of the Lord with song and extol him with my thanksgiving"—69:31; Salmon refers this psalm to exilic times). In the Rabbanite communities, too, there were those who ignored Saadiah's ruling, as can be inferred from Avenary's citations ("Genizah," p. 161) from the travelogues of Benjamin of Tudela and Petaḥia of Regensburg, who visited Saadiah's city of Baghdad in the second half of the twelfth century. Benjamin tells about the dean of a yeshiva who claimed descent from the Koraḥides: "he and his brothers know how to chant the melodies as did the singers who performed [variant reading: the singers and musicians] when the Temple was standing."[65] From Petaḥia's report it is clear that they actually did chant the psalms in this fashion, apparently as part of the prayer service: "There is a youth with a pleasant voice; he sings the psalms in a pleasant voice. On the intermediate days of the festivals they sing psalms with musical instruments, since they have a tradition about which melodies [are to be used]."[66] We see that Saadiah's prohibition was directed, not only against the Karaite pretensions to transform the divine service of the Temple into the Jewish liturgy for all generations, but also against the preservation of certain remnants of the Temple ritual even after the Destruction, a custom that apparently existed in his day as well and which he deemed to be forbidden.[67]

How is Saadiah's strong assertion that the psalms are not prayers and that they may not be sung outside the Temple compatible with the plain fact that many psalms are an integral part of the Rabbanite prayerbook and thus are also included in the *siddur* he himself compiled? Louis Ginzberg discussed this in his edition of a Genizah fragment of an early Karaite *siddur*, wherein he found an echo of Saadiah's statements on the topic, namely: "They say that our ancestors used to pray over their sacrifices with these songs and psalms, and that today we may not pray with these songs until the days to come." Ginzberg attempted to resolve the problem through a rather far-fetched reconstruction of Saadiah's position on the subject, based on his opponents' statements: "I have no doubt that Saadiah's adversaries misrepresented his position, and that he never said that now we may not use David's song in our worship. . . . What he did say was that now we use the Psalms only in the introductory psalms of the Morning Service *(P^e^suḳei d^e^-Zimrah)* and the *Hallel* (Pss. 113–118), while the service proper is in the language and style ordained by the Sages. In the world to come the essence of prayer will be the praises and songs in the Book of Psalms."[68] However, Saadiah's argument in his introduction to Psalms shows that the distinction he drew was not one of prophetic prayers to be said when the Temple stood versus non-prophetic prayers to be said after the Destruction, but of the psalm as a "special song" chanted and performed exclusively in the Temple versus prayer, the means for fulfilling, in ages past as well as in the present, the commandment to "provide yourself with words" (Hos. 14:3).[69] Shunari's proposal that "Saadiah was opposed to the *principle* of using biblical verses in general and Psalms in particular as the *sole* components of the order of prayer" (*Methods*, p. 17, emphasis in original) is incompatible with what Saadiah actually says and does not solve the problem posed by the inclusion of *complete psalms* in the prayerbook, despite Saadiah's declaration that scriptural passages that seem to be prayer are not really so, "since they are juxtaposed with commandments, admonitions, promises, and threats in each and every chapter [i.e., psalm]" (*Siddur*, p. 10).[70]

The starting point for solving the problem must be Saadiah's own words concerning the introductory psalms of the morning service: "Our nation takes it upon themselves to read *(biḳraʾa)* psalms from the Book of the Praises of the Lord (*tasbiḥi ʾlḳuddus*), with two benedictions, before and after them'' (*Siddur*, p. 32). He goes on to explain why a blessing is recited before and after a non-obligatory act: ''They ordained that we do so because the believer makes a blessing for everything that happens to him from his awakening until the time of prayer'' (ibid.). Saying the psalms precedes proper prayer, and thus one does not fulfill the obligation of prayer by reciting them. Voluntarily the Jews have taken upon themselves to *read* psalms as an addition to the required prayer. In the passage on the service for the New Moon, Saadiah carefully distinguishes between ''praying'' the *ʿAmidah* and ''reading'' the *Hallel:* ''We are obligated to *pray* (*nuṣalli*) four prayers (*ṣalawat*) on every New Moon: the evening, morning, additional, and afternoon services. . . . After the morning prayer we *read (jakraʾ)* part of the *Hallel*'' (*Siddur*, p. 128; emphasis added). He also has recourse to this terminology in his remarks on the recitation of Hallel on Passover (p. 153). This distinction between ''prayer'' in the strict sense of the word and the ''reading'' of the psalms fits well with the reiterated distinction in his introduction to Psalms between ''singing'' the psalms in the Temple, to which the five conditions apply strictly, and ''reading'' them, on which there are no restrictions. He repeats this distinction no less than five times: once he uses the Arabic verb *karaʾa* ''to read,'' as in the *siddur* (p. 33 at the bottom), three times the verb *tala* ''to recite'' (pp. 27, 30, 33), and once both verbs side by side: *ʾel-kiraʾa waʾt-tilawa* (p. 32). It seems that this terminological variation is needed to express Saadiah's complex conception of Psalms so that it is permissible not only to read the chapters of the ''book of guidance'' for edification but also to read the psalms of the ''book of praise'' as part of the synagogue liturgy. This is the narrow path that Saadiah attempted to tread—between the absolute rejection of the psalms as prayer and the recognition of their function in the Temple service, and between the absolute ban on their ritual use today and the recognition of their secondary liturgical role in the synagogue. The path is straitened by the polemical constraints that trap Saadiah between the desire to draw a clear distinction between the contents of the book (''commandment and admonition'') and its form (''praise and exaltation''), on the one hand, and the necessity to bridge the gap between them by acknowledging the roles that were and continue to be associated specifically with that form, on the other.

IV. The Exegetical Application: Radical reinterpretation

The first sentence of the next passage in the introduction, which considers the exegetical implications of recognizing the true nature of the book, is a good reflection of the inner tension of Saadiah's theory: ''To believe that it is a book of guidance for human beings, even though it is a book of praises *(kitabu ʾt-tasbiḥ)* and its purpose and goal are commandment and admonition . . .'' (p. 33). The ritual oriented information in the headings having been neutralized via the five conditions, he can return to the main issue and show us how to read the book in light of his radical reinterpretation, which transforms all appeals to the Lord into the Lord's word to man. Saadiah exemplifies this by explicating four passages (131:1; 132:1–2; 51:3; and 39:13), of which the last two are also used as examples in the parallel passage in the short introduction (p. 53). He summarizes this topic with a general methodological principle that can assist the reader of the psalms in identifying the verses that are not to be understood literally: ''Everything that is commandment or admonition, promise, threat, or narrative of the past or future [i.e., the six basic methods of instruction that operate directly] is to be understood literally; everything that is in the language of prayer and spiritual arousal and the like [i.e., the two indirect methods of edification] must be modified [and understood as] the word of the Lord, as we have explained'' (p. 34). It must be emphasized that Saadiah did not adopt this principle as the basis of his *Tafsir,* where he translates literally also the ''prayer and spiritual arousal'' that constitute the bulk of the book. For example, the four passages referred to above, which he used to show how to deviate from the literal meaning, are translated word for word in the *Tafsir.* In his detailed explication of the first four psalms, appended to the introduction as a sort of guide to reading the book, we find a good deal of theology, but no transmutation of prayer into commandment. Saadiah resisted the temptation to impoverish the literary form of the psalms and trade away their stylistic eloquence (which he praised so highly in his remarks on the eighteen rhetorical modes) for a clear but pallid paraphrase.[71] Thus the task of discerning the inner meaning of the psalms was left to the intelligent reader, who must make do with the explanation and guidelines presented in the two introductions, supplemented by some ten short notes scattered throughout the commentary.[72]

In some of these short notes he summarizes the theological message of the psalm (10:1; 139:1); in most, though, he warns against a literal understanding that would cast moral or theological aspersions on the prophet David (boasts about his innocence—17:3; 26:1; 73:1; his desire for revenge against his enemies—69:28; 109:1; complaints against the Lord—79:1). All agree that Psalm 119 is not a prayer, even though almost all its verses are phrased in the first person and in conspicuously personal terms. This is apparently why Saadiah considers it necessary to preface this psalm with a reminder of what he had written in the two introductions: ''This entire psalm is phrased as if spoken by the righteous servant, but the import is the Lord's command to his servants to do everything said in it, so that they may say such words and be just'' (p. 250). Given this transformation of earnest entreaties to be able to follow the just path into commandments to follow it, we can only rejoice that Saadiah refrained from imposing his conception on the *Tafsir* and mentioned it so few times in his commentary. Moreover, his fidelity to the style and format of the Book of Psalms was also expressed in a number of comments in which he relates to a psalm as a prayer or entreaty without the slightest hint that it is forbidden to understand it as ''the words of the servant.'' An example of this is his comment on the beginning of Psalm 43: ''The preceding chapter was a complaint (*šakwa*) about the sufferings of the nation, and this one is thanksgiving for their rescue'' (p. 125).[73] Thus once again we see that while Saadiah's conceptual framework is quite radical, its exegetical application is moderate and careful. Just as the absolute denial of the ritual nature of the psalms in his day left room for their liturgical use in the synagogue, so the total rejection of their devotional nature was not forced upon the reader through the translation and commentary, but presented as an exegetical method that he should apply for himself.

Saadiah next attempts to provide a strong methodological foundation for his exegetical principle by citing parallels from prophecies not found in the Book of Psalms. In the short introduction (p. 53) he had compared the stylistic variation that, in his view, characterizes the psalms with the frequent switches of speaker and person in *Ha'azinu* (Deut. 32:1–42). Here he repeats this comparison, stressing that if we find this in a poem that all agree is the word of the Lord there is clearly no aesthetic or rhetorical defect in varying the mode of expressing the divine word in the Book of Psalms either. He buttresses his argument with a similar analysis of two prophecies by Isaiah and Jeremiah, where such shifts are also found, but whose structural unity testifies, in his view, that they are clearly the word of the Lord. Thus Isa. 33:1–6 begins with a divine warning to the oppressors of his nation, but ''the second verse is placed in the mouth of the people, as if they were praying to the Lord.'' In his view, though, this prayer is really an indirect way of proclaiming the Lord's promise that ''I will have mercy upon all who hope for Me and will help them each morning and be their salvation from all trouble'' (p. 35). Saadiah goes on to explain four more addresses of Isaiah, all of which he explains in a similar fashion as indirect expressions of God's message to his prophet.[74] Even more far-reaching is the proposed interpretation of a prophecy by Jeremiah (17:7–14). He unhesitatingly appends to it the prophet's entreaty, ''Heal me, O Lord, and I shall be healed, save me and I shall be saved, for you are my glory'' (v. 14), as a sort of coda, while detaching it from the rest of Jeremiah's ''personal psalm'' (vv. 15–18). The decisive consideration for Saadiah is the internal unity of the passage; on this ground we are asked to see the petition as merely a rhetorical device intended to express God's word indirectly. This is how the verse sounds in his paraphrase, which purports to convey its true meaning: "I am He who when someone asks Me to heal him—I will heal him, and if he asks for My salvation—I will save him; in Me all who glorify shall be glorified" (p. 36).[75] Only such a drastic exegesis—which identifies request with answer—can convert the prophet's prayer into a prophecy of salvation, and the psalms of David into treatises of commandment and admonition.

The last part of the introduction, in which Saadiah searches, with extreme philological caution, for the principle underlying the arrangement of the individual psalms within the book, stands in sharp contrast to this exegetical passage. Reference to the headings of four psalms that contain biographical-historical information (3, 51, 52, and 54) proves that the order is not chronological. Thus one can assume that the order is related to their use in the Temple and reflects the various conditions regulating the performance of the psalms therein. It may be that the psalms are arranged in accordance with the places where they were sung, their special times, and the Levite families to whom they were assigned. All this is phrased tentatively; still, Saadiah feels a need to sum up with a clear warning: "Any of these explanations about the compilation of the book may be correct, but not definitively so" (p. 38). Saadiah was surely tempted by the opportunity to see the absence of chronological order as indirect proof of his theory of the five conditions, most of which are not made explicit in the text. But his caution induced him to add the warning that this idea is no more than a hypothesis, and it might be better not to rely too much on the correlation between a proof from silence and extremely fragmentary information.

In the absence of certainty another possibility remains—finding a topical connection between the psalms and showing that their order is not related to the ritual aspect of the "book of praise" but to the didactic nature of the "book of guidance." In his detailed commentary on the first four psalms, appended to the long introduction, Saadiah makes a concerted effort to explain the topical connection between each psalm and its predecessor and to elucidate the conceptual and literary logic of their order (pp. 47–49). While he adopts a confident tone—"the link between this fourth psalm and the third is very clear" (p. 49)—he also demands caution of anyone who attempts to apply this principle to the entire book: "If I were to do this for each psalm my book would be much too long. But I have given you a sort of key, which every reader of my book can ponder; he will then be able to understand how the rest of the book is put together, but as a hypothesis and not with certainty" (p. 50). This is followed by a sentence that is incomprehensible in Kafiḥ's translation, and most interesting in Rivlin's version: "This idea is in addition to the three previous ideas about the arrangement" ("Prefaces," p. 427).[76] In other words, the theory of a topical arrangement is separate from that of a ritually determined one, with its three components (the local, temporal, and personal conditions). The two theories cannot be integrated into a unified system applying to the entire Book of Psalms. At most one can say that part of the book is ordered according to one principle and the rest according to the other. It would be more reasonable to choose one of them, but Saadiah did not do so. It seems that by offering both of them to his readers he was declaring that he lacked sufficient information to decide which of them is the principle ordering the book, which, in his view, has two faces, as remote from each other as the distance between hymns of praise and moral exhortation.

V. Polemic and Truth: To what extent is Saadiah's approach to Psalms anchored in his thought?

Having concluded our discussion of Saadiah's unique understanding of the Book of Psalms and the bold arguments employed to endow it with verisimilitude, we ought to inquire to what extent these are anchored in Saadiah's thought, as expounded in his other works. Does his approach to the Book of Psalms deviate from his method of explaining other biblical books to such an extent that we must attribute it to the exigencies of the Karaite controversy? We shall endeavor to answer this question as regards three major issues in which Saadiah's unique approach is particularly evident: the ritual issue—the theory of the five-fold condition; the rhetorical issue—the eighteen modes of expression; and the literary issue—the attribution of all 150 psalms to David.

Lacking a firm foundation in Scripture and the Oral Law, the five conditions, which in his view regulated the singing of the psalms in the Temple, hang by a thread. Not only did Saadiah stretch the few hints in the headings and in Chronicles far beyond the actual text, he wove them together into a single interdependent system. What seems to be at most a performance instruction is presented as a necessary and mandatory condition. This assertion is so far-reaching that it is difficult to believe that it should be attributed solely to his polemical interest in conferring upon the chanting of the psalms in the Temple such an exclusive (and nontransferable) status. Indeed, what we see as assigning disproportionate importance to the precise musical performance of the psalms apparently results from the common medieval concept of music.

For us today the power of a musical creation lies primarily in its aesthetic-expressive aspect, and is thus dependent on its unique qualities as a work of art; but for the savants of the Middle Ages its influence was almost physiological, deriving from its ability to affect the soul through the senses. We stress the beauty of music, which we consider to be a marvel whose wonder stems precisely from its irrationality; they emphasized the utility of music, considered to be a realm of knowledge, whose glory lay in its wondrous integration with the other sciences. As the Faithful Brothers put it: "The musician philosophers limited themselves to four strings for the *ʿud*, no more, no less, so that their productions would be comparable to the natural things, that are under the lunary sphere and in the image of the science of the Creator, may He be exalted" (*Epistle*, p. 43). Accordingly, not only does the ratio among the diameters of the strings correspond with that among the celestial spheres, each of the four strings also parallels one of the four elements, one of the four humors, one of the four cardinal points, one of the four seasons, one of the four ages of man (infancy, childhood, maturity, old age), one of the four powers of the soul (memory, understanding, imagination, attention), one of the four postures of the soul (arrogance, generosity, sadness, humility), and similarly for the powers of the body, ethical traits, flavors, combinations of colors and odors, etc. Thanks to this parallel between the notes of each string and so many components of existence, musical harmony also corresponds to the mathematical harmony at the core of the universe, as Ibn Ezra wrote in his mathematical work, *The Book of Numbers:* "The science of music is a very wonderful science, for its ratios are composed of arithmetical and geometric proportions."[77] Just as the science of music is exceedingly wonderful, so too is the beneficial influence of instrumental music in softening the hearts of worshippers, in encouraging warriors, in healing the sick, in comforting mourners, in stimulating laborers, in rejoicing revelers, and even in taming animals (*Epistle*, p. 17). This power is explained by the fact that the notes produced by a particular string strengthen the powers of the soul that correspond to it, and weaken the others.

From this point we can rely on Saadiah's own words in *Beliefs and Opinions* (10:18), where he uses the "doctrine of the musical ethos" (i.e., the medieval theory of the influence of music on ethical behavior) to support his argument for a way of life that represents a harmonious balance of character traits and activities. He divides the eight rhythmic modes into four categories (of unequal size), characterizes their meters, and indicates which humor (phlegm, blood, choler, or black bile) each category affects and which qualities of the soul (dominance, courage, timidity, happiness or sadness)[78] it stimulates. Now he reaches the crux of the matter: "It is the practice among rulers so to blend these different modes as to harmonize them, the purpose being that the impulses stimulated by hearing these modes may put their souls in the proper disposition for conducting the affairs of the government. It should prevent them from being unfair by evincing either excessive mercy or severity or by showing undue courage or cowardice or either too much or too little cheerfulness and gaiety'' (p. 404). Saadiah wanted to use this intimate relationship between music and human nature to prove the blessing of moderation and the curse of excess; we learn from it how great a power he attributed to a particular rhythmic mode to effect a specific and predictable change in the soul. In his discussion of the instrumental condition in his long introduction to Psalms he mentions that Elisha was consoled for his parting from Elijah and enabled to prophesy by a particular *laḥn* played on a particular instrument (p. 31). The case of Elisha is mentioned only incidentally, but the manner of its presentation points to the theoretical link between the five conditions and the doctrine of the musical ethos. We can broaden this link beyond the instrumental and musical conditions with the aid of what the Faithful Brothers write about music therapy. To relieve the suffering of the sick and even heal them one must not only play melodies opposed to the nature of the illness; ''these melodies are used during the various parts of the day and the night whose nature is opposed to that of the illness and ailments in force . . .'' (*Epistle*, pp. 43–44). This need to consider the changing quality of time is repeated often in the *Epistle* (pp. 16–17, 25, 65),[79] and is supplemented by one reference to the influence of location on the power of music (p. 26). It is not explained how and why places differ, but this is clearly one of the aspects of geographic determinism at the basis of the theory of the seven climates, which was central to the thought of the Faithful Brothers,[80] and which al-Kindi used to explain the uniqueness of the ethnic music of each nation.[81] While there seems to be no direct reference to the climate theory in Saadiah's work,[82] we can assume that Saadiah had no reason to differ with its musical conclusions—the need to match the melody to the special qualities of each place.

Our attempt to reconstruct the musical background of the five-fold condition is still only partial. From Saadiah's own words we have shown that he adopted the doctrine of the musical ethos and used it to explain Elisha's prophesying in a way that could provide scriptural support for the dependence of psychological influence on the proper instrument and melody. Arab scholars of music supplied us with an appropriate foundation for the temporal and local conditions. But we have still found no parallel for the personal condition. While the Faithful Brothers link the unique qualities of ethnic musical traditions to the differences in the natures of different nations (p. 25), this is still remote from making the effect of music depend on the genealogy of its performer. We might say that precisely this condition required no outside reinforcement, since it is much better documented in the scriptural text than any of the other conditions.

It remains to ask how Saadiah explains the role of music in the vocal performance of the psalms in the Temple according to the doctrine of the musical ethos: whose soul was it supposed to influence? Did he see music as an integral part of the praise addressed to the Lord, as in the verse, "You shall sound short blasts on the trumpets, that you may be remembered before the Lord your God" (Num. 10:9)? Or did he perhaps believe that it was intended for the ears and souls of those who thronged to the Temple precincts? The Faithful Brothers often discuss the liturgical and ritual use of music (*Epistle,* pp. 16–17, 39–40, 56–57, 65–67). In this context they describe its basic role as engendering timidity and humility (mainly through a special mode called "the saddening") and turning the soul to the spiritual and exalted. Saadiah shares this general idea that music used in ritual affects man; but for him its use in the Temple was in the opposite direction—to gladden the soul. In his comment on "Praise him with *minnim* and *ᶜugav*" (150:4) he writes: "I derive *minnim* from the word *lᵉ-mino* ['of its kind' (Gen. 1:11)] . . . and therefore translated it [in the *Tafsir*] 'kinds of happiness.' All these kinds [of melodic modes] were used only in the Temple, so that the worshippers would be gladdened by them, as it is said: 'Worship the Lord with gladness' (Ps. 100:2) and the like" (p. 287).[83]

In this impressive fusion of an acceptance of the verities of musicology with its sovereign application to Scripture we have an answer to our question. It seems that Saadiah allowed himself to develop the theory of the five conditions with so little scriptural evidence because of his prior certainty, based on Greco-Arabic music theory, of the essential validity of his concept. It was self-evident that the sacred poetry sung in the Temple in Jerusalem must have been regulated no less strictly than the liturgical or therapeutic music of the Arabs. When the existence of at least four out of the five conditions is taken for granted, minute scriptural hints are more than adequate to prove conclusively that the psalms were sung in Solomon's Temple in accordance with all five of them.

We shall now proceed to the rhetorical issue. This daring theory, according to which the eighteen modes of expression appear in the Book of Psalms for the purpose of edification, seems to shatter the barrier that Saadiah himself erected against the unrestrained detaching of scriptural texts from their plain meaning. As is well known, in order to prevent metaphorization of the commandments and of the verses concerning the resurrection of the dead he attempted to establish clear and objective guidelines for determining when non-literal interpretation (*taᶜwil*) is required. This view of metaphorization has two facets: just as it is forbidden to resort to metaphor whenever it is not absolutely necessary, so is it forbidden to refrain from it when it is clear that the verse cannot be understood literally. Why does Scripture use so much figurative language and so much concrete description of the spiritual and abstract? Saadiah asks this question in *Beliefs and*

Opinions, in his discussion of anthropomorphism. His answer there is quite similar to his statements in the two introductions about the stylistic richness of the psalms, whose benefit (enhancing the power of persuasion) is greater than its damage (concealing the true nature of the psalms):

> And if someone were to ask: "But what advantage is there in this extension of meaning that is practiced by language and that is calculated only to throw us into doubt? Would it not have done better if it had restricted itself to expressions of unequivocal meaning and thus have enabled us to dispense with the burden of discovering the correct interpretation?" My answer should be that, if language were to restrict itself to just one term, its employment would be very much curtailed and it would be impossible to express by means of it any more than a small portion of what we aim to convey. It therefore preferred rather to extend its use of words so as to transmit every meaning, relying for the correct interpretation upon reason and acquaintance with the texts of Scripture and with history [here *ʾal-ʾaṯar* means Tradition]. Were we, in our effort to give an account of God, to make use only of expressions that are literally true, it would be necessary for us to desist from speaking of Him as one that hears and sees and pities and wills to the point where there would be nothing left for us to affirm except the fact of His existence. (*Beliefs*, II, 10, p. 117)

There is no escape from rhetorical richness and variety; while reason (which dismisses the absurd), comparison of verses (which prevents contradictions and mistakes), and tradition (which supplements our information) must serve as a barrier against error. Saadiah's confidence that understanding the Book of Psalms as a book of edification does not violate the sound rules of *taʾwil* is based not only on proofs drawn from reason, Scripture, and tradition that the psalms are not prayers, but also on his rhetorical theory, according to which edification must shun direct discourse and rely on many stylistic stratagems for the sake of persuasiveness.

Had Saadiah limited this assertion to the Book of Psalms, we could say that his purpose is merely to confute the Karaites. But this is not the case. On the contrary, the perplexing gap between the content of a scriptural book and its stylistic form is a topic discussed in all the extant introductions to his commentaries. According to Saadiah's didactic theory, edification is the purpose, not only of the Pentateuch, but of Proverbs and Job as well;[84] he must perforce explain why so much in these two books of guidance is not "commandment and admonition." In his introduction to the *Tafsir* on the Pentateuch he deals with this question (which resembles in its assumptions the famous question of R. Isaac cited by Rashi at the beginning of his commentary on the Pentateuch). As in the introductions to Psalms his answer is based on his theory of persuasion: to be effective, guidance cannot employ only commandments and prohibitions; often it must incorporate promises of bounty and threats of chastisement, on the one hand, and narrative exemplification of the rewards granted to the good and punishment inflicted on the wicked, on the other. For him this is a pedagogical-literary rule with general validity, which necessarily applies to the Bible as well, since its purpose is to guide the lives of men in the language of men. "Therefore the Wise One, may He be blessed, saw fit to give us His book, meant for edification of humanity, and included in it these three methods of persuasion, so that it should suit its aim most perfectly" (Saadiah, *Commentaries*, p. 159).[85]

Saadiah called his long commentary to Proverbs "The Quest for Wisdom" (*Proverbs*, p. 22); the extended introduction is devoted primarily to bridging between this name—which refers to the purpose of the biblical book—and the name "Proverbs"—which refers to its literary form. Here too the question of the frequent use of concretion appears, and here too his answer is that the style has to be adapted to the needs and limitations of the readers: "For them, sense perception is more accessible and simpler than reason. . . . Consequently they need parables, so as to draw an analogy between the demands of reason with the demands of the senses. . . . This is the advantage of parables—that they bring the decisions of reason closer to nature and show their resemblance to sense perceptions. In consequence it was decided to call this book 'Proverbs,' since it contains these [literary] kinds . . ." (p. 13). He bases this stylistic theory on a detailed psychological analysis of the relationship between "nature" and "reason" in the human psyche and upon an exhaustive study of the process of learning and the intellectual faculties implicated therein. This is followed by a detailed discussion of the rhetoric of Proverbs, with a list of twelve rhetorical modes he discerned in the book. As in the Pentateuch and Psalms these include command and admonition, reward and punishment, and narrative, as well as such devices as comparison of the unknown to the known and the phrasing of a conditional statement as a general truth. Proverbs also contains "language that might be thought of as narrative, but is actually command or admonition" (p. 20). This is an exact parallel to what Saadiah found in Psalms—"the speech of the servant" must be understood as the "command of the master." Since the discrepancy between the form of Proverbs and its content is not as great as in Psalms, the need to deviate from the literal meaning is also much less.[86] But the basic exegetical approach is one and the same, and helps explain how Saadiah could arrive at his revolutionary concept of the psalms.

The introduction to the commentary on Job, too, is primarily dedicated to preventing an erroneous interpretation of the book. "Many of the nation see this book as if it were arcane and hard to explain and understand" (*Job*,

p. 19). The difficulties responsible for this are then enumerated: (1) the identity of the Adversary and the meaning of his incitement; (2) the justification of the sufferings of the righteous prophet; (3) elucidation of the theological stance of each participant in the debate; (4) revealing the arguments stripped of their stylistic embellishments; (5) the elucidation of the doctrine latent in God's final response. Since these difficulties are essentially theological rather than linguistic or stylistic, the harm that he attempts to avert is in the realm of beliefs and opinions: "I saw that these five topics are difficult for many people, to the point that many attribute a variety of sins to Job and the others, so that this book, contrary to the original purpose of the Wise One, who intended it to be a book for the edification of His servants, became a stumbling block" (p. 20).[87] In other words, this is by no means a book of protest and complaint against heaven, as many think, but the "book of justification" (p. 19)—i.e., a theodicy—intended to prepare men's hearts to accept suffering with humility and discipline (see pp. 15 and 28) and to learn that injustice must not be attributed to the Lord, since "none of these five men made such an assertion" (p. 16). In the body of the commentary he shows that the Adversary was human (pp. 26–29), and systematically softens Job's complaints, turning them into questions and entreaties.[88] This could be done with the usual exegetical methods, without drastic deviations from the plain meaning, based on a specific rhetorical theory.

We see, then, that in his introductions to Psalms, Proverbs, and Job, Saadiah was fighting against "outward" approaches that focus on form and miss the content. With Job, intellectual and theological arguments were adequate to prevent mistaken interpretation. This was not the case with Proverbs and Psalms, so he provided his readers with a sophisticated rhetorical theory to guide them to the correct exegesis. But whereas in the introduction to Proverbs he merely justifies the use of the parable (whose Hebrew name, *mašal*, shows that it points to something beyond itself), in the introduction to Psalms he attempts to prove that the liturgical form of this prophetic book does not accord with the content, since the roles of speaker and listener have been reversed. This claim is so novel and daring that no later exegete could accept it. In Saadiah's eyes, however, it was merely expanding the scope of his rhetorical theory to encompass another biblical book.

We still have to examine the attribution of each and every psalm to David against the background of Saadiah's approach to the question of authorship of other scriptural books. As mentioned above, Saadiah utterly rejects the Talmudic view that David's name is attached to the Book of Psalms because he collected his own psalms along with those by other poets. In accordance with this approach we might expect Saadiah to prefer the view that Moses himself, and not Joshua, wrote the last eight verses of the Pentateuch (see BT Baba Baṯra 15a). Yet the Karaite Jacob al-Kirkisani reports that, according to Saadiah, the Lord dictated the Torah to Moses word for word "from 'In the beginning' through 'but you shall not cross there' (Deut. 34:4)."[89] It seems that this view is more typical of Saadiah, for despite his view of Proverbs as a prophetic book in all respects[90] he does not hesitate to say that its last two chapters are not by Solomon:

> The plain meaning (*basiṭu ʾn-nasḳ*), which our sages call "*pᵉšuto šel miḳraʾ*," is that there was a man named Agur, and his teacher was named Ithiel; the student received these sayings that follow from his teacher, just as the school of Hezekiah received the previous sayings [i.e., chaps. 25–29) in the name of Solomon, and Lemuel received from his mother the admonition with which she admonished him (chap. 31), and it was well known among the people.[91] It is also possible to say that Agur, Ithiel, and Lemuel are pseudonyms for Solomon. . . . [Here Saadiah presents more convincing etymologies for these names than those found in *Šir ha-Širim Rabba*, 1,10.] But although all of these explanations are correct and possible, to me it seems preferable to leave the Hebrew names in their present state (*biḥaliha*); thus I do not assert that they are all Solomon's and leave the verse as it is (*biʾajn*) [or *bibasiṯ*, "simply"), namely, that Agur was the disciple of Ithiel his teacher, who taught him what he retold. (Comm. on 30:1; *Proverbs*, pp. 244–45)

In this deliberation between the theological advantages of the first view versus the philological advantages of the second he clearly, albeit cautiously, decides in favor of the literal interpretation. We may infer that he had no serious problem with the idea that a number of authors (evidently all prophets) contributed to a single book, which is nevertheless commonly ascribed to the most important among them.

The same cautious approach is adopted with Job. In the introduction to his commentary Saadiah raises that book to prophetic status,[92] although in his gloss on 1:1 he admits that there are no unequivocal scriptural proofs of when and where "the prophet Job" and his friends lived or of the identity of the person who committed their speeches to writing (as Solomon has done for the first twenty-four chapters of Proverbs):

> I say that all that [those who believe that Job was an Israelite and even a priest] rely on is no more than inference. . . . I have found it sufficient to rely in this [matter] on the tradition that he was not an Israelite, nor were his friends, as I have already explained their lineage. As for when Job lived, even though it is not made explicit by Scripture, our Tradition states that he lived during the time that our ancestors were in Egypt, and that it was Moses who wrote this book at God's behest and gave it to the nation. This is the correct answer. . . . (pp. 23–24)

Hence we can conclude that on the issue of authorship Saadiah's stance on the Book of Psalms deviates significantly from his general method. His ideas about other scriptural books could help us to understand his approach to the ritual and rhetorical issues in Psalms; but they are of no avail with regard to the literary issue, where his method is inconsistent. To Psalms he took a maximalist approach, while for the other two books, not subject to the tug-of-war of the Karaite controversy, he took a minimalist stance, in one case basing himself on tradition (Job) and in the other deviating from it (Proverbs). Evidently Saadiah attributed greater importance to seeing the Book of Psalms as the vision of a single prophet, since unity of authorship strengthens the validity of his rejection of the book's ostensible nature as a collection of prayers and hymns.

It was typical of Saadiah to adopt an extreme position in response to the needs of his age. He was acutely aware of his personal responsibility to stand in the breach, because of the special talents the Lord had bestowed upon him. As he wrote in *Sefer ha-Galui*: "God does not deny His nation a scholar in every generation, whom He instructs and enlightens, so that he in turn may instruct and teach them and their situation be ameliorated. The reason for this is what I have seen in my soul of the grace that [God] has granted me and them" (p. 154, lines 2–6; see also p. 158, lines 7–13). He wrote in a similar vein in his introduction to *Beliefs and Opinions*, in a direct reference to his polemical endeavors:

> My soul was stirred on account of our people, the children of Israel. For I saw in this age of mine many believers whose belief was not pure and whose convictions were not sound, whilst many of the deniers of the faith boasted of their corruption and looked down upon the devotees of truth although they were themselves in error. I saw, furthermore, men who were sunk, as it were, in seas of doubt and overwhelmed by waves of confusion and there was no diver to bring them up from the depths nor a swimmer who might take hold of their hands and carry them above. But inasmuch as my Lord had granted me some knowledge by which I might come to their assistance, . . . I thought that it was my duty to help them therewith. . . . Something of this order was also expressed by the saint: "The Lord God hath given me the tongue of them that are taught, that I should know to sustain with words him that is weary . . ." (Isa. 50:4), although I do acknowledge that my learning is far from perfect. . . . (pp. 7–8)[93]

Such awareness of the danger and of the obligation to save his brethren from drowning in a sea of doubt explains the strength of polemical and apologetic considerations in his exegetical decisions. Ibn Ezra showed great understanding of Saadiah's attitude even while vehemently opposing its consequences. In his commentary on Gen. 2:11 he warns against the uncritical acceptance of the translations of *realia* terms in the *Tafsir:*

> There is no proof that *Pišon* is the Nile; and he translated *ḥawilah* according to his own needs, since he had no tradition [to rely on]. He did the same with clans, countries, animals, birds, and stones. Perhaps he saw them in a dream. In some cases he was wrong, as I shall explain in the appropriate places. We shall therefore not depend on his dreams. Perhaps he did so for the glory of God—for he translated the Torah into the Arabic language and alphabet—so that the Arabs would not say that there are commandments we do not understand.

This supposition—that Saadiah was apprehensive that the dominant religion would make nefarious use of any Jewish admission of limited understanding of the Bible—is in and of itself not reasonable;[94] but the allusion to Saadiah's responsibility to the community is no doubt correct. A similar case involves Ibn Ezra's assumption of the motives underlying Saadiah's vigorous opposition, in his commentary on Job, to the view of the Adversary as an angel. Dunash ben Labrat had contested this in his *Criticism of Saadiah* (p. 21, §67), and Ibn Ezra sided with him: "I have offered a proof that supports R. Adonim [i.e., Dunash] in my commentary on Job. Perhaps the Gaon [Saadiah] said this to keep the masses from understanding the truth, for only one out of a thousand understands the mystery, thus it is difficult for him to say that angels of the Lord are adversaries" (*Defense,* §63, emended according to MS Parma 314). Ibn Ezra himself, in his commentary on Job 1:6, offers an astrological solution to the problem of the Adversary's revolt; consequently his assumption that Saadiah preferred to conceal this answer in a book designed for a mass readership rests on the shaky foundation of attributing his own views to his great predecessor. Nevertheless, the great importance that Saadiah attached to theological and apologetic considerations is evident in the impassioned language in his own commentary on this verse: "I have heard about a heretic who disagreed with this to the extent that he imagined that this Adversary is an angel. . . . He omitted no defect or corruption in his descriptions of the angels, . . . and invented all these strange things because of his lack of knowledge of the meaning of the words in the language" (*Job,* p. 28).

In his introduction to *Sefer ha-Galui* Saadiah explains his concern with messianic computation in the fifth part of the book (which is not extant) as due to "the great need of the nation for such things" (p. 154, lines 6–9). He reckons the end of days in a separate section of *Beliefs and Opinions* (8:3; pp. 295–98) and in his commentary on Dan. 8:14 (ed. Kafiḥ, pp. 155–57). While in *Beliefs and Opinions* he merely resolves the contradictions in the Book of Daniel concerning the date of the redemption, in the commentary he gives a definite date for the coming of the Messiah. Poznanski found that according to Saadiah's explanation of the dates revealed to Daniel the Messiah was to have come in 968 CE (i.e., in the near future, which Saadiah would have lived to see had he survived to the age of eighty-six).[95] The boldness is commensurate with the potential danger of frustrated expectations; so it is not surprising that someone like Ibn Ezra would express himself so acerbically in his short commentary on Daniel: "His entire commentary on Daniel follows his desires, and he does not pursue the meaning of the words, as I shall show" (ed. Matthews, p. 3). When one of Saadiah's glosses is tendentious instead of philological, it is invariably wrong (according to Ibn Ezra): "In general I will say that Saadiah's four explanations for 'two thousand three hundred' (Dan. 8:14) and for 'time, times' (12:7), and for the two last verses of the book (12:11–12)—all is vanity, and their time has passed many years ago!" (ed. Matthews, p. 6). In contrast, Maimonides treated this issue with great understanding, and presented it as an extraordinary measure taken with supreme consideration for the needs of the age:

> As for R. Saadiah's Messianic calculations, there are extenuating circumstances for them though he knew they were disallowed. For the Jews of his time were perplexed and misguided. The Divine religion might well nigh have disappeared had he not encouraged the pusillanimous and diffused, disseminated and propagated by word of mouth and pen a knowledge of its underlying principles. He believed in all earnestness that by means of the Messianic calculations, he would inspire the masses with hope for the truth. Verily all his deeds were for the sake of heaven. Consequently, in view of the probity of his motives, which we have disclosed, one must not decry him for his Messianic computations. (*Epistle to Yemen*, Hebrew, p. 65; English, pp. xii–xiii)

"The nation's needs" have many aspects; one of them was the great perplexity caused by the Karaites' attacks on the Oral Law. One of the main issues in this fierce controversy, whose implications were manifold for the Jewish way of life, was the question of the sanctification of the New Moon. The Karaites claimed that this could be done only by actual observation, since calendrical reckoning has no scriptural basis. Saadiah took an extreme stance on this issue also, as is well explained by Israel Davidsohn:

> It is known that Saadiah, because he wished to defend sanctification of the New Moon by reckoning, exaggerated, and said that calendrical reckoning was revealed at Sinai, and that already in the days of the Mishnah they would reckon the New Moon calendrically, and that the postponements for those days on which it should not fall were already in force. Salmon ben Yeruham brings scores of proofs from Scripture and the Talmud against this. Indeed he is correct, for not only the Karaites opposed this view, but

several Rabbanite scholars as well. (Introduction to Salmon, *Wars of the Lord*, pp. 14–15)[96]

Following the same method, Saadiah adopted an extreme position in the controversy over the nature and status of the Book of Psalms, with the same result: the Karaites had no trouble refuting his claims (as we shall see in the following chapter), and the Rabbanite scholars too rejected his bold view. Except for the theory of the five conditions, of which we find a weak echo in Yefet ben ᶜAli's commentary and a stronger one in Ibn Ezra's introduction to the First Recension. Saadiah's basic approach to the Book of Psalms left no mark on Jewish exegesis.

Notes to Chapter 1

1. In his long introduction (Saadiah, *Psalms*, p. 37) Saadiah refers to "what others have already written by way of commentaries (in Arabic: *min tafsir*) on this book"; but evidently Abraham Ibn Ezra was already unfamiliar with these translation-commentaries, which had been shunted aside and overshadowed by Saadiah's great exegetical achievement. Fragments of a Hebrew commentary on the Book of Psalms by the ninth-century Karaite Daniel al-Kumissi are extant (Al-Kumissi, "Fragments"), but I have found no real echoes that could prove Saadiah's acquaintance with this commentary in the latter's explanations of those psalms.

2. Saadiah is not mentioned at all in Ibn Ezra's introduction to his standard commentary, while in the introduction to the fragmentary commentary his name appears four times in the "Fourth Enquiry," where Ibn Ezra demurs from Saadiah's method of linking the psalms with one another and from three of his explanations of musical terms found in the headings.

3. The two introductions have twice been translated into Hebrew—by Rivlin in 1942 (Rivlin, "Prefaces"), and in 1966 by Kafih, who also reedited the original Arabic and printed it alongside his Hebrew translation (Saadiah, *Psalms*). M. Zucker wrote a critical review of the text and translation of the introductionspresented in this edition (Zucker, "Notes"). A Genizah fragment from the Cambridge collection, which fills in most of the extensive lacuna in the long introduction (Saadiah, *Psalms*, p. 31, note 72), has been published by H. Avenary, accompanied by an English translation and a musicological discussion (see: Avenary, "Genizah"). Y. Shunary discusses both introductions in the second and third chapters of his dissertation (see: Shunary, *Methods*). Moshe Sokolow translated the long introduction into English: see M. Sokolow, "Saadiah Gaon's Prolegomenon to Psalms," *Proc. Am. Acad. for Jewish Research* 51 (1984), pp. 131–74.

4. See the description of the manuscript in J. Aumer, *Die arabischen Handschriften der K. Hof-und Staatsbibliothek in München* (Munich, 1899), p. 76, and Saadiah, *Psalms*, p. 14. Because of its inclusion among the Arabic MSS in the

Munich library, the Institute of Microfilms of Hebrew Manuscripts does not have a photocopy of the Munich MS; hence I was unable to examine it. S. Eppenstein, who published the Arabic original of the two introductions in *Zikkaron le-Abraham Elijahu* [Harkavy Memorial Volume] (St. Petersburg, 1908), pp. 135–60, printed the long one and then the short one, followed by the extensive commentary to Psalms 1–4. He does not explain this deviation from the order found in the MS, nor give any reason for separating the long introduction from the commentary on the four psalms, which clearly belongs with it. Apparently this is a consequence of his assumption that "the short preface is a summary of the long one."

5. Kafiḥ, too, associates the short introduction with the *Tafsir,* and emphasizes that it contains "no allusion or reference to the long commentary" (p. 10). He takes the long introduction to be an independent work, apparently because the translation included in it is not the same as the translation referred to by the commentary. In my view, however, these differences are better explained as resulting from the different exegetical needs of the introduction and the commentary; this solution is better than leaving the long commentary with an introduction of only a few lines—as Kafih's view does (see: Saadiah, *Psalms,* p. 54). Shunary's contention (*Methods*, chapter two, note 1), that there is no justification for talking about a "third introduction" and hence these lines are actually the beginning of the long commentary on Psalm 1, is persuasive.

6. BT Baba Batra 15a; *Midrash Tehillim*, 1; *Šir Ha-Širim Rabba* 4,4; etc.

7. On the contrary, it is most difficult to reconcile Saadiah's claim with the explicit rhetorical differentiation reflected in the Talmudic controversy over the first-person speaker of the psalms: "The sages taught: all the songs and praises which David said in the Book of Psalms, R. Eliezer says, concerning himself he said them; R. Joshua says, concerning the community he said them; the Rabbis say, some concern the community and some are said about himself; the ones formulated in the singular concern himself, the ones said in the plural concern the community" (BT Pesaḥim 117a).

8. See Y. Rosenthal, "History of sectarianism at the time of Saadiah," *Horeb* vol. 9, no. 17–18 (spring 1946), pp. 21–37 (Heb.); Zucker, *Translation*, pp. 12–142.

9. Confirmation that Saadiah calls the Karaites *baʿaḍun min ʾummatina* is found in his long commentary on Genesis, where he refers to them as follows: "There are those among them who think it possible to argue against tradition by saying that part of the nation (*baʿaḍu ʾl-ʾumma*) denies it" (Saadiah, *Genesis:* Arabic p. 17, Hebrew p. 190).

10. In accordance with this identification of those who err Zucker translates the verb *jatawahhamun* as "who uphold the false belief" and the noun *ʾelmuwahhim* as "the false belief."

11. Saadiah, *ʾEśśa Mešali*, ed. B. M. Lewin (Jerusalem, 1943), p. 42, lines 22–36.

12. Saadiah, *Siddur,* p. 10. I have followed Zucker's interpretation of the passage, which seems more accurate and reasonable than Joel's. See also B. M. Lewin's opinion in his introduction to *ʾEśśa Mešali*, p. 9, and S. Abramson, "A New Fragment of the book *ʾEśśa Mešali,*" *Tarbiz* 32 (1963), pp. 166–67. Both compare the passage in *ʾEśśa Mešali* with a longer section in Saadiah's *The Obligation of Prayer* (printed as an introduction to the *Siddur,* pp. 9–10). There Saadiah argues that "the speech of servant to his Master must be different from the speech of the Master to his servant," and cites various prooftexts from the Pentateuch and Psalms to show that the latter consists of commands, admonitions, promises, and threats. His conclusion is: "But the servant cannot address his Master with these kinds of words, because he would be rebelling against Him were he to command, prohibit, promise, and threaten Him. . . . Therefore the Lord commanded worshippers to select the sort of words that are suitable for a servant coming before his master, as it is said: 'Provide yourself with words' (Hos. 14:3)." This prooftext from Hosea is adduced in *ʾEśśa Mešali* as well (lines 22–24): "Our God commanded us: provide yourself with words / of supplication spoken by you / as from [a servant] to the lord of the realm."

13. Even the passages cited from Karaite works given by Shunari in note 28 use the terminology "the prayers of the prophets" and "the words of the prophets"; on this topic see further below.

14. The assumption that Saadiah presented the Karaite view inaccurately is supported by his statement that "they imagine that this book was said by David the prophet," while Al-Kumissi, Salmon, and Yefet, not unlike the Talmudic Sages, maintained that some of the psalms were composed by other prophets.

15. Ibn Ezra considers the possibility of prophetic prayer in his two introductions (see below, Chapter Four), while Maimonides characterizes the nature of the prophetic inspiration under which the psalms were composed as the second degree of prophecy, "which consists in the fact that an individual finds that a certain thing has descended upon him and that another force has come upon him and has made him speak; so that he talks in wise sayings, *in words of praise,* in useful admonitory dicta, or concerning governmental or divine matters—and all this while he is awake and his senses function as usual. Such an individual is said to *speak through the Holy Spirit*. It is through this kind of *Holy Spirit* that David composed Psalms, and Solomon Proverbs and Ecclesiastes and Song of Songs" (*Guide*, part II, Chapter 45, p. 398).

16. Published by Mann, "Karaite Commentaries," p. 474. In the extant fragments of Daniel al-Kumissi's Psalms commentary (on Pss. 17, 73–82; see: Al-Kumissi, "Fragments") he does not deal with this issue; nevertheless it is quite clear that the commentary is securely based on the assumption that the authors of the psalms were prophets, whose prophetic prayers relate primarily to the present exile and the future redemption. Wieder deals at length with this aspect of Daniel al-Kumissi's exegetical approach to Psalms ("Qumran," pp. 103–104; *Scrolls,* pp. 119–202).

17. One can infer from the limited information about the laws of prayer in the extant fragments of Anan's *Book of the Commandments* that the early Karaite prayerbook upheld the strict exclusivity of biblical prayer, and only for the blessings on food the verses are accompanied by a paraphrase. See: J. Mann, "Anan's Liturgy and his Half-Yearly Cycle of the Reading of the Law," *Journal of Jewish Lore and Philosophy,* 1 (1919), pp. 329–53, and compare Wieder, "Qumran," pp. 112–13. Also in the introduction to an early Karaite prayerbook, fragments of which as well as parts of the text were published by L. Ginzberg (*Ginzei Schechter,* New York, 1929, pp. 435–42), the call is heard "Let us return to the prayers of the prophets as recorded in the Pentateuch and Prophets and Writings," as well as the demand to cease praying in rhymed *piyyuṭim* (pp. 439–40). See Wieder's remarks on this topic, "Qumran," pp. 275–77.

18. In his commentary on the Minor Prophets, too, Al-Kumissi attributes the sufferings of the exile to the sin of perversion or substitution *(ḥilluf).* See his remarks on Hosea 5:10 and 13:2. Only the first page of Saadiah's Hebrew polemic against Al-Kumissi survives; nonetheless, we can surmise that he dealt with the charge of perversion of the commandments in general, and perhaps with the substitution of prayers in particular. In any event, in his opening lines, when Saadiah discusses Al-Kumissi's halakhic treatise, he repays the compliment in kind and calls him "the fabricator" (Schechter, *Saadyana,* §13, pp. 41–42).

19. Kirkisani is cited here on the basis of A. Scheiber, "Siddur," p. 27. Scheiber also quotes the Arabic original (*Kitab uʾul-ʾanwar waʾalmaraḳib*, ed. L. Nemoy, vol. 1 [New York, 1939], pp. 15–16) and notes that Kirkisani has slightly misquoted his prooftext, which reads "to praise the Lord."

20. See A. Scheiber, "Siddur," p. 35; S. Asaph, "From the Order of Prayer in Palestine" (Heb.), *Dinaburg Festschrift* (Jerusalem, 1949), pp. 123–24.

21. *Kitab uʾl-anwar waʾlmaraḳib*, vol. 3 (New York, 1941), p. 608; cited according to Scheiber, "Siddur," p. 28.

22. In *On the Source of the Revealed Precepts*, whose fragments were published and translated by Zucker ("Fragments," pp. 405–406), Saadiah alludes to seven arguments he had previously raised against this principle of "national consensus," and adds five arguments against the illogical use the Karaites made of it. As we shall see below, however, he himself had recourse to the *ʾiǵmaʿ* to prove David's authorship of all the psalms.

23. This tenet is clearly presented in *The Garden of Eden* by the Karaite scholar Aaron ben Elijah of Nicomedia (d. 1369): "David instituted these praises and thanksgivings, which all who wished to pray sang and recited, as it is said: 'In the words of David and Asaph the seer' (2 Chron. 29:30). . . . All these were instituted by King David, the Messiah of the Lord of Jacob and the pleasant singer of Israel, composed and made available [to satisfy] *the needs of every seeker.* Proof of this is the psalm, 'O God, heathens have entered Your domain' (79:1), which is intended for the exiles, and many similar psalms." (Gozlow, 1866, p. 71a, col. 1).

24. Conjectural emendation proposed by B. M. Lewin, *Ozar ha-Geonim*, Tractate Berakot, vol. 1 (Haifa, 1928), p. 142.

25. A. E. Harkavy, "R. Pinkas Head of the Academy" (Heb.), *Ha-Zofeh le-ha-Magid*, vol. 23, no. 45 (19 Nov. 1879), pp. 358–59. It has been re-edited by Nemoy, *Kitab u'l-anwar wa'lmarakib*, vol. 3, p. 609.

26. S. Poznanski, *The Karaite Literary Opponents of Saadiah Gaon* (London, 1908), p. 10 (repr. in P. Birnbaum, ed., *Karaite Studies* [New York, 1971], p. 140). I. Davidson (*Mahzor Yannai* [New York, 1919], English introduction, p. xliii, n. 87) also offers without demurral Harkavy's identification of the anonymous polemicist with Saadiah; whereas B. Klar (critical review of Saadiah's *Siddur, Kiryat Sefer* 18 [1941], p. 345) and S. Abramson ("A New Fragment," *Tarbiz* 32 [1963), p. 167) feel that the matter requires further study.

27. See the introduction to Saadiah's long commentary on Genesis (Arabic pp. 13–15; Hebrew pp. 181–84). See also Halkin ("From the introduction," pp. 152–53) who provides a Hebrew translation of Saadiah's proofs for the necessity of tradition, as cited by Kirkisani in *Kitab u'l-anwar.* In *The Origin of the Revealed Precepts* (Zucker, "Fragments," p. 404) Saadiah gives a stylistic proof as well: The allusive language of the Pentateuch clearly refers to what was revealed orally to Moses. To exemplify this he cites the allusion to the duty of prayer—"He is your praise" (Deut. 10:21)—which necessarily refers to known prayers.

28. The bitter intra-Karaite controversy on the issue of supplementing prayer with *piyyuṭim* was described and adjudicated in the middle of the fourteenth century by Aaron ben Elijah of Nicomedia (*The Garden of Eden,* p. 71a, col. 2), and again by Elijah ben Moses Bashyachi, the great fifteenth-century Karaite authority (*ʾAddereṯ ʾEliyyahu* [Odessa, 1870], p. 97b, cols. 1–2). Both authorities decided that *piyyuṭim* were permissible in prayer.

29. This is *The Obligation of Prayer,* an independent work appended to the *Siddur* as a sort of long introduction. See Joel's remarks in his introduction to Saadiah's *Siddur,* p. 42, n. 3; and note 12 above.

30. In *The Obligation of Prayer* Saadiah enumerated no fewer than twelve reasons (of which only three or four have come down to us) for the excellence of the number eighteen (with reference to the nominal eighteen benedictions in the daily *ʿAmidah*). He emphasized that "in the days of our ancestors," too, there were eighteen benedictions, but instead of the benedictions 'Who gathers in the remnants of his nation' and 'Rebuilder of Jerusalem,' "they used to request that the kingdom endure and that they vanquish their enemies, according to the needs of each generation" (*Siddur*, p. 6). Thus the exilic background of some parts of the liturgy is no argument against the antiquity of the prayerbook.

31. In his *Beliefs and Opinions* (III, 3; p. 145), Saadiah asks why a prophetic tradition is necessary for the rational precepts as well, and begins his answer with the example of the commandment of prayer: "Reason calls for gratitude to God for

His favors, but does not define how this gratitude is to be expressed, nor at what time, nor with what content. Consequently we had need of messengers who defined it and designated it as 'prayer,' and assigned it set times, a particular *formulation*, and a specific posture and orientation.'' Saadiah says almost exactly the same thing in *The Obligation of Prayer*, in a newly discovered fragment recently published by Zucker (''Fragment,'' p. 34): ''The *messengers* and *tradition* [!] came and defined it, called it 'prayer,' and established set times, *a particular text*, a specific orientation, and a specific posture.'' To this should be compared: ''One hundred and twenty elders, among them several prophets, composed the Eighteen Benedictions'' (BT Megillah 17b).

32. The *Tafsir*'s rendering of these verses (Ps. 68:27; 71:14; 106:2) shows clearly that Saadiah did not understand them as referring to the composition of new religious poetry.

33. In 2 Sam. 24:9 their number is given as only 800,000. In *Beliefs and Opinions* (III, 10; p. 174) Saadiah explained this contradiction by hypothesizing that the difference between the two figures represents the size of David's standing army. It is astonishing that in this demographic argument Saadiah quite ignored the additional half-million strong contingent from Judah, mentioned in the second half of the verse cited from 1 Chronicles. Perhaps he was dazzled by the round number—1,100,000—and by the fact that it parallels the 1,100,000 talents of gold and silver consecrated by David, discussed immediately afterwards.

34. This was the approach taken by many exegetes, from the Karaites Al-Kumissi (see note 16 above), Salmon, and Yefet (see the following chapter) through Abraham Ibn Ezra (in his two introductions to Psalms) and David Kimhi (in his introduction to Psalms).

35. Perhaps Saadiah saw fit, in light of the unequivocal evidence of the ancient prayer recited by all, to interpret the *baraiṯa* on the authorship of Psalms (BT Baba Baṯra 14b) in accordance with the technique of *ta'wil* (a method of nonliteral exegesis borrowed from Arab commentators), or denigrated it to the status of one possible exegetical opinion. In any case, he had no qualms about disagreeing with the *baraiṯa* also on Moses' inclusion among the ten elders and referred Psalm 90, with absolute certainty, to Moses' descendants, as explained below.

36. Compare the statement in *Sifra* (''Vayikra'' 1), on the verse ''The Lord called unto Moses and spoke unto him'' (Lev. 1:1): ''unto him—to exclude Aaron. R. Judah ben Beteira said: The Torah includes 13 statements made to Moses and Aaron, and 13 corresponding exclusions. This comes to teach us that they were not said to Aaron, but to Moses for him to say to Aaron.'' (ed. M. Friedmann [Breslau, 1915], pp. 33–34). See also *Sifre* (''Koraḥ,'' §117) (ed. M. Friedmann [Vienna, 1867], p. 37a); *Meḵilta* (''Bo'' 1) (ed. Horowitz and Rabin [Breslau, 1930], p. 1. Kafih (p. 28, n. 41) points out that R. Abraham the son of Maimonides, in his gloss on Exod. 7:1 (*Commentary on Genesis and Exodus*, ed. E. Wiesenberg [London, 1958], pp. 246–47) quotes Saadiah's remarks on this topic from his (lost) long commentary on the Torah. See also his gloss on Exod. 6:13 (same page), where

R. Abraham attests that Onkelous too did not translate those verses literally: "And the Lord spoke with Moses and to Aaron" (this is the version in Sperber edition). Cf. his commentary on Exod. 20:1 (pp. 314–15). Thus on this point there was a substantial consensus (nevertheless Ibn Ezra did not subscribe to it, see his long commentary to Exod. 7:7, 12:1, 31:18; Lev. 10:8).

37. Steadfast to his theory that none of Psalms antedates David, Saadiah must stress that the songs of praise recited during the consecration of the Tabernacle in the wilderness are not those found in the Book of Psalms. See his fragmentary commentary on Leviticus, published and translated by Zucker ("Saadiah's Commentary," p. 337): " 'When all the people saw it they shouted for joy' (Lev. 9:24) means that they recited praises, even though [the text] does not specify what they were. . . ."

38. In the *Tafsir* Saadiah does not translate this verse literally; in his commentary there he explains that a literal translation is impossible because many prayers found in the rest of Psalms are explicitly attributed to David. In his view, then, the verse can be adduced to prove that Psalm 72 was written by David (and not by Solomon) even if understood as he translates it: "when the prayers of David son of Jesse will be fulfilled."

39. Here only four restrictions (what Saadiah calls "conditions") of the "special song" are enumerated; later, though, five are listed. Evidently a scribal error, due to homoeoteleuton, resulted in the omission of "at a particular time." Since, however, the order of the conditions here does not correspond with the detailed discussion following, the original location of these words cannot be determined.

40. Ibn Ezra was willing to accept the idea that *ha-gittiṯ* referred to the name of a family (commentary on Ps. 8:1), but rejected out of hand that *ben* could be a proper name (ibid. 9:1). See below, pp. 244–248.

41. In *Ba-midbar Rabba* ("Bamidbar" 5:1) it is deduced from Num. 4:18–19 that in the Tabernacle Aaron and his sons were required to divide the holy vessels among the Levite porters, in order to prevent potentially disastrous quarrels among them. In BT ʿAraḵin 11b, Num. 3:10 and 18:3 are cited to prove that a gatekeeper who sings is punishable by death; others hold that the action is prohibited, but not a capital offense (Maimonides rules that the penalty is less severe—death by God's hand [*Mishneh Torah*, *The Laws of the Temple Vessels* 3:11). Not only do these sources fail to expand this prohibition to the realm of vocal and instrumental music; in Mishnah ʿAraḵin 2,4 the Sages disagreed about who stood on the platform and played the flute while the Levites were singing. R. Meir stated: servants of the Priests; R. Yosi: Israelites whose daughters married Priests; and R. Ḥaninah: Levites. Maimonides (ibid., *halakhah* 3) accepts R. Yosi's opinion that some of the musicians were Israelites of traceable lineage. It is clear, however, that Saadiah decided in favor of R. Ḥaninah, since he considered that the prohibition on exchanging tasks also applied to the assignment of musical instruments to the various Levite families, as will be explained below. The plain meaning of 1 Chron. 15:16, 19–22;

16:5, 42; and 2 Chron. 7:6 seems to support the theory that instrumental music was the province of the Levites. This was also the understanding (or testimony) of Josephus (*Antiquities*, VII, 12, 3) and the opinion of Rashi (comm. on Hab. 3:19), Ibn Ezra (introduction of the First Recension on Psalms, lines 18–19), and David Kimḥi (comm. on Ps. 4:1).

42. In MS Munich these verses are quoted without the bracketed words; we have inserted them since they provide the essential proof (as was seen by Rivlin, "Prefaces," p. 410, n. 134).

43. See Avenary, "Genizah," pp. 146–47 and 152–53. In the following discussion I occasionally depart from the English translation done by N. Allony and A. Shiloah for Avenary.

44. See Farmer, *Saadiah*, pp. 14, 31–35, and 68–69; and cf. Werner-Sonne, "The Philosophy," pp. 300–306. Among Arabic writers, too, the term *laḥn* is used in both senses; see "Epistle," pp. 58–59.

45. Ibn Ezra twice cites this explanation by Saadiah of *bi-n^eginot̲* anonymously: "The meaning of *bi-n^eginot̲* is a song with two melodies" (comm. on Ps. 4:1); "*la-m^enaṣṣeaḥ bi-n^eginot̲*—with different melodies" (ibid. 76:1).

46. On this topic Yefet ben ʿAli uses the same terminology as Saadiah; his unambiguous statements in his commentary on Ps. 67:1 (see below, p. 87) strengthen the interpretation presented here. Further support can be found in Zunz, *Poetry*, p. 116, where (although with reference to a later period) he reports the existence of Rabbanite and Karaite manuscripts with the note "another melody" in the middle of a *piyyuṭ*.

47. In the latter half of the tenth century a large encyclopedia called *The Epistles of the Faithful Brothers* was composed in Baghdad. It comprises fifty-two "epistles," of which one is devoted to music theory. See the chapter on mutations in Shiloah's English translation (*Epistle*, pp. 64–65). Farmer (*Saadiah*, pp. 88–89) quotes a similar passage, "Concerning the Method of Modulations from (one) Rhythm to (another) Rhythm" from *The Epistle on the Various Branches of Music* by the great Arabic philospher Yaʿqub al-Kindi, who lived in Baghdad in the second half of the ninth century. Saadiah composed *Beliefs and Opinions* in Baghdad in 935; there is great similarity between his description of the eight modes and the parallel description by Al-Kindi (see Farmer, *Saadiah*, pp. 12–26).

48. Ibn Ezra's introduction of the First Recension permits reconstruction of more of the lacuna—Saadiah's reliance on the correlation between the high-pitched *laḥn* designated *maʿalot* and the relative brevity of the fifteen psalms labeled *širei ha-maʿalot̲:* "The Gaon said that [*ha-maʿalot̲*] is the opposite of *ʿal ʿalamot̲* (46:1), because this [psalm] is to be sung in a loud and high voice, which is why these psalms are short" (lines 154–55 discussed below, p. 224).

49. See the description of the rhythmic modes given by Al-Kindi (Farmer, *Saadiah*, pp. 17–26) and by the "Faithful Brothers" (*Epistle*, pp. 58–60).

50. Compare: "R. Judah son of R. Ilai said: How many strings are there on a *kinnor*? Seven, as it is said: 'Seven times each day I praise you' (Ps. 119:164). But in the days of the Messiah—eight, as it is said: 'For the leader on the *šᵉminiṯ*' (12:1); and in the world to come it will have ten, as it is said: 'with a ten-stringed harp' (92:4)" (*Midrash Tehillim,* Ps. 81, par. 9). Similarly, the *Targum* on Ps. 6:1 reads: "on an eight-stringed lyre."

51. In addition to the reference given in note 49 above, see E. Werner, "The Origin of the Eight Modes of Music (Octoechos)," *HUCA* 21 (1948), pp. 211–55. Werner shows that the strong link between the number eight and music dates at least to the beginning of the first millennium BCE in Mesopotamia, and that the system of eight modes—documented in all Near Eastern cultures—did not develop from empirical observation of the actual number used by performers, which was generally larger, but from an abstract conception derived from cosmological-calendrical- arithmetic considerations. We find that the "Faithful Brothers" gave high praise to "the excellence of the number eight," relying on arguments from arithmetic (eight is the first cube), astronomy (the harmonious proportion between the diameters of the celestial spheres and those of the earth and air is based on eight), astrology (the eight aspects created by the respective positions of the planets), poetics (the eight meters of Arabic poetry), cosmology (the eight elementary qualities in nature: warm-wet; cold-dry; cold-wet; warm-dry), etc. (*Epistle,* pp. 45–47).

52. At the end of the chapter on the eight rhythmic modes, the "Faithful Brothers" point out that their description relates only to Arab music, and not to the rhythms of other nations, such as Persia, Byzantium, and Greece. But they immediately add that there are universal musical principles, since their declared intention was to achieve a universal musical theory (see *Epistle*, p. 60, and pp. 26 and 48). Saadiah's firm belief that Israelite music of the biblical period had eight rhythmic modes is reflected not only in *Beliefs and Opinions* and in the commentary on Psalms, but in his own poetry as well. In a *piyyuṭ* for the weekly portion *Šᵉmini* (M. Zulay, *Saadiah's Poetry,* p. 154) he writes: "You chose of the eight cymbals the melody *ʿal ha-šᵉminiṯ*," which the editor glosses: of the eight melodies used in the Temple (here represented by the cymbals), *ʿal ha-šᵉminiṯ* is the most excellent. Zulay cites a parallel assertion of the superiority of the eighth melody from Judah al-Ḥarizi's *Taḥkemoni* (Book XVIII; ed. Y. Toporowsky [Tel-Aviv 1952], p. 183). Werner-Sonne ("The Philosophy," pp. 551–52) cites a parallel from the section on music in *Ginzei Ha-meleḵ* by Isaac Ibn Latif (thirteenth century, Spain); Neubauer ("The Titles," p. 36) quotes Tanḥum Yerushalmi's Arabic commentary on Ps. 6:1, which expresses the same opinion, albeit with some reservations.

53. Avenary ("Genizah," p. 152) adds the word "eight" twice: in the sentence under discussion, which appears in lines 5–6 of the MS and is completely preserved (aside from a blurring of the word *ʾalḥan*, which leaves no room for an insertion); the second addition not only relies squarely on the previous insertion, but is itself not reasonable since it vitiates the logical structure of the argument (as explained below).

54. The translation and explanation of this sentence are based on Saadiah's use here of the same terminology as used above to note the opposite of the designation "in one *laḥn*." At the beginning of the discussion of the second condition he writes, *biʾalḥan kaṯiratu [ʾt]taḫalluf* (= in many different *ʾalḥan*); here, *[bi]ʾalḥan muḫtalifa* (= in different *ʾalḥan*). Clearly, here too the reference is to singing the psalm in a combination of *ʾalḥan*, not to exchanging them (as Avenary renders it).

55. Arabic *bibaʿḍi ʾl-ʾalḥan*. Rivlin and Kafih's translation, "of some of the *leḥanim*" blurs, to my mind, Saadiah's meaning.

56. Saadiah did not try to solve this problem by explaining the enigmatic words found in the headings as names of instruments. We have already encountered his glosses on *ha-gittiṯ*, *šᵉminiṯ*, and *ʿalamoṯ*. His explanations of the other words glossed by at least one other exegete as the names of instruments are as follows: *nᵉḥiloṯ* (5:1) is a description of the singers "who entreat [*mᵉḥalim*] the Lord"; *šiggayon* (7:1) is "a poem requesting victory" (according to the subject of the psalm): *ʾayyeleṯ ha-šaḥar* (22:1) means "at sunrise" (literally, the strengthening of the morning, from Hebrew *ʾeyal*, "strength"); *maśkil* (32:1) designates a psalm whose "purpose is to teach people wisdom," i.e., a didactic poem (Hebrew *maśkil* 'makes wise'); *yᵉdidoṯ* (45:1) is "a description of the qualities of lovers of the Lord" (Hebrew *yᵉdid*; "friend" or "lover"); *yonaṯ ʾelem rᵉḥoḳim* (56:1) "concerns assistance for the distant communities"; *ʾeduṯ* (60:1) is "for the community" (Hebrew *ʿedah* 'congregation'). A helpful though incomplete survey of interpretations of the headings, from the Septuagint to Menaḥem Meiri, is found in Neubauer, "Titles," pp. 33–57.

57. This number also includes Psalm 88, whose heading caused him many problems. Two families of Levites, playing on different instruments, are mentioned there: The sons of Koraḥ are explicitly said to play the *maḥalaṯ*, while Saadiah inferred from 1 Chron. 15:19 that Heman played only the *mᵉṣiltayyim*. The solution is found, according to him, in the word *lᵉ-ʿannoṯ*, which he explained in his commentary on 88:1 as derived from "response," and so translated it in the *Tafsir:* "And the sons of Heman the Ezrahite answered responsively." Thus the psalm was chanted by two groups of Levites, who sang in turn while playing different instruments.

58. This sentence is hopelessly corrupted in the translations by Rivlin and Kafih, since they translated *wabaʾl-huda* at the beginning as "quietly." However, it should be understood as meaning "in the proper way" (in the religious sense; my thanks to Prof. Michael Schwartz for his important remark on this point).

59. Not so Ibn Ezra, who, not subject to the heavy Karaite pressure that Saadiah faced, could base the temporal condition on the heading "A Psalm, a song for the Sabbath day" and on the rabbinic tradition: "The Sages, their memory for a blessing, handed down which song the Levites used to say in the Temple on each day" ("First Recension," lines 23–24). The Septuagint includes temporal indications not only in the heading of the psalm for the Sabbath (92) but also in those of

four additional psalms (24, 48, 93, and 94), which agree with the designations in the Mishnah.

60. Saadiah refers to the temporal condition at the end of the introduction as well (p. 38). There he mentions, aside from those psalms said on the Sabbath and holidays, a special psalm for the New Moon. This is apparently an example of a temporal condition whose source is in the Oral Law: see BT Sukkah 54b and tractate *Sof^erim* 17,11. His statement about specific psalms for the holidays may refer to the list of psalms for the holidays preserved in *Sof^erim* 18, 2–3.

61. In the Arabic original the first word in the sentence is *thumma*, rendered by Kafih as "and so" and by Rivlin as "afterwards." I prefer Rivlin's version, since it emphasizes that according to Saadiah two separate activities are described, as explained below.

62. Saadiah calls the Temple both *baitu ʾl-maḳdas* (*Beliefs and Opinions*, VIII, 8; pp. 254–56, several times) and *ʾl-ḳuds* (ibid., VIII, 9; p. 259; *Siddur*, p. 2).

63. Salmon ben Yeruḥam refers to Saadiah's claim in the introduction to his commentary on Psalms (see next chapter); it is clear from his text that he had Saadiah's introduction in front of him. He too uses the term *ʾl-ḳuds* once, but later twice explicitly writes "the House of the Lord" (in Hebrew!). According to Salmon, only performance with instrumental accompaniment, as in the Temple, is forbidden outside its precincts. As proof he offers a verse that Saadiah could have used for the local condition: "All these were under the charge of their father for the singing in the House of the Lord, to the accompaniment of cymbals, harps, and lyres, for the service of the House of God" (1 Chron. 25:6).

64. Saadiah even inverts this principle and rules that, just as it is forbidden to sing these psalms with other instruments, so too "one may not use [these instruments] to sing praises except to the Lord himself, and to no other" (p. 288). He offers no proof for this double prohibition; we may surmise that he derived it analogically from the biblical strictures regarding the exclusive sacred use of the oil of consecration and the incense (Exod. 30:31–33 and 37–38). Saadiah was forced to use the names of contemporary musical instruments to translate the name of those mentioned in the psalms, but when a verse speaks of performance in the Temple he specifies in the *Tafsir* that a special instrument is meant: e.g., *ʾal maḥalaṯ* (53:1) as *biṭubul fiʾl-ḳuds*, "with the Temple drums" (see also on 57:9 and 150:3). Kafih (Saadiah, "Psalms," pp. 105, 212) and Avenary ("Genizah," pp. 155–58) emphasize that Saadiah was very inconsistent in rendering the biblical musical instruments into Arabic. Avenary (p. 158) seems to be correct when he attributes this lack of precision to Saadiah's fundamental method, according to which performance on these instruments was permissable only in the Temple, so that their precise identification can be left to the messianic era.

65. *The Itinerary of Rabbi Benjamin of Tudela*, edited and translated into English by M. N. Adler (London, 1907), p. 39.

66. *Die Rundreise des R. Petachjah aus Regensburg*, edited and translated into German by L. Gruenhut (Jerusalem and Frankfurt a.M., 1904–1905), p. 24.

67. In the introduction to his *Siddur* (pp. 10–11) Saadiah reports that his shock at "the neglect, additions, and omissions" in the prayer rites in the Jewish communities he had visited was his prime motivation for compiling the book.

68. L. Ginzberg, *Ginzei Schechter*, vol. 2 (New York, 1929), pp. 435–42.

69. See Saadiah, *Siddur*, pp. 9–10; cf. Saadiah Gaon, *Sefer ha-Misvoth* [The Book of Commandments], with a commentary by Yeruham Fischel Perla, Part 1 (Warsaw, 1914). The commandment of prayer is listed as the second positive commandment: "The Lord your God you shall fear, and Him you *shall worship*—in *prayer*" (p. 32). See also the discussion on the source of the obligation in the commentary, pp. 54b ff. See also Saadiah, *Psalms*, p. 43, n. 62. Compare further Salmon ben Yeruḥam's statement (*Milḥamot ʾAdonai*, p. 48, lines 70–73) with Saadiah's remarks in the introduction to his long commentary on Genesis (Arabic p. 14; Hebrew p. 183), and with the reply by one of Saadiah's students to Salmon ben Yeruḥam (Halkin, "Introduction," p. 157).

70. This definitive pronouncement is based on the literary principle of the compositional unity of any work. This principle is so evident to him that he uses it as a reliable yardstick for detecting spurious additions to the text of the prayers. For example: "I have banned the recitation of whatever negates the main intention; as for whatever does not negate it, I have nonetheless noted that it has no basis in the tradition" (*Siddur*, p. 11); similarly: "As for those who add, in the prayer for rain, 'and make it for your nation a year of redemption and salvation,' if they say so it is harmful, since they transfer the prayer from sustenance to redemption, and the mention of the year becomes secondary" (p. 22). See also p. 37, n. 6. And compare J. Heinemann, "Saadiah Gaon's Attitude to Changes in the Text of the Prayers" (Hebr.), *Bar Ilan* 1 (1963), pp. 220–25.

71. There are good reasons for the three exceptions to this rule: (a) In the *Tafsir* on 91:1 he translates "He who dwells in the shelter of the Most High" as a direct address: "you who dwell in the shelter of the Most High"; in the next verse he renders "I say to the Lord: my refuge and my fortress" as: "I say to you in the name of the Lord, Who is my refuge and my fortress . . . that He will save you." This changes the direct address to the Lord into an announcement in his name; but the reason for this change is the difficulty in distinguishing among the different speaking voices in the psalm. It is not clear who says the first verse; in the second verse the Lord is apparently addressed; but in the third it is clear that he is being discussed. No doubt this difficulty is why Ibn Ezra adopted Saadiah's interpretation of these two verses (including the analogy from Exod. 14:3, which provides a philological basis for understanding "say to" in the sense of "say about"). (b) In both the appendix to the introduction (p. 49) and the commentary on 4:4[3] (p. 59) he notes that in the *Tafsir* he changed the first person pronoun in the verse—"The Lord hears when I call to him" to the third person—"when he calls to him." The reason given, however, is not the general rule stated in the introduction (which would have him make similar modifications in vv. 1–3), but something specific to this verse: the need to make the second half of the verse match the third person reference in the first half ("Know that the Lord singles out the faithful for Himself"). (c) In the commentary on Ps. 22:2 (pp. 87–88) he notes that in the *Tafsir* he altered "Why

have You abandoned me'' to ''Do not abandon me'' so as to make it more suitable to the context (we might add: also in order to remove a complaint against the Lord; cf. pp. 67, 189, 215). In any case the supplication remains one.

72. It is interesting to compare this restraint with his method in translating those terms that he perceived as mandating a nonliteral rendering because, as they stand, they contradict the senses, reason, a biblical statement, or a rabbinic tradition (see *Beliefs and Opinions*, VII, 2 [pp. 265–67]; Introduction to the long commentary on Genesis [Arabic pp. 17–18; Hebrew pp. 191–92]; Zucker, *Translation*, pp. 229–32). As a rule he translated nonliterally only when there was a danger of error or misunderstanding, but even in such cases there is a discernible effort to maintain the form of the verse (cf. Zucker, *Translation*, p. 266, n. 109*). His remark on Ps. 5:2(1) is illuminating: ''As for 'hear' (v. 4[3]), 'hearken' (v. 3[2]), and 'give ear' (v. 2[1]), when said with reference to the Lord, all the terms that are common usage in Arabic I have left as is, and whatever is not I have changed'' (pp. 59–60). Here the text is clearly a prayer, but Saadiah is concerned only about the problem of anthropomorphism, and explains that as long as these verbs can be translated directly into Arabic he sees no need to deviate from the plain meaning. We learn that in this matter too Saadiah relied on his readers' intelligence, albeit to a lesser extent, given the theological dangers of a misunderstanding.

73. See also his commentary on the following verses: 28:3; 30:7; 39:5; 44:1; 66:18; 68:1; 115:1.

74. Just how forced this interpretation is can be discerned by a comparison with Ibn Ezra's commentary on these verses. For him the prophet is the speaker throughout the prophecy; in vv. 2–3 he is presenting the future prayer of the righteous of the nation, as he hears it with his prophetic ear.

75. Ibn Ezra's commentary on Jeremiah is not extant, but he refers to Jer. 17.14 in his commentary on Ps. 12:4 (see p. 197).

76. See Shunari (''Methods,'' p. 25, n. 15), who enumerates the advantages of Rivlin's rendering of this sentence.

77. *Sefer Ha-Mispar—Das Buch der Zahl*, ed. and tr. into German by Moritz Silberberg (Frankfurt a.M., 1895; repr. Jerusalem, 1970), chap. 6 (Hebrew p. 46; German p. 48). See also the remarks on Gen. 4:21 in his two commentaries on Genesis.

78. The attribution of opposing influences—sometimes happiness and sometimes sadness—to the modes that affect black bile is not clear. Farmer (*Saadiah*, pp. 36–37) relates that in the same context Al-Kindi writes ''sometimes happiness and sometimes joy,'' and surmises that the text of *Beliefs and Opinions* is corrupt.

79. Avicenna (980–1037), too, demands that one adapt the melody to the hour, and enumerates the twelve modes that correspond to the twelve hours of the day.

See: H. G. Farmer, *A History of Arabian Music to the XIIIth Century* (London, 1929 [1973]), p. 197.

80. See: F. Dietrici, *Die Propaedeutik der Araber im zehnten Jahrhundert* (Berlin, 1865 [repr. Hildesheim, 1969], pp. 98–99); cf. A. Altmann, "The climate theory of Yehuda Halevi" (Hebr.), *Melilah* 1 (1944), pp. 1–17, esp. pp. 6–8.

81. See A. Shiloah's introduction to the *Epistle,* p. 8.

82. So states Altmann, in the article cited above (note 80), p. 11. In N. Allony's article, "*Sefer Ha-ʾegron vis-à-vis the ʿArabijja*" (Hebr.), *Shazar Jubilee Volume* (Jerusalem, 1973), pp. 465–74, the climate theory, which was one of the basic principles of the *ʿarabijja*, is not mentioned.

83. A. Shiloaḥ, in his article "Shem Tov ibn Yosef Falaquera's sources for the chapter on music in his *Ha-Mebakkeš*" (Hebr.), *Proceedings of the Fourth World Congress of Jewish Studies*, vol. 2 (Jerusalem, 1968), pp. 373–77, proved that the dialogue on music in this Hebrew work by the poet Ibn Falaquera (Spain, thirteenth century) is based almost entirely on the *Epistle on Music of the Faithful Brothers.* Falaquera adopts the Muslim view that the role of liturgical music is to "depress the heart until the hearer changes direction and repents his sins and returns from them" (p. 376). However, when he attempts to add a Jewish coloration to the dialogue the charm of scriptural rhetoric introduces the opposite notion here too. The "Seeker" addresses the "Musician" as follows: "You, my master, who serve [variant reading: who gladden] the Lord and people with all [or: with instruments of] song . . ." (ibid.). The incorporation of Judg. 9:13 lends credence to the reading "who gladdens."

84. This also applies to Isaiah, as we learn from the name of his commentary: *kitabu ʾl-istaṣlaḥ*, "the book of preparation." This name is mentioned in the passage from the introduction to Saadiah's commentary, published by Schechter from an extremely damaged Genizah fragment (*Saadyana,* p. 55). Cf. Saadiah, *Proverbs,* p. 8, note 1.

85. He returns to this briefly in *Beliefs and Opinions* (III, 6; p. 155). There too his statement is phrased as a rule with general validity: "When we examine all the books written by the prophets and the scholars of all peoples [!], however great their number might be, we discover that they all embrace no more than three basic themes. The first in rank is that of commandment and prohibition. . . . The second theme is reward and punishment. . . . The third [theme consists of] an account of the men that lived virtuously in the various countries of the world and were, therefore, successful, as well as of those who dealt corruptly in them and perished as a result. The interests of human well-being [probably *ʾistaṣlaḥ* here means 'guidance'] can be served completely only by a combination of these three [themes]." Only parts of Saadiah's long commentary on the Pentateuch survive. It seems most likely that, in addition to the topic of metaphorical language, the rhetorical issue was discussed there as well.

86. Nonetheless he interprets Prov. 31:10–31 as "a parable about the good woman, whom every wise and upright man resembles" (*Proverbs*, p. 268), since "for every verse that the sage [Solomon] said about the qualities of the woman, the wise and upright person has similar traits" (ibid., p. 269).

87. Kafiḥ (p. 20, n. 1) remarks that Saadiah is apparently alluding to the rabbinic statements in BT Baba Batra 16a, where strong criticism of Job is expressed. Still, we would do better to assume that the many to whom the Book of Job brought harm instead of aid were contemporaries of Saadiah. See also Saadiah's sharp polemic against a sectarian who thought that the Adversary was an angel (p. 28).

88. Thus, for example, he renders "yet I will defend my ways to His face" (13:15) as "in all my needs I will turn to Him," defending in the commentary this translation (p. 90).

89. See Halkin, "Introduction," p. 152, who translated the passage from the Arabic text of *Kitab uʾl-anwar* (ed. Nemoy, vol. II, §14 [= Saadiah, *Genesis*, Arabic p. 15, Hebrew pp. 185–86]). Kirkisani's own view on the question of the last eight verses is different: in the introduction to his "Book of Gardens" (Nemoy, *Anthology*, p. 60) he states that Moses wrote the Torah from beginning to end (see Ben-Shammai, "Review," p. 403).

90. As he states in his introduction to Proverbs (pp. 10–11): "Therefore the Wise One, may He be exalted, put into writing (*ʾan jarsuma fihi*) a book in the language of the sage Solomon son of David. . . ." In *Sefer ha-Galui* (p. 162, lines 11–12) Saadiah mentions Proverbs, Ecclesiastes, and Esther as examples of prophetic works; in the Arabic introduction to his *Ha-ʾegron* (p. 149, line 11) he attributes to "the prophets" passages taken from Proverbs.

91. Saadiah found it difficult to accept the idea that the sayings of Lemuel originated with a woman. Hence he emphasizes here, and in greater detail in his remarks on 31:1, that his teachings "were not received exclusively from this woman; rather it must be that a group among the people transmitted them faithfully, but Lemuel attributed them to the last one from whom he heard it . . ." (p. 264).

92. Saadiah, *Job*, p. 16; "Afterwards [the Lord] recorded for us the history of one of the righteous men whom He tested and who stood up to the test; He praised him for this and promised him eternal joy in the next world and in this world gave him all that he hoped for; this man is the prophet Job." Similarly (ibid., p. 19): "Therefore the Wise One, may He be exalted, recorded their words for us and set them up as an example so that we might learn a lesson from them and discipline ourselves."

93. Zucker, *Translation*, p. 8, n. 19, provides additional references on this topic, along with parallels from both rabbinic sources and Muslim writings.

94. Zucker (*Translation*, p. 284, n. 3) claims that it is still unclear whether the *Tafsir* was originally written in Hebrew or Arabic characters, and adds that Saadiah did not hesitate to admit his inability to translate with certainty the names of the birds in Lev. 11:13 (see Saadiah, *Commentaries*, p. 188).

95. Poznanski, ''Saadiah,'' especially p. 517. Malter (''Messianic Computation,'' pp. 53–56), however, raised doubts concerning the authenticity of a passage in Saadiah's commentary on Dan. 8:14 which served as the basis for Poznanski's computations, suggesting that it was an interpolation by a learned scribe, who sought to clarify Saadiah's reckoning. He also admits, though (pp. 58–59), that Saadiah wanted to show that the messianic end was near, and that even if his starting-point is not made explicit it clearly dates to the short interregnum between the destruction of the First Temple and the construction of the Second.

96. Davidsohn documents this statement in notes 81–82. Here a short passage from Ibn Ezra's long discussion of the issue will suffice: ''What Saadiah said—that they relied on calendrical reckoning—is not true, for in the Mishnah as well as the Talmud there are proofs that Passover actually came out on Monday, Wednesday, or Friday [which contradicts the rabbinic rule]'' (comm. on Lev. 23:3).

2

The Karaite Approach: The Psalms as Mandatory Prophetic Prayers

In the tenth century three Karaite exegetes came to Jerusalem, where they apparently wrote their commentaries on the Book of Psalms. The first, Salmon ben Yeruḥam, was born in Palestine or Egypt at the beginning of the century (ca. 910); the second, Yefet ben ᶜAli Halevi, was evidently born ten or twenty years later in Basra, Iraq; and the third, David ben Abraham, author of the ᵓ*Egron*, was born in Fez, Morocco, around the middle of the century. All three wrote in Arabic, and prefaced a translation (*Tafsir*) to the detailed commentary, which combines philological gloss with topical explication. The commentaries of Salmon[1] and Yefet[2] are extant in their entirety, but only a seven-page fragment of David ben Abraham's commentary (on Ps. 27:6—29:2) is known.[3] The introductions to the commentaries by Salmon and Yefet reflect the Karaite reaction to the challenge issued by Saadiah concerning the nature and status of the Book of Psalms.

I. Salmon ben Yeruḥam: The Psalms as prophetic prayer for all ages: Monarchy, Exile, and Redemption

The controversy with the Karaites is evident in Saadiah's radical approach to the Book of Psalms, but in the manner of its exposition, which shows no signs of hostility. Unlike his practice in his arguments with his Rabbanite, Karaite, and sectarian opponents,[4] his two introductions to the Book of Psalms, the fragments of *The Obligation of Prayer*, and the introduction to his *Siddur* contain no references to the advocates of erroneous opinions, aside from a lone reference in the long introduction to "a few of our nation" who hold the false belief that the Book of Psalms was composed by David on his own (p. 24; cf. above, pp. 7f.). This characterization of his adversaries is so moderate and vague that, as mentioned above, their identity was unclear until Zucker alerted us to the polemical motivation of the introduction. Perhaps it is this moderate and restrained tone that made Salmon, in his arguments against Saadiah in his own introduction to Psalms, stick to the matter at hand and avoid the sharp ad hominem attacks found in his *The Wars of the Lord* (which earned him at Pinsker's hand the epithet "father of all abusers and scorners"—*Lickute*, II, p. 134). It is true that Poznanski ("Opponents," p. 221) saw a slur in the words, "I have seen in my time a man known as *al-Fayyumi*" (the lead-in to Salmon's debate with Saadiah in his introduction, p. 172), since he refers to Saadiah as to some unknown. To this can be added the pejorative "this man" (p. 175) and the phrase "was mistaken and erred" (Shunary, p. 173). But all of these are a far cry from the harsh language he uses against Saadiah in *The Wars of the Lord:* "the contemptible and filthy scoundrel" (p. 74); "fatheaded" (p. 42 [literally a variant on Ps. 119:70—"their minds are thick like fat"]) and "I know his despicable replies" (p. 130). Perhaps differences in age, situation, and genre had their effect, for *The Wars of the Lord* was written by a young man eager to take on a famous and respected opponent,[5] while the commentary on Psalms—which is not essentially a polemical work—was composed thirteen years after Saadiah's death.[6]

Given his verbatim citation of a fairly long passage from Saadiah's introduction (p. 173 = Saadiah, *Psalms*, p. 29, line 16–p. 30, line 3) it is obvious Salmon had Saadiah's commentary on Psalms in front of him when he wrote his own introduction. Not only is the second part of the introduction explicitly devoted to refuting Saadiah's arguments, in the first part as well (in which Saadiah's name is not mentioned) the confrontation with Saadiah's basic theory, as well as with his arguments and proofs, is discernible. Salmon begins with a discussion of the essential nature of the book, explaining that its name, *Tillim*,[7] is derived from the same root as *tel* (mound), *taltallim* (curls), and talul (steep), and like them refers to something high, exalted, and respected. The greatness and glory of the book lies in its striking similarity to the Pentateuch. This similarity he documents over eight pages with no fewer than sixty-four features common to the two works. In Psalms, as in the Pentateuch, we find encouragement to worship the Lord (119:1) and to do good (31:20), warning against punishment (1:5), the principle of commandment and admonition (78:5), threats of exile (106:27), and promises of redemption (85:2; 107:2–3). Moreover, there are many descriptions of historical events: Creation (104), the adventures of the Patriarchs (105:9–15), the enslavement in Egypt (105:25), the Song at the Sea (106:12), the expulsion of the Canaanites (44:3), the division of the land among the tribes (78:55), the kingdom of David (78:70) and the selection of Jerusalem (78:69). Salmon is not disturbed by the fact that most of these references are to be found in a small number of historical psalms, and that even these, in both literary terms and their approach, are remote from the historiographic chapters of the Pentateuch. For him, the astonishing number of parallels is sufficient to demonstrate "that there is no root or branch of the Torah that is not included in this book," and to make the leap from this to another thesis, namely, that "it also contains most of the consolations that were written by the prophets in all their aspects and particulars; and were it not for my dislike of verbosity I would enumerate them" (p. 169). Yet there is no need for this, since in his view—which is expressed throughout the commentary—most of the psalms are prophecies of the exile (that following the destruction of the Second Temple) and of the future redemption.

The beginning of Saadiah's long introduction, too, compares the Book of Psalms and the Pentateuch, dwells on the parallels between the two, and is phrased in the same way: "The Torah says . . . and this book says . . ." (pp. 18–22). For Saadiah, however, this comparison is essentially stylistic and rhetorical, and its purpose is to prove that the Book of Psalms, as the "quintessence of edification" (p. 22), requires the same eighteen rhetorical modes employed by the Pentateuch, and for that matter by all of Scripture. Salmon's comparison, however, deals essentially with ideas and content; since, unlike Saadiah's, it does not deal with formal criticism, it is much less precise. Salmon's parallels serve his own less ambitious purpose of demonstrating the lofty status of the psalms and their thematic closeness to the Pentateuch and the Prophets. He apparently attempted to avoid borrowing Saadiah's parallels, in order to demonstrate (to himself and to his fellow Karaites) his ability to find new ones. Apart from these differences, the great similarity of approach and method is clear; but hereafter their paths diverge. While in Saadiah's eyes the Book of Psalms is a second Pentateuch, given to Israel when they settled peacefully in their inheritance as a supplement to the "first book" (p. 18), for Salmon the Book of Psalms is distinctly unique. For him too it is a book of edification and guidance,[8] but with a specific purpose: instruction in the commandments of praise and exaltation (p. 169). As proof he cites twenty-four verses containing twenty-seven different verbs indicating praise and exaltation, all phrased in the imperative mood: *hodu*, *halᵉlu*, *šabbᵉḥuhu*, *širu*, *zammᵉru*, *baḳḳᵉšu panaw*, *hištaḥawu*, *sollu*, *ʿivdu*, etc. (thank, praise, extol him, sing, chant, seek his presence, bow, glorify, worship). While Saadiah saw these commands as decisive proof of the fact that the Book of Psalms is the "speech of the Master," which cannot be obeyed by repeating those same commands,[9] Salmon offered three proofs that the Book of Psalms, alongside the command, contains its fulfillment as well.

The first proof is the frequency in Psalms of the nouns referring to prayer (*ʾaṣ-ṣala*), such as *tᵉfillah* (prayer), *tᵉḥinnah* (pleading), *šawʿah* (cry), *zᵉʿaḳah* (scream), and *dimʿah* (tears). The second proof is citation of more than twenty verses in which the same verbs previously cited in the imperative mood appear in the first person: "From *hodu—ʾodekka* l^{e}-*ʿolam* (I shall thank You for ever: Ps. 52:11[9]) . . . from *širu—ʾaširah* (I shall sing: Ps. 104:33)," etc. (pp. 169–70). Salmon makes no explicit reference to Saadiah's assertion that all "the words of the servant" in Psalms are to be understood as the "words of the Master," but this constitutes his answer to it. One who rejects Saadiah's narrow definition of the concept of "prayer" and his exaggerated claim of thematic unity in a literary work need give no direct response to Saadiah's rhetorical theory; quite enough is the plethora of quotations in which the "words of the servant" are found side by side with the "words of the Master" and thus can be understood as "the practical implementation of the commandment" (ibid.). This explanation is so simple and reasonable that it hardly requires a sophisticated theoretical grounding.[10]

The third proof is that in addition to the many terms of entreaty (*ʾaṭ-ṭaliba*), pleading (*ʾaš-šafaʿ*a), and prayer (*ʾaṣ-ṣala*) in the Book of Psalms, there is direct documentation for the use of the psalms in the regular liturgy in which both Levites and Israelites participated. The first exhibit is the description of the Temple service as ordained by David: "To stand every morning to thank and praise the Lord [and likewise at evening]" (1 Chron. 23:30). Should one claim, as did Saadiah, that this refers to the Levites and has no connection with the prayers of the people, Salmon proves that "this refers to the singers and the congregation" by citing the description of the reinauguration of Temple worship in Ezra 3:11: "They chanted praise and thanksgiving to the Lord; ['For He is good, His steadfast love for Israel is everlasting,' and all the people raised a great shout praising the Lord]" (p. 170). Similar descriptions are found in 2 Chron. 29:27, Neh. 11:17,[11] and in Psalms itself. Psalm 106:47 reads, "Deliver us, O Lord our God, and gather us from among the nations that we may give thanks to Your holy name," followed by the people's response: "Let all the people say: Amen! Hallelujah!" (v. 48). Moreover, the parallel text in 1 Chronicles adds a word to the first verse that makes it explicit that we are dealing with an "imperative command": "*And say*: Deliver us, O God of our salvation" (16:35). Yet this verse is truly astonishing: how could David and the other psalmists, who lived in conditions of peace and political independence in the Land of Israel, utter phrases like "Deliver us . . . gather us"? Salmon's clinching answer is: "Must we not understand this verse and similar texts in this book as instructions *to the people of the Exile* to pray to and entreat the Merciful One to restore them and gather them to His Temple?" (p. 170). We may conclude, then, that not only did the congregation participate in the Temple liturgy, the prayers themselves were intended to be said outside the Temple as well, since their content is clearly appropriate also to the situation of the exiles. To reinforce this assertion Salmon cites thirty-five more texts of supplication from situations of collective and personal suffering, all of which relate, in his view, to the poverty, misery, and mourning of the present Exile.

Salmon summarizes the conclusions to be drawn from his argument thus far: "The purpose in the revelation (*tanzil*, 'bringing down') of this book is that we pray from it. Therefore all of it is instruction and guidance for the people of the Exile, teaching them how to repent—to weep, fast, and wear sackcloth, and beseech the Merciful One for salvation . . ." (p. 171).[12] He hastens, however, to make it clear that the Book of Psalms is not intended only for the Exilic era, since it also contains prayers appropriate to the needs of Israel living in freedom on its own land: "It is also prayer for those living under the Monarchy (*ʾahlu ʾad-daula*, the opposite of *ʾahlu ʾǵ-ǵalija* 'the people of the Exile') and for the king, with regard to thanksgiving and praise, the profession of God's unity and description of His power, acknowledgement of the commandments, admonitions, statutes, and ordinances, . . . the description of the Lord's mercy and goodness, . . . confession of sins, . . . pleas for forgiveness and atonement and victory over the enemy . . . and the attraction to the good and rejection of evil . . ." (ibid.). Since the Book of Psalms fulfills all the needs of worshippers, whenever and wherever they live, there is no logical reason to supplement it with prayers written by men, which necessarily contain mistakes. The Psalms, however, were composed by the "holy spirit" (*ruaḥ ha-ḳodeš*—p. 171 [the original employs the Hebrew term]), as is proven by the fact that their authors were prophets: "Moses the man of God" (Ps. 90:1), "David king of Israel" (2 Chron. 29:27), and the other authors mentioned in the headings, as stated explicitly in 1 Chron. 25:1. The exclusive status of the psalms as the liturgy of Israel follows not only from the consideration that human compositions ought not be used when prophetic prayer is available, but is evident from Scripture as well. The very act of committing the Psalms to writing shows that they were viewed as commandments (*furuḍ*, in Islamic terminology = Koranic commandments, i.e. divine Law)—"just as all the commandments were written down" (p. 171). Moreover, the prophets themselves prayed using this book, and showed thereby that it should serve as the liturgy for future generations. In short, given the perfection of the Book of Psalms (both from the point of view of content and origin) there is no need to supplement it with anthropogenic prayer.

Only now does Salmon turn to overt and direct confrontation with the man "known as al-Fayyumi," with whom the argument is no longer the legitimacy of *supplementing* the psalms but rather of *replacing* them with nonbiblical prayer. He summarizes Saadiah's position in a few words: "this book is not meant to be used for prayer except in the Temple and with musical instruments'' (p. 172). It is hard to say whether this inaccuracy was intentional, since we have seen that others too failed to understand Saadiah's complex position, according to which even in the Temple the psalms were not used for prayer, while today too they are only ''read'' within the prayer service.[13] In any event it is clear that ignoring the two distinctions made by Saadiah—between ''chanting'' and ''praying'' on the one hand, and between ''praying'' and ''reading'' on the other—made it much easier for him to argue, against Saadiah's position, that ''Scripture itself and the consensus of all segments of the nation—both the faithful and the heretics [meaning Karaites and Rabbanites]—refuted this opinion'' (ibid.).

His first proof from Scripture is that David himself set the precedent for using Psalms in prayer outside the Temple, as we see from the superscriptions of nine psalms, which relate the occasions of their utterance. Seven of them were said after the holy spirit rested upon him, following his anointment (as recorded in 1 Sam. 16:13) but prior to his coronation: ''when he was in the wilderness of Judah'' (Ps. 63:1), ''when he escaped from Saul, in the cave'' (57:1), ''when Saul sent men to watch his house in order to kill him'' (59:1), as well as 142:1, 54:2, 56:1, and 34:1; the other two were composed after his enthronement in Jerusalem: ''When Nathan the prophet came to him'' (51:2) and ''when he fled from Absalom his son'' (3:1). Not only did David pray these psalms before the Temple was built, he even composed some of them outside the borders of the Land of Israel, and thereby ''taught the nation how to plead before the Lord in the exile'' (p. 172): ''A *mikhtam* of David, for instruction to teach. When he fought with Aram-Naharaim and Aram-Zobah. . . . O God, You have rejected us'' (60:1–3; cf. his commentary on these verses—Salmon, *Psalms*, p. 65). As mentioned above, Saadiah anticipated this problem and asserted that the Book of Psalms, like the Torah itself, was revealed ''scroll by scroll,'' and these headings refer to the places where David was granted revelation (see above, p. 13). Instead of arguing that Saadiah's solution is forced and implausible, Salmon concealed from his readers that he had dealt with this problem. In any event Salmon has a good explanation of the biographical headings: they are not merely indications of time and place, but descriptions of the events that led David to utter his prophetic prayer.

Next Salmon undermines Saadiah's strongest proof for the geographical condition—Psalm 137. The ''prophets' '' refusal to sing on alien soil stems from the fact that they were asked to sing it ''with lyres and harps as was obligatory in the Temple'' (p. 172), as shown by the words, ''we hung up our lyres'' (137:2). This was indeed forbidden, for from 1 Chron. 25:6 as well we learn that the musical performance of the psalms was restricted to the Temple. ''But as to prayer, it is an obligation to pray from it everywhere!'' (ibid.). He cites verses from Psalms to prove the obligation of reciting them in prayer everywhere (66:4; 96:1) and at all times, even during the Exile (74:21; 69:31[30]). He is careful to choose those verses in which the roots *z.m.r.*, *š.i.r.*, and *h.l.l.* (chant, sing, praise) appear, in order to contradict Saadiah's distinction (which he passes over in silence) between (conditional) singing and (unconditional) reading. These proofs are valid as long as we assume that the verses containing these imperatives refer to the singing of psalms. This assumption, however, is the crux of the debate.

The second proof is based on the general consensus (*ʾiǵmaᶜ*): ''The entire nation, in all parts of the world, prays (*tuṣalli*) from it and with it in all its assemblies'' (p. 173). True, the Rabbanite communities ''appended the Eighteen Benedictions to it,'' but the Talmud itself relates that 120 elders (he conveniently overlooks the prophets among them) gathered and composed them, and ''something composed that way is unacceptable to us'' (ibid.). While there is no *ʾiǵmaᶜ* concerning the nonprophetic prayer that was superadded later, there is general consensus that the psalms are used in prayer. The proof is that if we ask the Rabbanite communities of Byzantium, France, and the Far West what they pray in addition to the Eighteen Benedictions, they will testify that they ''pray from the psalms'' on the Sabbath and other days, and that on the night of the Day of Atonement it is even obligatory to recite the entire book.[14] Ultimately, then, ''it has been demonstrated that the one who said that they should be used in prayer only in the Temple was mistaken'' (p. 173). We should note that had Saadiah referred to the ''reading'' of *pᵉsuḳei dᵉ-zimrah* (the preliminary psalms in the Morning Service) and *Hallel* (Pss. 113–118) in the synagogue in the introductions to his Psalms commentaries, Salmon would have been hard put to cite the Rabbanite custom as clinching his assertion that all agree that the psalms are prayers in every sense of the term.

This concludes that part of the debate with Saadiah with a direct bearing on the Karaite-Rabbanite controversy over the use of Psalms as a prayerbook. Salmon saw no need to mention the theory of the five conditions, which occupies a central position in Saadiah's introduction, and made do with undermining its relevance by rejecting the distinction between singing the psalms with instrumental accompaniment in the Temple and singing them a capella (or with other instruments) outside the Temple. His comments on the performance instructions in the headings of the psalms show that his conception of the Temple music and singing was quite different from Saadiah's. We can assume that as a Karaite he did not share Saadiah's interest in erecting a barrier between the sacred hymns of the Temple and synagogal prayer. Thus it is not to be expected that he would adopt those interpretations that reinforce the idea that the singing of the psalms in the Temple was a special ritual, constrained by stringent conditions, which—inter alia—bar its continuation elsewhere (similar to the strict prohibition against sacrifice outside the Temple). His encounter with Saadiah's conception is evident in his comment on the heading of Psalm 4: *bi-n^{e}ginot̠* shows that this psalm is to be sung in several different "rhythmic modes and melodies" (*biʾalhan wanaġamat*), in contrast to (*ʿal n^{e}ginat̠* (61:1), which indicates a single melody. This statement is close to Saadiah's on the subject, as is his explanation of the role of instrumental accompaniment: "to encourage the people to worship the Lord with gladness, as it is said: 'worship the Lord with gladness' (100:2)."[15] This is not the case, however, for the melodic condition itself; whereas Saadiah assumed that Scripture and Oral Tradition prescribed exactly which mode is appropriate for a given psalm, Salmon held that the performance instructions refer only to the obligation to use one or more modes suited to the particular nature of the psalm. Musical harmony is required, but not fixed. He returns to this issue with greater clarity in his comment on "Raise a song, sound the timbrel, a melodious lyre and harp" (81:3[2]): "Perform the melody (*ʾan-naġma*) and the words of praise (*ʾat-tamġid* = the words of the psalm) in the beat (*ʾiḳaʿ*) of the instruments so that the words are not separate from the beating [of the drum]. As is written on this matter: 'First come singers, then musicians' (68:26[25])." This triune concord of rhythmic mode, instrumental beat and words has a tremendous effect on the players, as he explains later in his remarks on Ps. 4:1: "When they play the instruments a prophetic spirit will rest upon them, as is stated: 'Who prophesied to the accompaniment of lyres, harps, and cymbals' (1 Chron. 25:1), and as is said of Elisha: 'As the musician played, the hand of the Lord came upon him' (2 Kings 3:15)."

Note that while Saadiah cited the incident of Elisha as proof of the instrumental condition (see above, p. 19), for Salmon it indicated that music has the capacity to engender prophetic inspiration even in the Temple. Unlike his predecessor, then, he clearly inclines to general inferences and prefers thematic to musical explanations for the headings. Thus, in his commentary on Ps. 6:1 he ignores Saadiah's interpretation that *ʿal ha-š^{e}minit̠* refers to the eighth rhythmic mode and prefers (without mentioning his source) a rabbinic midrash: "Some explain *ʿal ha-š^{e}minit̠* as a musical instrument, referring to the eight-stringed *ʿud*, as is written: 'with lyres to lead on the *š^{e}minit̠*' (1 Chron. 15:21), and in the Messianic era it will be enlarged and have ten strings, as is written: 'with a ten-stringed lyre' (Ps. 92:4), 'I will . . . sing a hymn to You with a ten-stringed harp' (Ps. 144:9)."[16] In his commentary on Ps. 53:1 he attributes to "some say" Saadiah's gloss of *maḥalat̠* as the name of an instrument, just like *maḥol*;[17] but he also cites an anonymous opinion that *maḥalat̠* refers to the kingdoms of

Edom and Ishmael, relying on the verse, "And Esau went to Ishmael and took Maḥalath the daughter of Ishmael . . . as his wife" (Gen. 28:9). He does not decide in favor of either explanation; a similar indeterminacy marks his presentation of the two opinions he cites concerning *ʾel ha-nᵉḥilot̲* (5:1), which he explains as either the name of an instrument or as the heartache that afflicted Israel. This is apparently his method concerning *ʿal šošanim* (45:1) as well: "Some say a musical instrument that is round like the lily (*šošan*), others that it means the true remnant of Israel, which is compared to a lily, as it is said: 'Like a lily among thorns . . .' (Cant. 2:2)." When he takes up the subject again, however, in his commentary on *ʿal šošan* (60:1) and *ʿal šošanim* (69:1), he cites only the second, metaphorical interpretation. This clear decision against the musical interpretation is also found in his commentary on *ʿalmut̲ labben* (9:1). First he offers the opinion that *ʿalmut̲* is a musical instrument, and that *labben* refers to one of the chief choristers, Ben, who is mentioned in 1 Chron. 15:18. (This, it will be recalled, was also Saadiah's understanding of *labben*, but he glossed *ʿalmut̲* as the name of a rhythmic mode.) Next he offers his own opinion, namely, that *ʿalmut̲* means a venial sin, as in "You have set our iniquities (*ʿalumenu*) before You" (Ps. 90:8), or that it is derived from *ʿelem* 'youth' and refers to youthful indiscretions (at Ps. 48:15, too, he glosses *yᵉnahagenu ʿalmut̲* in the sense of "He will return us to the days of our youth"). Either explanation fits in well with his gloss of *labben* as a verb in the imperative mood: "That is, cleanse us and blanch us of sin." Immediately after this nonmusical explanation Salmon protests against the illegitimate custom, apparently widespread among the Karaites, of omitting the headings of the psalms when praying. This sheds light on his preference of the thematic interpretation (which connects the heading to the subject matter of the psalm) to the musical one (which gives the heading merely informative and antiquarian interest).

Salmon's clear reservations about Saadiah's strenuous effort to underscore the musical sophistication of sacred poetry go along with his different conception of the regulations that governed its performance in the Temple. In his view, not only were the Levites free to choose whatever rhythmic mode they felt was appropriate, they even allowed Israelites and women to take part in the singing and musical accompaniment. From his detailed description in his remarks on the verse, "First come singers, then the musicians, among maidens playing timbrels" (68:26), the following picture emerges: in the Inner Courtyard stood the musicians, with the choristers behind them—both groups being Levites. The other tribes, who stood in rows in the Outer Courtyard, joined their song, accompanied by musical instruments. From the verse, "You who fear the Lord, bless the Lord" (135:20), Salmon infers that the worshippers in the Outer Court also included converts. Surrounding these stood the choruses of young women holding musical instruments, as is written in the verse under discussion, just as during the song of the Sea (Exod. 15:20) and as will occur in the days to come (Jer. 31:12[13]). He stresses, though, that the women were permitted to play only the *tof* (timbrel) and *maḥol* (large two-headed drum), since only these two instruments are mentioned in the verses upon which he bases himself. Their location on the periphery of the Temple precincts he derives by analogy from the situation in the wilderness: "from the mirrors of the women who performed tasks *at the entrance* to the Tent of Meeting" (Exod. 38:8). It is quite likely that he emphasized these two limitations—the instrumental and the local—because of their halakhic and practical implications for the place and role of women in the synagogue of his day. In any event it is clear that this idea that minimal restrictions applied to the singing of the psalms in the Temple facilitates the assertion of a direct continuity between it and their liturgical use in the exilic synagogue. He states this very clearly in his commentary on the next verse, "In assemblies bless God, the Lord, O you who are from the fountain of Israel" (68:27[26]: "The phrase 'from the fountain of Israel' means the places that are the fountain of Israel and its gathering, namely, the Temple. These words encourage *us* as well to gather in order to praise the Lord in concert, as it is written: 'Let them exalt Him in the congregation of the people' (107:32), and 'in assemblies I will bless the Lord' (26:12)."[18]

Salmon devotes the last part of the introduction to a discussion of the authorship of the psalms. The form he chose for this was an overt attack on Saadiah's view, perhaps because this enabled him to undermine Saadiah's standing as a reliable exegete. He summarizes Saadiah's view accurately, in these words: "Everything in the Book of Psalms is exclusively the prophecies of David, which were given over to the sons of Moses and the sons of Levi to use for praise" (p. 173). This paraphrase is followed by a long verbatim quotation from Saadiah's arguments in his introduction about "of Moses" (90:1) and "of Solomon" (127:1) (see above, pp. 13f.). Salmon asserts that he cannot pass over these statements in silence, since this view denies Moses and the other prophets mentioned in the Book of Psalms their prophecies and attributes them to another prophet—and on the basis of an untenable theory. He proceeds to a systematic assault on all facets of Saadiah's position. Saadiah's argument that Scripture refers to descendants collectively by the name of their ancestor is true only for "Israel" and the twelve tribes. This unique custom is based on Jacob's blessing to his sons (Gen. 49); its exclusivity is apparent in the fact that later descendants were never given the name of the father of the tribe. Saadiah attempted, as will be recalled, to bolster his theory with two verses from 1 Chronicles, and Salmon now sets out to refute him.

The first verse is: "But Aaron and his sons made offerings . . ." (1 Chron. 6:34[49]). For Saadiah the fact that the context refers to David's time proved that "the reference is to the descendants of Aaron" *(Psalms,* p. 29). Salmon devotes a page and a half to demonstrating that this conclusion is too hasty and that the verse necessarily refers to Aaron himself. Since Saadiah had relied on the context, Salmon scrutinizes the structure of the pericope that begins at 5:27 [6:7]. In modern terms we would say that he found a repetitive and chiastic structure, since the section begins with a genealogical list of the Priests (5:27–41 [6:1–5]), continues with the genealogy of the Levites (6:1–33 [6:16–48]) and concludes with the genealogy of Aaron and his sons the Priests (6:34ff. [6:49ff.]). The second paragraph of the lists of Levites recounts the appointment of the three singers by David (6:16[31]); analogously, the second list of the Priests commences with the appointment of Aaron and his sons to offer the incense and sacrifices on the altars (6:34[49]). From this parallelism we learn that, just as the division of Levitical tasks originated with *David*, the description of the Priestly tasks necessarily goes back to the initial consecration of Aaron and his four sons "as ordained by the Lord" (p. 174), namely, by *Moses* in the wilderness. Moreover, not only does the context show that verse 34 does not relate to David's time; the very juxtaposition of "Aaron and his sons" is enough to refute Saadiah's claim. For "how can the word 'Aaron' refer to Aaron's sons, when the verse states 'Aaron and his sons'!?" (ibid.).

Saadiah's second prooftext, which clearly refers to David's sojourn in Ziklag, includes the words "Jehoiadah, the chief officer of Aaron" (1 Chron. 12:27), which he interprets as "chief officer of the Aaronides." The context is clear, and the stylistic argument (that "Aaron" can not mean "the sons of Aaron") is irrelevant. Nevertheless Salmon states categorically that Saadiah is wrong, since here *l*^{e}*-ʾAharon* does not mean "of Aaron" but "from Aaron" (the man). His proof is that the prefix *lamed* means "from" in other passages as well, as for example: "who had come from the war" (*la-milḥamah*) (Num. 31:21), "and Solomon came from the high places" (*la-bamah*) (2 Chron. 1:13). Salmon was not the first to discover this usage, which Saadiah himself accepted, as we see both from the *Tafsir* on Lev. 11:24 and Num. 31:21 and from his gloss on Lev. 11:24 in the long commentary.[19] Still, we can ask whether the application of this usage to our verse is reasonable, or merely serves the needs of the controversy. The Karaite David ben Abraham, too, cites this usage at the beginning of the entry for *lamed* (Al-Fasi, *Dictionary,* II, pp. 141–42), as does Ibn Ganach *(Ha-Riḳmah,* pp. 55–56). The former exemplifies the usage with eight verses (one of them is 2 Chron. 1:13); the latter cites seventeen verses (beginning with Num. 31:21 and 2 Chron. 1:13, supplemented by two others quoted and thirteen not quoted by his predecessors). Neither mentions the verse in dispute here.[20]

After this refutation of Saadiah's claim that "of Moses" means "of the sons of Moses," Salmon attacks Saadiah's view that "of Solomon" means "concerning Solomon" (see above, p. 14). His first argument is that Solomon was undoubtedly a prophet, as is demonstrated by his two prophetic works, Proverbs and the Song of Songs; none would dream of attributing them to David. He adds a stylistic proof: just as the incipit of the Songs of Songs uses a prefix *lamed* to designate the author of the book (and not its topic), so too the psalms headed *li-š^{e}lomoh* (72:1 and 127:1) "are entirely the prophecy of Solomon" (p. 175). Salmon returns to this issue in his commentary on Ps. 42:1, the first mention of the sons of Koraḥ. He must clarify the identity of these; are they the sons of Koraḥ ben Yiṣhar who rebelled against Moses and Aaron, or their remote descendants in the age of David (mentioned in 1 Chron. 9:19, 12:6, and 26:1)? His answer:

> It is known that where it is written in this book "of David," "of Moses," "of Asaph," these are the famous and well-known individuals [of those names]; so we must necessarily say that "the sons of Koraḥ" undoubtedly refers to the famous and well-known ones, as it is said: "The sons of Koraḥ: Assir, Elkanah, and Abiasaph" (Exod. 6:24). This shows that they prophesied [this psalm] in the wilderness.

The inclusion of earlier prophecies in a later work should not astonish us, for Moses' prophetic prayers, too, are included partially in the Pentateuch and partially in the Book of Psalms. The former concern the Israelites in the wilderness (e.g., Exod. 32:11ff.; Deut. 9:26ff.; Num. 14:13ff., 16:22, and 12:13), while the latter concern "the exile and redemption." Since the seven Koraḥide psalms are also prophecies of the exile and the messianic days they were included in the Book of Psalms.

How does his conception of multiple authorship fit in with the verses adduced by Saadiah as proofs that Scripture itself ascribes the entire Book of Psalms to David (Saadiah, *Psalms*, p. 28)? Saadiah based his argument on three verses (Neh. 12:24; 2 Chron. 7:6 and 8:14); Salmon, because he accepts Saadiah's interpretation of these verses, mentions only one of them (2 Chron. 7:6). He does, however, demur with regard to Saadiah's inference from them. The fact that the book as a whole is ascribed to David does not mean that it contains no psalms by other prophets. Even Moses' Pentateuch includes prophecies by Noah, the three Patriarchs, and many others (p. 175). It remains for him to refute Saadiah's assumption that two prophets cannot prophesy one prophecy and his conclusion that when two individuals are mentioned in the heading of a psalm at least one of them was not the author-prophet but the singer (see above, pp. 13f.). Salmon is incensed that "this man deprived Aaron of his prophecy, as he deprived Moses of his prophecy in the Book of Psalms" (p. 175). True, Aaron's prophecy was through the intermediacy of an angel, while Moses' was direct. But we may assume that the simultaneous revelation to the two prophets occurred in the following manner: the Lord created a voice which Moses and the angel heard directly, and the angel then transmitted the message to Aaron, so that both of them received the prophecy (Lev. 11:1–2). This may also have been the case with Asaph and Jeduthun (Ps. 77:1)[21] and with the three sons of Koraḥ—Assir, Elkanah, and Abiasaph. This is why they sometimes employ the plural—"We have heard with our ears, our fathers have told us" (44:2)—although not always (42:2). Ultimately, depriving Moses of the authorship of "the prayer of Moses" (90:1), as Saadiah would do, entails denying David of "a prayer of David" (17:1 and 86:1), since there is no difference between them!

Thus Israel's mandatory book of prayers is called by David's name, but some of the psalms were composed by other prophets. Salmon ben Yeruḥam made a concerted effort to uncover the thematic connection between each psalm and its predecessor, since he assumed that the prophetic nature of the book rests not only upon the fact that all of the psalms (including their headings) are prophecies, but upon their prophetic ordering as well. As he says: "The psalms are all linked to one other; this was ordained by the command of Him who handed them down from heaven" (commentary on Ps. 46:1).

II. Yefet ben ʿAli: The Psalms as prophetic prayers, perfect in form and content

Yefet frequently quoted the opinions and interpretations of his predecessors; and in his introduction (p. 10) he underscored their significant contribution to his commentary.[22] Yet he almost never provides names or sources. Consequently Yefet's introduction contains no explicit references or allusions to Saadiah, although it is clear that he had firsthand knowledge of Saadiah's view of the Book of Psalms (and not only from Salmon ben Yeruḥam's commentary). For one thing, Yefet's remarks on Ps. 62:20 are based—though, as is his wont, with no attribution—on Saadiah's commentary on that verse, which is not quoted by Salmon. Moreover, Yefet's commentary on Ps. 136:4 clearly echoes Saadiah's remarks on the same psalm.[23] While, as we shall see, he confronts Saadiah's theory in his introduction, he avoided any direct attack on his arguments and proofs. Yefet contented himself with presenting and consolidating the Karaite position; consequently the latent controversy with his adversary is perceived only by those who are familiar with Saadiah's view. Evidently Yefet was not afraid that the Karaite reader might be exposed to Saadiah's arguments, and was not inclined to employ their refutation as ammunition in the bitter struggle that continued to rage between the two camps.[24]

Yefet's commentaries on Scripture are extremely long-winded. Anxious, then, lest he weary his reader, he interpolates frequent promises to be brief; this may be the motive for the somewhat extraordinary practice of splitting the introductory discussion between the formal preface (found at the beginning of the commentary before the *Tafsir*) and his commentary on the first few verses of the book. His commentary on each biblical book is preceded by a discussion of the themes of that book, its lessons, and why it was written; of its literary genre, structure, and characteristic terminology; of the identity of the author, his time, and his prophetic status; and of related issues. This broad conception of the purpose of the introduction seems to have collided with hesitation to expatiate in essay-like lectures; consequently he was inclined to infiltrate his treatment of these topics, to the extent possible, in his thematic and philological glosses of words and themes found in the superscription of the book and its own "introduction."[25] This tendency reaches its acme in his commentaries on Nahum, the Song of Songs, and Ecclesiastes, which have no separate introductions; the prefatory discussion comes only after the *Tafsir* of the first verses, at times with no evident link to the words of the scriptural text.

Yefet's commentary on Daniel exemplifies the opposite pole; here the prefatory discussion is confined within the bounds of the not-overlong introduction that precedes the *Tafsir.* In his commentaries on the Minor Prophets, Proverbs, and Ruth,[26] however, the preface overflows the introduction and is continued in the body of the commentary. The same is true (and to an even greater extent) of his Psalms commentary: the introductions to Psalms 1 and 3 completed the thematic discussion in the long preface. The absence of a heading to Psalm 1 provides a suitable occasion for a comprehensive discussion of the issue of authorship of the Psalms and the principle of their sequential arrangement, while the superscription "A psalm of David" prefixed to Psalm 3, and the accompanying biographical note ("when he fled from Absalom his son") open the door to surveys of the terminology of genres and of the historical information found in the headings and their significance. Our discussion of Yefet's introduction to the Psalms must, therefore, also consider its supplements in the commentary on Psalms 1 and 3.

As in his other introductions, in the introduction to Psalms Yefet attempts to equip the student with a comprehensive summary of the topics covered in the scriptural book being considered. He does this by defining the twelve "gates" (*ʾabuab*) that support the Book of Psalms.[27] We can summarize this survey as follows: a record of the wonders of the Lord and his goodness, in the Creation and throughout history (gates 1–3); an account of the sins of Israel, their punishment and repentance (gates 4–6); supplications that the Lord grant knowledge, provide assistance in time of trouble, and hasten the redemption (gates 7–9); and descriptions of the end of days: the acceptance by all nations of the One God; their submission to Israel and its Messiah; and the reign of comprehensive peace throughout the world (gates 10–12). After this "table of contents" Yefet returns to each "gate" and presents a detailed list of the complete psalms and individual verses devoted to each topic. The reader may wonder about the purpose of this thorough documentation, which occupies about a third of the introduction, and whose utility for a reader of the Book of Psalms is unclear. The wonder is dispelled by the sentence with which the section concludes: "These twelve gates must be included in the obligatory prayers morning and evening" (p. 6).[28] Thus Yefet is not offering a quasi-scientific description of the themes of the book, intended for exegete and student, but rather a classified index of verses for the Karaite worshipper, who is to find in Psalms both the twelve obligatory elements of prayer and their prescribed wording.

Yefet strengthens this viewpoint with the following argument: prayer is essentially a rational obligation, since reason suggests that one praise his benefactor, recognize his greatness, and recount his favors and wonders. However, the Lord's mercies to his creatures fall into two categories: general and perpetual, on the one hand, and personal and temporary, on the other. For those favors that are granted to all persons at all times we ought really to express perpetual thanks; but since this is impossible, we must mention all of them (i.e., all "twelve gates") on regular occasions—in the obligatory morning and evening prayers. When it comes to favors to an individual, each of us must thank the Lord when he enjoys—when eating and drinking, after rescue and convalescence, after the birth of children, etc. Aside from this difference in timing, the two types of thanksgiving are distinguished by their wording: "An obligatory prayer (*ṣalatu ʾl-farḍ*) cannot be composed by an individual, but must be expressed in the words ordained by Heaven (*ʾal munazzal*), while the second type does not have to be expressed in words ordained by Heaven" (p. 7). The reasoning behind this distinction follows: "Since the obligatory prayer is a ritual (*ʿibada*) like all the commandments (*ʾl furuḍ*), it must be prophetic (*munazzala*) just as they are. The other way, however, is not like other rituals and consequently can be taken from both prophetic and other sources" (ibid.). This emphasis on the dispensation to express personal thanks for occasional mercies in nonscriptural language is meant to reinforce the scriptural nature of the obligatory prayer, and indirectly to cast aspersions on Rabbanite law, which specifies that both obligatory prayers and the "Blessings on Enjoyment" are to be said in the words laid down by the Sages.

Yefet next refers his reader to his commentary on Ps. 136:1, where he expands on this topic. There he begins with the assertion that "one must know that thanks for His mercy is an obligation on both the community and on the individual, and that a man must enumerate these things in the obligatory prayer."[29] This combination of the obligation itself, which can be derived from reason, with the manner of its fulfilment, as ordained in a prophetic book,[30] is already familiar from the introduction; the innovation here lies in Yefet's attempts to prove from Scripture that this psalm was part of the public "obligatory prayer" in the Temple, where the Priest stood in front of the choruses and chanted the beginning of each verse and the congregation responded with the refrain, "His steadfast love is eternal." He finds proof of his theory in a rather enigmatic verse included in the list of "the heads of the province who lived in Jerusalem" in Nehemiah's time: "Mattaniah son of Micha son of Zabdi son of Asaph was the head; at prayer, he would lead off with praise . . ." (Neh. 11:17). Yefet explains that Mattaniah "said to the congregation 'Praise the Lord,' and he is the one who recounted God's marvels and mercies, while the congregation said only: 'His steadfast love is eternal.'" As mentioned above, this verse was one of six prooftexts cited in Salmon ben Yeruḥam's introduction to support his claim that the psalms were used in regular prayer (see above, p. 62); Yefet for his part cites only this verse and omits it from his introduction. This paucity of quotations is another reflection of the lowered polemical tone that characterizes Yefet's Psalms commentary.

Continuing his introduction, Yefet moves from the content of the Book of Psalms to its style: "After mentioning these twelve gates, we deem it right to mention the terms used in it to praise the Lord, and they are ten" (pp. 7–8). He lists ten Hebrew nouns meaning praise, each exemplified by a verse in which the same root appears as a verb in the imperative or future: *zimrah*, *širah*, *hodayah*, *hallel*, *t*^{e}*ruʿah*, *rinnun*, *šebaḥ*, *rom*^{e}*mut̠*, *g*^{e}*dullah*, *b*^{e}*rak̠ah*.[31] Next he classes them in two categories—six terms of praise also used in secular life versus four used only to praise the Creator (*zimrah*, *širah*, *t*^{e}*ruʿah*, *rinnun*).[32] This distinction evidently relates to the problem that "Scripture speaks in human language," and is intended to make the reader aware that in the final analysis the problem of homonymity is only partial. As will be recalled, in his long introduction Saadiah distinguished between the meaning of certain expressions when spoken by human beings and their meaning when uttered by the Lord (see above, p. 4). This parallel is not coincidental; the emphasis on the terms of praise used in Psalms represents Yefet's indirect answer to the complicated rhetorical theory developed by Saadiah in order to ground his theory that Psalms is a "book of edification." Ironically, the Karaite scholar could draw on rabbinic sources for his view, while Saadiah had to forge his own path.[33]

Yefet's introduction, read this far, raises two questions that are actually one: Is Karaite prayer really based exclusively on praise, with no admixture of request that the Lord grant one's needs? Are not at least three of the "twelve gates" that Yefet holds to be obligatory in prayer requests—for knowledge, assistance, and redemption? The rest of the discussion of style in fact addresses our question. Yefet indicates that, in addition to the ten terms of praise (*ʾat-tasbiḥ*), ten terms of supplication (*ʾat-taliba*) are also found in Psalms: *tᵉfillah*, *šawᶜah*, *ḥallot̠* (from the root *ḥ.l.h*, as in Ps. 119:58), *tᵉḥinnah*, *ḳᵉriʾah*, *ṣᵉᶜaḳah*, *zᵉᶜaḳah*, *dᵉrišah*, *baḳḳašah*, and *šᵉʾelah* (p. 8). Yefet emphasizes that just as the terms of praise are not all synonymous, each of the terms of supplication has a specific meaning, which he will explain in the body of the commentary. The importance of this semantic point for the Karaite claim that Psalms is a book of prayer is evident in his next statement: "These twenty terms all (refer to) oral expression. In the obligatory prayer [the tongue] must be assisted by other organs" (pp. 8–9). There follows a list of the six physical activities that are part of the Karaite prayer ritual, in addition to speech: standing (on the legs), bowing (inclining the head and neck), bending (inclining the back), kneeling (going down on the kneees), prostration (complete descent to the ground until the shanks are under the buttocks), and stretching out the hands. He documents all this with verses from Psalms,[34] thereby not only proving the correctness of the Karaite *halakhah*, but also implying what Salmon ben Yeruḥam had asserted openly—namely, that the Book of Psalms includes both the text of the prayers and their regulations.

Only in its last paragraph does Yefet provide a hint (for those in the know) of the polemical dimension of his introduction. Two concerns motivated him, he says, in his selection of topics for discussion: first, the need to clarify the purpose of the Book of Psalms; second, the need to survey the terminology used in it. The thematic analysis showed that Psalms is a book of prayer (*diwan ʾeṣ-ṣala*); the stylistic analysis revealed which terms of praise and supplication "one is obliged to use in prayer" (p. 10). This, then, is Yefet's twofold answer to Saadiah: Psalms is not a "book of edification" but a "book of prayer" whose form is appropriate to its content, and whose form and content together are entailed upon the worshippers of all generations.[35] This general claim requires further detail and clarification, and these are left for the prefaces to Psalms 1 and 3. The rest of the introduction is devoted to a sort of apology for his audacity in attempting to add his own novellae to the glosses of his predecessors, which, he says, constitute the majority of the commentary. He is well aware of the danger of error and begs the Lord's forgiveness for them at the outset. But even in this he follows the footsteps of "the wise men of our nation," who did not refrain from writing down their opinions despite the danger of error. Had they done so, knowledge would have been forgotten![36] The way to prevent the entrenchment of error is not the avoidance of new ideas, but the criticism leveled by each generation at the ideas of its predecessors, so that learning advances from generation to generation. Yefet concludes his introduction by citing a number of verses to prove the validity of this method, for example: "The wise man shall hear, and increase in learning" (Prov. 1:5); "I have gained knowledge more than all my teachers" (Ps. 119:99); and "I understand more than the aged" (Ps. 119:100).[37]

Yefet displays great originality in his treatment of the authorship of the 150 psalms, to which the bulk of the preface to the commentary on Psalm 1 is devoted. Unlike Salmon ben Yeruḥam (who argued at length with Saadiah's claim that all the psalms were written by David), Yefet presumes from the start that the book had a number of different prophetic authors, some of whose names are listed in the headings: David, Solomon, Asaph, Jeduthun (whose other name, according to Yefet, is Ethan)[38] and Moses.[39] Just as he does not deem it necessary to prove that they were all prophets, he sees no cause to refute Saadiah's arguments, perhaps because Salmon had already done so. He is interested primarily in the problem of the anonymous psalms, which has only an indirect connection with the controversy with Saadiah. In order to round out the survey, he mentions first the psalms that bear explicit attributions. Then, before discussing the anonymous psalms, he deals with an intermediate category: the eleven psalms attributed to the family of the Koraḥides. He cites anonymously the opinion that the reference is to Assir, Elkanah, and Abiasaph, mentioned in Exod. 6:24 as the sons of Koraḥ. He supplements this opinion (held by Salmon, see above p. 70), which dates the composition of these psalms to Moses' time, with another opinion, which makes the Koraḥide psalmists contemporaries of David: "Someone said that 'the sons of Koraḥ' is Heman alone, like 'The sons of Dan: Ḥushim' (Gen. 46:23)." In other words: since we find the plural used for one person, we can identify "the sons of Koraḥ" with "Heman the Ezraḥite" (frequently mentioned in Chronicles as one of the Levite singers who served in the Temple in David's time, and who shares the attribution of Psalm 88 with the Koraḥides). Both opinions are founded on a dislike of anonymity, which Yefet does not share. According to him, the collective designation "the sons of Koraḥ" refers to groups of prophets living in different periods, who, because of their large number, were not mentioned individually.[40] Following this admission of the partial anonymity of "the sons of Koraḥ," Yefet turns to a detailed and fundamental examination of the anonymous psalms.

He begins with a statistical survey, stating that there are forty-six psalms with no explicit attribution, namely: 1, 2, 10, 33, 43, 71, 91–100, 102, 104, 106, 107, 111–118, 120, 121, 123, 125, 126, 128, 129, 130, 132, 134, 135, 136, 137, 146–150;[41] to these he adds Psalm 119 and Psalms 66 and 67 (pointing out that the last two are the only ones whose superscriptions read "for the leader" without naming the author). Several times thereafter he refers to the number 46, and it is not clear why he did not add these three to the total.[42] Next Yefet proposes that the authors of five of the anonymous psalms can be identified, since each had originally been part of the preceding (explicitly attributed) psalm and had been detached from it by the editor (*ʾal-mudawwin*), for reasons to be explained in the commentary on the psalms in question.[43] Yefet's reasons for joining Psalms 9 and 10, 32 and 33, 42 and 43, 70 and 71, and 103 and 104 seem to be stylistic and thematic; so far as I have been able to check, he did not have biblical manuscripts in which these psalms were joined.[44] According to him, Psalm 10 completes Psalm 9 (attributed to David), since the first has an alphabetical acrostic (its verses beginning with the letters *alef* through *kaf*), whose partial continuation can be found in the latter psalm (*lamed*, *ḳof*, *reš*, *šin*, *taw*). In the preface to his commentary on Psalm 9 (as well as to Psalm 119) Yefet treats the theme of alphabetical acrostics in some depth. He offers a theoretical explanation for this stylistic phenomenon and endeavors to explain missing or out-of-order initial letters in the alphabetical psalms by phonetic (letters with similar sounds may replace one another) and thematic explanations (similar in principle to the method used by the rabbis to explain the omission of the letter *nun* from Ps. 145).[45] There is nothing in the commentaries of Saadiah and Salmon about a structural link between Psalms 9 and 10 (or between any of the other twinned psalms). From Yefet's choice of words it is clear that the idea was original with him; the union of Psalms 9 and 10 is not obvious, given the fragmentary nature of the acrostic in Psalm 10 (neither Ibn Ezra nor David Kimḥi mention it in their commentaries).

Yefet then points out that from a thematic perspective Psalm 33 completes Psalm 32 (attributed to David), a point that he briefly reiterates in the commentary to Psalm 33. The merger of Psalm 43 with its predecessor (attributed to the sons of Koraḥ) is given a distinctly structural explanation (accepted by modern commentators, but not found among his predecessors nor among the Jewish exegetes of Spain and Provence): "This speech has three parts (*fuṣul*). At the end of each part he says, 'Why so downcast [my soul'] (42:6, 12; 43:5), because in each part he complains about his enemies and yearns for God's Temple and His salvation. This is why he ends each part with 'why so downcast'" (comm. on 43:5). The thematic connection between Psalm 70 (attributed to David) and Psalm 71 is so obvious that Ibn Ezra, too, notes it, and compares it to the formal link betweenPss. 103 and 104 (see his commentary on Pss. 71:1 and 104:1). Here too Yefet is the originator, the first to view Psalm 104 as the continuation of Psalm 103 (attributed to David), primarily because of their common structural feature: both psalms begin and end with the words "Bless the Lord, O my soul."[46]

With a lesser degree of certainty it is possible, according to Yefet, to identify the authors of two additional groups of psalms, attributing each group to the author of the eponymous psalm with which it begins. Thus one can assume that the ten psalms 91–100 are by Moses, since they follow "A prayer of Moses, the man of God" (Ps. 90). In the introduction he says no more than this, but it is clear that he was influenced by the rabbinic tradition expressed, among other loci,[47] by R. Levi in the name of R. Ḥaninah: "The eleven psalms composed by Moses were written in the style of the prophets. Why were they not included in the Torah? Because those are the words of the Law, and these are words of prophecy [and one does not interrupt the Law for the words of prophets]" (*Midrash Tehillim* 90,4).[48] The second group comprises the five psalms 146–150, which he designates collectively as "the last praise" (*hallel*), and is inclined to attribute to David because they follow *t^ehillah l^e-Dawid* (145). We can infer from the designation "the last praise" that he viewed them as a group composed by a single author because all of them begin and end with the word *hall^eluyah*. The reason for attributing Pss. 66–67 to David is different: these are the only two psalms bearing the superscription *la-m^enaṣṣeaḥ* whose author is not named; therefore it is plausible that they are not truly anonymous and should be ascribed to David (on the evidence of the fifteen earlier *la-m^enaṣṣeaḥ* psalms, which are attributed to him, and the three that follow), or to another author (the Koraḥides or Jeduthun, who also composed *la-m^enaṣṣeaḥ* psalms).

In this way Yefet managed to rescue seventeen psalms from anonymity. Regarding the thirty-two that remain[49] he states that "it is impossible to attribute them to a specific person or time, and it seems reasonable that they were composed in different generations, and by a group (*ǵamaʿa*), which is why they were not attributed to a a particular person." In other words, we must resign ourselves to the anonymity of one-fifth of the psalms and understand it in the same way we understand the partial anonymity of the Koraḥides. Their anonymity does not detract from their prophetic status, since it is not the result of the editor's ignorance of their authors' identity. Rather, it is because there is no point in listing many names in the heading of what was a group prophecy. Again (as in the statement about "the sons of Koraḥ" in note 40 above) we must differentiate between the explanation given for the anonymity, and the assumption—which is independent of it—

that these psalms were not composed by a single group that lived in a particular generation, but by various groups who prophesied in different ages.

Without any transitional words Yefet now turns from the question of authorship to a consideration of how the psalms were recited in the Temple. He devotes only one sentence of the introduction to this subject, which interests us because of its centrality in Saadiah's introduction. Since this single sentence is followed immediately by further attention to the problem of the authors and their time, we should finish our discussion of this issue before delving into the ritual matter.

In a self-justifying tone similar to that in the introduction itself, Yefet now explains why he must consider the question of authorship in the preface to Psalm 1. The reason is his predecessors' unacceptable identifications of the author of this psalm, "which lacks a heading and which has no preceding psalm that does have an attribution." Some say the author was Adam, others argue it was Moses, and most of the commentators attribute it to David (just as they attribute to him all the psalms without headings, except for the ten by Moses).[50] None offered any serious proof of his opinion, nor even support of its plausibility, so he sees no point in "mentioning their proofs and refuting them." Saadiah's unique position (that all 150 psalms were composed by David) is not mentioned at all, as Yefet evidently felt that the reservations of both the Rabbanite and Karaite scholars were sufficient to discount it. Yefet cannot share the dislike of anonymity and the attempt to fill in the blanks with unfounded hypotheses. Instead he does three things: (1) he shows legitimate ways to reduce the scope of the phenomenon; (2) he faithfully notes the degree of certainty in his identification of the author of the various psalms; (3) he suggests a comforting explanation of the fact that about some psalms we have absolutely no information about the identity and date of the author.

Yefet concludes his discussion of authorship with a chronological summary: "If we examine the length of the period during which this book was completed (*ʾinḫatama*) we find that it lasted for more than four hundred years—from Moses to Solomon." Among the psalmists named in the headings, Moses is the earliest and Solomon the latest; but how do we know that the anonymous or semi-anonymous psalms were not composed after Solomon's death? Apparently, Yefet's statement means only that his examination of the 150 psalms disclosed none antedating Moses or postdating Solomon. A consideration of Yefet's approach to the historical aspect of the psalms must be deferred to our discussion of his preface to Psalm 3, where he surveys the biographical information in the headings and deals with their implications. For now we can wind up our investigation of his treatment of the subject of authorship by citing Yefet's statements in other places about the prophetic status of the psalmists.[51]

In his commentary on the verse, "Not so with My servant Moses, he is trusted throughout My household" (Num. 12:7), Yefet considers the difference between Moses' prophecy and those of all the other prophets; to this end he grades prophecy in six levels. The first, "face to face," is exclusive to Moses, while the second, "the holy spirit," is common to "Moses and many other prophets" (Ben-Shammai, *Doctrines* I, p. 258; II, p. 173). The prophets who were granted inspiration by "the holy spirit" are not named here, but are enumerated in Yefet's commentary on Zech. 1:8, where he deals with the nature of Zechariah's prophetic dream and locates it in a scheme of five levels of prophecy. Here too "the holy spirit" is the second level, but is defined in greater detail: "This is the rank of the 'singers' (*mešorerim*—Ezra 2:41), in other words, Moses, David, Solomon, the sons of Koraḥ, Asaph, Heman, and Jeduthun" (ibid. I, p. 277; II, p. 232).

"Face to face" prophecy is exclusive to Moses, for through it the commandments were given; but Moses also partook of prophecy by "the holy spirit," not only in that he composed some of the psalms but also because the Pentateuch itself contains his poems alongside the commandments. Yefet explains these two facets of Moses' prophecy in his commentary on "A prayer of Moses, the man of God" (Ps. 90:1): "the words 'man of God' here mean that Moses said these psalms [i.e., 90—100] by the 'holy spirit,' just as he uttered [the blessing in Deut. 33]. For there are seven levels of prophecy, of which the most exalted is 'face to face,' followed by 'the holy spirit.' All the commandments transmitted by God to Moses on Sinai were spoken 'face to face,' while the blessing [in Deut. 33] and the psalms were by 'the holy spirit.' Similarly, what is said about David 'the man of God' (Neh. 12:24; 2 Chron. 8:14) has the same meaning. The verse, 'the spirit of the Lord spoke by me, and His word upon my tongue' (2 Sam. 23:2) means that the 'holy spirit' rested upon him and he uttered what the Lord revealed to him." As a psalmist Moses' rank is no higher than David's, and this is also true concerning Moses' poems included in the Pentateuch.[52] Or, to reverse this statement: as a psalmist David "the man of God" is in no wise inferior to Moses "the man of God," and this apparently applies to the other psalmists as well. In the passages devoted to the degrees of prophecy Yefet does not explain how the *mešorerim* of the second rank are superior to prophet-messengers like Samuel, Isaiah, and Ezekiel, who are assigned to the third and fourth degrees of prophecy. The prophetic rank of the latter is stressed in the discussion of the sin of the Waters of Contention (comm. on Num. 20:12), where he claims that the prophets sent to mediate between the Lord and the nation resemble Moses in that they report the words of the Lord as they heard them, without addition or omission. He proves this from the explicit scriptural comparison, "I will raise up a prophet for them from among their own people like yourself: I will put My words in his mouth and he will speak to them all that I command him'' (Deut. 18:18), and from his own comparison of what is said about Moses—''[he] addressed the Israelites . . . in accordance with all the instructions'' (Deut. 1:3) with Ezekiel's statement—''I told the exiles all the things that the Lord had shown me'' (11:25). Furthermore, prophecy is protected not only from distortion by the messenger but also from oblivion, for ''he taught us that the Lord strengthens the memory of his prophets so that they can remember their message from beginning to end, remembering all the words in order.''[53] Yefet does not accord this word-for-word revelation of the prophet-messenger to the psalmist, as emerges from Ben-Shammai's summary of the nature of the second degree of prophecy:

> The holy spirit is not a sort of speech or vision that the prophet hears or sees and transmits to his audience; it is an inspiration that causes the possessor of the holy spirit to do certain things, to act in a certain way, or to say certain things, chiefly words of song and praise. (p. 270)

Ben-Shammai bases this generalization, inter alia, upon Yefet's remarks about the prayer of Hannah (comm. on 1 Sam. 2:1). We shall quote this passage because of its importance for understanding his conception of prophetic prayer:

> She said this prayer (*ʾaṣ-ṣala*) by the holy spirit, like ''A prayer of Moses'' (Ps. 90), ''[a prayer] of Habakkuk'' (Hab. 3). Her prayer can be divided into two parts: one describes [the Lord's] deeds at all times, and the other [describes the Lord's] deeds that are uniquely for Israel at the time of the redemption. The Lord saw fit to inspire her with this prayer so that she could know her rank with him. (p. 271)

There seems to be a fundamental difference between prayer, which is man's address to the Lord, and prophecy, which is the Lord's word to man. When prophets pray, however, this opposition disappears, because of the holy spirit, which descends from heaven and inspires the prophet's address to the Lord. The comparison of Hannah's prayer with those of Moses and Habakkuk is meant to show that the introductory words ''she prayed'' (1 Sam. 1:10) do not negate the prophetic quality of her utterance. The prominence within her prayer of her vision of future events provides a positive confirmation of the prophetic nature of her prayer. But it is precisely the prediction of Israel's future redemption that goes beyond the definition of prayer and must therefore be linked with the personal situation in which it is spoken. This is why Yefet connects the last verse of the prayer with a distinctly individual purpose—revealing to Hannah her exalted prophetic status with the Lord! Yefet does not say that Hannah's prayer will ultimately serve as a harbinger of Israel's redemption and an encomium sung by His worshippers about the Lord's righteous sovereignty over human destiny. Nevertheless, as we shall see from his explanations of the biographical headings of certain psalms, the link between the prophecy, "He will give power to His king and will raise the horn of His anointed one" (1 Sam. 2:10), and the personal celebration of the barren woman who has borne a child does not nullify the role of personal prophetic prayer in the public sphere as both prayer and prophecy.[54] On the contrary, it seems that precedence given to the psalmists over the prophetic messengers must be attributed to the importance of the psalms as Israel's obligatory prayers for all generations, which for Yefet evidently outweighed the significance of prophetic reproofs and predictions. It is in any event clear that the classification of the psalmists' prophecy as by the "holy spirit" and the relation of some psalms to a specific personal situation do not in any way detract from their divine and absolute truth. The difference between the word-for-word revelation conveyed by the prophetic messenger and the inspiration of the holy spirit that rests upon the prophetic psalmist involves only how the word of the Lord comes to man and not the value of the divine words that he speaks. Thus while Saadiah saw the psalms as prophecies in every respect, some of which were phrased as prayers, Yefet viewed them as actual prayers, which resembled prophecies per se in that they were uttered by the holy spirit.[55]

Another difference between prophecy per se and the "holy spirit" is their historical duration, according to Yefet. Just as "face to face" prophecy was limited to the days of Moses, so too the "holy spirit" was not vouchsafed throughout the prophetic age, that is, until the beginning of the Second Temple period. As will be remembered, Yefet concluded his discussion of the authorship question with the remark that his investigations indicated that the Book of Psalms was composed during the four hundred years between Moses and Solomon. This lower boundary is mentioned again in his commentary on the verse "to seal both vision and prophet, and to anoint the holy of holies" (Dan. 9:24). He explains "vision" as "prophecies relating to the future, like the prophecies of Haggai, Zechariah, and Malachi," and "prophet" as referring to prophetic utterances relating to the present. He continues: "Some scholars say that the 'holy spirit' came to an end in the days of Solomon, and that there remained only singers (*m^{e}šor^{e}rim*) who said (*jaḳulun*) the songs and psalms, as was said concerning the time of Hezekiah the king of Judah: 'and he said, etc.'"[56] Yefet is evidently referring to the verse, "King Hezekiah and the officers ordered the Levites to praise the Lord, in the words of David and Asaph the seer, so they praised rapturously, and they bowed and prostrated themselves'' (2 Chron. 29:30); from this he infers that in Hezekiah's time the Levites sang the psalms but no longer composed them. Yefet then offers an alternative explanation of the words ''to seal both vision and prophet'': the meaning is not the end of prophecy, but rather the closure of the scriptural canon of twenty-four books. This alternative interpretation has no effect on the validity of the incidental statement about the scholars who say that the ''holy spirit'' was withdrawn after Solomon's death, many generations before Malachi, the last of the prophets. Yefet neither agrees nor disagrees with this view; but the correlation between this generalized assertion and the results of his investigation concerning the dating of the psalms cannot be overlooked. Were it not for the distinct theological benefit of an early dating for the cessation of the ''holy spirit,'' Yefet would probably not have pointed it out in at least two places. True, Yefet did not adopt Kirkisani's view that Jeroboam I was the father of the Rabbanite schism and the instigator of sectarian strife in Israel.[57] Nonetheless, it seems plausible that someone who was so concerned with the prophetic status of the psalms, even while acknowledging the anonymity of many of them, would prefer to say that the canon was completed during the glorious period of the institution of the Temple ritual by David and Solomon. Moreover, to counter the Rabbanite claim that the Eighteen Benedictions were composed by anonymous prophets and elders at the end of the prophetic period (''one hundred and twenty elders, among them some prophets, ordained the eighteen blessings in their order''—BT M^{e}gillah 17b), Yefet and his predecessors raise the historical and theological argument that the ''holy spirit'' had departed from Israel long before that![58]

What is the relationship between the cessation of ''the holy spirit'' in Solomon's time, and the opinion of the Karaite scholars that ''there remained only singers who said the songs and the psalms'' (as proven by the description in 2 Chron. 29 of Hezekiah's renewal of the Temple service)? This distinction between composing and performing the psalms would seem to be self-evident, and require underscoring only for the benefit of those who adhere to the belief—which Yefet frequently repeats—that the recitation of the psalms in the Temple service was a sort of secondary (or repeated) prophecy, it too under the influence of ''the holy spirit.'' Consequently, he must supplement the assertion that the ''holy spirit'' was withdrawn after Solomon's death with the reservation that this refers to authors but not to singers, upon whom ''the holy spirit'' still rested in Hezekiah's reign and afterwards. This reservation is necessary not only because of the ambiguity of *m^{e}šorer* as used in Scripture (both poet and performer), but also because Yefet's use of the Arabic verb *ḳala* 'said' is ambiguous, denoting both initial composition and later performance. This homonymity is intentional and expresses the essential kinship between the two activities, which were often the province of the same individuals: just as we find Asaph described as a poet (in Pss. 50, 73–76, and 78–83, whose superscriptions contain only his name), we also find him performing a psalm by someone else. This is how Yefet explains the perplexing heading, "for the leader; on Jeduthun, of Asaph. A psalm" (77:1): "The prophecy was Jeduthun's, and it descended in a state (*ʾalḥal*) of the holy spirit upon Asaph, who said it at the [appointed] time; thus Jeduthun was the author of the prophecy, but it was recited by Asaph." He explains the heading of Psalm 88 in the same fashion: the Koraḥides are the "authors of the hymn, i.e., those who said it initially," while Heman the Ezraḥite was its leader (*m^e naṣṣeaḥ*), because he was the head of the Levite watch at the time designated for its recitation in the Temple. For the heading of Psalm 39, however—"For the leader; for Jeduthun, a psalm of David"—Yefet proposed two alternative explanations: (1) "The psalm is essentially David's, and Jeduthun encouraged [i.e., directed] the singers to chant it at appropriate times"; (2) "David said (*kala*) this psalm during Jeduthun's watch. If so, David said the psalm after he had ordained the order of singers." Both explanations posit David as the author of the psalm, but according to the first he may have composed it before the institution of the Temple service, and the heading—which indicates that in the Temple this psalm was to be led by Jeduthun—was added later.[59] According to the second explanation, however, the psalm and its heading both postdate the institution of the Levite watches, since David himself assigned his psalm to Jeduthun. Yefet's method here is similar to that of Salmon ben Yeruḥam.[60] Both (unlike Saadiah) believed in th possibility of simultaneous revelation to a number of prophets, but nevertheless preferred to explain the headings that include more than one name as referring to individuals with different functions, all of whom were inspired by the "holy spirit" but fulfilled different roles.

This inherent similarity between the original "saying" (i.e., composition) of the psalm and its "saying" (i.e., performance) in the Temple is why the lone sentence about how the psalms were recited in the Temple crops up in the discussion of authorship. His remarks about the collective inspiration of the anonymous authors led him to consider the collective inspiration of the Temple choristers:

> Those of the watch had hymns which they said (*jaḳulunha*) standing. The holy spirit would rest upon them[61] at the [appointed] time and they recited this psalm according to its order (*niẓamuhu*), its rhythmic mode (*laḥnuhu*), and its structure (*tartibuhu*) without a change. (p. 15)

This sentence apparently summarizes Yefet's response to Saadiah's idea of the "five-fold condition" (see above, pp. 15–27). We must examine where they agree and where they differ.

There is no dispute between them concerning the first condition—the personal. Yefet too believes that each Levite watch was assigned certain hymns. This is evident not only from the beginning of the passage just quoted, but also from Yefet's explanation of those headings with multiple names (see above). Saadiah never mentions the obligation to say the psalms standing—Yefet's second condition—apparently considering it to be self-evident in light of the ban on sitting in the Temple precincts, which applies to everyone except for kings of Davidic lineage (and even they may sit only in the Courtyard).[62] Yefet may have stressed this condition because of the importance of physical actions in Karaite prayer (see above, p. 75); if so, standing is only one detail that exemplifies the whole. Indeed, from his commentary on the verse, "come let us bow down and kneel, bend the knee before the Lord our maker" (Ps. 95:6), it is not clear whether he thought that only the congregation in the Temple bowed and knelt, or also the Levites who invited them to do so (as seems to be the case from the first person plural of the verse). The prooftext he cites—"When the offering was finished the king and all who were there with him knelt and prostrated themselves" (2 Chron. 29:29)—is itself ambiguous.

Yefet's third requirement—the temporal—parallels Saadiah's fourth condition. Its wording is obscure, for Yefet says only "the holy spirit rested upon them at the time (*fi-ʾl-wakt*)." The noun "time" is preceded by the definite article but has no modifying adjective, so in the translation above I added the word "appointed," on the basis of parallel sources wherein Yefet uses the same wording, but in a clearer context. In his remarks on Ps. 77:1 (discussed above) he writes: "The prophecy was Jeduthun's, and it descended in the state of the holy spirit upon Asaph, who said it at the time (*fi ʾl-wakt*)"; here it is clear that the meaning is at the appropriate time designated for it. In his commentary on Ps. 88:1 he says that the heading distinguishes the Koraḥides who composed the psalm from "Heman who was the leader and the head of the watch at the time" (*fi ʾl-wakt*), meaning at the time appointed to sing this psalm.[63] We learn the appointed time for reciting the psalms from his commentary on Ps. 92:1, where he remarks that Moses (the author of the "Psalm for the Sabbath day") ordained that the psalm be said in the Tabernacle on the Sabbath, apparently while the Additional Sacrifices were being offered. He deduces the temporal link between the psalm and the sacrificial ritual from the description of Hezekiah's activities (2 Chron. 29:27–29): "[The text] informs [us] that the song began 'when the burnt offering began' (ibid. 27)" (comm. on Ps. 95:6).[64] His explanation of the heading "a psalm for thanksgiving" (100:1) offers two options; according to one of them these words mean that the psalm was chanted when the thank offering was made. In the prefaces to the six daily psalms (24, 48, 81, 82, 93, and 94) he says nothing about their having been recited during the morning sacrifice on weekdays. Psalm 81, however, he connects with the New Moon: "It seems that it was said on every New Moon, when Israel gathered in the House of the Lord." The cautious language which he uses is surprising in light of the explicit reference to the New Moon in v. 4 ("Blow the horn on the new moon"), but he uses the same terminology in his preface to Ps. 68: "It is reasonable that it be said on the festival of Pentecost, because it mentions the day of Mt. Sinai (v. 9) and the revelation of the Divine Glory (v. 8)." Thus Yefet deduces from the "Psalm for the Sabbath day" that the psalms corresponded with particular days and festivals; from the description of the Temple worship during Hezekiah's time he concludes that they were recited at specific times, in conjunction with the sacrificial offerings. When it comes to specifying the exact time assigned to a particular psalm, however, he limits himself to cautious hypotheses.

It is difficult to understand the nature of the fourth requirement—saying the psalm according to its order (*niẓamuhu*). The noun *niẓam* means "order" and can apply to many things. We can infer the intended signification here from Yefet's frequent use of it in his discussion of the thematic link between the psalms, which is the reason for their serial arrangement. When he explains, for example, why the Book of Psalms was not arranged chronologically, he uses the term *niẓamu ʾez-zaman* "order of times" (end of preface to Ps. 1: p. 15), and similar uses are common throughout the commentary. Yefet seems to have assumed that the thematic ordering, in which the beginning of a psalm is usually linked to the conclusion of the previous one, applied not only to the arrangement of the psalms in the edited anthology but also to the order in which they were chanted in the Temple. Saadiah advanced no similar claim, but the idea is far from strange: the Rabbanite prayerbook, too, incorporates groups of psalms in the order of their appearance in Scripture, such as the psalms of the *Hallel* (113–118), the introductory psalms of the Morning Service (145–150), and, to some extent, the psalms for the Inauguration of the Sabbath (95–99, 29; 92–93).

The fifth requirement parallels Saadiah's second condition—the melodic: the psalm must be sung according to a particular rhythmic mode *(laḥn)*. This requirement stems from the performance instruction found in some of the headings; Yefet's glosses on them reflect his view. Thus (like Saadiah and Salmon) he comments on the heading of Psalm 4 that "*bi-n^eginoṯ* is in the plural, which means at least two, but can be more. There are also psalms that are chanted in [only] one rhythmic mode, as is written: *ʿal n^eginaṯ l^e-Dawid* (61:1)." This statement is ambiguous—like Saadiah's in his introduction (p. 31)—and it is difficult to say whether the meaning is that the rhythmic mode should be changed during a single performance of the psalm or that one performance may be in one mode and a subsequent performance in a different one. Yefet's gloss on the heading of Psalm 67 clarifies his intention: "*Bi-n^eginot̠* indicates that the psalm should be sung in different (*muḥtalifa*) modes even though it is short." Apparently it is split into two sections because it deals with two subjects: "They chanted in one mode as far as *yiśm^eḥu wi-y^erann^enu* (verse 4), and after that chanted it in another mode from there on." The cautious and noncommittal language in the last two passages quoted is characteristic of Yefet in general, including his statements about the vocal and instrumental performance of the psalms. He is not interested in proving a specific musical thesis, or in refuting Saadiah's thesis, but in explaining the verses. He probably did hope that a by-product of his cautious exegesis would be the undermining of the textual basis of Saadiah's view, which the latter, as will be recalled, had proposed with great confidence. Yefet says, for instance, that the term *mizmor* refers to a psalm that incorporates praise (*tamǵid*) of the Lord and which is performed with a melody and instrumental accompaniment (84:1, 88:1). Yet he is somewhat hesitant about applying this rule to Psalm 63, because of the circumstances in which it was composed: "It is, however, difficult to assume this with regard to 'A psalm of David when he was in the Wilderness of Judah,' although it is possible that initially it was simply recited, and only later was its recitation accompanied by song and instruments" (preface to Ps. 3). In other words, not all of the psalms were sung and accompanied by music, only those whose headings indicate this; and even among these there were some that, at least initially, were not sung.

Like Salmon he prefers thematic explanations to musical ones; unlike his predecessor, though, he does not even mention musical explanations when he glosses *ʿal maḥalat̠* (53:1) as referring to Mahalath daughter of Ishmael (see Gen. 28:9), *ʿal ha-š^eminit̠* (6:1) as concerning the "eighth horn" (i.e., the kingdom of Ishmael), and *ʿal šošannim* (45:1) as referring to the remnant of Israel who is "like a lily among thorns" (Cant. 2:2). Like Salmon, Yefet does not hesitate to read "in choruses bless the Lord" (68:27[26]) as indicating that the male choruses in the court of the Israelites sang along with the Levites, and "amidst maidens playing timbrels" (ibid., verse 26[25]) as meaning that the women participated in the instrumental accompaniment. He, too, finds it necessary to offer a scriptural proof that the women stood in a separate place from the men,[65] but fails to specify that they were permitted to play only on the "timbrel and drum" explicitly mentioned (comm. on Ps. 68:26). Thus while Salmon ben Yeruḥam grapples with the impressive musical theory proposed by Saadiah and adopts those parts that are compatible with the Karaite view, none of it survives in Yefet's commentary, except for the idea that the Levites in the Temple were required to comply with the performance instructions contained in the headings, according to a very cautious interpretation.

The sixth and last requirement that was incumbent upon the members of the watch of Levites, according to Yefet, was that the recitation of the psalm not deviate from its structure (*tartib*). Yefet uses the Arabic verb *rataba* to render the Biblical *k.w.n.* in verses like "He has set up (*konen*) His throne for judgment" (Ps. 9:8[7]) and "set it upon the rivers" (24:2); he employs the noun *tartib* to mean a chronological order (comm. on 24:1 and 39:1) or textual sequence (comm. on 107:3). We might infer from these uses that his intention is that it is forbidden to deviate from the way in which the psalm is set up and ordered, i.e., from its textual sequence. Much as the Mishnah M^{e}gillah (2,1) bans switching the order of the sections during the ceremonial reading of the Scroll of Esther, Yefet apparently assumed that it was forbidden to sing the end of the psalm before its beginning, to skip verses, or to repeat them several times, as well as to make other changes in its "structure." Saadiah stated no corresponding requirement, perhaps because it was self-understood. On the other hand, Yefet has no parallel to Saadiah's fifth condition—the obligation to say each psalm in the place designated for it in the Temple—perhaps because the scriptural basis of this condition is particularly tenuous (see above. pp. 22ff.)

But beyond their similarities and differences, there is an essential gap between Saadiah's five-fold condition and Yefet's six requirements. The former presents the "conditions" as normative requirements that regulated the Levites' duties in the Temple. The Karaite scholar, however, lists his requirements as preconditions for the descent of the holy spirit upon the Levites. Saadiah's approach is legal, while Yefet's is prophetic. The first is designed to erect a solid barrier between the singing of the psalms in the Temple and their recitation in the synagogue, while the second is intended to exalt and glorify the sacred hymns of the Temple as a model for partial imitation in the synagogue and as an aspiration for the messianic future.

From Yefet's point of view the entire introduction to the commentary on Psalm 1 is devoted to a single topic—the question of authorship; therefore he concludes it with a short note on a related topic—the editing of the book: "Having explained this matter, we should mention why the book was not written down (*judawwan*) in chronological order; our answer is that there is greater benefit in associating topics than dates, particularly [with regard to] the needs of the people of the exile" (p. 15). In other words, grouping the psalms according to topic confers greater benefit for students and worshippers, particularly during the exile, when the biographical and historical aspect of the psalms has lost some of its importance (see below on this topic). Yefet does not identify the editor of Psalms at this juncture, and throughout his commentary he generally refers simply to the *mudawwin* (literally: he who writes down a composition *[diwan]*). From several of these references one can deduce that he does not mean David or one of the prophetic poets named in the headings. Thus, for example, his commentary on Ps. 56:1 implies that the detailed heading is not an essential part of the psalm (as Salmon believed—see his commentary on this verse), but is a later addition: "When he writes *ʿal yonat ʾelem* he is referring to David, who said of himself 'O that I had the wings of a dove [*yonah*]!' (Ps. 55:7); *ʾelem r^eḥoḳim* refers to a place near Gath, where the Philistines kept him tied up [deriving *ʾelem* from *ʾalummah* 'bundle']. The *mudawwin* states that this psalm is by David, who was held captive by the Philistines in a distant *[raḥoḳ]* place." Just as here the *mudawwin* provides us with information about the identity of the psalmist and the situation in which he composed the psalm, so too in the heading of Psalm 22 the *mudawwin* informs us that David said this psalm, and adds that the utterance was inspired by the holy spirit and addressed to *ʾayyelet ha-šaḥar*, meaning a group of people in the distant future who will be in great distress (comm. on 22:1). Yefet also understands the two opening verses of Ecclesiastes as a heading supplied by the *mudawwin*, who relates to us the appellations and genealogy of the author, and summarizes in his own words the topic (*ġarḍ* = purpose) of the treatise: "Utter futility!—said Koheleth—utter futility! All is futile!" (Yefet, *Ecclesiastes*, p. 5, lines 12–15; English translation p. 147).

This attribution of the informative headings to the *mudawwin* is so obvious to Yefet that he sees no need to note this fact with regard to every psalm and merely glosses the meaning of the superscription. Sometimes the heading supplements the identification of the psalmist with that of the leader charged with supervising the recitation of the psalm in the Temple (see comm. on 77:1); sometimes, in addition to defining the theme of the psalm, it also indicates the literary genre (*šir, mizmor*) and even provides musical instructions to the performers (see comm. on 88:1). Moreover, when the term *maśkil* (savant) appears in a heading, Yefet interprets this as "guidance and instruction for the people of the exile to use it [the psalm] in worship and proclaim [through it] their troubles to the Lord and beg for redemption and salvation and the fulfillment of the promise and the hastening of the deliverance (ibid.).[66] In other words, the *mudawwin* added both personal and biographical information as well as instructions for the psalm's performance in the Temple and the appropriate situations for using it in prayer.[67]

In the closing note of his introduction to Psalm 1—in which he deals briefly with the *mudawwin* (quoted above, p. 88)—Yefet attributes the ordering of the psalms as well to the *mudawwin;* earlier, in his discussion of the anonymous psalms, he says in an aside that the *mudawwin* split what were originally five psalms so that we now have ten (see above, p. 77).[68] In his remarks on 42:1 he notes that the *mudawwin* divided the 150 psalms into five books,[69] in each of which he collected and arranged the psalms with attention to unity of subject and authors: "Since the chapters by the sons of Koraḥ have similar subjects, the *mudawwin* collected them and arranged them one after another, separating them from David's psalms" (see also comm. on 84:1 and 100:5).[70] Like Saadiah and Salmon, Yefet attaches great importance to the juxtaposition of consecutive psalms. Sometimes he finds a distinctly theological reason for it, which adds an additional stratum of meaning to the psalms: "The *mudawwin* placed it after the previous psalm to tell us that the Lord accepted the prayers of those who desire [to return to] His land and holiness" (comm. on 85:2, and see also 110:1).

How did Yefet view the status of this *mudawwin*, who left so large an impress on the Book of Psalms? Are those who see the *mudawwin* as the "editor" (in the sense intended by modern biblical scholarship) correct? I have found no answer to these questions in Yefet's commentary on Psalms, so we must rely on statements about the *mudawwin* in his commentaries on other biblical books. In his remarks on the verse, "These too are the proverbs of Solomon, which the men of King Hezekiah of Judah copied" (Prov. 25:1), Yefet says that the words "these too" mean that the proverbs that follow are a supplement to the two earlier sections of the book (chapters 1–9 and 10–24), and that the word "copied" means that "they copied (*naḳaluha*) them [and added them] to the two existing parts. These [additional proverbs] were in separate sections, and Hezekiah's men transcribed them into the *diwan* [that already contained the first] two parts." In other words, Hezekiah's men did not write down Solomon's proverbs, previously transmitted orally, but merely collected separate written collections and appended them to the manuscript that already contained the first two sections. While Yefet attributes to Hezekiah's school only the technical crafts of appending and transcribing, he quickly emphasizes that "when the text says 'the men of Hezekiah' it means the prophets of [Hezekiah's] time before the exile of the ten tribes; thus they took them [the proverbs] with them [into exile] joined into a single book. This was done at the command of the Lord (*biʾamr ʾilahi*), may He be exalted and His name praised" (MS New York-Jewish Theological Seminary, Adler 102, vol. 2, pp. 57b–58a). Such assertions of certainty are rare in Yefet, and must be understood as a polemical retort to Saadiah's impressive argument, based on this verse, for the legitimacy of the commission of the Oral Law to writing during the Mishnaic and Talmudic periods.[71] Saadiah writes in his commentary on Proverbs *ad loc.*: "The words of this book teach us that many things remained that our forefathers transmitted one to another over a long period without writing them down, until they were written down later. For it says explicitly that Solomon said these proverbs but they long remained unwritten until they were written down (*dawwanaha*) by Hezekiah's men." Later Saadiah cites Jer. 17:22 to prove that laws, too, were transmitted orally, and concludes that "it was possible for our ancestors to transmit from one to another many of the commandments that they heard from Moses and did not write them until the Mishnah was written and the Talmud was written" (p. 194).[72] Yefet, by contrast, reads "these too" as meaning that the last group of proverbs were written down just like the first, and deduces that the two *diwans* could be combined only by prophets who had received an explicit divine commandment to do so.[73]

Had Yefet endowed only "Hezekiah's men" with prophetic status, we could view it as an uncharacteristic statement spurred by polemical needs; we find, however, that he grants a similar status to the *mudawwin* of the Book of Joshua. In his remarks on the verse, "The children of Judah could not oust the Jebusite inhabitants of Jerusalem, and the Jebusites dwell with the children of Judah in Jerusalem *until this day*" (Josh. 15:63), Yefet writes: "He tells us that the Judahites did not overpower the Jebusites who dwelled in it, and this was after the death of Joshua, but the *mudawwin* wrote this by divine ordinance."[74] In light of the information in Judges 1:8 about the capture of Jerusalem and its burning by the Judahites, one must say that the verse in Joshua refers to the period between the death of Joshua and the city's recapture by David. Since Yefet assumes that the *mudawwin* wrote the words "until this day" not long after Joshua's death, he must make it plain that the information in the verse was written prophetically. Similarly, Yefet seems to have held that the *mudawwin* of Ecclesiastes was active in Solomon's time, for in his commentary on Eccles. 1:12 he points out that Solomon himself employed the appellation *ḳohelet̠* used by the *mudawwin*, and adds: "it is likely that he called himself 'Ecclesiastes' first, and that the *mudawwin* called him that following his lead" (Yefet, *Ecclesiastes*, p. 19; English pp. 166–67). That "it is likely" leaves room for the opposite conclusion—namely, that the name was first used by the *mudawwin* and later adopted by Solomon—something possible only if they were contemporaries. The Karaite reluctance to admit the possibility that scriptural books were transmitted orally and later written down underlies Yefet's assumption that the *mudawwin* was always a contemporary of the author.

Furthermore, Yefet assigned prophetic status to the *mudawwin* not only in order to endow his deeds (the transcribing enterprise of the "men of Hezekiah") with absolute authority and in order to explain his access to information about the future ("until this day"), but mainly because in his view the *mudawwin* had a major share in the book's composition. True, in the Book of Psalms and Ecclesiastes his function is that of an editor, collecting and classifying the material, arranging it and adding on his own headings and colophons; in the historical books, however, he is an author-narrator, responsible for everything that is not the direct speech of one of the characters, and for even more than that. Yefet comments on the verse,

"And the captain of the Lord's hosts said to Joshua: Remove your sandals from your feet" (Josh. 5:15), that "the *mudawwin* called him 'the captain of the Lord's host as he had called himself" (Marwick, "Yefet," p. 448, note 11). This is meant to direct the reader's attention to the descriptive sequence: in verse 13 the narrator uses indefinite language—"and behold *a man* was standing before him"; in verse 14 the man identifies himself—"I am the captain of the Lord's host"; and thereupon the *mudawwin*-narrator also starts to designate him by that name—"and the captain of the Lord's host said to Joshua" (v. 15). Similarly, Yefet notes that the words "And the people were faint" (1 Sam. 14:28) are supplied by the *mudawwin* (Marwick, ibid.). By this he means that the evaluation of the situation is the narrator's, and not that of the soldier who told Jonathan about his father's vow.[75] Moreover, Yefet also took note of the opposite phenomenon: in the summary of his commentary on the story of the Witch of Endor (1 Sam. 28:8–25) he cites six cases where the *mudawwin* expresses in ostensibly factual language the subjective point of view of the protagonists. For example, "the people chased them by way of the Jordan" (Josh. 2:7) does not describe the true situation, since the spies were still in Rahab's house; hence we must conclude that "the writer reported what the king and the [towns]people believed."[76] The chronological data about Saul's reign (1 Sam. 13:10) are also attributed by Yefet to the *mudawwin* (Marwick, ibid.).

On the basis of the foregoing we might conclude that Yefet understands whatever is not the direct speech of an actor—prophet or otherwise—as coming from the *mudawwin*'s pen. In fact, he goes even further and offers the bold hypothesis that the *mudawwin* modified the actual words of his characters when stylistic concerns so dictated. Two such cases are the indefinite phrasing of David's words to Ahimelech the Priest of Nob ("I have directed my young men to such and such a place"—1 Sam. 21:3),[77] and the elliptical address of Joab to the Tekoite woman ("'Go to the king and say to him thus and thus.' And Joab told her what to say"—2 Sam. 14:3). Yefet even formulates an extremely important stylistic principle: "The *mudawwin* did not relate Joab's words to the Tekoite woman in full, relying on the woman's account to the king. This is done in the opposite way as well—he relates (*dawwana*) Jacob's words to the messengers (Gen. 32:5–6) but omits that the messengers repeated [those words] to Esau. Similarly, in Balak's message to Balaam, the first time he relates (*dawwana*) Balak's words to the messengers (Num. 22:5–6) and omits the messengers' repetition [of the words] to Balaam [v. 7: "they gave him Balaam's message"]. The second time he did the opposite [i.e., in vv. 16–17 the speech of the second group of messengers is given, with no prior mention of Balak's commanding them to say it]" (Marwick, ibid.).[78] Finally, as Ben-Shammai has demonstrated ("Review," pp. 403–405), Yefet's introduction to Genesis and his commentary on Gen. 1:1 imply that Moses was the *mudawwin* of the Torah, "responsible for the wording and arrangement of the text."

Given this far-reaching concept of the function of the narrator-editor, it is not surprising that Yefet considered the *mudawwin* of each scriptural book to be a prophet in his own right. The task of collecting the prophecies also required a prophetically inspired *mudawwin*. In his commentary on Hosea 1:1 Yefet explains that just as the books of Chronicles and Kings describe only selected historical incidents, so too only those prophecies of Hosea and Micah that have relevance for the exilic age were written down.[79] It is the prophetic selection of prophecies and psalms to be preserved for posterity that justifies and validates the Karaite *pešer*, since it obligates one to interpret the verses as alluding to the present situation of the exiles and what the future holds in store for them.[80] Moreover, as a prophetic writer who was contemporary with the prophetic speaker, the *mudawwin* was also the source of the written "transcript" (*naḳl*) and responsible for its authority and accuracy.[81] It follows that the clear distinction between the words of the eponymous prophet and those of the anonymous *mudawwin* who wrote them down, and that between the words of the psalmists and those of the *mudawwin* who collected and arranged them and supplied them with headings, were in no way meant to confer a subsidiary status on the *mudawwin*'s words. These distinctions have only an exegetical import—to permit maximum understanding of the structure of the book and its stylistic layers. Yefet makes no attempt to lift the veil of anonymity from the *mudawwin*, because his precise identity is of no importance; but at the same time, a clear notion of his activity is useful for a stylistic, literary, and thematic grasp of Scripture, including the Book of Psalms.[82]

Psalm 3 is the first that has a heading, and allows Yefet to continue the prefatory discussions as part of his commentary on verse 1. The first half ("A psalm of David") is the occasion for a consideration of psalmic genres; the second half ("when he fled from his son Absalom") leads into the question of historical background and chronology. Yefet begins by enumerating seven terms that indicate a literary genre—*mizmor*, *šiggayon*, *mik̲tam*, *šir*, *maśkil*, *tᵉfillah*, and *tᵉhillah*—followed by the number of times each appears in the headings of the book, either alone or associated with others. For example: "The word *mizmor* is frequently used in the headings, a total of 47 times. The word *šir* [appears] 29 times, and is associated with *mizmor* 12 times." Next he attempts to explicate each term and define the genre designated by it. He concludes the discussion by noting that *hallᵉ-luyah*, *hodu*, and *la-mᵉnaṣṣeaḥ* do not indicate genres and consequently are not glossed here. The desire for system, expressed primarily by classification, and the strong tendency to statistical summary, which are also found in the writings of Saadiah and Samuel ben Hophni, are attributes of the scholarly tastes of that age. Today we are no longer impressed by such details, not only because concordances have made them accessible to all, but chiefly because they have no meaning in and of themselves. Ibn Ezra already viewed them as superfluous and misleading, because of their superficiality, as is evident from his fierce reservations about the Torah commentaries by the "scholars of the Talmudic Academies in the Islamic countries": "Samuel ben Hophni, too, garnered a handful [*ḥofen*] of wind, for in his commentary on 'Jacob went out' he multiplied words, mentioning each prophet by name and how many times he exiled from his home, and explaining the great benefit of travel. But there is no benefit in this commentary, just long-windedness" (introduction to the standard commentary on the Pentateuch, First Path).[83]

The short biographic-historical excursus that follows is called by Yefet "matters concerning the enemies mentioned in this book." He starts with David's personal enemies—Absalom, Saul, Doeg, and the Philistines—listing the psalms in which they are mentioned, separately and collectively. Next he surveys "the enemies of Israel and of the righteous servant," classifying psalms by the number of enemies to whom they refer. Some psalms refer to only one enemy (for example, Gog alone: 2, 27, 40, 48, 68; Edom alone: 31, 71, 53); others relate to two enemies (for example, Ishmael and Edom: 5, 9, 140); while others mention three, four, or more (83). He goes on to distinguish between Psalm 35, which relates to "Gog, Edom, Ishmael, and the enemies of the righteous servant," Psalm 69, which refers to "the three kings and the enemies of the righteous servant among Israel," and Psalm 109, which refers to "the enemies of the righteous servant alone." The beginning of his commentary on Psalm 109 clarifies that the "righteous servant" who is persecuted by both gentile kings and domestic enemies is actually none other than the Karaite community. Alongside the idea that David often prophesied about the enemies of Israel in the countries of its exile, the Karaite *pešer* also took it as given that the original purpose of certain psalms was to describe the Rabbanite-Karaite schism. Reading the verse, "like a lily among thorns, so is my beloved among the maidens" (Cant. 2:2), the Karaite minority identified itself with the complimentary term "lily"; reading the verse, "and the knowledgeable (*maśkilim*) will be radiant like the bright expanse of sky and those who lead the many in righteousness will be like the stars forever and ever" (Dan. 12:3), it cast its own scholars as the "knowledgeable." Thus it is not surprising that both Salmon and Yefet interpreted the psalms whose headings have *šošan* "lily" (60) or *šošannim* "lilies" (69) as referring to the Karaites, nor that the term "blameless" at the beginning of Psalm 119 endowed this psalm with a central status in the consciousness of the Karaites and in their prayers.[84]

By contrast, the heading of Psalm 109 provides no indication of its topic; Yefet must have linked it to the Karaite-Rabbanite controversy not only because of its thematic similarity to Psalm 69, but primarily because of the vehemence of the persecuted worshippers' entreaties for revenge. We should note that Saadiah felt obliged to stress that "The sense of this psalm is not that the prophet prays for evil to befall his enemies or curses them, just as Moses, when he said, 'pay no regard to their presentation' (Num. 16:15), did not intend a prayer for evil to befall those persons; rather, both are a proclamation by the Lord, who told His prophets what would happen to the wicked" (*Psalms*, p. 238; see also p. 168, on Ps. 69). Yefet, for his part, did not hesitate to explain "may his children be orphans and his wife a widow" (109:9) literally, and had no qualms about understanding the text as directed against the Rabbanite opponents of his sect: "This psalm includes a remonstrance against the situation of the knowledgeable of the exile at the hands of the shepherds of the exile, who mislead Israel, are the guardians of the walls, oppose the knowledgeable, and harm them in every way." The frequent interpolation of scriptural codewords contorts the syntax of the Arabic sentence, but the intention is clear: this psalm expresses the complaint of the Karaite scholars of the exile, who are the faithful guardians of the walls, against the stubborn opposition of the shepherds of the exile (the Rabbanite leadership), who lead Israel astray. Yefet proceeds to ground this identification of the terrible enemy reviled in the psalm with the dominant majority in his contemporary Jewish communities by means of an analogy with the violent persecution of the "righteous prophets," Micaiah, son of Imlah, and Jeremiah, by Zedekiah, son of Chenaanah, and Pashhur. The prophets of the Lord were beaten because they contradicted the suave deceptions of the false prophets (after Isa. 30:10) and their soothing prophecies (Jer. 6:14), and because they dared "to declare to Jacob his transgressions and to Israel his sin" (Mic. 3:8). Like the "prophets who lead My people astray" (Mic. 3:5), "the shepherds of the exile who mislead" lightened the burden of the commandments on Israel "and permitted them food and drink, contamination and purity, Sabbath and festival, and forbidden sexual relationships." Like those "concerned about His word" (Isa. 66:5) in ages past, today's knowledgeable of the nation confront them and reprove them for their sins. As in the past, the reproof brings upon its deliverers a violent reaction—hatred, bodily harm, and excommunication—so that they must pray for divine assistance in order to be able to withstand it.

While Saadiah's conception of Psalms as a book of edification, valid for all time, protected him against the temptation to exploit the psalms for the transient exigencies of the internecine Jewish quarrel by means of topical identifications of the worshipper and his enemies, the Karaite view of the psalms as prophetic prayers naturally led them into the trap of specific identification. Thus Saadiah says of Psalm 91 that "this text concerns the righteous servant" (*Psalms*, p. 211), without associating the psalm with specific persons or a defined historical time; whereas Yefet cannot refrain from an exclusive and unequivocal identification of the "righteous servant" with the Karaites. From the exegetical perspective, these identifications seem extremely forced to us today; but we must recognize that Yefet and the other Karaite exegetes of the Book of Psalms performed a great service for the Karaite synagogue. Not only did they assert that Karaite prayer was superior to Rabbanite, since it alone is prophetic; by virtue of their *pešer*, Moses and David, Asaph and Heman, the Koraḥides and the other psalmists became the prophets of consolation to the latter-day "sons of Scripture" who anticipated a speedy redemption.[85]

After his survey of enemies domestic and foreign Yefet lists all the headings that contain a temporal designation, such as "when he fled from his son Absalom" (3:1). He concludes that there are eleven psalms whose time of composition is indicated; in his opinion Psalms 7 and 18 should be added to this number, even though they contain less precise temporal information. The association of these thirteen psalms with specific events in David's life would seem to disqualify them as prayers for the use of later generations. Consequently, Yefet must make it clear that even though the prayers were uttered by David in particular personal circumstances, as prophecies they were originally intended to provide a vehicle by which the Jews could express themselves in analogous historical circumstances: "This psalm is one of those that David said about himself, and he taught Israel how to pray to the Lord in situations similar to his. He said it by the holy spirit, and the choristers in the House of the Lord repeated it, as we have explained the meaning of the term *mizmor*" (end of commentary on Psalm 3). Yefet strives to anchor this view in the text itself. From the contiguity of Psalms 2 and 3 he infers that the *mudawwin* placed Psalm 3 (written in response to a personal danger in the present) immediately after Psalm 2 (which refers to a national danger in the future) not only because of the seriousness of the two dangers, but primarily so that we would "compare the incident of Absalom with that of Gog." First he explains the nine verses of Psalm 3 as referring to David and his kingdom—the request to be saved from Absalom's large army (vv. 1–3); the Lord's response, which is made known to David through prophecy (vv. 4–7); and an additional request to save him and his nation in future wars with external enemies (vv. 8–9). At the end of this explanation Yefet adds: "We have promised to return to each verse of this psalm and show the similarity between the case of Israel and Gog and what happened to David at the hands of Absalom." But since he finds parallel language only in the opening verses of the two psalms ("O Lord, my foes are so many!" [3:2(1)]—"Kings of the earth and regents"

[2:2]; "many are those who attack" [3:2(1)]—"nations . . . and peoples" [2:1]), he must resort to non-psalmic texts to demonstrate that the balance of Psalm 3 also has a national dimension ("a shield about me" [3:4]—"In that day, the Lord will shield the inhabitants of Jerusalem" [Zech. 12:8]; "my glory" [3:4]—"Bowing before you, shall come the children of those who tormented you" [Isa. 60:14]; "He who holds my head high" [3:4]—"Now is my head high over my enemies roundabout" [Ps. 27:6], etc). This exegetical enterprise is justified only by the basic assumption that the very inclusion of the personal psalms in the Book of Psalms is evidence that they were meant to be used for congregational prayer in the future.

This future must also include the present of the Karaite exegete, faithful to the belief that the commandment of prayer is fulfilled primarily by the recitation of psalms. For Saadiah, the permanent value of the psalms rests in their message. Thus the reference to the rebellion of Absalom in Psalm 3 is only "an example from which to learn" about God's punishment of the wicked (*Psalms*, p. 48). Consequently he need not detach Psalm 137 from the historical era for which it was intended; he does this by interpolating the words "the people of the exile will say" (*jaḳul ʾahlu ʾaǵǵalijah*) at the beginning of the *Tafsir* on that psalm. Yefet, too, in the introduction to his commentary on Psalm 137, writes that "this chapter is the utterance (*ʾaʿraba*) of the exiles";[86] but he feels obliged to add an explanation of the status of this prophetic prayer (which refers to a future that has now become the past) for the present exile: "He wrote it down (*dawwana*) in this book to be a lesson for the people in exile—they should use it in prayer and remember what happened in Jerusalem and not forget it." For the Karaites, this is the force and authority of prophetic prayer. Its capacity to break through the mists of the future and match the needs and situation of a distant generation comes from its prophetic nature,[87] while its eternal authority as obligatory prayer is entailed by its inclusion in Scripture.

Notes to Chapter Two

1. The complete commentary of Salmon ben Yeruḥam to Psalms was not available to me, since I had access to only four sources: (1) MS Leningrad-Firkovich, II, 1345 (dated 1515), which contains the introduction and the commentary on Pss. 1—72; (2) MS Leningrad-Firkovich, I, 555 (dated 1391), which contains the introduction (minus the first page and two pages in the middle) and the commentary on Pss. 1—89 (the second volume of this MS is MS Firkovich, I, 556, which contains the commentary on Pss. 90—150. There is no microfilm of this MS at the Institute of Microfilmed Hebrew Manuscripts in the Jewish National and University Library, Jerusalem. Pinsker had access to both volumes, and described

them briefly [see *Lickute* II, pp. 130–34]); (3) Marwick's edition of the commentary on Pss. 42—72, based on MS Firkovich, II, 1345, which lacks an introduction, notes, and variant readings (see Salmon, *Psalms*); (4) Shunary's edition of the introduction, which is also based on this MS (see Shunary, "Salmon"). Unless otherwise stated, all the quotations from the commentary herein are from MS 1345. Passages from the introduction are referenced according to the pagination in Shunary's edition; those from the body of the commentary are referenced by chapter and verse.

2. I had two sources for Yefet's commentary on Psalms: (1) MS Paris-Bibliothèque Nationale, Héb. 37, dated 1612–1614, which includes the introduction and the complete commentary (except for pp. 50 and 136, which are missing); (2) Bargès' edition, which contains the introduction and commentary on Pss. 1—2 with a Latin translation (see: Yefet, *Psalms*). References to the introduction and Psalms 1—2 are according to the pagination in the Bargès edition; those to the rest of the commentary are by chapter and verse. For a description of the other eight extant manuscripts (all partial) see Ben-Shammai, *Doctrines,* II, pp. 14–17. On the relatively late date of the MSS of Yefet's commentaries written in Hebrew letters and the additions and changes found in them see Ben-Shammai, "Yefet's Commentaries," pp. 20–32.

3. See Marwick, "Al-Fasi." This short fragment does not provide sufficient basis for a discussion of David ben Abraham's approach to the Book of Psalms.

4. Cf. Malter, *Saadiah,* pp. 260–71; Poznanski, "Opponents," pp. 215–16.

5. See Salmon, *Wars,* pp. 2–6.

6. The commentary was written in 955, as we learn from his remarks on Ps. 102:14 (published by Poznanski, "Saadiah," pp. 519–29, based on MS Vienna-Rabbinical seminary 39, written out by Pinsker, which was lost during the Second World War. Since both volumes of MS Firkovich I, 555–56 were borrowed by Pinsker [see *Lickute*, II, p. 130], it can be assumed that this was his copy-text).

7. Regarding the weakening of the laryngeals and pharyngeals in Palestine, under the influence of Greek, and in Babylonia, under the influence of Akkadian, see E. Y. Kutscher, *The Language and Linguistic Background of the Isaiah Scroll* (Leiden, 1974), pp. 505–11; A. Bendavid, *Biblical Hebrew and Mishnaic Hebrew*, vol. II (Tel Aviv, 1971), p. 440, §13 (Hebrew). In biblical Hebrew the plural of *t^ehillah* is *t^ehillot*; only in rabbinic Hebrew do we find *t^ehillim* and *tillim* (JT Sukkah, 3, 10; BT Pesaḥim 117a).

8. He uses the same Arabic root—*zalaḥa*—as Saadiah.

9. In *The Obligation of Prayer* he expresses this while discussing the benediction *Modim ᵓanaḥnu lak̲* (we give thanks unto You) in the *ᵓAmidah* prayer: "After these [prayers] concerning our needs come thanks for the Lord's mercies in the *Modim*, as the Lord said: 'Give thanks unto the Lord for He is good' (Ps. 136:1), to

which the response is 'we give thanks unto You'; but the response is not this very same [imperative]: 'Give thanks unto the Lord for He is good'!'' (Saadiah, *Siddur,* p. 5).

10. Saadiah's argument that the words of commandment found in the Book of Psalms cannot be used for prayer must have greatly disturbed the Karaites: in his commentary on Ps. 9:1 Salmon finds it necessary to inveigh against the mistaken custom of many Karaite worshippers: ''They also mutilate the received [grammatical] form of the prophetic text (*ʾat-tanzil*); when they pray *hodu* (thank!) (105:1; 136:1) they say: *ʾodeh* (I shall thank); if they find *zammᵉru* (sing!) (9:12) they say *ʾazammᵉrah* (I shall sing); if they find *halᵉlu* (praise!) (113:1 et passim), they say *ʾahalᵉlah* (I shall praise); and so throughout the entire book. But they are mistaken.''

11. Salmon mentions the verse without glossing its difficult text. From his argument, though, we may infer that he understood it to mean that the head of the Levites recited the praises first, after which the congregation repeated them. This is how Yefet explained this verse in his commentary on Ps. 136:1 (see below, p. 74).

12. In another context Salmon shows how the laws of prayer should be learned from the Book of Psalms: ''When I saw that in two places the prophets concluded their prayers with the verse 'Deliver us . . . and gather us' (Ps. 106:47 and 1 Chron. 16:35) [I understood that] this was done to teach us that we too should finish each section of the liturgy with the verse 'Deliver us . . .' '' (pp. 171–72). In the *Prayerbook according to the Customs of the Karaite Jews*, 3 vols. (Ramle, 1962–1963), the verses ''Deliver us . . .'' are not the regular ending, either of sections of the service nor of an entire service. Nevertheless they are the conclusion of certain prayers: the evening and morning services for the New Moon (I, pp. 30 and 71) and the morning service for the Sabbath (I, p. 220); at times, however, they are inserted in the middle of the service as well: in the morning service for the New Moon (I, p. 67) and for the Sabbath (I, p. 220) and in the evening service for Festivals (II, p. 40).

13. See above, pp. 24–27.

14. See *Tur ʾOraḥ Ḥayyim*, Laws of the Day of Atonement, §619: ''In Ashkenaz the righteous men have the custom of standing all night and all day. . . . They also had the custom of spending the night in the synagogue, reciting hymns and praises all night long.'' Thus Salmon was overstating the facts when he spoke of a universal duty to recite all 150 psalms, but it is hard to know whether he was misinformed or trying to mislead his readers.

15. Compare Saadiah's remarks, cited above, p. 34.

16. See above Chapter One, note 50.

17. Salmon links *maḥalaṯ* and *maḥol* with the *ḥalil*, too, but without identifying the instrument by giving its Arabic name. By contrast, he renders both *maḥol* (30:12) and *maḥalaṯ* (88:1) as *ṭubul*, a large two-headed drum. This was also Saadiah's rendering of these two words in his *Tafsir* on Psalms; while *ḥalil*, not found

in Psalms, he translated in the *ʾEgron* and in the *Tafsir* on Isaiah (5:12) as *naʾi*, "flute, oboe" (see Saadiah, *ʾEgron*, p. 228).

18. Similarly he derives (in his commentary on Ps. 5:1) from the verse "But I, through Your abundant love, enter Your house, I bow down in awe toward Your holy Temple" (Ps. 5:8[7]) the current ruling that "bowing and prayer must be towards the direction of the Temple." In BT Berakot 30a this rule is derived from verses of Solomon's prayer in its two versions (1 Kings 8:35, 44, 48; 2 Chron. 6:32).

19. Regarding the *Tafsir* on these verses, see Saadiah, *Torah Commentaries*, pp. 97 and 130. On p. 192 a fragment of the long commentary on the weekly portion *Šᵉmini*, which refers to Lev. 11:24, is given in Hebrew translation.

20. R. David Kimḥi, in his commentary on 1 Chron. 12:27, interprets it as Saadiah does—"the descendants of Aaron"—though in 1 Chron. 6:34 he refers to Aaron himself.

21. Later Salmon notes his own belief that the prophet-author of Psalm 77 is Asaph alone, since the text reads "of Asaph" (*le-ʾAsaf*) but "about Jeduthun" (*ʿal Yᵉdutun*). Both here in the introduction and in his commentary on 77:1 and 62:1 he explains *ʿal Yᵉdutun* as "concerning the prophecy of Jeduthun," without explaining his meaning further. Psalm 39:1 reads *la-mᵉnaṣṣeaḥ li-Yᵉdutun mizmor lᵉ-Dawid*; in his commentary on this verse Salmon notes that some hold that the two prophesied together (as he explained in his introduction), while others understand it as only David's prophecy, while Jeduthun was the singer-conductor charged with chanting it in the Temple.

22. In the Hebrew preface to his commentary on the Song of Songs Yefet writes: "With the aid of He who enlightens all teachers I shall begin to interpret the Song of Songs; my ears have heard from its interpreters who instructed and taught the people of the exile" (p. 1 on the right side of the book). See also Yefet, *Hosea*, pp. viii–ix; Yefet, *Ruth*, p. 7; Yefet, *Daniel*, pp. 86–87.

23. See below, note 29. Since Saadiah's commentary on the Minor Prophets is not extant, Birnbaum (Yefet, *Hosea*, pp. xx–xxiii) was forced to use indirect methods to assess the degree of Yefet's dependence upon his Rabbanite predecessor. According to him, of fourteen glosses attributed to Saadiah by R. David Kimḥi in his commentary on Hosea no fewer than twelve are identical with Yefet's commentaries *ad loc*.

24. From the plethora of arguments directed against Saadiah's interpretations in Yefet's Pentateuch commentaries, and their scarcity in his commentaries on the Prophets and Hagiographa, Hirschfeld (Yefet, *Nahum*, pp. 5–6) infers that for this Karaite commentator the anti-Rabbanite polemics had been carried far enough in his exegesis of the Pentateuch, and that elsewhere he was concerned mainly with explaining the text for its own sake.

25. Yefet classifies Eccles. 1:1–2 and Prov. 1:1–7 as "prefaces" (*ṣadr*) that precede the beginning of the books themselves. See the end of his remarks on

Eccles. 1:2 (*Ecclesiastes*, p. 5; English translation p. 147) and the end of his commentary on Prov. 1:7 (*Proverbs*, p. ix).

26. Yefet's commentary on Ruth, chaps. 1—2, was translated into English by Nemoy (*Anthology*, pp. 84–107; 344–48). An early Hebrew translation of the entire commentary—mistakenly attributed to Salmon ben Yeruḥam—was published by Y. D. Markon ("A commentary on the Scroll of Ruth by the Karaite Salmon ben Yeruḥam," *Poznanski Memorial Volume* [Warsaw, 1927], pp. 78–96). L. Nemoy pointed out the error in his article "Did Salmon ben Jeroham Compose a Commentary on Ruth?," *JQR* 39 (1948), pp. 215–16.

27. Here Yefet seems to be following in the wake of Saadiah, who, in his preface to Proverbs, enumerates "twelve excellent topics [taken] from the gates of wisdom" (*Proverbs*, pp. 19–21). The resemblance, however, is illusory, since Saadiah is writing about twelve rhetorical devices (or exegetical modes), whereas here Yefet is referring to twelve topics. Yefet's preface to Proverbs has no similar survey.

28. Anan ordained only two daily prayers, one at sunrise and the other at sunset, corresponding to the daily sacrifices in the Temple. Later the Karaites recognized the obligation of the afternoon prayer as well, but set its time at noon (see Nemoy, *Anthology*, pp. 271–72). Yefet apparently held a middle view. In his commentary on "Evening, morning and noon I complain and moan" (Ps. 55:18[17]) he writes: "Next he proclaimed that each day he prays (*juṣalli*) to the Lord three times. . . . At these three times Daniel prayed [as well], as is written: 'three times each day . . .' (Dan. 6:11[10]). If so, he prayed the obligatory service (*ṣalatu ʾl-farḍ*) evening and morning, accompanying his prayer with a plea to God for rescue; and at noon, too, he entreated the Lord to save him. . . ." In other words, in the morning and evening the supplications were appended to the obligatory prayers, while at noon he uttered only his voluntary entreaties.

29. Saadiah writes, in his commentary on 136:7: "This psalm includes the three reasons for the obligation to worship the Lord." The statements are essentially the same, but Yefet changed general "worship of God" into specific "obligatory prayer." Saadiah proceeds to list these three reasons: (1) the mercies of the Lord in creation, (2) in the history of Israel, and (3) at the end of days. There is a distinct echo of this in Yefet's remarks on "who alone works great marvels" (v. 4): "These marvels are of three types; all are the work of the Creator, may He be blessed. The first type are His creatures [= no. 1 in Saadiah's list]; the second type is His continuous providence [a reference to v. 25—"Who gives food to all flesh"]; and the third type are the miracles that He performs from time to time . . ." [= no. 2 and 3 in Saadiah's list]. The influence of Saadiah's commentary is strong, although not overpowering; even while maintaining the external framework of the argument Yefet attempts to improve its content.

30. In this, too, the influence of Saadiah's statements in *Beliefs and Opinions* (III, 3), as well as in his other works, is discernible; see the previous chapter, note 31.

31. Compare: "R. Joshua ben Levi said: with ten terms of praise the Book of Psalms was said—*niṣṣuaḥ*, *niggun*, *maśkil*, *mizmor*, *šir*, *ʾašrei*, *tᵉhillah*, *tᵉfillah*, *hodaʾah*, *hallᵉluyah*" (BT Pesaḥim 117a). The two lists have only four terms in common, because R. Joshua refers only to terms in the headings while Yefet refers to the verbs in the psalms. Yefet could have easily added other terms (such as *siḥah*, *ḳᵉriʾah*, *zᵉḵirah*); the fact that he did not do so indicates his desire to preserve the traditional structure of ten terms. This tendency to preserve his predecessors' patterns even while modifying the content was mentioned above.

32. A check reveals that the other six terms are in fact applied to human beings. For example: "You, O Judah, your brothers shall praise (*yoduḵa*)" (Gen. 49:8); "Let the mouth of another praise you (*yehallelḵa*)" (Prov. 27:2). Of the four terms said to apply exclusively to the Lord, this is certainly true with regard to *zimrah*; for *rinnah*, *teruʿah*, and *širah*, however, objections can be raised, such as: "A shout (*rinnah*) went through the army" (1 Kings 22:36); "the Philistines came shouting (*heriʿu*) to meet him" (Judg. 15:14); "Sweetly play, make much music (*šir*)" (Isa. 23:16). Thus when Yefet asserts that these verbs do not apply to human beings he must mean that they do not do so with the sense of praise.

33. Saadiah too was initially faithful to the number ten; in his short introduction he enumerates precisely ten modes of expression used to guide man (Saadiah, *Psalms*, p. 51). He later abandoned it for the eighteen modes presented in the long introduction (see p. 4).

34. He promises to return to this topic at the beginning of the psalm "Praise the Lord for He is good," but we find no mention of it in his commentary on the four psalms that have this heading (106, 107, 118, 136).

35. When Yefet (in his commentary on Hos. 11:10 and 14:5) describes the prayers of the *maśkilim* (learned ones) and *šaḇei pešaʿ* (repenters), both designations meaning the Karaites, he puts into their mouths verses from Psalms: "My God, My God, why have You abandoned me" (Ps. 22:2) and "Accept, O Lord, my free-will offerings" (Ps. 119:108).

36. This argument is presented in Salmon ben Yeruḥam's introduction to Psalms as well (p. 4a).

37. This inquisitive and non-authoritarian position and the deliberations that accompany it can be illustrated by two passages from Yefet's works. The first is from his commentary on Zech. 5:8, where he vehemently attacks the rabbis and accuses them of, inter alia, representing their own words as the Oral Law and "forcing Israel to obey and fulfil them, and decreed death for their opponents, instead of saying, this is what we think and believe, and you, O Israel, search as we did! Had they done so, they would be saved from being arraigned before Divine justice! This is what Anan did, who said: 'Search ye well in the Bible [and do not rely on my opinion].' Benjamin [an-Nahawendi] said at the end of his book: 'I Benjamin am one of a million and one of a hundred million, nor am I a prophet or the son of a prophet.' So too each Karaite scholar follows this path, and writes what he sees as

truth, and commands people to examine and experiment. Thus it happens that a brother differs with brother and son with father, but the father does not say, why do you take issue with my words? And so too the student with his teacher. Thus they emerge innocent and are saved before the Lord, even though they err in some of their opinions and books. They have a great reward for opening and enlightening people's eyes and leading them from darkness into the light.'' Poznanski (''Anan,'' vol. 44, pp. 184–85) published the Arabic original of this passage (on the basis of MS British Library Or. 2401) with a French translation. The second passage is from Yefet's commentary on Job 42:8 (cited by Ben-Shammai, *Methods*, I, p. 5, note 18): ''This is what I believe to be the correct opinion concerning Job and Elihu. May the Lord forgive me if I have decided without adequate thought, for one of my predecessors already said what I have said about Elihu. The controversy among the scholars over this matter was great; some upheld Elihu's words and did not uphold Job's words, while others did not uphold Elihu's words. I have interpreted [the passage] according to the opinion that seemed to me the more cogent of the two.''

38. The introduction fails to explain this identification of Jeduthun with Ethan, but in the commentary on Ps. 39:1 Yefet provides a detailed discussion of this assumption, which helps him resolve two contradictory verses in 1 Chronicles.

39. Heman (to whom Ps. 88 is attributed) is not mentioned here, either in Bargès edition or in MS Paris 286–289; but he is included in the list of psalmists found in Yefet's commentary on Zech. 1:8 (Ben-Shammai, *Methods*, I, p. 277, and II, p. 232). In the preface to Ps. 88 Yefet attributes it to the sons of Koraḥ, and sees Heman merely as the ''leader.'' We must conclude that the failure to mention Heman here is not a scribal omission, but reflects a revision of Yefet's opinion since the composition of his commentary on the Minor Prophets. This change fits his general viewpoint concerning the authorship of the Psalms, as will be explained below.

40. In his commentary on 42:1 Yefet adds that ''the sons of Koraḥ prophesied at different times and are thus different people. This is why they are called 'sons of Koraḥ' without any further designation.'' The internal logic of these assertions is elusive unless we add two tacit assumptions, stated by Yefet elsewhere: (1) In his commentary on Num. 11:25 he refers to the prophecy by the seventy elders in the desert as a collective prophecy, similar to that in the Psalms (cited by Ben-Shammai, *Methods*, I, 269). In his commentary on Ps. 84:2 he clearly mentions the collective prophecy of the sons of Koraḥ: ''It seems that when the Temple was being built and the people were rejoicing, the Lord made the sons of Koraḥ prophesy this psalm.'' (2) The conclusion that the sons of Koraḥ prophesied at different periods is not deduced from the fact that the reference is to a family, but stems from various exegetical and historical considerations. In his commentary on Ps. 84:1 he explains the division of the Koraḥide psalms into two groups (42 and 44—49 in the second ''scroll,'' and 84—85 and 87—88 in the third ''scroll of Psalms'') by the fact that the former were composed prior to the construction of the Temple and the latter afterwards.

41. He ignores another anonymous psalm—105. Apparently he attributed it to David on the basis of the fact that 105:1–15 = 1 Chron. 16:8–22, and there (v. 7) it is written: "On that day, David ordained to thank the Lord, through Asaph and his brothers." In the preface to his commentary on Psalm 105 as well, Yefet does not refer to the question of its authorship.

42. This is quite strange, since the question of the authorship of Psalms 66 and 67 is discussed and partially solved later in the introduction (see below), while Psalm 119 is never mentioned again. Nor is the issue of authorship raised in his preface to Psalm 119.

43. For Yefet it was apparently self-evident that the psalms were collected, arranged, and given headings by someone other than David; otherwise he could not mention the *mudawwin* in an aside, here and elsewhere, as if the reference was obvious. At the end of his preface to Psalm 1 he says a bit more about the *midawwin's* activities. We will discuss this issue in detail, see pp. 88 ff.

44. The lists of variae lectiones in medieval Biblical manuscripts, edited by B. Kenicott (Oxford, 1776–1780) and by de Rossi (Parma 1784/5) mention one manuscript (Kenicott 245) in which four out of these five psalms are joined, and four MSS (Kenicott 97; 133; 156; de Rossi 670) in which three of them are joined. Psalms 9 and 10—combined into one in the Septuagint—are not joined in any of these manuscripts, but are joined in four other MSS (which do not, however, join any of the other pairs) and by the Tosaphists on BT M^{e}gillah 17b, s.v. "and David." It is clear that the copy of the Book of Psalms used by Yefet for his translation and commentary had 150 psalms, and that Yefet regarded the joining of these psalms as a prior state before they had been edited. Nevertheless, it is hard to ignore the coincidence between the conclusions of his literary considerations and the ancient textual tradition transmitted to us via later manuscripts. We should therefore not dismiss the possibility that Yefet had heard of this tradition and used it as the springboard for developing his views even while denying its reliability and authority. See also tractate *Sof^{e}rim* 16,11: "The 147 psalms that are written in the Book of Psalms correspond to the years of Jacob's life."

45. Yefet deals with the absence of the letter *nun* in the introduction to Ps. 145 and in his commentary on verse 14 there. He does not mention the explanation of R. Yoḥanan cited in BT Berak̲o̲t 4b, and offers two of his own explanations. One is that the *nun* was omitted in order to give expression to man's inability to praise the Lord in the complete manner worthy of Him, for the Lord is "exalted above all blessing and praise" (Neh. 9:5). The second, that the omission of the *nun* is meant to express the inability of the people in exile to praise and exalt the Lord with musical instruments and the Holy Spirit as in the Temple.

46. While Yefet joins Pss. 103 and 104 (see his commentary on 104:35) because of their shared inclusio, the Sages had preceded him in joining Psalms 1 and 2, because this creates an inclusio: " 'Happy is the man' and 'Why do the nations assemble' are a single chapter. . . . R. Yoḥanan said: Every chapter of which David was especially fond he began with 'happy' and ended with 'happy.' He began with

'happy,' as is written: 'Happy is the man' (Ps. 1:1); he ended with 'happy,' as is written: 'Happy are all those who take refuge in Him' (2:12)'' (BT Berakot 9b–10a).

47. In JT Šᵉvuᶜot 1,5, *Numbers Rabba* 12,3, and parallel sources, there are various homilies attributing one or another of these psalms to Moses. Apparently the tradition attributing these eleven psalms to Moses precedes the homilies; see *Midrash Tehillim* 90,3: ''Moses composed eleven psalms corresponding to eleven tribes,'' followed by the homilies associating Psalm 90 with the blessing of Reuben, 91 with the blessing of Levi, 92 with Judah's, 93 with Benjamin's, 94 with Gad's, and 95 with Issachar's. The homilies concerning the five remaining psalms are missing; in their place the statement of R. Joshua ben Levi is cited: ''Thus far I have heard; from here on figure it out yourself.'' Ben-Shammai (''Review,'' p. 406) noted the possibility that this tradition reached Yefet through Kirkisani, who cites Ps. 94:9 as ''Moses' words'' in his commentary on Gen. 1:1 (quoted by Ben-Shammai, *Doctrines*, II, p. 23, line 81).

48. The bracketed words are found in only some manuscripts (see Buber's edition [Vilna, 1891], p. 194b).

49. Adding the three that were not included in the count of forty-six anonymous psalms and subtracting the seventeen Yefet succeeded in assigning to an author leaves us with thirty-two.

50. In Midrash Tehillim on Ps. 1 there is no direct reference to the question of authorship, but various identities are suggested for the righteous man who is the subject of the psalm: Adam (§9), Noah (§12), Abraham (§13), the Levite tribe (§14), the sons of Koraḥ (§15). Only fragments survive of Daniel al-Kumissi's Hebrew commentary on Psalms (Al-Kumissi, ''Fragments'') and they contain no discussion of the problem of anonymity; neither does Salmon ben Yeruḥam deal with this question in his introduction or his commentary on Pss. 1—2.

51. See Ben-Shammai's extremely interesting chapter, ''Prophet and prophecy'' (*Doctrines*, I, pp. 259–78). Yefet's statements borrowed from there will be cited according to the Arabic originals in vol. II and the Hebrew translation in vol. I.

52. Deut. 33 is cited as only one example, since in his commentary on Exod. 15:1 Yefet uses the term ''holy spirit'' concerning the Song of the Sea.

53. Cited by M. Zucker, ''Can a prophet sin?,'' *Tarbiẓ* 35 (1966), pp. 163–64 (Heb.).

54. See pp. 96–97.

55. Yefet's approach agrees in essence with the statement of R. Eliezer: ''Wherever it says ''a psalm of David''—he played and then the holy spirit came to rest upon him; [wherever it says] ''of David, a psalm''—the holy spirit rested upon him and then he would play'' (*Midrash Tehillim* 24,3).

56. See: Yefet, *Daniel*, Arabic p. 100, English p. 50.

57. The first chapter of Kirkisani's *Kitabu ʾl-ʾanwar*, which is devoted to the history of sectarianism in Israel, opens with Jeroboam's schism (English translation by Nemoy, *Anthology*, pp. 45–49). Yefet—in his commentary on Zech. 5:8—dates it to the Tannaitic age (the Arabic original of Yefet's commentary on the Minor Prophets is preserved in MS British Library, Or. 2401, and a medieval Hebrew translation in MS Leiden-University Library, Warner 12).

58. According to the *baraiṯa* cited in BT Sanhedrin 11a and in Tosefta Soṭah 13,3, "the holy spirit departed from Israel" with the deaths of Haggai, Zechariah, and Malachi. Our assumption that there is a link between the Karaite tendency to assert the early cessation of "the holy spirit" and their assertion of the non-prophetic nature of Rabbanite prayer is strengthened by the parallel link between their expressions of sorrow over the cessation of prophecy at the beginning of the Second Temple period and their assertion of the non-prophetic nature of the Oral Law, which they represented as the purely human endeavor of the rabbis (see the appendix to Wieder's *Scrolls*, "The Cessation of Prophecy in Karaite Ideology" (pp. 259–63). On the symmetry between the Karaite arguments against the Mishnah and against the Rabbanite Siddur, see above, pp. 10f.

59. Yefet attributed such headings to the "editor": see pp. 88–89.

60. See above, pp. 66 and 70–71.

61. In Bargès' edition the words "upon them" are missing, but they are found in MS Paris Héb. 37.

62. See BT Yoma 25a, JT Pesaḥim 5,10, and *Midrash Tehillim* 1,2.

63. See also the passage from his commentary on Ps. 39:1, quoted above, p. 84, where he explicitly states: "Jeduthun encouraged the singer to chant it at appropriate times (*fi baʿdi ʾl-ʾawḳat*).

64. The Sages learned this from Num. 10:10: "You shall sound the trumpets over your burnt offerings" (see BT *ʿArakin 11b*). Which song is referred to in 2 Chron. 29:27–29 Yefet deduced from a close study of the terminology in the headings of the Psalms. In his commentary on Ps. 88:1 he says that the word *šir* indicates that a psalm "was recited over the daily sacrifice or over the additional sacrifice."

65. An anonymous anti-Karaite tract discovered in the Cairo Genizah and designated by scholars "Ancient questions concerning the Bible" includes a satirical description of the prayers and lamentations of the Karaite "Mourners for Zion," which concludes on the same note: "Their wives sit separately and mourn / with wailing and lamentation" (See A. Scheiber, "Unknown Leaves from *šeʾelot ʿattiḳot*," HUCA 27 [1956], pp. 299–300). Despite its gross polemical character, the description is clearly factual, as it is not too remote from that provided by Yefet himself in the passage introducing his commentary on Ps. 119, originally written in

Hebrew, and published by Bargès (Yefet, "Song of Songs," pp. 187–88) and by Wieder ("Qumran," pp. 289–90). The Karaite Sahl ben Maṣliaḥ, too, attests to the role of Karaite women in a passage cited by Wieder (*Scrolls,* p. 206, note 2).

66. Wieder ("Qumran," pp. 102–13; Scrolls, p. 200) shows how throughout the generations the Karaites identified the scriptural *maśkilim* with their scholars in the Diaspora. In this context, Yefet's remarks on Dan. 12:3 are particularly instructive: he associates the *maśkilim* of future generations with the servant of the Lord in Isa. 52:13ff., a prophecy that depicts the sorrows and tribulations of the *maśkil* along with his wide knowledge and righteousness (Yefet, *Daniel,* Arabic p. 140, English p. 77).

67. According to Yefet, the headings also include words of prayer, like *ʾal tašḥeṯ* (which he paraphrases as "do not abolish, O God, the lineage of David, from whom the righteous judge will be enthroned"—58:1) and *ʿalmuṯ labben* (which he interprets as a plea that the Lord purify and cleanse Israel of those unconscious sins committed in error—9:1). From his introduction to the commentary on Psalm 57 we may infer that he attributed these words of prayer to the leader or to David rather than to the *mudawwin.*

68. In his commentary on these ten psalms Yefet proves their original unity at length (this is perhaps his most important innovation) and sees no need to offer a fundamental explanation of why the *mudawwin* separated them. The most detailed explanation is found in his commentary on 9:2: "The reason for dividing it into two chapters (*faṣlain*) is that from its beginning to its middle—i.e., the letter *lamed,* which is the beginning of the second half of the alphabet—it concerns both Edom and Ishmael, while in the second half it deals with Ishmael alone" (at the end of the introduction to Psalm 10 he gives an alternative explanation). Evidently Yefet accepted the *mudawwin's* authority to divide David's psalms in two so as to clarify their meaning as self-evident and requiring no justification and explanation.

69. Similarly Yefet attributes to the *mudawwin* the exclusion of Ruth from the Book of Judges and its placement as the first of the five Scrolls (see the translation of his commentary on Ruth 1:1 in Nemoy, *Anthology,* p. 86).

70. In accordance with this view, in his remarks on 72:20 he considers the possibility that "End of the prayers of David son of Jesse," is a colophon added by the *mudawwin.* See further below, note 82.

71. The severity of the Karaite claim on this topic is clearly evident from Salmon ben Yeruḥam's blunt attack: "You say that God gave two Torahs / one written and the other oral; / if it is as you say / your actions are false and rebellious. // The Holy One gave you an Oral Torah / in order that you recite it with your mouths— / for such in His wisdom was a fitting commandment: / Why did you engrave it in ornamental writing? // The Merciful one, had He wished to write it down / would have done so by Moses' hand! / It was given orally for study, / and not to be set down in a book! // They altered things and wrote that down / and transcribed it from the oral reasoning and set it down. / Now how can their words be

believed after they have committed such an abomination / and from this path cannot return!'' (*Wars*, pp. 38–39).

72. In a note the editor refers us to similar statements made by Saadiah in his commentary on *Sefer Y^eṣirah*, at the end of the introduction: from the body of this book and from rabbinic statements we can deduce that *Sefer Yᵉṣirah*, was composed by Abraham but written down only many generations later. Oral transmission is thus not a rare phenomenon; we also find ''that the Mishnah was transmitted and not written down, and even part of Scripture remained for many years transmitted and not written down (*manḳula gajr maktuba*), like 'the proverbs of Solomon which were copied by the men of Hezekiah king of Judah''' (Saadiah, *Commentary on Sefer Yᵉṣirah*, ed. and tr. into Hebrew by Y. Kafih [Jerusalem, 1972], p. 33). Compare to this the distinction made by Ibn Giath (*Ecclesiastes*, p. 166) between Solomon the author of Ecclesiastes (*ṣaḥib haḏa ʾed-diwan*) and the *mudawwin*—Hezekiah and his men who wrote it down after generations of faithful oral transmission.

73. I do not know why Yefet stressed that the various groups of proverbs were joined into a single collection before the destruction of the Northern Kingdom. Perhaps his meaning is that the consensus (*ʾiǵmaʿ*) of the exiles from both Israel and Judah with regard to the scope of the Book of Proverbs stemmed from the fact that Hezekiah's school acted with prophetic sanction before the exile of the Ten Tribes. See Ben-Shammai (''Review,'' p. 406), who buttresses this assumption by means of Al-Kumissi's gloss on Amos 5:2 (*Minor Prophets*, p. 35).

74. Cited by Marwick (''Yefet,'' p. 448, note 11) as one of twelve passages in Yefet's commentaries on the Early Prophets and Esther in which the *mudawwin* is mentioned.

75. In Tosefta Soṭah 9,2–9 distinctions are drawn between the speeches of different characters (''the entire passage is a medley of speeches; he who said this did not say that'') and also between the characters' speeches and the words of the ''holy spirit.'' The nine scriptural examples discussed there can be supplemented by two more found in *Sifre* Numbers, Bᵉ-*haʿaloṯᵉḵa*, §88. An examination of Rashi's commentary on these eleven loci reveals that he adopts these distinctions only when he finds them compatible with the plain meaning of the text, and even this with a significant modification of phrasing. The Tosefta, discussing the incident of the manna, reads: ''The Israelites say: 'Nothing but this manna to look at!' (Num. 11:6); God comes to conciliate all his creatures by telling them what all the discontent is about: 'Now the manna was like coriander seed' (v.7).'' Rashi writes: ''The Holy One blessed be He caused to be written in the Torah. . . .'' The Tosefta, discussing the passage of the beheaded heifer, reads: ''The elders say: 'our hands did not shed this blood nor did our eyes see it done' (Deut. 21:7); the priests say: 'Absolve, O Lord, Your people Israel whom You redeemed etc.' (8a); and *the Holy Spirit* says: 'They will be absolved of bloodguilt!' (8b).'' Rashi writes: ''*the text proclaims* to them that because they have done so the sin will be absolved.'' Rashi applies such distinctions also in passages not mentioned in the midrashim (e.g., his

glosses on Judg. 5:32 and Ezek. 1:1). Ibn Ezra considered Moses to be the *mudawwin* of the Pentateuch. This emerges mainly from his remarks concerning anachronistic verses (e.g., "'Horeb, the mountain of God'—Moses wrote this," in the long commentary on Exod. 3:1; see also his remarks on Gen. 11:26, 12:5, 28:11: Num.13:24), and from his distinction between the speeches of the actors and the contributions by the narrator (see his commentary on Gen. 20:16 and the fragmentary commentary on Gen. 11:5).

76. This aspect of the *mudawwin's* task was clarified by Ben-Shammai ("Review," pp. 405–406). Ibn Ezra cites two of Yefet's six examples in his short commentary on Exod. 7:11, and a third in his comment on Psalms 78:36 and in the long commentary on Exod. 20:3 (see also his two commentaries on Gen. 2:22; comm. on Ps. 68:5 and 74:4). Another of Yefet's examples—"he saw the bush burning" (Exod.3:2) is omitted by both Ibn Ezra and Ibn Ganach in their discussions of that passage (*Ha-Riḳmah*, p. 329) but it is one of the foundations of the chapter on "Point of View" in Adele Berlin, *Poetics and Interpretation of Biblical Narrative* (Sheffield, 1983), pp. 66–67.

77. Ibn Ezra, too, assumes that Boaz's "Come over and sit down here, So-and-so!" (Ruth, 4:1) is a paraphrase rather than a literal rendition of what he said (comm. on Ruth 3:13). It is also very likely that Rashi's comment ("his name was *not written* because he did not want to perform the Levirate marriage") reflects this view. On the other hand, Ibn Ezra takes issue with the daring assumption of Jeshuah ben Judah the Karaite that Moses modified the actual words of the Lord (long commentary on Exod. 6:3; and see also on 8:22).

78. This rare insight was not taken up by later biblical exegesis, and awareness of this fundamental stylistic phenomenon was lost, to be revived only lately thanks to the article by J. Muilenberg, "A Study in Hebrew Rhetoric: Repetition and Style," *SVT* 1 (1953), pp. 97–112.

79. See Yefet, *Hosea*, pp. 7–8.

80. The use of the term *pešer* to characterize one aspect of Karaite exegesis, which closely resembles the *pešer* of the Judean desert sect, was introduced by N. Wieder (see "Qumran"; "Exegesis"; and *Scrolls*, pp. 213–99). He has shown how the two sects used "prognostic exegesis," which finds in certain prophecies and psalms a direct reference to the situation of the sect in the present and to its messianic expectations.

81. Ankori (*Karaites*, pp. 224–28) shows that while Saadiah uses the Arabic term *naḳl* to mean oral tradition, the Palestinian Karaites of Yefet's generation used it only for the written transmission of the books of the Prophets and Hagiographa.

82. The application of these assumptions about the manner in which the Book of Psalms was originally written down for a distinctly exegetical purpose can be seen in Yefet's detailed discussion of the problematic verse, "End of the prayers of David son of Jesse" (Ps. 72:20). He offers three alternative explanations. According

to the first two these are "the words of the *mudawwin*," who is telling us that this is the last psalm that David composed (although it is not the last in the book) or that from now on a large part of the book will contain psalms not by David. According to the third possibility these are "Solomon's words," meaning that the author of Psalm 72 himself is expressing his gratitude that the prayers of his father David are hereby concluded, in the sense that all his requests had been fulfilled and there was nothing more to ask for. Yefet attributes the first two opinions to "certain of our scholars," which implies that the concept of the *mudawwin* was not new with him. In his commentary on Esther (end of chapter 7), too, he offers (in the name of his predecessors) the hypothesis that the name of God in not found in that book because "the *mudawwin* wrote it down from the version which Esther wrote, and Esther's composition contained no reference to the Lord" (cited by Marwick, ibid.). A similar notion of a prophetic author who is not identical with the prophetic protagonist of the book is found in Saadiah's introduction to his commentary on Job: "Therefore he wrote down the sufferings of Job, his tribulations, and his words and the words of his friends, what each asserted, and Elihu's answer to them" (p. 15). As for the identity of this prophetic *mudawwin,* Saadiah, following the Sages, writes: "The generation in which Job lived, although not stated in Scripture, is explicated by Tradition; it was the generation when our forefathers lived in Egypt, and Moses was the one who composed this book (*dawwana kitabahu haḏa*) at the Lord's commission and gave it to the nation" (p. 24).

83. In a similar vein, in his first commentary on Psalm 1 Saadiah mentions that there are twenty-four additional occurrences of the word *ʾašrei* in Psalms and seven in other scriptural books (*Psalms*, p. 41; the editor notes that the word actually occurs thirteen times outside Psalms).

84. See Wieder, "Qumran," pp. 97–113, 289–91; *Scrolls,* pp. 206–13.

85. For another important aspect of the messianic *pešer*—the Karaite belief in the central role played by the sect in hastening the coming of the Messiah—see the chapter on Ibn Ezra, pp. 206 ff.

86. Wieder ("Qumran," p. 282, note 94; *Scrolls*, p. 199, note 2) discussed the use of the Arabic expressions *ʾaʿaraba* and *ʿala lisan*, and their Hebrew parallels *ba-ʿabur* and *ʿal lᵉson*, by Karaite scholars from Daniel al-Kumissi through Judah Hadassi and by Rabbanite scholars from Ibn Ezra to Maimonides. Saadiah should be added to his list: in his *Tafsir* on Ps. 102:1 he interpolates the words *ʿala lisan*— "This prayer is said *in the language* of the weak man when he implores" (*Psalms*, p. 222); see also in the long introduction to Psalms, p. 35).

87. Yefet's commentary on Psalm 137 exemplifies how far, in his view, the prophetic power of a psalm can go. In his prophetic vision the psalmist, who lived in David's time, saw the Chaldean soldiers besieging Jerusalem, overhearing the lyres and hymns in the Temple, ordering their Levite captives to take their musical instruments with them into exile and, after their arrival in Babylonia, commanding them to play and sing the songs of Zion in the temples of Bel and Marduk. The poet puts into the mouths of the Levites the words of refusal "how can we sing" and the

vow "if I forget you, Jerusalem." Next he turns to the more distant future and prays that God revenge the destruction of the Second Temple at the hands of the Edomites and Greeks (whom he explicitly identifes with the Romans): "Remember, O Lord, against the Edomites" (cf. the words of Rav, BT Giṭṭin 57b). At the end he again refers to Babylon and puts in the mouths of the Israelites, who will have their vengeance when it falls at the hand of Persia, the triumphant shout: "a blessing on him who repays you in kind what you have inflicted on us." This far-reaching preview of the future is not sufficient reason for including Psalm 137 in the Psalter; it was written there only for the sake of the exiles throughout the generations, who must recite the psalm in their prayers and vow never to forget Jerusalem, like the Levites who hung their lyres on the poplars by the rivers of Babylon.

3

Moses Ibn Giqatilah: The Psalms as Non-prophetic Prayers and Poems

Moses Ibn Giqatilah's introduction to his Arabic commentary on the Book of Psalms is no longer extant; we must reconstruct his fundamental approach to Psalms from the few fragments of the commentary that have reached us. His position holds great interest for us because it represents a significant departure from the approach of his predecessors, and because of Abraham Ibn Ezra's intensive interaction with it.

Ibn Giqatilah was born in Cordoba at the beginning of the eleventh century, was active in Saragossa towards the middle of the century, and spent some time in southern France, where he translated two of Judah Ḥayyuj's grammars from Arabic to Hebrew. His importance as a grammarian is attested by the fact that Abraham Ibn Ezra includes him among the sixteen "Elders of the Holy Tongue" surveyed in the preface to his own Hebrew grammar, *Moznayim*. There he mentions Ibn Giqatilah's Arabic *Book of Masculine and Feminine*[1] and stresses its originality: "He also added topics unknown to the ancients" (fol. 2a). The extent of Ibn Ezra's appreciation of Ibn Giqatilah is indicated by the fact that when he disagrees with him in the body of his book he refers to him as "the greatest of the grammarians" (p. 13b) or as "one of the great commentators" (p. 5b).[2] Moses Ibn Ezra, too, praises him as a scholar, philologist, poet, and preacher: "Rabbi Moses Ibn Giqatilah . . . was one of the leading scholars (*ʾahlu ʾl-ʿilm*) and masters of the language (*riǵālu-ʾl-luġa*), one of the greatest savants and most famous of authors, and in the front ranks of the speakers and poets in both languages [i.e., Hebrew and Arabic], despite the intellectual confusion (*lawṯa*) from which he suffered and which cost him his high place among the great" (Moses Ibn Ezra, *Discussions*, pp. 67–69). It may well be that the social difficulties to which Moses Ibn Ezra alludes stemmed from the excessive intellectualism that underlies Ibn Giqatilah's commentary on the Bible, expressed in many ways: his tendency to restrict to the minimum the deviation of miracles from natural law (attacked by his younger opponent R. Judah Ibn Balaam as one of "his deceptive and corrupt opinions");[3] his attempts to establish the date of prophecies and make them refer to historical events that occured in proximity to their utterance rather than to the messianic era (on this account he was accused by Ibn Balaam of tending to undermine the faith in the future redemption);[4] his free use of Christian commentaries and translations of the Bible, while objecting strongly only to Christological interpretations;[5] and his view of the psalms as prayers and poems rather than prophecies—the subject of our present discussion.

The strong personal rivalry between Ibn Balaam and Ibn Giqatilah (reflected in the great acerbity of the former's attacks on the latter, which are not by any means limited to matters of faith and belief)[6] compels caution in any evaluation of the magnitude of the innovation in Ibn Giqatilah's method and the extent to which it was thought to go beyond the pale. Thus we should also consider what later generations had to say about him. Alongside the two Ibn Ezras, who displayed great respect for him, he was also praised by Abraham Ibn Daud in the *Book of Tradition* (written in Toledo in 1161) as one of the scholars "who wrote books, liturgies [*piyyuṭim*], hymns, and praises to our Creator, His Name be Praised, and consolations for Israel to encourage them in the lands of their exile."[7] In the course of his discussion of the metaphorical interpretation of "the wolf shall dwell with the lamb" (Isaiah 11:6) Maimonides notes that "our understanding of this matter has been anticipated by rational commentators (*ʾahlu ʾt-taḥṣil min ʾl-mufasirīn*) such as Ibn Giqatilah and Ibn Balaam".[8] However, Naḥmanides has sharp criticism for the view that the book of Obadiah and the eleventh chapter of Isaiah refer to the times of Hezekiah, upheld by "the stubborn Rabbi Moses ha-Kohen," whom he also calls "the deceitful priest."[9] In a similar vein, Isaac Abarbanel attacks Ibn Giqatilah's linkage between Joel 3 and events in the times of Jehoshaphat as the direct result of "the lack of faith of that same Rabbi Moses ha-Kohen and those who follow him with regard to the coming of the Messiah, until they had to distort the words of the prophets and have them refer to the past, and make the signs and future wonders they were foretelling into events that had already happened."[10] Naḥmanides' and Abarbanel's far-reaching inferences from the fragmentary glosses of Ibn Giqatilah quoted by Abraham Ibn Ezra are incompatible with Ibn Daud's remark about the important role played by Ibn Giqatilah's poetry in consoling the Jews and encouraging them in their lands of exile. The few poems by Giqatilah that have come down to us do in fact confirm Ibn Daud's evaluation of the man and his poetry.[11] In the *piyyuṭ* "Mi-tigraṯ kapeḵa" the worshippers' hope of salvation rests on their identification with the suffering servant of God, as described in Isaiah

53:4–5: "Comfort him who awaits / the salvation of his Master // Plagued and stricken, / crushed by his sins." In the *piyyuṭ* "ʾAḳdišah l^{e}-ʾEl b^{e}-noʿam šinnuni," the supplication to speed the coming of the Messiah is based on Moses' prophecy (Deut. 30:3–5): "Speed a redeemer to redeem your people / on whom your furious wrath rested; // Fulfill and consent to the prophecy of your faithful one: / 'The Lord your God will restore your captives.'" To Ibn Giqatilah it was clear beyond all doubt that Moses is referring to the distant future, and thus can be seen as a firm foundation for the belief in the coming of the redeemer. Abraham Ibn Ezra's gloss on Numbers 24:17, then, faithfully reflects the opinion of his predecessor, and may have even been drawn from Ibn Giqatilah's lost commentary on the Torah: "Those who lack knowledge may think that the interpretation that refers 'a star rises' to David denies the coming of the Messiah. Heaven forbid! For the Messiah is clearly indicated in the prophecy of Daniel, as I have interpreted [it]. . . . There is no need for any prophet whatsoever, given what Moses said, which is the cornerstone of the matter[12]—'if your outcasts are at the ends of the sky' (Deut. 30:4), then 'the Lord your God will restore your captives' (ibid., 3)." Note that this master of the plain meaning is not content with stating that Moses' prophecy of redemption applies to the exiles living in the Far West; he *proves* that this is the case by emphasizing the circumstances in which the prophecy applies, as made explicit in the text: "If your outcasts are at the ends of the sky."

Given the paucity of information available to us, we cannot determine whether Ibn Giqatilah was better understood in Muslim Spain where he grew up than he was by later generations, or whether his contemporaries were even more put off by his innovations. The polemical language employed by Abraham Ibn Ezra in the passage cited above indicates the nature and severity of the argument that was being waged in Spain a century after Ibn Giqatilah's death. Those who wanted to historicize the prophecies of consolation were accused of a lack of faith; Abraham Ibn Ezra retorts by accusing the accusers of a lack of knowledge. There are many signs that a spiritual struggle of this sort between two groups of scholars—at one in their desire to unify faith and knowledge but divided in how best to accomplish this—accompanied Spanish Jewry from the time it set forth on its unique path. The interpretative enterprise of Moses Ibn Giqatilah is one of the most original expressions of this fruitful spiritual ferment, as evidenced by the long debate that focused upon it.

Because of the shift of demographic and cultural centers that has been so frequent in the long and vacillating history of the Jewish people, intellectual endeavors written in the vernacular have generally been doomed to oblivion, unless translated into Hebrew. The operation of this cruel decree on Spanish Bible exegesis is only too evident. While most of the commentaries of Abraham Ibn Ezra, Naḥmanides, and Don Isaac Abarbanel, who wrote in Hebrew, are extant in manuscript and abundant printed editions, almost all of the commentaries by Samuel Ha-Nagid, Moses Ibn Giqatilah, Judah Ibn Balaam, Isaac Ibn Samuel Al-Kanzi, and others have been lost. Were it not for the scanty remnants found in the Cairo Genizah we would not be able to properly evaluate the nature and scope of the contribution by Iberian Jewry to the understanding of the Bible. But because Abraham Ibn Ezra was so lavish in his quotations of Moses Ibn Giqatilah we have a narrow opening onto his method of interpretation. The labor of gathering these scattered citations was begun by L. Dukes (Stuttgart, 1844) and B. Z. Bacher (Budapest, 1881; German tr. Strassburg 1882), and was continued with great diligence and thoroughness by S. Poznanski in his dissertation (Leipzig, 1895), where Ibn Giqatilah's glosses were collected from the literature of commentaries and grammar texts from Ibn Balaam through Joseph Ben David, the author of *Mᵉnoraṯ ha-Maʾor* (end of the thirteenth century), and explained and analyzed. Whereas Bacher found 137 of Ibn Giqatilah's glosses on Psalms (*Ibn Ezra,* p. 139) in Abraham Ibn Ezra's commentary on Psalms, Poznanski was able to locate 156 (including seven from other sources). Two years after the appearance of this monograph—which won immediate praise in the scholarly reviews and remains the only summary of Ibn Giqatilah's method of interpretation—Eliahu Harkavy informed Poznanski of a discovery he had made in the Firkovich collection in St. Petersburg, which ought to have marked the dawn of a new age in the study of Ibn Giqatilah's Bible commentaries. As he wrote to him, inter alia, in a postcard dated May 15, 1897: "I hope to cheer you with the good news that I have found more than 80 folios (and I am sorry to say that they are worn) from Moses Ibn Giqatilah's commentary on Isaiah, and I see that almost everything that Ibn Balaam and Abraham Ibn Ezra said about this book is as it were merely an abridgement of Ibn Giqatilah, even in places where they do not mention him; and in general this commentary is a great treasure of our ancient literature."[13] Poznanski did not keep copies of his own letters, so his reply has been lost. On December 12, 1897, Harkavy has another important announcement: "I am happy to inform you that I found a large part of Ibn Giqatilah on Psalms in which his *Kitābu ʾat-taḏkīr wʾat-taʾnīṯ* is cited. Abraham Ibn Ezra borrowed from him a number of times even though he did not mention his name" (no. 27, p. 213). We can imagine how great was Poznanski's desire—until then he had had to content himself with Ibn Giqatilah's words cited at second and third hand—to examine the writings themselves; but in Tsarist Russia a Jewish scholar living in Warsaw was not permitted to visit the Imperial Library in St. Petersburg. Thus Poznanski had to wait three years until a local copyist was found who agreed to transcribe the manuscripts for him.

During the next two years the matter is not mentioned at all in Harkavy's postcards; Poznanski was evidently seeking help from others. His archives include a letter dated August 1, 1900 and a postcard dated September 24, 1900 from the St. Petersburg bibliographist Samuel Wiener, warmly recommending Kalman Dov Horowitz, ''who has all of the qualifications enumerated by scholars for copyists,'' that is, understanding, diligence, devotion, and reliability, as well as experience in copying Arabic manuscripts in Hebrew letters. The connection was made, and we can follow it through five letters from Horowitz found in the Poznanski archives.

In Horowitz's second letter (November 6, 1900) he deals mainly with the commentary on Psalms, which indicates that Poznanski was chiefly interested in this. It is a fair assumption that the reason for this preference was that Harkavy had already proved Ibn Giqatilah's authorship of this commentary on the basis of the mention of his grammatical work on masculine and feminine forms. Horowitz describes in detail the form, contents, and flaws of the 120-folio unpaginated manuscript. He adds a transcription of three passages from different places, so that Poznanski can judge his ability as a copyist and also the ''the physical and spiritual condition of the original manuscript.'' These passages include the commentary on Psalms 3; 4:1–9a; 5:11–13 (in this fragment more has faded than survives); and 8. He also reports that Ibn Giqatilah's Isaiah commentary was then being examined by the student Yiẓḥak Duber Markon, who had expressed his willingness to make it available to the copyist whenever he so requested. The condition of this manuscript is much worse than that of the Psalms commentary, however: ''There is no undamaged spot in any of its pages, and it resembles a heap of old and worn rags.'' At the end of the letter he mentions that another manuscript, eighteen pages of a commentary on the last chapters of Psalms, has been made available to him; he stresses that it was Harkavy who had written Ibn Giqatilah's name on it, followed by a question mark.

Poznanski must have been very eager to hold the commentary on Psalms in his hand, and Horowitz must have been diligent in doing his job: by January 19, 1901 the copy of Ibn Giqatilah's commentary had been sent to Warsaw. In the accompanying letter Horowitz writes that, in accordance with Poznanski's instructions, he is also enclosing a copy of the second eighteen-page commentary, and proposes copying Ibn Giqatilah's Isaiah commentary as well. This manuscript, written in 1381, contains eighty-seven pages, in very poor condition; he provides two samples (on 11:10–15a and 51:4b–6). Only two weeks later (February 4, 1901) Horowitz acknowledges receiving payment for the transcription and Poznanski's dissertation, which he had been so bold as to request. He also sends him a transcription of the last page of Ibn Giqatilah's commentary on Isaiah, which includes the copyist's colophon.

As was his wont, Poznanski was quick to reply; from Horowitz's fifth letter (February 18, 1901) we can infer that Poznanski was not interested in a transcription of the Isaiah commentary, because he had learned that its author was not Ibn Giqatilah but Tanḥum Yᵉrušalmi. In his disappointment Horowitz showed the letter to Harkavy, but he "hardly had anything to say to me on the subject," merely advising him to send Poznanski a sample from Ibn Giqatilah's commentary on the minor prophets. Horowitz did so, and transcribed the section on Zephaniah 2:9—3:18 from Ibn Giqatilah's commentary on the minor prophets, which consists of thirty-one pages, and also enclosed a sample of Ibn Balaam's commentary on the minor prophets, which consists of twenty-nine pages—on Hosea 13:12—14:3.

How was Poznanski able to determine that the Isaiah commentary was by Tanḥum Yᵉrušalmi so quickly and with such certainty? The answer is found in an article he published that same year on the manuscripts of Tanḥum's commentaries.[14] There he writes (p. 186) that he was convinced that the commentary was written by Tanḥum Yᵉrušalmi as soon as he examined the fragments he received from the copyist. In these short segments he did in fact find only one (almost word-for-word) parallel to a known gloss by Tanḥum (*mišmaᶜtam* in Isaiah 11:14 compared with *mišmaᶜto* in 2 Sam. 23:23); but for him the didactic style and neo-Platonic terminology are enough to prove with certainty that the commentary was written by Tanḥum, the "Ibn Ezra of the Orient." To convince the reader of this he includes the two fragments sent him by Horowitz in the article.

Poznanski reached the same conclusion with regard to the fragment of the Psalms commentary that Harkavy had ascribed to Ibn Giqatilah (albeit with a question mark), and which Horowitz had already copied for him. In a previous article in the same series,[15] Poznanski includes this manuscript (No. 3676, some eighteen pages long) among those of Tanḥum's commentary. He bases this determination on three parallels to other commentaries by Tanḥum, and on a number of citations that are characteristic of the later author's style. Finally he notes that Simon Eppenstein had agreed to edit the entire manuscript. This fragment of Tanḥum's commentary on Psalms (Psalms 16 through 29) was later published by Eppenstein, accompanied by a German translation, with expressions of profound gratitude to Poznanski for having made available the copy of the Petersburg manuscript that had been prepared for him.[16] Incidentally, Poznanski (p.187, note 5) and Eppenstein (p. 287) both found it necessary to express their doubts as to the faithfulness of the transcription; these suspicions may have contributed to the fact that Poznanski stopped relying on Horowitz. In any case, with regard to the Ibn Balaam commentary, he found another source, both more reliable and free of charge. Jacob Israelson (a student of the Iberian Arabic-language Bible exegesis who had previously studied at the university in St.

Petersburg) generously loaned Poznanski the annotated transcription he had prepared from manuscripts in St. Petersburg of Judah Ibn Balaam's commentaries on the Former Prophets, Jeremiah, and the Minor Prophets. The clear superiority of Israelson's transcriptions can be inferred from Poznanski's praise: "With his breadth of understanding and great knowledge of Arabic he has gone over the commentaries and corrected their mistakes and even added references to the other loci in Scripture and sayings of the Sages cited therein."[17] On the basis of these transcriptions Poznanski brought out Ibn Balaam's commentaries on Joshua (1903), Judges (1906), and the Minor Prophets (published posthumously in 1924–25). For Ibn Balaam's commentaries he relied thus on Israelson; but it remains surprising that he did not ask Horowitz to prepare a transcription of Ibn Giqatilah's commentary on the twelve minor prophets, a sample of which he had sent to him on the advice of Harkavy. I have not found a reference to this commentary anywhere; perhaps this silence implies that Poznanski, after having refuted two attributions by Harkavy, preferred not to write to the aged and honored scholar his opinion of the third. In any case, it is clear that he soon concluded that the commentary on the Minor Prophets in question was not written by Ibn Giqatilah, given the total lack of correspondence between the passage on Zephaniah 2:9—3:18 and the glosses cited by Abraham Ibn Ezra ad locum.[18] Poznanski's four surveys of the Ibn Giqatilah fragments—found in articles that he wrote later[19]—fail to mention the commentary on the Minor Prophets.

Only one of the four announced discoveries of Ibn Giqatilah manuscripts in the Firkovich collection in St. Petersburg proved to be genuine—the Psalms commentary. To our great astonishment, however, Poznanski did not edit this commentary for the next decade, despite the energy and rapidity with which he had obtained the transcription. Later, in 1912, he published an initial review of Ibn Giqatilah's Psalms commentary, at the end of which he provides the entire commentary on Psalm 8 by way of example. He stresses the temporary nature of this publication and his intention to edit and publish the entire manuscript (Poznanski, "Psalms," p. 41); but he never managed to do so before his sudden death in 1921, at the age of 57. In his archives, acquired by the National Library in Jerusalem in 1931,[20] I have not found any preliminary drafts for this edition,[21] nor, to my great disappointment, the Horowitz transcription. Thus the relic of Ibn Giqatilah's Psalms commentary, characterized by Poznanski as "one of the most important monuments of Spanish commentary during its Golden Age" ("Psalms," p. 58) has been lost to us. St. Petersburg became Leningrad, but we are still unable to photocopy the unique manuscript of Ibn Giqatilah's Psalms commentary that has survived in the Firkovich collection. In this chapter I have therefore been forced to rely on amputated and largely indirect documentation: the citations from Abraham Ibn Ezra's commentaries amassed by Poznanski in his dissertation, five citations from the Tanḥum Yᵉrušalmi's Psalms commentary transcribed for him by Israelson,[22] the commentary on Psalms 3, 4, 5:11–13, and 8 that Horowitz copied out as a sample, and the few truncated quotations included by Poznanski in his review, drawn from the transcription he possessed and which has gone astray. It is true that in 1926 Yehoshua Finkel acquired a transcription of the commentary on two psalms (apparently made from the actual manuscript in the Leningrad library), but as luck would have it these are the very same psalms that have been found in Poznanski's archives—chapters 3 and 4. Finkel added the commentary on Psalm 8 (which, as has been said, Poznanski appended to his survey), and published all three of them accompanied by a Hebrew translation and notes.[23] The Cairo Genizah, where nine fragments have so far been discovered, fills in the lacuna only slightly. N. Allony identified two fragments in the Musseri Collection,[24] and recently Dr. Maᶜaravi Perez found seven additional fragments, which he most graciously placed at my disposal even before he published them.[25]

To sum up, were we not in possession of an additional previously unpublished introduction to Psalms by Abraham Ibn Ezra (the "First Recension")—which includes important information on Ibn Giqatilah's approach—we would be unable to make any progress beyond what Poznanski wrote on the subject.

Ibn Giqatilah's name is not mentioned in the description of the debate among the commentators regarding the nature of the Book of Psalms, found in Ibn Ezra's introduction to his standard commentary. For this reason, Poznanski's summary of Ibn Giqatilah's position (*Giqatilah*, pp. 31–32) is based exclusively upon analysis of Ibn Ezra's citations of Ibn Giqatilah within the body of his commentary. In Poznanski's opinion, Ibn Giqatilah's major innovation in the interpretation of Psalms was his willingness to openly and explicitly date many psalms to the Babylonian exile. True, the statement, "this Psalm was written in Babylonia" is quoted by Ibn Ezra in Ibn Giqatilah's name only on 42:1 and 47:1; but Poznanski could conclude with a high degree of certainty that this was also the case for Psalms 102 and 106, since at 102:15 Ibn Ezra reports Ibn Giqatilah's opinion that this verse refers to the rebuilding of the desolate land in the days of the return to Zion, while at 106:47 he says that "one scholar said that the author of this Psalm lived in Babylonia." It was clear to Poznanski that this anonymous scholar was Ibn Giqatilah, because "he is practically the only early commentator known to us who held that some psalms were written in the Diaspora" (p. 176). From this supposed uniqueness of Ibn Giqatilah's approach Poznanski also infers that "the Spanish scholar" referred to by Ibn Ezra on Psalms 51:20, who believed the last two verses of this psalm were an addendum written in Babylonia, is certainly Ibn Giqatilah (p.32).[26] Poznanski notes that the need to assume that these two verses were written later proves that Ibn Giqatilah did not assign a late date to the body of the psalm, because David's name appears in its ascription. He believes that another expression of this position can be found in the forced interpretations proposed by Ibn Giqatilah to make Psalms 30 and 122 fit the age of David.[27] At the same time, Poznanski adds (p. 32, note 2) that Ibn Giqatilah held that the heading *le-Dawid* can also be understood to mean that the psalm was written about David by some anonymous poet contemporary with him, just as *li-Š^{e}lomoh* indicates, not that Psalm 72 was composed by Solomon, but rather that it is about him.[28] To sum up, when the subject matter of a psalm so requires, Ibn Giqatilah allows himself to deny David and Solomon the authorship of psalms *le-Dawid* and *li-Š^{e}lomoh,* but not to attribute them to a later era.

Poznanski does not explain the basic conception underlying Ibn Giqatilah's assignment of a late date to certain psalms, because he found no explicit statement on this matter. Such a statement seems to appear in Ibn Ezra's introduction to the standard commentary: "Others say that this book contains no prophecies about future events" (lines 22–23), and hence assign a late date not only to Psalm 137 but also to many other psalms "referring to the exile" (line 27). With regard to the identity of these commentators, Poznanski states that they were contemporaries of Ibn Ezra and aparently assumes that they took this position under the influence of Ibn Giqatilah, who paved the way for it (p. 32, note 1). Thus Poznanski would have the critical statements, attributed by Ibn Ezra in the body of his commentary to a single scholar, refer to Ibn Giqatilah, whereas he relates the plural reference in the introduction to later commentators who followed in Ibn Giqatilah's path. This cautious distinction does not permit a determination as to the extent to which Ibn Giqatilah shared the anonymous principle stated in the introduction and the weighty conclusions entailed by it. The answer to this can undoubtedly be found in the body of the commentary, but Poznanski did not deal with this topic in his 1912 survey of the manuscript in his possession (see Poznanski, "Psalms"), apparently preferring to discuss this fundamental question at greater lengths in the preface to the edition he hoped to publish in the near future. In the narrow scope of his article he considered only four topics: the history of research and the condition of the manuscript (pp. 38–42), additional proofs that Ibn Giqatilah was indeed the author of the commentary (pp. 42–47), a few lines to characterize the method of the commentary (pp. 47–52), a list of the scholars cited in the commentary (pp. 52–58), and, as an appendix, the commentary on Psalm 8 with annotations (pp. 59–60). From all of this we will consider here only what is relevant for us.

The manuscript consists of 120 loose and unnumbered pages, of which a few are illegible, begins with the commentary on Psalm 1 and concludes with the commentary on 144:3. Because many pages from the end of the manuscript have been lost, as well as some from the middle and apparently also from the beginning, the commentary on only eighty psalms survives (and a quarter of them are truncated). An exact list of the psalms and partial psalms for which the commentary survives can be found on page 42 of Poznanski's article; particularly distressing is the absence of the introduction and of the colophons (author and copyist?) at the end. For this reason the author's name is not mentioned in the manuscript, but Harkavy had already concluded that the commentary was written by Ibn Giqatilah from the fact that the author relates to the *Book of Masculine and Feminine* as to his own work. Poznanski adds many other proofs, of which the most important is the correspondence between the text of the commentary and passages in Arabic quoted by Ibn Balaam, Tanḥum Yᵉrušalmi, Isaac Ibn Samuel Al-Kanzi, Isaac Ṣar-Šalom, and Isaac Ibn Barun and attributed by them to Ibn Giqatilah. Most of the quotations were actually paraphrases, but some were literal. This was also the method of Ibn Ezra, whose quotations (translated into Hebrew) have proven to be reliable,[29] and whose dependence on his predecessor is much greater than might be concluded from the explicit citations. Poznanski has very little to say about the nature of the commentary: it is almost continuous, concise, and has few excursuses (one of them is devoted to a strong attack on Ibn Ganach's methods of word replacement). Occasionally there are historical clarifications, mainly in connection with the headings of the psalms. Poznanski notes that questions about the editing of the book are also discussed, such as why Psalms 3 and 30 are included in the first book despite dealing with a later stage in David's life; but he does not quote Ibn Giqatilah's answers to such questions. From Ibn Ezra's commentary on Psalm 110:3–4 we already knew that Ibn Giqatilah did not ascribe Psalm 72 to Solomon, but to another poet writing about him; from the commentary on 127:1 (quoted by Poznanski, p. 49) we learn that he held that Psalm 127, too (*šir ha-maʿalot li-šᵉlomoh*), was written not by Solomon but by his father David. In order to prove his points and illustrate his assertions Poznanski quotes from various places in the commentary; we shall rely on a number of these short citations for our own purposes.

Even though we are still unable to examine those parts of Ibn Giqatilah's commentary that survive in MS Leningrad, we can again consider his basic approach to the Book of Psalms, because we can now be certain, on the basis of Ibn Ezra's introduction to the first recension of the Psalms commentary, that the anonymous opinions presented in great detail in the introduction of the standard commentary are in fact those of Ibn Giqatilah himself. The plural "others say" in the introduction to the standard commentary may well apply to a single commentator; according to Poznanski (*Giqatilah*, p. 55, note 12), Ibn Ezra may in one place quote a particular opinion in the name of "and many say" (*Defense of Saadiah*, §20), yet elsewhere cite the very same opinion and ascribe it to Ibn Giqatilah (*Ṣaḥot*, p. 16b).[30] Moreover, Ibn Ezra gives a plural attribution to the first position in the "major controversy" as well—"some say that the entire book is by David" (lines 10–11); but it is clear that this is merely the radical position of Saadiah Gaon, since to date no other commentator who holds it has come to light. In the first introduction, however, Ibn Ezra chose a slightly different path: there the opinion of Saadiah is presented both anonymously and in the plural (integrated with a number of opinions of the Sages), whereas the opposing viewpoint is cited in the name of its holder: "R. Moses ha-Kohen (his soul rests in Paradise) said" (line 49).

Abraham Ibn Ezra's two introductions to Psalms differ in their structure and mode of presentation, so there is also a significant difference in how Ibn Giqatilah's position is presented. This difference makes it possible for us to broaden our knowledge about it. Whereas in the first introduction the question of the authorship (discussed in the "first inquiry") and the question of the prophetic status of the psalms (to which the "third inquiry" is devoted) are treated separately, the standard introduction considers these two interrelated questions together. Thanks to this integration the debate is set clearly on its fundamental principles. Despite this undeniable advantage of the standard introduction, we shall first consider what Ibn Ezra wrote about Ibn Giqatilah's position in the first introduction, both because it was written earlier[31] and because only there is this position explicitly ascribed to Ibn Giqatilah.

In the "first inquiry" of the first commentary (lines 35–79), two contradictory answers are initially given to the question whether the entire book is by David. The first position—which anonymously represents Saadiah, who had given a resolutely affirmative answer to the question—requires coming up with an explanation for all of the names found in the headings other than David (which always indicates the author). The explanation is that Asaph, the sons of Koraḥ, and Jeduthun were singers in the time of David; "*l^e-Mošeh*" indicates the original father or ancestor of the family of musicians to whom David assigned the task of singing the psalm; while "*li-Š^elomoh*" indicates neither the author nor the singer, but the person about whom David was prophesying. The holder of the second view—Ibn Giqatilah—is also rather flexible in his interpretation of the preposition *l^e-* that precedes the names, and applies it even to psalms that are ascribed to David, because, according to his minimalist position (lines 49–50) "most but not all of the psalms bearing the ascription *l^e-Dawid* are by

David'' (and *a fortiori* those not attributed to him). Ibn Ezra does not state explicitly what motivated Ibn Giqatilah to deny David's authorship of a number of the *l^e-Dawid* psalms, and mentions only two of them—Psalms 20 and 110. An examination of these yields the conclusion that in this case the motive was apparently stylistic, since they speak of the king in the third person. Later Ibn Ezra reports Ibn Giqatilah's opinion as to the identity of the authors of the psalms not ascribed to David, while tending to preserve the order in which these names were discussed in his presentation of the first position.

In total contrast to Saadiah, who saw Asaph and the sons of Koraḥ as choristers contemporary with David, for Ibn Giqatilah these names designate their later descendants, who actually wrote the psalms attributed to them. He does not give a reason for this astounding assertion, which explodes the accepted chronological framework of the Book of Psalms and opens the door to dating them much later. Ibn Ezra continues and reports that, on the other hand, Ibn Giqatilah understood *l^e-Mošeh* literally, that is, as indicating the ancient author of Psalm 90; whereas *li-Š^elomoh* he interpreted, like Saadiah, as indicating ''about or concerning Solomon''; but, in contrast to Saadiah, he ascribed it not to David but to some anonymous poet who wrote about Solomon during the latter's reign. Here Ibn Ezra cites Ibn Giqatilah's opinion about two names not mentioned in the first part of the introduction (because they were obviously considered to be musicians): ''The attributions to Ethan (89) and Heman (88) are to be taken literally, though he had doubts about the psalm 'I will sing of the Lord's steadfast love forever' (89:2)'' (lines 58–59). From the context we can infer that ''literally'' means that Psalms 88 and 89 were written by Ethan and Heman rather than about them, and that Ibn Giqatilah's doubts with regard to Psalm 89 were that perhaps it was not in fact written by Ethan the Ezraḥite, but by some king descended from David (this hypothesis follows from the first-person pronoun in verse 51), and was merely given to Ethan to play.[32] There is only one name that Ibn Giqatilah did not view as denoting an author: ''But *li-Y^edutun* (39) means [for Jeduthun] to perform'' (line 59). This exception is evidently to be explained by the fact that Jeduthun always appears in the headings of psalms alongside someone else: twice with David (39 and 62) and once with Asaph (77). Ibn Ezra does not explain how Ibn Giqatilah solved the difficulty raised by his view of Asaph as a later poet—how could Jeduthun have been a musician both in his time and in that of David? In his own commentary on these three psalms Ibn Ezra does not mention Ibn Giqatilah's opinion on the subject. Thus we can only surmise that Ibn Giqatilah believed that just as the Asaph mentioned in the headings of Psalms 50 and 73–83 was a descendant of the Levite Asaph who was David's contemporary (1 Chron. 6:24), so too the Jeduthun in the first verse of Psalm 77 was a later musician descended from the Jeduthun who played Psalms 39 and 62 for David.[33]

Finally, Ibn Ezra presents Ibn Giqatilah's opinion about the anonymous psalms. In contrast to Saadiah, who ascribed them all to David (line 36), Ibn Giqatilah saw the very anonymity as proof that they could not be attributed to David: "As for the Psalms without a name [in the heading], we do not know who wrote them" (lines 59–60). This also applies to the partial anonymity of the sons of Koraḥ—"we do not know which of them wrote these psalms" (line 61).[34] Ibn Ezra adds to this a specific note about one of the psalms attributed to the sons of Koraḥ: "[Ibn Giqatilah] also said that '*a maśkil.* A love song' (45) is to be taken literally as said about David, as are 'Daughter of Tyre' (ibid., 13 [12]) and 'take heed, lass, and note' (ibid., 11[10])" (lines 61–63). In his commentary on these verses Ibn Ezra is uncertain whether this royal psalm "was said about David or about the Messiah his son" (45:2); it is clear, then, that when he says here, in his terse and enigmatic style, that Ibn Giqatilah interpreted it "literally as said about David," he means that even though Ibn Giqatilah gave a late date to all the Koraḥide psalms, he did not feel compelled to understand this psalm as referring to the messianic Son of David, but took it in the plain sense as referring to David and his Tyrian wife, that is, to the poet's past rather than his future.

This concludes his presentation of Ibn Giqatilah's approach; thereafter Ibn Ezra summarizes his own stance with regard to the authorship of Psalms (which we shall discuss below in Chapter 4, pp. 178–82). Even though his position is much closer to Ibn Giqatilah's than to Saadiah's, he finds it necessary to begin with an explicit reservation about the former: "Many arguments can be made against him" (line 64). He explicitly states only one of these here, that regarding anonymous authorship: Psalm 105 is unattributed, but its first fifteen verses are attributed to David in 1 Chron. 16:7–22: "Then David first commissioned Asaph and his kinsmen to give praise to the Lord" (v. 7). As is his wont, Ibn Ezra is extremely concise; but this question can evidently also be raised with regard to the rest of the psalm celebrating the transfer of the Ark of the Covenant to Jerusalem found in 1 Chron. 16, which is parallel to psalms and parts of psalms that all appear anonymously in the Book of Psalms—verses 23–33 are parallel to Psalm 96:1–13 and verses 34–36 to Psalm 106:1, 47–48. Ibn Ezra winds up the subject with a possible rebuttal by Ibn Giqatilah, though he considers it weak: "though it would seem he can rebut this argument weakly, claiming that only what is ascribed to David in Chronicles is by him" (lines 66–67). In other words, Ibn Giqatilah could have argued that his assertion that it is impossible to identify the authors of anonymous psalms does not apply to psalmic material attributed to David in 1 Chronicles. Ibn Ezra thereupon tries to demonstrate that this is not the only exception, and that the authors of a number of additional psalms can in fact be identified on the basis of a formal or topical connection between an anonymous psalm and its predecessor.[35]

Continuing the presentation of his own position, Ibn Ezra adopts Ibn Giqatilah's opinion and sees all the names in the headings (except for Jeduthun) as indicating authors rather than musicians; but he clearly disagrees with their late dating. Just as he previously failed to explain what motivated Ibn Giqatilah to assign a late date to them, now he gives no grounds for his flat assertion that the Asaph, the sons of Koraḥ, and Heman mentioned in the headings were the contemporaries of David and not their descendants. The reason must be that he preferred to avoid an open discussion of Ibn Giqatilah's basic assumptions, knowing that Italian Jewry was not so receptive of innovation as their Spanish brethren and that the readers of his commentary would not recognize the religious legitimacy of Ibn Giqatilah's approach. Consequently, he sheltered his predecessor by presenting his conclusions as one possible interpretation (which he personally rejected) rather than as a principled position.[36] He provides only an indirect hint for readers who insist on knowing the reason for assigning these authors to a later period.

In the "third inquiry" he raises a seemingly unconnected question: "Are these words of David and the other poets veritable songs, psalms, and prayers, or were they said through the Holy Spirit? Do some refer to incidents that have already occurred and some to those that will yet come to pass?" (lines 82–84). With exceeding caution the two opinions are here presented as theoretical alternatives rather than as the stances of two schools of interpretation, as in the "first inquiry." But the careful reader will ask whether this is a continuation of the argument over the identity of the authors, and will even hypothesize that Ibn Giqatilah, who assigned a late date to most of them, is the one who holds that the psalms were not inspired by the Holy Spirit. There is in fact a close connection between the two positions: someone who views the psalms as prophetic can attribute all of them to the time of David (although he need not do so); whereas someone who believes that they are merely "songs, psalms, and prayers" must assign a later date to some of them, since as such they cannot anticipate the historical situation reflected in them. Thanks to the introduction to the standard commentary this is not a mere assumption, since there the two issues are integrated from the start: "Some say that the entire book is by David, who was a prophet. Their evidence: 'by the ordinance of David the man of God' (Neh. 12:24)" (lines 10–12); while "others say that this book contains no prophecies about future events, which is why the Sages transcribed it with Job and the Scrolls, and this is attested by [the terms] 'psalm,' 'song,' and 'prayer.' They say that 'by the rivers of Babylon' (137) was written by one of the poets in Babylon'' (lines 22–25). Note that the first argument deals with the nature of the psalms, and this leads into the second arguement about the identity and date of the authors. The point of departure for the first opinion is the prophetic character of the psalms, which it seeks to prove on the basis of texts that describe David as a prophet; while the second opinion starts off from the non-prophetic character of the psalms, as attested by the literary terminology in the headings thereof. Making the date of composition of a psalm correspond to its historical background is presented as a direct result of viewing it as a prayer like all other prayers. Hence if the unpublished introduction explicitly attributes the late dating of Psalms to Ibn Giqatilah, it follows that he also viewed them as non-prophetic.

From the introduction to the standard commentary it is clear that this is not simply a hypothetical position and that some commentators actually supported it; there seems to be an allusion to this in the introduction to the first recension as well. Ibn Ezra devotes the greater part of the''third inquiry'' to citing proof texts that ''the correct answer, given by the Sages, is that the Book of Psalms was said through the Holy Spirit'' (lines 84–85). He does not limit himself to passages in which David, Heman, Asaph, and Jeduthun are given prophetic attributes, but also endeavors to prove ''the holiness of these songs and psalms'' (lines 92–93) on the basis of 1 Chron. 9:22 and 2 Chron. 5:13, that is, that the prophecies of David and his colleagues were indeed collected in the Book of Psalms. As against all this he raises a basic question that he places in the mouth of a hypothetical opponent: ''What is the meaning of prayer uttered under divine inspiration?'' (lines 94–95). In the standard introduction (line 36) this same difficulty (''why are they surprised by the word 'song'?'') is attributed to ''others say''; but even were this not the case, we could conclude with a high degree of certainty that this question was one of the cornerstones of Ibn Giqatilah's original conception of Psalms, and apparently was included—in terms similar to the two formulations presented by Ibn Ezra—in the (lost) introduction to his commentary.[37]

There is no doubt that Ibn Giqatilah did not disagree with the accepted belief that David was a prophet. Had he done so, it is reasonably certain that Ibn Ezra would not have mentioned his position without explaining how he interpreted those texts where David is described with prophetic attributes. We do not need to limit ourselves to this tacit proof, however, because we can see from Ibn Giqatilah's gloss on Psalm 32:7–8 that in this Davidic psalm he found an echo of a prophetic revelation of quasi-prophetic revelation experienced by its author: '''You surround me with the joyous shouts of deliverance'—Rabbi Moses said: 'You surround me'—this is a transitive verb that takes two direct objects [i.e., you cause me to be surrounded by] angelic voices that I escape . . . and they will reprove me and say: 'Let me enlighten you [and show you] which way to go' (v. 8)'' (cited by Ibn Ezra *ad loc.*). Had Ibn Giqatilah denied that David was a prophet, he could have easily explained these texts (as did, for example, Rashi and David Kimḥi) without attributing to David the ability to hear angels announcing salvation to him and adding words of reproof and counsel. Moreover, just as Ibn Giqatilah saw Psalm 32 as a description of a past revelation, so too he viewed Psalm 101 as a prayer to merit revelation in the future. In this psalm, ascribed to David in its heading and written in the first person, the poet addresses God with a request: ''When will You come to me'' (v. 2). Ibn Ezra explained this as a prayer to merit to walk continually in the ways of God, but nevertheless found reason to cite the commentary of his predecessor as well: ''Rabbi Moses said: 'When will You come to me'—this is like 'God came to Balaam' (Num. 22:9)—that the Holy Spirit shall rest upon him in his house when he is apart from other people and their contentions and arguments.'' In fact, both of them explain David's request in the psalm of repentance over his sin with Bathsheba—''Do not take Your holy spirit away from me'' (51:13)—in the same vein. Ibn Giqatilah writes (in the fifth Genizah fragment) that ''he feared that he would be deprived of prophecy because of the sin he had committed.'' Similarly, and perhaps following in his footsteps, Ibn Ezra writes: ''He was afraid that he would fall from the rank of those who bear the Holy Spirit; and we find that at the end of his life he said, 'the spirit of the Lord has spoken through me' (2 Sam. 23:2).''

Thus we may conclude that neither the identity of its author nor its content, but rather its literary form, determines whether a psalm is a prophecy or a prayer. Despite the description of revelation in Psalm 32 and the request for prophecy in Psalms 51 and 101, Ibn Giqatilah saw these as prayers rather than prophecies, because of their pronounced psalmic form (and also because of the absence of prophetic figures of speech such as ''thus says the Lord''). When Ibn Ezra, in the introduction to the standard commentary, sums up Ibn Giqatilah's position, according to which ''this book contains no prophecies about future events'' (line 23), he does not mean that the 150 psalms do not contain many verses that could easily be interpreted as prophetic statements, but that the designations ''psalm,'' ''song,'' and ''prayer,'' and the literary genres that they designate, clearly exceed the bounds of prophetic literature. Like other exegetes of the plain meaning (*p*^{e}*šaṭ*), who strive to restore the original import of the text, it is most important for Ibn Giqatilah to show that he too relies on the Sages. Thus he stresses that the ''sages'' who ''wrote down'' the Book of Psalms in the Hagiographa thereby demonstrated that it is not part of the prophetic literature.[38]

Because the psalms are not prophecies, it follows that their authors should be considered to be poets, whether or not they personally merited prophetic visions. Consequently, Ibn Giqatilah calls the later descendants of Asaph, Ethan, and the Koraḥides poets, without detracting thereby from their religious and spiritual status. The lofty religious status of non-prophetic prayer in the Bible, as he sees it, is proven by Ibn Giqatilah's intense efforts to blunt the sting of the sharp words directed against Heaven in Psalm 89:39–50. Ibn Ezra (in his commentary on Psalm 89:2) tells us that "there was a great and pious savant in Spain who found this psalm difficult, and he could neither read it nor listen [some MSS add: to it] because the poet spoke harshly against God.[39] [Saadiah] Gaon did not mention explicitly [some MSS: in his commentary] the correction [*tiḳḳun*] of this psalm, while Rabbi Moses ha-Kohen went on at great length about this subject." Thus for Ibn Giqatilah the fact that, in his view, the psalms were not written under the influence of the holy spirit did not solve the problem of the lack of faith expressed in this psalm, and he searched for a way to explain the text so that he could find a way of "correcting" it[40] that would be compatible with the inclusion of this psalm in the Holy Scriptures. To sum up, Ibn Giqatilah saw the psalms as non-prophetic prayers written by men of lofty religious and spiritual standing, which are to be read and heard with full spiritual and fideistic identification.

This idea—which stems from a literary perspective on the nature of the psalms rather than from a theological recognition of the status of their authors—entails the necessary late dating of psalms with a post-Davidic historical background. But while there is no problem in assigning a late date to anonymous psalms such as "By the rivers of Babylon" (137) and "Happy are those whose way is blameless" (119), how is it possible to do this with regard to psalms that are attributed to poets contemporary with David? Ibn Giqatilah solves this problem by means of a bold assumption, namely, that "Asaph, too, is the name of a poet who lived in Babylon, and is not [the same as] Asaph the chief musician who lived in the time of David" (standard introduction, lines 28–29); the same hypothesis holds for the Koraḥides and Ethan the Ezraḥite. From a purely formal perspective he was anticipated in this argument by Saadiah Gaon, who, in order to postpone the composition of Psalm 90 from the time of Moses to that of David, interpreted and even translated *l*^{e}*-Mošeh* to mean "the sons of Moses." Ibn Giqatilah was apparently influenced[41] by this precedent, but deviated from it slightly, when he hypothesized that the poet who lived in the Babylonian exile actually had the same name as the head of the important family who had served in the Sanctuary in the time of David.

This interpretation of the names found in the headings of certain psalms makes it possible to assign a late date to them, but does not require it. Ibn Ezra does not cite Ibn Giqatilah's grounds for giving a late date to various poets, and provides no more than partial and almost enigmatic information on the subject. First of all he reports that Ibn Giqatilah said that "*all* the *livnei Koraḥ* psalms are by one of the descendants of Heman who lived in Babylon, and they are referring to the exile" (ibid., lines 25–27). It is not clear from this whether all of the Koraḥide psalms deal with the exile, but even if this is not the case Ibn Giqatilah did not assume that the "sons of Koraḥ" sometimes refer to a poet contemporary with David and sometimes to a later poet. In the second part of this sentence Ibn Ezra writes that "this cannot be found in David's writings" (lines 27–28)—i.e., Ibn Giqatilah found an impressive (albeit partial) correlation: while an exilic background cannot be found in any psalm explicitly ascribed to David, such a background appears in at least some of the psalms explicitly attributed to the sons of Koraḥ. He adds that this also applies to the psalms of Asaph, as well as to that by Ethan the Ezraḥite (89). He notes that this last was written "at the fall of the House of David in the time of Zedekiah" (lines 29–30), and relies on the reader to infer the grounds for this dating from the text of the psalm (see especially vv. 37–40). He provides no specific proof for assigning a late date to the twelve Asaph psalms (50 and 73–83), nor an answer to whether any of them (or of the eleven Koraḥide psalms) must be ascribed to the time of David.

Some of what Ibn Ezra omitted from the introduction he supplied in the body of his commentary. We have already noted that in the commentary Ibn Ezra attributes the late dating of four psalms to Ibn Giqatilah. He states this explicitly about two of the Koraḥide psalms (42 and 47); Poznanski inferred it from Ibn Ezra's text, with a fairly high degree of certainty, with regard to two anonymous psalms (102 and 106). We can now add to these another eight psalms, for which a late date is reported by Ibn Ezra through a direct or indirect mention of the opinion of the late-daters mentioned in the introduction (which has lost its anonymity for us, because it is attributed to Ibn Giqatilah in the introduction to the first recension). Thus he writes at the beginning of his commentary on Psalm 79 (which is ascribed to Asaph in its header and speaks of the destruction of Jerusalem and the Temple in the past tense): "I mentioned the disagreement among the commentators at the beginning of the book." In almost identical terms he refers the reader to his introduction at the beginning of his commentary on the two anonymous psalms—119 and 137—mentioned in the introduction as examples of psalms with a Babylonian background. In his commentary on two of the Asaph psalms he indirectly alludes to Ibn Giqatilah's position and mentions the uncertainty in determining the date of its author: "*If* this poet Asaph is the one who lived in the time of David" (78:54; and, phrased almost identically, 81:12). Speaking of the two psalms attributed to the sons of Koraḥ he even presents Ibn Giqatilah's position as an alternative of equal status:

"If this Koraḥide lived in Babylonia . . ." (84:3); and again: "by one of the grandsons of Samuel, or their descendants" (87:1). Psalm 87 does not have any obviously Babylonian background, so it may be that this time "one of their descendants" indicates an author who lived before the destruction. Something along these lines is stated of another psalm ascribed to the sons of Koraḥ: "Some say that this poet was a descendant of Koraḥ [who lived] in the time of Hezekiah when Sennacherib retreated" (46:1). By contrast, we read in the introduction that "they say that all the *livnei Ḳoraḥ* psalms are by one of the descendants of Heman who lived in Babylon" (lines 25–27). Since we have no knowledge of another commentator who assigned a late date to psalms because he did not see them as prophetic, it is reasonable to assume that the opinion cited in the commentary on 46:1 is Ibn Giqatilah's, and that the phrasing of the introduction is not precise. Ibn Ezra should have written that for Ibn Giqatilah "the sons of Koraḥ" always indicates a poet who lived later than David, though not necessarily one who lived in the Babylonian exile.[42] In any case we cannot doubt that Ibn Giqatilah assigned a late date to Psalm 46, because it includes a clear reference to the rescue of Jerusalem in the time of Sennacherib (see especially verse 6: "God is in its midst, it will not be toppled; by daybreak God will come to its aid"). The only question is whether he saw it as a song of thanksgiving written by a poet who personally experienced that salvation, or as a song of praise composed by a poet who lived in Babylonia and cited that past act of salvation as a portent of God's activity on behalf of his people. The first possibility seems to me better suited to Ibn Giqatilah's method, even though it involves the assumption that he was not afraid to claim that "the sons of Koraḥ" refers to more than one poet. The problem with this hypothesis is that it makes it more difficult for us to understand Ibn Giqatilah's consistent failure to explain "the sons of Koraḥ" literally, that is, as referring to a poet contemporary with David. We will return to this question below; here we will offer another proof that Ibn Giqatilah tended to interpret the names in the headings with a certain flexibility, in order to permit a closer link between the time of their composition and their historical background. From what Ibn Ezra writes on Psalm 76:4 we may infer that Ibn Giqatilah understood the designation *l^eAsaf* in the first verse of the psalm as referring to a poet who lived after David, although not necessarily during the Babylonian exile: "Rabbi Moses said that this psalm was said about the war of an enemy who besieged Jerusalem and was weakened."

On the basis of explicit statements, some of them direct but most of them indirect, we have been able to identify fourteen psalms to which Ibn Giqatilah assigned a late date. These, according to author, are as follows: by the sons of Koraḥ—42, 46, 47, 84, and 87; by Asaph—76, 78, 79, and

81; by Ethan—89; anonymous—102, 106, 119, and 137. Additional late psalms can be identified through a more precise application of Ibn Giqatilah's various reasons for assigning a late date to psalms. Because of its conspicuously Babylonian background he assigned a late date to another Asaph psalm, 74 (principally because of verse 7—"They made Your sanctuary go up in flames; they brought low in dishonor the dwelling place of Your presence"); to the anonymous "Song of ascents. When the Lord restored the fortunes of Zion we were like dreamers" (126); and apparently also to Psalm 43 (vv. 2–3: "Why must I walk in gloom, oppressed by the enemy? Send forth Your light and Your truth; they will lead me; they will bring me to Your holy mountain, to Your dwelling place"). With regard to the late dating of Psalms 43 and 126 we do not have to rely purely upon our own judgment, since even Ibn Ezra, who did not assign a late date to them, was forced to make them refer to the future (see his commentary to 43:3 and 5 and to 126:1).

Another possible reason for assigning a late date to some psalms can be found in the justification cited by Ibn Ezra for "one of the Spanish savants" who denied David's authorship of the last two verses of Psalm 51: "He had to do this because it was not known that Zion was the chosen place until David's old age" (comm. on 51:20). We can understand why he does not postdate the body of the psalm: it is explicitly attributed to David, phrased entirely in the first person, and is clearly dated—"when Nathan the prophet came to him after he had come to Bathsheba" (v. 2). But the last two verses of the psalm are incompatible with this early date, because they speak of Zion as the place designated for offering sacrifices, whereas the sanctity of the Temple Mount was revealed to David only in his old age, when the plague was arrested on the threshing floor of Ornan the Jebusite, as it is written: "David said, 'Here will be the House of the Lord and here the altar of burnt offerings for Israel'" (1 Chron. 22:1). Before that time David could not have sung of righteous sacrifices, burnt offerings and whole offerings on Zion. This is why that anonymous Spanish scholar had to conclude that these two verses were written by "one of the pious men who was in Babylonia" who, in his total identification with David's psalm of repentance, appended to it a contemporary dimension—a prayer for the rebuilding of Jerusalem and the renewal of the sacrificial service. All the same, this argument is based on the assumption that David's psalm is a prayer and not a prophecy; Ibn Ezra could therefore answer briefly that there is no anachronism for anyone who assumes that the psalm is prophetic: "It is also true that [the psalm] was said under the inspiration of the Holy Spirit." By contrast, Ibn Giqatilah ascribed to the literary assumption that the psalms are not prophecies, so it is not surprising that Poznanski proposed to identify him with the Spanish scholar whose name Ibn Ezra failed to mention (see above, pp. 120f.). Now that we have Ibn Giqatilah's commentary on Psalm 51:7–21 before us (in the fifth Genizah fragment), however, we learn that he resolved the anachronism without postdating the two verses: "As for his saying afterwards 'May it please You to make Zion prosper' (v. 20)—this was because he knew that he was in the favored place for offering sacrifices, and there would be no other when it was built. And this in contrast to the situation that existed during the period of the Sanctuary in the times of David, when it was permissible to offer sacrifices in other places as well." The knowledge that Zion is to be "the place that will be chosen" is indeed prophetic, but it does not refer to the exact location of the Temple, which will later be revealed to David when the plague is arrested on Ornan's threshing floor. And whereas, according to Ibn Ezra, the anonymous scholar assumed that "Zion" means the Temple Mount (apparently on the basis of Psalm 132:13, and see Ibn Ezra *ad loc.*), Ibn Giqatilah must have identified "Zion" with the entire City of David (on the basis of 2 Sam. 5:7; 7:12–17; and 1 Kings 8:1). Consequently, he saw no difficulty in the fact that David the prophet, who brought the Ark of the Covenant to Jerusalem and offered sacrifices before it, and was aware of the future exclusivity of that site for the divine service, prayed for its peace and its construction.

References to Jerusalem as the holy city and even to the House of God and its courts is very frequent in psalms that are explicitly attributed to David; Ibn Giqatilah had to resolve all these anachronisms. He did this in four different ways, which, taken together, indicate how strongly he held to his non-prophetic view of the Davidic psalms. The first way is to interpret the text not literally but metaphorically. The heading of Psalm 30, "A psalm of David. A song for the dedication of the House," poses a problem because of its anachronistic reference to the dedication of the Temple, and because of its discordance with the body of the psalm, which is a song of thanksgiving for recovery from illness. Ibn Ezra begins his commentary on this psalm by mentioning the opinions of various commentators, who solved the first problem by assuming that David wrote the psalm for the dedication of the First Temple, the Second, or even the Third, and some of whom suggested a metaphorical solution for the second problem—"the days of exile resemble the days of illness." He then proceeds to offer his own solution, which holds fast to the plain meaning of the text: the reference is not to the dedication of God's House, but rather to the dedication of David's palace, which must have taken place at the same time as the king arose from his sickbed. Finally he offers Ibn Giqatilah's opinion, which aims at integrating the resolution of the two difficulties—even if at the price of excessive metaphorization: David's illness was spiritual rather than physical, caused by his pain at the announcement by Nathan the prophet that he, David, would not build God's House because of the great amount of blood that he had shed (1 Chron. 28:3). But when the prophet informed him that his son Solomon would build the Temple (v. 6) his mourning turned to joy, and he composed a psalm of thanksgiving that permission had been given for dedication of the house.[43]

Ibn Giqatilah had a different explanation for the anachronism in "A Song of ascents. Of David. I rejoiced when they said to me, 'We are going to the House of the Lord'" (122). This time he relied on the method he had rejected for Psalm 30: "Rabbi Moses said that David wrote this song to be sung in the Temple after it was built." Relating the psalm to the future is compatible in and of itself with his view, so long as it does not involve a prophetic anticipation of as-yet unknown future events. Just as David amassed materials for building the Temple, it is reasonable that he composed poems to be sung in it. Ibn Ezra continues and cites a prophetic solution as well—"some say it refers to the Third Temple"—which contradicts Ibn Giqatilah's view, and after that another non-prophetic solution, attributed to Yeshuᶜah (a Jerusalem Karaite scholar contemporary with Ibn Giqatilah). According to Yeshuᶜah, the psalm does not refer to the Temple to be built by Solomon, but rather to the "house that David himself erected in Zion," i.e., the tent pitched by David to shelter the Ark of the Covenant when he brought it to Jerusalem from Ḳiryaṯ Yᵉᶜarim (2 Sam. 6:17). As we shall see below, Ibn Giqatilah adopted a solution of this sort for other psalms; he apparently rejected it for Psalm 122 because he preferred to assume that this song of praise for the sanctity of Jerusalem was composed, not after the Ark was transferred to the capital city at the king's initiative, but following the prophecy of Gad the Seer regarding the selection of Jerusalem as the Holy City. Deferring its composition to David's old age (not possible for the last two verses of Psalm 51, because of the earlier date included in its heading) is the tacit assumption that lends plausibility to a view of Psalm 122 as intended to be sung in the as-yet unbuilt Temple. Thus this solution rests on two methods: postponing the date of its composition, on the one hand, and referring the content to the near future, on the other.

The third method is to assume that the psalm was dedicated to David rather than written by him. In the first introduction Ibn Ezra reports that Ibn Giqatilah held that Psalm 110, headed *lᵉ-Dawid*, was written by "one of the musicians *about* David" (lines 50–51). In his commentary on 110:1, Ibn Ezra writes that it is indeed possible to explain the psalm as written by David about Abraham—principally because of what seems to be a reference to Melchizedek, the ancient priest of ʾEl ᶜElyon, in verse 4[44]—but that "'Zion' [verse 2], which was David's city, makes this problematic; and we can explain it in a somewhat farfetched manner." Unfortunately he does not specify how it may be possible, albeit with difficulty, to make the phrase "the Lord will stretch forth from Zion your mighty scepter" compatible with the time of Abraham;[45] evidently this is because he agreed with Ibn Giqatilah, who held that the psalm was not by David but about him (and thus not about Abraham.[46] In Ibn Ezra's opinion, an anonymous poet composed "this psalm when David's men vowed: 'You shall not go with us into battle any more' (2 Sam. 21:17)." This biographical explanation of the phrase "The Lord said to my lord, 'Sit at My right hand while I make your enemies your footstool' " (v. 1) involves assigning a late date to the psalm, and thereby also solves the problem of the anachronistic reference to Zion as God's dwelling place. Even though he does not say so explicitly, we may assume that this was also Ibn Giqatilah's opinion, since in his commentary on verse 4 Ibn Ezra reports that Ibn Giqatilah, too, ascribed the psalm to David's old age: "Rabbi Moses said—because you are a righteous king, as [is attested by] 'and David executed true justice among all his people' (2 Sam. 8:15). The [implied] meaning is that you have waged war enough, because God aids your right hand and 'He crushed kings in the day of His anger' (v. 5) by means of you."[47]

The fourth way—already mentioned above, with regard to Psalm 122, in the name of Yeshuᶜah the Karaite—is to have the mention of God's dwelling in Zion refer to the recent past, that is, to the day when the Ark of the Covenant was brought up to Jerusalem by David from Kiryat Yᵉᶜarim a short while after Jerusalem became the City of David (2 Sam. 6). We have no direct information as to how Ibn Giqatilah interpreted the reference to the House of God in the past tense in David's prayer: "My zeal for Your House has been my undoing; the reproaches of those who revile You have fallen upon me" (69:10). But it is reasonable to assume that the two alternatives proposed by Ibn Ezra in his commentary on this verse reflect the fundamental debate over this matter between himself and his predecessor: "The meaning of 'my zeal for Your house' is that enemies were reviling the house where the Ark was. A more reasonable explanation is that this psalm was said by the inspiration of the Holy Spirit and refers to the Exile, as is witnessed by '[the Lord] will rebuild the cities of Judah' (v. 36)." Because of the reference to the destruction of the Temple at the end of the psalm Ibn Ezra preferred to relate it to the period of the Exile, but a commentator like Ibn Giqatilah who will not admit that the psalm is prophetic can explain that the enemies' insults were directed against the temporary dwelling that David had erected to shelter the Ark.[48] With regard to Psalm 138 as well (which is attributed to David and phrased throughout in the first person) Ibn Ezra proposes two ways to resolve the fact that God's Temple is spoken of as if it already exists: "'I will bow down [toward Your holy temple]'—some say that 'Your holy temple' refers to the heavens, but this is hard to accept because of 'I will bow down.' The correct explanation is that it refers to the place where the Ark was'' (commentary on 138:2). It is quite possible that Ibn Giqatilah adopted here the second alternative (which Ibn Ezra preferred for exegetical reasons), which coincides with his approach, as we have reconstructed it, concerning Psalms 69, 14, and 20.[49] If not, we must attribute to him a fifth method for resolving anachronisms—that is, understanding ''Your holy temple'' as indicating God's heavenly residence.

The situation changes fundamentally when David's name does not appear in the psalm. For Ibn Giqatilah a reference to the Temple or the Holy City is no longer anachronistic when the psalm itself is viewed as being of later date. Ibn Ezra, on the other hand, must still rely on the various explanations we have enumerated or on the assumption that the statement is prophetic. A good example of this can be found in Psalm 84, ascribed to ''the sons of Koraḥ,'' in which we read: ''I long, I yearn for the courts of the Lord'' (verse 3). In his commentary there Ibn Ezra summarizes with extreme terseness three ways to understand ''the courts of the Lord,'' of which the first is undoubtedly Ibn Giqatilah's: '' 'For God's courts'—if this Koraḥide was living in Babylonia; or he may be one of the Koraḥides in the time of David—[and means] the courts surrounding the Tent of the Lord; or it may be a prophecy.'' The first option makes sense only if we integrate the initial quotation with it, that is: one who assumes that the poet is one of the Korahides who lived in Babylonia will interpret ''God's courts'' literally; whereas one who assumes that the poet lived in the days of David must adopt the fourth method of explanation and say that the reference is to the courts surrounding the tent erected by David over the Ark of the Covenant, or assume that the ancient poet was speaking prophetically of the longings of a later generation for the courts of Solomon's Temple. Assigning a late date to the poet (in accordance with Ibn Giqatilah's method) or understanding the psalm as a prophetic reference to the future absolves the commentator of the need to take ''God's courts'' metaphorically. On the other hand, dating the poet to the time of David and seeing the statement about the Temple as non-prophetic requires us to understand it metaphorically, by means of one of the methods of ''correction.''[50]

The following picture emerges from the information we have gathered from Ibn Ezra's commentary and his two introductions about Ibn Giqatilah's approach to the psalms.[51] Ibn Giqatilah found a Babylonian background in psalms attributed to the sons of Koraḥ (42, 47, 84, [85],[52] and [87]); to Asaph ([78], 79, and [81]);[53] to Ethan [89]; and to anonymous poets ([43], 102, 106, 119, [126], and 137,[54] but not in any psalm attributed to David (composed by or about him). This also applies to a historical background later than David but antedating the destruction of the First Temple; this too he found only in psalms that are not by David—one by the sons of

Koraḥ (46) and one by Asaph (76). In contrast to the total absence of anachronistic references to later events and situations in the Davidic psalms—which undoubtedly impressed him greatly and provided the foundation for his late dating of an author when he found such anachronisms in a number of his psalms—he had to wrestle strenuously with the references to Zion as the Holy City and to the Temple as currently standing in psalms that clearly belong to David's time. Of the five methods to resolve this phenomenon mentioned by Ibn Ezra, we have found explicit evidence that Ibn Giqatilah had recourse to two (with regard to Psalms 30 and 122), and can reconstruct with a high level of certainty his use of two or three of the others (with regard to Psalms 14, 20, 69, 110, and 138).

We can infer from Poznanski's survey that the manuscript of Ibn Giqatilah's Psalms commentary does not contain any dispute with Saadiah Gaon's fundamental approach on the one hand, and with the Karaite interpretation on the other. There is no point in hypothesizing whether Ibn Giqatilah took issue with the maximalist view of Saadiah in his lost introduction (as seems to be implied from its presentation as "a major controversy" in the introduction to Ibn Ezra's standard commentary). We may assume, however, that in view of the fundamental innovation represented by his approach Ibn Giqatilah would have had to present it to his readers in a well-grounded form. His argument was basically literary: the nature of the psalms as addresses to God, the poetical terminology in their headings, and the non-inclusion of the Book of Psalms among the prophetic writings are evidence that these are prayers rather than prophecies. Even the prayer of prophets cannot contain foreknowledge of future events, because the essence of prayer is the aspiration to deflect the future in the direction desired by the worshipper. For Rabbi Moses ha-Kohen Ibn Giqatilah, the biblical commentator and liturgical poet, the sanctity of the psalms was based on their religious and spiritual elevation, on their inclusion in the Holy Scriptures, and on their being the sincere prayers of great spiritual leaders, from Moses, the master of all the prophets, and David, the prophet-king, through Asaph and the Koraḥides, pious poets living in the Babylonian exile.

Notes to Chapter Three

1. See P. Kokovtsov, "The Surviving Fragments from the *Kitābu ʾat-tadkīr wʾat-taʾnīt* of Rabbi Moses Ben Giqatilah," in his book *Nowiye Materyali . . .* (Petrograd, 1916; repr. Jerusalem, 1970), pp. 59–66 (Russian); N.Allony, "Fragments of the Book of Masculine and Feminine by Rabbi Moses ha-Kohen Ibn Giqatilah," *Sinai* 24 (1949), pp. 34–67 (Hebrew).

2. Poznanski (*Giqatilah*, p. 55, notes 10 and 11) proved that these anonymous designations refer to Ibn Giqatilah.

3. In Ibn Balaam's commentary on Josh. 10:12–13 (ed. S. Poznanski, in *Berliner Festschrift* [Berlin, 1933], p. 103; Hebrew translation by M. Goshen-Gottstein, in H. I. Gad, ed., *The Book of the Ten Great Luminaries* [Johannesburg, 1953], p. 36 [Heb.]). From Ibn Giqatilah's commentary on Num. 20:8 (cited by Ibn Ezra in his commentary *ad loc.*), however, it is clear that he was very far from a fundamental denial of the possibility of miracles.

4. See Ibn Balaam's commentary on Zech. 9:9, cited by Poznanski (*Giqatilah*, pp. 157–59).

5. See Poznanski, "Psalms," pp. 57–58; Ashtor, *Moslem Spain* 2, pp. 261–262.

6. Poznanski (*Giqatilah*, pp. 51–54) collected and classified these attacks.

7. See Ibn Daud, *Tradition*, p. 73 (Hebrew section). It may be, however, that alongside the overt praise Ibn Daud's writings also contain covert polemics directed against Ibn Giqatilah. G. D. Cohen, the editor of Ibn Daud's book, hypothesizes that under the guise of a war against the Karaites Ibn Daud is here battling the radical intellectualism of the extreme literalists in the rabbinic camp, whose understanding of the prophesies of consolation struck him as erroneous and harmful (English section, pp. 300–303).

8. Maimonides, *Treatise on Resurrection*, ed. Y. Finkel (New York, 1940), p. 21. On p. 19 Maimonides describes the literalists as "the Andalusian savants and commentators." W. Bacher (*Die Bibelexegese Moses Maimunis* [Budapest, 1896], p. 143, note 7) pointed out additional references by Maimonides to Ibn Giqatilah. In the *Guide to the Perplexed*, Part 2, Chapter 35, the miracle of the sun's standing still (Joshua 10:12) is discussed. It is evident from his phrasing that Maimonides adopted the rationalist and minimalistic interpretation of Ibn Giqatilah and was not impressed by the counterclaims of Ibn Balaam (see note 4 above). In my opinion we can assume that the rationalization of the miracle of the resurrection of the widow's son by Elijah—mentioned by Maimonides without agreement but without any refutation in principle—refers to Ibn Giqatilah (see *Guide*, Part 1, Chapter 42).

9. Naḥmanides, *Book of Redemption* (Heb.), ed. H. D. Chavell (Jerusalem, 1963), 1, pp. 274–75.

10. In his commentary on Joel 3, gloss beginning "the general intention," corrected according to MS Escorial G-I-11.

11. See H. Brody, "From the Poems of Rabbi Moses ha-Kohen Ibn Giqatilah" (Heb.), *Bulletin of the Institute for the Study of Hebrew Poetry* 3 (1937), pp. 67–90. Y. Razhabi, "A Liturgical Poem by Rabbi Moses Chiquitilla" (Heb.), *Sinai* 24 (1949), pp. 288–89.

12. This means that fundamentally the prophecy of the first of the prophets, Moses, is all that is required, because his unique status (see Numbers 12:8) endows his prophecies with special status and validity.

13. Seventy-one postcards from Harkavy to Poznanski are preserved in the Poznanski archives in the Manuscript Department of the Jewish National and University Library in Jerusalem (No. 4°1180). They were published by S. Asaph, "A Memento of the Last Generation—Letters from E. Harkavy to S. Poznanski" (Heb.), *Ḳoveṣ ʿal Yad,* n.s., 11 (1936), pp. 191–243. The postcard in question, number 22, is found on pp. 209–10.

14. S. Poznanski, "Weiteres aus Tanchum Jeruschalmi's Commentaren," *ZfHB* 5 (1901), pp. 184–89.

15. S. Poznanski, "Tanchum Jeruschalmi's Psalmen-Commentar," ZfHB 5 (1901), pp. 122–26.

16. S. Eppenstein, "Ein Fragment aus dem Psalmen-Commentar des Tanḥúm Jerusalem," *ZAW* 23 (1903), pp. 287–325.

17. S. Poznanski, "A Commentary on the Book of Joshua by Rabbi Judah Ben Balaam" (Heb.), in *Berliner Festschrift* (see above, note 3), p. 92.

18. The two explanations, cited by Ibn Ezra and attributed to Ibn Giqatilah in his commentary on Zephaniah 3:8–9, are missing in the fragment copied by Horowitz; on the other hand, the gloss on *moreʾah wᵉ-nigʾalah* (Zeph. 3:1) cited by Ibn Ezra in his name is totally different from what is found in the fragment. The commentary on Hosea 13:12—14:3 transcribed by Horowitz also does not resemble in the slightest Ibn Balaam's commentary on the Minor Prophets as published by Poznanski on the basis of Israelson's transcription.

19. See the previously cited edition of Ibn Balaam's commentary on Joshua, p. 91; Poznanski, "Psalms," p. 41, note 4; S. Poznanski, "The Arabic Commentary of Abu Zakariya . . . Ibn Balʿam on the Twelve Minor Prophets," *JQR* 15 (1924/25), pp. 1–2. Idem, "Moses Ibn Chiquitilla as Poet," *HUCA* 1 (1924), p. 599.

20. See *Kiryat Sefer* 7 (1930/1931), p. 317; 9 (1932/33), pp. 139–40.

21. There may be all sorts of reasons why he put off this important task, and it is better to refrain from idle hypotheses, aside from the possible reluctance entailed by the need to rely on Horowitz's transcription and the hope he may have entertained that when things calmed down in the Soviet Union it would be possible to acquire a photocopy of the manuscript itself (see note 11 in his edition of Ibn Balaam's commentary on the Minor Prophets, note 19 above).

22. S. Poznanski, "Tanhoum Yerouschalmi et son commentaire sur le livre de Jonas, Appendice: Tanhoum Yerouschalmi et Moïse Ibn Chiquitilla," *REJ* 41 (1900), pp. 45–61.

23. See Finkel, "Psalms." From our survey of Poznanski's study of Ibn Giqatilah's writings we learn that the information reported by Finkel in the name of S. L. Skoss regarding two or three manuscripts of Ibn Giqatilah's Psalms commentary is incorrect. Evidently this information is based on a quick glance at the Firkovich collection or its temporary catalogue.

24. N. Allony, "Fragments of the Commentaries of Rabbi Moses Ha-Kohen Giqatilah" (Heb.), *Sinai* 24 (1949), pp. 138–47. Both fragments are part of a single manuscript, and include the commentary on 34:10–14 and 35:10–13.

25. The seven fragments (parts of three different MSS) are as follows: (1) JTS ENA 2819 (4:1–8); (2) Cambridge T-S ar. 21,23 (4:9—5:9); (3) Cambridge T-S ar. 1c,3 (9:17—10:13); (4) JTS ENA 2934, ff. 29–30 (35:23–25; 36:1–17; 40:9–16; 41:1–5); (5) British Library Or. 5562D (51:7–21; 52:1–6; 60:2–7); (6) Oxford Heb. 3. 99 (55:19–23; 56:3; 58:4–10); (7) JTS ENA 2464, II, ff. 45–46 (75:1–11; 77:19–20; 78:1–9). The attribution of the seven fragments to Ibn Giqatilah is unquestionable. In addition to the style and method of commentary, there are three convincing proofs: (1) The complete correspondence (aside from small textual variants) between the commentary on Psalm 4 found in fragments 1 and 2 and the commentary in the Leningrad manuscript (based on Horowitz's transcription and Finkel's publication); (2) the congruence between three of the citations included in Poznanski's review (the glosses on 10:2, 55:22, and 75:3) and the commentary on these texts found in fragments 3, 6, and 7: (3) five glosses by Rabbi Moses ha-Kohen cited in his name in Ibn Ezra's Psalms commentary (10:3,5,9; 36:7; 55:23) are to be found in fragments 3, 4, and 6. True, there is no textual proof for the attribution of fragment 5 to Ibn Giqatilah, but there is paleographic proof: the handwriting and format (19 lines to the column) indicate that fragments 4, 5, 6, and 7 all derive from the same manuscript.

26. The argument is reasonable in and of itself, but the recently discovered Genizah fragment dealing with this verse contains no hint of a late dating, and an explanation of their attribution to David is provided (see below).

27. According to the passages cited in Ibn Ezra's commentary on the first verses of these two psalms, Psalm 30 does not refer to recovery from a physical illness but to rescue from spiritual distress: David's mourning over the prohibition against his building the Temple turned into joy in the wake of Nathan's announcement that the Temple would be built by his son Solomon. Psalm 122, on the other hand, which deals with the joy of the pilgrimage to God's house, was written by David to be sung "when the House was built."

28. See the quotation in Ibn Ezra's commentary on Ps. 110:3–4, according to which Ibn Giqatilah gave a similar interpretation to the designation *L^{e}-Dawid* in the headings of Psalms 20 and 21 as well.

29. Poznanski ("Psalms,"pp. 44–45) shows on the one hand that the midrash cited by Ibn Ezra in his commentary on Psalm 1:1 is borrowed from Ibn Giqatilah's commentary, and on the other hand that the quotation in his commentary to 9:7 is so abridged that it was not understood correctly.

30. It may be that this usage of the plural even when a single person is intended is an Arabism, since in Arabic the word *ba^{c}ḍu* in its partitive sense means both "one" and "several," so that it is possible to translate *ḳala ba^{c}ḍu ᵓlmufassirīn* as either "one of the commentators said" or "a number of commentators said." In

fact, Rabbi Judah Ibn Tibbon translated *baᶜdu* sometimes in the plural and sometimes in the singular, as Wilensky notes: "Ibn Ǵanach" (Heb.), *Riḳmah*, p. 23, note 9.

31. The first recension of Ibn Ezra's Psalms commentary, of which only the fragment has survived, was written in Italy between 1140 and 1143; whereas the standard commentary was written in Northern France in 1156. For details, see below, chapter 4.

32. There is no additional information on Psalm 88, neither in the introduction to the standard commentary nor in Ibn Ezra's commentary *ad loc.*, but the mere fact that this psalm too is attributed to the sons of Koraḥ suffices for him to assign a late date to it. Concerning Ibn Giqatilah's position on Psalm 89, Ibn Ezra writes in the standard introduction: "thus too [as with the late dating of Asaph] Ethan the Ezraḥite wrote a Psalm [89] at the fall of the House of David in the time of Zedekiah" (lines 29–30). This discrepancy between the hypothetical language of the first introduction and the definitive language of the introduction to the standard commentary cannot be properly resolved as long as we lack the body of the first recension.

33. The heading of Psalm 39 is *li-Yᵉdut̲un*, whereas in Psalms 62 and 77 it is *ᶜal Yᵉdut̲un*. Ibn Giqatilah may have relied upon this difference in order to avoid the need to distinguish between an earlier and a later Jeduthun; as Ibn Ezra notes in his commentary to 62:1: "As for its being an instrument—this is rather far-fetched." If indeed this anonymous opinion was Ibn Giqatilah's, then *ᶜal Yᵉdut̲un* indicates not a man but a musical insrument (like *ᶜal ha-šᵉminit̲*).

34. Compare the stand of Yefet ben ᶜAli on the sons of Koraḥ (above, p. 78). In accordance with the general nature of the introduction to the standard commentary, this opinion about the anonymous psalms is also presented in a terse formulation—the meaning is not that the later commentator was unable to discover the identity of the authors, but that the editors of the Book of Psalms did not know it, as attested by their silence on the matter (lines 47–50); we shall return to this question below.

35. Ibn Ezra may have learned this from Yefet ben ᶜAli (see above, pp. 77–78), but Ibn Giqatilah apparently did not know Yefet's commentary on Psalms. Poznanski (*Giqatilah*, p. 48) did note five correspondences between Ibn Giqatilah's and Yefet's commentaries on Psalms, but they could have arrived at these independently.

36. In his commentaries on the Pentateuch and on Isaiah, also written in Italy, Ibn Ezra had to resort to extremely veiled allusions to his own critical opinions. For greater detail, see below, pp. 152ff.

37. In the Fourth Inquiry of the first introduction—which is devoted to the clarification of literary questions—Ibn Ezra quotes three specific glosses of Rabbi Moses ha-Kohen (on *mizmor*, *ʾayyelet̲ ha-šaḥar*, and *yonat̲ ʾelem rᵉḥoḳim*). These

glosses have no connection with Ibn Giqatilah's fundamental approach to the Book of Psalms, and hence there is no need for us to consider them here.

38. Only a handful of quotations from Ibn Giqatilah's commentary on Daniel have survived, and it is impossible to conclude from them how he related to this book, also considered to be prophetic. The same applies to his commentary on the Song of Songs. In the opinion of Ibn Ezra, both of these books contain prophecies about the future (see the prefatory poem to his long commentary on Daniel and the introduction to the standard commentary on the Song of Songs).

39. Some believe that the reference is to Judah Halevi (see Ben Menachem, *Ibn Ezra*, p. 230, note 29).

40. For Ibn Ezra, the verb *tiḳḳen* also means "to interpret a text not according to its primary meaning" (in order to resolve a certain difficulty). Compare his second introduction to the Pentateuch, the Fourth Path (Weiser, *Ibn Ezra,* 1, p. 139); and the Fifth Path (ibid., p. 141); and the long commentary on Exodus 20:1 (ibid. 2, p. 127).

41. Saadiah Gaon gives a detailed reason for this interpretation of *l^{e}-Mošeh* both in his introduction (Psalms, p. 29) and his commentary on 90:1 (ibid., p. 208), and correspondingly also translates in the *Tafsir*: "And this prayer will be sung by the sons of Moses, the messenger of God." Poznanski ("Psalms," pp. 54–55) found a number of anonymous references to the *Tafsir* on Psalms in Ibn Giqatilah's Psalms commentary, and at least two explicit mentions of "Al Fayyumi" and "Al Maphsar," which also refer to the *Tafsir.* We can thus assume that Ibn Giqatilah knew Saadiah's approach to these matters from the *Tafsir*, but we have no proof that his arguments were also known to him.

42. In fact this seems to be the meaning of the formulation of the first introduction: "Similarly the Koraḥides are not the sons of Heman (who lived in the time of David) but their later descendants" (lines 54–56).

43. In addition to the short paraphrase of Ibn Giqatilah's words in Ibn Ezra's gloss on 30:1, we also have a portion of his gloss on this verse in the original: Poznanski, "Psalms," p. 49, note 2.

44. Rabbi Ishmael (BT N^{e}darim 32b) and, following his footsteps, Saadiah Gaon (*Psalms*, p. 241), and Rashi explained it in this way.

45. We may hypothesize that Ibn Ezra assumed that receiving God's strength from Zion is reasonable for Abraham, given the fact that after his victory over the four kings Abraham was blessed by Melchizedek King of Salem, to whom he in turn gave a tithe of everything (Gen. 14:17–20).

46. In the first introduction (line 51) this opinion is given without grounds; obviously he held this view because of the second- and third-person pronouns in the psalm.

47. Postponing the composition of a psalm to a later situation in the life of the author (whose authorship cannot be denied) has also been suggested as a solution to the problem of Jonah's prayer. Ibn Ezra so reports in his gloss on Jonah 2:2, in the names of "commentators"; it is a reasonable assumption that he meant Ibn Giqatilah, who was very strict in distinguishing between an author's being a prophet and the non-prophetic nature of the prayer. Ibn Ezra's reservations about this solution will be discussed below (pp. 189f.).

48. Ibn Ezra also suggests these two possibilities in his gloss on the verse "O that the deliverance of Israel might come from Zion!" (14:7) found in a psalm attributed to David. While there he does not decide in favor of the second alternative ("it refers to the future"), Ibn Giqatilah is compelled to choose the first alternative ("because the glory was with the Ark in the days of David").

49. On "May He send you help from the sanctuary, and sustain you from Zion" (20:3), Ibn Ezra explains "from the site of the Ark"; it is quite reasonable that Ibn Giqatilah gave a similar explanation of the reference to the holy place in this psalm, which in his opinion was written about David (see the first introduction, lines 50–51).

50. See a similar comment on Psalm 78, attributed to Asaph (Ibn Ezra on 78:54).

51. In the references that follow, brackets indicate those psalms for which the information is inferred rather than explicit.

52. We have included Psalm 85 in the list (even though we have no direct information about it), relying on the fact that Ibn Ezra asserts with certainty that "this psalm refers prophetically to the Babylonian exile as well as to our own exile" (commentary on verse 1).

53. Perhaps we should add Psalms 74 and 80 to this list, since we learn from Ibn Ezra's remarks that he himself saw them as prophecies about future events (see his commentary on 74:9 and 80:8).

54. Ibn Giqatilah did not assign a late date to all of the anonymous psalms. Not only were Psalms 20 and 110, in his opinion, written about David during his lifetime, and Psalms 72 and 127 about Solomon, neither did he refrain from attributing the anonymous Psalm 116 to David on the basis of a biographical detail. In this psalm, which is entirely in the first person, we read: "I said rashly, 'All men are false'" (verse 11). In his commentary *ad loc.* Ibn Ezra quotes Ibn Giqatilah: "*B*^{e}*-ḥofzi* ['rashly']—this refers to the event about which it was written 'David was making haste [*neḥpaz*] to elude [Saul]' (1 Samuel 23:26). The meaning of 'all men are false'—this refers to Samuel, who made a promise to him, or *kozeḇ* ['false']—like '[whose waters] do not fail [*y*^{e}*ḵazz*^{e}*ḇv*]' (Isaiah 58:11) and the meaning is—cut off, because he thought that he would be killed." Note: the fact that at the end of the psalm there is a reference to bringing a thanks-offering "in the courts of the

house of the Lord'' (verse 19) did not deter Ibn Giqatilah from ascribing it to David. It seems likely that he explained it in this way by integrating the third and fourth ways—dating the psalm to David's old age, after he had already built the altar on the threshing floor of Ornan and transferred there the Ark of the Covenant and the temporary ''House of the Lord'' that sheltered it.

4

Abraham Ibn Ezra: The Psalms as Prophetic and Sacred Poetry

I. Abraham Ibn Ezra's two commentaries on Psalms

Comparing two commentaries by Abraham Ibn Ezra on a single biblical book is a double blessing—not only does it clarify his meaning, it also opens up a window into his study. Writers have had many, varied, and complex motives for rewriting their works: some saw a need for a corrected and expanded edition to replace the first version,[1] while others were content merely to correct and improve the original;[2] some made fundamental changes in the format of the book in order to make it suit the needs of a different readership,[3] while others had to remake their creations for a new audience that did not have access to the original version.[4] But whatever their motivation, all such revisers have in common the desire to make the new version reflect what they had learned in the interim, so we must not imagine that they intended for their readers to place the two versions side by side and compare them. This, however, is what we intend to do, because juxtaposing variants and tracing the changes that occurred in their opinions is the best way to elucidate difficult passages in the writings of ancient authors and understand how they thought. This is particularly true with regard to the commentaries of Abraham Ibn Ezra. On the one hand they require much more deciphering and glossing than the writings of other biblical commentators, because of their terse and associative nature, the hasty and allusive mode of composition, and the obscure style that tends to rhetorical flourishes while giving short shrift to clarity of expression.[5] On the other hand, as if to compensate us for these special difficulties, Ibn Ezra's nomadic life and his alert and ever-innovative spirit frequently caused him, more than any other commentator, to go back and write a second commentary on a biblical book. Until recently we knew of two commentaries by him on five books—Genesis, Exodus, the Song of Songs, Esther, and

Daniel;[6] two more can now be added to this list: the Minor Prophets[7] and Psalms. All the same, our great joy at finding another recension of Ibn Ezra's Psalms commentary is tempered by the fact that so far only a small fragment of it has surfaced: the introduction and the commentary on Psalms 1 and 2 (through verse 5).

Our remark about Ibn Ezra's hasty habits of composition is not merely an impression based on the large number of commentaries he wrote, but is also based on explicit information that has reached us on the astounding rapidity with which he wrote them. The long commentary on Daniel was completed—according to the author's colophon preserved in the first printed edition (Venice, 1524–25)[8]—"in Marheshvan of the year 4916" (October, 1155). He had finished writing the standard Psalms commentary by the end of the same year, as can be concluded by the colophon in three of the twelve complete manuscripts that have survived (Paris, Bibliothèque nationale Héb. 1222; Rome, Angelica 72; Parma, 510), where we read: "I, Abraham the son of R. Meir the Spaniard, glossed the Book of Psalms and completed the work in the middle [15th] of Elul *anno mundi* 4916" (September 2, 1156). From mid-October to the beginning of the following September no more than ten and a half months passed; this is the longest possible span for the composition of the Psalms commentary. But since we know only when he finished the book, not when he started it, we cannot know how long it really took him to write the Psalms commentary. We can learn something about this, however, by considering the information we have about how long it took to write the standard commentary on the Minor Prophets. In its colophon, preserved in five manuscripts and in the first printing (Venice, 1524–25), we read: "I the author Abraham the son Meir Ben Ezra the Spaniard, wrote a commentary on it in the year 4917 on the first day of the month of Tevet" (December 16, 1156) (MS London, Montefiore 34). In British Library MS 24.896, this commentary on the sixty-four chapters of the Minor Prophets runs to thirty-two folios; it was written in no more than three and a half months. Since the commentary on the 150 chapters of Psalms in the same manuscript is not quite twice as long (sixty-one folios), it is very possible that it was written in less than ten months.[9]

The colophons of the commentaries on Daniel, Psalms, and the Minor Prophets add a location after the date. I omitted it from the quotations above, because the many variants found in the manuscripts make it extremely difficult to identify the city where the commentary was written. The abundance of variants stems first of all from the perplexing fact that the name of the city contains three letters that can easily be interchanged because of their graphical resemblance in semi-cursive Italian Hebrew script: *dalet/resh*, *resh/dalet*, and *samekh*/final *mem*. Thus we find in the various manuscripts (including the author's colophon to the long commentary on Exodus, written in the same place in the year 1153) different and strange variants of the name of the city: Dros, Redos, Derom, Radom, Rodos, Rodno. Scholars have long pondered over the identity of the city concealed behind this elusive name, and four places have been proposed: the island of Rhodes; the city Rhodez in Provence; Dreux, which lies west of Paris in Normandy; and Rouen, the capital of Normandy, on the banks of the Seine. The research on this question was surveyed at length in 1932 by I. L. Fleischer, who decided for Dreux.[10] Recently, however, N. Golb has reconsidered this issue in his Hebrew monograph, *History and Culture of the Jews in Rouen in the Middle Ages* (pp. 1–5, 21–31, 45–66). On the basis of an analysis of newly available historical and literary sources, a comprehensive examination of the textual data, and clarification of the modes of Hebrew transcription of French geographic names, Golb reaches the persuasive conclusion that all of the different variants derive from ''Radom.'' This is documented as a transliteration of the French Rothom(a)/ Rodom(a) which is a shortened form of the Latin Rothomagus. The extraordinary multiplicity of errors made by the copyists is to be explained not only by the graphic similarity between the letters *dalet* and *resh,* and *samekh* and final *mem,* but also by the assumption that the name Radom was unknown to them, since by the thirteenth and fourteenth centuries the name had already been changed to Rouen. Even those who do not accept Golb's far-reaching conclusions about the nature of the relations between Ibn Ezra and the Rashbam (neither mentions the other in his commentaries, although they apparently both taught the Bible according to the plain meaning [*pᵉšaṭ*] in the same city at the same time)[11] must see the identification of the place where the printed Psalms commentary was written with Rouen as quite reasonable. In addition to this clarification of the city mentioned in the various colophons, we also have direct proof that this and the other commentaries were indeed written in northern France, which Ibn Ezra calls simply *Ṣarefaṯ.*[12] Thus in his long commentary to Daniel 1:15 Ibn Ezra compares the nature and qualities of the peas ''found in *Ṣarefaṯ*'' with those of the peas ''found in Spain and Egypt and Rome and Provence'' (i.e., southern France); and in the standard commentary on Zechariah 1:1 he expresses his reservations about a certain idea he had seen in ''the books of the scholars who lived in *Ṣarefaṯ*''; and in his commentary to Psalms 64:7 he notes that ''defective-*ʿayin* verbs'' are called ''by the scholars of *Ṣarefaṯ* doubles'' (that is, having a bi-consonantal root).[13]

True, there are eight references to Ibn Ezra's Psalms commentary as a finished work in the short commentary on the Pentateuch (introduction, Fourth Way [Weiser edition, vol. 1, p. 8]; Genesis 14:18; short commentary on Exodus 22:15 and 33:4; Numbers 12:1; Deuteronomy 1:41, 32:3, and 33:2), and six more times in the long commentary on Exodus (7:7, 14:20,

20:8, 33:4, 34:11, and 36:5). The short commentary was written in Lucca in central Italy before 1145,[14] and the long commentary on Exodus was completed in Rouen in 1153, as we have said; how, then, can the reader be referred to a Psalms commentary that was not written until 1156? Although we could assume that these references were added later by the author himself or by diligent copyists,[15] Friedlaender and Fleischer hypothesized that Ibn Ezra was referring to an early version of the Psalms commentary, which he must have written in Italy.[16] But because the Psalms commentary is also mentioned twice in the future tense ("I will explain") in Ibn Ezra's commentary on Isaiah (2:14 and 26:4)—which, according to the author's colophon, was written in the year 1145 in Lucca—Friedlaender was forced to assume that the Psalms commentary was written immediately after the Isaiah commentary, and that when it was finished Ibn Ezra corrected and completed the short commentary on the Pentateuch, adding the references to the Psalms commentary. Fleischer, on the other hand, rightly claims that it is hard to see a later addition in the reference found in the rhymed introduction of the short commentary on the Pentateuch, because it is well-woven into the rhyme scheme (and, I would add, into the thematic argument as well). Moreover, in the commentary on Isaiah 12:2 we read: "The explanation of half of the Name is in the [commentary on the] Book of Psalms, and *zimraṯ* is explained in the [commentary on] the Pentateuch." The word *zimraṯ* is in fact glossed in the short commentary on Exodus 15:2.[17] As to the reference to the Psalms commentary, Fleischer says: "What can we do if we have gone over the entire Psalms commentary and not found a gloss on the Divine Name *YH?* R. Yiẓḥaḳ Shrim testifies the same fact in his supercommentary *Hadar ʿEzer*" (p. 173). From this Fleischer concludes that the Psalms commentary mentioned by Ibn Ezra here must be a different version, where the topic in question is actually covered. Totally ignoring the two references in the future tense found in the Isaiah commentary, and basing himself on the many mentions in the past tense found in the two commentaries on the Pentateuch, Fleischer concludes that the first version of the Psalms commentary preceded both the Pentateuch and Isaiah commentaries.

The evidence is truly perplexing; we can only say that Fleischer's hypothesis seems simpler and more reasonable than Friedlaender's, even though it requires an additional assumption: that the two references in the Isaiah commentary, which are in the future tense, were added by a copyist who knew only the second Psalms commentary, and therefore placed the future tense "I will interpret" in the mouth of his author (indeed the topics referred to are discussed in the standard Psalms commentary). On the other hand, we have additional evidence of the early date of Ibn Ezra's Psalms commentary, unavailable to Friedlaender and Fleischer because of the poor state of the text in Lippmann's edition of *S^e^fat Yeter*. In this book, which ought to be called the "Defense of Saadiah Gaon" (see further, below, note 39), and which was written in Lucca before 1145 (see Fleischer, "*S^e^fat Yeter*," p. 166) paragraph 41 contains the following reference: "As I explained in [my commentary on] the Book of Psalms" (the complete text—on the basis of two manuscripts—is quoted and explained below, pp. 244–45). This reference is undoubtedly reliable, not only because it was clearly written by Ibn Ezra himself, but also because it must have been written when the book itself was composed, since the reference comes in place of an explanation, without which the argument is incomprehensible (see there). Moreover, we now have a real remnant of Ibn Ezra's other Psalms commentary. Given the shortness of our fragment, we cannot be certain that the many references do indeed refer to this commentary. All the same it would appear that the proofs offered by Fleischer and the additional evidence we have supplied are adequate to demonstrate that the other Psalms commentary was written before the standard one, and was composed at the beginning of Ibn Ezra's stay in Italy, before he wrote his commentaries on the Pentateuch and Isaiah and the *Defense,* i.e., in 1140–43 in Rome or Lucca.[18] Not much time is available for the composition of a commentary on the 150 chapters of Psalms during this period when Ibn Ezra wrote so many books (listed in note 18, to which we must apparently add his translation from Arabic to Hebrew of three grammatical works by Judah Ḥayyuj).[19] Thus this commentary, like its later cousin, must have been written in great haste.

Friedlaender[20] attempted to find the characteristics distinguishing the commentaries written in Italy from those written a decade later in France: sharp reservations about Talmudic homiletic exegeses (compared to a more cautious and moderate tone in France); referring to the Sages as "our ancestors" (*ḳadmonenu*), "our Sages" (*ḥakamenu*), or "the Transmitters" (*ha-maᶜtiḳim*) (versus the more traditional designation "our Rabbis, their memory for a blessing" [*rabbotenu z''l*)] he employed in France); little reliance on parallels from Arabic (compared to their relative frequency in France); the designation of Ibn Ganach as Rabbi Jonah (Rabbi Marinus in France); the many glosses cited in the name of Ibn Giqatilah and the small number of citations from Yefet ben ᶜAli the Karaite (the ratio was reversed in France). But there is little benefit in this sort of characterization, since it does not provide a common denominator for the various phenomena and does not even explain them individually; its principal use is as an aid in dating Ibn Ezra's writings. Moreover, its validity is rather doubtful. Friedlaender himself noted occasional significant deviations from these distinctions (accompanied by rather far-fetched attempts to explain them),[21] and even admitted that they do not apply to the two commentaries on the Song of Songs (p. 181). Nevertheless, these characterizations have become established in the scholarly literature,[22] and should be investigated on their own merits before we turn to considering the contribution of the fragmentary Psalms commentary, written in Italy, to the question.

The distinction drawn between two periods in Ibn Ezra's career seems to be a hasty generalization drawn by Friedlaender on the basis of a comparison of the two commentaries on Exodus. It is true that Ibn Ezra's reservations about homiletical exegesis (*d*ᵉ*raš*) is expressed with great vehemence in the introduction to the short commentary on the Pentateuch ("The end of the matter is: there is no end to homiletics"—Fourth Way), whereas in the introduction to the long commentary he adopts a much more moderate tone (even though here too he repeatedly refers to the Sages as "our ancestors"; and see below, note 33). It is also true that in the short commentary he always speaks of "Rabbi Jonah," whereas in the truncated commentary on Genesis and the long commentary on Exodus he always writes "Rabbi Marinus." Astonishingly enough, Yefet is evidently never mentioned by name in the short commentary on the Pentateuch, whereas he appears frequently (some thirty times) in the long commentary on Exodus, and even more frequently (around sixty times) in the commentary on the Minor Prophets. It is clear that Ibn Ezra was relying on his memory when he borrowed from Yefet's Arabic commentaries (to which he had had access only in Islamic countries before his arrival in Italy). He also quotes him anonymously in the short commentary,[23] and it is hard to say that he started to cite him by name in France because of a change in his attitude toward the Karaites: his attacks on Yefet in the long commentary are no less fierce than those in the short commentary. A partial explanation for this phenomenon may be found in Ibn Ezra's general tendency to be extremely selective in citing other commentators by name in the short commentary. All the same, the evidence does not support Friedlaender's assertion (p. 152) that Ibn Ezra departed from this habit with regard to Ibn Giqatilah by citing him frequently in the short commentary but infrequently in the long one. On the contrary, there are eleven explicit references to Ibn Giqatilah in the long commentary, but only three in the short one.[24]

Bacher (*Ibn Ezra*, p. 25) saw the consistent references to Ibn Ganach in *Safah B*ᵉ*rurah* as "Rabbi Marinus" as proof that it was written in France, even though he himself found (contrary to what Friedlaender wrote [*Essays*, p. 151 n. 1]), that in *Sefer Ṣaḥot̲*, written in Mantua in 1145, Ibn Ganach is referred to both as Rabbi Jonah and as Rabbi Marinus. He endeavored to explain this discrepancy in similar vein to Friedlaender's tactic on the Psalms commentaries: "Perhaps this is because he revised it in France" (p. 22, n. 1). However, Wilensky discovered that the alternation of names in *Sefer Ṣaḥot̲* is much more comprehensive than Bacher had assumed, and that in the *Defense* as well, written in Italy, there is a reference to "Rabbi Marinus" (§67). Consequently he sees the appellations of Ibn Ganach as an unreliable index for dating Ibn Ezra's works (preface to *Safah B^{e}rurah*, p. 277). Fleischer accepted Wilensky's rejection of Friedlaender's rule of thumb, and saw no reason to deny, despite the exclusive use of "Rabbi Marinus," that *Safah B^{e}rurah* was written in Verona between 1146 and 1148.[25] We can add that, like the alternation of the two appellations in the Psalms commentary (see above, note 21), the commentary on the Minor Prophets (also written in Rouen) refers to "Rabbi Marinus" sixteen times alongside a single reference to "Rabbi Jonah" (Nahum 2:5). To sum up, despite a certain amount of inconsistency, we cannot ignore Ibn Ezra's clear tendency to prefer one appellation in Italy and another in France.[26] Deviations from this tendency are natural in and of themselves, and can be ascribed merely to Ibn Ezra's temperament, his hasty manner of writing, and perhaps to emendations made by copyists. Thus we cannot determine where Ibn Ezra's undated works were written on the basis of this tendency, nor can we rest far-reaching assumptions about the editing or revision of his works on supposed deviations from it.

Nor does the new-found first recension of the Psalms commentary attest to Friedlaender's supposed Italian markings. True, Ibn Giqatilah is mentioned by name in the first introduction no fewer than five times (lines 49, 74–75, 111, 150, and 156), and this is the evidence that allows us to state now that the commentator who held the second opinion expounded at great length in the standard introduction, but without attribution ("and others say"—line 22), was in fact Ibn Giqatilah. But this is no more than apparent confirmation of the contention that the "Italian" writings reflect greater reliance on Ibn Giqatilah, which is refuted by a comparison of the two versions of the commentary on Psalm 1. In the first recension on 1:1, Ibn Ezra offers an interpretation in his own name, but in the standard commentary the very same interpretation is presented as that of Ibn Giqatilah; whereas at verse 3 the situation is precisely the opposite: the first recension cites the interpretation as that of Ibn Giqatilah, whereas in the standard commentary Ibn Ezra writes "some say." We cannot know what was Ibn Ezra's practice in this regard in the rest of the Italian commentary,[27] and whether he did in fact mention Ibn Giqatilah more than the 150 times he is mentioned in the standard commentary (see note 21 above). In any case it seems reasonable to assume that the same inconsistency found in the two interpretations of Psalm 1 was to be found in the rest of the first recension, a habit that is typical of how Ibn Ezra cited the interpretations of his predecessors.[28]

Because of the truncated nature of the fragment we cannot determine whether the first recension of the Psalms commentary was shorter than the second, and whether its relation to the standard commentary is similar to that of the short commentary on Exodus to the long commentary on the same book. The commentary on Ecclesiastes—Ibn Ezra's first exegetical work in Rome—can by itself refute the common assumption that Ibn Ezra originally wrote short commentaries, starting to write the longer ones only in his more mature exegetical phase in France. The Ecclesiastes commentary shares the approach of the long commentary on Exodus with regard to its thorough explication of linguistic and textual matters and the relative clarity of the style,[29] but it also resembles the short commentary in its extreme paucity of references to the commentators and grammarians on whom Ibn Ezra relied to such a great extent.[30] While the introduction to the long commentary on the Pentateuch is almost twice the length of that of the short (standard) commentary, the situation is reversed with regard to the two Psalms commentaries: the first introduction is three times as long as the second one. Of course this does not necessarily mean that the Psalms commentary written in Italy was longer than that written in France: the standard commentary on the first two Psalms is longer than its parallel in the first recension.

It is more important to refute the common belief that in Italy Ibn Ezra was able to give freer expression both to his reservations about the Sages' homiletic interpretations as well as to his more critical opinions, whereas in northern France he had to take into account the proximity of scholars from the school of Rashi and the Tosafists. First, we must remember that in the twelfth century Italy too was an important Talmudic center.[31] Second, we must take into account that the significant difference in tone between the two introductions to the Pentateuch and between the two commentaries on Exodus could well have to do with the personality and opinions of the patron for whom the long commentary was written.[32] In any case, a comparison of the two introductions to Psalms clearly contradicts the assumption that Ibn Ezra's modes of expression correspond to the accepted images of a more liberal Italian Jewry vis-à-vis a more conservative community in northern France. Rather, it is the introduction written in northern France that presents the position of those commentators who denied the prophetic character of the Book of Psalms and postdated a number of the psalms to the time of the Babylonian exile as a legitimate possibility. True, this position is rejected by Ibn Ezra, but in a very moderate fashion ("But I tend to agree with the Sages, . . ." line 35), without any dogmatic arguments being brought to bear against it. In the introduction written in Italy, on the other hand, this position is presented in so murky and partial a fashion that its critical sting is taken from it; if only this introduction survived we would have no idea of the severity of the fundamental argument regarding the nature and character of the Book of Psalms among the Spanish Bible commentators. Also, given how Ibn Ezra wrote, his silence provides no criterion for measuring the extent to which he was trying to conceal from his readers an opinion contradicting one of their firmly held beliefs, since what was omitted here may have been discussed in the body of the commentary. So long as we have only this small fragment, we should rest content with stating that the presentation of Ibn Giqatilah's position in the Italian introduction is very similar to the extremely allusive language with which Ibn Ezra veiled his own critical opinions in two other commentaries he wrote in Italy: the short commentary on the Pentateuch (see particularly on Deuteronomy 1:2) and the Isaiah commentary (see Simon, ''Medievalism''). In Italy, then, there were many limitations on how Ibn Ezra expressed himself; perhaps we can learn something about the atmosphere that caused these limitations from his poem ''*Nedod hesir oni*,'' written in Italy. In his bitter complaint against the rabbi from Greece who incited the community against him, he says: ''He reviled a Torah scholar / and all who know the Scriptures, / for which reason those who fear God / are covered in sackcloth. // And how can he call heretics / faithful sons / pious ones and *geonim*, / and all who hear him remain silent?!'' (Ibn Ezra, *Poems*, p. 92). Casting aspersions of heresy on those who interpreted Scripture according to the plain meaning (which Ibn Ezra emphatically applies also to the exegetes of the plain meaning among the Babylonian Gaonites) did not arouse his audience to protest, because of the cultural gap between Spanish and Italian Jewry— ''In Edom there is no glory / for any scholar who lives / in the country of the sons of Kedar / and they jeer at us'' (ibid., p. 90). Thus we see that we must interpret and evaluate what Ibn Ezra says in the first recension in complete detachment from any presuppositions nurtured by the common view of the nature of the commentaries written in Italy—a view for which we have found no substantial basis.[33]

Because of the truncated nature of the fragment we cannot know whether the complete manuscript concluded with an author's colophon, in which the date and place of composition were indicated. For the moment we must be content with the indirect proofs mentioned above about the time and place of composition, since extensive efforts to locate an additional manuscript of the first recension of the Psalms commentary have so far failed to bear fruit. Examination of the facsimiles of the twelve complete manuscripts and four partial manuscripts of Ibn Ezra's Psalms commentary in the possession of the Institute of Microfilms of Hebrew Manuscripts— the Jewish National and University Library, Jerusalem—revealed that all of them contain the standard commentary. However, MS Rome-Angelica Or. 72 and MS Mantua 13 contain a short addendum, which represents an additional mention of the existence of the first recension: before the published prefatory poem they incorporate the prefatory poem found in our fragment as well. The dozens of fragments of anonymous manuscripts of Psalms commentaries in the possession of the same institute disappointed our hopes; for now we must make do with a small portion of the first recension, extant in two short fragments from a unique manuscript (except for the prefatory poem, for which, as has just been mentioned, there are two additional sources).

The first and larger fragment is to be found in the Verona Municipal Library, MS 204 (82.4) (No. 23 in Tamani's catalogue).[34] It is published here with the gracious permission of that library, on the basis of the microfilm in the collection of the Institute of Microfilms of Hebrew Manuscripts (sigil: S32678). According to Tamani's description (pp. 239–40), the manuscript, consisting of 1 + 112 folios, was written on paper, with page dimensions of 286x220 mm, by two different scribes (the first wrote thirty-five lines per page while the second only thirty-four). I do not know on what basis the cataloguer determined that the manuscript dates from the fifteenth century; in any case there is no direct evidence for this, since the names and dates of the two copyists—whose semicursive Italic scripts are quite similar—are not mentioned anywhere in the codex. Of the five items in the codex, the first three are fragments (each ending in the middle of a sentence at the end of the verso of a page). The first two fragments are of substantial length (a Hebrew translation of Maimonides' commentary on Hippocrates, twenty-three folios long, and an anonymous commentary on the medical canon of Avicenna, seventy-one folios long). The third fragment—the only known copy of Ibn Ezra's Italian Psalms commentary—is only two folios long. It is followed in the codex by two complete works: an article on medicine and astrology by David ben Yom-Tov Ḥoumi (three folios), and a commentary on Esther by Ibn Ezra, which is also unique in being a rather successful integration of his two commentaries on this book (seven folios). The handwriting of the second copyist (who produced all but the Maimonides fragment) is well-formed and legible, but not necessarily accurate. There are around thirty mistakes in the two pages of the Psalms commentary, some of which can be corrected by reference to the biblical verses cited, but most of which can be emended only conjecturally. Whether the errors are due to earlier copyists or to the present scribe's carelessness, it is clear that he was not thinking about what he was writing. On the other hand, it is clear that he proofread his own work, since he not only blotted out extraneous words and letters while working (by means of dots or lines through them), he also jotted a few corrections in the margin. He may also be the source of the corrections of transposed words (a dot above the word that should come first, and two dots above the word that should follow it). The left margin was justified by graphical fillers (dashes and dots, stretching or contracting letters), and not by orthographical means (abbreviation, word division, anticipation of the next word), which usually make for more mistakes. The scribe wrote catchwords at the bottom of every verso, but evidently added no headings or colophons to Ibn Ezra's commentaries. At the beginning of Ibn Ezra's Psalms commentary (f. 100ʳ), though, the author's prefatory poem ("In the name of God Whom I call my desire to fulfill") is preceded by a copyist's rhyme introducing a supplicatory verse: "In the name of the God Who is great over all divinities / I begin a commentary on the Book of Psalms. / 'Hear, O Lord, and have mercy on me; O Lord, be my help!' (Ps. 30:11)." But since there is no analogous invocation at the beginning of the Esther commentary, we can assume that the scribe found these two preambles in the manuscript from which he was copying. In any case, Ibn Ezra's name appears in the body of both commentaries in the first person—in the Psalms commentary, right after the prefatory verses ("Thus says Abraham, the son of R. Meir his soul rests in Paradise Ibn Ezra the Spaniard"), and in the Esther commentary both in the prefatory verses ("May He command strength to Abraham son of Meir") and immediately thereafter ("the words of Abraham the Spaniard, known as Ben Ezra"). In addition to these unmistakable marks, the language and content of the fragment bear clear witness that this commentary was written by Abraham Ibn Ezra.

The second fragment was discovered by Benjamin Richler, the deputy director of the Institute of Microfilms of Hebrew Manuscripts, a few months after the appearance of the original Hebrew edition of this book, in which the first fragment was published. It is included in MS Leipzig University Library (formerly the Municipal Library), number XL (BH 2° 14). It appears here with the gracious permission of that library on the basis of the Institute's microfilm (sigil: S30745). The catalogue of the Leipzig Municipal Library, whose Hebrew manuscripts were described by Franz Delitzsch,[35] does not identify the author of the fragment. Mr. Richler discerned that the style resembles that of Abraham Ibn Ezra, and that the fragment is the immediate continuation of the fragment published by me. He kindly made the text available to me for the preparation of a scholarly edition,[36] for which favor he has my profound gratitude.

The first fragment ends with the catchword *rᵉšaʿim* (at the bottom of the verso of the second folio), while the new fragment begins with what is left of this same word—[*rᵉ šaʿi*]*m*. The beginnings of the lines were covered over by a strip of paper, used to fasten the folio into the codex. Later someone pulled part of this strip off in order to read what was written beneath it, and this may be how some letters were erased even beyond the strip (start of the third line). Perhaps it was this reader, who displayed interest in the fragment, who inscribed above it, in a later hand, the words *ʾEven ha-ʿEzer* (1 Sam. 7:12), thus alluding to the identity of the author. By contrast, it is quite clear that whoever glued on the strip of paper without worrying that he was covering over part of the text did not insert the page into the codex because he thought its content important, but rather so as to be able to write on the blank verso.

There is no doubt that the fragment contained in the Leipzig MS was copied by the same scribe responsible for the two leaves of the Verona MS: the letters are formed identically, the average number of letters per line is the same, and the manner of writing the lemma of each gloss and making it stand out by leaving a blank underneath it. Moreover, the two manuscripts use the same graphical devices both to left-justify the lines and to mark the end of a gloss. Since textually the new fragment is the direct continuation of the first one, it is clear that they were not only written by the same copyist but also originally formed a single continuous manuscript.

The new fragment begins with the last words of the commentary on Psalm 1, followed by the commentary on Ps. 2:1–5. Only the initial words of the gloss on 2:5 are included, and the fragment concludes in the middle of a sentence, with the word *y*^{e}*ʾabbed*. This is the only word on the last line of the fragment, and rather than being placed at the start of the line it is indented some five or six words from the right margin. This is a clear sign that the copyist did not leave off here by chance, intending to continue at some later date, but was forced to stop work because his sourse also broke off here; in order, then, to have a more festive ending, he wrote the last word near the center of the line. The clear inference to be drawn is that the two fragments constitute a complete copy of an earlier fragment that contained only the introduction and commentary through 2:5 (middle). It may be that that earlier fragment ended at the bottom of a verso page, like many loose folios. In any case, our own scribe copied it onto four and one-third pages, leaving the remainder of folio three blank. The copying of so small a fragment from a much longer work ought not to surprise us, since we also have four manuscripts of Ibn Ezra's second ("fragmentary") commentary on Genesis, three of which end in mid-sentence with the same word, and the fourth even earlier, and thus derive from a single truncated source. Before the days of printing, then, students of Torah were interested in comparing Ibn Ezra's parallel commentaries, and took the trouble to copy them over even if they were incomplete. For us, of course, this means that there is no chance of finding the rest of the manuscript that has come down to us in two parts, and that our only hope is to find some other independent manuscript containing the First Recension of Ibn Ezra's Psalms commentary.

II. Echoes of Ibn Ezra's predecessors in his commentaries on Psalms

There is no doubt that Ibn Ezra knew Saadiah's *Tafsir* and commentary (including the long introduction) on Psalms, as well as Ibn Giqatilah's

Psalms commentary. By contrast, Ibn Ezra's two Psalms commentaries contain no substantial echoes of the *Tafsir* and commentary by Salmon ben Yeruḥam, nor is it clear whether he had access to Yefet ben ʿAli's *Tafsir* and commentary.

In his two introductions Ibn Ezra presents Saadiah's view on the authorship of Psalms, as propounded in the latter's long introduction, in great detail, but without explicitly attributing the view to him. In addition, at the beginning of the introduction to the First Recension Ibn Ezra enumerates the five conditions that, according to Saadiah, governed the recitation of the psalms in the Temple, again without noting that he is borrowing from a predecessor. But whereas Saadiah's name is never mentioned in the introduction to the standard commentary, Ibn Ezra explicitly refers to him four times in the later part of the earlier one while demurring at his position, and twice more anonymously (lines 133 and 142). A seventh reference comes at the end of this introduction (lines 159–162), where he presents his own interpretation of the term *šir ha-maʿalot̠*, and offers Saadiah's opinion that the term designates a psalm to be sung in a fine and high voice, concluding with the note that "our Sages, their memory for a blessing, said that there were fifteen steps in the Temple, to which these songs correspond". In his commentary on Psalm 120:1, however, Ibn Ezra ascribes the explanation that *maʿalot̠* means steps to Saadiah. Thus it is evident that in the thirteen to fifteen years that elapsed between the writing of the first and second commentaries Ibn Ezra both changed his mind about a number of points and forgot that this explanation has its source in the Mishnah Sukkah (5,4) and that Saadiah did not mention it at all (see Saadiah, *Psalms*, p. 260). Since copies of the Mishnah were of course to be found in all Jewish communities, one may be astonished at such a mistake, especially by a scholar like Ibn Ezra.[37] On the other hand, it is not surprising that he had forgotten Saadiah's commentary, as he had been unable to reread works written in Arabic since he left Spain in 1140, some sixteen years before he wrote the second commentary. Evidence of Ibn Ezra's reliance on his memory for Saadiah's commentary is provided by a short work he wrote several years after he came to Italy, intended, as he stated in his preface, "to save the *Gaon*'s words from a harsh master" (with a pun on Dunash's Hebrew name, Adonim, and *ʾadon* "master"), that is, to respond to Dunash's *Criticism of Saadiah.*[38] In this book (erroneously designated *Sᵉfat̠ Yet̠er*, it should be called the *Defense of Saadiah Gaon*)[39] Ibn Ezra generally relies on Dunash's own citations of Saadiah. For example, when Dunash, out of respect for Saadiah, refrains from citing the latter's commentary on Proverbs 25:2, with which he disagrees (*Criticism of Saadiah*, §17), Ibn Ezra is forced to admit (*Defense*, §16): "I have forgotten how Saadiah explains this."[40] When, however, he agrees with Dunash's criticism, Ibn Ezra endeavors to defend Saadiah by assuming that his reasons may have involved the context rather than the etymology: "Perhaps Saadiah was not speaking of the root, but of the subject matter" (§43).

Similarly, Ibn Ezra had no access to Ibn Giqatilah's Arabic commentary in Italy and France, but nevertheless quotes it much more frequently than he quotes Saadiah. While Ochs ("Reconstruction," p. 211) found eleven explicit references to Saadiah in the printed commentary, Poznanski (*Giqatilah*, pp. 105–16) located 150 mentions of "Rabbi Moses ha-Kohen" (including direct references to the book itself: "Rabbi Moses ha-Kohen dealt with this matter at length, but I read his book a number of times and could not understand what he had to say"— Ibn Ezra on Ps. 89:2). The main reason for this clear preference of the later commentator over his great predecessor (whom Ibn Ezra called, in the preface to *Moznayyim,* "the first and foremost speaker in every place") is that, unlike Saadiah, Ibn Giqatilah could build upon the advances in scientific Hebrew linguistics begun by Judah Ḥayyuj and Ibn Ganach. Ibn Ezra does raise this historical perspective when he defends Saadiah against Dunash (*Criticism of Saadiah*, §88) with regard to the ungrammatical forms used in the former's liturgical poems: "I would answer him: we know that the *piyyuṭim* of all the Easterners are like this, as are most of the *piyyuṭim* of the Westerners, and it is their habit to hunt out strange and difficult words. Nor should we wonder at this, because the grammar of the Holy Tongue was not known until the time of Rabbi Judah son of Rabbi David [Ibn Ḥayyuj], the first of the grammarians" (*Defense*, §74).[41] When it came to philological explanations, then, Ibn Ezra had to exercise great caution in his use of the *Tafsir* and commentary, since their author was ignorant of the triliteral root of Hebrew verbs. To this was added another limitation—what Ibn Ezra saw as Saadiah's fundamental adherence to the interpretations given by the Talmudic sages:

> In everything that a student says in the name of his teacher, and his teacher in the name of his teacher, it is appropriate to question only the original teacher. I know that Saadiah was the least of the students of the Talmudic sages, while the greatest of them was the least of the scholars of the Mishnah. Thus what is Saadiah's sin? Why do you quarrel with him? Arise and dispute with the mountains that are the foundations of the earth, the scholars of the Mishnah who originated this explanation! Moreover, we find that in many places in his works Saadiah said: Even though it appears that according to grammar the meaning is not in (MS Parma 314: like) the words of the Sages, we shall rely upon them and put aside our opinion, which is of small weight next to theirs (*Defense,* §1; and compare also §§7, 9, and 31).

This forceful demand that Saadiah's critic should not ignore the guidelines and fundamental principles of the subject of the critique does not mean that he must accept them. On the contrary, reading between the lines it is clear that Ibn Ezra has reservations about adopting the Sages' interpretations when they deviate from grammatical principles. True, more than once he accedes to the Sages' view because "their knowledge is broader than ours" (e.g., in his gloss on Lev. 25:45; Num. 5:7, 31:23; Deut. 10:1–3; and in his preface to the short commentary on Daniel), but when he does this he is referring to the tradition which they transmitted and not necessarily to their own interpretations that accompany it.[42] For him, their additional knowledge is superior chiefly by virtue of the reliability of the information transmitted to them, and only secondarily by virtue of the extra understanding with which they were individually endowed. While their reliability on matters of information is absolute, the superiority of their keen minds and profound understanding is merely relative, since "the spirit of God formed all of us, and we and our ancestors were formed from the same clay (after Job 33:4–6) and 'the ear tests words' (Job 12:11)" (commentary on Eccles. 5:1). Consequently, he does not dismiss his own opinions because of theirs, but treats what they said just as Saadiah had actually done—his own understanding will determine whether the Sages' interpretations present the literal meaning or are merely "allusions" and proof texts, and whether their statements are to be understood literally or "as parables and riddles" (Commentary on the Torah, second recension, Fourth Way).

Here too Ibn Ezra is much closer to Ibn Giqatilah, the Spanish literalist, than to Saadiah Gaon, whom he describes as belonging to the school of the Talmudic sages. This can be made more concrete through a comparison of their approaches to the order of the verbs *hlk*, *ʿmd*, and *yšv* in the first verse of Psalm 1. Saadiah explained that they were arranged in ascending order (see *Psalms*, p. 41), and here he was undoubtedly following Rabbi Shimon ben Pazi: "If he walks he will eventually stand, and if he stands he will eventually sit, and if sits he will eventually come to mock" (BT Avodah Zarah 18b). Ibn Ezra begins his standard commentary with a paraphrase of this interpretation and notes that "Rabbi Moses ha-Kohen gave the opposite interpretation," i.e., that the adjectives appear in descending order of severity: the "wicked" are worse than the "sinners," who are in turn worse than the "mockers." Ibn Ezra himself, however, found it difficult to decide about this matter. In the First Recension on Psalm 1 he adopted Ibn Giqatilah's method (without explicit attribution), while acknowledging that the Sages' interpretation "is also correct." On the other hand, in the standard version he rejected Ibn Giqatilah's explanation, and even offered support of his own for the "opinion of our ancestors." We might conclude that Saadiah preferred to follow the Sages whenever possible, whereas Ibn Giqatilah and Ibn Ezra, because they saw the plain meaning as the essence, both felt quite free to accept or reject midrashic interpretations. It is clear in any case that Ibn Ezra exaggerated and sharpened Saadiah's basic position, since the latter did not refrain from deviating from midrashic exegeses, especially when compelled to do so by his polemic needs.[43] We should recall that Saadiah did this with regard to the authorship of the Book of Psalms as well;[44] and whereas Ibn Giqatilah's position was even farther from that of the Sages, but in the opposite direction, Ibn Ezra's stance on this issue was rather close to theirs.

According to Ochs (''Reconstruction,'' p. 212), Salmon ben Yeruḥam is not mentioned in Ibn Ezra's writings; nor have I found any significant echo of the arguments of this Karaite scholar about the nature of the Book of Psalms in Ibn Ezra's introductions and commentary. By contrast, Friedlaender (*Essays*, p. 171) found four references to Yefet Ben ᶜAli in Ibn Ezra's Psalms commentary (8:7, 11:7; 71:19; 78:47).[45] True, the first three have no parallel in the extant version of Yefet's commentary, and the fourth has only a partial parallel (see note 45). A similar phenomenon exists, however, with regard to quotations from Yefet that appear in other works by Ibn Ezra. Several hypotheses have been proposed to explain this: Yefet wrote two commentaries on the same book (Poznanski, ''Catalogue,'' p. 306; ''Opponents,'' pp. 229, 231); Ibn Ezra quoted from memory and sometimes ascribed glosses by other commentators to Yefet (Birnbaum, in Yefet, *Hosea*, p. xliii); Yefet's commentaries were substantially reworked when transliterated from Arabic to Hebrew characters (Ben Shammai, ''Yefet's Commentaries,'' pp. 17–22). In the absence of a systematic examination of the extent to which Yefet's glosses on Psalms are incorporated into Ibn Ezra's commentary, we can say only that, despite the paucity of direct references and the problematic nature of those that exist, there is a significant proximity of both general lines and details[46] between the approaches of Ibn Ezra and Yefet. The reason why Ibn Ezra omitted Yefet's intermediate path from the description in his two introductions of the exegetical debate over the nature of Psalms must be that his own path was so close to Yefet's. This ought not to surprise us, since Ibn Ezra followed a similar course in the introductions to his two Pentateuch commentaries, in which he discusses at length the four approaches he does not follow and passes over in total silence the Spanish literalists from whom he learned the fifth path that is his own way. This silence is not to be faulted, because Ibn Ezra had no intention of surveying the history of exegesis or of expounding the various exegetical approaches, but merely of clearly defining his own approach by criticizing alternative ones.[47] He follows the same tack in his Psalms introductions, where he omits the opinion of the Talmudic Sages in favor of Saadiah's more radical position, and contrasts this with Ibn Giqatilah's diametrically opposite approach. In the broad territory between these two legitimate options he places his own method, whose legitimacy is guaranteed and reasonability underscored by its location between the two extremes. We can perhaps infer from Ibn Ezra's failure to mention Yefet's approach that for him the Rabbanite-Karaite dispute over the place of the psalms in the prayerbook had lost its sting. The axis of debate had thus shifted from the fundamentally halakhic dispute between Saadiah and the Karaites over the nature of obligatory prayer to the exegetical argument between Saadiah and Ibn Giqatilah with regard to the nature of the psalms—are they divine writ or human prayer? Ibn Ezra tended to answer this question as both the Sages and the Karaites had done—prophetic prayer; but to do this he had to show that this answer could indeed withstand Ibn Giqatilah's literalist criticism.

III. The prologue to the First Introduction: The musical and thematic superiority of the Psalms as divine songs

Ibn Ezra begins the introduction to the First Recension with a discussion that makes up a quarter of the whole (lines 1–34) and has no parallel in the introduction to the standard commentary. This prologue deals with the superiority of the psalms as sacred poetry sung to the accompaniment of instrumental music, with complete harmony between the poem and the melody, instrument, performer, place, and time. The discussion begins with praise of God who endowed man with an ear, the organ that permits him to understand any utterance by virtue of its inner link with the "higher soul," which is man's superiority over the animals. He goes on at length in praise of the ear, and enumerates the four advantages of hearing over seeing: (1) The ear hears by day and by night, unlike the eye, which requires light; (2) the ear can pick up sounds from all directions, whereas the eye sees only straight ahead; (3) the ear hears through physical obstructions that block off the line of sight; and (4) the ear is the precondition for speech, whereas the eye is not required for intersubjective communication.[48] This kind of comparison between the senses was a commonplace among medieval Muslim and Jewish scholars; despite the masses of material available to us it is difficult to estimate the extent of Ibn Ezra's contribution to these debates.[49] In other contexts Ibn Ezra stressed the eye's great advantage over the ear—it can see far and absorb impressions immediately and even simultaneously, while the ear—which depends upon the air to carry the sound—lags behind.[50] Moreover, in his commentary on Isaiah 11:3 he notes the superiority of the sense of smell over both the eye and the ear: whereas optical and acoustic illusions are quite possible, "only the sense of smell cannot go astray." It is evident that Ibn Ezra saw nothing in these relative advantages to undermine the well-grounded primacy of the ear. Here this primacy provides him with a suitable scientific basis for his discourse on the power of verbal communication and the possibility of strengthening it immeasurably though poetical expression and musical accompaniment.

Communication takes place through the medium of sound; but by no means can one identify a sound or even a word with the message. He asserts as a fundamental principle that "the words are like bodies and the meanings like spirits" (line 9). This distinction between speech, a physical and sensible phenomenon, and meaning, which is spiritual and abstract, and the comparison of the first with the body or vessel and of the second with the soul or inside, are regularly used by Ibn Ezra to explain why one subject appears in Scriptures in different formulations.[51] Here, however, the distinction is not cited for exegetical purposes, but in order to explain the nature of speech and poetry as sounds that carry meaning and generate an impact. As Dan Pagis saw so well, in Spanish poetics, essentially classical-ornamental in nature, form and content are not apprehended as being intimately linked, as they are in the romantic-expressivist poetics of our own day.[52] Still, even if language and poetry were totally separated and distinguished from the content, to the point of being compared to its attractive vessels,[53] great confidence was placed in their power and influence. Ibn Ezra goes on to explain how acoustic influence increases in proportion as the artistry is more sophisticated and more complex: the sounds themselves can cause the soul pleasure or pain; more powerful than these is prosaic speech with a sublime content, which can make an enemy of a friend and a friend of an enemy; more powerful still is poetry, and when poetry is accompanied by music "then will marvels be beheld." Two scriptural proofs of music's wondrous power are offered: music dispelled Saul's evil spirit, and music brought the prophetic spirit to Elisha.[54] If all this applies to profane poetry, how much the more so for sacred poetry.

He still must demonstrate that the psalms are truly divine sacred poetry, and that their musical performance in the Temple was in fact sublime. One proof of the exalted status of the psalms is found in the fact that the Levites who were exiled to Babylon designated the "Song of Zion"—i.e., the songs that had been sung in the Temple—as "the Lord's song" (Ps. 137:4). Proof of the manner in which they were performed is found in 1 Chron. 16:4–7 and 37–43, which describes David's actions after he had brought the Ark of the Covenant from Kiryat Yeʿarim and placed it in a tent in the City of David. The king appointed singers "to invoke, to praise, and to extol the Lord God of Israel" before the Ark (verse 4), and other singers "before the Tabernacle of the Lord at the shrine which was in Gibeon" (verse 39) "to give praise to the Lord, 'for His steadfast love is eternal'" (verse 41). As part of this regulation that the psalms be sung at these two sites of divine worship until the Temple be built, David and Samuel also determined how they would be performed in the future, as we read: "David and Samuel the seer established them by their faith'' (1 Chron. 9:22). From this verse the Sages learned that David and Samuel instituted the twenty-four watches of priests and Levites (BT Taᶜanit 27a), while Ibn Ezra rests on it his own version of the five conditions according to which—in the opinion of Saadiah—the recitation of the psalms in the Temple was regulated (see above, Chapter 1, §III). From the word ''established'' Ibn Ezra deduces that David ''established five principles'' (line 17)[55] which he then proceeds to enumerate, without tying himself to Saadiah's definitions and proofs and also without mentioning him by name.

Like Saadiah, Ibn Ezra begins with the principle of *personal correspondence*; unlike his predecessor, however, he does not base this on the headings of the psalms but on the historical information found in Chronicles. There are two reasons for this. First, since Saadiah considered David to be the author of all of the psalms, he had to see all the names in the headings (including ''Moses''!) as those of singers. Ibn Ezra, on the other hand, who interpreted each name individually, with a clear awareness of how difficult it is to decide among various possible interpretations, required external proof that would be both unequivocal and applicable to *every* psalm attributed to a particular poet. Second, whereas Saadiah wanted to prove that every psalm was allotted to a particular Levitical family ''and it was forbidden for any others to recite it'' (*Psalms*, p. 30), Ibn Ezra was content with a much more moderate version of the personal condition—''only Levites could perform music [in the Temple]'' (line 19). His proof is drawn from 1 Chron. 15: 16–21, where we read that in response to David's command the ''princes of the Levites'' appointed their brothers Heman, Asaph, and Ethan (who belonged to the three Levitical families) to lead the singers. Thus Ibn Ezra—who had no polemical axe to grind—was free to make sure that his argument did not go beyond what could in fact be proven from Scripture.

In Saadiah's introduction *local correspondence* is the fifth condition, whereas Ibn Ezra presents it second. Saadiah may have left this concept for last because he found it hard to prove from scriptural passages, whereas Ibn Ezra moved it closer to the beginning because he was able to do so. Saadiah demonstrated from three texts (Ezra 3:8; Isa. 38:20; Ps. 137:4) that it was permissible to sing the psalms only in the Temple; but he had to rely upon a rather farfetched analogy between the gatekeepers and the singers when he sought to prove that there was also a restriction of location within the holy precincts (see above, pp. 22f.). Ibn Ezra, however, relied simply on 1 Chron. 6:16–32, where we read that when the Ark of the Covenant reached its resting place in Jerusalem David determined how the singers would stand ''to carry out their duties as prescribed'' (verse 17): the Kehathites, led by Heman, would stand in the center (verse 18); to their right would be the Gershonites led by Asaph (verse 24); and to their left the Merarites led by Ethan (verse 29). To reinforce this Ibn Ezra added that the placement of the families of singers was "just as the Levites were encamped around the Tabernacle" (line 22). His reference must be to the third chapter of Numbers, where we read that the Gershonites encamped west of the Tabernacle (verse 23), the Kehathites to its south (verse 29), and the Merarites to its north (verse 35). At first sight this analogy is astonishing, since according to the text in Numbers the Gershonites were encamped in the center, whereas 1 Chron. places the Kehathites in the center. The enigma can be resolved, however, by having recourse to the complex explanation offered by Ibn Ezra for the arrangement of the Levitical families in the wilderness, found in his commentary on Numbers 3:29:

> Because the Kehathites are the most honored of all of the Levites, Kehath was placed to the right [which is the south], for this is a more honored position than the left [i.e., the north][56] and the rear [i.e., the west], and only the east is more honorable. Because Gershon was the first-born of Levi he has primacy over Merari, for he bears more sacred objects than does Merari [i.e., the burden of the Gershonites—the hangings of the Tabernacle and the tent, the covers and the gate curtains—are more sacred than the burden of Merari—the boards, the latches, the pillars, and the sockets]. Therefore, Gershon encamped in the west adjacent to the flag of Ephraim, and Merari in the north adjacent to the flag of Dan, who was the first-born of the handmaiden [and therefore his status is less than Ephraim's]. And the Kehathites—adjacent to the flag of Reuben; that is why Koraḥ joined forces with Dathan and Abiram [of the tribe of Reuben].

Ibn Ezra's words indicate that although the order in which the Levitical families were arranged was indeed different in the two cases, nevertheless their ranking was the same—the Kehathites outrank the other two, followed by the Gershonites, with the Merarites bringing up the rear. How is this? In the wilderness the hierarchy is expressed by the different ranks of the cardinal *directions* (first the south, then the west, and finally the north), whereas in the City of David the hierarchy is expressed by the different ranks of the three *positions* (the center is the most honorable, followed by the right side and then the left). It would seem that Ibn Ezra's efforts to provide a common denominator for the two descriptions were intended not only to reveal the inner significance of the arrangement of the Levitical families, but also to buttress the validity of the local condition.

Temporal correspondence has a more restricted applicability than the former conditions. Whereas the first two principles can be formulated in absolute terms—only the Levites were permitted to sing in the Temple, and this only in fixed places—the third principle refers only to certain psalms, intended to be sung at designated times. Moreover, Ibn Ezra's careful formulation contains no hint of the exclusivity of these times—"there was a prescribed song for a given day" (line 23). In fact Saadiah too argued for no more than this, but Ibn Ezra brings only one of the former's proofs—the heading of Psalm 92, which designates it for the Sabbath Day. He may have simply forgotten Saadiah's other proofs, but it is also possible that he did not consider them to be convincing. Instead he relies on the rabbinic tradition that assigns the other six daily psalms, which Saadiah could not cite in a dispute with the Karaites (who did not accept the authority of Talmudic sources).

The fourth principle is that of *instrumental correspondence*: every musician (and his descendants for all time) was assigned a particular instrument, and this also determined the ratio of the different groups of instruments that made up the ensemble. Ibn Ezra proves this from 1 Chron. 15:19–21, which lists the names of those who performed on each instrument. When he refers to this text he highlights the number of musicians—three on the *m^eṣiltayyim*, eight on the *nevel*, and six on the *kinnor*. Saadiah too relied principally on these verses, but, as was his wont, he wanted to apply this information to as many psalms as possible (see above, pp. 20–21). Ibn Ezra, by contrast, went no further than this demonstration that there was a compulsory link between performer and instrument.

Ibn Ezra also proved the fifth principle—*melodic correspondence*—from the same verses. Two of the three instruments listed in 1 Chron. 15:19–21 are accompanied by designations which Ibn Ezra understands as designating "melodic performance." No doubt he was guided here by the fact that these designations also appear in the headings of certain psalms (as such he will later gloss them individually at the end of this introduction). But whereas Saadiah based the melodic condition of the musical terminology in the headings, Ibn Ezra preferred to prove it from these verses, in which they are clearly linked with an instrument and melody—the *nevel* with *ʿal ʿalamoṯ* (cf. Ps. 46:1), and the *kinnor* with *ʿal ha-šeminiṯ* (cf. Ps. 6:1 and 12:1).

In conclusion, whereas Saadiah adopted halakhic language when proving that it was *forbidden* to perform the psalms without observing the "five conditions," Ibn Ezra relied exclusively upon historical-descriptive terms to prove that the divine songs were indeed sung in God's House in full perfection: that is, with total harmony among the factors that the doctrine of musical ethos considered to be influential—performer, place, time, instrument, and melody. As a commentator on the Book of Psalms, Ibn Ezra had a double goal here: the five principles exalted and adorned the recitation of the psalms in the Temple, but they also explain and justify the astonishing inclusion of personal and musical information in the headings of psalms. Anchoring this information in the musical theory of his day allowed Ibn Ezra to propose his own interpretations for the musical terminology in the headings; while explaining this terminology as instructions to the performer about the performance of the psalms in the Temple allowed him to avoid giving an explanation when he felt he lacked sufficient data to do this. In the last part of the introduction he proposes a highly original explanation for the method by which the melody is designated in the headings, based on the musical custom of his day; on the other hand, he generally refrains from identifying the biblical instruments with those of his own age, given the multiplicity and variety of the latter.

These two contradictory trends find appropriate expression in the commentary on Psalm 150. In contrast to Dunash, who glossed *minnim* in verse 4 as the name of a musical instrument, Ibn Ezra, like Saadiah, understands the word as the plural of *min* (type), and explains, "praise Him with *minnim*—with many [types of] instruments and one melody." Evidently he means that the different instruments should play—unlike the normal practice—in a single melodic mode. A proof that his understanding of *beminnim* as a performance instruction was indeed taken from the practice of his own day can be found in his comment on this word in the *Defense of Saadiah*: "If so, it means playing on many instruments unlike other [reading *kiš^{e}ʾar* for *kaʾašer* (MS Parma: *ken š^{e}ʾar*)] melodies, *and this is also known today*" (§95). On the other hand, he tends to rely on internal evidence from the biblical text with regard to the names of musical instruments. Of *nevel* in 150:3 he writes, in the Psalms commentary: "it has ten holes";[57] while of *ṣilṣ^{e}lei šamaʿ* (verse 5) he writes: "these are the cymbals mentioned in Chronicles (1 Chron. 15:19)" and adds: "This is the general rule: there is no way to know what these musical instruments were, because many of the musical instruments found in the Islamic countries have never been seen by the Christians, and in the Christian countries there are instruments that have never been heard by Arab scholars."[58] His wanderings had permitted him to note the great variation between the musical instruments of Moorish Spain and those of Christian Italy and France; from this he inferred the absurdity of any analogy from present to past in this realm. This did not apply to musical theory, however, since, like all the scientifically oriented scholars of his generation, he had no reason to doubt the eternal and universal validity of the Greco-Arab doctrine of music.

Ibn Ezra opens this musicological prologue with an expression of thanks to God for endowing human beings with hearing and understanding; he concludes it by thanking God for sanctifying His people Israel and singling them out among all the nations as that nation whose poetry is sacred poetry. Ibn Ezra composed a short poem (Schirmann, *Hebrew Poetry* 1, p. 578) on this subject, of which a prose paraphrase is given here, much like the paraphrase of his poetic debate among eye, ear, and tongue found at the start of the prologue (see note 48 above). The nations of the world had developed the various branches of secular poetry: the Arabs, love poetry; the Christians, sagas of war and knightly valor; the ancient Greeks, poems of wisdom and philosophy; and the Indians, parables and riddles. Israelite poetry, however, was sacred poetry: "Only the poetry of Israel [is dedicated] to show them that He is their God alone" (lines 32–33). Only with regard to Israelite poetry is there a significant distinction between the prose and poetical versions, perhaps stemming from two scribal errors that may have crept into the introduction (which is full of them). The last line of the poem reads: "And the Israelites—with songs and praises to the Lord of Hosts"; and if we assume that we should emend the text in the introduction to read "to give thanks [*le-hodot*] to God" (instead of "to tell [*le-horot*] them"), we obtain a smoother sentence and also bring the text closer to the last line of the poem: i.e., only the poetry of Israel [is devoted] to God who is their only God. On the other hand, we must remember that Ibn Ezra holds that the psalms have a strong theological and philosophical element (see below, pp. 211–17), and that the doxological and didactic aspects are intimately connected. Evidence of this is the third—eschatological—formulation of the uniqueness of Jewish poetry. In his commentary on the verses "*All the kings of the earth* shall praise You, O Lord, for they have heard the words You spoke. They shall sing of the ways of the Lord, 'Great is the majesty of the Lord!'" (Ps. 138:4–5) he writes: "They will not have love songs or martial epics, only poems about the ways of God and retelling His deeds." Thus David, in his song of thanksgiving, anticipates that as a result of the news of the many wonders that God has done for His people, the songs of the nations too will become sacred poetry, just like those of Israel.

In the context of an introduction to Psalms commentary, the contrast between Israel's sacred poetry and gentile secular poetry means that, in addition to the sublimity of the musical performance of the psalms in the Temple, their content too is exalted beyond comparison. The condemnation of profane poetry is of course intended only to magnify the merits of sacred poetry, but all the same we may wonder how it is compatible with the great pride that the Jewish poets of Spain took in their outstanding achievements in all branches of profane poetry, here described as the not very honorable lot of the Gentiles. Ibn Ezra himself wrote a few love poems like the Arabs, many philosophical poems like the Greeks, and very many riddle poems like the Indians; and if he did not write war poetry like the Christians, he certainly had a high regard for what Samuel ha-Nagid had done in this genre. Nor did he fail to acknowledge wholeheartedly that metrical theory was developed by the Arabs,[59] and that Hebrew poetry of the biblical period was neither metrical nor rhymed.[60] Still, it would seem that precisely because this marvelous creativity of the Iberian poets was accompanied by a clear awareness that they were borrowing from the Gentiles—and even by doubts as to the legitimacy of this borrowing[61]—they felt a need to buttress the elevated status of biblical poetry. Because the psalms lack meter and rhyme—which in Spain were considered to be the distinctive marks of poetry—Ibn Ezra could not glorify their form, and therefore had to praise their content.[62] He did not mean to deny that Muslims and Christians also wrote sacred poetry, and that Jews also composed secular poetry, but merely to say that each nation excelled in its own particular realm and that the special talent of Israel, in the past as in his own time, lay in its fervent devotion to its God.[63] Thus far Ibn Ezra has been arguing that the ''Israelite poems'' in the Book of Psalms are ''divine poetry'' with regard to their content; later in the introduction (the Third Inquiry) he will consider whether they are divine poems with regard to prophetic inspiration as well.

The link between the glorification of the Levites' performance of the psalms in the Temple and the deprecation of gentile poetry will be understood better when we compare this passage at the beginning of the introduction of the First Recension with its parallel in the book by Moses Ibn Ezra, *Maḳālatu-l-ḥadīḳā fī maʿna-l-maǵaz wa-l-ḥaḳīḳa (The Book of the Garden—Metaphorical Language and Reality*). As the book's title indicates, it is devoted to clarifying the relationship between the primary and metaphorical meanings of words. The expansive survey of biblical metaphors which it includes evidently indicates that its double goal was to prove that Scripture contains actual metaphors that must not be understood literally, and also that the Jews preceded the Arabs in the development of metaphorical language, which is one of the foundation stones of poetry and rhetoric. It may well be that Abraham Ibn Ezra was familiar with this book (as well as with *The Book of Studies and Discussions*, written soon afterwards), since Moses Ibn Ezra died only a few years before Abraham Ibn Ezra left Spain in 1140. The work on metaphors has been translated into Hebrew a number of times, once by Yehuda Alḥarizi, who called it—following the author himself[64]—*Sefer ʿArugat̠ ha-Bośem*. The Arabic original, extant in two manuscripts, has yet to be edited and published, while only selections and fragments of the Hebrew translations (none of which survives *in toto*) have been published.[65] No Hebrew version of the musicological passage in which we are interested has survived; the original was published in part by Adler (*Writings*, pp. 159–64) on the basis of MS Sassoon 412 (now Jewish National Library MS Heb. 8° 570), and again by Shiloaḥ with many additions and an English translation.[66] Even if Abraham Ibn Ezra never saw *ʿArugat ha-Bośem*, the closeness in their opinions is evidence of the influence of the *Zeitgeist* on two of the greatest scholars and poets of Jewish Spain.

A page-long lacuna[67] makes it difficult to analyze the structure of the fragment. In general we can summarize it as follows: (1) an acoustic-phonetic discussion of the production of sounds and how they serve in the expression of emotions and in human speech; the lacuna; (2) successive citations of eight philosophical passages on the blessed influence of music on the soul (all but one of which are found, as Adler and Shiloaḥ demonstrate, in the "Epistle on Music of the Faithful Brothers") and a description of the correspondence between the four strings of the *ʿud* (lute), the four elements, and the four humors (also found in the "Epistle"); and (3) a description of the exalted status of music in the Scriptures, beginning with the appointment of the Levites in the desert, through the period of the First Temple and Babylonian exile, and concluding with the Second Temple period. Quite a similar order of topics marks the much shorter treatment by Abraham Ibn Ezra: (1) praise of the ear; (2) the power of music; (3) a description of the performance of the psalms in the Temple. But whereas Abraham Ibn Ezra brings in music as a way to adorn the psalms, for Moses Ibn Ezra the psalms are mentioned to exalt music. Both authors avoided an assertion of the aesthetic superiority of ancient Hebrew poetry over Arabic poetry; [68] but just as Abraham Ibn Ezra asserted the topical superiority of the psalms over the poetry of the nations, Moses Ibn Ezra asserted the antiquity of music and musical theory among the Jews.

Before launching his historical survey of the status of music among the Jews, Moses Ibn Ezra incorporates among the passages from the philosophers scriptural proofs that Isaiah anticipated Thabet Ibn Kura and Al Farabi in rejecting music that pleases the senses, as evident from the prophet's rebuke in 5:11–12 (sentence 1); that Jubal, "the ancestor of all who play the *kinnor* and the *ʿugav*" (Gen. 4:21), was the inventor of those musical instruments that have a beneficial effect on the soul (sentence 11); and that even the improvement made to the *ʿud* by doubling its strings from the original four to the present eight is already documented in the Bible: "on the *š*^{e}*miniṯ*" [*š*^{e}*monah* = eight] (Ps. 12:1) (sentence 17); and that the Bible even refers to a solution of the problem caused when text and melody are of different lengths—"Enter singers after musicians" (Ps. 68:26), which he understands to mean that a musical prelude should introduce the vocal song (sentence 21).[69] The first sentence of Moses Ibn Ezra's historical survey clearly attests to his far-reaching aim: "Doubtless, this great science [i.e., music theory] and its noble inherent meaning are anchored in the fundamental laws of Moses the prophet, peace be upon him" (sentence 23). His first proof is that musical performance was specifically assigned to the "sanctified tribe" (i.e., the Levites), is called "service" (*ʿavodah*—

Num. 4:47), and was strictly limited—in the Tabernacle, according to the Torah (Num. 8:25–26) to those below the age of fifty, or in the Temple, according to the Oral Law, to those in good voice (sentences 24–25).[70] The first proof offered is identical to the "personal correspondence" of Saadiah and Abraham Ibn Ezra's introductions, but the second proof is closer to their principle of "temporal correspondence"—that poetry and music accompanied the sacrificial service on certain days such as Sabbaths, Festivals, and New Moons (sentence 26). Moses Ibn Ezra then moves on to the period of David and stresses that the watches of the Levitical musicians were instituted according to God's instructions "to the prophet sent by him for this matter" (sentence 27), i.e., Samuel.[71] Not only was the selection of the singers prophetically inspired, their performance too is defined as a prophetic activity—"who should prophesy with *kinnoroṯ*" (1 Chron. 25:1) (sentence 28), and the chief singers Asaph, Jeduthun, and Heman are described with prophetic attributes (1 Chron. 25:2–5) (sentence 29). Moses Ibn Ezra translates this to the terminology of his own day: "Undoubtedly the revelation of these prophets is due to what God concealed in their nature of this noble science; consequently, they expressed it in word and demonstrated it in practice" (sentence 30). He does not explain what he means by "word" and "practice," but the former would seem to refer to the composition or singing of the psalms, and the latter to instrumental performance. The composition of the psalms is not central to the topic of music, so it receives no more than passing mention here. By contrast, it is essential in the introduction to the Psalms commentary, which is evidently why Abraham Ibn Ezra refrained from citing these texts to strengthen his assertion of "personal correspondence" and preferred to quote them later in the introduction (in the Third Inquiry) to prove the prophetic status of Asaph, Jeduthun, and Heman as performers-composers.

Later in his argument Moses Ibn Ezra discusses David, not as the author of Psalms but as a musician who magnified the glory of music by rising early in the morning and playing in order to reach a higher pitch of devotion in his prayer: "Awake, O my soul! Awake, O harp and lyre! I will wake the dawn" (Ps. 57:9) (sentence 30). Music helped Elisha when his emotional state prevented him from prophesying (sentence 31), and the exiles in Babylon when they accompanied their dirges of the *kinnor* (proven, in his opinion, by Ps. 137)[72] (sentence 32). Whereas he seems to have been the originator of the proof taken from the exiles, that based on Elisha is conventional. Saadiah used it to prove the "instrumental condition," and Abraham Ibn Ezra to demonstrate the power of music; but Moses Ibn Ezra wanted to use the information about David, Elisha, and the exiles to show that in addition to the sacred song of the Temple, music had many noble functions in ancient Israel—in prayer, prophesy, and mourning.

The chronological arrangement of his survey prevented Moses Ibn Ezra from classifying his proofs by subject; thus he returns to the "personal correspondence" when he reaches the period of the Return to Zion. From Nehemiah 12:24 he proves that in the Second Temple the order of the Levitical watches was reinstituted in accordance with David's regulations (sentence 33). From this he turns to describing the division of tasks among the Levitical families inaugurated by David and Samuel (1 Chron. 9:27–29) in order to highlight the fact that musical performance was the exclusive province of those Levites designated for this function, whereas the others were charged with guarding the gates, maintaining the ritual objects, keeping the food stores, and the like (sentence 34). Just as not every Levite was privileged to sing, neither were all musical instruments appropriate, since "not all musical instruments are made to stir the rational soul" (sentence 35)—as is proven by the fact that Scripture is careful to designate precisely which musical instruments were used by David and the whole House of Israel in their rejoicing before the Lord when the Ark was brought to Jerusalem from Kiryat Yᵉᶜarim: "with . . . *kinnoroṯ*, *nᵉvalim*, *tuppim*, *mᵉṣiltayyim*, and *haṣoṣᵉroṯ*" (1 Chron, 13:8). Since his topic is "instrumental correspondence," he mentions a number of verbs derived from the names of instruments, and identifies the biblical *kinnor*—through the Arabic word *kinnār*—with the *ᶜud* or *ṭunbūr* (sentences 36–37). This slight detour allows him to conclude his general argument by quoting the hypothesis of one or more of the Sages that *šiddah* and *šiddoṯ* (Eccles. 2:8) refer to "wonderful musical instruments which ceased to exist with the end of the state [destruction of the Second Temple]" (sentence 38). This is a fitting conclusion to his proofs of "instrumental correspondence" and of the achievements of Israelite music: not only did the Levites play appropriate instruments, but the word *šiddah* may even indicate a wondrous instrument possessed exclusively by the Israelites when they lived in their own land, today unknown to the savants and musicians of the Gentiles![73]

How does his campaign to demonstrate the antiquity and lofty status of music in ancient Israel fit in with Moses Ibn Ezra's willingness to recognize the clear superiority of the Arabic language over the Holy Tongue and of Arabic poetry over scriptural poetry? Indeed, just as Moses Ibn Ezra proved from the Bible that the ancient Israelites possessed a developed and sophisticated musical tradition that dwindled away after the destruction of the Second Temple, his contemporaries endeavored to prove that there was metrical and rhymed poetry in the time of the First Temple, lost along with all the other works whose names alone are preserved in the Bible. As he writes in *Discussions,* with clear reservations: "The Bible tells us that Solomon [wrote] poetry and prose that are proverbs: 'he composed three thousand proverbs' (1 Kings 5:12)—this is the prose; 'and his songs numbered one thousand and five' (loc. cit.)—this is the poetry. Some scholars believe that these are *kaṣīdas* [rhymed metrical poems], but I know nothing about the nature of these compositions and poems and their very existence, and nothing of them survives, not even fragments'' (p. 47).[74] Again we must ask: why doesn't he accord Solomon's poetry the same formal perfection as David's aubade? There are two possible reasons for Moses Ibn Ezra's ironical demurral at the naive endeavors of certain scholars to save the glory of ancient Israelite poetry. First, there are many more scriptural proofs for the antiquity of a musical culture in Israel than can be found for the antiquity of Arabic-style Hebrew poetry.[75] Second, it is not reasonable to assume that Solomon's 1,005 poems had greater formal sophistication than the Song of Songs, which Moses Ibn Ezra did not view as a poem, despite its name, since ''the word *šir* also applies to works in prose [*ʾal-manṯūr*] like the Song of Songs, 'Let me sing for my beloved' (Isa. 5:1), and others'' (p. 21, and see also p. 47).[76]

It would seem, though, that the decisive reason for Moses Ibn Ezra's refusal to deal with language and poetry in the same way as music is to be sought not in the interpretation of scriptural texts but in his recognition of reality. The relative poverty of Hebrew vis-à-vis the astonishing richness of Arabic was a fact of life; while palliative explanations could be found for this, a poet and critic like himself had to confront it head on and endeavor to reduce its impact on poetic and prosaic creativity. It was also hard to ignore the fact that the development of Hebrew grammar in Iberia was thanks to the example of Arabic linguistics; even though Moses Ibn Ezra may not say this explicitly, his recognition of this obligation underlies his enthusiastic description of how the secret of the Hebrew language and its grammar was revealed to the Spanish scholars after they had mastered the Arabic language (p. 57). Nor is there any doubt that all acknowledged, willingly or not, that the great flowering of Hebrew secular and liturgical poetry in Spain was made possible by the adoption of Arabic meters and by conscious imitations of Arabic models. We need merely recall the title of the eighth and most important chapter of *Discussions*—''To Guide You on the Best Path in Writing Hebrew Poetry According to the Arabic Rules (*ʾal-ḳanūn*)''—to demonstrate that Moses Ibn Ezra was convinced that imitation of Arabic models was the only way a Hebrew poet could progress, and that even Hebrew rhetoric and poetics—which he was the first to develop—had to be founded upon their Arabic older sisters.

Neither A. Halkin nor N. Allony approved of this attitude. They saw it as slavish adulation of the glitter of the majority culture, as accepting the chauvinistic claims of the Arabist movement (*ʿarabiyya*), which championed not only the absolute superiority of Arabic language and poetry, but also the climatic superiority of the Arabian peninsula, the ethnic superiority of the Arab nation and of Mohammed its chosen son, and the religious superiority of the Koran and Islam.[77] However, Moses Ibn Ezra's enthusiastic endeavor to demonstrate the great achievements of ancient Israelite music requires that we reconsider the nature and motives of his attitude toward the dominant culture. All acknowledge that he utterly rejected the religious foundations of this ideology, as is attested both by what he has to say about the sanctity of Israel, its Torah, its prophets, and sages (pp. 35–37) as well as by his implicit demurral at the Muslim tenet of the Koran's miraculous eloquence, inimitable by mere mortals (pp. 37–39). After depriving Arabism of the religious realm, where Israel and its Torah had the merit of being based upon revelation, he has no qualms about acknowledging the superiority of the Arabs over other races in the other two realms—language and poetry. He links this excellence, quite naturally, in what was then considered to be the scientifically verified theory of climates (pp. 29–35). He supplements the scientific argument (p. 39) with prooftexts from the Bible: "Kedar, who lives in open towns, the inhabitants of Sela will sing [*yaronnu*], from the peaks of the mountains they speak eloquently [*yiṣwaḥu*]" (Isa. 42:11; see also Dan. 7:20). The recourse to these texts is evidently an attempt to find scriptural legitimacy for Arabism, a way of sanctioning unhesitating Jewish recognition of its veracity with regards to language and poetry. Still, this recognition is *a priori* restricted to these areas, and is accompanied by an insistence that in other fields the Arabs too are merely epigones and translators, since philosophy and the sciences are the special province of the Greeks. For this too he finds a traditional prooftext, this time a talmudical one: "The Sages said (BT Megillah 9b) that 'May God enlarge Japheth' (Gen. 9:27) is an allusion to the Greek scholars, since the Greeks are descended from Japheth" (p. 41). In accordance with this idea he sketches out in the Hebrew poem prefaced to *ʿArugat ha-Bośem,* the curriculum for an enlightened Jewish scholar:

> He will give thanks to the One who placed His Word / In his mouth to strengthen him / When he learns His Holy Tongue / And the visions of His prophets / And the Jewish speech / As it is spoken in accordance with its ways / And the strength of the speech of the Arabs, / Their poems and eloquence, / Whose benefit is in counsel, / Knowledge, and rhetoric; / And the wisdom of the Greek tongue, / Its parables and its riddles.[78]

This basic scheme, according to which Torah and prophecy are the province of Israel, language and poetry of Arabia, and philosophy and science of Greece, does not stem from a blind acceptance of Arabism, but is the fruit of a sober and even bold view of the historical and literary evidence on the one hand, and of the possibility of the development of a new

Hebrew culture on the other. Moses Ibn Ezra, like his predecessors, could explain the Arabs' linguistic superiority by the fact that trials of exile had led to the neglect of Hebrew; but for the absence of rhymed and metrical poetry among the Israelites, in the age when their poetry blossomed on their own land, the only explanation involved a cautious and critical application of the theory of climates in its Arabist version. The palliative theory that the Hebrew *ḳaṣīdas* had been lost might have reinforced national pride, but it would not have obviated the need to adopt the Arabic aesthetic canon, without which classicist poetry cannot succeed. For the Hebrew poets of Spain the Bible was the exclusive authority for poetic language (what is permitted and what forbidden in vocabulary and grammar) and as a fertile source of poetic ornaments[79] and rhetorical insertions and allusions; but they could not take it as an example for the poetic genres in which they desired to write, nor as a poetic and rhetorical canon (defining what is appropriate and beautiful in poetry). The force and benefit of the canon depend on its having full and exclusive authority, which is why Moses Ibn Ezra demands that it be obeyed in full, even though he candidly admits that its rules "are conventional rather than proven" and that their validity is purely pragmatic: "We must agree with them as they are and in accordance with our ability, since it is not right for us to follow them in some parts and not in others" (p. 223). In other words, it was not the intoxicating charm of Arabism but rather a voluntary decision to write modern Hebrew poetry in borrowed meters and rhyme schemes that induced poets like the two Ibn Ezras to acknowledge the superiority of the sophisticated meters of the Arab *ḳaṣīdas* over the simple rhythms of the psalms. To see this as a distortion of judgment caused by the looming shadow of a proud and powerful culture is both to ignore the reciprocal relationship between creativity and poetics (which Moses Ibn Ezra analyzed so well on p. 223) and to demand that the members of that classicist school subscribe to historical and relativist standards quite alien to their spirit.

Thus Moses Ibn Ezra was afraid that the benefit of strengthening Jewish national pride might be offset by the potential damage to creativity. He had no such fear in another realm where, unlike poetry and science, there seemed to be no significant implications for his contemporaries—music. Consequently in *ʿArugat ha-Bośem* he endeavors to prove that it was not Pythagoras who was the father of music, as the Greeks believed,[80] but rather Jubal, "the ancestor of all who play the *kinnor* and the *ʿugav*" (Gen. 4:21), and that this art reached the acme of its development among the Israelites many generations before the birth of that Greek philosopher, thanks to its role in the Temple ritual and to musicians endowed by God with superhuman talent, such as the Levite poets and the orant King David.

Before we draw any conclusions from Moses Ibn Ezra's remarks on music regarding the passage on music in Abraham Ibn Ezra's introduction, we ought to examine the position of a third poet of that age who expressed his opinion on this matter—Judah Halevi. Since he completed the *Kuzari* in the year that Abraham Ibn Ezra left Spain (1140), the passage on music was written between Moses Ibn Ezra's *ʿArugat ha-Bośem* and Abraham Ibn Ezra's first Psalms commentary. In the context of the rabbi's assertion of the high status of the sciences in ancient Israel, he speaks of agriculture, botany, zoology, physiology, and astronomy, and then of music:

> Imagine a nation esteeming music to such an extent that it entrusts its performance to the most respected of the people, the Levites, who engaged in music in the Holy House during the Holy Season. They did not have to work for their upkeep, for they were satisfied with the tithes, as they had no occupation other than music. This art is venerated by mankind as long as it is not abused and degraded, how much the more so when it is practiced by a group with the noblest pedigree and the most refined talent, whose masters were David and Samuel. Therefore have no doubts as to whether their knowledge of music was thorough. (2, 64–66; pp. 123–24 [here and below, translation modified])

The pagan king must admit that the performance of music as part of the sacred ritual in the holiest place and on the holiest occasions by the most important of the people (led by men of the stature of David and Samuel) must necessary yield outstanding results. He reaches this conclusion despite the inferior status of Jewish music in the present:

> Al Khazari: There can be no doubt that at the Holy Place this art reached perfection, and that there it touched the souls, as people say that it changes the humor of a man's soul to its opposite. It is impossible that it should now reach the same high level. It has deteriorated, for today it is practiced only by servants and unworthy people. Truly, Rabbi, it sank from its greatness in spite of its nobility, as you have sunk in spite of your nobility.

Whereas the two Ibn Ezras glorified and exalted only ancient Israelite music, Judah Halevi makes it the archetype of the other arts and sciences, and even of language and poetry. In all of these the Israelites attained perfection in the epoch of the First and Second Temples, as the rabbi explains:

> What is your opinion of Solomon's accomplishments? Did he not, with the assistance of divine, intellectual, and natural power, converse on all sciences? The inhabitants of the earth travelled to him, in order to carry

> forth his learning to the nations as far as India. Now the roots and principles of all sciences were handed down from us first to the Chaldeans, then to the Persians and Medes, then to Greece, and finally to the Romans. On account of the length of this period, and the many transmitters, it was not mentioned in the books of science that they had been translated from the Hebrew, and so they were ascribed to the Greeks and Romans. To Hebrew, however, belongs the first place, both as regards the nature of the language and the fullness of meanings.

Later (§§67–81; pp. 124–34) the rabbi endeavors to prove the absolute superiority of the Hebrew language and biblical poetry, since Judah Halevi's integrative approach could not admit of a prophet who was not a philosopher, just as his ontological approach to the Holy Tongue does not allow him to grant primacy to any other language or to non-Jewish forms of liturgical poetry.[81] Because he does not assign the sciences to the Greeks and language and poetry to the Arabs he must also vigorously reject the superiority of Arabic meters and argue that their absence from biblical poetry is a sign not of its inferiority but rather of its superiority. For by its very nature biblical poetry does not aspire to beauty of expression but to didactic clarity, and therefore requires its own unique metrical system—the cantillations. Notwithstanding these proud remarks, of course, Judah Halevi did not write poems according to the biblical cantillations; nor could the impressive apologia for biblical poetry presented here be applied to actual poetic composition. The two Ibn Ezras sought to escape this problematic internal contradiction by a critical acceptance of one part of Arabism.

Among the three poets and theoreticians, then, only Abraham Ibn Ezra returned in full to the five conditions of Saadiah. Moses Ibn Ezra was content with personal, temporal, and instrumental correspondence, while personal, local, and temporal correspondence sufficed for Judah Halevi; and both of them preferred to ignore the specifically musical question—melodic correspondence. Abraham Ibn Ezra must have adopted Saadiah's full conception, albeit in a more moderate version—because writing a commentary on the Book of Psalms required him to examine it in detail, and this in turn led both to a more cautious formulation of the five conditions and to grounding them more firmly on scriptural passages. Indeed, Abraham Ibn Ezra was interested in the musical aspect of the Book of Psalms chiefly from the exegetical perspective, whereas his three predecessors exploited the musical discussion for polemic and apologetic purposes. Saadiah was caught up in the throes of the war against Karaism; while Moses Ibn Ezra and Judah Halevi, each in his own way, sought to buttress Jewish culture in its competition with Arabic culture. Abraham Ibn Ezra, however, built upon the accomplishments of his predecessors while being largely unfettered by their motives. Unlike Saadiah, he did not require the five conditions for polemic purposes, but rather as a background for clarifying the information found in the headings of the psalms; and unlike Moses Ibn Ezra and Judah Halevi, he did not have to glorify Israelite music in order to repel the onslaught of Arabism, but rather for the sake of a balanced appreciation of the poetical nature of the psalms. Unlike Judah Halevi, he could not praise the form of the non-metrical and unrhymed psalms, and therefore emphasizes the superiority of content held by biblical sacred poetry over the profane poetry of the various nations. But as a faithful son of an aesthetically oriented culture, he could not rest content with a superiority on content, and endeavored to prove that, from the aesthetic perspective as well, the psalms attained perfection—whatever is lacking in their inner form was counterbalanced by the exquisite musical performance.[82] Regarding both religious content and musical perfection, the psalms that were sung by the Levites in the Temple are "the songs of God."

IV. The First Inquiry: Who wrote the Psalms?

Abraham Ibn Ezra's introduction to his standard Psalms commentary does not contain even one sentence that parallels the prologue of the introduction to the First Recension, which deals with the excellences of the Book of Psalms. We should not infer from this silence that with the passage of time Ibn Ezra had changed his opinion about the quality and function of music or how the psalms were sung in the Temple, since these topics are dealt with in the body of the standard commentary. His silence stems simply from the concise nature of this commentary, written in great haste (see above p. 146), which leaves him time to discuss in its introduction only two interconnected issues—the question of authorship and the holiness of the psalms. By contrast, the first introduction has greater scope, and its structure is directly or indirectly influenced by that of Isaac Ibn Giath's Arabic commentary on Ecclesiastes. Ibn Giath's introduction starts by asserting the legitimacy of commentaries on the Bible and the particular need for a commentary on Ecclesiastes, given its enigmatic character and its richness. He follows this with the main part of the introduction, which discusses the "eight things that the student must know" (Ibn Giath, *Ecclesiastes*, p. 165). Ibn Ezra starts the main part of his introduction by stating that "we must undertake four inquiries" (line 35). The similarity between the two prefaces is obvious when we juxtapose the arrangement of topics in them.

Ibn Giath's Introduction	**Ibn Ezra's Introduction**
1. Identity of the author	1. "Is the entire book by David?"
2. Meaning of the book's name	[No clarification necessary for Psalms]
3. Identity of the writer (ʾ*al-mudawwin*) and his time	2. "Who wrote down this book?"
4. The question of holiness	[Not in doubt for Psalms]
5. The source of its authority: the author's wisdom or the Holy Spirit?	3. "Are these . . . veritable songs, psalms, and prayers, or were they said through the Holy Spirit?"
6. Innovations in the book vis-à-vis the Torah and prophecy	4. Elucidation of the literary and musical terms in the headings and the question of the psalms' autonomy as separate poems
7. Theoretical foundations of the book	
8. A summary of its lesson: The limits of the asceticism presented in it	

Ibn Ezra's first three "inquiries" are essentially parallel to Ibn Giath's first five points, but thereafter their paths diverge because of the difference between the ethical and philosophical nature of Ecclesiastes and the liturgical and poetical nature of Psalms, such that Ibn Giath had to expatiate on matters of content while Ibn Ezra had to discuss matters of form. In the introduction to the standard commentary, however, Ibn Ezra bypassed all of this and dealt only with the questions of authorship (discussed in the First Inquiry of the first introduction) and sanctity (discussed in the Third Inquiry). When he abandoned his predecessor's format Ibn Ezra was also wise enough to liberate himself from it and treat the two questions together, thereby illuminating the internal connection between them. Thus the loss incurred due to the abridgement was to a certain extent balanced by the gain derived from greater clarity (see above, p. 127). Here we shall deal with Ibn Ezra's two introductions at the same time, wherever they are parallel, and will then return to consider the rest of the first introduction, whose topics, although lacking parallels in the second one, are discussed at various places in the body of the standard commentary.

In the first introduction Ibn Ezra defines the subject of the First Inquiry by asking: "Is the entire book by David?" (lines 35–36). In the later introduction, however, he prefers to point to problematic elements in the headings of various psalms, which had engendered a major controversy among the commentators: "This Book of Psalms contains some psalms in which the name of the poet or author is found in the heading, and many others where the name of the poet is not mentioned, such as Psalm 1, and also Psalm 2, and 'O you who dwell in the shelter of the Most High' (91) and the one after it" (lines 7–10). If we add another element to the perplexing scenario (though Ibn Ezra does not mention it until the end of this introduction)—"the book does not begin [with the heading] 'the prophecy of David' " (line 51)—we can rephrase his questions as follows: Not only does the book as a whole and many of the psalms within it lack a heading, even when the header to a psalm does contain a name it is difficult to know whether the reference is to a musician or to an author. Moreover, we see from Ibn Ezra's discussion (principally in the first introduction) that the problem, whose roots lie in the paucity of information and the obscurity of what there is, is exacerbated by the extreme sophistication of the exegetical methods. All agree that the *lamed* before a personal name in the header of a psalm can be interpreted in four ways, which lead to five or six different conclusions: the reference can be to an author, to a musician, to the descendants of an author or musician, to the subject of the psalm, or even to his descendants. The fundamental argument about the nature of the psalms is based on a selective and even contradictory application of these exegetical possibilities. In the first introduction Ibn Ezra shows how the proponent of the opinion that all of the psalms were written by David (meaning Saadiah), resorted to these methods in order to "neutralize" all the other names found in the headings. But even Saadiah's great disputant Ibn Giqatilah, who systematically understood the names in the headers to refer to different authors, had to rely on the same methods. This permitted him to interpret a number of the *l^e-Dawid* psalms as being about David (which he wanted to do for purely exegetical reasons), and, more significantly, allowed him to understand *l^e-ʾAsaf* and *livnei Ḳoraḥ* as referring to the descendants of Asaph and Koraḥ who lived in the Babylonian exile. Each tugs the anonymous psalms in his own direction, too: Saadiah holds that all were composed by David, whereas Ibn Giqatilah insists that we do not know who wrote them (and thus they are certainly not by David).

Ibn Ezra's exposition of his own position in the First Inquiry of the first introduction begins with criticism of Ibn Giqatilah's position: the anonymity is not absolute, and therefore cannot be a matter of principle. His proof is that 1 Chron. 16:7–37, which is explicitly ascribed to David, is merely a medley of psalms and parts of psalms that are all included anonymously in the Book of Psalms: 105:1–15, 96:1–3, and 106:47–48. On the other hand, Ibn Ezra does not consider it essential to refute the extreme opinion that all of the anonymous psalms are by David, nor even to demur at it, because it is obviously unprovable. But precisely because he shares Ibn Giqatilah's allegiance to the plain meaning of biblical texts he feels obliged to speak out against whatever he views as a deviation from the facts as given, since otherwise we are merely substituting one dogmatic opinion for its opposite. Ibn Ezra goes on to show that cautious attempts can be made to identify the authors of other anonymous psalms (see above, p. 125, and below, pp. 218–220). Here we can already discern the fundamental principle of his method—the aspiration to reduce every daring hypothesis and every marginal method to the *absolute minimum.* Hence a literal understanding of the prefix *lamed,* that is, as indicating the author of the psalm, should *a priori* be preferred; recourse should be had to less probable methods of interpretation only when there is no alternative. Consequently Ibn Ezra agrees with Ibn Giqatilah that the text provides no support for Saadiah's distinction between David's name and all other names in the headings; thus we must assume that they too indicate authors, provided there is no special reason to prevent us from doing so (for example, with regard to Jeduthun: see below).

Ibn Ezra recognizes another method for depriving names of their primary meaning—understanding them as a reference to descendants of the person named. He demurs at Saadiah's application of the method to *l^{e}-Mošeh,* and equally from Ibn Giqatilah's application of it to *l^{e}-ʾAsaf* and *livnei Ḳoraḥ.* In the introduction to the First Recension he fails to mention when, in his opinion, the method is valid. We find this in the second introduction, accompanied by two proofs: " 'Of Solomon' (72, 127) is by someone who prophesied about Solomon, or about the Messiah his descendant, who is called [by] his name [like] 'My servant *David* their prince for all time' (Ez. 37:25), which is like 'have no fear, My servant *Jacob*' (Jer. 30:10 and 46:27)" (lines 44–47).[83] In the standard commentary Ibn Ezra proposes the messianic interpretation for the two *li-š^{e}lomoh* psalms and for one *l^{e}-Dawid* psalm (see his commentary on 21:11); it is hard to be certain whether his silence in the first introduction indicates that this interpretation was a later development or—what seems more likely—that his silence stems from the fact that neither Saadiah nor Ibn Giqatilah resorted to the messianic interpretation: the former, because he wanted to link the psalms with Davidic authorship in every possible way; the latter, because he did not view the psalms as prophetic.

This principle of the minimal application of a legitimate method is also applied by Ibn Ezra to the interpretation of *li-š^{e}lomoh* in the sense of "about Solomon," and even more so to the denial of Davidic authorship of *l^{e}-Dawid* psalms and their attribution to anonymous poets who sang about him.[84] In the first introduction, too, Ibn Ezra asserts that Psalm 72 may well be about Solomon, and if so is anonymous; but he adds that it may nevertheless be possible to identify the author—"though it may be by David, because of the conclusion: 'End of the prayers of David son of Jesse' (72:20)" (line 76).[85] Ibn Ezra does not explain why he is willing to understand *l^e-Dawid* as "about David" in only "some of the psalms" (line 77); but if we examine his approach to the *l^e-Dawid* psalms throughout the standard commentary we discover that in his view there are only a few psalms whose content and especially style attest that David was their subject rather than author.[86] It is true that Saadiah adopted this method only with regard to the two *li-š^elomoh* psalms (because he wanted to attribute psalms to David rather than deny their Davidic authorship); Ibn Giqatilah too made but slight use of this tactic (apparently because with respect to historical dating it makes no difference whether a psalm is attributed to David or to a contemporary of his).

The opposing viewpoints of Saadiah and Ibn Giqatilah converge in one point—the function of Jeduthun, named at the beginning of Psalms 39 and 62 along with David, and in the heading of Psalm 77 along with Asaph. Both concluded that Jeduthun was a musician, who received Psalms 39 and 62 from David (for Ibn Giqatilah's opinion of Psalm 77 see above, p. 124). But whereas Saadiah saw Jeduthun as the archetypical case for all names found in the headings of psalms—except for David—Ibn Giqatilah viewed him as a single exception. He could have assumed that Jeduthun was also a poet who wrote these psalms about David; but because these two psalms are in the first person such a theory seems to be rather farfetched. Ibn Ezra apparently agreed with this judgment, since he notes that these two psalms should be ascribed not to Jeduthun but to David (lines 78f.), although he never says how he himself understands *li-y^edutun* (39) and *ʿal y^edutun* (62). This is merely a deferral, however, which stems from the fact that Ibn Ezra cannot offer his interpretation before he develops, in the Fourth Inquiry, his original theory of the musical terminology used in the headings. Still, despite the charm of this hypothesis—in accordance with which he does indeed interpret the name Jeduthun in the standard commentary on 39:1, 62:1, and 77:1—in the first introduction Ibn Ezra acknowledges that the argument is not definitive, and that another possible interpretation is that David "may have given this Psalm to Jeduthun" (lines 152f.).

We have endeavored to uncover behind Ibn Ezra's definitive assertions a clear and consistent line; it seems that he thought of his readers as learned individuals who could abstract and generalize independently from his opinions, which are practically unaccompanied by grounds. These opinions are more or less identical in the two introductions (except for the addition of the messianic interpretation in the later one, discussed above, p. 180); the difference between them is merely in the order of exposition. The clear advantage of the second introduction is that linking the exegetical and philosophical disputes eliminates the apparent arbitrariness of the commentator's conclusions. But the first introduction too has an advantage, at least for those interested in problems of methodology. By concealing the fundamental positions that guided the disputants Ibn Ezra can consider the exegetical questions per se, and first propose a methodological solution that does not depend on his own fundamental stance.

The general rule to be inferred from Ibn Ezra's opinions is an operative rule: to the extent possible the commentator must avoid interpreting the text other than according to its primary meaning. Given that he cannot reduce the number of legitimate exegetical methods used by his predecessors, he demands, for the sake of probability, maximum restraint in their application. Giving preference to the basic literal meaning as a matter of principle and making any deviation from it depend on some urgent need is merely one more important application of the principle of restricting metaphorization (*taʾwīl*) that Ibn Ezra inherited from Saadiah and discussed at length in his two introductions to the Pentateuch. With regard to metaphorization it was possible to try to define the three or four cases in which the law of contradiction requires us to understand the text other than according to its basic literal meaning; but when it comes to interpretations of the prefix *lamed* and many other exegetical methods the only limit is the law of maximum probability. It is difficult to persuade others by means of such a flexible rule, which is why Ibn Ezra frequently goes no further than the characteristic assertion "but there is no need for this," which means that in his opinion it is perfectly possible to understand the text according to its basic literal meaning, and hence farfetched hypotheses and questionable methods should be avoided.[87] This is not a solution to the problem—whose source is the paucity of data and multiplicity of methods—but it is an important contribution to limiting it.

V. *The Second Inquiry: Who edited the Book of Psalms?*

The Second Inquiry is very short, because Ibn Ezra dismisses the question "Who edited [*ḥibbᵉruhu*] this book" with the excuse that the Sages provided a clear answer to this. In his words: "There is no need to answer this, since the Sages, their memory for a blessing, handed down to us that the men of the Great Assembly edited it, and this satisfies us" (lines 80–81). Since he has already dealt with the question of authorship in the First Inquiry, it is clear that *ḥibbᵉruhu* refers to what we would call "editors," that is, those who gathered the psalms and wrote them down in a particular order. Not only does *m^e^ḥabb^e^r* have two meanings for him, he often uses them both in the same context. Thus, for example, in the introduction to the standard commentary, while presenting Ibn Giqatilah's position, he writes: "As for those psalms that have no explicit attribution, the editors [*m^e^ḥabb^e^rim*] of this Book of Psalms did not know the name of the author [*m^e^ḥabb^e^r*]" (lines 30–31).[88] The gap between original writing and editing did not loom so large to the Spanish scholars as it does to us, because of their different approach to the whole question of originality.[89] Even an author-creator bases himself on older material, whether in raw or literary form, which he molds and works into a new entity.[90] Like him, the author-editor gathers material and writes it down; Ibn Ezra designates both activities by the word *ḥibbur*. In his commentary on Eccles. 1:16 he writes: "The meaning of 'I have grown in wisdom and added to it' is that he collected [*ḥibb^e^r*] and learned the wisdom of the ancients and added to it." On the other hand, consider his commentary on Eccles. 12:11: "'ᶜbaᶜalei ʾasuppot'—these are those who gather from many books and write [*y^e^ḥabb^e^ru*] collections." When Ibn Ezra wants to underscore the aspect of composition in the editor's work he refers to him as a "writer" (*kotev*), as in the introduction to the standard commentary, where he discusses the position of the Book of Psalms in the canon: "the Sages transcribed it [*kat^e^vuhu*] with Job and the Scrolls" (lines 23–24). Because of this blurring of distinctions Ibn Ezra also uses *kotev* and *maᶜtiḳ* to designate what we would call a narrator. When, for example, he deals with anachronistic texts or distinguishes between speeches by the actors and the narrator's voice, he speaks of Moses as the *kotev* of the Pentateuch (see Chapter 2, note 75), on the one hand, and of the *maᶜtiḳ* of the Book of Job, on the other.[91] So when Ibn Ezra, in the Second Inquiry, asks who composed (*ḥibb^e^r*) the Book of Psalms, what he really means is what is called *mudawwin* in Arabic, one who performs all the literary tasks except for the original creation of the text (cf. above, pp. 88–93). This also has implications for Ibn Ezra's original understanding of the headings of the psalms, discussed in the Fourth Inquiry.

This distinction between one who speaks a prophecy and one who writes it down is anchored—as Ibn Ezra notes—in the words of the Sages. The *baraita* in Baba Batra 14b–15a, which deals with the order of the biblical books and the identity of their authors, mentions the editorial endeavors of the men of the Great Assembly: "The men of the Great Assembly wrote [down] Ezekiel, the Minor Prophets, Daniel, and Esther." How, then, can Ibn Ezra say that "the Sages . . . handed down to us that the men of the Great Assembly edited it [the Book of Psalms]" (lines 80–81)? If we answer that Ibn Ezra's memory led him astray and he confused Psalms, in which poems by many authors are collected, with the Minor Prophets, where the words of many prophets were collected, it is still hard to explain how he could have totally forgotten the continuation of the same *baraita*, where we explicitly read that "David wrote [down] the Book of Psalms, [which was composed][92] by ten elders."[93] The matter is perplexing; the only solution seems to be that this is simply further evidence that Ibn Ezra's command of Talmud—especially *aggadah*—was not great, whether because he failed to review what he had learned in his youth or because he had originally learned only from secondary sources (cf. note 37). His overlooking of the Talmudic reference to David as the "writer" of the Book of Psalms was aided, naturally enough, by Saadiah's failure to mention it in his own introduction to Psalms. This silence ought not to surprise us, given Saadiah's strenuous efforts to prove that the Elders mentioned in the headings, whom the Sages considered to be the authors of the psalms, were only musicians. Ibn Giqatilah may have avoided citing this *baraita* for the opposite reason: the Sages' view of David as the final editor of the entire book made it impossible to give a late date to those psalms not explicitly attributed to him.[94]

It is in any case clear that neither Saadiah nor Ibn Giqatilah viewed the *baraita* as an obligatory tradition. Why, then, does Ibn Ezra present what he remembered as the words of the Sages on the subject as "transmission" to be accepted without question (as he says: "There is no need to answer this") and with no additional proof ("this satisfies us")?[95] Furthermore, in the introduction to his standard commentary on the Song of Songs he relies in analogous fashion on the unappealable authority of the tradition: "Heaven forbid that the Song of Songs deal with carnal matters; it is an allegory, and were it not for its great merit it would not have been included in the Holy Scriptures; nor is there any disagreement that it 'defiles the hands' [i.e., is holy]." This argument, too, does not accord with what we find in Tractate Yadayyim 3, 5 about the Sages' debate concerning the sanctity of the Song of Songs; it is merely an echo of the words of Rabbi Akiva there, which Ibn Ezra remembered out of context—"Rabbi Akiva said: Heaven forbid! No Israelite ever disagreed that the Song of Songs defiles the hands."[96] Our question becomes even more acute by virtue of the fact that Ibn Ezra did not follow a similar course with the Book of Ruth and Lamentations, which the *baraita* in Baba Batra 14 attributes without any disagreement to the prophets Samuel and Jeremiah respectively. In his commentary on Ruth he does not consider the question of authorship at all; he even seems to have avoided an indirect identification of the author with the prophet Samuel by employing anonymous terms in his commentary on 3:13: "Some say that *Tov* was the redeemer's name, but if this were the case, why should the text say in the scroll [this is the version in a number of manuscripts, but others read "the author of the Scroll," and this is obviously the correct text]: 'Come over and sit down here, So-and-so' (4:1)?''[97] He is more explicit in his reservations about the attribution of Lamentations to Jeremiah. In his commentary on Lam. 3:1 he writes: '' 'I am the man'—our ancestors said that Jeremiah wrote this scroll, in which case he is the one who says 'I am the man'; but any other man of Israel might say this'' (that is, an anonymous author is speaking for all the mourners). Note carefully: he does not say ''transmitted''—as for the Book of Psalms—but ''our ancestors said,'' despite the fact that he is referring to the same Talmudic source! Evidently the origin of this difference is that Ibn Ezra felt obliged to reject two scriptural proofs offered by the Midrash to establish the connection between the Book of Lamentations and Jeremiah. In the preface to his commentary on Lamentations he demonstrates that ''this is not the Scroll that was burned by Jehoiakim (Jer. 36:23)'' (see introduction to *Lamentations Rabba*); while in his gloss on Lam. 4:20 (''The breath of our life, the Lord's anointed, was captured in their traps'') he writes: ''Some say (see Tosefta Taᶜaniṯ 2,10) that Jeremiah was mourning for Josiah, which is proven by: ['Jeremiah composed laments for Josiah . . .] and they are included among the laments (2 Chron. 34:25)' but this is not correct, because the troubles began after Josiah's death, and here he said: 'Your iniquity is expiated [O Daughter of Zion; He will exile you no longer] (Lam. 4:22)'! My opinion is that he was speaking of Zedekiah, whom the king of Babylonia appointed over Jerusalem, and he was at the end of the exiles [emending the printed ''exile'' on the basis of the MSS].'' In Ibn Ezra's opinion Jeremiah may well have been the author of Lamentations; but given the anonymity of the book and the improbability of these proofs he preferred to assume that the Sages' attribution of the book to Jeremiah was based on these quasi-textual proofs and not necessarily on received tradition.[98] Thus he seems not to have accepted every assertion of the Sages as *a priori* indisputable. In order to understand why he wrote ''they said'' here but ''they transmitted'' elsewhere we must try to reconstruct his train of reasoning in each case.

An advocate of the plain meaning of the text like Ibn Ezra cannot easily ignore the absence of the author's name in a biblical book. Since he is not certain whether the Sages' identification was a received tradition he prefers to leave the question of authorship open (as he did for Ruth and Lamentations, and also Job—see his commentary on Job 2:11).[99] For the Song of Songs, however, what was at issue was not its authorship but its sanctity; and Ibn Ezra, from his apprehension that it be understood as dealing with carnal love (that is, that it was no better than Arabic poetry),[100] saw the supposed absence of a halakhic disagreement on the subject as a clear proof that the core of the allegorical interpretation had been handed down to the Sages in a direct and reliable line from Solomon the author of the work (as he phrases this in the preface to the standard commentary: "The truth is what our ancestors transmitted, namely, that this book deals with the congregation of Israel").[101] His stance on the authorship of the anonymous Scrolls is the same as on the authorship of psalms that do not contain the name of a poet-author, as we have already seen from his explicit remarks in the First Inquiry (see above, pp. 178–181). Only when information is available from the text of a psalm or from its location in the book does he make a cautious attempt to identify its author; in those cases he sometimes cites the Sages' identification of the author as supportive but not conclusive evidence: "[Psalm 91] may also be by Moses—which is what the Sages said" (first introduction, lines 70f.). This does not apply to the editorship of the entire Book of Psalms, where he classifies the Sages' answer as "transmission." He remembered that the Sages had handed down, without giving any justification, that the men of the Great Assembly "composed it." On the other hand, he could find nothing in the text that provided a foothold for juxtaposing Tradition with Scripture, except perhaps for the astonishing negative datum that many psalms lack the name of an author. According to Ibn Ezra in the later introduction, Ibn Giqatilah explained that their identities had simply been forgotten over time ("As for those psalms that have no explicit attribution, the editors of this book of Psalms did not know the name of the author"—lines 30f.). Ibn Ezra proves that this does not necessarily apply to all the anonymous psalms, but he too explains the phenomenon in this way, and saw it as one proof for assigning a later date to the editors. Had Ibn Ezra remembered the *baraita* correctly he would probably have found it difficult to consider the assertion that David wrote the book according to ten elders to be a matter of transmission, since so renowned and important an exponent of the *halakhah* as Saadiah Gaon had not done this. On the other hand, viewing the men of the Great Assembly as the editors of the Book of Psalms allows him to see the great debate between Saadiah and Ibn Giqatilah with regard to the authorship of the psalms as legitimate. A late date for the editing of Psalms seemed reasonable to Ibn Ezra; furthermore the assumption that the (supposed) attribution by the Sages was a matter of transmission excused him of the need to discuss a topic on which he could offer no new ideas (and which he also evaded in the introduction to the First Recension). If this was his line of reasoning, the motive at work here was the opposite of that for the Song of Songs. In that case his concern for the sanctity of the book led him to rely on the absolute authority of rabbinical transmission, whereas here what he saw as the insignificance of the issue and his inability to add anything to what the Sages had said or call it into question led him to stress their authority in such a way that he could cut the matter short with "this satisfies us."

VI. *The Third Inquiry: Are the Psalms prayers or prophecies?*

A. *The answer of the introduction: Prophetic prayers*

Ibn Ezra also presents a complex answer to the source of the authority of the psalms, the subject of the Third Inquiry. The question is "Are these words of David and the other poets veritable songs, psalms, and prayers" (lines 82f.), or whether their form and content do not match, so that their nature is not to be inferred from their literary form, and external evidence must be cited to show that they were "said through the Holy Spirit." In the first introduction he does not make it clear that the disputants whose positions are described in the First Inquiry (see above, pp. 178–179) disagreed about this as well, but provides his own answer straight away: "The correct answer, given by the Sages, is that the Book of Psalms was said through the Holy Spirit" (lines 84f.).[102] When Ibn Ezra says "the correct answer" he means one that is "reasonable" and "compatible with the plain meaning of the text," not necessarily that it has exclusive validity.[103] Because the scriptural proofs he was about to cite struck him as extremely probable but not necessarily conclusive, he goes no further than noting the agreement between his own opinion and the "answer given by the Sages." In the standard introduction, however, he openly acknowledges that "there is a major controversy among the commentators" (line 10), and that his own conclusion is merely a well-grounded personal opinion: "But I tend to agree with the Sages, their memory for a blessing, that this entire book is divinely inspired. Why are [those who hold the opposite opinion] surprised by the word 'song'?" (lines 35f.).

The cautious language of the second introduction seems to be particularly appropriate, since the fact that all of Ibn Ezra's prooftexts for the prophetic character of the Book of Psalms are external to that book indicates that the problem is real and difficult. His argument in the first introduction is more comprehensive, since there he is endeavoring to prove not only that Scripture describes the psalmists as prophets, but also that the poems collected in the Book of Psalms are their prophetic utterances. Thus he demonstrates that David is called "the man of God" (Neh. 12:24) and even says of himself, "The Spirit of the Lord has spoken through me" (2 Sam. 23:2); he also shows that Heman is called "the seer of the king" (1 Chron. 25:5), that Asaph "prophesied by order of the king" (25:2), and that Heman and Jeduthun "prophesied" (25:1). This list of authors of psalms omits Moses and Solomon on the one hand, and Ethan and the sons of Koraḥ on the other; Ibn Ezra obviously believed that just as no proof is needed that Moses and Solomon were prophets,[104] so too the absence of such texts about the Koraḥides and Ethan is no indication that they were not prophets.

By contrast, it is more difficult to demonstrate that the psalms are more than personal and non-prophetic poetry by these prophets. To do this Ibn Ezra is constrained to twist the plain meaning of the verse "David and Samuel the Seer established them [*hemmah*] in their faith" (1 Chron. 9:22): he understands the word *hemmah*, which refers to the Levites appointed by David and Samuel, as meaning "the poems" (line 86); in addition, he begs the question by glossing the word *be-ʾemunaṯam* (in their faith) as meaning precisely what he seeks to prove: " 'By their faith' means by the faith of the Holy Spirit" (line 87).[105] His second proof is not much better than the first: in 1 Chron. 28 we read that David gave his son Solomon "the plan of the porch and its houses, its storerooms and its upper chambers and inner chambers; and of the place of the Ark-cover" (verse 11), as well as "the plan of all that he had by the spirit" (verse 12). This expression is followed by more architectural items—courtyards, chambers, and treasuries—but there may also be an indirect allusion to the sacred songs—"the divisions of priests and Levites" (verse 13). Ibn Ezra does not rely explicitly on this mention of the Levites, since he was more impressed by the use of the term "by the spirit" (which he quotes, whether by mistake or with paraphrastic liberty, as "by the Holy Spirit"); he views this as analogous to the verse about David's prophecy—"the Spirit of the Lord has spoken through me" (2 Sam. 23:2). The third proof is certainly better than its predecessors: "It was because of the holiness of these songs and psalms that in Solomon's time the Temple was filled with the glory of God" (lines 92f.), as described in 2 Chron. 5:12–14. This is actually a supplemental proof for the broader argument presented at the beginning of this introduction that the psalms are exalted as sacred poetry, because of their content and how they were sung in the Temple; but it does not prove that the psalms were divinely inspired. Ibn Ezra omits these three proofs of the prophetic nature of the psalms in his second introduction, and perhaps we may see this omission as evidence that he too was not happy with them.

By contrast, the introduction to the standard commentary does offer the proofs that the psalmists were prophets. The two verses about David (Neh. 12:24 and 2 Sam. 23:2) are cited in the first section, in which Saadiah's position is reported anonymously. In fact, in his long introduction (page 28) Saadiah too relies on Neh. 12:24 as well as on the similar passage in 2 Chron. 8:14 and on 2 Chron. 7:6, but does not cite Ibn Ezra's second prooftext—2 Sam. 23:2. We cannot know whether Ibn Ezra realized that he was adding another proof to Saadiah's position. But this is the end of their agreement, because Saadiah wanted to prove "that the entire book is by David, who was a prophet" (line 11), whereas Ibn Ezra, who agreed only with the second part of the statement, had to prove that the other psalmists were also prophets. This he does (in the section beginning "But I tend to agree with the Sages''—line 35) by means of the same passages cited in the first introduction, but omitting the proof about Jeduthun. He considered the proofs about David, Asaph, and Heman to be valid for the other psalmists as well, including those not mentioned specifically by name (he accordingly designates them ''poets prophesying''—lines 39f.).

Still, all of these external proofs that the various psalmists were prophets do not refute Ibn Giqatilah's argument about the distinctly non-prophetic literary form of the psalms. In the first introduction, at the end of the Third Inquiry, Ibn Ezra puts it this way: ''What is the meaning of prayer uttered under divine inspiration?'' (line 95). That is, prayer, which is essentially man's supplication before his God, cannot be prophecy, which is essentially God's message to man. In the second introduction, this argument is extended to those psalms that are not prayers, but which, as ''psalms'' and ''songs'' are not ''prophecies about future events,'' which is why the Sages included them in the Hagiographa ''with Job and the Scrolls'' rather than with the prophetic books (lines 23f.). Saadiah, in his attempt to prove that the Book of Psalms is a second Pentateuch, provided a radical answer to this argument: the human language in this book is merely an external garb, intended to facilitate human comprehension of divine speech. He strengthens this rhetorical theory with an analysis of Moses' song in Deuteronomy chapter 32 (short introduction, p. 53), as well as of the poems in Isaiah 33:1–6 and Jeremiah 17:7–14 (long introduction, p. 35): all acknowledge that these are the word of God, despite the frequent changes of speaker (God, the prophets, and the people). (See above, pp. 28–30.) Even though Ibn Ezra does not share Saadiah's approach to the Book of Psalms and does not accept his rhetorical theory, he relies on the same biblical passages in his own answer to Ibn Giqatilah's argument (end of the Third Inquiry):

> Should someone object—what is the meaning of prayer uttered under divine inspiration?—we can show him: ''A prayer of the Prophet Habakkuk'' (Hab. 3);[106] ''O Lord, be gracious to us! It is to You we have looked'' (Isa. 33:2); ''Heal me, O Lord, and let me be healed'' (Jer. 17:14).'' (lines 94–97)

Since the only argument raised here is that prayer is not prophecy, he merely mentions three prophetic prayers; in the second introduction, however, where Ibn Giqatilah's argument is cited at greater length, he writes: ''Why are they surprised by the word 'song,' when the song of Moses (Deut. 32:1) proves [that this term can refer to prophecy]'' (line 36), and proceeds to refer to Habakkuk's prayer, as in the first introduction, along with two additional proofs that we shall discuss later—Habakkuk 1:2 and Isaiah 63:17. Note that even though Ibn Ezra cites, inter alia, the same prophetic passages as Saadiah, he attributes no importance to the stylistic phenomenon of changing speakers and relates only to the problematic literary genre—prophetic prayer. Whereas Saadiah's argument is exclusively rhetorical, since he does not consider that actual prayers are involved, Ibn Ezra's argument is distinctly theological, because he must prove that prophetic prayer is indeed possible.

The two or three lines that Ibn Ezra devoted to this fundamental question in each of his two introductions do not permit the reader to fully appreciate his approach, and we must rely on what he has to say about this elsewhere in his writings. Consider, for example, his interpretation of Jonah's prayer, whose past tenses—"Yet you brought my life up from the pit" (2:7[6]) and "And my prayer came before You" (2:8[7])—give the impression that the prayer is one of thanksgiving for a past rescue rather than a request for rescue in the future. Ibn Ezra begins his commentary on Jonah 2:2 with a sharp demurral at such a solution to the problem of the lack of correspondence between the language of the prayer and the situation in which it is presented: "The commentators, endeavoring to offer an original interpretation, ignored the plain meaning of the text, [and said that] Jonah prayed only after he reached dry land. [They said this] because the text reads 'from the belly' (2:2[1]) rather than 'in the belly'." This, we may recall, is precisely what Ibn Giqatilah did with the psalms: on the basis of their language he reconstructed the historical or biographical situation in which they were composed, not hesitating to give them a late date but never denying any explicitly ascribed authorship (see above, pp. 129–130). It seems reasonable that here, too, as in his second introduction to Psalms (see above, pp. 122–123), Ibn Ezra wanted to protect Ibn Giqatilah even while rejecting his interpretation by referring to him with a hazy plural—"the commentators." Ibn Ezra criticizes this postponement of the prayer until after the fish had vomited Jonah onto dry land as being an interpretation made only for the sake of the novelty,[107] because it involves the farfetched assumption that the circumstances in which the prayer was uttered are described in extremely elliptical language—"Jonah prayed to the Lord his God [after he escaped] from the belly of the fish," while the text as given is plain and clear when we understand it as parallel to "from the belly of Sheol I cried out" in the prayer itself (verse 3[2]). So too "You heard" (verse 3[2]) and "my prayer came before You" (verse 8[7]) attest that Jonah prayed before he was saved, just as the description of God's response, which comes after the prayer (verse 11[10]) proves that the prayer preceded the response.

Following this refutation of the drastic solution, Ibn Ezra offers his own, based on the same principle that underlies his conception of the psalms (and which has no place in Ibn Giqatilah's method): "Now pay attention and see

[that] every prayer or blessing by a prophet is [inspired] by the prophetic spirit [MS Montefiore 34: "the Holy Spirit and the prophetic spirit"]. Jacob said, 'which I took from the Amorites' (Genesis 48:22), because that which has been decreed to be is spoken of in the past tense." This is followed by five additional citations, quoting Jacob, Balaam, and Moses to demonstrate that the prophetic past is quite common in Scripture.[108] Next he draws a parallel between David's "He answered me from His holy mountain" (Ps. 3:5) which anticipates God's response during the very distress of flight, and Jonah's "But I shall indeed look upon Your holy Temple" (verse 5[4]); the latter, though expressed in the future tense, reflects the same faith found in the former that the prayer has already been answered (especially if we assume that the reference is to the heavenly sanctuary, as Ibn Ezra does). He concludes with an additional proof that Jonah's prayer is future-oriented: "Deliverance is the Lord's!" (verse 10[9]) is to be understood as an elliptical expression of hope—"that he was hoping, like: to beg for the Lord's deliverance."

To sum up, prophets' prayers and blessings are uttered with prophetic inspiration (or, according to the reading of the Montefiore manuscript—which is the best manuscript of Ibn Ezra's commentary on the Minor Prophets—some were inspired by the "Holy Spirit" and some by the "prophetic spirit"); thus they may very well be a herald of the response to come, which the prophet had the merit of hearing while he was still addressing God. If Jonah describes his rescue in the past tense while he is still praying to God from the belly of the fish, we should not be surprised that the psalms reflect future situations: they too are prophetic prayers inspired by "the Holy Spirit and the prophetic spirit."[109]

The distinction between "Holy Spirit" and "prophetic spirit" seems to be original with Ibn Ezra, but it does not reflect well-defined levels of prophetic revelation. Ibn Ezra did not rest content with a general assertion that the prayers and blessings of prophets are prophecies, however, but wanted to determine the proportion of prophecy in each and every prayer and blessing. He notes, for example, that the designation "Moses the man of God," found in the heading of Moses' blessing of the tribes, is intended "to make known that he blessed them prophetically" (commentary on Deut. 33:1). By contrast, an understanding of Isaac's blessings for Jacob and Esau is linked with "a number of difficult questions," of which the most serious is: "If this blessing was a prophecy, how is it that [Isaac] did not know whom he was blessing?" (see commentary on Gen. 27:40). After demurring at the answers given by his predecessors, he cautiously offers his own answer: "I think the correct answer is that a prophet's blessing is a sort of prayer, and God heard his prayer, because the thrust of this blessing refers to their (one MS reads: his) descendants." In other words: Isaac was indeed a prophet, but his failure to discover the identity of the recipient of the blessing proves that his blessing was not inspired by the spirit of prophecy nor by the Holy Spirit. His failure to see the present demonstrates that the blessing was not accompanied by a vision of the future; thus it was simply a normal prayer, which was answered by virtue of God's special relation to those for whom Isaac prayed. Whereas supplication and response are almost simultaneous in Jonah's prophetic prayer from the belly of the fish and David's while fleeing from Absalom, there is no expression of the fact that Isaac, for all that he is a prophet, is aware that his blessings will indeed be conferred on the descendants of their recipients. This combination of limited human knowledge with prophetic influence is somewhat astonishing, so Ibn Ezra reiterates that "a prophet does not know hidden things unless God reveals them to him" (commentary on Gen. 32:9; cf. short commentary on Ex. 4:20 and long commentary on Dan. 8:13 and 25). Accordingly, in the long commentary to Ex. 7:1—while discussing the verse "Restore the man's wife, for he is a prophet" (Gen. 20:7)—he defines prophecy by separating two aspects thereof: first, "that I reveal My secrets to him, on the lines of 'without having revealed His secret to His servants the prophets' (Amos 3:7)"; second, "He delights in Me and therefore 'he will intercede for you and you shall live' (Gen. 20:7)." "He delights in me" (*hu mit̲ʿanneg ʿalai*), which is a clear allusion to "Take delight [*we-hit̲ʿannag*] in the Lord and He will give the desires of your heart" (Ps. 37:4), allows Ibn Ezra to explain the efficacy of a prophet's prayer as the direct result of his intimacy with God.

In order to understand Ibn Ezra's conception of prophetic prayer we must also consider the distinctions he makes among various types of prophecy. With regard to content there are three types: only Moses and Aaron were "Pentateuchal prophets" (long commentary on Ex. 12:1), while all the other prophets "are prophets of reproofs or of future events" (ibid., 7:7; and cf. the commentary on Ps. 99:7). We have already seen that Ibn Ezra's laconic assertions were never intended to exhaust the matter at hand; here too we must add prophetic praises of the Lord to commandments, reproofs, and visions, as he himself notes in his commentary on Ecclesiastes 1:1, while touching on Solomon's proverbs and poems mentioned in 1 Kings 5:12: "It is in the nature of poetry to be praise [following the reading of seven MSS] or [to be about] events that will occur in the future." Ibn Ezra viewed the lost poems by the prophet Solomon as being in the mold of the psalms by his father David: both were divinely inspired and both comprised praises and visions. There are two subtypes of prophecies about future events—short term prophecies (which by now have already been fulfilled) and long term prophecies (which refer to the messianic era). As Ibn Ezra puts it (in the prefatory rhyme at the beginning of the long commentary on

Daniel): "This is the book of the precious man / which speaks of weighty matters / and of prophecies passing and future." The terminology is not particularly successful, because "passing prophecies" are also "visions of the future," but the future to which they relate is already our own past. To be more precise, the "passing prophecies" refer to a temporal future (which happens to have passed already), whereas the "future prophecies" relate to the ultimate future, to the End of Days. In the Third Inquiry of the first introduction Ibn Ezra applies this distinction to the psalms as well, which "were . . . said through the Holy Spirit . . . [and] some refer to incidents that have already occurred and some to those that will yet come to pass" (lines 83f.). In these few words Ibn Ezra tells those who are familiar with Ibn Giqatilah's exegetical method that his debate with him is twofold—concerning both the fundamental possibility of prophetic prayer and the frequency of messianic prophecy. The importance of these distinctions for exegetical decisions is illustrated by what Ibn Ezra writes at the beginning of his commentary on Psalm 47: "This Psalm [refers] to the Messianic era; Rabbi Moses said that it was written in Babylonia. But some say [it was written] in the time of David when they brought the Ark up [to Jerusalem], [for which] the evidence is: 'God has gone up amidst acclamation' (47:6[5]). But this is not correct, because of 'He will choose our heritage for us' (verse 5[4]) [the point is that the verb is in the future tense, as he stresses in his commentary *ad loc.*: "He will choose—either in Babylonia, or in the Messianic era when Israel returns to its inheritance."]. This commentator responded that this is an allusion to Mount Moriah, for it was still unknown [as the Holy Mount] when this Psalm was said." The chronological argument (when the psalm was written and to what period it refers) is linked with the argument about the literary genre: according to the anonymous commentator, who attributes it to the time of David, this is a hymn of praise (with an element of prayer—a supplication that the final resting place of the Ark be chosen); according to Ibn Giqatilah, who postpones the composition of the psalm to the Babylonian exile, it is a prayer for the return to Zion; and according to Ibn Ezra, who believed that the Koraḥides lived in the time of David, it is a prophetic prayer about the future redemption.

By its very nature prophetic prayer would seem to belong to the passing type of prophecy, since the prophet's request or supplication obviously refers to some current distress. Nevertheless, Ibn Ezra holds that there are prophetic prayers that relate to the distant future, since given the prophet's innate vision of events yet to come he may serve as the mouthpiece for the prayers of a future generation. This is not Ibn Ezra's innovation; he even uses the same term to designate this phenomenon that had been used in biblical exegesis since Saadiah's day—"he spoke in the words of . . ." (see above, chapter 2, note 86). Saadiah and Yefet ben ᶜAli made use of the assumption that prophecies may contain the direct speech of future generations to solve difficult anachronisms, such as the attribution of "By the rivers of Babylon" to David (or at least to the First Temple period). Here too Ibn Ezra followed in their footsteps, as is attested by his remark on Psalm 137:1: "At the beginning of this book I mentioned the opinion of the commentators about this Psalm [he is referring to what he wrote in the introduction to the standard commentary: "They [viz., Ibn Giqatilah] said that 'By the rivers of Babylon' was written by one of the poets in Babylon"]. This Psalm was written in the voice of the Levite musicians in their exile about [MS: to] Babylonia." The relevancy of a long-term prophecy about a situation that has no meaning for the prophet and his contemporaries—which is one of the fundamental questions of the new biblical criticism—bothered Ibn Ezra no more than it did his predecessors (including Ibn Giqatilah).[110] In any case it is clear that the fundamental controversy between Ibn Ezra and Ibn Giqatilah did not revolve around this question, which is essentially theological (what are the nature and purpose of prophecy?), but around another question, of which one facet is theological (is prophetic prayer possible?) and the other literary (do the psalms truly resemble the form and language of prophecies?). Collecting the membra disjecta we have discussed reveals that Ibn Ezra's answer to the theological-literary argument underlying Ibn Giqatilah's approach was as follows: The fulfillment of Isaac's blessings of his sons and of Moses' blessings of the tribes attests that, despite their human limitations, the blessings of prophets are not merely fervent hopes (see also Ibn Ezra on Gen. 49:28). God's speedy response to the prayers of his prophets (such as that of Abraham in Gerar) permits us to infer that knowledge of the imminent salvation may come before the supplication is completed, and that by way of further emphasis that salvation is sometimes even described as already accomplished (via the "prophetic past"). True, on purely stylistic grounds those who say (as we hypothesize, Ibn Giqatilah) that Jonah's psalm is one of thanksgiving and not of supplication are correct. But since the psalm is quite clearly anchored in a situation of distress, and since it is uttered by a prophet, Ibn Ezra felt that he had no choice but to assume that it represents a unique literary genre—prophetic prayer.

In order to prove that such a literary genre can indeed be found in Scripture Ibn Ezra first of all relies, in both Psalms introductions, on the juxtaposition of terms in "a prayer of the prophet Habakkuk" (Hab. 3:1). Because of Ibn Ezra's terse style this proof seems to be purely formal, but there is no doubt that this was not his intention. In the Fourth Inquiry of the first introduction, in his discussion of literary terminology, he demonstrates in passing the justification for seeing Habakkuk's prayer/prophecy as the archetype for understanding the psalms, because of the great stylistic similarities between them: "The word *la-m^enaṣṣeaḥ*—we find this word only in the writings of David, and in [other] psalms and in the prayer of Habakkuk, which is in the style of the Book of Psalms, for '*ʿal šigyonoṯ*' (Hab. 3:1) is like '*šiggayon l^e-Dawid*' (Ps. 7:1); at the end [of Habakkuk's prayer] '*bi-n^eginoṯai*' (Hab. 3:19) is like '*ʿal n^eginaṯ l^e-Dawid*' (Ps. 61:1); and the word *selah* [appears] in three places in Habakkuk (3:3, 9, 13)" (lines 124–28).[111] According to Ibn Ezra, this impressive stylistic similarity calls into question Ibn Giqatilah's form criticism and demonstrates that there is no sharp generic division between psalm and prophecy. In other words, if the prayer of a prophet is phrased just like a psalm, it follows that the psalms of David may also be the prayers of prophets.

Habakkuk's psalm also calls into question Ibn Giqatilah's theological distinction between prayer and prophecy, if one can explain properly why it is called "a prayer of Habakkuk" (3:1). There is no difficulty in understanding how Jeremiah's personal supplication, "Heal me, O Lord, and I shall be healed" (17:14), and Isaiah's collective supplication, "O Lord, be gracious to us! It is to You we have looked" (33:2)—the two prayers mentioned by Ibn Ezra in the Third Inquiry (lines 96–97)—are prayers. But what motivates Habakkuk's prayer, and what in fact is his request? Ibn Ezra explains this in his commentary on the Minor Prophets (written right after he finished writing the standard commentary on Psalms), in his gloss on Hab. 3:1: "This prayer was uttered with prophetic inspiration; he is prophesying about a famine that will occur, as becomes clear at the end of the prayer [verses 15–17], when Israel will not have the strength to withstand its enemy." In his commentary on verse 2 Ibn Ezra explains that the words "O Lord, I have heard the report" mean "that God informed him concerning the famine," whereas the words "Your deeds in the midst of the years revive him" indicate "that Israel will live in the midst of those years." The prophet foresaw, then, not only the famine and the enemy attack connected with it (see his commentary on verse 15), but also God's help to his people in their double distress. Thus, according to Ibn Ezra, we should not view verse 16 as the prophet's prayer, but must refer the first person of "I heard and my bowels quaked" to the collective I of those suffering starvation—"The prophet speaks this prophecy on behalf of Israel" (end of gloss on verse 15). Only at the end of the chapter (verses 18–19) does Habakkuk speak in his own voice, and this too is prophecy (rather than a personal statement): "The prophet said in his prophecy that for this reason he will not worry; rather, his heart rejoices because he has confidence that God will save him" (commentary on verse 18). Those who are astonished that Ibn Ezra has no hesitation to split the prophecy between two voices can find Ibn Ezra's explanation in his commentary on Psalm 118, which he understands as a dialogue between the priests on the Temple Mount and the pilgrims: "Do not be surprised that at the beginning those who are speak ing are not identified, because this is a form of poetic eloquence, like 'I have taken off my robe' (Cant. 5:3) and many other texts'' (118:28).[112]

We see, then, that in order to explain Habakkuk's psalm as prophetic prayer Ibn Ezra had to have recourse to four far-reaching assumptions: (1) the psalm refers to a future situation (not linked to current events); (2) the supplication is placed in the mouth of the future generation (who are not sure of God's salvation); (3) the promised response is expressed by the prophet's personal confidence in God's salvation; and (4) the attribution of the two passages of direct speech to different speakers is reasonable in light of the frequency with which biblical poetry omits any indication of the speaker's identity.

This willingness to accept multiple hypotheses and exegetical methods, which deviates from the principle of exegetical necessity to which Ibn Ezra held (see above, pp. 180–181), gives the commentator a dangerous liberty. He is liable to resort to arbitrary manipulation of exegetical methods in order to impose a rigid theological-literary conception on the various psalms. Still, Ibn Ezra's Psalms commentary attests that its author was well aware of this danger and guarded against it by limiting his reliance on the generalizing assumptions made by his predecessors to the minimal extent possible. A good example of his cautious manner can be found in his commentary on Psalm 3. In his gloss on verse 1 he formulates the position sketched out in the introductions: ''*Mizmor*—prophetically [i.e., this is a prophetic psalm]; he prophesied that he would be victorious, [therefore] (added according to one MS) 'and He answered me from his holy mountain' (verse 5[4]), is like Jonah's prayer, 'and my prayer came before You' (2:8[7]).'' He accordingly explains the entire psalm as a prophetic prayer; but when he reaches the concrete requests at the end—''Rise, O Lord! Deliver me. . . . Your blessing be upon Your people! Selah'' (verses 8–9[7–8])—he explains them as a request that God assist David's men who are fighting on his behalf against Absalom's army, and notes: ''he *prayed* that God bless them and that he would not lose a single man in war, or he *prophesied*.'' Even though David already knew by prophecy that he would be victorious, prophetic knowledge leaves room for human uncertainty; thus Ibn Ezra does not reach an unequivocal decision as to whether the additional supplication at the end of the psalm is a true request (indicating ignorance of the fate of the request) or an additional prophecy (which is merely phrased in supplicatory terms). Also instructive is his note on ''He answered me from His holy mountain'' (which he explained in his gloss on verse 1 as the prophetic core of the psalm): '' 'From His holy mountain'—because the Ark was in Zion it was called the Holy Mount, and this preceded the incident with Aravnah the Jebusite'' (commentary on 3:5). David was indeed informed that his request would be answered from Zion; but we must not expand this prophetic revelation and apply it to matters not related to the concrete situation of the psalm by assuming that at the same time David was also told that Mount Moriah was destined to be the site of the Holy Temple. Thus Ibn Ezra must emphasize that the language in which the prophetic annunciation is phrased is an appropriate reflection of what David knew at the historical moment when—in Ibn Ezra's opinion—he composed the psalm.[113]

In general, proposing alternative interpretations is evidence of exegetical caution; here it reflects also sensitivity to the uniqueness of each psalm and each situation. Even though it perplexes readers who are looking for an unequivocal guide to the meaning of the psalms,[114] it is one of the distinguishing marks of Ibn Ezra's Psalms commentary. For example, he offers no fewer than three alternative interpretations of the supplication, "Arise, O Lord, judge the earth": "a prayer by the poet himself, or he may be speaking on behalf of those who cry out against injustice, or he may be speaking prophetically" (comm. on Ps. 82:8). The alternatives seem to be offered in descending order of probability: the first is compatible with the text (which is phrased as a request in the first person), while the second requires us to assume that there has been a change of speakers and the third that the prophet's request essentially expresses the message of its fulfillment. Thus his confidence that prophetic prayer is indeed possible did not lead Ibn Ezra to apply this concept indiscriminately to every psalm and every passage within a prophetic psalm. A good example of this is his hesitation over the precise meaning of the verse, "The Lord will cut off all flattering lips, every tongue that speaks arrogance" (Ps. 12:4[3]). He had nothing to say about the cry, "Help, O Lord! For the faithful are no more" in verse 2(1), evidently because this is clearly a prayer, whereas verse 6 he confidently defines as God's response—" 'I will act now, says the Lord'—[this is uttered] prophetically." But he is of two minds about the intervening verses 4–5(3–4): "*yakhret* [may mean 'He will cut off,' and be] a prophecy like 'Heal me, O Lord, and I shall be healed' (Jer. 17:14), or [it may be] a prayer ['may He cut off']." According to the first interpretation, verse 4 is the beginning of the prophetic response, and the future tense indicates a factual description of what is going to happen; according to the second interpretation, it is a continuation of the psalmist's prayer, and the future tense expresses a wish. Citing the passage from Jeremiah in support of the prophetic explanation is strange, for two reasons: the verb is in the imperative mood rather than a future tense; and the context is generally viewed as distinctly one of prayer. Nevertheless, for Ibn Ezra the verse at hand and his prooftext are analogous, because he recognizes no clear distinction between the imperative and future in Biblical language: "There is an imperative that should have a futurial prefix, like 'Ascend . . . and die on the mountain' (Deut. 32:49–50) which means 'and you will die on the mountain' " (*Moznayim*, p. 47a). Since God obviously did not command Moses to die on Mount Abarim, but told him what would happen there, we must inquire of every imperative form whether it is replacing a future tense.[115] Thus Ibn Ezra had no problem referring to Jeremiah 17:14 as an outstanding example of prophetic prayer (not only here, but also in the first introduction, lines 96f.), because he understood *r^{e}fa᾿eni* ("Heal me") grammatically as an imperative with a future sense, and stylistically as a prophetic future. Just as we find it difficult to share Ibn Ezra's confidence that this interpretation is correct, so should we esteem the fact that he refrained from making it the archetype for his interpretation of Psalms.[116]

One of the most striking expressions of Ibn Ezra's willingness to offer many alternative exegeses and acknowledge the difficulty of choosing among them[117] is his presentation of Ibn Giqatilah's position on the authorship of the psalms. Despite the fact that he was convinced that he had successfully demonstrated that the Bible contains prophetic prayer, Ibn Ezra realized that he had not proven that a particular psalm necessarily belonged in this category. Consequently, he not only refrained from denying the doctrinal and exegetical legitimacy of giving a late date to the psalms in his two introductions, he even reiterated in the body of the standard commentary the possibility that certain psalms were composed during the Babylonian exile, an alternative that he never accepts, even though he rarely rebuts it. Sometimes he mentions the opinion of the late-daters by referring the reader to the introduction, where it is presented and explained (79:1; 119:1; 137:1); elsewhere he offers it in the name of Ibn Giqatilah (42:1; 47:1; 76:4) or as "some say" (46:1); and at other times he prefaces it with "if" or "or," which gives it the status of an equally valid alternative (78:54; 81:11; 84:3; 87:1; 89:2).[118] Even when he writes, "I think that the correct opinion is . . ." (106:47) he is only stating a preference, as if acknowledging that no clear-cut decision is possible on the basis of the text itself, so that his preference is based on his general principles whose applicability to the case at hand cannot be proven. Only when he has tangible proof that a psalm is truly prophetic in nature does he adopt absolute terms ("The correct opinion is . . . as is demonstrated by . . ." [102:1]), and sees no need to mention the opinion of the late-daters: "This psalm is about the Babylonian exile and also about our own exile, [and was spoken] prophetically" (85:1; and see his detailed proofs throughout the commentary on that psalm).[119] This insistence on a cautious ranking of the degrees of certainty, and his far-reaching intellectual fairness with regard to an opinion that neither his mind nor heart could accept reflect the clarity of thought typical of Ibn Ezra, who always endeavored to distinguish the hypothetical from the proven and to separate doctrinal and exegetical verdicts.

The authorship controversy between Ibn Ezra and Ibn Giqatilah can be summed up as follows: they agreed that almost all the *l^e-Dawid* psalms were written by David and a few about him; but they disagreed about the dating of the other poets, Ibn Giqatilah assigning them to the Babylonian exile and Ibn Ezra to David's age. Ibn Giqatilah also gave a late date to anonymous psalms when he believed that their historical background so required, whereas Ibn Ezra avoided this by virtue of his view of the psalms as prophetic prayers. Still, while he does not give a late date to any anonymous psalm, he rather surprisingly wants to postpone Psalm 65, ascribed to David—albeit only to the time of Solomon. To quote his commentary on verse 2: "[If (supplied on the basis of most MSS)] this psalm was written by David, then [he wrote it] when the Ark was in [Zion (supplied from five MSS)], or it was written by one of the musicians when the Temple was built, and I think this is the correct opinion." It is very difficult to know why here Ibn Ezra adopted the method of Ibn Giqatilah (who obviously must have assigned a late date to this psalm and postponed its composition to the time of the construction of the Temple). From Ibn Ezra's commentary on the body of the psalm we see that he was impressed not only by the repeated references to the Temple, but also by the similarity of the ideas found in the psalm and in Solomon's prayer of dedication for the Temple. "To You shall all flesh come" (verse 3[2]) is parallel to the prayer of the non-Jew who comes to Jerusalem from far off (1 Kings 8:41–43), while "Our transgressions prevailed" (verse 4[3]), which he reads as the poet's confession of his and the people's sin that caused the drought and siege alluded to in "You visited the earth and watered it" (verse 10[9]), corresponds to the passage on famine, siege, and confession in Solomon's prayer (1 Kings 8:37–40). Still, the interpretation is surprising: Ibn Ezra could have easily asserted that this was uttered prophetically; and what is stranger still, it totally fails to explain how the heading of this ostensibly anonymous psalm composed when the Temple was dedicated attributes it to David. I can only hypothesize that for Ibn Ezra the attributive *lamed* in *'l^e-Dawid'* could mean not only that the psalm is about David, but also that it was composed in his honor or dedicated to his memory; similarly, he concludes that Psalm 127 does not deal with future actions by Solomon but was written in his honor (see commentary *ad loc.*).[120] Whatever the explanation may be, we can deduce from this astonishing deviation from his general line that, as befits a true exegete, Ibn Ezra was more interested in the unique nature of each individual psalm than in buttressing the validity and consistency of his exegetical method.

B. *The answer in the body of the commentary: Prophetic prayers with abundant theological lore*

More can be said about these two interwoven questions: the authorship of the psalms and their prophetic nature. In the first chapter of his book *Y^e^sod Mora᾿* (The Foundation of Reverence), written in London in 1157 or 1158, Ibn Ezra makes statements about Psalms that seem to contradict the approach found in his two introductions and commentary on Psalms. To quote him: ''If we knew [the whole secret of (supplied on the basis of three MSS)] the Book of Psalms, which is all songs and prayers, even though it was uttered with divine inspiration *it does not contain any prophecies of future events.*''[121] What he seems to mean is that even a perfect understanding of the Book of Psalms would not provide any information about future events, because even though the psalms are prophetic prayers they do not refer to our own future. Not only is this view incompatible with Ibn Ezra's messianic interpretation of a not insignificant number of psalms, its application, in the very next sentence, to the five Scrolls (''likewise Job and the books by Solomon and the Scrolls and Ezra'') does not mesh with his explicit statement at the beginning of the standard commentary on the Song of Songs: ''This is the most excellent of all the songs by Solomon, and it contains hidden and arcane secrets, from the days of Abraham until the times of the Messiah.'' In order to correctly understand what Ibn Ezra wrote in *Y^e^sod Mora᾿* we must investigate the context and background of his remarks there.

Y^e^sod Mora᾿ was written to clarify the nature of the commandments and elucidate their meaning. In its eighth chapter Ibn Ezra explains that every Jew is obligated to perform the commandments even before he understands them, since otherwise ''he would remain without Torah,'' but on the other hand, ''the learned man can know many meanings of the Torah that are clearly understood, while others are understood by only one man out of a thousand.''[122] Later in this section he surveys the first type of meanings (those presented explicitly in the Torah); in the ninth chapter he uses allusive and veiled terms to discuss the hidden meanings of many commandments, relying on a broad variety of sciences—astronomy, astrology, arithmetic (according to the Pythagorean symbolistics), the natural sciences, linguistics, etc.[123] Moreover, he saw the study of these sciences as necessary not only to arrive at a full understanding of the commandments, but also to attain ''knowledge of the Most High,'' which one can acquire by understanding God's works as they are described in the Torah and reflected in nature. He explains this in the brief introduction to this volume, where he asserts that man's superiority over the animals is ''in the higher rational soul,'' which, before ''it returns to God who gave it'' is brought down to earth to dwell in a body ''and be shown [God's miracles (supplied from two MSS)] . . . in order to learn the works of its Master and to keep His commandments.'' How is this learning accomplished? ''All wisdom gives life to those who acquire it; there are many sciences, and each of them is useful, and each is like a rung on a ladder ascending to knowledge of the truth. Happy is he whose mental eyes have been opened, and whose destiny is to stream to the Lord and His goodness.''[124] Since spiritual and religious perfection cannot be attained without mastery of all the sciences, any one-sided concentration in a single branch of knowledge is merely false scholarship and cannot lead to the goal.

In order to prove this thesis, Ibn Ezra devotes the first chapter to a critical description of four types of ''Jewish scholars,'' whose restriction to a single field of scholarship prevents them from attaining true knowledge. The first are the Masoretes, whose utility in preserving the text of Scriptures is indeed great, but since they do not delve deeply into the content of the Scriptures they are like ''a camel carrying silk; he does nothing for the silk, nor does the silk benefit him.'' The second are the grammarians, who practice ''a glorious science,'' which helps us write clear and eloquent prose and poetry and understand the texts correctly, but exclusive preoccupation with grammar is turning the means into an end: ''Heaven forbid [that someone] deal always with the craftman's tool and never make the vessel itself.''[125] For now we will skip over the third group (which interests us) and proceed directly to the fourth. These are the scholars of the Talmud, who shower great blessings on themselves and on the public when their goal is ''to know the forbidden and the permitted,'' and when they rely on knowledge of Scripture (to understand the biblical passages cited in the Talmud), grammar (to understand passages that the Sages did not explain), astronomy (to determine the calendar), and geometry (to understand the measurements and dimensions prescribed by the *halakhah* and to recognize God's wisdom in creation), as well as psychology, cosmology, and logic. At the same time he expresses his reservations about two types of Talmudic scholars who, he says, were common in his own day. The first of these are those ''who are erudite in the Midrashim and come up with new [homiletical interpretations] and search out a meaning for every plene and deficient spelling,'' while ignoring the fact that the scriptural texts are not at all careful about the exact words (and certainly not of their spelling) but only about the accuracy of the meaning, as is proven, in his opinion, by the two versions of the Decalogue and similar repetitions. The second type of Talmudic scholar whose learning misses the mark is the one who specializes in the law of torts. True, he is highly honored and finds employment as a teacher and judge, but his knowledge has no intrinsic spiritual significance, since "if all of Israel were righteous there would be no need for the order Nezikin."[126]

Now we shall turn our attention to Ibn Ezra's third category; his remarks about it are not as clear as those about the other groups. These scholars "always ponder the Pentateuch, the Prophets, and the Hagiographa, as well as their Aramaic translations, and believe that because they search after their meaning in accordance with their ability they have ascended to the highest level." At first sight this seems to refer to those who interpret Scripture according to the plain meaning; but from the sequel it is clear that he does not mean Spanish commentators like Judah Ibn Balaam and Moses Ibn Giqatilah, and certainly not French commentators like Rashi and Rashbam, for Ibn Ezra offers against them the classic anti-Karaite objection: "No learned man has the capacity to know [even] one complete commandment from the Torah without basing himself on the Oral Law." The proofs he proceeds to offer for this assertion are quite similar to those brought in his argument against Karaite exegesis in his two introductions to the Pentateuch; the term "search" is perhaps intended as an allusion to the well-known saying attributed to Anan, the founder of the Karaites—"Search ye well in Scripture."[127] On the other hand, it is far from obvious against whom Ibn Ezra's next arguments are aimed; moreover, they are astonishing in and of themselves. We shall cite him at length:

> It is also good to know the *miḳra*ʾ [scriptures, i.e., the Prophets and Hagiographa] because many commandments can be learned from them, such as "You shall not eat [any flesh] with its blood" (Lev. 19:26) from what Saul did [see 1 Sam. 14:32–35], and "the fathers shall not be put to death on account of the children" (Deut. 24:16) from what Amaziah did [see 2 Kings 14:5–6]. But there is little benefit for the great effort required to learn the names of the cities of Israel, and the deeds [most MSS: names] of the judges and kings, and the construction of the First Temple [see 1 Kings 6], and of the [Third Temple] to be built [see Ezek. 40–42], and prophecies that have passed by in part [i.e., have already been fulfilled], while some of them are visions of the future that we can investigate, and with others we grope as blind people [feel] a wall—one says it is one thing and another something else. If we knew [the whole secret of (supplied from three MSS)][128] the Book of Psalms, which is all songs and prayers, even though it was uttered with divine inspiration it does not contain any prophecies of future events. Likewise Job and the books by Solomon and the Scrolls and Ezra. Thus we cannot know when the end [of days] will come from the Book of Daniel, because he [himself] did not know this, as I wrote in my commentary there [see the long commentary on Daniel 11:30 and 36]. If we examined all these day and night we would not gain any knowledge of a commandment on whose account we can

inherit the life of the world to come. This is why they [five MSS: the Sages] said of the study of *miḳra*ʾ: "it is meritorious and it is not meritorious."[129] It is good for a knowledgeable man to learn the rules of the holy tongue from the *miḳra*ʾ, because this leads to understanding the foundation [most MSS: secret] of the Torah and the secret of reverence. The Aramaic translation is beneficial, too, even though it is not always according to the plain meaning of the text.

Ibn Ezra's statement that the study of the prophetic books can lead to a better comprehension of the commandments is sincere rather than ironical; in his commentary on Lev. 19:26 he explains "with his blood" by means of "a trustworthy witness—the deeds of Saul"; in his commentary on Deut. 24:16 it is clear that he is relying on Amaziah's behavior, even though he does not mention him explicitly (as did Ibn Balaam[130] and Rashbam, who gave similar explanations). But he limits this statement with the assertion that this utility is not sufficient justification for an intensive preoccupation with the prophetic writings and Hagiographa, because they are full of geographic, genealogical, and architectural information which is of no help in elucidating the commandments. Moreover, most books of the Hagiographa contain no commandments whatsoever; even from the prophetic writings we can learn very little about our own future, since some prophecies have already been fulfilled, and as for the others—some are so vague that it is quite impossible to extract from them what the Jews can anticipate will happen to them, and only some are "visions of the future that we can investigate." This applies with even greater force to the psalms, which, although written with divine inspiration, contain no prophecies of future events. It is no wonder, then, that the Sages warned against excessive preoccupation with the Scriptures. Even a man who won his reputation inter alia by virtue of his commentaries on the Prophets and Hagiographa can offer only one additional justification for studying them, a justification that further underscores their secondary status—the utility of acquiring knowledge about the language of the Torah.

Given Ibn Ezra's usual habits in polemic disputations of this sort, we may assume that rather than attempting a precise formulation of his position he was trying to dramatically strengthen his argument about the uselessness of one-sided specialization, and incidentally also to undermine the position he opposed.[131] In order to verify this hypothesis we must prove that in the balance of his assertion of the absolute need to supplement the Written Law with the Oral Law (whose anti-Karaite nature is abundantly clear) Ibn Ezra attacks three other aspects of Karaite belief regarding the exclusivity of the scriptural books as a source of knowledge for Israel.

The Karaites found it extremely difficult to base a complete halakhic canon on the Pentateuch alone, and thus could not adhere to the principle that all of the commandments can be deduced from the written Torah. But instead of augmenting it with a reliable oral tradition (as they later did, at least partially, via the principle of *sevel ha-y^eruššah* [unwritten transmission]), they sought to supplement it from a more reliable source—the prophetic books and the Hagiographa. This is explained very clearly in two Karaite sources written in Byzantium in the eleventh and twelfth centuries and which were probably not known to Ibn Ezra. Nevertheless we can rely on them, because, as is the custom with Karaite literature, they repeat with only minor variations a classic Karaite argument that Ibn Ezra could well have known from earlier sources.[132] One source is *ʾEškol ha-kofer*, by the Karaite scholar Judah Hadassi, written in Hebrew in Constantinople starting in 1148. Hadassi enumerates and explicates the methods for expounding the plain meaning of the Torah; of the seventh of these he writes:

> We learn by way of a seventh method—a subject that is not explicated where it appears but is explicated elsewhere,[133] like the arcane or allusive statements by Moses the father of the prophets, which were explained by the prophets later. For these had been transmitted from generation to generation; moreover, realizing that knowledge was waning in Israel, one generation would explain them to another. For example, he wrote, "In the beginning God created the heavens and the earth," but Moses did not explain the creation of the angels or when they were created, because he included them in the statement "In the beginning God created etc.," and we must ask and inquire and search diligently. And then King David came and said "Praise the Lord from the heavens, praise Him on high, praise Him all His angels . . ." (Ps. 148:1–2), and this on the first day when the upper heavens were created. This was also stated by the scholars and by the Greek savants, that the beginning of creation was the creation of the angels and His servitors. (page 64a, col. 1)

This is followed by many additional examples, including the two commandments cited by Ibn Ezra—using Saul's action to explicate "You shall not eat with the blood" (Lev. 19:26) and the leniency of Amaziah son of Joash king of Judah to explicate "Parents shall not be put to death for children" (Deut. 24:16). In another context Hadassi brings prooftexts for this Karaite view of the prophetic books and Hagiographa as the only authentic supplement to the Torah:

> The Torah and Prophets and Hagiographa are all three called "Torah," as it is written: "And we have not obeyed the voice of the Lord our God by following His teachings [*toroṯ*] which He set before us by His servants the *Prophets*" (Dan. 9:10), and the wisest of all men said about them: "Indeed, I wrote down for you a three-fold love, in wise counsel" (Prov. 22:20) in the Holy Spirit of your God. (page 70a, col. 2)

This view of Scripture takes issue with the Talmudic sages' designation of the halakhic status of the Prophets and Hagiographa as "transmitted tradition," but the two camps agreed that commandments could be learned from them and they could assist in understanding the Pentateuch.[134] The Karaites seized on this partial agreement in their campaign to undermine the reliability of the Oral Law. Thus Hadassi attacks the laws of the Mishnah regarding the *sukkah* and the four species (of plants used on the Feast of Tabernacles): "Shall we abandon what the Prophets say [i.e., Neh. 8:14–16] and grasp external writings [i.e., the Mishnah] like your interpretation, to which our Torah never alluded?!" (page 86b, col. 2). Similarly, he attacks the multiplicity of rabbinic interpretations of "You shall not eat [any flesh] with its blood," and praises the Karaite interpretation, which confidently rests on the words of Saul (1 Sam. 14:32–35) and Ezekiel (33:25), whose reliability cannot be doubted, since "had this interpretation not been transmitted from generation to generation, from Moses down to King Saul . . . , Saul and his wise men would never have invented something new on their own initiative" (page 87a, col. 1).

A variation on this polemic argument can be found in our second source, an as-yet unpublished Hebrew Karaite commentary on Exodus and Leviticus, written in Byzantium in 1088. For this anonymous author, not only does the Sages' disagreement over the meaning of "you shall not eat [any flesh] with its blood" clearly attest that their religious rulings are not an oral Torah that was received by Moses on Sinai, but moreover:

> The Lord disclosed their deceitfulness through this verse, making known that everything they say is on their own initiative and not the word of the Lord. For it is not reasonable that Moses did not make known to Israel the meaning of this verse and that the Prophets did not know it. Therefore God, His name be blessed, expounded this verse for us by means of Saul. The fact that they offer many different interpretations of this verse reveals that most of what they say consists of lies; only when they forget themselves did they speak the truth. This verse is like "And you shall take on the first day the fruit of *hadar* trees" (Lev. 23:40). (Leiden University MS Werner 3, p. 369$^{r\text{-}v}$)

Ibn Ezra was familiar with this rather standard Karaite argument, as is attested by his direct reference to it in his commentary on Lev. 23:40. He begins his gloss with a declaration of faith: "We believe in the words of the Sages, for they would not contradict Scripture. . . . Also they transmitted that the fruit of the *hadar* tree is the *ʾetrog* [citron]." He continues by bringing pertinent proofs, and closes by rejecting the opinion of the "Sadducees" (i.e., the Karaites) that the commandment is not to hold the Four

Species in the hand but rather to use them in constructing the festival booth by refuting the interpretation by these "blind-hearted ones" of the verse in "the Book of Ezra" (i.e., Neh. 8:15) upon which they base themselves.

This, then, is the controversy behind both Ibn Ezra's acknowledgement in *Y^e sod Mora^ɔ* "that we can learn many commandments from Scriptures" as well as the accompanying assertion that the historiographic nature of the Early Prophets and the wisdom-literature aspect of most books of the Hagiographa do not justify presenting these two units as a halakhic supplement to the Torah. If we change our modern phrasing for one more in keeping with how Ibn Ezra and his contemporaries spoke, we would ask: how is it possible to understand the plural reference to more than one Torah in Dan. 9:10 as applying to the Prophets and the Writings, when in fact they contain long sections without any reference to the commandments? The inference to be drawn from Ibn Ezra's words is that the Karaites responded that wherever religious commandments are lacking something no less important is present—prophecy. Indeed, the spiritual world of Karaism had two foundations: exact knowledge of the commandments and their precise fulfillment, and perfect knowledge of the Messianic age and bringing it closer through vigils of prayer and lamentation, fasting and mourning.[135] Against this presentation of the prophecy of the end of days as the second main subject of the Prophetic Writings and Hagiographa, alongside explication of the commandments, Ibn Ezra makes the same quantitative claim he had made earlier about the commandments. Those prophecies that have already been fulfilled cannot be considered to be prophecies about the End of Days; but what is more, even those that have not yet been fulfilled are in part so veiled that "we grope like blind people [feel] a wall—one says it is one thing and another something else." Here Ibn Ezra is hoisting the Karaites on their own petard: they claim that the Sages' disagreements recorded in the Mishnah and Gemara are evidence that *halakhah* does not rest on tradition and transmission; in the same vein he argues against them that the commentators' disagreements about the meaning of the prophecies about the future are decisive proof that tearing away the veil from the secrets of the end is not the main task of the Prophetic Writings and Hagiographa. Moreover, most books of the Hagiographa contain no prophecies about the future; we cannot even know when the end will come from such an essentially eschatological book as Daniel, because Daniel himself did not know. True, Yefet ben ᶜAli (in his commentary on Daniel 12:4, 8, 9, 12) also stresses that the End of Days is indeed hidden and sealed and will not be revealed until just before the redemption (his explanation: had so remote a time been recorded in the Book of Daniel many would have despaired and abandoned their religion).[136] On the other hand, Yefet does not refrain (glosses on vv. 7, 9, and 10) from giving a detailed rendering of the stages of the redemption and a confident identification of those who bring it nearer (the Karaites, "those whose way is blameless") and those who defer it (the Rabbanites, "those who act wickedly toward the covenant"). Even if Ibn Ezra had not seen Yefet's Psalms commentary and was not aware of how far he went (by way of the prognostic *pešer*) in making the psalms refer to the struggles of the Karaite sect and its brilliant victory (see above, pp. 94–97), he certainly knew about Yefet's approach from the latter's commentary on Daniel and the Minor Prophets, which he certainly had seen. Similarly, even if Ibn Ezra did not know the last chapter of *ʾEškol ha-kofer*, in which Hadassi enumerates one by one the seventy-seven marvels that God will work for his people when the Redeemer comes—each of them documented by an abundance of texts garnered from all corners of Scripture—he certainly was familiar with the depictions of the Messianic era in the works of the Karaite sages from whom Hadassi derived his position.[137] Against this background we should see Ibn Ezra's quantitative argument that only some prophecies are "visions of the future that we can investigate" as fundamentally qualitative—an appeal against the exegetical validity of the Karaite prognostic exegesis.

In other words, there are very few certain prophecies of the End of Days, and the efforts of the Karaite *pešer* to multiply them tenfold is vain, as the disagreements among their commentators prove. These disagreements stem first of all from the fact that the Karaite method of prognostic interpretation, like all allegorical approaches, is based on identifying key words in the text with personalities and concepts not stated there explicitly, which can therefore be discovered only by means of a metaphoric reading. "Roses" (Ps. 45:1) and "blossoms" (Cant. 2:12) refer to the Karaites and their scholars with the same degree of certainty as the non-metaphorical designations "those whose way is blameless" (Ps. 119:1) and "the knowledgeable ones" (Dan. 12:3, 10). Clearly anyone who wishes to refute the *pešer* must first attack this system of identifications, whose artifical and arbitrary nature is evident to anyone who is not an adherent of the sect.[138] Furthermore, it is not only the exegetical debate between the Rabbanite and Karaite scholars that detracts from the validity of the *pešer,* but also, and even more so, the disagreements among the Karaite sages themselves. Ibn Ezra had already raised a similar claim against their halakhic exegesis in his first introduction to the Pentateuch ("The Second Way," Weiser ed., vol. 1, p. 2): "How can they rely in [fulfilling] the commandments on their own devising, when every moment they switch from side to side as their thought impels them." These internal disagreements, which did indeed in large measure stem from the non-authoritative nature of their exegetical labors (cf. above, Chapter 2, note 37), embarrassed the Karaite scholars more than a little.[139] They endeavored to limit them to the bare minimum, although they did not exaggerate the seriousness of the problem as did their rivals. Still, we should stress that this was not simply one more polemical shot for Ibn Ezra; when he uses the first person plural—"we grope like blind men against a wall"—he is referring to a genuine problem that troubled him frequently: the partial nature of the information available to us, which prevents us from giving a full interpretation of scriptural texts. Given our imperfect command of biblical language and especially the absence of adequate historical and biographical information in Scripture he rejects Saadiah's homiletical exegeses of names ("Pay no attention to what the Gaon says about names, for [even] if we knew the entire Holy Tongue how could we know everything that happened, like the meaning of 'Moses' and 'Issachar' [where the events that explain their names are known to us]" (Ibn Ezra on Gen. 4:16, and cf. on Isa. 40:12). By the same token he argues against attempts to identify the events referred to by Jacob's blessings of his sons (commentary on Gen. 49:19) and the visions of Zechariah ("Were we to find some ancient book that told us what wars occurred in those days, we would grope like blind men against a wall and say 'perhaps the prophecy referred to this,' but as things stand we have nothing upon which to rely" [introduction to the commentary on Zechariah;[140] and cf. his glosses on Zech. 12:11; Hag. 2:22; Ps. 78:2]). So too he rejects all of the Sages' attempts to identify the prophets Joel and Obadiah with personalities whose dates are known (commentary on Joel 1:1; introduction to Obadiah). Ibn Ezra's consistent opposition to such manifestations of overinterpretation within his own camp is based on the very same considerations (the uncertainty caused by a lack of information on the one hand and the intentional vagueness of scriptural texts on the other) and is sometimes even phrased in the same terms ("like blind men against a wall," "if we knew") that he uses in his arguments against the Karaite *pešer.* This similarity gives his polemic argument, phrased as a factual but ungrounded assertion, great methodological credibility.

Furthermore, we saw above (pp. 197ff.) that one of the conspicuous lineaments of Ibn Ezra's Psalms commentary is his strong tendency to offer the reader alternative definitions of the nature of the psalm being discussed—is it prayer or prophecy? Is the prophecy messianic or not? A number of explanations for this behavior, which is liable to perplex many readers, have been offered above; to these we can now add Ibn Ezra's desire to show his readers how uncertain is the explication of the Book of Psalms in general (as he puts it: "If we knew the whole secret of the Book of Psalms") and especially of prophecies about the End of Days. This desire to define the solid core of messianic prophecy stemmed from his own spiritual needs, and should not be understood simply as an expression of a tendency to reject Karaite *pešer.* These discussions, found throughout the standard commentary, lack any tinge of polemicism; and in his two introductions as well he never mentions or quarrels with the Karaite approach. Still, for him too the Book of Psalms contains not only prophetic psalms that have already been fulfilled (e.g., Psalm 137), but also conspicuously messianic psalms (e.g., 43, 82, and 102); thus, to return to our initial question, how could he have written, in *Yᵉsod Moraʾ*: "If we knew the whole secret of the Book of Psalms, which is all songs and prayers, even though it was uttered with divine inspiration *it does not contain any prophecies of future events*"?

If we have correctly reconstructed the polemic context in which this sentence is to be located, we may assume, not only that it is directed against the Karaite view, but also that the concept of "prophecies of future events" is used as understood by the Karaites. In other words, Ibn Ezra is here arguing, first, that our understanding of the Book of Psalms is far from being as complete and comprehensive as the Karaites claim, and second, that it contains only poems and prayers, which, for all that they are prophetic, are not—because of their nature as prayers and poems—future-oriented prophecies in the sense of detailed prognostic prophecies of the Messianic era, as the Karaite *pešer* would find in them. In Ibn Ezra's commentary the prophetic dimension never deprives the psalms of their literary quality as psalms, but on the contrary is always anchored in and interwoven with it. Sometimes the prophetic poet prays "in the words of" (i.e., on behalf of) the exiled Children of Israel who find themselves in distress, and sometimes he announces their future rescue and redemption; but he does not describe the stages of their redemption, something that is found, even according to Ibn Ezra, in a number of prophecies of future events included in the prophetic writings and the Book of Daniel.[141]

How wide is the gap here between the views of Ibn Ezra and of Karaite commentators like Yefet is shown by their different approaches to Psalm 22. From the designation *ʾayyeleṯ ha-šaḥar* (hind of the dawn) in the heading Yefet infers that David was prophesying about what will befall Israel in "a time of distress" (i.e., in exile), and therefore identifies "many bulls surround me" (13[12]) with the kingdom of Edom (Christians), a "tearing, roaring lion" (14[13]) with the Ishmaelites, "dogs surround me" (17[16]) with the violent inhabitants of the desert, and "you who fear the Lord" (24[23]) with the descendants of Jacob returning from exile.[142] By contrast, it is clear to Ibn Ezra that here David is praying about his personal distress (see his commentary on verses 2, 4, and 19), and that there is no sense in trying to identify the historical event that provided the background for the composition of this psalm. This is equally valid for the Song of Songs, which Ibn Ezra allegorizes as referring to the history of Israel "from the days of our father Abraham to the Messianic era" (introduction to the standard commentary). Even though he is quite liberal in his historical and conceptual metaphors (for example, ''your two breasts—these are the two laws, the Written Law and the Oral Law, because the breasts give milk, as it is said 'Come, buy food and eat' [Isa. 55:1, and see his commentary ad loc.]''—The Third Way on 4:5), he nevertheless avoids any sort of prognostication in the manner of the Karaite *pešer,* and goes no further than a few basic and simple statements about the Messianic era.[143]

Thus the Prophets and Hagiographa provide insufficient information on the commandments and on future events that we can investigate to justify the intensive study of these books; the only benefit to be derived from studying them is linguistic—''to learn the rules of the holy tongue from Scriptures.'' Still, the polemic context in which this bleak conclusion is presented allows us to assume that it does not really reflect Ibn Ezra's attitude towards the study of the Prophets and Writings, but refers solely to the Karaite approach and is intended as an ironic thrust at yet another aspect of the Karaite position. If this is truly the case, we must discern what important element, which escaped the Karaites' notice, was discovered by Ibn Ezra in the Book of Psalms. The answer to this must be found in the Psalms commentary; before we turn to it, however, we can rely on the principal directive to be found in the last section of the first chapter of *Y^e^sod Mora*ʾ. Following his criticism of the four types of scholars, he presents his own approach in a positive vein (as he does with the Fifth Way in his two Pentateuch introductions). He expresses the ultimate goal of study, derived from the true purpose of life, as follows: ''Man must perfect himself and know the commandments of God who created him and prepare his [all MSS: understand His] deeds; *then he will know his Creator.*'' As proof that man indeed has a duty to endeavor to know God, Ibn Ezra cites verses from the Torah (Ex. 33:13; Deut. 4:39), the Prophets (Jer. 9:22–23), and the Hagiographa (1 Chron. 28:9), and also relies on the fact that the Sages ''knew the secret of the chariot and of the Divine stature.'' Knowledge of the Creator can be attained only through self-knowledge (''The general rule is, how can a man seek to know what is above him when he does not know his own soul and body?''); and self-knowledge cannot be attained without mastery of all of the sciences (six of which he lists).[144] The intelligent man must therefore perfect himself in the secular sciences in order ''to be able to ascend to the higher level and know the secret of the soul, the angels, and the world to come [and the good in store for him there]'' [completed from one MS]. Once having achieved this higher level, he will have to advance further through a profound study of all of the Scriptures and sacred writings, since ''from the Torah and the words of the Prophets and the words of the Talmud he will gain wisdom and understand deep secrets that have escaped many, some of which I will explain'' (emended on the basis of many MSS). Thus, in addition to the commandments and future events that are the chief component of the Pentateuch and prophetic writings, all three sections of Scripture are intended to serve educated individuals with the necessary scientific training as a source of metaphysical and theological truth.[145]

The seventh chapter of *Yᵉsod Moraʾ* can serve as an excellent example of how Ibn Ezra applied this fundamental concept in practice. There he deals with the various aspects of an important theological issue (free will), relying on texts drawn from all over the Bible, a few references to the Talmud, and allusions to the natural sciences. For us, what is most striking is the significant proportion of theological exegeses in Ibn Ezra's Psalms commentary, found principally in his glosses on those psalms he defines as "important."[146] Personal psalms (such as 16 and 25), which a commentator like Rashi understood according to their plain sense as referring to the fulfillment of physical and spiritual needs, the forgiveness of moral and ritual sins, and the yearning for a life of fulfilling the commandments and learning Torah, were elevated by Ibn Ezra from the individual and biographical to the theological and metaphysical plane. For him, these psalms deal mainly with spiritual and intellectual needs, warn against deviations from the true path, and teach that the eternal life in the world to come is a direct result of cleaving to God in this world. In the "important" psalms—but not only in them[147]—he hears warnings against the pursuit of physical pleasures (17:14–15; 19:10–11; 23:5; 49:6, 12, 17, 18; 73:17) juxtaposed with promises about the reward of the righteous in the world to come (16:11; 49:1, 16, 20–21; 73:1, 24)—just as can be found in the moral poetry of Spain, particularly in the genre known as *toḵaḥah* (reproof).[148] Alongside these two he finds in these psalms strikingly speculative statements—such as are found in his own and his predecessors' philosophical poetry[149]—about the ways of acquiring truth and the obligation of teaching it (19:2; 23:5), about the certainty of the truth of the Written and Oral Laws (19:8–9), about the nature of the soul (49:16), and about knowledge of God (73:28). Since comprehension of all of these depends on prior study of the sciences, he occasionally finds it essential to allude to "psychology" (17:15), "astronomy" (19:2), and "natural science" (148:8).[150]

Given this exegetical approach and the scholarly and intellectual ideal that underlies it, it is not astonishing that Ibn Ezra (in the long commentary on Exodus 31:18) fiercely attacks the approach based on a totally different scholarly-intellectual ideal:

> The *empty-headed* may wonder: what did Moses do on the mountain for forty days and forty nights? They do not understand that if he stood there with God this number of years or even four times this number he would not be able to know one part in a thousand of God's works and the secret

> of all of the commandments that He gave to him. They think that the deed is the main thing; but this is not so, but the [commandments of the] heart [are the main thing], while the deed (and the heart)[151] and the tongue are meant to habituate [one], as it is written: "In your mouth and in your heart to observe it" (Deut. 30:14). As the Sages said: "God wants the heart" (BT Sanhedrin 106b). The root of all of the commandments is that one should love God with all of one's soul and cleave to Him; but this cannot be complete unless one knows God's deeds in the celestial and the sublunary spheres and knows His ways. This is what the prophet meant: "But only in this let him who glories glory—that he understands and knows Me" (Jer. 9:23 [AV 24]). Then he will discover that the Lord "acts with kindness, justice, and equity in the world" (ibid.). One cannot know God if one does not know one's own soul and body; for if one does not know the nature of his own soul, of what benefit is knowledge to him? Moses, who prophesied for forty years in the wilderness and understood many secrets that God revealed to him on Mount Sinai, said before his death: "You have only begun to show Your servant Your greatness" (Deut. 3:24—and see Ibn Ezra *ad loc.*); [we see that] He [only] began to show him the greatness of God, and this is the truth, for "His greatness is unsearchable" (Psalm 145:3).

It is reasonable that Moses' long stay on Mount Sinai should astonish (and perhaps even worry) those who believe in the exclusivity and absolute autonomy of the Written Law, i.e., the Karaites. For if the Written Law is supposed to be interpreted from internal evidence alone, with no reliance on external information, why did God have "to speak with him" (Exodus 31:18) for forty days and forty nights? Obviously any Karaite scholar had to reject out of hand the rabbinic answer to this question, namely, that on Mount Sinai Moses received the central principles of the Oral Law;[152] on the other hand, it would seem that the "aggressive anti-intellectualism" (in the words of Vajda, *Two Commentaries,* p. 73) of most of their scholars prevented them from giving a theological and scientific answer to the question of the sort proposed by Ibn Ezra in the passage quoted above. In fact, Daniel al-Ḳumissi's struggle for the fundamental exclusiveness of the biblical canon incorporates an absolute rejection of "a commandment of men learned by rote" (i.e., the Oral Law) side by side with the vigorous rejection of "alien wisdom." Thus, for example, al-Ḳumissi describes (commentary on Hosea 5:13) the sins of "the exiles": "They did not return to God to learn from the Law of Moses, but wandered among the nations and [followed] their customs and learned their writings, which are vain writings, alien wisdom, an abomination to God. They did not realize that it was not proper for them to rely on those who smite them, that they would never find any remedy from them, 'and he will never be able to cure you.' . . .

Far worse and more serious than all of these is that they erred and relied on the shepherds of exile in the *taḳlid* [i.e., on uncritical observance of tradition], like the broken reed of a staff'' (al-Ḳumissi, *Minor Prophets*, pp. 8–9; see also p. 4, note 23, which refers to his other statements on the subject). In a Hebrew manifesto that al-Ḳumissi sent from Jerusalem to his brothers in the Diaspora, too, he links these two demands: ''Do not err in alien wisdom, the false alien wisdom and follies that are abominations to God, because alien wisdom has corrupted many until this very day. . . . Leave behind the commandments of men learned by rote, which do not come from the Torah, and accept nothing from any man except for what is written in the Torah'' (Mann, ''Tract,'' pp. 273–74; see also ibid., p. 262, note 115, on al-Ḳumissi's opposition to determining the new month according to astronomical calculations, an opposition whose source is halakhic but whose implications are anti-scientific, as the phrasing attests: ''We are not permitted to determine the Lord's months and festivals by the calculations of enchanters and astrologers''; cf. his commentary on Micah 5:11). All the same, he who urges a critical rejection of the rabbinic tradition on the basis of denying the *taḳlid* ought not to go beyond opposition to alien wisdom and should avoid applying his anti-intellectual approach to intellectual analysis per se and rational exegesis of the Scriptures. In fact, in an Arabic Karaite propaganda tract published by M. Zucker and attributed by him to Daniel al-Ḳumissi or one of his circle, we find the demand to engage in ''the science of unity'' and to base oneself on proofs derived ''from ideas that are deduced by the mind by examination of Scriptures'' alongside a reproof of studying ''alien wisdom [which is] 'vain and an abomination' ''—a demand that rests on a confident rejection of one of the fundamentals of Greco-Arabic science: ''Know that the philosophers said that the world is based on four qualities: heat, cold, humidity, and dryness; but this is not true, because it is according neither to the Torah nor to what we apprehend with our eyes'' (Zucker, *Translation*, pp. 179–80; see also ibid., p. 175, note 680).[153]

Just how widespread and important was this position among the Karaites is attested by the fact that Kirkisani found it necessary to refute it in detail in the introduction to his commentary on the non-halakhic portions of the Pentateuch; he explains the need to do this as follows:

> We shall do this because some of our scholars, upon hearing an interpretation interspersed with a matter pertaining to philosophical speculation, are frightened away from it, regarding it as superfluous and unnecessary; indeed, some of them consider it improper and even forbidden.[154]

Kirkisani goes on to explain that this position stems from ignorance; not only is there no contradiction between the Torah's description of creation and the laws of philosophy and nature, the sciences are a tool for the correct (i.e., intellectual) understanding of Scripture. Still, his logical arguments and many proofs from Scripture apparently did not persuade the Karaite scholars who followed him to view the study of the sciences as the fulfillment of a religious obligation. In any case the two commentators on Psalms, Salmon and Yefet, continued to cleave, to a greater or lesser extent, to the approach of Daniel al-Ḳumissi. Salmon ben Yeruḥam evidently feared principally the deleterious influence of heretical literature on belief in God and His Torah and the observance of the commandments, but he also rejected the mere study of alien wisdom by undercutting its veracity:

> When you want to know that the wisdom of the Gentiles and their philosophy is vain and empty and fruitless and false, consider that they have no true root and no true growth that two of them can agree on. . . . Also, all of their knowledge deals with the unseen by way of hypothesis, as you will find in [Ptolemy's] *Almagest* and the book of Euclid, to the point that they attempt to prove the existence of the spheres and the measurements of each of them, and the measurements of the sun and the moon and the stars in the upper spheres, just the opposite of what is found in God's Law, where it says, "God set them in the expanse of the sky to shine upon the earth" (Gen. 1:17). Woe unto him who wastes his days in alien wisdom and abandons the words of the Lord of Hosts, which are pure and distilled, compounded of truth and righteousness. (commentary on Psalm 102:5)[155]

Just as sharp a statement directed at the very best of Gentile science can also found in Yefet ben ʿAli's Job commentary, on the verse, "Who is this who darkens counsel, speaking without knowledge" (38:2):

> He says "darkens" because they argue that they knew the secrets of the world in their wisdom, and considered matters that are hidden from men. In their eyes simple men are like asses; they tell them arcane matters and pretend. These are the wise men of the Gentiles, may the Lord destroy their memory and blot out their name, such as Plato and Aristotle and their ilk. He said "darkens counsel" because they assert that they "enlighten counsel," but their words are false, and the truth is the opposite of what they say. (Ben Shammai, *Doctrines*, vol. 1, p. 106)

From Ben Shammai's analysis we can infer that Yefet too was motivated by a fear of heretical thought and slack observance of the commandments; at the same time, though, he did not reject the intellectual path, seeing it as an essential means for understanding the Scriptures, and was not opposed to a cautious and controlled investigation o.ˆ the meaning of the commandments and of the theological statements, to the extent that both were in fact explicated in Scriptures. For our purpose here what is important is Yefet's unequivocal stance on the exclusivity of Scripture and its autonomy, as expressed, inter alia, at the end of his commentary on Prov. 30:1–6:

> After that Solomon said, ''Do not add to His words'' (verse 6), which means—do not add to what He wrote in His Torah, [because] it is greater and more marvelous than [the understanding] of men. This [prohibition] includes: not to add to His commandments, as it is written, ''You shall not add anything [to what I command you]'' (Deut. 4:2); but he abbreviated and did not mention subtracting from it, as it says about the Torah: ''or take anything away from it'' (loc. cit.), because they add [in all] the topics we have mentioned.[156] [Solomon] included in this section the unity [of God], and the Torah and the Day of Judgement, which includes reward and punishment. About reward he said ''a shield to those who take refuge in Him'' (verse 5), and about punishment he said ''lest He indict you and you be proved a liar'' (verse 6), to teach us that *God will demand His due from him who adds to His words and makes assertions that [he can] not prove, and then he will lose what he has.* And after [this] loss [will come] punishment without a doubt. (Ben Shammai, *Doctrines*, vol. 2, p. 276)

The words in italics express the principle that underlies the Karaite opposition to studying the sciences: the only way to arrive at true knowledge of the Creator and his creation is through God's word; thus anyone who adds (that is, who makes assertions that cannot be proven from Scripture) is detracting from the truth of God's word, and merits punishment as one who errs and leads others astray.

In conclusion, vis-à-vis the Karaite belief that all who add to Scripture lose even their basis in Scripture, Ibn Ezra holds the opposite view, namely, that one who goes no farther than Scripture loses even Scripture itself. There is no way to observe the commandments without the Oral Law, just as it is impossible to attain knowledge of God and understand the meaning of His commandments without prior knowledge of the sciences. Since the details about future events that the Karaite *pešer* claimed to extract from the Prophetic Writings and Hagiographa had an extremely flimsy exegetical base for Ibn Ezra, only one rationale for their intensive study of the Prophets and Writings remained for him—learning the holy tongue in order to understand the Torah. Still, how can Ibn Ezra ignore, in this sharp and cruel argument, the supreme importance that the Karaites attached to the Book of Psalms as the obligatory prayerbook of Israel? Ibn Ezra certainly knew about the use of the Book of Psalms in the Karaite liturgy, if not from direct contact with them then at the least from Saadiah's introductions to Psalms (which, it will be recalled, he knew very well), where this fact is a major axis of the discussion. Evidently Ibn Ezra quite ignored this aspect of their connection with the psalms because the first chapter of *Yᵉsod Mora*ʾ deals, not with the initial study of the entire congregation of worshippers, intended to bring them to a simple linguistic and thematic understanding of the psalms used in prayer, but rather with the profound intellectual study of the "knowledgeable," which requires additional justification. All the same, his silence here is not to be understood as agreement with Saadiah's position, since both as an exponent of the plain meaning and as a liturgical and secular poet he knew full well that Saadiah's attempt to prove that the psalms are not the prayers of the servant but the law of the Master cannot withstand criticism. Consequently he could not deny the lyrical and liturgical nature of the psalms, neither in the pursuit of a halakhic controversy over the legitimacy of the Rabbanite prayerbook (which evidently did not preoccupy him as it had Saadiah) nor to strengthen his exegetical argument about the theological and cognitive aspect of the psalms (which interested him very much). It would seem that the strong philosophical nature of many of the poems and *piyyuṭim* composed in Spain made it easier for him to assert the honorable rank of the psalms as containing "important" information, and at the same time to render abundant praise (in the introduction to the First Recension) of their merit as sacred poetry that had been sung in the Holy Temple with musical accompaniment of the highest caliber. An outstanding expression of this linkage of the two aspects that Ibn Ezra found in the psalms can be found in the prefatory poem to the standard Psalms commentary (see below pp. 330–331). In its first lines he uses astronomical imagery to exalt the wondrous dominion of the Lord of Hosts over the heavens: "His breath turns all the spheres / and impels all His hosts in their courses; / All the angelic bands perform His will"; at its close, speaking in the first person, he defines the ethos of the liturgical poets: "It is my heart's delight to entreat my Creator / and my entire desire to devise prayers to Him." When a liturgical poet of Ibn Ezra's stature prefaces a statement like this to his commentary on the Book of Psalms, it is tantamount to a declaration that he sees himself as continuing, in some sense, the work of the liturgists whose poetical prayers are incorporated in Scripture.[157]

VII. The Fourth Inquiry: Editorial matters—the order of the psalms and the terms used in their headings

A. The five books of psalms in comparison to Iberian anthologies

The Fourth Inquiry begins by setting forth two questions dealing with editorial matters. What is the nature and significance of the strange terms found in the headings of the psalms? What principle governed the order of the individual psalms in the book, and is there any link between adjacent psalms? Because these questions are interrelated, Ibn Ezra skipped over the first and proceeded directly to the second question, apparently out of an aesthetic inclination for chiastic order.[158] His discussion begins with an extremely concise summary of Saadiah's affirmative answer to this question: there is indeed a strong thematic link between adjacent psalms. Psalm 3, for example, comes right after Psalm 2 because it is a historical exemplification (the bitter end of Absalom who raised his hand against David) of the general warning to gentile kings not to attack God's anointed, voiced in Psalm 2. Ibn Ezra rejects this link by categorizing it as "a homiletical explanation" (line 103); by this he evidently means that such a theory has no substantial basis in the text. Not only is there no thematic sequence, neither is there any chronological order; this is proven by the fact that Psalm 3 (which refers to David's flight from Absalom) precedes Psalm 142 (which refers to his flight from Saul).[159] This should not astonish us, because even in the Pentateuch there is no chronological sequence, as the Sages taught us, and as is proven by the fact that what occurred "on the first day of the second month in the second year" (Num. 1:1) comes before what happened "on the first new moon of the second year" (Num. 9:1). Thus there is no escape from the conclusion that "every psalm stands by itself" (lines 109f.).

With these words Ibn Ezra concludes his discussion of this question; but the elliptical phrasing makes it hard to understand what he means. Nor is the analogy between the absence of the chronological order in the Book of Psalms and its absence in the Pentateuch, which is reinforced by the formal comparison "this book is divided into five parts, like the Pentateuch" (lines 103f.) obvious. The deviations from chronological order in the Pentateuch are not so drastic, and when they do in fact go beyond the bounds of the narrative Ibn Ezra endeavored to provide grounds why "it had to be said this way" (comm. on Gen. 38:1) and even to explain the literary function of these deviations (loc. cit.; cf. the second recension on Gen. 11:32, the long commentary on Ex. 16:15; 18:1, 19:1, 32:11; Lev. 25:1; and on Num. 8:26). Thus when Ibn Ezra compares the absence of chronological order in the five divisions of the Book of Psalms with the situation in the five books of the Pentateuch, where chronological sequence is generally observed, the analogy is not meant to be taken very far; he merely seeks to buttress his claim by virtue of the fact that the Book of Psalms, too, is divided into sections. He states his meaning more clearly in his commentary on Psalm 3:1: "This Psalm is included in the first Book—for there are five books—so we must not wonder that in the fifth we find 'while he was in the cave; a prayer' (142:1), which occurred before the incident with Absalom."

Whereas the differences between Psalms and the historical portion of the Pentateuch are significant, it may be reasonable to compare them with its legal portions, about which Ibn Ezra made a similar, albeit not identical, comment. At the beginning of his commentary on the weekly portion *Mišpaṭim* he writes: "I will tell you a general rule before I begin my commentary: every law or commandment stands by itself. If we can find a reason why one law follows another, or one commandment another, we will establish the linkage with all our might; but if we cannot, we must attribute this to our own lack of knowledge" (long commentary on Ex. 21:2). On the one hand he states unequivocally that, from a legal perspective, each statute is quite autonomous; but on the other hand he is confident that from the literary point of view it is not possible that the laws are enumerated in the Pentateuch in an arbitrary order with no thematic link among them. The way out of this dilemma is the cautious assumption that "there is a sort of proof to the sequence of the verses" (short commentary on Ex. 21:1), or, as he puts it elsewhere, "there is a sort of homiletic explanation to the sequence of the sections" (comm. on Deut. 16:18). This acknowledgment of the homiletical nature of any account of the sequence of the sections allows him to knock out the plain-meaning underpinning of Karaite glosses (which were frequently based on the juxtaposition of sections—see his commentary on Deut. 22:13 and 24:6), without giving up the attempt to discover some thematic continuity in distinctly halakhic sections.[160] Still, while he favors a cautious linkage of the statutes in the Pentateuch and is prepared to acknowledge the quasi-homiletical nature thereof, he rejects Saadiah's corresponding endeavors with regard to the psalms because, given their evident detachment one from another, they are merely homiletical. That this was in fact his meaning can be proven from the parallel utterance in his commentary on Psalms 3:1 "Saadiah Gaon wanted to link all of the Psalms with one another, and said after 'Why do nations assemble' (Ps. 2) that their fate would be like that of Absalom (Ps. 3), *but the commentator is unable to make such a connection.*"

Thus Ibn Ezra has two reasons for not linking the psalms: the lack of chronological order (which demonstrates that the arrangement of the psalms does not reflect the order in which they were written) and the absence of conclusive linkages in the text of the psalms themselves. When he concludes that "the truth . . . is that every psalm stands by itself" he means that the autonomy of the psalms—which were written by many poets over an extended period of time—is essentially different from that of the commandments in the Pentateuch. He can accept this fact because, unlike Saadiah, he does not see the Book of Psalms as a single unified work like the Pentateuch, but as five collections of psalms, which were gathered, assembled, and written down by the Men of the Great Assembly many years after their composition (see what he says in the Second Inquiry, discussed above, pp. 181–182). Just as he agrees with Ibn Giqatilah that the anonymity of many psalms stems from the fact that the identity of their authors had been forgotten by the time of the editors (see above, p. 186), so too he evidently assumes that the editors wrote them down in the order they found them, without any fixed editorial principle to guide them.[161] We may hypothesize that this is how he conceived of the editorial process, since, despite his unequivocal assertion of the fundamental isolation of the psalms from one another, he occasionally permits himself to draw guarded conclusions based on the sequence of some of them. In his discussion of the anonymous psalms in the First Inquiry he writes: "In my opinion, while we do not know who wrote a psalm that lacks a name, it is possible that it is attached to the one that comes before, like 'Bless the Lord, O my soul' (104) to the other psalm [with the same heading] (103) and also to the one after it, 'Praise the Lord; call on His name' (105)" (lines 67–69). As is typical of Ibn Ezra, he is quite laconic here, and only slightly more voluble elsewhere. He does not explain upon what basis it is possible to link Psalms 103 and 104, perhaps because he left this for the (lost) commentary on those psalms; but he does do so in the standard commentary on 104:1: "One can infer that this psalm, too, is by David, because its beginning and end are like the previous one." This means that the formal similarity between these two adjacent psalms, both of which employ the inclusio "bless the Lord, O my soul," may be purely coincidental; but it is more reasonable that it attests to their having been written by the same poet. In the passage quoted above from the introduction he buttresses this line of reasoning with another consideration—the attribution of Psalm 104 to David is strengthened by its location between two explicitly Davidic psalms—103, ascribed to him in its heading, and 105, which Ibn Ezra had previously attributed to David (lines 68–69) on the basis of 1 Chron. 16:7. A common subject and thematic continuity—clearly evident in Psalms 70 and 71—can demonstrate that adjacent psalms really are associated, as he proposes in his commentary on 71:1: "I think the correct answer is that this psalm [too (reading with MS)] was composed by David, like the psalm 'Bless the Lord, O my soul' (103), and 'O Lord my God you are very great (104:1)—they are linked." Moreover, even when there is no formal or thematic similarity, a certain weight must be given to the very fact that two psalms are juxtaposed, as Ibn Ezra says in the First Inquiry (the continuation of the above quotation): "The same is true for 'A prayer of Moses' (90), which is by him, and [is followed by] 'O you who dwell in the shelter of the Most High' (91), which may also be by Moses—as the Sages said" (lines 69–71). It may be that in the First Recension, in his commentary *ad loc.*, he gave reasons for this partial adoption of the Sages' opinion (the attribution of Psalms 90–100 to Moses); in the Second Recension, which has come down to us, we find only an even more hesitant variant on this assumption:

"It may be that this psalm too is by Moses, or by one of the singers" (commentary on 91:1). It would seem, then, that here too Ibn Ezra anticipated that the erudite reader would understand how he arrived at this far-reaching assumption. As is known, the Book of Psalms contains blocks of psalms that are attributed to a particular author (44–49 to the Koraḥides; 73–83 to Asaph); this opens the way to assuming that certain anonymous psalms follow one another because they were written by the same poet. Who, in Ibn Ezra's opinion, put together the explicit and presumed groups of psalms? From the fact that the editors did not add many psalms whose authors are named explicitly to such groups, preferring to arrange them separately (just as they did not arrange the psalms in chronological order), he evidently inferred that they preferred to write down the psalms as they came to hand—those that they found as a unit, in a single unit, and those that came to hand separately, separately.[162]

The absence of a principle of arrangement is no commendation for an anthology of poems; this makes its hard to accept the conclusion that the Men of the Great Assembly did not do a thorough job of editing the psalms. Ibn Ezra could evade this conclusion and argue—along the lines of the passage quoted above about the commandments in the Pentateuch—that the absence of a connection between most psalms is not really a flaw in the book, but a direct result of our inability to discover the connection: "we must attribute this to our own lack of knowledge." He refrained from doing this because he recognized the essential difference between Psalms and the legal sections of the Pentateuch, and apparently also because his expectations about the editing of the Book of Psalms—as about the terminology employed in the headings, to be discussed below—were influenced by contemporary Iberian practice with regard to poetic anthologies.

The *diwans* of the Hebrew poets of Spain that have reached us in whole or in part, as well as those about which we have only indirect information, are arranged according to various principles, which resemble those of the Arabic *diwans.*

(1) *Alphabetical order,* intended to make it easy to find a poem on the basis of its first line. In the collection of Moses Ibn Ezra's poems in the Oxford MS (Neubauer catalogue No. 1970) the poems are arranged alphabetically by the last syllable of the line, which determines the rhyme (see Schirmann, "Poets," p. 125); whereas in Samuel ha-Nagid's *Ben Kohelet* and *Ben Mišlei* they are arranged alphabetically by the initial letter of the line, while within each letter the poems are arranged by their meters (see Yellin,

"Metrical Forms," p. 186). Since they lack rhyme and meter, the psalms could have been arranged only according to their initial letters. A purely technical arrangement of this sort, however, is alien to the spirit of the Scriptures; and since its absence is immediately evident, Ibn Ezra had no need to even mention this possibility.

(2) *Classification by poetic forms,* and arrangement of the poems in decreasing order of their poetical value. The first section contains poems with the same rhyme and meter throughout; the second, strophic poems; and the third the "prosaic" poems, that is, metrical and nonmetrical liturgical poetry, *maqamas,* and rhymed epistles. To date this classification has been found only in the *diwans* of Abraham Ibn Ezra and of Judah Halevi, edited by Yeshuah ben Elijah Halevi, whose time and place remain unknown, but who certainly lived many years after the deaths of these two poets.[163] In his collection of Abraham Ibn Ezra's poetry he arranged the poems within the three sections by subject (see Ibn Ezra, *Diwan*, pages xviii–xx), whereas in Judah Halevi's *diwan* he arranged the poems in the first section alphabetically by rhyme, began the second section with the poems collected by the previous editor and followed them with those added by himself (see Judah Halevi, *Diwan,* pp. 5–6). I do not know whether Ibn Ezra was familiar with this editorial approach, but it clearly cannot be applied to the psalms, since by Iberian standards they all belonged to the inferior third category (see above, pp. 168ff.). Still, we may be interested in the fact that even an editor with so strong a tendency to systematic classification preserved an older collection as a separate block within the second section of Judah Halevi's poems; we shall return to this point later.[164]

(3) *Classification by topics and the genres* appropriate to them: love poems and drinking songs, satire and invective, elegies, and so forth. This classification is used in the *diwan* of Judah Halevi mentioned above, and is also attested to by the ascriptions preceding the poems in the surviving fragments of Moses Ibn Ezra's *diwan* (see Schirmann, "Poets," p. 125). Saadiah, Salmon Ibn Yeruḥam, and Yefet all

sought a thematic arrangement of this sort in Psalms, but Ibn Ezra argued that there was simply no evidence for one in the book.

(4) *Chronological Order,* based on when the poems were written. Yehoseph, the son of Samuel ha-Nagid and editor of *Ben T^{e}hillim,* writes at the end of his preface to that work: "I did not worry, in what I collected, whether a poem was earlier or later, but arranged them as I found them." This apologia attests—as the modern editor, D. Jarden, notes—that he felt that chronological order was superior. In fact, Jarden's analysis revealed that only seven of the seventy poems in *Ben T^{e}hillim*, are out of chronological order, for those poems where the event described can be dated. This means that Yehoseph wrote down the poems in the order that they reached him from his father's campaigns, so that for the most part they were arranged quite naturally by the date of composition (see Samuel ha-Nagid, *Ben T^{e}hillim,* pp. 30–31). Chronological order is appropriate for the Book of Psalms, at least for those psalms with biographical headings, which is why Saadiah and Ibn Ezra both call attention to its astonishing absence. But whereas Saadiah concluded that other principles of arrangement must therefore be found, Ibn Ezra concluded that the editors wrote down the Psalms in the same fashion as had Samuel ha-Nagid's son—"as they found them."

(5) *In the order of their discovery.* Like Yehoseph ha-Nagid, Tadros Abulafia apologized in the preface to his own collection of poems that he had not arranged them properly (Tadros, *Gan ha-M^{e}šalim,* vol. 1, p. 2): when the poet collected his scattered poems, he transcribed them in the *diwan* as he found them arranged in his own manuscripts and those written by others. He apologizes that the lack of chronological and thematic order results in songs coming with dirges, love poetry with poetry of thanks, and later works with early ones. In fact the anarchy was not total, as can be seen from the comparative tables of the placement of the poems in the manuscript with that in Yellin's edition, which is arranged thematically (ibid., vol. 1, pp. 135–37; vol. 2, pp. 160–63; vol. 3, pp. 111–13). Yellin leaves quite a few poems (among those collected by

> the poet himself) in their original order, whether because they constitute coherent groups or because they had in any case been grouped with their comrades, as dealing with a common topic or a single event or constituting part of an exchange of poems. Such an arrangement of poems—in the order they were found by the editor—is found not only in the *Gan ha-M^{e}šalim* (edited at the end of the thirteenth century) but also in *diwans* written before the time of Abraham Ibn Ezra: *Ben T^{e}hillim* (whose composition began—according to Yehoseph in his preface—in 1044), and the *diwan* of Isaac Ibn Ḥalfon, of which the two manuscript fragments discovered in the Cairo Genizah were almost certainly copied in the early twelfth century.[165] These two fragments together contain twenty-six poems; Hayyim Schirmann concluded from them that "Ibn Ḥalfon's *diwan* was not arranged by topic or by rhyme scheme, as was the custom in most Arabic *diwans*." [166]

In fact, arranging the contents of a *diwan* in an appropriate order was not the principal task of an editor. Priority, in terms of time and importance, was taken by many other difficult labors: gathering the scattered poems, verifying their attribution to the poet, clarifying the circumstances of their composition, and identifying the people to whom they were addressed. To the extent possible, and in accordance with his capacity, the editor might also endeavor to establish the correct text of the poem and determine the meter, melody, and literary genre. Schirmann calls attention (in the article cited in note 166) to two references to Ibn Ḥalfon in *Sefer ha-Riḳmah*, whence much can be learned about the wide circulation of poetry, both orally and in manuscript, about mistaken attributions of poems made even during the lifetime of their authors (see Ibn Ganach, *Ha-Riḳmah,* p. 320), and about grammarians' pretenses to emend texts to eliminate not only errors of transmission but also solecisms committed by the poets themselves (ibid., pp. 226–27).[167] The greater the distance in time and place between editor and poet, so much more difficult was it for the former to verify the latter's authorship of poems attributed to him. This is evidenced not only by the fact that the manuscripts attribute many poems to the wrong poets, but also by the doubts about the poet's identity found in the headings of many poems,[168] as well as by Yeshuah ben Elijah's uncertainty about finding any internal criterion for identifying an author other than the acrostic, which, given the multiplicity of poets with the same first name, can hardly be relied upon.[169] Moreover, it is even more difficult to fulfill these tasks when we are speaking not of a collection, which limits itself to poems by a single author, but of an anthology (*maǵmūʿat šiʿr*), which incorporates poems by many authors. Such anthologies were known among the Arabs since ancient times,[170] and were also widespread among the Jews of Spain (see Schirmann, "Poets," p. 126). It seems quite plausible that Ibn Ezra had them in mind in his attempt to understand the problems involved in editing the Book of Psalms.

Ibn Ezra ignores two questions: first, how were the psalms transmitted to the Men of the Great Assembly—orally or in writing? Second, what were their criteria for deciding which psalms should be included in the book and which should be discarded? It is clear in any case that for him the exalted status of these editors was a complete guarantee both of the textual accuracy of the psalms[171] and of the fact that all were composed with divine inspiration.[172] He takes these points as given despite his acknowledgement of the fact that the editors had no information about the identity of many poets and about the circumstances in which many psalms were composed. Consequently they did not arrange the psalms in chronological order, nor did they classify them by author (as should be done in an anthology of the works of multiple poets); instead, they wrote them down one after another in five books, evidently according to the order in which they found them. If this is an accurate reconstruction of Ibn Ezra's position, he probably held that the incomplete nature of the information that reached the Men of the Great Assembly did not undermine the reliability of the tradition they had inherited; on the contrary, it strengthened it, because their failure to arrange the psalms and complete their headings—as might be expected from top-flight editors—is indirect evidence that the information that is contained in the book (from the sanctity of the psalms and the reliability of their text through the details conveyed by their headings) is not their own invention or opinion, but a received tradition handed down from their predecessors. Unlike the *diwan* and anthology, reliability is preferable to thorough editing when it comes to the Holy Scriptures. True, the psalms are not linked, but there is no doubt about their sanctity.

B. Two different explanations of the problematic term mizmor

Ibn Ezra's conclusion that "every psalm stands by itself" leads him to consider the meaning of the word *mizmor* before that of *la-mᵉnaṣṣeaḥ*, with which he had intended to begin his discussion of the terminology used in the headings. At first glance it would seem obvious that *mizmor* indicates poetry and song (*zimrah*) and refers to songs of praise and thanksgiving; but the fact that this designation is also found in the headings of poems of complaint and supplication (such as psalms 3 and 79) requires a different explanation. As is his wont, Ibn Ezra begins with a concise and not particularly lucid presentation of a solution that he does not accept: "The word *mizmor*, in the opinion of Rabbi Moses ha-Kohen, is related to 'you shall not . . . prune [*tizmor*] your vineyard' (Lev. 25:4), i.e., something that is severed and stands by itself, as with the word for poem in Arabic'' (lines 111f.). Also Ibn Ezra holds that every psalm stands by itself; but is their autonomy so essential to their nature that one can say that *mizmor* means ''something that is severed and stands by itself''? Did it originally belong to a cluster of psalms, so that it can be said to have been severed from them? Furthermore, the Arabic *mazmūr* does indeed designate a poem, but the root *zamara* means playing the flute, not cutting and severing. How, then, could Ibn Giqatilah rely on the analogy with Arabic? In his commentary on Ps. 79:1 Ibn Ezra again mentions his predecessor's opinion; even though there too his phrasing is terse and laconic it may help us understand the matter. There he writes: ''some say that *mizmor* [means] something that is cut off and severed from many, perhaps they were dirges.''[173] The superiority of this formulation is that it allows us to infer that Ibn Giqatilah actually did mean severing in the sense of detaching, and that in his opinion a poem called a *mizmor* originally belonged to a collection of poems or to a comprehensive unit composed of many parts. Because this comprehensive unit could be devoted to any subject, happy or sad, he assumes that Psalm 79, being a dirge, was detached from a cycle of dirges. In fact we know of large compositions comprising individual *piyyuṭim,* both in classical liturgical poetry, where they are known as ''verse *piyyuṭim*'' and ''word *piyyuṭim*'' (see E. Fleischer, *Poetry,* p. 170), and in Spanish liturgical poetry, such as the *maᶜamad* for the Day of Atonement, which consisted of dozens of separate *piyyuṭim* of various sorts closely interwoven into a single framework, which was ultimately dismembered because of its size (ibid., p. 377). Even though we have not found an Arabic etymological parallel to the derivation of *mizmor* from a root meaning ''sever,'' there is a semantic parallel: the nouns *ḳiṭᶜa* and *maḳṭūᶜa*, which mean a section or chapter (of a melody, song or text), a short poem, or a refrain,[174] are derived from the root *ḳaṭaᶜa* 'cut'. Thus Ibn Giqatilah's suggestion that *mizmor* means something cut off seems much less astonishing when grounded on the Arabic parallel, which, according to Ibn Ezra's precise wording, is literary rather than linguistic—''as with the word for poem in Arabic.''

Since Ibn Ezra does not rebut his explanation, we must assume that he thought it reasonable and possible. But he at once proposes his own solution, which he prefaces with a typical formula of personal preference—''but in my opinion the correct answer is. . . .'' This opinion is that the word *mizmor* is derived, as is conventionally assumed, from *zamar* ''sing''; his innovation is that as a literary term he defines it as: ''a poem [performed] in accordance with the musical art, and adapted fully to its purpose and time, be it for joy or sadness. We have thus:'[*mizmor* l^e*-Dawid*] when he fled from his son Absalom' (3), [on the one hand, and] '*Mizmor l*^{e}*-ʾAsaf.* O God, heathens have entered Your domain' (79), [on the other]'' (lines 112–16). Although the wording of the original is difficult, its meaning is clear enough: the word *mizmor* indicates both happy and sad poems, since originally the sense is not a poem of happiness but a poem that is chanted, i.e., a poem whose distinguishing characteristic is that it is intended from the outset to be sung, so that its words and melody must correspond fully. In the language of the Spanish Jews *ʾamar* (influenced by the Arabic *ḳāla*) also means ''compose poetry''; accordingly the words ''adapted fully to its purpose and time'' refer to the subject of the poem, which is not limited *a priori* but reflects the nature of the moment of its composition—a happy poem in a time of joy, a sad poem in a time of woe.

From the end of the definition we shall return now to the beginning of the sentence (which we have translated as ''a poem [performed] in accordance with the musical art''), which contains two rare and difficult words—*maʿareḵeṯ* and *maṯkoneṯ*. For Ibn Ezra the noun *maʿareḵeṯ* indicates, inter alia, a ''row'' or ''series'' (comm. on Gen. 49:12 and Lev. 24:6), an ''order'' or ''category'' (comm. on Lev. 27:8), and specifically a ''constellation'' (comm. on Gen. 6:2–3; Deut. 5:26; and Job 38:7). *Maṯkoneṯ* too has this astrological sense of a group of heavenly bodies (comm. on Job 2:14 and Eccles. 3:1), as well as the senses of ''natural law,'' ''essence,'' ''nature'' (Ibn Ezra, *Religious Poems*, vol. 2. p. 90, line 9; long commentary on Ex. 25:40 and long commentary on Daniel 2:2) and ''measure'' or ''proportion'' (long commentary on Ex. 30:32 and Isa. 40:12). Accordingly the sense of the sentence in question is something like this: poem is called *mizmor* when it (i.e., its words) coincides with a musical system (*maʿareḵeṯ*) and creates with it a unified complex or ensemble (*maṯkoneṯ*). This explanation of the word *mizmor* is compatible with the theoretical concept that Ibn Ezra developed in the musicological section at the beginning of the first introduction, whose core is ''when instrumental music is joined with the poem, then will marvels be beheld'' (line 11; see the discussion above, pp. 162–168). Moreover, a presentation of the psalm as a unified musical and linguistic ensemble provides a sort of preamble to his great innovation (in the Fourth Inquiry) about the melodic codes found in the headings of the psalms. Both the concept of poetry and the exegetical applications thereof are deeply rooted in the poetical practice with which Ibn Ezra was familiar in Spain—the blossoming of girdle poems, whose subjects were quite varied, and which were originally intended to be sung to an instrumental accompaniment, as is attested, inter alia, by the melodic directives found in their headings (see below, pp. 251–57).

All the same, Ibn Ezra offers another solution to the enigmatic appearance of the word *mizmor* in the heading of psalms like 3 and 79, whose subject matter does not seem to be appropriate for song. "Some say" that the descriptions of distress and the entreaties for divine salvation found in these psalms are not to be understood literally, because the poets, who as prophets are endowed with an infallible view of the future, can "speak as they wish," that is, they can deviate from customary forms of speech and describe future events in the past tense.[175] Ibn Ezra notes that he has already explained this matter of the prophetic past, but since he does not say where, this is hardly a reference to a particular locus in his earlier writings.[176] It would seem, then, that "as I have explained" is intended to free him of the need to present multiple examples of this stylistic phenomenon (he makes do with "Jeshurun grew fat and kicked" [Deut. 32:15], which he cites as an example of the prophetic past in his commentary on Jonah 2:2 as well); at the same time, it must be emphasized that there really is a solid and independent linguistic underpinning to this solution of the problem of *mizmor.* Over the years Ibn Ezra even came to think more highly of this solution, since in the standard commentary on Psalms 3 and 79 he presents it while omitting the solution offered in the first introduction. In the standard commentary on Psalm 3:1 he offers only one solution, which is identical with what "some say" in the first recension:"*mizmor*—prophetically, [i.e.,] he prophesied that he would be victorious, hence 'and He answered me from His holy mountain'(3:5), [which is] like Jonah's 'and my prayer came before You' (Jonah 2:8). In other words, because the prayer for salvation was answered while it was still being uttered, it ceases being a prayer and becomes a song of thanksgiving and praise that does indeed merit the designation *mizmor.* Ibn Ezra does not feel any need to indicate that this response was expressed by means of the prophetic past, merely mentioning the analogous phenomenon in Jonah's prayer (which is in fact explained there). In his commentary on 79:1 he first offers, under the rubric "some say," Ibn Giqatilah's hypothesis (cited and discussed above); then, instead of the two alternatives offered in the first introduction, he proposes only that "the meaning of *mizmor* is that he saw by the Holy Spirit, because of what he wrote at the end, that Israel is His nation and His inheritance." This is quite similar to what he had said about Psalm 3; from the wording of the first introduction, however, it is clear that the meaning is somewhat different. In the first introduction he does more than merely quote verse 13 to prove that Asaph saw by the Holy Spirit that God would save his nation and flock; he also argues that "heathens have entered Your domain" is prophetic past. Indeed, for someone who believes, like Ibn Ezra, that Asaph was a contemporary of David, it follows that the distress of "they turned Jerusalem into ruins" (79:1) cannot be understood as the actual distress of the worshipper, but as a prophetic description of future woes. Thus we must say that Psalm 79 not only concludes with a prophecy, like Psalm 3, but also begins with one; if so, it is even more appropriate that it be called *mizmor*, i.e., a song praising God, who promises to save his people from troubles that have not yet befallen them.

We cannot say that Ibn Ezra held fast to his previous conception of the meaning of *mizmor,* and merely failed to apply it to Psalms 3 and 79, because "prophetically" (comm. on 3:1) clearly attests that when he wrote the standard commentary he believed that *mizmor* meant a song of praise. No reason or explanation is given for this return to the conventional view; any attempt on our part to explain it must begin and end with the fact that abandoning his novel opinion about the neutral character of the designation *mizmor* was bound up with his emphasis on the prophetic nature of the two psalms in question. Whereas it is only with difficulty that a view of these psalms as dirges and complaints can be made compatible with understanding them as prophetic, it certainly contradicts perceiving them as prophecies of salvation. So long as we do not have Ibn Ezra's first commentary on Psalms we cannot know whether he there interpreted Psalms 3 and 79 in accordance with the sense of *mizmor* presented in the introduction. In any case, some years later he clearly attached great importance to interpreting them as songs in praise of God who had saved his people, even at the cost of conceding his original explanation of the term *mizmor* as a musical and liturgical rather than thematic designation.[177]

In a sort of appendix to his discussion of the word *mizmor* Ibn Ezra notes that he sees no difference between *mizmor le-David* and *le-David mizmor.* His proof is that " 'ḥayyim tifśum' and 'tifśum ḥayyim' (1 Kings 20:18) both mean 'take them alive' " (lines 122f.). This is obviously directed against the Sages' distinction that "*l*^e*-Dawid mizmor* means that the Divine Spirit rested upon him and then he composed the poem, whereas *mizmor l*^e*-Dawid* means that he composed the poem and after that the Divine Spirit rested upon him" (BT Pesaḥim 117a); he insists that there is no basis for this distinction in the plain meaning of the text. Still, he discusses this issue in other contexts as well, e.g., in the standard commentary on 48:1: "We cannot distinguish between *šir mizmor* (loc. cit.) and *mizmor šir* (30:1 et passim), nor between *mi-ṣur ḥalamiš* (Deut. 8:15) and *mi-ḥalmiš ṣur* (Deut. 32:13)" (cf. his commentary on Deut. 32:13 and Ps. 89:44). Thus it would seem that this linguistic question interested him for its own sake, apparently because the answer also had implications for the definition of acceptable practice in the language of liturgical and secular poetry. In his criticism of the faulty language of the liturgical poets (commentary on Eccles. 5:1) he cites the example of the defective style of a French liturgical poet, who had written: "For Your name is in You, and in You is Your name." This is absurd, according to Ibn Ezra, purely with regard to the content; furthermore "once he said 'for Your name is in You'—that is the very same thing as 'in You is Your name'! For what is the difference between *šalom ʿaleḵa* and *ʿaleḵa šalom;* between *Reuben ʾattah* or *ʾattah Reuben*; between 'ḥayyim tifśum' and 'tifśum ḥayyim'; or between 'may the Lord bless you and preserve you' (Num. 6:24) and 'may the Lord preserve you from all evil' (Ps. 121:7)?! This is not a prayer, but a joke!'' Ibn Ezra brings two proofs from everyday speech and two from Scripture to prove that the order of words has no effect on the meaning. This conclusion is compatible with his fundamental understanding that ''the words are like bodies and the meanings like spirits,'' so that the content does not change when synonyms are substituted for one another, auxiliaries are deleted, or the internal order of the components is modified for some reason (see his detailed argument in the long commentary on Exodus, introduction to chapter 20). It is not astonishing, then, that the tautologous style of the French liturgical poet strikes him as illegitimate and that he attacks it so vehemently. By contrast, it is somewhat surprising that he uses moderate language—''in my opinion''—when he refers to the very same linguistic issue in the first introduction (written not so long after the Ecclesiastes commentary). It seems likely that respect for the Sages, or consideration for the sentiments of his readers, led Ibn Ezra to moderate his criticism of what he considered to be an illegitimate stylistic distinction, by omitting explicit identification of its adherents and by presenting his own view as a personal conclusion (though accompanied by a strong proof from Scripture).

C. Two explanations of la-mᵉnaṣṣeaḥ

Following his discussion of the word *mizmor*, which is the first ''technical'' term found in the heading of a psalm (3:1), Ibn Ezra takes up the next such term—*la-mᵉnaṣṣeaḥ* (4:1 et passim). Before clarifying its meaning he discusses its provenance: ''we find this word only in the words of David, and in the [other] psalms and in the prayer of Habakkuk, which is in the style of the Book of Psalms'' (lines 124f.). There can be no doubt that ''in the words of David'' refers to the many psalms ascribed to David whose superscriptions include the word *la-mᵉnaṣṣeaḥ*. Hence the somewhat astonishing phrase ''and in the [other] psalms'' must refer to the eight Koraḥide psalms and the four by Asaph, which also are introduced by the term *la-mᵉnaṣṣeaḥ* (we have consequently supplied ''other'' on the assumption that it may have been accidentally omitted by the copyist). In any case Ibn Ezra had obviously gone from indicating the author to indicating the genre, to make it plain that all these are poetry. In fact, the only occurrence of *la-mᵉnaṣṣeaḥ* outside thc Book of Psalms comes at the end of Habakkuk's prayer (Hab. 3:19), whose essentially poetic nature he proves (in the continuation of the sentence quoted above as well as in the standard commentary on Ps. 3:3 and Hab. 3:1) by citing three additional psalmic terms found in it—"ᶜal šigyonot" (3:1), "bi-nᵉginotai" (verse 19), and "selah" (verses 3, 9, 13). Thus its provenance demonstrates that *la-mᵉnaṣṣeaḥ* must be a poetic or musical term.

The commentators were divided as to the meaning of *la-mᵉnaṣṣeaḥ;* as in many other places Ibn Ezra first presents an opinion he considers to be wrong—that *mᵉnaṣṣᵉḥim* are "the officers in charge of the singers" (lines 129f.). This sense, says Ibn Ezra, can be inferred from the ratio of fifty to one between the 153,600 aliens conscripted by King Solomon (2 Chron. 2:16) and the 3,600 "supervisors to see that the people worked" (verse 17), which clearly attests that the latter were appointed over the former. Though I have not found a similar reliance on arithmetical computation in the writings of Ibn Ezra's predecessors, it is easy to identify the advocates of this interpretation. Salmon ben Yeruḥam and Yefet ben ᶜAli rendered the word *la-mᵉnaṣṣeaḥ* in the headings of the Psalms as *li-l-mustaḥitt* 'to the repetiteur'. Yefet explains its use in his commentary on Ps. 4:1: "In our opinion, with regard to every psalm with *la-mᵉnaṣṣeaḥ* in its heading, the meaning is that the head of the [Levitical] division led the singers of that division in repeating this psalm; it may be that they repeated it a number of times, as might be necessary at the moment." David al-Fasi, too (*Dictionary*, s.v. *nṣḥ*), explains it as meaning "to coach," but distinguishes between two sub-meanings. When it is the psalmist himself who "coaches" the singers, his role is to teach them how to declaim it, which is why the *mᵉnaṣṣeaḥ* is also called *mevin* 'master' (cf. 1 Chron. 25:8: "master and apprentice alike"). But when some other *mᵉnaṣṣeaḥ* is mentioned alongside the poet (as in the superscription of Psalm 39: "For the *mᵉnaṣṣeaḥ;* for Jeduthun. A psalm of David"), the second *mᵉnaṣṣeaḥ* is responsible for the actual performance of the psalm by the singers. In contrast to these three Karaite scholars, Ibn Ganach (*Dictionary*, s.v. *nṣḥ*) glossed the term as meaning an officer responsible for the service in the Temple (1 Chron. 23:4; Ezra 3:9) or for the performance of the psalms (1 Chron. 15:21; Ps. 4:1; Hab. 3:19)—precisely the first opinion cited by Ibn Ezra. Similarly, Ibn Giqatilah (comm. on Ps. 4:1; see "Psalms," p. 157), translates "la-mᵉnaṣṣeaḥ bi-nᵉginot" as the "master of the musical instruments," and explains that the reference is to the musician who performs the psalm composed by David.

The second opinion Ibn Ezra offers and adopts as his own: "Some say—and I think they are correct—that the word is derived from *neṣaḥ* [forever], and that *la-mᵉnaṣṣeaḥ* means 'to a musician who always plays' " (lines 133f.). According to this, *mᵉnaṣṣeaḥ* means someone who plays all the time; in order to anchor this temporal meaning of *mᵉnaṣṣeaḥ* in the circumstances in which the psalms were chanted in the Temple, he cites the musicians' exemption from all other duties so that they would always be free to sing: "Now these are the singers, the chiefs of Levitical clans, who remained in the chambers free of other service, for they were on duty *day and night*" (1 Chron. 9:33). Ibn Ezra strengthens this argument in favor of the second opinion by refuting the first one. The proportion of fifty to one found among the builders of the Temple does not apply to the musicians, since, out of 38,000 Levites counted late in David's reign, some 24,000—more than half—had "charge of the work of the House of the Lord" (1 Chron. 23:3–4); so large a number must be the performers themselves rather than foremen supervising the work of others. It hardly seems likely that Ibn Ezra knew that the Septuagint and Vulgate understand *la-m^{e}naṣṣeaḥ* in the temporal sense of *neṣaḥ*—eternity; he must have thought that this derivation originated with Saadiah, since he attributes it to him in the standard commentary on Ps. 4:1: "The Gaon said that this psalm is by David, who gave it to one of the musicians to perform it all the time, like *la-neṣaḥ*." In fact, in Saadiah's *Tafsir* on Psalms *la-m^{e}naṣṣeaḥ* is frequently rendered "wasabbaḥa bihi ʾal-muwāẓibīn": "those who do [something] all the time will sing it." It is not clear *what* they do all the time; Rabbi Ḳafiḥ, in his back-translation to Hebrew, expands it to "those who are always on their watch." From Ibn Ezra's paraphrase—"a musician who always plays"—we can infer that he understood Saadiah to mean those who *sing* all the time. Ibn Ezra employs a singular noun, corresponding to the number of *la-m^{e}naṣṣeaḥ;* Saadiah's use of the plural evidently indicates that he understood the term as a collective reference to the Levitical choir.

Saadiah is more explicit about the meaning of *la-m^{e}naṣṣeaḥ* in his long introduction to Psalms, in his description of the two aspects of the Levites' performance of the psalms—initially to accompany the construction of the Temple, and thereafter as part of the Temple ritual ("Psalms," pp. 26–27). Because this explanation seems to be very different from his translation of the term in his *Tafsir,* we cite the passage in full:

> One of the things connected with the construction of the Temple is that the Levites used it [i.e., the Book of Psalms] to encourage [*yuhiṭṭu*] the work until it was completed; for we find *la-m^{e}naṣṣeaḥ* in this book many times, and Chronicles explains that it means encouraging the work, as it says: "Of these there were 24,000 to urge the work [i.e., the building] of the House of the Lord" (23:4); similarly in Ezra: "They appointed Levites from the age of twenty and upward to urge the work [i.e., the building] of the House of the Lord" (3:8). The members of the watch chanted it [i.e., the Book of Psalms] all night and all day, each group what [i.e., that portion of the Book] that was assigned to it, as it says: "Now these are the singers, the chiefs of the Levitical clans, who remained in the chambers free of other service, [for they were on duty day and night]" (1 Chron. 9:33).

Not only is there nothing here about the derivation of *la-m^enaṣṣeaḥ* from *neṣaḥ;* twice Saadiah had recourse to the idea of encouragement, which seems to coincide with how Karaite exegesis understood *la-m^enaṣṣeaḥ* (see above). In order to resolve the contradiction between the introduction and the *Tafsir* we must carefully follow the argument in the former. According to it, the obscure indication *la-m^enaṣṣeaḥ*, found in the heading of many psalms, is to be interpreted on the basis of two scriptural passages—1 Chron. 23:4 and Ezra 3:8—where we read that the Levites were charged *l^e-naṣṣeaḥ* during the construction of the First and Second Temples. In Saadiah's opinion this recurring language implies that the Levites were charged with using the psalms to assist in the construction work; it is clear to him that this means that they sang to encourage the workers.[178] Saadiah reached this conclusion, not through a philological investigation of the derivation of *la-m^enaṣṣeaḥ,* but through a semantic inquiry after the common denominator of its various appearances. He also implicitly assumes that the numerous *la-m^enaṣṣeaḥ* psalms were sung by the Levites as part of the divine service even after the construction of the two Temples was completed, so that *la-m^enaṣṣeaḥ* must have a meaning in this ritual context as well. Here too, however, Saadiah does not explicitly assert that it is derived from *neṣaḥ* in the sense of eternity or persistence, although at the end of the passage he cites 1 Chron. 9:33, which he takes to mean that the singers were exempted from other forms of service "for they were on duty day and night," i.e., they had to sing all the time, and chant the specific psalms allocated to each family. Note that at the end of the passage he no longer speaks of encouragement, but rather of the sense of chanting day and night; hence even at the beginning of the passage he cannot see encouragement as the fundamental meaning of *la-m^enaṣṣeaḥ*. Furthermore, the fact that in translating the headings of the psalms Saadiah generally supplemented *la-m^enaṣṣeaḥ* with the verb *yusabbiḥu* "sing praises" indicates that, following Rabbi Joshua ben Levi (BT Pesaḥim 117a), he considered *niṣṣuaḥ* to be one of the ten terms of praise used in the Book of Psalms. It seems likely, then, that for him *l^e-naṣṣeaḥ* means "to sing all the time," whether in order to encourage the builders or as part of the Temple service.

From this excursus we learn that Ibn Ezra's first proof in the first introduction (drawn from 1 Chron. 9:33) was borrowed from Saadiah, while his second proof (based on 1 Chron. 23:3–4) is evidently his own original contribution. Still, despite Ibn Ezra's acceptance of Saadiah's idea and his attempts to strengthen it, he eventually abandoned it. In the standard commentary on 4:1 he wrote: "Others said that the *m^enaṣṣeaḥ* is the supervisor over the singers, like 'supervising them' (2 Chron. 2:1), and this is correct.[179] The *lamed* of *la-m^enaṣṣeaḥ* has a *pataḥ* because it represents the definite article." Since the reason for this surprising change of opinion is never made explicit, we can only hypothesize why he abandoned Saadiah's interpretation. We can start from the passage cited as a proof—"supervising them" (2 Chron. 2:1). First, this verse (like 2 Chron. 2:17) speaks of *m^{e}naṣṣ^{e}ḥim* who are not Levites; hence it is only logical that they had nothing to do with singing and playing, but with supervision and management. Second, this text (like the others) links the verb *naṣṣeaḥ* with the preposition *ʿal* "over"; while this suits the sense of supervision and control, it is incompatible with the meaning of constant performance. As against these two considerations, the large number of Levites who had "charge of the work of the House of the Lord" (1 Chron. 23:4), raised by Ibn Ezra as proof of Saadiah's interpretation, remains a problem. One possible answer is that the next verse—"four thousand for praising the Lord with instruments I devised for singing praises"—makes clear that the 24,000 *m^{e}naṣṣ^{e}ḥim* had nothing to do with singing and musical performance. Thus we are forced to conclude that they supervised the construction of the Temple or were responsible for its maintenance.

D. The enigmatic expressions in the superscriptions as melodic indications

The discussion of *la-m^{e}naṣṣeaḥ* in the first introduction is followed by that of "la-m^{e}naṣṣeaḥ bi-n^{e}ginoṯ" (which first appears in the superscription of Psalm 4). This time he does not start with his predecessors' opinions, but proceeds straightaway to present his own interpretation of most of the enigmatic expressions found in the headings of the psalms:

> In my opinion, the Israelites had many melodies before the time of David. Here he indicates the melody by quoting the first word of the song, which is "bi-n^{e}ginoṯ," and similarly: "ʿal n^{e}ginaṯ l^{e}-Dawid" (61:1); the proof being that [the word *n^{e}ginaṯ*] is in the construct case and the *taw* is [preceded] by a *pataḥ*. The same is true for "ʿal maḥalaṯ l^{e}-ʿannoṯ" (Ps. 88:1)—[*maḥalaṯ*] is a construct derived from "any disease [*maḥalah*]" (1 Kings 8:37) as I will explain, although many have explained that it is derived from *maḥol* [= dance]. (lines 138–142)

It is hard to distinguish between the two terms *n^{e}ginoṯ* and *n^{e}ʿimoṯ* which he uses in the first sentence, because Ibn Ezra glosses "bi-n^{e}ginot" in the heading of Psalm 4 as "it has two *n^{e}ʿimoṯ*," whereas he glosses the same word in the heading of Psalm 76 as "with different *n^{e}ginoṯ*," and his meaning is clearly identical in the two places. Moreover, while there is no doubt that for him the word *noʿam* (in the second sentence of the passage cited above) is synonymous with the Arabic *laḥn*,[180] he uses the plural form *n^{e}ʿimoṯ*[181] in various senses: as a synonym for *n^{e}ginoṯ* (as in this passage) and also to mean musical tones or notes (commentary on Ps. 150:6: "R. Judah [Ḥayyuj] said, [this is] because the musician played *neʿimoṯ* on the lyre, which changed according to the length of the breath and the shortness of the sound, its pitch (treble or bass), or its speed, which is why he concluded, 'let all that breathes praise the Lord')."[182] Indeed, not only is Ibn Ezra not terribly consistent in his use of musical terms, to increase our perplexity he frequently uses them in a tautological medley. It is in any case clear that in the first sentence of the passage quoted above Ibn Ezra is saying that even before the composition of most of the psalms Israel had a well-developed musical culture. Some of these older melodies, composed for secular songs, were adopted for the performance of the sacred poetry; the melody in question was indicated in the superscription of the psalm by means of the first word(s) of the song whose melody was being borrowed, e.g., "bi-n^{e}ginoṯ" in Psalm 4 and "ʿal n^{e}ginaṯ" in Psalm 61. That "n^{e}ginaṯ" is in the construct state (as shown by the *pataḥ* under the *nun* and the final *taw*) proves, according to Ibn Ezra, the correctness of his view, since a construct with no supporting noun is clearly a truncated quotation.[183] Another proof is the construct noun without a noun in the absolute state in "ʿal maḥalaṯ l^{e}-ʿannoṯ" (88:1), since, in opposition to the view of many, "maḥalaṯ" is not the feminine form of the musical instrument *maḥol*, but rather the construct state of *maḥalah* "illness".[184] He cannot apply these proofs to "bi-n^{e}ginoṯ," the starting point for his exposition of this opinion, however, because in the plural there is no difference between the construct and absolute states; thus it is perfectly possible to understand "*bi-n^{e}ginoṯ*" as standing by itself as an instruction to the performer. In fact, in his commentary on Psalm 4:1, where he first presents this idea in the standard commentary, he initially offers two variants on this alternative understanding:

> The meaning of "*bi-n^{e}ginoṯ*" is that it has two melodies; but some say [it refers to] a musical instrument called "*n^{e}ginoṯ*." In my opinion, the Israelites had many melodies and songs, and the meaning of "*bi-n^{e}ginoṯ*" is that this was the beginning of a song, and the melody for this psalm is indicated in this way.[185] Similarly, [we have] "*la-maʿaloṯ*" (121:1) and "*ha-maʿaloṯ*" (120:1 et passim), "*ʿal ʿalamoṯ*" (46:1), "*ʿal ʾayyeleṯ ha-šaḥar*" (22:1), "*ʿal yonaṯ ʾelem*" (56:1), and "*al maḥalaṯ*" (53:1 and 88:1).

The first opinion, that "bi-n^{e}ginoṯ" indicates that the psalm should be played with "two melodies," is phrased somewhat differently in his gloss on the heading of Psalm 76: " '*bi-n^{e}ginoṯ*'—with different melodies." The second formulation clearly attests that this view originated with Saadiah, who not only translated the six occurrences of "*bi-n^e^ginoṯ*" as "*biʾalḥān*" "with melodies" (Yefet used the identical rendering, while Salmon ben Yeruḥam employed the similar "*bi-n-naǵamāt*"), but also explained in his long introduction (*Psalms*, p. 31) that this musical indication means that the melody should be changed while the song is being sung. The advocates of the second opinion, namely, that "neginoṯ" is the name of a musical instrument, are Menaḥem Ben Saruk and Moses Ibn Giqatilah. In his *Maḥbereṯ* (s.v. *gaṯ*) Menaḥem explained that "n^e^ginoṯ" is a musical instrument; Ibn Giqatilah, in his commentary on Ps. 4:1, wrote that the designations *n^e^ginoṯ*, *š^e^miniṯ*, and *gittiṯ* indicate on which instrument the *m^e^naṣṣeaḥ* performed when the psalm in question was sung (Finkel, "Psalms," pp. 157 and 161). In contrast to all these, Ibn Ezra offers his own original interpretation, according to which "bi-n^e^ginoṯ" is not a performance instruction, whatever the meaning, but rather the first word of a well-known song, whose citation serves to indicate its melody. He brings six additional examples of such melodic cues, garnered from all over the Book of Psalms, not in the order of the psalms themselves and apparently with no thematic or systematic arrangement. These six are all mentioned in the first introduction, as part of the survey of the other thirteen cues (in addition to the three already discussed—"bi-n^e^ginoṯ," "ʿal n^e^ginaṯ," and "ʿal maḥalaṯ"), which are enumerated there in order of their appearance in the book.[186] Since we cannot explicate his rather terse language in the introduction on the basis of what he may have added in the body of the lost commentary, we must rely on what he wrote about them in the standard commentary *ad loc*.

1. "*ʾEl ha-n^e^ḥiloṯ*" (5:1): Ibn Ezra adds nothing on this cue in the introduction, but in his commentary *ad loc.* he proves that the prepostions *ʾel* and *ʿal* are used interchangeably in Scripture, and that "ha-n^e^ḥiloṯ" is "the beginning of a poem" and is cited to indicate the melody. He adds a cautious hypothesis about the derivation and form of the word: namely, that "n^e^ḥiloṯ" is like *n^e^ḥaloṯ*, and the plural form with a medial *yod* may indicate a singular form *n^e^ḥilah*, on the pattern of *ʾaḵilah*. Because of the fundamental importance of this issue Ibn Ezra also discusses it in his *Defense* of Saadiah (§64), even though Dunash had not attacked Saadiah on this point. There Ibn Ezra begins with precise information: "ʾEl ha-n^e^ḥiloṯ—Saadiah said: this word connotes prayer, from [the same root as] 'and Moses implored [*wa-y^e^ḥal*]' (Ex. 32:11), but Dunash said nothing about it." Ibn Ezra continues (since the text of the Lippman edition is corrupt, we cite according to MS Parma 314): "In my opinion the correct answer is that it is the beginning of a psalm, like a *piyyuṭ*, and the meaning is according to a certain melody."[187] That is: "Ha-n^e^ḥiloṯ" is the first word of another

psalm,just as in Ibn Ezra's own day it was customary to include in the superscription of one liturgical poem the opening words of another *piyyuṭ*, as a means of indicating the melody identified with the latter. We shall return later to discuss this reliance on the conventions of twelfth-century Spanish poetry; for now we must consider the interesting aside at the end of his remarks: "If we knew where to find that psalm, we could inquire about the meaning of "nᵉḥiloṯ"; perhaps it is a plural form of *nᵉḥaloṯ*."[188] Since the psalm to which the melodic indication refers has been lost, we possess insufficient information to uncover the literal meaning of the term in its original context. Moreover, this elucidation is quite unnecessary because it has no bearing on the exegesis of the text at hand—as a cue such words relate to the forgotten melody of the psalm and not to its content. True, Ibn Ezra is willing to offer a cautious hypothesis about the form and meaning of "nᵉḥiloṯ," merely as a contribution to biblical lexicography rather than as exegesis. Here Ibn Ezra discloses the fundamental point of his theory of melodic indications: it makes no attempt to explicate their literal meaning, for only their function is at issue, thus divorcing them from the body of the psalm and any link with its content.

2. "*ʿAl ha-šᵉminiṯ*" (6:1; 12:1): Here, and in his commentary on the heading of Psalm 6, Ibn Ezra notes that "some say" that *šᵉminiṯ* is a musical instrument with eight strings, just as *nevel ʿasor* is a ten-stringed lyre. We have already seen that this is the opinion of Menaḥem and of Ibn Giqatilah;[189] to them should be added Moses Ibn Ezra, who used "*ʿal ha-šᵉminiṯ*" to prove that the ancient Israelites were familiar with the eight-stringed *ʿud* (see above, p. 169). In the continuation of his commentary on Ps. 6:1, Ibn Ezra writes: "Or [it may mean] a liturgical poem with eight melodies, which is why it says '*bi-nᵉginoṯ*,' referring to the eighth melody." This seems to be taken from Saadiah, who translated the phrase in both psalms as "*bi-l-laḥn ʾṯ-ṯāmin*" 'to the eighth melody' and even explained this in his commentary on 6:1: "*ʿal ha-šᵉminiṯ* tells us that the Levites in the Temple had eight melodies, and each group was responsible for one of them" (*Psalms*, p. 61). On the other hand, his use of *piyyuṭ* indicates that Ibn Ezra is expressing his own opinion, namely, that the reference here is to another poem. It seems likely that "beginning of" or "melody of" has dropped out before the word "*piyyuṭ*," and his meaning is that "*bi-nᵉginoṯ*" refers to a poem that was sung to eight different melodies (whether it was inscribed as a musical indication at the beginning of that poem or was its first word), whereas "*ʿal ha-šᵉminiṯ*" indicates that our psalm is to be sung to the last of the eight melodies of that poem. Ibn Ezra briefly returns to this topic at the beginning of his commentary on Psalm 12: "*Ha-šᵉminiṯ*"—melody, poem, or string." The first suggestion repre-

sents Saadiah's opinion that this is the name of a melody; the second is Ibn Ezra's own opinion, namely, that this is an indirect reference to the melody via the name of a poem identified with it; while the third possibility represents the opinion of Menaḥem and Ibn Giqatilah that we are dealing with the name of the instrument characterized by the number of its strings. The failure to make a clearcut decision among these three options stems from the fact that since "*ha-šᵉminiṯ*" can certainly stand alone as a direction for performance Ibn Ezra saw no necessity to interpret it as a truncated quotation.

3. ["*Šiggayon*" (7:1)]: This term is skipped or was dropped unwittingly (see note 186) in the first introduction; in the standard commentary *ad loc.*, however, Ibn Ezra writes: "I think the correct answer is that it refers to a melody whose beginning is '*šiggayon* (concerning Cush')."[190] First, though, he cites two alternate explanations, whose common denominator is that the word indicates the genre of the psalm. According to the first opinion, the psalm is a love song to God (similar to the Ibero-Hebrew genre *ʾahavah*), since *šiggayon* means "pleasure, as in 'be infatuated [*tišgeh*] with love of her always' (Prov. 5:19)" (or as Ibn Ganach puts it in *Shorashim*, s.v. *šagah*: "joy and sweetness"). According to the second opinion this is a prayer for forgiveness, like the genre *sᵉliḥah*, since *šiggayon* is derived from *šᵉgagah*, "error." *Šiggayon* can certainly stand by itself, and Ibn Ezra found it plausible that the genre might be indicated in the superscription of a psalm (see below, §7), so he has no argument with those who so understand the term. The direction "*ʿal šigyonoṯ*," found at the beginning of the psalm of Habakkuk (3:1), closely resembles the melodic cues, and in his commentary *ad loc.* Ibn Ezra merely refers the reader to his Psalms commentary.

4. "*ʿAl ha-gittiṯ*" (8:1; 81:1; 84:1): In the introduction Ibn Ezra mentions two possible opinions without refuting them, whereas in his commentary *ad loc.* he mentions three and demurs at two of them. The first opinion presented in the introduction "derived at *gaṯ* [= winepress], as in 'like one who treads a press' (Isa. 63:2)"—is somewhat difficult to understand, so we shall leave it for the end of our discussion. The second interpretation offered in the introduction is identical to the first interpretation presented in the body of the commentary; in the introduction, though, it is attributed to Saadiah, whereas in the commentary it is both offered as Ibn Ezra's own suggestion and given the same degree of probability as his melodic cue theory: "This Psalm was given to the family of Obed-Edom the Gittite (2 Sam. 6:10–12), who was a Levite, like "*li-Yᵉduṯun*" (39:1)[191] [the correct reading, found in some MSS, is "*ʿal Yᵉduṯun*" 62:1; 77:1)] or

[perhaps there was] a *piyyuṭ* that began 'the Gittite [family] boasts' or something similar.'' Saadiah does not rely on the neat parallelism between ''*ʿal ha-gittiṯ*'' and ''*ʿal Yᵉduṯun*,'' nor is it mentioned in Ibn Ezra's first introduction. It seems likely, then, that Ibn Ezra discerned it later, and this is what motivated him to adopt Saadiah's suggestion. Understanding ''*ha-gittiṯ*'' as a reference to a melody absolves him of the need to gloss the word itself; on the other hand, it would be nice to provide it with some plausibility as the first word of a poem. To this end Ibn Ezra offers the hypothesis that the lost poem began, ''the Gittite [family] boasts'' or in similar vein. The third opinion, offered in the name of Ibn Giqatilah, is phrased in almost the same words used by Ibn Giqatilah in his commentary on Ps. 8:1: '''Gittith' [is] an instrument attributed to Obed-Edom the Gittite'' (Finkel, ''Psalms,'' pp. 158 and 162). Still, Ibn Ezra rejects this interpretation, because there is no biblical support for naming an instrument for those who play it—'We cannot find such an attribution.'' His demurral at the fourth opinion is much sharper: ''The praters say: to the melody [used by] those who trample in the winepress''; and at first glance it seems that he is rejecting out of hand the idea that psalms might have been sung in the Temple to tunes borrowed from secular songs. Not only is such a stance incompatible with his general theory about the adoption of the melodies of secular songs, he is quite explicit in his commentary on the superscription of Psalm 22 that the melody indicated there was borrowed from ''a poem dealing with amorous matters.'' If his opposition is not a matter of principle, then, it must be one of method,[192] and can be understood correctly once we have identified the interpretation it was aimed against. The object of his criticism seems to have been Yefet ben ʿAli, who wrote, in his commentary on Ps. 8:1: ''Some say that *gittiṯ* is a dance with leaping steps, because the singers leaped while chanting this psalm, much as people jump up and down in a winepress.'' Yefet prefers this opinion to others, because ''we have seen that David, peace be upon him, was leaping and dancing before the Lord [a reference to 1 Chron. 15:29],'' and concludes that ''it seems likely that they did not accompany the dance with a long drawn-out melody [*laḥn*], but [used] a staccato one appropriate for dancing and jumping.'' Even though Ibn Ezra himself believed that ''ha-gittiṯ'' refers to a melody, he saw this attempt to infer something about the nature of the melody and the choreography of the psalm from the derivation of the word as totally illegitimate. David al-Fasi, too (*Dictionary*, vol.1, p. 355) demurs at this interpretation, but whereas he says calmly that ''some say, with no proof, that the reference is to a dance,'' Ibn Ezra defines those who hold it as ''praters.'' Now we return to the first opinion in the introduction, which is also based on the assumption that *gittiṯ* is derived from *gaṯ*. It may be that the words ''as in 'like one who treads a press,' '' which seem to be superfluous, are intended merely to tell us that the reference is to the common noun *gat̲* "winepress," and not to the city of Gath (which is the assumption shared by Saadiah, Ibn Giqatilah, and Ibn Ezra, who all believe that "*ha-gittit̲*" is the name of a Levitical family from Gath). It is still not clear what "*ʿal ha-gittit̲*" means if this is its derivation; perhaps Ibn Ezra is alluding to an interpretation attributed by Ibn Giqatilah (in his commentary *ad loc.*) to "Christian commentaries": an instrument shaped like a winepress.

5. ["*Mik̲tam*" (16:1; 56:1; 57:1; 58:1; 59:1; 60:1)]: This term is not discussed in the Fourth Inquiry, despite Ibn Ezra's promise, at the beginning of that inquiry, to elucidate it. If this is not a case of the copyist's eye skipping ahead (see note 186), perhaps Ibn Ezra planned to defer his discussion of this word, and its partner *maśkil*, to the end of his survey, wanting to treat them separately because of their problematic nature, only to forget about them when he got there. In his commentary on Ps. 16:1 he writes: "A *mik̲tam* of David—this important psalm is like 'finest gold [*ke-t̲em paz*]' (Cant. 5:11), or [the reference may be to] the melody of a poem that began 'mik̲tam.' " Both interpretations are based on the assumption that "mik̲tam" refers to gold; but whereas the second interpretation sees it as the first word of a poem, serving to indicate a melody like all the other melodic cues, the first interpretation represents a new possibility—the excellence of the psalm is indicated in its superscription. The idea itself was not original with him; in his commentary on Ps. 80:1, he offers this concept in the name of Ibn Ganach: "Rabbi Marinus said that '*ʿedut̲*' is like '*ʿadi*' [= jewel], something excellent, and is also like 'the crown and the insignia [*ha-ʿedut̲*]' " (reading, along with many MSS, in accordance with 2 Kings 11:12). This is taken from Ibn Ganach (*Dictionary*, s.v. *ʿadah*) who even compares *ʿedut̲* and *mik̲tam:* "In my opinion 'and placed upon him the crown and the insignia' (2 Kings 11:12) comes from this root; [*ʿedut̲*] means ornament, and has the same vocalic pattern as '*teʾut̲ laveš*' (Ps. 93:1); another occurrence is '*ʿedut̲* of Asaph, a psalm' (80:1), which is like '*mik̲tam* of David' (16:1), which in turn is related to 'the finest gold [*ket̲em*] of Ophir' (Job 28:16), (and the meaning is that it is a precious saying),[193] just as the Arabs say that their most excellent poems are 'gilded' [literally: the Arabs call the pearl of their poetry 'gilded']." The analogy from Arabic poetry heightens the plausibility of the suggestion that the headings of the psalms also contain figurative praises of their excellence; the importance of such analogies for Ibn Ezra will be discussed below. It is clear in any case that he agrees with Ibn Ganach's gloss on "*ʿedut̲*," and even sees the application of the same reasoning to "*mik̲tam*" as of equal validity with his own opinion. No doubt this is because in its other five appearances in the

superscriptions of psalms (56–60) "*mik̲tam*" is accompanied by what are in his view unquestionably melodic indications. Consequently, in his commentary on 56:1 Ibn Ezra writes: "To the melody of a poem that began '*yonat̲ ʾelem reḥoḳim*,' while '*mik̲tam*' is a poem more excellent than fine gold [*ket̲em paz*]." Since here and in the other psalms the meaning and function of "*mik̲tam*" is quite clear, it is almost certain that it always has the same significance. This would seem to be the consideration that kept Ibn Ezra from casting his vote in favor of his own opinion even with regard to Psalm 16, where he could certainly have done so.

6. "*ʿAl ʾayyelet̲ ha-šaḥar*" (22:1): Both in the introduction and in his commentary *ad loc.* Ibn Ezra asserts absolutely that his interpretation—that this is clearly an indication of the melody—is the correct one. No proof of this is offered in the introduction, whereas in the body of the standard commentary he offers a most interesting explanation of the meaning of these words as the first line of the lost song: "This is the beginning of a psalm in the form of a love song, like 'a loving hind [*ʾayyelet̲*]' (Prov. 5:19)." That is, just as we find that the Book of Proverbs uses the hind as a metaphor for a woman in love, so too this image could have introduced an ancient ritual poem. In the introduction Ibn Ezra offers the opinion of "many" that the image of the woman-hind is here an allegory for the Jewish people: just as the hind pines through the night for her love, so do the Jewish people, through the darkness of their exile, yearn for the dawn of redemption. I have not located this idea in the midrashim; and Rashi, who conveys it in very similar terms ("about the Jewish people, who are 'a loving hind' [Proverbs 5:19] 'that shines through like the dawn' [Cant. 6:10]"), does not report this in the name of the Sages. Since Rashi's influence is not to be found in the standard commentary on Psalms, which was written in the north of France, *a fortiori* Ibn Ezra could hardly have relied on his commentary while he was still in Italy. Moreover, two *ʾahavah* poems (which Ibn Ezra probably wrote before he left Spain) attest to the wide dissemination of this idea and to the strength of its hold on Ibn Ezra's consciousness. The first lines of one of them, "ʾAyyelet̲ ʿal dod ʿag^{e}vah" (see *Religious Poems*, vol. 1, p. 220; see also vol. 2, p. 601) incorporates the entire image—Israel is compared to a hind, constantly yearning for her lover during the night of her wandering. What the poet could accept wholeheartedly, however, the commentator had to reject; and what was cited but rejected in the introduction to the First Recension is not even mentioned in the standard commentary.

In the first introduction he quotes also Ibn Giqatilah to the effect that "*ʾayyelet̲* is related to 'like a man with no strength [*ʾeyal*]' (Ps. 88:5)," but he does not say what the verse would mean according to this interpretation.

If he did not supply this in the lost commentary *ad loc.* he must have relied on his reader's capacity to infer his meaning. We, however, would not easily understand what the strength of the dawn is doing in the heading of this psalm, had he not explained in the standard commentary *ad loc.* that the intention is to designate the hour at which this psalm was recited in the Temple—"when he sees the strength of daybreak." This is exactly what Saadiah said in his commentary on this psalm: "I glossed '*ʾayyeleṯ ha-šaḥar*' as daybreak, because I derive its root from *ʾeyal* and *ʾeyaluṯ*, which mean capability" (*Psalms,* p. 87). Ibn Ezra, on the other hand, offers this opinion in the standard commentary with no attribution, and in the first introduction even credits it to Ibn Giqatilah. In the standard commentary he cites another solution: "Some say it is the name of a musical instrument"; I have no idea who may have made this suggestion before him (other than Rashi). At once, though, he returns to the first opinion and attacks its linguistic basis: given that the *yod* in "ʾayyeleṯ" has a *dagesh*, whereas in "ʾeyaluṯi" (Ps. 22:20) and "ʾeyal" (ibid. 88:5) it has none, the derivation does not seem plausible. Ultimately, since it is clear to him that "*ʿal ʾayyeleṯ ha-šaḥar*" is not an indication of time, and because he finds it difficult to see these words as symbolizing the theme of the psalm or as a picturesque name for some musical instrument, he can assert definitively: "the correct interpretation is what I said above" (line 151).

7. ["*Maśkil*" (32:1; 52:1; 53:1; 54:1; 55:1; 74:1; 78:1; and 88:1)]: This term, like *mikṯam*, should have been discussed in the Fourth Inquiry, and it too is more problematic that those that are discussed. in his gloss on its first appearance (32:1) Ibn Ezra adopts cautious language: "It may be that this psalm is [to be sung to] the melody of a poem that began '*maśkil*,'[194] or [that he used the word] because he says 'let me enlighten you [*ʾaśkilᵉʾḵa*]' (verse 8)." In other words, if "maśkil" does not indicate a melody it indicates a genre, defining the psalm as being didactic or ethical. To prove that this designation is appropriate to the psalm, Ibn Ezra quotes verse 8: "Let me enlighten you and show you which way to go." The rabbis of the Midrash and Ibn Ganach preceded Ibn Ezra in finding indications of its genre in the heading of a psalm—this is how they understood *šiggayon*. It is true that Ibn Ezra did not accept this interpretation, but he cited it without expressing any fundamental reservations (see above, §3). With regard to "maśkil," however, he offers this interpretation as fully plausible in his commentary on 78:1 as well: "A *piyyuṭ* that begins 'maśkil,' or enlightens [*maśkil*] the listener"—i.e., *maṣkil* may indicate a melody, or it may be a fitting designation for this psalm, because it enlightens its hearers. In the commentary on 52:1, however, only the musical explanation is offered: "[This indicates] the melody of a poem that began 'maśkil,' and the

meaning is to attest that the wicked meet a bad end.''[195] Ibn Ezra does not explicitly link these two assertions—that the psalm was accompanied by a melody called ''maśkil'' and that the subject of the psalm is the doctrine of retribution (like the Ibero-Hebrew genre *tokaḥah*); but their conjunction may imply that he thought there was an internal correspondence between the melody of the psalm and its ethical theme. Although I do not know why he felt he could make a definitive decision here, it is easy to understand how he did so with regard to the superscription of Psalm 53, where ''maśkil'' is accompanied by an obvious melodic cue, and therefore must designate a genre: ''The correct answer is that it [was sung] to the melody of a poem that began 'maḥalat'; as for 'maśkil'—I have already glossed this.'' Such double designations are also found in the headings of Psalms 54 and 55, where he must also have understood *maśkil* as indicating the genre.

8. ''*L^e-hazkir*'' (38:1 and 70:1): formally, ''l^e-hazkir'' resembles ''l^e-lammed,'' found in the heading of Psalm 60. But whereas at its two appearances Ibn Ezra simply defines ''l^e-hazkir'' as designating a melody, without offering an alternate interpretation, he takes another tack in his gloss on ''l^e-lammed'': ''The meaning of 'l^e-lammed'is that he ordered the musicians to teach it, to alway recall [*l^e-hazkir*(!)] God's mercy, when he prevailed in a battle after being close to defeat.'' According to this, ''l^e-lammed'' instructs the Levite musicians that they must teach this psalm to the Israelites, so that they will know it well and will be able always to praise God for his mercy to David their king. This is how Saadiah interpreted *la-m^{e}naṣṣeaḥ* as a performance direction, and Ibn Ezra agreed with him in the first introduction, although he had changed his mind by the time he wrote the standard commentary (see above, p. 232). Why, then, did Ibn Ezra fail to gloss ''l^e-hazkir'' in this way? It would seem that the difference between the two formally analogous words is that ''*l^e-lammed*'' is the third term at the beginning of Psalm 60, after the melodic cue ''*šušan ʿedut*'' and the generic designation ''*miktam*,'' whereas ''*l^e-hazkir*'' is the only term found in the two headings where it appears. In the absence of any external constraint, then, Ibn Ezra preferred to assume that the superscription of a psalm contained an indication of the melody with which it was to be accompanied in the Temple.

9. ''*ʿAl Y^{e}dutun*'' (62:1 and 77:1): This term should have been discussed immediately after ''*ʿal šošannim*,'' first mentioned in Psalm 45; this single deviation from the order of the psalms is evidently because the heading of Psalm 39 contains the term ''*li-Y^{e}dutun*,'' and Ibn Ezra's intention was to discuss the linguistic variants of this designation here. In fact, alongside the interpretation of *Y^{e}dutun* as a melodic cue (which works quite

well, since it follows the preposition *ʿal*, which is typical of melodic cues), he mentions with no reservations an alternative interpretation, which goes better with "li-Yᵉdutun": "or he may have given this Psalm to Jeduthun" (line 152). The problem of Jeduthun had already been discussed in the First Inquiry, where he sought to identify the various psalmists. Ibn Giqatilah and Saadiah were in agreement on this point (lines 38f.): David wrote all three "Jeduthun" psalms and gave them to Jeduthun to perform (line 59). Ibn Ezra, by contrast, did not state his position there, contenting himself with the assertion that these psalms were composed by David (lines 78f.) with no explanation of the additional name found in their headings. Here, too, in the Fourth Inquiry, he does not explain how a proper noun can serve as a melodic cue; we can infer that he did so in the lost commentary *ad loc.*, as he later did in the standard one. In his commentary on 39:1, he writes as follows: " '*La-mᵉnaṣṣeaḥ li-Yᵉdutun*'—as I mentioned at the beginning of this book [he was one of the chief musicians (reading with MS Parma 584)]; in my opinion there was a song well-known in that generation written by Jeduthun, or written in praise of him, which began '*li-Yᵉdutun*.' " First he repeats what he had presented in the second introduction (lines 14f.) in the name of the advocate of the first opinion (i.e., Saadiah), namely, that "*li-Yᵉdutun*" indicates the name of the performer. But he demurs at this and expresses his opinion that it indicates the melody. How can this be? According to the first option, the melody is called "*li-Yᵉdutun*" after the indication of authorship, inscribed by some editor above Jeduthun's poem. According to the second option, however, this melodic cue—like all of the others—is simply the first word of the first line of a song of praise written by some other poet in honor of Jeduthun. These two possibilities are presented in slightly different wording in the gloss on "*ʿal Yᵉdutun*" (62:1): "The melody of a poem that began '*li-Yᵉdutun*,'[196] written by Jeduthun the musician, or which someone wrote about him; [the suggestion] that it is an instrument is rather farfetched." Here, too, "began" has two possible senses: if Jeduthun wrote the lost poem the indication of authorship must precede its first line, whereas if another poet wrote it in his honor "*Yᵉdutun*" must be the first word of the poem itself. Except for Rashi, I do not know who may have suggested that "*Yᵉdutun*" is the name of a musical instrument. In any case, Ibn Ezra rejects as unreasonable this astonishing interpretation, which ignores the inclusion of Jeduthun as one of the musicians mentioned in 1 Chron. (16:41 et passim).

10. "*ʿAl šošannim*" (45:1; 69:1; 80:1): The picturesque word *šošannim* [= lilies] is so appropriate for the beginning of a poem that Ibn Ezra has absolutely no doubt that it is a melodic cue.[197] Therefore he wastes no effort, either in the first introduction or in his commentary on three headings

that contain it, on refuting the allegorical interpretation that sees "*šošannim*" as a reference to Israel (Midrash Tehillim), to the Sanhedrin (Targum Jonathan) or to the Karaite remnant (Yefet ben ʿAli; see above, pp. 94f.), or on discussing the view of Saadiah, who, following a totally different chain of reasoning, concluded that *šušan* is a figurative name of a melody (see above, pp. 17f.).

11. "*ʿAl ʿalamot*" (46:1): Ibn Ezra agrees with Saadiah that this is the name of a melody, but disagrees with him as to the meaning of this name. This disagreement is not reflected in the prologue to this introduction, where he describes how the psalms were sung in the Temple and relied on evidence external to the Book of Psalms to prove that "*ʿal ʿalamot*" is the name of a melody: "The fifth principle: [a prescribed] melody—those who played the *nevel*—[the tune of] *ʿal ʿalamot* (1 Chron. 15:20)—and those who played the *kinnor*— *ʿal ha-šeminit* (ibid. verse 21)" (lines 27–29). By contrast, his survey of the melodic cues is the appropriate context for his exegetical argument: "the Gaon, his memory for a blessing, said that [*ʿalamot*] means a quiet [*neʿelam*] voice, but there is no need for this" (line 154); and again, when speaking of the melodic cue "*ha-maʿalot*," he notes: "The Gaon said that it is the opposite of "*ʿal ʿalamot*" (46:1), because this [psalm] is to be sung in a loud and high voice, which is why these psalms are short" (lines 159–61). In these two sentences Ibn Ezra faithfully summarizes what Saadiah says in his long introduction (*Psalms*, p. 31; see above, p. 17). Ibn Ezra prefers not to relate to this gloss on "*ʿalamot*" and to argue simply that "there is no need" for it; it is superfluous—and therefore also dangerous—to carry hypothetical derivations too far, when one can readily conclude that the term indicates a melody simply by assuming that " '*ʿalamot*' is the name of a poem" (as he says laconically in his commentary on 46:1). Certainly he also saw no need to interpret *maʿalot* as meaning a high and sweet voice, although he demurs at it neither in the first introduction nor in the standard commentary on 120:1.

The fact that the discussion of " *ʿal ʿalamot*"in the survey of the melodic cues comes between those of "*ʿal šošannim*" (45:1) and "*yonat ʾelem reḥokim*" (56:1) seems to indicate that the reference is to "*ʿal ʿalamot*" in the heading of Psalm 46 rather than to "*ʿal-mut*" in the superscription of Psalm 9. Yet this conclusion does not sit well with what Ibn Ezra wrote on the subject in the *Defense* of Saadiah (§41). Because the text in the Lippmann edition has been corrupted past all comprehension, we cite it here according to the clear version of MS Parma 314:

> "ʿAl-mut labben" (9:1)—Saadiah said that the *lamed* is a prefix and has a *pataḥ* under it as in "*la-yišhar*";[198] the reference is to Ben, one of the

> Levites, as is written in Chronicles (1 Chron. 15:18). Dunash said it was the name of a Gentile king who made war on David, but he offered no proof. In my opinion "*ʿal-muṯ*" is [to be read as] a single word, like "*ʿalamoṯ šir*," which is the beginning of a poem, as I explained in [my commentary on] the Book of Psalms. But Saadiah did not say that [the text meant that] Ben died, because for him ["*ʿal-muṯ*"] was a single word.

In the last sentence Ibn Ezra is not arguing with Dunash but correcting an error of fact: Saadiah did not say that "*ʿal-muṯ*" is to be read as two words indicating someone's death [*maweṯ* = death; the normal construct form is *moṯ*]. Whereas Saadiah glossed "*ʿalamoṯ*" as a single word designating a quiet melody, the implication of what Dunash writes (*Criticism of Saadiah*, §44) is that he believed that his dispute with Saadiah focused exclusively on the morphology and meaning of "labben":

> He wanted to understand "*ʿal muṯ labben*" (9:1) as about the death of a man whose name was Ben, one of the Levites. This is an error, because if this is the meaning of the text it should read "ʿal muṯ Ben" and not "*labben*"! For we say "*ʿal mot šem we-ḥam*" rather than "*ʿal moṯ lᵉ-šem u-lᵉ-ḥam.*" David made clear the flaw in this explanation when he afterwards said "You blast the nations; You destroy the wicked" (9:6). I say that the *lamed* is intrinsic to the word, like "laban" (Gen. 24:29) or "lashaʿ" (Gen. 10:19), and that "*labben*" [is the name of] a man, a Philistine or Edomite, who made war on David and was killed in battle, or died or drowned (see verse 16). And of him it was said: "You blast the nations; You destroy the wicked." Understand this and learn!

Eventually Dunash himself realized that he had erroneously attributed his own opinion about "*ʿal muṯ*" to Saadiah, since later in his book (§69) we find a new criticism of Saadiah's interpretation thereof: "He made '*ʿal muṯ*' (9:1) into a single word, meaning a quiet voice."[199] It may be that Dunash considered his criticisms of Saadiah to be a literary form useful for composing his own novellae, and thus saw no need to correct what he had written in §44 and make his criticism of Saadiah correspond to what Saadiah had really said. Ibn Ezra did not condemn this; he merely set matters straight.

From the end of Ibn Ezra's remarks let us now return to their beginning. Not only does he express no explicit disagreement with Saadiah's interpretation, he even adds his own proof for it from the form *la-yiṣhar.* At the same time he raises an objection to Dunash's criticism based on history: he "offered no proof" for his assumption that a king named Labben waged war against Israel in the time of David. Consequently, Ibn Ezra prefers to understand "*ʿal-muṯ*" as a single word, parallel in meaning and function to "*ᶜalamot šir.*" He avoids the need to offer his own interpretation of the difficult combination "*ᶜalmut labben*"; seeing them as the initial words of some forgotten poem can in and of itself make the combination reasonable and clear (for example, "*ᶜAlamot, la-ben tᵉnu kavod!*" [*ᶜalamot*, honor the son!]). Neither does he mention his theory of melodic cues here in the *Defense* (he does allude to it in §64, discussed above), merely referring the reader to his commentary on Psalms. Since the *Defense* was written in Italy (see note 39), it is clear that the reference is to the first recension rather than to the second. In fact, we can infer from the standard commentary on 9:1 that in the interim Ibn Ezra had totally revised his opinion on the matter. There he not only fails to apply his theory of melodic cues to the superscription of Psalm 9, he even explicitly adopts the previously rejected interpretation of Dunash:

> "*La-mᵉnaṣṣeaḥ ᶜal mut labben*"—these are two words, and the one who said it is like "*ᶜalamot šir*" (46:1) was wrong. Furthermore, why should it be followed by a prefix *lamed*? The one who said that "labben" was the name of a musician, like "Ben and Jaᶜaziel" (1 Chron. 15:18) was also wrong, because it is not in accordance with the language to say "*la-yiṣḥak*" or "*la-yaᶜakov*" with a *pataḥ* under the prefix *lamed* before a person's name, because a proper noun is [itself (added from MS)] definite, as I explained in *Sefer Ha-šem*.[200] Some say that "labben" is "naval" backwards; or [that it is] about the death of the champion [understanding *labben* as alluding to *ʾiš ha-benayim*, i.e., Goliath, 1 Sam. 17:4 and 23]; or [about] the death of his son. The correct answer is what Dunash wrote, [namely,] that it was the name of some prince of the Gentiles who oppressed Israel, as is made clear in the psalm.

Without explicitly naming Saadiah, Ibn Ezra raises three arguments against him. The third, that a personal name cannot be preceded by the definite article, is not new; it can be found in *Moznayim* (24a), which was written before the *Defense* (see Fleischer, "Rome," pp. 169–71).[201] But the first argument is diametrically opposed even to his own opinion, as expressed in the *Defense*: it is a mistake to compare "*ᶜal mut*" written as two words with "*ᶜalamot*" written as one! It is not logical that in this instance Ibn Ezra changed his mind on the basis of textual information that had come to his attention during the interim (something he does report to have happened in the long commentary on Ex. 25:31); he could have known from Ibn Giqatilah's commentary (see note 200) that "*ᶜal mut*" is written with a hyphen. Moreover, in his commentary on 48:15 he has no hesitation about explaining "*ᶜal mut*" in the sense of "*ᶜolamit*," while noting that "the Masoretes said that they are two words." His other discussions of this phenomenon—already mentioned in the post-Talmudic tractate Soferim

(7,3) under the rubric of "writing one word and reading two" and "the reverse"—attest that his considerations here are exegetical and not textual.[202] Thus it seems reasonable that when he says "they are two words" Ibn Ezra is not arguing that it is forbidden to explain the crux as one word, but rather that this may be done only in the case of a genuine need, since it is preferable to interpret the Scriptures as written. One "who says that it is like *ʿalamoṯ šir*" (as Ibn Ezra himself said in the *Defense*!) "erred" only because it is possible to offer an explanation for the text as written that is no less reasonable. In the wake of this fundamental argument, the second and third arguments are intended to undermine the plausibility of Saadiah's explanation.

Not only does Saadiah fail to give a correct explanation of the prefix *lamed,* which according to him intervenes between the melodic cue "*ʿalamoṯ*" and the name of the musician Ben (in fact Saadiah did not translate it in the *Tafsir*, and was hard-pressed to explain it in his commentary *ad loc.*); the fact that it is vocalized with a *pataḥ* makes it quite impossible to understand "ben" as a proper noun. Although these two arguments do not apply to his own explanation of "*ʿalamoṯ labben*" as a melodic cue (as we explained above), the first argument does. On the other hand, "*ʿal muṯ*" can be explained as two words only if it is glossed in a way that satisfactorily accounts for the person whose death is spoken of. Ibn Ezra enumerates three identifications proposed by his predecessors, which he does not believe even require refutation.[203] The first is that "*labben*" is "nevel" backwards (see *Midrash Tᵉhillim* 9,17); David al-Fasi, *Dictionary*, s.v. *ben,* says there is no need to rebut this interpretation, while Dunash too rejects it out of hand: "it cannot be explained as a palindrome." Second, the reference may be to the death of Goliath (see Targum *ad loc.* and David al-Fasi). Third, the reference could be to David's son (see *Midrash Tᵉhillim* 9,4); David al-Fasi argues the impossibility of a song of thanks on the downfall of an enemy being written about the death of Absalom or of Bathsheba's son, whereas Dunash reiterates his argument that were the death of Absalom involved, the noun should be a direct object, "*ha-ben,*" not an indirect object, "*la-ben.*" Ibn Ezra now accepts Dunash's suggestion as correct. In the *Defense* he rejected it because there is no proof of the existence of a king of some enemy country named "Labben," whereas here he has no difficulty assuming that the psalm speaks of "one of the Gentile princes who oppressed Israel," despite the fact that he is not mentioned anywhere else in Scripture. This assumption accords with Ibn Ezra's view of the extreme paucity of historical information in the Early Prophets (see above, p. 208); moreover, it is also compatible with the content of the psalm— "as is made clear in the psalm." Dunash, it will be recalled, said much the same thing, relying on verse 6; Ibn Ezra follows suit, writing in his commentary on that verse: " 'You destroy the wicked'—this is Labben." Thus we see that he was willing to yield the interpretation of a particular expression as a melodic cue when he was convinced that it could be explained in some other fashion without resorting to extraordinary explanations, which are legitimate only when absolutely necessary.

12."*Yonat ʾelem r^e^ḥoḳim*" (56:1): This phrase seems to be particularly supportive of the theory of melodic cues, given its obviously lyrical character on the one hand and its clear truncation on the other. Ibn Ezra must have been encouraged in this assumption by the fact that a poet contemporary with him, Yehudah Halevy, began two of his poems with these charmed words: "*Yonat ʾelem ṣ^e^ḳi laḥašek*" and "*Yonat r^e^ḥoḳim nagg^e^ni heṭivi*" (Yehudah Halevy, *Diwan*, p. 25, poem 66, and p. 2, poem 6). It is true that in these poems the mute dove stands for the people of Israel, which clearly echoes the alternative interpretation of the heading of this psalm, to which, according to Ibn Ezra, most of the commentators subscribed (the Aramaic Targum, Salmon ben Yeruḥam, David al-Fasi, *Dictionary*, s.v. *ʾ.l.m.*). By contrast, Ibn Giqatilah preferred to understand the dove as a metaphor for David the poet (in this he was preceded by Yefet) and interpreted "ʾelem r^e^ḥoḳim" as the continuation of an image drawn from the life of birds: David held prisoner by the Philistines in Gath "likened himself to a dove that lives inside a distant sheaf" (line 156). Obviously Ibn Ezra cites this interpretation because of its originality, particularly conspicuous vis-à-vis the perplexity of Ibn Ganach, who proposed no fewer than three far-fetched glosses for "*yonat ʾelem reḥoḳim*" (*Shorashim*, s.v. *ʾ.l.m.*).

13. "*ʾAl tašḥet*" (57:1, 58:1; 59:1; and 75:1): In the standard commentary on 57:1 Ibn Ezra writes: "To the melody of a poem that began '*ʾal tašḥet*.' " This explanation is repeated word for word in his gloss on the heading of Psalm 75, evidently because of the distance between the two loci. On the other hand, he feels no need to explain the term in Psalms 58 and 59. All four psalms seem to be entreaties for rescue from the hands of an enemy; nevertheless, Ibn Ezra refrains from glossing "*ʾal tašḥet*" in their superscriptions as the beginning of the request for assistance found in the body of the psalm, and does not mention that this is how Saadiah translated the phrase in the *Tafsir* and how Yefet glossed it in his commentary *ad loc*. Evidently he rejected their interpretations because of the obvious ellipsis—"*ʾal tašḥet*" has no object—which he saw as reinforcing the idea that these words are the beginning of a poem (like his own poem that begins with a similar request, "Do not bring Your servant in judgment and remember Your mercy" [Ibn Ezra, *Religious Poems*, vol. 1, p. 420]).

14. "*šušan edut*" (60:1): *šušan* is very similar to *šošannim* (see §10); the advantage of the theory of melodic cues is that he has no need to gloss the word "*ᶜedut*," since he can simply assume that "*ᶜal šušan ᶜedut*" means "to the melody of a poem that began *šušan ᶜedut*" (standard commentary *ad loc.*). He goes on to mention what "some say," which, so far as we know, is a synthesis of what Saadiah said about *šušan*—"a musical instrument"—with what Ibn Ganach said about *ᶜedut*—"like *ᶜadi*" (i.e., an indication of the excellence of the psalm; see above in §5 on *miktam*).

15–16. "*šir la-maᶜalot*" (121:1) and "*ha-maᶜalot*" (120:1; 122–134): Ibn Ezra does not think he has to explain the inclusion of "*la-maᶜalot*" and "*maᶜalot*" in the list of melodic cues, and sees nothing wrong with concluding the first introduction with the anticlimatic explanation of these words. Saadiah viewed them as the name of a particular melody, which, in contrast to "*ᶜalamot*" (see beginning of §11), was performed in a "loud and high voice." According to Ibn Ezra, however, the Sages said that these fifteen psalms were written to correspond to the fifteen steps in the Temple (and evidently were intended to be said on them).[204] By the time Ibn Ezra came to write his second commentary his memory of the subject had become somewhat hazy, and in his gloss on 120:1 he attributed both explanations to Saadiah, despite their incompatibility, as is even evident from his wording:

> Saadiah said that these fifteen poems correspond to fifteen steps; he also said that perhaps [they were to be sung] in a high voice. I already mentioned at the beginning of the book what [I think] is the right answer—that this is the [beginning][205] of a *piyyuṭ*, and that this poem should be performed to the melody *ha-maᶜalot*.

The reference to the beginning of the book alludes to the commentary on 4:1 (discussed above, pp. 234f.), where the theory of melodic cues is first expounded in the standard commentary, and, inter alia, "*ha-maᶜalot*" and "*ᶜal ha-maᶜalot*" are mentioned. Evidently Ibn Ezra repeats his exposition of the theory here because of the long gap between Psalm 120 and Psalm 88, the last time it had been applied to the superscription of a psalm. It also is apparent that he returns to the topic in his commentary on the heading of the next psalm in order to make it clear that the fourteen psalms with the heading "*ha-maᶜalot*" were all sung to the same melody, whereas Psalm 121, with the superscription "la-maᶜalot," was sung to a different tune: "*Šir la-maᶜalot*"—[to] the melody of a poem that began 'la-maᶜalot.' "

These two melodic cues complete the list in the first introduction. The standard commentary provides no additional references to the designation of the melody for a psalm by the opening words of a lost poem.

Just as we examined (above, pp. 220–24ff.) how and to what extent Ibn Ezra's ideas about the editing of the Book of Psalms were influenced by the manner in which *diwans* and anthologies were compiled in Spain, we should also consider the possible impact of contemporary practice on his theory of melodic cues. But whereas Ibn Ezra never explicitly indicates that on the subject of editorial activity he drew an analogy between the poetry of his own time and biblical poetry, he does make such a clear statement, in his commentary on Psalm 7, with regard to melodies:

> ''šiggayon''—some gloss it as pleasure, as in 'be infatuated [*tišgeh*] always' (Prov. 5:19), and some say, ''about his error [*šigᵉgato̱*].'' I think the correct answer is that it is [to be sung] to the melody of a poem that began ''šiggayon [concerning Cush],'' [206] as the Spanish writers of *piyyuṭim* do: above the *piyyuṭ* they indicate the melody (reading with five MSS: ''noᶜam'') of a known *piyyuṭ*.

The explanation of ''šiggayon'' as a melodic cue was discussed above in the fifth paragraph of our survey of melodic cues, along with Ibn Ezra's stand on the two alternative interpretations. Here we must consider the analogy he drew from the conventions of Spanish poetry to prove the plausibility of his most original theory. Note that Ibn Ezra says that ''Spanish writers [*ko̱tᵉvei*] of liturgical poems'' indicated the melody by inscribing above the first line of a *piyyuṭ* the opening words of another *piyyuṭ*. Since Ibn Ezra uses *ko̱tev* as the Hebrew equivalent of the Arabic *mudawwin* (see above, pp. 182–185), he clearly means that in Spain the melodic cues were added by the editor who gathered the *piyyuṭim* and collected them in a *diwan,* and not by the poet himself earlier or the performer later. In fact, the Arabic inscriptions prefaced to many of the Hebrew poems written in Spain speak of the poet in the third person—not only when they append a blessing for the dead to his name (see, for example, Ibn Gabirol, *Secular Poems*, vol. 1, pp. 1 and 50), but even when they associate his name with a blessing for the living (as with the poems of Yehudah Ibn Giath and Joseph Ibn Ṣaddiḳ that have survived in Genizah fragments; see the facsimile in Schirmann, *Hebrew Poetry*, vol. 1, facing p. 513). This is the situation whether an anonymous editor uses impersonal terms (as in all of the superscription in Ibn H̱alfon's *diwan*; see the Mirsky edition, mentioned above, note 166), or whether an indentified editor like Yehoseph the son of Samuel ha-Nagid writes in the first person (see Samuel ha-Nagid, *Ben Tehillim,* pp. 34–41). At first glance Tadros Abulafia's *diwan* seems to be an exception to the rule, but in fact it confirms it; only those poems collected by the poet himself are introduced by rhymed Hebrew inscriptions in the first person (see Tadros, *Gan ha-Meshalim*, vol. 1, Notes, p. 16), whereas the superscriptions to poems collected by other persons are generally in Arabic and the third person (ibid., vol. 2, Notes, p. 18). The Ibero-Hebrew poetry that has come down to us thus confirms Ibn Ezra's assertion that the informative headings prefaced to poems were generally written by the editors rather than by the poets themselves.

This conclusion apparently applies also to indications of melody (*laḥn*) or meter (*wazn*) by citing the opening of well-known poems. Abramson ("Letter," p. 403), however, argued that they were not written by the editors of the *diwans*, but were added by the copyists or owners of the manuscripts. His proof is that in Ibn Ezra's *diwan*, extant in a single manuscript (MS Berlin 186), these inscriptions were added later, since "the handwriting is not that of the copyist of the *diwan*." From this he infers a specific conclusion about the *wazn* indication prefaced to one of Ibn Ezra's poems: "All that can be inferred from this inscription is that whoever wrote it knew the Arabic poem 'ma la<u>dd</u>a etc.,' and that its meter is similar to that of Ibn Ezra's poem" (ibid.). If so, it follows that an indication of a melody does not mean that the poet himself directed that his poem be sung to the particular Arabic melody, or that a well-informed editor was so attesting. Is this indeed the situation Ibn Ezra has in mind when he draws an analogy between the melodic cues in the headings of the psalms with those found in the Spanish *diwans?* In other words, it is clear that comparing the melodic cues in the Book of Psalms with those of "the Spanish writers" detaches the words glossed as melodic cues from the body of the psalm and even from the psalmist's quill; but are we meant to infer also that the ascription of the melody to the psalm was done later and at second hand?

In his guidelines for a poet seeking "the very best way in Hebrew poetry according to the rules of Arabic," Moses Ibn Ezra writes as follows: "If someone wants to learn music—there is nothing wrong in learning it after grammar, since both are involved in the creation of poetry" (*Discussions*, p. 137). If music is not an obligatory study for a poet, he must believe that the musical element in the creation of a poem is not expressed in the musical aspect of the meter, but in writing the words so that they will scan to a given melody. We cannot really know what proportion of Ibero-Hebrew poety was *a priori* written to be sung, but we do have evidence that at least some of Samuel ha-Nagid's poems were sung during his own lifetime. In his preface to *Ben Tehillim,* his son Yehoseph writes as follows: "What I have collected in this *diwan* includes his metrical poetry and the poems in different meters *that were sung in his presence*" (Samuel ha-Nagid, *Ben Tehillim,* p. 1). These words seem to be echoed in what Moses

Ibn Ezra wrote about *Ben Tehillim*: "The supplications and prayers meant to be sung, which are found in *Ben Tehillim,* have poetic meters" (*Discussions,* p. 63). It follows, then, that the poems to be sung included liturgical poetry as well; this conclusion also seems to follow from the superscription to the poem "My God, I entreat You on the day of my fear," which also contains a reference (as was shown by Allony)[207] to the preface of *Ben Tehillim*: "The long poems have been completed, praise to God, may He be blest. Now I will begin the short poems with the help of the Rock. These poems were sung in his presence when he was relaxing, and are those that were mentioned at the beginning of the book" (*Ben Tehillim,* p. 344). The secular and religious poems sung for Samuel ha-Nagid may have been set to music by others; but it is also possible that the poet himself wrote them to fit well-known melodies. The latter possibility is particularly plausible for a literary genre that was *a priori* intended to be performed with musical accompaniment—the girdle poem (Arabic *muwaššaḥ*). There is direct evidence of this in an anecdote cited by Ibn Ḫaldun: a girdle poem by Ibn Bāǧa (a native of Saragossa and contemporary of Moses Ibn Ezra) made a strong impression on the ruler of the city—for whom it was sung under the direction of the poet-composer—because of the close correspondence between the words of the song of praise and its melody (see Stern, "Poetry," p. 44; Rosen-Moked, "Girdle Poem," pp. 57–58). The fact that these elaborate strophic poems were meant to be sung is expressed not only in the melodic cues given in the superscriptions of many of them, but also in their very structure. The secular girdle poem (both Hebrew and Arabic) generally concluded with one or two lines in the vernacular (spoken Arabic or Arabic mixed with Old Castilian), frequently borrowed from another girdle poem. Thanks to this borrowing of the conclusion of the final girdle—known in Arabic as *ḫarǵa* (exit)—it was predetermined that the meter and rhyme scheme of all the girdle stanzas (from the "guide" at the beginning of the poem to the "conclusion" at its end) would duplicate those of the original poem; this made it easy to borrow its melody as well.[208] Not only was this imitation (Arabic *muʿāraḍa*) of the meter and rhyme scheme considered to be legitimate, it even was seen as a challenge to demonstrate the virtuosity of the imitator; this is attested, inter alia, by stories about parties where each poet tried his hand at imitating a given model (see Abramson, "Letter," pp. 399–402). Stern associates the great frequency of imitation in girdle poems with the fact that they were meant to be sung: given the intimate connection between melody and meter, the poet could easily overcome the problem of setting the words to music by adopting the structure of a poem that fits a popular and beautiful melody (see Stern, "Imitations," pp. 166–76; Rosen-Moked, "Girdle Poem," pp. 65–79).

We can learn a lot about the relationship between *ḫarǵa* and melody from Tadros Abulafia's girdle poems, because he edited his own *diwan* and himself provided the indications of Arabic melodies at the beginning of each poem, as he informs us in his rhymed preface ("Girdle Poem," p. 5). All the melodies were indicated by a cue: he cites the first words of an Arabic song, preceded by the Arabic word *laḥn*. Of the forty-seven girdle poems in the *diwan*, forty-five conclude with a vernacular *ẖarǵa*. The two poems (6 and 7) with a Hebrew conclusion are the only ritual ones in the collection; their superscriptions define them as *ʾahavah* poems, but they too are to be sung to Arabic melodies, at least one of which (that for poem 6) is obviously taken from a well-known love song: "Melody: 'he has captivated me, the fair one.' " Thus there is no necessary link between the borrowed *ẖarǵa* and the melody, since even without such a borrowing the poet could adopt a well-known melody and with it, apparently, the meter of the poem that gave its name to the melody. This conclusion is strengthened by two findings: (1) Poems 10 and 36 have the same melodic cue but different *ẖarǵas*; (2) the *ẖarǵa* of poem 1 is not taken from the Arabic poem mentioned in the melodic cue (which was identified by Stern, "Imitations," p. 179). By contrast, in about half of Tadros's girdle poems there is an extremely close connection between the *ẖarǵa* and the melodic cue; in twenty-one of them the melodic cue in the heading is identical with the *ẖarǵa* that concludes the poem. Stern hypothesized that the first line of the model was frequently used as the *ẖarǵa* instead of the last line; he was able to prove this for poems 10 and 40 by identifying the two Arabic girdle poems whose opening lines are both *ẖarǵa* and melodic cue in Tadros Abulafia's poem (ibid., pp. 183–84). Still, one must not ignore the possibility that sometimes the melody was indicated by the last line of the poem imitated, as seems to be the case with poem 13, whose melody is indicated by the *ẖarǵa* of a poem by Ibn Ḳuzmān, also identified by Stern (ibid., p. 182).

Thus even when the poet himself did not write melodic cues above his poems—as was in fact generally the case—the editor could legitimately see the *ẖarǵa* as a trustworthy starting point for identifying the poem whose melody had been adopted, or at least for identifying the melody shared by songs with the same *ẖarǵa*. We can buttress this cautious conclusion from Stern's illuminating findings about Abraham Ibn Ezra's imitations of his predecessors' girdle poems.

Yeshuʿah ben Elijah, the editor of Ibn Ezra's *diwan* (see above, p. 221), devoted the second half of the *diwan* chiefly to girdle poems. In his introduction to this section (*Diwan*, pp. 13–14), he writes about the headings as follows:

> I will give the poems of this section one after another and indicate the meters (*ʾawzān*) of some of them by means of the openings of Hebrew and Arabic poems, where they are known to me, and sometimes even by means of another poem in this section.

This testimony by an editor corresponds with what Ibn Ezra tells us about the practice in Spain in his own day, namely, that the melodic cues were added by the editor rather than written by the poet. In light of this correlation, it is rather perplexing that in the only extant manuscript of Ibn Ezra's *diwan* (MS Berlin 186) the metrical and melodic indications clearly seem to be a later addition, since the copyist did not leave enough space for them. As a result they are written in tiny letters and a cursive script between the poems and even in the margins. On the other hand, the poems themselves, as well as the editor's introductions, are written in a fine semi-cursive script with much attention to the use of space. Somewhere in between these two extremes are the indications of authorship, centered over the first line of the poem and written in large letters, despite a certain tendency in them to a cursive hand (e.g., poems 28, 40, 46, and 77, in Egers' numbering). These cursive letters allow us to determine that the tiny letters were also written by the copyist of the *diwan* (see especially poem 100). Were the Berlin manuscript Yeshuᶜah's autograph it would be a major problem to resolve the contradiction between the editor's declaration in his preface about the metrical indications and the fact that they were added later. But since the manuscript was copied by someone else, we can hypothesize that this later copyist added the indications from a second manuscript, because they had been omitted from the first manuscript from which he had copied the body of the *diwan* (as Eger himself was later to omit them). Thus there is no reason to doubt that the metrical and melodic indications in the *diwan* were indeed contributed by Yeshuᶜah ben Elijah.

Stern ("Ibn Ezra," p. 384) stresses that Yeshuᶜah's goal was to indicate the meter by means of the opening words of other poems with the same meter, and not necessarily to identify the poems that had actually served Ibn Ezra as a model for imitation. At the same time, he believes it almost certain that Yeshuᶜah did in fact indicate the original poem for poems 95, 191, and 198. To these we can add the poems that Stern was able to prove had borrowed *ẖarǵas,* since they are already found in Arabic girdle poems prior to Ibn Ezra. We can begin with poem 191 (*Diwan,* p. 84). This secular girdle poem, with its copious praise for a rich man named Isaac, concludes with a *ẖarǵa* in literary Arabic (as is customary in panegyric poems). In the header, written in large letters, we read, "and he also said, his memory for a blessing," and in small letters, "he wrote this in the meter of 'Bi-abi ʾaḥwā.' " Stern ("Imitations," pp. 176–77; "Ibn Ezra," pp. 374–75) found a girdle poem by Ibn Bāḳi (from Cordova or Toledo, died around 1150), which contains both the *ẖarǵa* that concludes Ibn Ezra's poem and the opening words cited by his editor. This *ẖarǵa* is also found in a girdle poem by Ibn Ḳuzmān (Ibn Baḳi's younger contemporary), who says explicitly that he had imitated Ibn Bāḳi's poem. True, one can assume that Ibn Ezra borrowed the *ẖarǵa* from Ibn Ḳuzmān, and that Yeshuʿah knew only the poem by Ibn Bāḳi and therefore used it to indicate the meter; but it is more reasonable to assume that Ibn Ezra borrowed from the original poem and not from its imitation. Finally, if the editor of Ibn Ezra's *diwan* did not rely on some external information available to him, he could have reached his conclusion that Ibn Ezra "wrote this in the meter" of Ibn Bāḳi's poem on the basis of internal evidence drawn from the poem itself—the borrowed *ẖarǵa*.

In the letter from Yehudah Halevy to Moses Ibn Ezra, which begins "šalom rab̲ w^{e}yešaʿ y^{e}ḳareb̲" (its first part was discovered by Davidson, and the second by Abramson; see: Abramson, "Letter"), the younger poet tells the older how the poets of southern Spain gathered at a party had worn themselves out trying to imitate Moses Ibn Ezra's panegyric for Joseph Ibn Ṣaddiḳ, which begins "*lel maḥašab̲ot̲ leb̲ ʾaʿirah*," and had urged him to try his hand at it. Although the task seemed impossible to him, he eventually succeeded, and appends to his letter a panegyric for Moses Ibn Ezra, which begins "ʾAḥar gallot̲ sod mah ʾaṭmin," which borrows the prosody of "lel maḥašab̲ot̲ leb̲ ʾaʿirah." This sequence of events is alluded to in the inscription that precedes Yehudah Halevy's poem in his *diwan*, whose ultimate editor was also Yeshuʿah ben Elijah (MS Oxford 1971, formerly owned by S. D. Luzzatto): "This is his [Yehudah Halevy's] about Abu Harun Ibn Ezra and is the poem he alluded to in his letter that begins 'šalom rab̲ w^{e} yeša y^{e}ḳareb̲.' " There is further confirmation of this in the text of Yehudah Halevy's poem: the name Moses in line 20, the total identity of prosodic structure and rhyme scheme in the two poems, and the identical Arabic *ẖarǵas* that end both of them. Initially Stern ("Imitations," pp. 168–71) was confident that Moses Ibn Ezra borrowed the *ẖarǵa* from a girdle poem by ʾAbu Bakr al-ʾAbiaḍ (executed by the ruler of Cordova some time after 1130), of which only two stanzas have survived as a quotation in a book by Ibn H̲aldun. This assumption, which relied on the identity of "so typical, complex, and uncommon a rhyme" (p. 169), was confirmed when Stern located the complete text of al-ʾAbiaḍ's poem in the manuscript of an anthology edited by Ibn Bušrā[209]. Now he had before him not only the very same *ẖarǵa*, exactly as it appears in the poems by Moses Ibn Ezra and Yehudah Halevy, but also the first line of al-ʾAbiaḍ's poem, which begins "Ma lad̲d̲a lī šarb ʾar-rāḥ." This also confirmed Brody's assertion (*Diwan Jehuda ha-Lewis*, notes to vol. 1 [Berlin, 1899], p. 222) that Abraham Ibn Ezra's poem, "ʾel dod b^{e}šem lo kinniti" (*Religious Poems*, vol. 1, p. 129) is written in the same meter and rhyme scheme as Yehudah Halevy's girdle poem "ʾaḥar gallot̲ sod." At the time he noted this Brody did not know that in the manuscript of Abraham Ibn Ezra's *diwan* (MS Berlin 186) the meter of this poem is in fact indicated by reference to al-ʾAbiaḍ's poem: "wazn 'Ma ladda lī šarb ʾar-rāḥ.' " At the beginning of the next poem in the manuscript—"ʾorḥot ʾEloah ʿamadu" (*Religious Poems*, vol. 1, p. 131)—we read: "In the same meter as the previous one." In fact this poem too, like its predecessor, is a faithful imitation of the common prosodic structure of the secular poems by al-ʾAbiaḍ, Moses Ibn Ezra, and Yehudah Halevy. Thus we see that even though Ibn Ezra's two poems lack an Arabic *harǵa* (inappropriate for liturgical poetry), their meter was correctly identified with that of al-ʾAbiaḍ's poem, which is the root of this chain of imitations.[210] What was clear to the editor—or to whoever preceded him in this—must have also been clear to a poet like Abraham Ibn Ezra, who had before him the famous *harǵa* incorporated in the much-praised imitations by Moses Ibn Ezra and Yehudah Halevy.[211]

In Yeshuʿah ben Elijah's introduction to the second part of Abraham Ibn Ezra's *diwan* (quoted above, p. 253), he promises to indicate the meters of the poems whenever he knows them, but does not say that he will also indicate their melodies. Evidently he lacked reliable information about these; in fact, the few melodic indications nevertheless found in the *diwan* seem to be quite secondary.[212] On the other hand, Ibn Ezra's analogy between the headings of the psalms and those of poems written in Spain is based precisely on *melodic* indications, since, given his view of the psalms as non-metrical poetry (see above, p. 168), the indications in their headings cannot refer to meters. True, the borrowing of meter and melody are interrelated in Iberian poetry; nevertheless, a certain elucidation is provided by the evidence of a direct borrowing of a melody probably by Ibn Ezra himself.[213]

A Genizah fragment discovered by H. Brody preserves a liturgical girdle poem by Abraham Ibn Ezra, "šur lᵉbabi bᵉka mᵉśoś ruḥi." The Arabic superscription indicates the *melody* by means of two words, later identified by Stern as the opening of a girdle poem famous in Spain for the excellence of its words and melody. Written by the philosopher-poet Ibn Baǵā, called by Ibn Haldun "the author of the praiseworthy melodies" (see above, p. 252), it was also the model for Judah Ibn Giath's girdle poem "sammᵉkuni bᵉ-yen šᵉfat ʿofri" (the first line of the Arabic poem is the *harǵa* of the Hebrew poem). Stern subsequently identified four more imitations of this in Arabic poetry, one a secular poem and the others Islamic sacred poetry.[214] Given the extreme popularity of Ibn Baǵā's girdle poem and the praise for its melody, it is more than reasonable to conclude that the melodic indication at the beginning of Ibn Ezra's poem not only reflects full identity of the rhyme scheme and meter of the two poems, but also Ibn Ezra's intention to write the poem so that is would match the melody of his model.

We can conclude, then, that when Ibn Ezra explains the melodic indications in the headings of the psalms according to the literary custom of

Spain, his intention must be that the melodic indication in the heading of a psalm is a compulsory instruction to the Levites of how it should be sung in the Temple, because melody and text form a single linguistic and musical entity. That this was in fact his idea can be seen from a number of sources; his praise of the perfection of the musical performance of the sacred poems in the Temple, with which he begins the first introduction; his definition of the term *mizmor* at the beginning of the Fourth Inquiry; and what we have discovered about the intimate connection that existed in Spain between borrowing the melody of a well-known poem and imitating its structure. A final proof is the fact that Ibn Ezra stressed, at the beginning of his explanation of the theory of melodic cues in the Fourth Inquiry, that in the biblical period the melodies pre-existed the Psalms: "in my opinion, the Israelites had many melodies before the time of David" (lines 138f.). Note that he does not assert that the melodies were original nor that they were written especially for the psalms. On the contrary, given the example of Jewish liturgical poets in Spain, who borrowed secular melodies (and even Arabic ones), he saw nothing wrong with the assumption that the prophetic psalms included in Scripture were sung to secular melodies in the Temple. We must conclude that in his eyes it was not the sacred origin of a melody or its originality that was essential, but the total correspondence between the words of the psalm and a given melody, accomplished by the psalmist himself. True, his view of the enigmatic words in the headings as melodic cues detaches them from the body of the psalm; at the same time, however, they are fully integrated with its musical performance. These difficult words remain unglossed, since they refer to a lost poem; but instead we are assured that the melodies selected from the wealth of music that flourished in Israel were appropriate to the prayers of the prophet-poets and were performed by the Levites with total adherence to all the demands of the musical art. Here Ibn Ezra's experience as a liturgical and secular poet served him in his attempt to discover the plain meaning of the headings of the psalms and provide a realistic description of the glory of the performance of the sacred poems in the courts of the Temple in Jerusalem.

Notes to Chapter Four

1. The archetype for this is the second edition of Levy ben Avraham's encyclopedic work *Liwyat Ḥen* (in manuscript), whose author's colophon reads as follows: "I acknowledge before every wise man that in the short while since I wrote this book I have changed certain passages and changed the order of many topics, corrected some matters, and added and innovated many things time after time. . . . I know that during this period many people copied this book; I hereby request

of anybody into whose hands one of these earlier versions came that he correct it according to this final version, or discard it in favor of this one'' (MS Vatican 192, 147a; cf. C. Sirat, ''Les différentes versions du *Liwyat Ḥen* de Lévi b. Abraham,'' *REJ* 122 [1963], pp. 167–77). A good parallel for this from Arabic culture is cited by A. S. Tritton, *Muslim Education in the Middle Ages* (London, 1975), p. 189: ''After I had read the *musnad* of Ibn Hanbal, I found that it was the first edition and there was written on the cover in the author's hand: 'This is the first copy which I wrote first and taught from it. Then I made changes in places, changing some traditions and providing *isnāds* for more. It was copied at my dictation as the definitive edition.' ''

2. This is what Maimonides did for his *Yad ha-Ḥazakah,* as we learn from his responsa (see *Maimonides' Responsa,* ed. Y. Blau, vol. 2 [Jerusalem, 1960], §287, p. 539). And cf. what Saul Lieberman wrote on the various editions of Maimonides' commentary on the Mishnah, in his *Laws of the Palestinian Talmud* (Heb.), (New York, 1947), pp. 6–12.

3. See Saadiah's preface to his *Tafsir* on the Pentateuch (Hebrew translation by Y. Ḳāfiḥ in Saadiah, *Torah Commentaries,* pp. 159–61). Saadiah explains that he wrote this commentary-translation in response to ''the request by one of my students . . . to devote a special volume to the plain meaning of the Pentateuch,'' a volume that would omit the linguistic, halakhic, and philosophic discussions found in the long commentary on the Pentateuch he had already written. The *Tafsir* is written with great terseness, so that ''there will not be too much trouble for someone who wants to know something from the Pentateuch''; at the same time, Saadiah refers readers who want a fuller and more fundamental discussion, accompanied by proofs, to his long commentary (whose surviving fragments have been collected and translated into Hebrew by Moshe Zucker [see: Saadiah, *Genesis*]).

4. At the end of his preface to *Safah B^{e}rurah* (ed. Wilensky, p. 295; ed. Lippmann, p. 15a), Ibn Ezra reports that when one of his students asked him to write a grammar book for him he tried to refer him to the three volumes on grammar he had already written in various cities in Italy. But the student replied that nobody who had a copy of one of those books was willing to lend it to him. Since Ibn Ezra no longer possessed a copy of these books he had no choice but to write a new work for ''the student mentioned at the beginning of the poems.'' In fact, the prefatory poem contains a dedication to ''Š^{e}lomoh.'' A total of eleven such dedicatory poems by Ibn Ezra are extant, while the prefatory poems to his other writings do not mention the names of students or patrons (see Ibn Ezra, *Poems,* vol. 1, pp. 16–85; vol. 2, pp. 47–48). Nevertheless, I tend to agree with those scholars who believe that Ibn Ezra's frequent travels and unrelieved dependence on patrons are the most important reasons for the frequency with which we find two versions of a single work by this wandering scholar. On the other hand, I am not persuaded by the hypothesis of R. Joseph Bonfils (*Ṣaf^{e}nat Pa^{c}neaḥ* 1, p. 185) that the first edition of Ibn Ezra's duplicated writings is merely a rejected first draft. It relies on an

invalid generalization ("every author writes two versions and keeps the second and discards the first") and is merely intended to buttress his argument (in itself unacceptable) against the reliability of the long commentary on Exodus.

5. See Simon, "Exegete," pp. 29–30.

6. The long commentary on Genesis (extant only through 12:11) was published by M. Friedlaender (London, 1877) and included in the Weiser edition (Jerusalem, 1976). The short commentary on Exodus was first published by I. S. Reggio (Prague, 1840) and later edited and provided with a supercommentary by J. L. Fleischer (Vienna, 1926); it is also included in *Meḥokekei Yehudah* and in the Weiser edition. The First Recension of the commentary on the Song of Songs was edited and translated into English by H. J. Mathews (London, 1874); the Second Recension of the Esther commentary was published by J. Zedner (London, 1850). The short commentary on Daniel was first edited by H. J. Mathews (London, 1877), and again, with an accompanying supercommentary, by A. Mondshine (Ramat Gan, 1977; provisional mimeographed edition).

7. The short commentary ("Second Recension") on the Minor Prophets (notes taken by someone who studied the biblical book with Ibn Ezra) has been published by me and is included in Ibn Ezra, *Minor Prophets.*

8. Since the eight surviving manuscripts of the long commentary on Daniel lack an author's colophon, it is here quoted from the *editio princeps.*

9. Ibn Ezra's seven astrological works were also written very rapidly one after the other and are therefore known as the Astrological Encyclopedia. The first of these—*Rešit Ḥokmah*—was finished "in the month of Tammuz 4908 [1148]," and the last—*Sefer ha-ʿOlam*—in "Marheshvan of the year 4909 [1149]." See *Sefer ha-Ṭeʿamim*, first version, ed. J. L. Fleischer (Jerusalem, 1951), pp. 5–7. If we relate only to the six works that were written from Tammuz until Marheshvan, and translate the ninety-seven pages they fill in MS Vatican 390 to the dimensions of the pages of the British Library MS mentioned in the text, we find that Ibn Ezra wrote six treatises whose total length is equivalent to forty pages of the British Library MS within four to five months. This pace is very similar to that for the commentary on the Minor Prophets, and provides further support for the assumption that the composition of the Psalms commentary did not occupy the maximum possible duration of ten months.

10. Fleischer, "France," §§ 8–12.

11. Golb bases his assumption that there was personal enmity between Ibn Ezra and R. Samuel ben Meir (Rashbam) (pp. 60–66) chiefly on the findings of A. Margoliouth in his article "The relationship between Rashbam's and Ibn Ezra's commentaries on the Pentateuch" (Heb.), *Asaph Festschrift* (Jerusalem, 1953), pp. 357–69. Material and chronological criticisms of this article can be found in my article, "Exegetic Method" (pp. 130–36), which Golb had not seen.

12. The verses that Ibn Ezra sent to R. Jacob ben Meir (Rabbenu Tam) begin "Who brought a poem to a *Ṣarᵉfaṯi* in his house" (Ibn Ezra, *Poems,* vol. 1, p. 144). See also Golb, *Rouen,* p. 4, note 12.

13. Ibn Ezra makes a similar statement in the long commentary on Exodus 7:1, also written in Rouen in 1153: "According to the scholars of *Ṣarᵉfaṯ* the root *nyb* is a biliteral, but according to the Spanish scholars it belongs to the category of those that elide the *ʿayin* [second letter of the root]."

14. Ibn Ezra mentions Lucca as his current residence in his comm. on Gen. 33:10. Fleischer presents definitive proof of the literary unity of the commentary on the Pentateuch and of its composition *in toto* in Lucca (Ibn Ezra, *Exodus [short comm.]*, pp. xxxiii–xxxix; Fleischer, "Lucca," pp. 186–92).

15. See (in a radical formulation that probably does not hold for a nomadic author like Ibn Ezra) Abramson, "Sefer ha-Tagnīs" (Heb.), *Ḥanoḵ Yalon Festschrift* (Jerusalem, 1963), p. 57; see also his article "From them and in them (a study in booklore)" (Heb.), *Sefer Shalom Sivan* (Jerusalem, 1980), pp. 14–16.

16. See Friedlaender, *Essays,* pp. 156–57; Fleischer, "Corrections and additions to my article on Ibn Ezra's Sefer *ha-ʿaṣamim,*" *Ha-Ṣofeh lᵉ-hoḵmaṯ Yisrael* 11 (1927), pp. 172–74; idem, "France," p. 220. Note that while in the first article Fleischer offers the hypothesis that this commentary on Psalms is part of the biblical commentary written by Ibn Ezra when he was still in Spain or North Africa, in the second article he accepts—with no explanation—Friedlaender's hypothesis that the first version of the Psalms commentary was written in Italy. If Ibn Ezra did indeed write commentaries while still in Islamic countries, there is no doubt that he wrote them in Arabic. One can hardly assume that in his Hebrew commentaries he would refer readers to a book written in a language they did not understand.

17. The commentary on the Pentateuch is mentioned five more times in the Isaiah commentary (19:4; 28:29; 38:10; 40:28; and 54:5), whence the conventional assumption that the short commentary on the Pentateuch known as *Sefer ha-Yašar* was written before the Isaiah commentary. On the other hand, there is one reference to the Isaiah commentary in the short comm. on Exodus (32:4); but this may be a copyist's addition, like two references in the future tense that will be discussed below.

18. From the table of cross-references in the commentaries drawn up by L. Levy (*Reconstruction des Commentars Ibn Esras zu den Ersten Propheten* [Berlin, 1903], p. x) we learn that the Psalms commentary is not mentioned in the books for which there is evidence of their composition in Rome: the commentaries on Ecclesiastes, Job, Song of Songs (Mathews edition), and Lamentations, as well as in the Hebrew grammar *Moznayim.* To the extent that we can rely on this negative datum, it is a proof of sorts that the Psalms commentary was written after these works, but before the commentaries on the Pentateuch and Isaiah, in which, as has been said, it is mentioned. The standard commentary on Esther was also written in Italy (as

proved by Zedner in his introduction to the "Second Recension," p. 15); this is also the case with the commentary on Ruth and the short commentary on Daniel, although we do not know exactly when and where they were written, and in any case they do not refer to the Psalms commentary. We can, however, be more precise with regard to the commentary on Ruth, since in his gloss on 1:16 Ibn Ezra speaks of the Isaiah commentary (on 47:3) in the future tense, whereas in the gloss on 1:15 he uses the past tense with reference to the Pentateuch commentary: "I have already explained it in the Pentateuch [commentary]" (according to the version of most manuscripts; the reference seems to be to his comm. on Deut. 25:5). Nevertheless, Fleischer ("Rome," p. 96) wanted to date the Ruth commentary before the Pentateuch commentary, on the assumption that this remark was added by a copyist, since he had been told that it is not found in MS Vatican 488. An examination of a photocopy of that manuscript, however, reveals that his information was erroneous.

19. Golb (*Rouen*, p. 24, note 72; pp. 55–56) believes that this labor, too, was done in Rouen; but this hypothesis is based on an erroneous interpretation of what Judah Ibn Tibbon wrote in the preface to his translation of Ibn Ganach's *Ha-riḳmah*, namely, that Ibn Ezra supposedly helped the Jews of *France* learn Hebrew grammar by continuing the translation enterprises started by Ibn Giqatilah. Ibn Tibbon clearly says, however, that Ibn Ezra's assistance was expressed in "short compositions, in which he included many precious things" (vol. 1, pp. 4–5), that is, in the composition of *original* grammatical works, which, as is known, Ibn Ezra was the first to write in Hebrew. Similarly, Golb ignores Fleischer's arguments ("Rome," §5, p. 170; §11, pp. 134–35) intended to strengthen the hypothesis that all three books were translated in Rome.

20. Friedlaender, *Essays*, pp. 143–44, 150–53, 161, 165, 169, 170–71, 176, 179, 181, 186, and 194.

21. In the standard commentary on Psalms, Ibn Ganach is (as expected) called "R. Marinus" at least six times (40:8; 74:8; 80:1; 111:2; 119:3; and 143:9), but also on two occasions "R. Jonah" (49:8 and 15). Moreover, in utter contrast to what might be expected, Yefet is cited only a few times, whereas Ibn Giqatilah is quoted more than 150 times (see Poznanski, *Ibn Giqatilah*, pp. 105–16). Friedlaender tried to explain this by assuming that this commentary is merely a reworking and expansion of the first commentary, written in Italy, and that it therefore has traits of both periods (*Essays*, p. 151, note 1; pp. 170–71). The fragment that we have now discovered totally refutes this assumption. In his commentary on Job Ibn Ezra frequently relies on examples from Arabic, and Friedlaender wanted to explain this deviation as due to the many linguisitic difficulties presented by Job (*Essays*, p. 176).

22. See lately Golb, *Rouen*, pp. 54–55.

23. An examination of Ibn Ezra's short commentary on Exodus on the twenty-seven verses where Yefet is mentioned in the long commentary reveals that Yefet is quoted in six of them: 3:3; 5:5; 7:29; 19:8: 25:4 and 17.

24. This is also the situation in his two commentaries on Genesis: in the twelve chapters of the truncated commentary Ibn Giqatilah is mentioned twice, but only once in the parallel chapters in the short (standard) commentary. He is mentioned four more times in the balance of the short commentary, twice in the commentary on Leviticus, seven times in the commentary on Numbers, and once in the commentary on Deuteronomy. (The following should be added to the references given by Poznanski [*Ibn Giqatilah,* pp. 95–98]: short commentary on Genesis 42:23; short commentary on Exodus 14:14; 15:2; and 28:4; long commentary on Exodus 14:14; 29:39; Numbers, 22:13; and Deuteronomy, 8:13. Obviously a systematic examination would uncover more references, but it is hardly likely that the proportions would change in any significant fashion.)

25. J. L. Fleischer, "When and where did Ibn Ezra Write his *Safah B^e rurah?*" (Heb.), *Ha-Ṣofeh l^e-ḥoḵmaṯ Yisrael* 13 (1929), pp. 82–88.

26. Wilensky returned to this topic in his article "Le nom D'Abou-l-Walid," *REJ* 92 (1932), pp. 55–58, where he argues that it is not reasonable that Ibn Ezra would call Ibn Ganach by an Arabic name in France, of all places, where this language was not understood. He consequently proposes that Ibn Ganach had only an Arabic name—Marwān Ibn Ganāch—and that in Italy Ibn Ezra referred to him by the Hebrew translation of his family name Ibn Ganach—R. Yonah; whereas in the French communities that were familiar with the Talmud he preferred the Talmudic name Marinus (BT Keṯuvoṯ 60a; BT Baba Baṯra 56a) as a Hebraization of his first name Marwān. To support this most interesting hypothesis he offers Ibn Ezra's habit of calling Dunash Ben Labrat by the Hebrew name R. Adonim. Ibn Ezra followed a similiar custom with regard to Abraham Ibn al-Faḫar, to whom he refers (in his long comm. on Daniel 10:17 and 11:30) as *ben ha-yoṣer,* "son of the potter" (the Hebrew translation of his Arabic surname). Nevertheless, these Hebrew names were not original with Ibn Ezra; as Bacher noted (preface to Ibn Ganach's *Dictionary,* p. ix), the name Marinus was also used by Abraham Ibn Daud, a Spanish contemporary of Ibn Ezra (*Tradition,* Hebrew portion, p. 73, line 420). The same is true of Dunash, who called himself by the Hebrew name Adoniah (*Criticism of Saadiah,* §6).

27. The name of the commentator has been erased in the manuscript of the fragmentary comm. to Psalm 2:1; it is possible that "R. Moses" is what was originally written (see my note *ad loc.*, line 35).

28. With regard to the nature and dimensions of this disorder, conclusions can be drawn from Galliner's statistics on references to Saadiah's commentary in Ibn Ezra's commentary on Job: Saadiah is mentioned by name only six times, although some 100 of Ibn Ezra's glosses coincide with Saadiah's glosses *ad loc.* Of these hundred instances, only forty are presented without attribution, while most are presented as Ibn Ezra's own opinion (see J. Galliner, *Abraham ibn Esras Hiobkommentar auf seine Quellen untersucht* [Berlin, 1901], p. 18).

29. A comparison of the Ecclesiastes and Isaiah commentaries (both written in Italy) with the commentaries on Psalms and the Minor Prophets (written in France),

included in British Library MS 24,896 (in the handwriting of a single copyist) discloses that the Ecclesiastes commentary is twice as long as the commentary on the same number of verses in the other three cases. This conspicuous length of the Ecclesiastes commentary is due only in part to the two long excursuses included in it (comm. on 5:1 and 7:3), which together run to five manuscript pages.

30. A systematic examination of the sources of Ibn Ezra's Ecclesiastes commentary performed by a student of mine, Ms. Herzliya Wagner, found very few explicit references: four to Judah Ḥayyuj, four to Ibn Giqatilah, three to Saadiah (two of them to his *Beliefs* and religious poetry); and one each to Adonim Ben Tamim, Samuel ha-Nagid, and Ibn Ganach.

31. See H. Vogelstein and P. Rieger, *Geschichte der Juden in Rom,* vol. 1 (Berlin, 1896), pp. 223–24 and 372; Fleischer, "Rome," pp. 98–100; E. E. Urbach, *The Tosafists* (Heb.), (Jerusalem, 1955^2), pp. 60–61; Y. Gottlieb, "The commentary of R. Isaac Ben Malchizedek of Siponto on Bikkurim, chapter 1" (Heb.), *Sinai* 76/77 (1975), pp. 97–99.

32. In the dedicatory poem to the long commentary on the Pentateuch (Ibn Ezra, *Poems,* vol. 1, pp. 55–56), Ibn Ezra dedicates the work to "R. Moses the son of Meir," whom he calls "my patron," who supported him during his serious illness. Alongside the warm words of gratitude there is also extravagant praise: "All wisdom was apportioned to Moses' share." We know nothing more about him. It should also be stressed that in the body of the long commentary on Exodus no difference in Ibn Ezra's attitude (thematic or stylistic) towards halakhic and aggadic midrashim is evident.

33. Ibn Ezra's two Psalms commentaries provide clear evidence that there is no basis for Friedlaender's classification of Ibn Ezra's designations of the Sages in his various compositions. In the introduction to the First Recension, written in Italy we find *ḳadmonenu* (three times), *ha-ḳadmonim, ha-ḥaḵamim z''l, ha-maʿtiḳim,* and *ḥaḵamenu z''l*, and *ḳadmonenu* in the commentary on Psalm 1. In the standard commentary, by contrast, there are few references, but the elegant variation remains: *ha-ḳadmonim* (twice) in the preface, and *ḥaḵamim* in Psalm 1. In his preface, the author of the supercommentary *Ṣafᵉnaṯ Paʿneaḥ* stressed that no element of demurral is implied by the term *ha-ḳadmonim*. In fact, it is merely a translation of the Arabic terms *ʾal-ḳudamā* and *ʾal-ʾawāyil*, used frequently by his Arabic-writing predecessors—Saadiah, Ibn Giqatilah, Ibn Balaam, and Ibn Giath.

34. G. Tamani, "Manoscritti Ebraici nella Biblioteca Comunale di Verona," *Rivista degli Studi Orientali* 45 (1970), pp. 217–43.

35. A. G. R. Naumann, ed., *Catalogus liberum manuscriptorum qui in Bibliotheca senatoria civitatis Lipsiensis asservantur* (Grimae, 1838), p. 303.

36. I published the fragment in *Ḳiryat Sefer* 57 (1982), pp. 709–14.

37. In his poem "Nᵉdod hesir ʾoni" (mentioned above, p. 153), Ibn Ezra mocks the pretensions of his adversary, who claims that he is an expert in four

orders of the Mishnah, when he does not know thoroughly even those passages that every householder knows from the Prayer Book, and who glorifies in his study of the order Tohorot, when he reads incorrectly and misunderstands scriptural verses that are familiar even to schoolchildren. Note that even in this polemic context Ibn Ezra presents himself as a student of the (written) Torah and one who knows Scripture (i.e., the Prophets and Hagiographa), and does not defend his knowledge of the Oral Law. In fact, not only did Ibn Ezra attribute a well-known passage from the Mishnah to Saadiah in his second Psalms commentary, in his first commentary he had quoted the same passage incorrectly. The Mishnah Sukkah 5,4 does not read—as he would have it—that David wrote the fifteen "Songs of Degrees" to correspond to the fifteen steps in the Temple, but quite the opposite—"the fifteen steps that descend from the Court of the Israelites to the Court of the Women correspond to the fifteen 'Songs of Degrees' in the Book of Psalms" (see also Mishnah Middot 2,5). E. Z. Melammed (*Commentators* 2, pp. 655–56) cites, in addition to the passage in question, eleven more places where Ibn Ezra attributes to Saadiah glosses whose source is the Talmudic sages. All this is merely supplementary proof to the conclusion that Ibn Ezra was not a great Talmudic scholar, as can be deduced from the instructive material gathered by Reifmann in "The Talmud and Midrash not seen by Abraham Ibn Ezra" (Heb.), in Jacob Reifmann, *Studies in Abraham Ibn Ezra* (Heb.), collected and edited by N. Ben-Menahem (Jerusalem, 1962), pp. 89–93. The Psalms commentary provides yet another example. In his gloss on 147:9, Ibn Ezra writes: " 'the raven's brood'—because the Gentile scholars say that their parents abandon them at birth." One may seriously doubt whether Ibn Ezra would have relied on non-Jewish naturalists had he remembered that the topic is discussed in BT Ketubot 49b. See further, p. 183f.

38. Recently, A. Sáenz-Badillos (ed., *Tešuboth de Dunaš ben Labrat* [Granada, 1980], p. xiii), joined the ranks of those who doubt whether Dunash was in fact the author of *Criticism of Saadiah.* Ezra Fleischer, on the other hand ("Dunash Ben Labrat, his Wife and Son" [Heb.], *Jerusalem Studies in Literature* 5 [1984], p. 189, note 4) offered two persuasive proofs of Dunash's authorship of this book. It is clear in any case that Ibn Ezra attributed it to Dunash: in the *Defense of Saadiah* he always calls his disputant R. Adonim; while in his comm. on Ps. 42:5, dealing with the subject discussed in the *Defense,* §41, he calls him Ben Labrat (this is the reading of the twelve extant manuscripts and the *editio princeps*). In his comm. on Ps. 9:1, which relates to the subject matter of §14 of the *Defense,* he refers to him as R. Dunash Halevi (the reading of *Miḳraʿot Gedolot* [Amsterdam, 1727], though all of the manuscripts have "R. Adonim").

39. See M. Wilensky, "On Abraham Ibn Ezra's *Sefer ha-Yesod* and *Sefer Sefat Yeter*" (Heb.), *Ḳiryat Sefer* 3 (1926), pp. 73–79; J. L. Fleischer, "On Abraham Ibn Ezra's *Sefer ha-Yesod* and *Sefat Yeter*" (Heb.), ibid., pp. 165–68. In the author's colophon, Ibn Ezra writes: "This book of R. Adonim's criticisms I found in the land of Egypt. There were many copyist's errors in it, because in these places our authors are not accustomed to verifying a copy made from another copy" (*Defense,* p. 34b). Wilensky (p. 79) reports that two manuscripts lack the word "Egypt"

while a third leaves a blank space (in fact, the word is missing in one manuscript, while three others leave space for four or five letters); he hypothesizes that Ibn Ezra wrote "in the land of the uncircumcised" or some other designation for Christians and the word was deleted due to censorship. Fleischer (p. 168) prefers to maintain the reading "Egypt," finding it difficult to assume that a copyist would add this on his own. In any case, given that copyists were in the habit of replacing the forbidden "Edom" and "Christians" with the names of distant lands (see W. Popper, *The Censorship of Hebrew Books* [New York, 1969^2], pp. 59 and 86), Wilensky would seem to be correct here. If so, Ibn Ezra was merely complaining about the uncritical approach of the scholars "in these places" towards the reliability of copies, which contributes to the corruption of the text, and which is particularly serious with regard to the sole exemplar of a Spanish book, which in Italy could be corrected only on the basis of conjecture (as Ibn Ezra in fact did). From this we may conclude that if Dunash's Hebrew book was so hard to find in Italy, *a fortiori* Arabic books by Spanish scholars were rare. This situation is reflected in Ibn Ezra's translations from Arabic into Hebrew: while in Rome he translated three of Ibn Ḥayyuj's works on grammar; in northern Italy or southern France, *Maša᾿allah's Book on the Eclipse of the Moon and Sun*; and in London, al-Mathni's *Ṭaᶜamei ha-luḥoṯ* (for more details, see Simon, "Exegete," notes 22, 23, 51, and 52).

40. In the long comm. on Dan 7:14 (written in Rouen in 1156), Ibn Ezra says that he is relying on his imperfect memory of a book he had seen in Spain: "I also saw this written in the Book of the Kings of Persia some forty years ago, but have forgotten the names of the cities." (He also relies on this book in ibid. on 6:1 and in the standard comm. on Esther 1:14 and 7:8.) He makes a similar remark concerning the location and regime of the land of Sheba: "This is to be found in the books, but I have forgotten their names" (long comm. on Dan. 11:6).

41. Nevertheless, in his commentary on Ecclesiastes, written in Rome a few years before the *Defense of Saadiah*, Ibn Ezra contrasted Saadiah's poetry with the liturgical poems of Eliezer Ha-kallir, which he denigrated to the point of forbidding their use in prayer: "The Gaon Rav Saadiah refrained from these four things in his two *baḳḳašoṯ*—unparalleled in the writings of any other poet!—and they are [written] according to the language of Scripture and the grammar of the [Holy] language, without riddles, parables, or homiletic interpretations" (5,1). These two statements are compatible, since this fulsome praise relates only to these two "petitions" (see Saadiah, *Siddur*, pp. 45–81), written, unlike Saadiah's *piyyuṭim*, in prose and in a lucid scriptural style. It follows that Ibn Ezra assumed that when Saadiah stuck to biblical language and avoided innovations of form and meaning he intuitively adhered to the grammatical rules as well, even though he could not have known them.

42. This rule applies mainly to the interpretation of the legal chapters of the Pentateuch, as is demonstrated, inter alia, by the fact that Ibn Ezra concludes the passage cited above from the first section of the *Defense of Saadiah* by referring the reader to Saadiah's commentary on Ex. 23:2 and 37:7.

43. M. Zucker (*Translation*, pp. 442–79) devoted a chapter (''The Translations that are not in Accordance with the Legal Homiletics'') to this subject. I rather doubt whether Ibn Ezra was accurate when he reported that Saadiah had written that we are obliged to rely on the Sages because of their superior knowledge. In any case, it is clear that when Saadiah wishes to divorce a passage from its plain meaning in accordance with the method of the *taʾwīl* in order to make it compatible with the Oral Law, he grounds this on the authority of tradition and not on the wisdom of its bearers (see Saadiah, *Beliefs*, 5,8 and 7,1; and the preface to his long commentary on the Pentateuch [Zucker, *Translation*, pp. 230–32]).

44. Ibn Ezra's vehement reservation from Saddiah's readiness to abandon the plain meaning of the text from considerations of polemic necessity was cited above, p. 40.

45. The reading of MS Parma 584 at Ps. 78:47 is ''the Gaon said,'' whereas all of the other manuscripts and the *editio princeps* (Venice, 5285 [1525]), read Ḥasan said '' (Ḥasan being Yefet's Arabic name, *ḥasan* = *yafeh* = beautiful). Ibn Ezra reports, in Ḥasan's name, that *ḥanamal* means ''a species of locust, while he himself glossed '*ḥanamal*' as two words.'' In Saadiah's *Tafsir* this word is translated as *ʾal-sakiʿ* (extreme cold), whereas in Yefet's commentary, as it has come down to us, there are two interpretations: locust; small hailstones. But not only does Yefet prefer the second interpretation, his text does not suggest splitting the word into two (an opinion offered in the name of Resh Lakish in Midrash Tehillim *ad loc.*).

46. One methodological parallel between Yefet and Ibn Ezra was mentioned above, chapter 2, note 75.

47. Cf. W. Bacher, *Abraham Ibn Esras Einleitung zu seinem Pentateuch Commentar* (Vienna, 1876), pp. 12–16. Bacher was still unacquainted with Ibn Ezra's second Pentateuch preface (in which the paths are presented in a distinctly nonchronological order); consequently he attributed also a historical inclination to Ibn Ezra—describing the history of Bible exegesis in its general lines.

48. These four advantages of the ear are found in the very same order and with slight changes in phrasing in the poem written by Ibn Ezra in Rome in honor of R. Menaḥem and his son Moses (see Ibn Ezra, *Poems*, pp. 124–26). As opposed to the clear preference expressed in the introduction, in the poem Ibn Ezra modestly leaves the decision among the arguments of eye, ear, and tongue to R. Menaḥem's great wisdom.

49. See the chapter ''The Argument between Seeing and Hearing,'' Kaufmann, *Senses*, pp. 139–43 (and cf. also pp. 117–18). Most of the scholars cited there champion the eye. Kaufmann, who was not acquainted with the First Recension, includes Ibn Ezra among them (on the basis of the passage referred to in the next note). In the *Faithful Brothers' Epistle on Music* we find a dispute between the champions of the eye and those of the ear, in which the latter clearly have the advantage (Shiloaḥ, *Epistle*, pp. 67–68). Moses Ibn Ezra, who also felt this way, says: ''Those authors who write about the senses have written untold volumes about

the superiority of hearing over the others'' (Moses ben Ezra, *Discussions*, p. 143). He does not cite these psychologists, and rests content with quoting the praise of ''a musicologist'' for hearing, cited word for word from the above-mentioned dispute in the *Epistle* (see the note by the editor of *Discussions*, A. S. Halkin). Abraham Ibn Ezra's four arguments do not have parallels in Moses Ibn Ezra, and only the third of them—that sight is restricted to straight lines—is found in the *Epistle*. There is impressive support for Abraham Ibn Ezra's fourth argument in a saying attributed to Helen Keller, who was blind and deaf, that deafness was the more severe of these two handicaps, because a blind person is cut off from objects, but the deaf person is cut off from society.

50. See the short comm. on Ex. 19:17 and 23:20, the long comm. on Ex. 3:6 and 20:1, and his *Sefer ha-ʾEḥad*, ed. Pinsker (Odessa, 1867, repr. Jerusalem, 1970), p. 55. Ibn Ezra's view of the immediacy of vision seems to have been influenced by Solomon Ibn Gabirol in *Sefer Tiḳḳun Middoṯ ha-Nefeš*, tr. Judah Ibn Tibbon (Riva di Triento, 1562), p. 4a, as quoted in Kaufmann, *Senses*, p. 117, note 55.

51. The classic example of this is the two versions of the Decalogue (see the long comm. on Ex. 20:1; Deut. 5:5; *Yᵉsod Moraʾ*, §1). Additional examples are discussed in the long comm. on Ex. 11:5 and 32:9; Isa. 36:1. He needs this axiom also to explain the ungrammatical nature of the midrashic explanations of proper names found in Scripture (*Safah Bᵉrurah*, ed. Wilensky, p. 288; ed. Lippmann, p. 4a), and to ground his evaluation of the Sages' homiletical interpretations as deviating from the plain meaning of the text (ed. Wilensky, loc. cit.; ed. Lippmann, p. 4b). His attitude on this matter is very similar to that of Moses Ibn Ezra, who also relies on his predecessors: ''It has been said: 'The meaning is the soul and the word is the body.' It has also been said: 'The prophet cannot fulfill his mission other than through words, of which some will be understood even if they are different from the words that he heard, and the idea is not changed thereby' '' (Moses Ibn Ezra, *Discussions*, p. 145). In another context (p. 43), Moses Ibn Ezra attributes the distinction between an object and its name to Galen; here too it seems likely that Moses Ibn Ezra was influenced by the *Epistle* (see Shiloaḥ, *Epistle*, pp. 35 and 41) and by his teacher R. Isaac Ibn Giath, who dealt with this matter at great length in the preface to his Ecclesiastes commentary (Ibn Giath, *Ecclesiastes*, pp. 161–62).

52. See the chapter on ''Poetry as ornamented speech'' in Pagis, *Secular Poetry*, pp. 35–54.

53. Of language viewed purely as a tool for communication, Ibn Ezra writes as follows: ''The core of speech is allusions; knowledge of language is not knowledge intrinsically, but only a means of mutual understanding'' (short comm. on Ex. 23:20). At the same time, common nouns are not arbitrary but essential: ''You see that he [Adam] gave names to all of the animals and birds according to the nature of each and every one of them, and he was a very wise man'' (comm. on Gen. 2:17). But whereas for Yehudah Halevy this supported his view that Hebrew is ''the language created by God, which he taught Adam and placed on his tongue and in his heart'' (*Kuzari* 4,25; p. 229), Ibn Ezra saw Adam as the creator of the Hebrew

language (second introduction to the Pentateuch, the "First Way": "According to the rules of the language established by Adam" [ed. Weiser, vol. 1, p. 137]); therefore he accorded the Hebrew language no more than the status of "the first language" (*Safah B^{e}rurah*, ed. Wilensky, p. 286; ed. Lippmann, p. 2a) and of a "lucid tongue," unique in that it is the holy tongue, since "only it contains the great Divine name" (comm. on Zeph. 3:8). His realistic understanding of the separation of the other languages from Hebrew at the time of the tower of Babel (see his two commentaries on Gen. 11:7) is compatible with this. Moses Ibn Ezra, too, stresses the conventional nature of language, rhetoric, and poetry—unlike music, which in his opinion is one of the exact sciences based on proof because of its affinity with mathematics (*Discussions*, p. 135).

54. Everything that Ibn Ezra says here in praise of poetry and music, and much else, is to be found in the *Epistle on Music* (Shiloaḥ, pp. 12–17). Isaac Ibn Giath (1038–1089) also writes of the power of music to restore the equilibrium of the soul, give it spiritual pleasure, and heal it (*Ecclesiastes*, p. 168).

55. In the Third Inquiry of the first introduction Ibn Ezra again cites 1 Chron. 9:22 as a proof that the psalms were written under the inspiration of the Holy Spirit: " 'by their faith' means by the faith of the Holy Spirit" (line 87). Later, however, he felt compelled to give up the assumption that "by their faith" indicates that the five elements were ordained by prophetic illumination (see the long comm. on Ex. 12:1, written many years after the first commentary on Psalms). Yehudah Halevy, too, believed that the establishment of the Levitical divisions by David and Samuel was a non-prophetic innovation (*Kuzari* 3,39; p. 172).

56. He stresses the superiority of the right over the left side in his comm. on Gen. 48:16 as well; the astronomical-astrological superiority of south over north is alluded to in his comm. on Numbers 1:19.

57. In his comm. on Isa. 5:12, too, he asserts with no proof that *nevel* is a wind instrument with ten holes. It is clear that he did not infer this from "nevel ʿaśor" (Ps. 33:2), as Saadiah, Yefet, and Ibn Giqatilah had done, since in his comm. *ad loc.* (as well as in *Ṣaḥoṯ*, p. 41b) he demurs at this interpretation by Ibn Giqatilah, who said that *nevel ʿaśor* means "a *nevel* with ten holes," and argues that *nevel* and *ʿaśor* are two separate instruments. It is clear from what follows that he was interested in the syntactic ellipsis and not in the identity of the instrument, to which he returns only in his ungrounded assertion in his commentary on Psalm 150. Perhaps he offered no support for the identification because he saw it as no more than a hypothesis (cf. the passage quoted in the next note).

58. In the long comm. on Daniel 3:5 (written the same year as the standard Psalms commentary) he glosses only two of the six Aramaic names of musical instruments found in the verse, and goes no further than the assertion that these are "musical instruments." By way of self-justification he adds that this is the state of affairs with regard to the holy tongue: "We do not know what *kinnor* and *maḥol* and *minnim* and *ʿugav* are, even though *ʿugav* is derived from *wa-taʿg^{e}vah* ["she lusted"—Ezek. 23:20] and *minnim* is two instruments and *maḥol* is a kind of flute

[*ḥalil*], and *kinnor* is shaped like a candelabrum [*m^enorah*]. But these are hypotheses without proof.'' In his two commentaries on Gen. 4:21, as well as in his glosses on Ps. 92:4 and Isa. 22:24, he also fails to identify *kinnor* and *ʿugav*.

59. The discussion of poetic meters in *Ṣaḥot* concludes by answering the anticipated question of the reader (who, of course, was not educated in Spain): ''Perhaps someone will ask: what is the point of the meters being the way you described them? Cannot I make an unlimited number of meters, placing a *yated* [metrical foot] after a *yated* and adding or taking away?! Perhaps this questioner will awake from his slumber of ignorance and learn the wisdom of the Arabs; then he will have full proofs of why [just] these meters were chosen and not others and will be satisfied'' (ed. Rodriguez, p. 31; ed. Lippmann, p. 11b). Moses Ibn Ezra went on at great length about this in *Discussions*, pp. 29–39 and 57.

60. In his comm. on Eccles. 5:1 Ibn Ezra asserts that ''we nowhere find that the prophets in their prayers speak in rhyme''; his opinion on the nature of the songs and poems not included in the Bible can evidently be inferred from his commentary on Amos 6:5: ''They knew how to write unmetrical [*ḥatukim*] poems to a melody, without rhyme.'' Just as separate grapes (*pereṭ*) are not connected to one another, so too they ''separate'' (*por^eṭim*) their poems (cf. his comm. on Lev. 19:10). Since the Spanish poets called metrical rhymed poetry *m^eḥubbar,* ''connected'' (a translation of the Arabic *manẓūm*) and unmetrical prose *m^eforad,* ''separated'' (a translation of the Arabic *mantūr*), it is understandable that Ibn Ezra (like Yefet in his commentary *ad loc.*) inferred from *por^eṭim* that the reference is to nonmetrical poetry. This interpretation of Ibn Ezra's most enigmatic statement is substantiated by his gloss on Amos 6:5 in the Second Recension (see *Minor Prophets ad loc.*). Ibn Ezra's meaning in the two commentaries is identical: they sing unrhymed and nonmetrical poems that are linked only by their melody, which gives them a rhythm. In his denial of Jewish anticipation of the Arabic meters he was preceded by Dunash, Menaḥem, and their disciples, whose fierce argument as to whether ''Arabic meters are proper in the Jewish tongue'' did not prevent their agreeing about historical fact (see Dunash, *Criticism of Menaḥem*, p. 31; Menaḥem's Disciples, *Polemics*, part 1, p. 27; part 2, p. 22). The same applies to Samuel ha-Nagid, who did not hesitate to praise a panegyric written in his honor for being ''balanced in the meter of the Ishmaelites / and supported by the wisdom of the Greeks'' (*Ben Tehillim*, poem 61, line 18; see also poem 53, line 14). Moses Ibn Ezra, too, gave a negative answer to the painful question—''was [rhymed and metrical] poetry known in our nation in the days of its kingdom and glory?'' (*Discussions*, p. 47), as did his contemporaries, Yehudah Halevy (*Kuzari*, 2,72–78; pp. 126–27) and the apostate Jewish philosopher Abu-l-Barakāt ʾal-Baġdādī (see Pines, ''Abu'l-Barakāt,'' p. 130), followed in the thirteenth century by Yehudah al-Ḥarizi (*Taḥk^emoni*, §18) and Moses Ibn Tibbon (in the preface to his commentary on the Song of Songs, Lick, 1874), and, at the beginning of the sixteenth century, by Don Isaac Abarbanel (beginning of his commentary on Ex. 15). For those who held the opposite view, see note 74.

61. For the apologiae by Samuel ha-Nagid and his son Yehoseph for the composition of love poetry, see Y. Ratzaby, ''Love in the poetry of Samuel ha-Nagid''

(Heb.), *Tarbiṣ* 39 (1970), pp. 146–47; for Moses Ibn Ezra's self-justification in the matter, see *Discussions*, p. 107; cf. Pagis, *Secular Poetry*, pp. 272–74. With regard to the tension between Yehudah Halevy's fundamental opposition to the adoption of Arabic metrics (*Kuzari* 2,70; p. 125) and his unbroken composition of metrical verse until the end of his life, see N. Allony, "R. Judah Halevy and the Theory of Poetry in the *Kuzari*" (Heb.), *Sinai* 9 (1942), pp. 168–83.

62. This is precisely what Ibn Ezra did in the introduction to his standard commentary on the Song of Songs: "This is an important and precious book, and its equal cannot be found in all of the poems of King Solomon—a thousand and five [see 1 Kings 5:12]; this is why it begins 'the Song of Songs of Solomon's,' because this song is superior to all others by Solomon, and it has a deep and hidden secret, for it begins with the times of our father Abraham [and continues] through the days of the Messiah." Nor does he praise the form elsewhere in the commentary. In his comm. on Eccles. 1:1, too, he discusses the poetry of Solomon mentioned in 1 Kings 5:12, and characterizes it exclusively in terms of its content: "It is in the nature of poetry to be a praise-psalm [reading with the MS *tᵉhillah* instead of *tᵉḥillah]* or [about] what will occur in the future [i.e., prophecy]."

63. This argument undoubtedly applies to Ibn Ezra's own poetical output, as can be inferred from the quantitative ratio between his religious and secular poetry. I. Levin, in his survey of the girdle poems in *Abraham Ibn Ezra,* enumerates 270 religious poems (pp. 252–99), versus only twenty-eight secular girdle poems (pp. 240–46).

64. This was pointed out by A. S. Halkin, the editor of *Discussions*, p. 73, note 69.

65. See M. Idel, "The identity of the translator of R. Moses Ibn Ezra's Sefer *ʿArugat̲ ha-Bośem*" (Heb.), *Ḳiryat Sefer* 51 (1976), pp. 484–87; S. Abramson, "The translator of R. Moses Ibn Ezra's *ʿArugat̲ ha-Bośem* was R. Yehudah al-Ḥarizi" (Heb.), ibid., p. 712; P. Fenton, "Gleanings from Mošhe Ibn Ezra's Maqálat Al-Ḥadiqa," *Sefarad* 36 (1976), pp. 285–89.

66. A. Shiloaḥ, "The Musical Passage in Ibn Ezra's *Book of the Garden*," *Yuval* 4 (1982), pp. 212–24.

67. The Sasson MS is missing a leaf between fols. 212 and 213, and a photocopy of the Leningrad MS was not available to the editors. For this reason Adler decided to begin his quotation of the musicological passage from fol. 213, even though it actually begins on 203, as Shiloaḥ demonstrated. Adler and Shiloaḥ divided the text into sentences and numbered them; these numbers will be used in the citations that follow below.

68. See note 60.

69. This problem is also mentioned by Yehudah Halevy (*Kuzari* 2, 69–77; pp. 125–27), but he makes quite different use of it and thus does not need this passage from Psalms. Neither Saadiah nor Abraham Ibn Ezra glossed the verse in this way.

70. See BT Ḥullin 24a: "A Levite from the age of thirty to the age of fifty is fit for the divine service, and age disqualifies him. To what does this refer?—to the tabernacle in the desert; but at Shiloh and the Holy Temple (where there is no labor of carrying) they are disqualified only by their voices." Here (and in another halakhic matter which does not concern us) his summary exactly corresponds with what Maimonides writes, *Laws of the Temple Vessels*, 3,7–8.

71. He goes no further than this allusion to 1 Chron. 9:22 (upon which Abraham Ibn Ezra relies too [see above, note 55]); immediately thereafter he relies on 1 Chron. 28:19 as an explicit proof that this was done at God's command.

72. Moses Ibn Ezra did not disagree with Saadiah, who added in his *Tafsir*, alongside "we hung up our lyres" the gloss "by way of putting them away"; he assumed, however, that the lyres were hung up in reaction to the captors' demand that Levites sing the songs of Zion (as is indicated by the word *ki*, "for," at the beginning of verse 3). It follows that until then the exiles had held their lyres in their hands and played on them while mourning for Zion.

73. Here Moses Ibn Ezra is quoting or paraphrasing his teacher, R. Isaac Ibn Giath, who offers this gloss in his commentary on Ecclesiastes *ad loc.* (p. 193).

74. It would seem that "scholars" refers inter alia—or perhaps chiefly—to Isaac Ibn Giath, who writes, in the introduction to his commentary on Ecclesiastes, that "I got myself male and female singers" (2:8) refers to "the knowledge of logic, rhetoric, grammar, languages, and prose and poetry, like metrical songs and the *tarǵīᶜ* and the *tarǵīz* (*Ecclesiastes*, p. 168). The spiritual need to adorn biblical poetry with the concepts of gentile poetry, considered to be superior, can already be found in the writings of Josephus, who, in accordance with the spirit of his times, attributed the Greek meters to the psalms: "David, being now free from wars and dangers, and enjoying profound peace from this time on, composed songs and hymns to God in varied meters—some he made in trimeters and others in pentameters. He also made musical instruments. . . . The forms of these instruments were somewhat as follows. . . . But now that our readers are not altogether unacquainted with the nature of the aforementioned instruments, let this much about them suffice" (*Jewish Antiquities*, 7,12,3, tr. H. St. J. Thackeray and R. Marcus [London and Cambridge, Mass., 1934]). By contrast, Saadiah (or someone from his school) had no qualms about acknowledging that even though the Bible contains *raǵaz* rhymes (e.g., Job 28:16 and 21:4; Isa. 49:1), this is not true poetry (*Ha-ᵓEgron*, p. 387). For three scholars later than Moses Ibn Ezra who vigorously insisted upon the antiquity of metrical poetry among the Jews, see Allony, *Scansion*, pp. 16–17.

75. The importance for Moses Ibn Ezra of this broad basis can be demonstrated by his note that he intends to take most of his examples of each poetical ornament from Scripture, "Lest they be thought to be few in number and someone say that in these too we have little vigor" (*Discussions*, p. 221).

76. If we did not know that Abraham Ibn Ezra agreed with Moses Ibn Ezra in his evaluation of the formal aspects of the Song of Songs (see above, note 62) and

denied that metrical and rhymed poetry were known in the biblical period (see above, note 60) we might have assumed, on the basis of his comm. on Numbers 21:14, that he was one of the scholars with whom Moses Ibn Ezra disagrees. There he writes: " 'In the Book of the Wars of God'—this was a separate book, in which the wars of God were transcribed for those who fear Him. Perhaps it goes back to the times of Abraham, since many books have been lost and cannot be found, like the 'History of Nathan' (1 Chron. 29:29), the 'Chronicles of Iddo' (2 Chron. 12:15), the 'Chronicles of the Kings of Israel' (1 Kings 14:19 et passim) and *the songs and proverbs of Solomon* (1 Kings 5:12)."

77. See I. Goldziher, "Die šuʿubiya unter der Muhammedanern in Spanien," *ZDMG* 53 (1899), pp. 601–620; S. A. Halkin, "Moses Ibn Ezra and Poetic Language: Arabic Criteria and Arabic Linguistics" (Heb.), *Molad* 5 (27), pp. 316–21; idem., introduction to *Discussions*, pp. 14–16; N. Allony, "R. Moses Ibn Ezra's Reaction to *Arabiyya* in *Discussions*" (Heb.), *Tarbiṣ* 42 (1973), pp. 97–112; idem. "The Hebrew *Egron* Versus *Arabiyya*" (Heb.), in: *Shazar Festschrift* (Jerusalem, 1973), pp. 465–74.

78. Moses Ibn Ezra, *Secular Poetry,* ed. H. Brody, vol. 1 (Berlin, 1935), poem no. 234, lines 131–33. See also poem no. 24, lines 23–24.

79. In this realm Moses Ibn Ezra even granted primacy to Scripture, since for him its priority in time is adequate proof that the Arabic poets must have imitated it in this regard (see *Discussions*, p. 225).

80. There were various opinions among the Arabs on this subject. The Faithful Brothers—whose approach to the subject was not at all chauvinistic and whose *Epistle on Music* was known, as has been said, to Moses Ibn Ezra—attribute the invention of musical instruments and the development of musical theory to "philosophers" (see *Epistle,* pp. 15, 32–33, 40). For Iberian Jewry's taste for Arabic music and their poets' dependence on Arabic melodies, we have the testimony of Tadros Abulafia (born in Toledo in 1247) in the prefatory poem to the *diwan* of his girdle poems, as summarized or paraphrased by the editor: "At the beginning of each of these songs I will indicate according to which scene [i.e., the melody of which song] it should be sung to. These are the melodies of Arabic songs, because it is now customary for those who perform music to sing according to the Ishmaelite instruments" (Tadros, *Girdle Poems*, p. 5, and glosses on p. 3). Still, we do have knowledge of Jewish composers in Spain (see Schirmann, "Poets," p. 134).

81. For the link between prophesy and wisdom in the philosophy of Yehudah Halevy, see Y. Silman, "Intellect, Revelation, 'Rational Being' and Prophet in the Kuzari of Y. Hallevi," in: M. Ḥallamish and M. Schwarcz, eds., *Revelation-Faith-Reason* (Ramat Gan, 1976), pp. 44–53 (Heb.). On the status of Hebrew as the divine tongue see Y. Silman, *Thinker and Seer* (Ramat Gan, 1985), pp. 87–88 and 246 (Heb.); cf. note 53 above.

82. Evidence of the high status accorded by Abraham Ibn Ezra to musical science is the fragmentary comm. on Gen. 4:21: "Musical wisdom is excellent, be-

cause it is based on [mathematical] proportions'' (ed. Weiser, vol. 1, p. 172; cf. the standard comm. *ad loc.*). Ibn Ezra also found scriptural support for Pythagoras' theory of the music of the spheres; see his comm. on Ps. 93:4 and Job 38:7. His remarks there agree with the Faithful Brothers (*Epistle*, pp. 35–38 and 45–47). On the other hand, Maimonides (*Guide to the Perplexed*, 2,8, p. 267) argues that in this matter we must accept the view of Aristotle, who denied the existence of the music of the spheres, even though the Sages believed in it, because in matters relating to physical nature our decision must be based on observation and experiment.

83. Ibn Ezra avoids relying on the prooftexts cited by Saadiah in his introduction for anchoring his argument that *l^e-Mošeh* means ''for the sons of Moses,'' against which Salmon ben Yeruḥam had raised serious questions. Even if one does not accept Ibn Ezra's conclusion that the Messiah is called ''Solomon,'' one must acknowledge that his prooftexts are valid per se. He also cites them in his standard commentary on the Song of Songs, the preface of the Third Way, as proofs that ''every 'Solomon' means King Solomon, except for 'You have the thousand, O Solomon' (8:12), which refers to the Messiah who is called Solomon because he is his son.''

84. In his comm. on Ps. 72:1 he provides philological grounding for this interpretation: ''It is [MS Oxford-Bodleian Lib. 364: For] the letter *lamed* means 'about,' as in 'about Levi he said' (Deut. 33:8), since 'Your Thummim and Urim' is addressed to the Lord.'' In his comm. on Deut. 33:8 he cites Gen. 20:13 as proof; in his commentary there he cites Ex. 14:3).

85. This proof, presented as a hypothesis by Ibn Ezra, is phrased as certain in Saadiah's introduction (see *Psalms*, pp. 29–30).

86. See his comm. on Ps. 20:1; 21:11 (and cf. 110:1); 28:1; and 65:2. In his comm. on 66:1 he formulates the stylistic criterion for attributing Psalms to David as follows: ''The name of the author is not mentioned; because it is spoken in the first person plural, which is not found in most of the Psalms that are by David, this Psalm, too, may be by one of the other poets'' (in this vein see also his comm. on 90:1).

87. An outstanding example of the rejection of an accepted method because it is not absolutely required can be found in Ibn Ezra's remarks in his first introduction to the Pentateuch, the Fifth Way: ''In the glosses based on the plain meaning, there is also no need for *tiḳḳun sof^erim* [a rabbinic method that assumes some textual changes]'' (ed. Weiser, vol. 1, p. 10). See also his comm. on Gen. 2:2; short comm. on Ex. 34:11; long comm. on Ex. 2:3; 15:27; 25:3; and on Deut. 25:4.

88. He also uses the word *m^ešorer* in two senses, relying on the reader to infer from the context which of these is meant. At the beginning of the later introduction he distinguishes between *m^ešorer* and *m^eḥabb^er* (''This Book of Psalms contains some psalms in which the name of the poet [*m^ešorer*] or author [*m^eḥabb^er*] is found in the heading''—lines 7–8), but later *m^ešorer* means either musician (''David wrote it [*ḥibb^ero*] about the Ark, and gave it to Asaph the singer [*ha-m^ešorer*]''—

line 50) or author (''Every psalm that says in its heading *l^e-Dawid* is by David, or by some [other] poet [*m^ešorer*] prophesying about David,''—lines 39–40). See above in the chapter on Yefet (pp. 83f.), who also uses *m^ešorer* in both senses.

89. See Pagis, *Secular Poetry*, pp. 101–105.

90. This is why he also uses the word *m^eḥabb^er* to indicate a creator who does not write books, like ''the *m^eḥabb^er* of the Holy Tongue'' (*Ṣaḥot*, p. 171; ed. Lippmann, p. 14a).

91. In *Sefer ha-Šem*, §8 (ed. Lippmann, p. 18b) he writes: ''The Tetragrammaton was known only to the few pious ones until the advent of our teacher Moses. Note that it is not to found anywhere in the colloquy of Job and his friends [i.e., in the speeches in the book]; one cannot argue from 'Fear of the Lord is wisdom' [Job 28:28], because here it is written as *adonai*. Nor can one argue from 'The Lord answered Job' (38:1; 40:1 and 6) because these are the words of the transcriber [*maᶜtiḳ*].'' True, in the opinion of Lippmann (in his note *ad loc.*), Friedlaender (*Essays*, p. 59, note 1) and Rosin (*Philosophy*, vol. 43, p. 25), Ibn Ezra is referring here to the translator of the book. In fact, in the preface to his standard commentary on Esther Ibn Ezra wrote that ''the Persians translated it [*heᶜtiḳuha*] and copied it in their royal chronicles.'' Generally, however, he uses the word *targum* about the Book of Job itself (comm. on Job 2:11), Saadiah's *Tafsir* (comm. on Gen. 2:11), and the Septuagint (long comm. on Ex. 4:20). But it is the essence that counts, not terminology. The fact that the Tetragrammaton appears a dozen times or more in the narrative portion of the story (and is even used by Job himself: ''The Lord has given and the Lord has taken away; blessed be the name of the Lord''—1:21) indicates that here Ibn Ezra was not using *maᶜtiḳ* in the sense of a translator who perhaps adds speakers' names of his own accord, but to refer to whoever transmitted the chapters containing the colloquy of Job and his friends to us by transcribing them and adding speakers' names and a narrative framework (in which he preserves the meaning but not the wording).

92. This is Rashi's gloss *ad loc.*

93. In the parallel passages in Canticles Rabba 4,3 and *Midrash Tehillim* 1,6 David is identified not as the one who ''wrote'' the book but as the first among its poets.

94. On the other hand, R. Maimon the *dayyan* (father of Maimonides, contemporary of Ibn Ezra, and one of the greatest Talmudists in Spain) related to the well-known *baraita* about the Book of Psalms in BT Baba Batra 15a as to a historical fact, albeit without defining it as an obligatory tradition. As he says in his *Letter of Consolation*: ''I pondered why this prayer [i.e., Psalm 90, written by Moses] was included in the Book of Psalms, and it was handed down by uncontended tradition until the time of David, who inserted it in his book of praises, with whatever else he had arranged of the prophecies of ten elders, some of whom preceded him and some of whom were his contemporaries'' (Hebrew tr. B. Klar [Jerusalem, 1945], p. 39).

95. Compare his similar expressions: "The tradition is strong and does not require reinforcement" (long comm. on Ex. 13:9); "since we have a tradition [in this matter] we do not need to inquire" (comm. on Leviticus 16:29). As for the obligation to accept the tradition and its epistemological reliability, he writes, in his commentary on "things we have heard and known, that our fathers have told us" (Ps. 78:3): " 'we have heard'—from many and righteous men, since the individual is *obliged* to accept what they have transmitted, so that tradition is like knowledge: this is the meaning of 'and known'; the sense of 'telling' (verse 4) is that those who told it loved us—viz., 'our fathers,' who have no desire to deceive us."

96. In his first commentary on the Song of Songs, written in Italy, Ibn Ezra used halakhic terms and thereby avoided the factual imprecision about the lack of a disagreement: "Were it not for its high status, in that it was uttered with divine inspiration, it would not defile the hands" (ed. Mathews, p. 9). Since for him the absence of a disagreement among the Sages is one of the salient features of an obligatory tradition, its existence is permission not to accept the words of the Sages as a historical fact: "The homiletical interpretation that one in five hundred came out [of Egypt] is the statement of a single person, while others disagree, and it is not tradition at all" (short comm. on Ex. 13:18).

97. In his gloss on 3:15, he uses more indefinite language: "Scripture tells. . . ."

98. This was not Ibn Ezra's procedure with regard to the legal portions of the Pentateuch, where he upheld tradition and tended to see the proofs not based on the literal meaning found in the Sages' homiletical interpretations as merely supporting texts: "What the Sages said about this is true, for they had received the tradition that a man is heir to his wife and defiles himself when she dies, and they taught this homiletical interpretation as a sign and reminder that it not be forgotten" (*Safah B^e^rurah*, ed. Wilensky, p. 289; ed. Lippmann, p. 5a-b).

99. Ibn Ezra expresses this subordination of obedience to the Sages' words to their being tradition as follows: "If this is the tradition, we accept it" (comm. on Gen. 22:4; long comm. on Ex. 15:22). It should be noted that Ibn Ezra passes over in silence the fact that in BT Baba Batra 15a the writing down of the Song of Songs and Ecclesiastes is attributed to Hezekiah and his circle. In his opinion, Solomon was both author and editor of Ecclesiastes (see his comm. on 1:12; 7:3; and especially 1:1, where he attributes to Solomon even the superscription of the book). Similarly, he ignores the fact that, according to the *baraita,* Esther was written down by the Men of the Great Assembly, and expresses his opinion on the subject in the preface to his standard commentary on Esther: "In my opinion the correct answer is that this scroll was written by Mordechai, and this is the meaning of 'he sent dispatches [*s^e^farim* = books]' (9:20), all of which were copies of a single book, namely, this scroll."

100. We have a certain amount of evidence about the background for Ibn Ezra's fears (collected in S. Salfeld, *Das Hohelied Salomos bei den jüdischen Erklärern des Mittelalters* (Berlin, 1879): (1) R. Joseph ben Judah Ibn Aknin was a

younger Spanish contemporary of Ibn Ezra who fled to North Africa because of anti-Jewish persecution. In the epilogue of his Arabic commentary on the Song of Songs, based on the arcane meaning (*Divulgatio Mysteriorum Luminumque Apparentia*, ed. and tr. into Hebrew by A. S. Halkin [Jerusalem, 1964], p. 49) he writes of a Jewish physician—whom we know as a friend of Yehudah Halevy—who met another Jewish physician at the court of the ruler of Marakkesh "interpreting the Song of Songs according to its plain meaning as a love poem; I rebuked that physician and criticized him in front of the king, to whom I said: 'This man is a boor and ignoramus and knows absolutely nothing about our Torah and its scholars, and does not understand the meaning of Solomon, son of David, peace be on both of them, and his intention in this book.' " At the beginning of the commentary (p. 3), too, he writes: "The masses stick to the plain meaning." (2) R. Joseph Kimḥi, another contemporary of Ibn Ezra who emigrated from Spain to southern France, writes in the preface to his commentary on the Song of Songs (MS Oxford-Bodleian Lib. 63): "The commentator who said that King Solomon wrote this poem in his youth as a love song meant to delight—not even crazy people will agree with him. . . . Heaven forbid that love songs and amorous poetry be included in the Scriptures" (cited by Salfeld, p. 53n.). (3) In the prefatory poem to the commentary on the Song of Songs erroneously attributed to Naḥmanides, but in fact written by his contemporary R. Ezra Girondi, we read: "I have seen that there are three groups holding three opinions about it: The first group did not understand and was not intelligent and slew many by saying that his writings are of desire and charm, of idolatry and vanity that are of no benefit. May their mouths be stopped up and their eyes rot. Were they correct, it would not have been written or included in the Holy Scriptures" (*The Writings of R. Moses Naḥmanides*, ed. C. D. Chavel, vol. 2 [Jerusalem, 1964], p. 480).

101. With regard to the transmission of an interpretation by the oral tradition, see his comm. on Deut. 31:19, "teach it to the Children of Israel." The parallel between the Song of Songs and the song of Moses in Deut. 32 is pointed out in the introduction to the standard commentary on the Song of Songs. The great distance between this conception of the historical sequence of events and that of the Talmudic sages themselves can be seen from the words of the Tanna Abba Shaul: "Originally, it is said, Proverbs, Song of Songs, and Ecclesiastes were suppressed; for since they were held to be mere parables and not part of the Holy Writings [the religious authorities] arose and suppressed them; [and so they remained] until the men of Hezekiah came and interpreted them" (*The Fathers According to Rabbi Nathan* 1,5, tr. Judah Goldin [New Haven, 1955], p. 5).

102. The source for this assertion is not clear. He may be referring to Rabbi Eliezer's statement in the *baraita* in BT Pesaḥim 117a, which ostensibly refers only to David: " 'To David, a Psalm' intimates that the Shechinah [Holy Spirit] rested upon him and then he uttered [that] song: 'A Psalm of David' intimates that he [first] uttered [that particular] psalm and then the Shechinah rested upon him" (tr. H. Freedman). See my hypothesis (pp. 3f. above) about Saadiah's similar remark in his short introduction to Psalms (which may have served as a secondary source for

Ibn Ezra here): "We must understand . . . everything in this book [as] . . . the word of the Lord and nothing [as] human discourse, as the faithful transmitters of our tradition have attested" (*Psalms,* p. 53). Cf. below, note 109.

103. In his comm. on Isa. 41:2 he uses the phrasing "this too is correct, but in my opinion . . ." where his meaning is that he prefers another interpretation even though he must acknowledge that the former is possible. In his comm. on Isa. 45:1 he offers two alternative interpretations, demonstrates that "both of them are correct" (i.e., possible), and finally interprets the prophecy according to the second alternative, which appears more likely to him. See also his comm. on Ps. 110:1.

104. On the other hand, he feels this is necessary in the standard commentary on the Song of Songs, end of the preface of the Third Way: "Since the verse attests that God appeared to Solomon twice (1 Kings 3:5; 9:2), why should we be surprised that he prophesies about a future event, since this book was written with divine inspiration? The same applies to Asaph and Heman, who also wrote poems under divine inspiration and are called 'prophets' and 'seers'."

105. He would later retract this interpretation (long comm. on Ex. 12:1).

106. His reliance on Habakkuk's prayer as proof that prophetic prayer is possible was anticipated by Yefet in his commentary on Hannah's prayer (1 Samuel 2:1), quoted above, p. 81.

107. Ibn Ezra's hesitations about innovative commentary seems to contradict our image of him. But we also find this in a nonpolemic context, referring to his own ideas: "Were it not for the fact that it is not proper to innovate, I would say . . ." (comm. on Isa. 57:19).

108. Ibn Ezra frequently relies on the prophetic past in his commentaries; see Bacher, *Ibn Ezra,* p. 127. In *Ṣaḥoṯ* (ed. Rodriguez, p. 315; ed. Lippmann, p. 43b) he offers it in the name of Samuel ha-Nagid.

109. Just as he relies here on Psalm 3, he also mentions Jonah's prophetic prayer in his comm. on Ps. 3:1; 6:2; and 28:6. In perceiving the psalms as prophetic Ibn Ezra is following the Sages, as he stresses in his two introductions. An outstanding example of the Sages' approach can be found in the words of R. Judah in the name of Rav about Ps. 137: "This indicates that the Holy One, blessed be He, showed David the destruction both of the first Temple and of the second Temple. Of the first Temple, as it is written, 'By the rivers of Babylon, there we sat, yea we wept'; of the second Temple, as it is written, 'Remember, O Lord, against the children of Edom [i.e., Rome] the day of Jerusalem (Ps. 137:1,7)" (BT Giṭṭin 57b, tr. I. Eppstein). The Karaite Yefet ben ʿAli also followed this route, both in his commentary on Psalms (see above, pp. 80f.) and in his commentary on Jonah 2:2–3 (MS Bodleian 2483): "He says 'You brought my life up from the pit,' which means—You brought my life up from this grave, i.e., 'the belly of the fish.' This is a prophecy: he knew that the Master of the world would rescue him from the belly of the fish and that he would return to the Land of Israel and see God's temple."

110. In *Midrash Tehillim* (Ps. 90, §4) this approach is phrased radically: "R. Eleazar taught in the name of R. Jose ben Zimra: None of the Prophets, as they uttered their prophecies, knew that they were prophesying, except Moses and Isaiah who did know. Thus Moses said: 'My doctrine shall drop as the rain' (Deut. 32:4); and Isaiah said: 'Behold, I and the children whom the Lord hath given me shall be for signs and for wonders in Israel' (Isa. 8:18). R. Joshua the Priest bar Nehemiah maintained that Elihu also prophesied and knew he was prophesying, for he said: 'My lips shall utter knowledge clearly' (Job 33:3). R. Eleazar taught in the name of R. Jose ben Zimra:

> Samuel, the master of prophets, as he uttered his prophecy did not know he was prophesying, as is said: 'And the Lord sent Jerubbaal, and Bedan, and Jephthah, and Samuel' (1 Sam. 12:11). Samuel did not say 'the Lord sent . . . me,' but 'the Lord sent . . . Samuel,' for he did not know that he was prophesying" (*The Midrash on Psalms,* tr. W. G. Braude [New Haven, 1959], vol. 2, p. 88).

In the preface to his commentary on Zechariah, Ibn Ezra explains that the levels of prophecy depend on the varying capacities of the prophets to absorb, and that this capacity diminished over the generations. In contrast to the prophets of the Second Temple, like Zechariah and Daniel, who required angels to decipher their nocturnal visions for them, he mentions an ancient prophecy that was totally clear: "When the glory still dwelt with Israel before they were exiled, there was no need to interpret prophecies, as in the case of 'a son shall be born to the House of David, Josiah by name' (1 Kings 13:2), and it was understood at once." We see that Ibn Ezra was concerned with the meaning of the name Josiah, and not with its significance and relevancy for those who heard it.

In his long comm. on Dan. 8:25 Ibn Ezra stresses that not everything was explained to Daniel and makes clear the purpose of incomprehensible prophecy: "Daniel, too, did not know the end, for he said 'I heard and did not understand' (12:8), and he also said 'seal the book until the time of the end' (12:4). 'But the knowledgeable will understand' (12:10) when the end comes, from the words of an angel." What was incomprehensible to Daniel and his contemporaries was intended for the wise and learned men of the generation of redemption, who would read the prophecy in the light of its fulfillment. The same applies to psalms that deal with future events, like 'By the waters of Babylon,' which were spoken in the voice of the exiles and intended for them rather than their ancestors (in this context see also his comm. on Zech. 11:11).

Ibn Ezra, who did not accept the principle that a future-oriented prophecy had to be relevant when uttered, acknowledged it with regard to past-oriented prophecy. He rejected Saadiah's interpretation of Belshazzar's dream: "[Saadiah said that] this vision is about the past, about what happened to Nebuchadnezzer. . . . This is not correct, in my view, because what is the sense of seeing what has passed and what is the benefit of recalling it?" (long comm. on Dan. 7:14). For the same reason he rejects the "decoding" of Zechariah's visions as referring to the past: "I have seen the volumes by French scholars [from Rashi's comm. *ad loc.* we may infer that the reference is to him] who interpreted Zechariah's visions retrospectively, as dealing with events that occurred before the time of this prophet, . . . but [from the imperative in 11:4 it is clear that] in the time of the prophet this was a prophecy of future events'' (preface to comm. on Zech.).

With no connection to the principle of relevancy, Ibn Ezra rejects any interpretation that goes beyond the situations prophesied about or that is not compatible with the meaning of the words as originally spoken. For this reason he sees nothing to prevent us from understanding Psalm 137 as a prophecy about the destruction of the First Temple, but he vehemently refuses to understand ''Remember, O Lord, against the Edomites the Day of Jerusalem'' (137:7) as referring to the destruction of the Second Temple, as he explains in his comm. *ad loc.*: '' 'Remember'—this does not refer to the exile by Titus, as many believed [see above, note 109], because afterwards he mentions 'the daughter of Babylon'; furthermore, Titus was not an Edomite; the Romans are of Greek descent.'' The ethnographic reason is not a matter of principle, but it was of great importance for Ibn Ezra (cf. his comm. on Gen. 27:40; short comm. on Daniel [ed. Mathews, pp. 3, 12–13; ed. Mondshine, pp. 12–13, 69]. On the other hand, the stylistic and situational reasons presented first are decisive: the fact that later the psalmist prays for vengeance on the daughter of Babylon proves that the subject is the destruction of the First Temple, and of that alone! But when a multi-layer interpretation is compatible with the text of a psalm Ibn Ezra has no reservations about it, as with Psalm 24, which he refers to the time of the First, Second, and Third Temples (see his comm. on 24:3, 9, and 10; 80:8; 85:1, 5, 6 and 10; 136:1, 23, and 24). On this issue in general, see Simon, ''Medievalism,'' pp. 257–68.

111. He also says something like this in his commentary on Hab. 3:1: ''This prayer resembles the manner of prayers (two MSS: psalms), which is why he wrote ''ʿal šigyonoṯ,' 'la-mᵉnaṣṣeaḥ,' and 'selah'; I glossed these words in the Book of Psalms.''

112. He also asserts this general rule in his commentary on Num. 23:7: '' 'Come, curse me Jacob'—the words 'he [i.e., Balak] said' are omitted; there are many verses like this in the Song of Songs, and it is a concise way of speaking.'' In fact, for the sake of clarity, Ibn Ezra frequently identifies speakers in his commentaries. See, for example, the standard commentary on the Song of Songs on 1:2, 8, 12, 15 (the Second Way); and on Micah 7:1, 5, 7, 14, 16, 18. Many convincing proofs of the validity of this rule were given by R. Gordis, ''Quotations as a Literary Usage in Biblical, Oriental and Rabbinic literature,'' *HUCA* 22 (1949), pp. 157–219. Most of his examples are from the prophetic and wisdom literature.

113. The varied exegetical methods employed by Ibn Ezra to explain anachronistic references to the Temple in Davidic psalms were discussed in the chapter on Ibn Giqatilah (pp. 132–136).

114. Then, as now, the vast majority of readers were those fleeing from doubt. Saadiah expressed the obligation of the responsible commentator to refrain from

presenting doubtful matters as certainties in the introduction to his long commentary on the Pentateuch: "Let no man scoff at the commandments of the Torah when he hears me say, in the commentary on the Torah, 'it may be,' 'perhaps,' or 'it is possible' " (*Genesis,* Arabic p. 24, Hebrew p. 204).

115. Ibn Ezra uses "you shall die on the mountain" as a standard example in many places. See his commentary on Gen. 1:22; 42:16; Num. 5:20; Ps. 2:11 and 37:27.

116. Ibn Ezra's reluctance to see all of Psalms as prophetic prayer is attested by his remarks on "the span of our life is seventy years, or given the strength, eighty years" (Ps. 90:10). One of Ibn Ezra's predecessors asked: "Didn't Moses live one hundred and twenty years? How could he say seventy years?" and suggested that the author of this psalm was not Moses Our Teacher but some other poet named Moses. After Ibn Ezra refutes this farfetched explanation he offers a simple answer: "The sense of this psalm is that Moses is speaking on behalf of every generation, including his own, through the present day." This is followed by another tentative answer: "Perhaps he wrote this prayer before he became a prophet, because he was eighty years old and his hands were heavy." That is: the psalm may be prophetic, in which case it deals with the permanent human situation; but one can also assert that it is a nonprophetic prayer, written by Moses before he became a prophet, and refers to his own age at the time. The second interpretation not only corresponds to Ibn Giqatilah's basic approach, but also to his methodology; it is thus reasonable to assume that it was borrowed from his commentary. See also Ibn Ezra on Ps. 125:4.

117. This is a sort of sober answer to the method of Judah Ibn Balaam, who called his Pentateuch commentary *Kītāb ʾal-triğīḥ* (The Book of Decision) because of his untiring efforts to make a reasoned and demonstrated choice among alternative interpretations. See Peretz, "Contribution," pp. 157–59.

118. Similarly, he offers the opinion of "a Spanish scholar" who saw the last two verses of Psalm 51 as an addition by some pious man living in the Babylonian exile, without deciding one way or the other, merely noting that "it is also true that it was spoken with divine inspiration" (comm. on Ps. 51:20; and see above, pp. 132f.). This is rather astonishing, since in his Pentateuch commentary Ibn Ezra avoided the common prophetic solution for the problem of anachronistic geographical designations ("in accordance with its later name"), preferring to see them as later additions (albeit prophetic—see *Ṣafᵉnat Paᶜneaḥ* on Gen. 12:6 and Deut. 1:2). Here, however, he cites his predecessor's similar solution for this psalm and merely presents it as a possible alternative to the prophetic solution. The answer must be that in the context of Psalm 51 a prophetic reference to the future status of Jerusalem as the holy city seemed more reasonable than for Moses to refer to the residence of the Canaanites in the Holy Land in the past tense and to Transjordan, where he was then standing, as Transjordan. This is because, unlike Ibn Giqatilah, Ibn Ezra did ascribe to David and his contemporaries psalms dealing with the exile of the Levites from Jerusalem to Babylon (137) and the return from it (126); conse-

quently, he had no difficulty assuming that in a psalm of personal repentance David might speak by divine inspiration of the rebuilding of the demolished walls of Jerusalem and the restoration of the sacrificial service.

119. He also refers Psalm 126 to the time of the Return to Zion (see his commentary on verse 1) and Psalm 43 to the messianic era (see his commentary on verses 3 and 5), never mentioning the alternative interpretation that these psalms were written later.

120. Alternately, one may assume that Ibn Ezra interpreted ''l^e^-Dawid šir'' as indicating the melody, just as he would later interpret ''ʿal Y^e^dutun'' in the Fourth Inquiry of the first introduction, line 152.

121. The citations from *Y^e^sod Moraʾ* are based on the standard printed edition, emended as required on the basis of manuscripts. I would like to thank Dr. Joseph Cohen for making available to me his collation of eleven manuscripts, prepared for his forthcoming critical edition of *Y^e^sod Moraʾ*.

122. With regard to the possibility of perfect understanding, see the long commentary on Ex. 20:2 (passage beginning ''the first commandment''; ed. Weiser, vol. 2, p. 131): ''If so, the learned man, whose eyes have been opened by God, can know the secret of all the commandments from the words of the Torah.'' He makes similar remarks in his commentary on Deut. 4:1, 5, 7; Ps. 119:6.

123. See the chapter on Ibn Ezra in Y. Heinemann, *The Meanings of the Commandments in Jewish Literature* (Jerusalem, 1954^2) (Heb.), pp. 65–72.

124. In his commentary on Lev. 18:4–5, too, he writes that eternal life in the world to come is conditional on observing and *understanding* the commandments in this world.

125. This analogy is missing in the eleven manuscripts that have been examined, in the Constantinople edition of 1530, in the Venice edition of 1566, and in modern standard editions, but is found in the Prague edition of 1793. In and of itself it sounds original; see the parallel in the next note.

126. This argument, already to be found in the short commentary on Ex. 23:20 (ed. Weiser, vol. 2, p. 305) is not original with him. It appears in Abraham Ibn Daud's *Book of the High Faith* (written in Toledo in 1161, that is, almost at the same time as *Y^e^sod Moraʾ*), attributed there to an Ishmaelite scholar. Jacob Guttman (*Die Religionsphilosophie des Abraham Ibn Daud aus Toledo* [Göttingen, 1879], p. 171, n. 1) identifies the Ishmaelite scholar as al-Ghazali (1058–1111) and refers the reader to his book *Mizan al-amal*, translated and reworked in the thirteenth century by Abraham Bar Ḥasdai and given the Hebrew title *Sefer Moz^e^nei Ṣedeḳ* (ed. J. Goldenthal [Leipzig and Paris, 1839], pp. 165–80). Whereas al-Ghazali's influence on Ibn Daud is evident both in the content and in the phrasing, Ibn Ezra's connection with his predecessor is less conspicuous, mainly because, following Bachya (as will be demonstrated in the next note), he transferred the discussion from the general intellectual realm to the specific arena of Judaic studies.

Al-Ghazali too stressed "that all the sciences help one another and are interconnected. . . . Thus it is not fitting that a learned person scoff at any type of wisdom; rather it is fitting for him to acquire every type of knowledge according to his capacity and to grant it its portion and level. For the different sciences, according to their degrees, accompany the slave to meet his God" (p. 165). He also demurs at the exclusive focus on linguistics and rhetoric: "Those who go no further than grammar, vocalization, poetry and knowing the pronunciation of the letters are settling for the husk. . . . This is like someone who, intending to go on a pilgrimage, buys a camel for his burdens and prepares provisions and all of his other needs, but then stays home. . . . There is no use for sword and spear and lance when they are not employed in battle and war" (pp. 172–73). He rates legal knowledge as superior to linguistic knowledge, but it too is merely utilitarian: "However, knowledge of laws and statutes is not like this, because it is required only because it is a necessity of the body, and the body has no existence and endurance without physiology, i.e., medicine, and jurisprudence, i.e., the laws, since men were created in such a fashion that no one can live alone like a beast of the field. . . . There is no doubt that when they are in a group they need honesty among themselves and known rules for their intercourse; otherwise there would be only quarrels and fights among them" (pp. 176–77). On this point there is conspicuous similarity between Ibn Ezra and Ibn Daud, both of whom go much further than al-Ghazali. Since they seem to have worked independently, it is a reasonable assumption that both were influenced by some book deriving from al-Ghazali (or perhaps even from his predecessors). Guttman (p. 24, note 1) points out the reservations about the purely utilitarian study of linguistics, poetics, rhetoric, astronomy, and astrology found in Bachya Ibn Paquda's *Duties of the Heart* (5,5; vol. 2, p. 31). To this should be added Bachya's fierce demurral at the excessive preoccupation of halakhic scholars with legal matters (introduction, vol. 1, p. 29; see also the description of the eighth level of learning in 3,4, p. 221). For chronological reasons, al-Ghazali is unlikely to have influenced Bachya directly; the many parallels between them have therefore been explained as the result of a common source (see D. H. Baneth, "The common theological source of Bachya Ibn Pakuda and al-Ghazali" [Heb.], *Magnes Anniversary Book*, ed. F. I. Baer, et al. [Jerusalem, 1938], pp. 23–30). In contrast to all this, in BT Berakhoth 6a we find a transfunctional evaluation of the labor of judges, considered to be equal on the spiritual plane to the study of Torah: "One might have thought that the reward for doing justice is simply making peace and that it does not call down the Divine presence, but we learn that doing justice is like learning Torah."

127. This combination of thorough study of the plain meaning of the biblical books with no reliance on the Oral Law is very similar to the characterization of the students of the fifth level described in Bachya's *Duties of the Heart* (3,4, p. 221). In addition to this material similarity, there is a structural similarity as well: the four types of scholars in *Y^{e}sod Mora*ʾ are described in the same order as the ten levels of study in *Duties of the Heart*: (1) those who know how to read the Pentateuch and the rest of the Scriptures without understanding (compared to an ass burdened with books); (2) Punctuators and Masoretes (Ibn Ezra's first category, compared to a

camel laden with silk); (3) those who know grammar (Ibn Ezra's second category); (4) those who study the plain meaning of the text and delve into content and style; (5) those who engage in intellectual investigation without relying on the tradition (Ibn Ezra's third category); (6–10) those who learn the Oral Law in various degrees (Ibn Ezra's fourth category, which most closely resembles Bachya's eighth level). Still, whereas Bachya multiplied the categories in order to attain the number ten and transcribed them in ascending order, from total lack of understanding through perfect comprehension (attained by the Men of the Great Assembly and the Talmudic sages), Ibn Ezra found four categories sufficient. Each of these has a positive and a negative aspect, and his corresponding praise and criticism are meant to aggregate into a description of the proper method of study. To this end his Pentateuch introductions also contain critical descriptions of the four types of commentators; in the second introduction the four paths are ranked in ascending order, like the four categories here.

128. "The whole secret" (*kol sod*) is found only in MS British Library 1073 (and as a marginal note in MS Berlin 79), but *kol* is found in all the MSS (although it was deleted from the *editio princeps*, Constantinople, 1530).

129. Ibn Ezra could rely on the adage of R. Simeon bar Yoḥai: "He who occupies himself with the *miḳra*ᵓ—it is meritorious and it is not meritorious" (JT Šabbat̠ 1,2, and, worded somewhat differently, JT Berak̠ot̠ 1,2 and JT Horayot̠ 3,2) only because he assumed that for the Sages, too, *miḳra*ᵓ refers only to the Prophets and Hagiographa. Since the discussions in which R. Simeon bar Yoḥai is quoted speak explicitly of the study of Torah, it seems likely that Ibn Ezra took his adage as an independent statement detached from its context and interpreted it in accordance with his own needs. It also seems likely that Ibn Ezra did not know or did not remember the statement of R. Simeon bar Yoḥai in full—"They who occupy themselves with the Bible [alone]—it is meritorious and it is not meritorious; with Mishnah, are indeed meritorious, and are rewarded for it; with Talmud—there can be nothing more meritorious" (BT Baba Meṣiᶜaᵓ 33a; JT Šabbat̠ 16,1)—since taken in context it is far from serving as a proof for Ibn Ezra's idea of the Jewish ideal of study.

130. See his commentary on Deut. 24:16, quoted by Peretz, "Contribution," p. 161.

131. See Simon, "Exegetic Method," pp. 106–111.

132. B. Klar ("Ben Asher," *Inquiries*, pp. 303–304) offers proofs of this from the writings of Anan ben David and Sahl ben Maṣliaḥ.

133. This is the seventeenth of the thirty-two methods by which the aggadah is expounded (see *The Mishnah of Rabbi Eliezer*, ed. H. G. Enelow [New York, 1933], p. 30). In his definition of the other methods, too, Hadassi made no attempt to avoid reliance on their Rabbanite versions.

134. B. Klar (*Inquiries*, p. 303), points out the difference between these approaches: "According to Rabbanite Judaism, the written Law comprises only the

Pentateuch, while the Prophetic Writings and Hagiographa are merely 'tradition.' A major axiom is that 'we do not learn the Law from tradition,' i.e., the exegetical methods used for the Pentateuch are not applied to the Prophets and Hagiographa.'' At the same time, it is clear that the Sages made use of this ''tradition'' to improve their linguistic understanding and broaden the thematic content of the Torah, just as they were careful to resolve any possible contradiction between them (see s.v. ''Divrei ḳabbalah,'' *Encyclopedia Talmudica* 7 [Jerusalem, 1956], pp. 106–114).

135. Wieder discusses this bipolarity in their outlook in the chapter on messianism in *Scrolls,* pp. 95–127.

136. At the end of his commentary on Daniel 12 (Margoliouth, *Daniel;* in Arabic pp. 151–52; in English pp. 86–87) there is a sort of appendix in which Yefet surveys the computations of the End of Days made by Rabbanite and Karaite scholars, which had been refuted by the failure of the Messiah to come at the calculated time. His vehement insistence that it is impossible to decipher this secret was probably influenced not a little by the repeated failures of his predecessors (of whom the most recent had been Salmon ben Yeruḥam).

137. Because of the frequent references to the anticipated downfall of the Christian kingdom and religion, the editors of the 1836 Gozlow edition deleted quite a bit from this chapter; Ankori edited it in full on the basis of two MSS (see his ''Studies''). Ankori discusses Hadassi's reliance on his predecessors for the topic of messianism, like other subjects in his book, *Karaites*, pp. 187–88 and note 11.

138. How far this exegetical dispute could be carried is attested by a fine example cited by Wieder (*Scrolls,* p. 103, note 3): In order to avoid the Karaite interpretation that ''my eyes forestalled the night watches'' (Ps. 119:148) refers to the vigils of the Mourners of Zion, Saadiah was forced to translate it as ''my eyes overcame their drowsiness.''

139. Cf. Yefet's presentation of his opinion against the background of his predecessors' opinions, appendix to his commentary on Daniel 12 (mentioned in note 136 above).

140. Here Ibn Ezra goes beyond asserting a lack of information and argues that in the absence of an explicit linkage of the vision with the event we cannot eliminate the uncertainty in the identification, even were we to find an external historical source. Thus the argument based on history is converted into a theological and literary one.

141. Instructive in this context is the axiom formulated in the long commentary on Dan. 11:4. Since ''there is no benefit now in knowing what happened in the past'' we must content ourselves with linguistic and thematic explanations of ''past prophecies.'' By contrast, he will provide a detailed explanation of the sequence of events described in ''future-oriented'' prophecies. This assertion of the lack of spiritual utility in knowledge of the past is quite similar to what he wrote in *Y^e^sod Mora*ʾ about the insignificant intrinsic value of the historical information contained in the Early Prophets; hence despite the polemical context, it seems to reflect his

true position. In the opinion of Saadiah, too, the religious importance of the chronological, genealogical, geographical, and demographic portions of the Torah is slight; but since "it is impossible that the Torah contains totally useless things" (*Genesis,* p. 175) he endeavors to show why they are necessary (p. 180) and even praises their continuation in the Oral Tradition (p. 184). On this issue, then, Ibn Ezra did not follow him; it seems likely that here too he was influenced by the position of Bachya, as expressed in the analogy to the three types of silk found at the end of the preface to *The Duties of the Heart* (vol. 1, p. 227). In this parable the historical narrative in the Pentateuch is compared to inferior silk, the halakhic and legal sections (the duties of the limbs) to silk of medium quality, and the spiritual and cognitive portions (the duties of the heart) to silk of the finest water. Awareness of this relative merit is more than just a precondition for recognizing the superiority of the duties of the heart (Ibn Ezra preaches this too, using similar terminology: "The commandments of the heart are the most important principles of all"—long comm. on Ex. 20:1, ed. Weiser, vol. 2, p. 131; see also comm. on Deut. 5:16 and 30, 30:10 and 14; 32:39; and *Y^esod Mora*ʾ, ch. 7); it is also a defense against overvaluing the historical and narrative sections while understanding them as underscoring hedonism, and against a utilitarian attitude towards the Pentateuch as a whole (the practice of the servants of God of the fourth and fifth levels, described in 3,4, vol. 1, p. 227).

142. See Yefet, "Psalm 22" on verses 1, 14, and 24. Judah Hadassi went furthest in denying a biographical and historical background to the psalms, arguing that the psalms were meant to be the liturgy of the Jews of the Diaspora: "Similarly, nothing happened to David, his memory for a blessing, that caused him to say, 'I afflicted myself with fasting' (Ps. 35:13), 'dogs surround me' (ibid. 22:17[16]), 'they divide my clothes among themselves, casting lots for my garments' (verse 19[18]) [followed by many more passages from Psalms of the same nature]. Did any of these things happen to King David, his memory for a blessing, or to Asaph or Ethan or Heman or Jeduthun or any other poet? Cries and supplications of this sort, phrased in the words [i.e., on behalf] of later generations, were prophesied by your poets; hence we are required to use them for prayer constantly, night and day, in our abjection" (*ʾEškol ha-ḳofe*, p. 39, col. 2; quoted by Wieder, *Scrolls,* p. 199, note 2).

143. See his glosses on 7:6; 8:3 and 12 (the Third Way.)

144. In his commentary on Eccles. 7:3, too, he emphasizes that comprehension of the "secret of the soul" depends on a thorough and comprehensive study of the sciences: "This book [i.e., his commentary on Ecclesiastes] is not intended to speak of the secret of the soul, for this is a very deep subject about which no one can understand the truth until he has read many books; were I not required to mention the parts of the soul for the sake of interpreting the verses I would not have alluded to the matter in general or in particular."

145. An outstanding expression of the centrality of cognitive effort to Ibn Ezra's outlook can be found in the following passage: "Only man's soul as given by

God is like a tabula rasa waiting to be written on, and when the writing on this tablet is a divine script—knowledge of created objects [i.e., the three types of creatures: inanimate, vegetative, and animate] of the four elements, and knowledge of the spheres and the throne of glory and the secret of the chariot and the highest knowledge—then the soul will cleave to God while it is still in man, and so too when its vigor separates from the body, which is its dwelling place'' (*Y^e^sod Mora*ʾ, ch. 10). See also his commentary on Hosea 6:3.

146. See his commentary on 16:1; 19:2; 23:1; 25:5; 49:1; 56:1; 73:1 (where the subject of the psalm is compared to that of Psalm 49); 68:2; 139:1; and 148:1.

147. Like his commentaries on 36:8–11; 84:3; 89:7–9; and 103:1.

148. On 49:5 he explicitly says ''I will reprove my soul'' just as he begins one of his reproofs, ''with my mouth I will reprove my spirit'' (*Religious Poems,* vol. 1, no. 208); later he writes, ''I will reprove my spirit'' (ibid., lines 27f). His interpretation of all of Psalm 49 is very close to a number of motifs in this and other of his *tok̲aḥah* poems (ibid., nos. 206, 214, 215, 216, 227, and 240).

149. See, for example, the *piyyuṭim* included in the chapter ''Thought and Art,'' Levin, *Ibn Ezra,* pp. 47–83. The close reciprocal relations between Ibn Ezra's religious poetry and his exegetical approach to the psalms is manifested not only in the commonality of subjects and ideas and the wealth of inlaid biblical phrases, but also in the fact that two of his *piyyuṭim*—''My God, You have investigated me and known me'' (*Religious Poems,* vol. 1, no. 10), and ''O Lord, You have investigated me and known me'' (ibid., no. 222)—are merely versifications of Psalm 139, about which he writes (comm. on verse 1): ''This is a very important psalm about God's ways; it has no peer in all five books of the Psalms. A man will comprehend its meaning in proportion to his comprehension of the ways of God and the ways of the soul.''

150. In his opinion a theoretical interpretation of this sort (one that relies on scientific knowledge and seeks to supplement it) is totally incompatible with the Song of Songs. See the preface to the standard commentary to the Song of Songs: ''Men of science have endeavored to interpret this book in accordance with the secret of the world and the union of the celestial soul with the body, which is at the lowest level. Others have interpreted it as dealing with the elements, but the wind will carry them away, for they are all empty. The truth is merely what our Sages transmitted, namely, that this book deals with the people of Israel.'' What is illegitimate there is permissible for the ''important'' (theological) psalms, because he finds the inquiring intent in the plain meaning of their text and also because in their case there is no obligatory exegetical tradition which specifies that the text must not be understood literally as well as the direction of the required allegorization.

151. The words in parentheses should be deleted, in accordance with six MSS and three early printings that have been examined.

152. See the homiletical interpretation of R. Simeon ben Lakish on Ex. 24:12 (BT B^e^rak̲ot̲ 5a), and the testimony of Ibn Ezra (long commentary on this verse)

about Saadiah's position, which is very close to that of Resh Lakish. On the other hand, we can infer from Ibn Ezra's remark there, and his commentary on Deut. 5:28, that he himself believed that both of these verses deal only with the Decalogue and most of the Written Torah.

153. How serious was Al-Ḳumissi's call to engage in intellectual inquiry has yet to be clarified adequately; see Ben Shammai, *Doctrines,* vol. 1, p. 10, note 12.

154. Cited by Ben Shammai (ibid., p. 8), who contributed a comprehensive and thorough discussion of the different positions of Kirkisani and Yefet on this matter (ibid., pp. 8–35 and 101–111). The English translation is that of Nemoy, *Anthology,* p. 55.

155. Quoted by Pinsker, *Lickute,* vol. 2, p. 134. See also the citation from his commentary on Eccles. 7:16 (vol. 1, pp. 27–28). This passage, and many others from Salmon ben Yeruḥam's commentary on Ecclesiastes, were translated into French by Vajda and included in his chapter on the anti-intellectualism of Salmon in *Two Commentaries,* pp. 78–87. He documents and discusses Yefet's opposition to the study of secular sciences in the chapter dealing with his approach to epistemology (pp. 118–57).

156. From Ben Shammai, *Doctrines,* note 17, we learn that here Yefet is wondering why there are two prohibitions in the Pentateuch—to add and to subtract, whereas in Proverbs the only prohibition is to add, and that his answer is that when it comes to commandments men both add and subtract, whereas when it comes to theological assertions they only add.

157. He was preceded in this by Samuel ha-Nagid, who, evidently himself entitled the *diwan* that includes his battle poetry *Ben Tehillim,* and related to this directly in dialogue form in his poem "š^{e}ᶜeh menni": "He says to me: 'Can you sing praises?' / I answered: 'I am the David of my generation!' " (see *Ben Tehillim,* pp. 33–34 and p. vi). For the various ways in which Samuel ha-Nagid linked his poems with the psalms, see D. S. Segal, *Ben Tehillim of Samuel Hanagid and the Book of Psalms: A Study in Esoteric Linkage* (Brandeis University diss. 1976; [Ann Arbor, 1977]).

158. A concise explanation of this stylistic principle and an exaggerated assertion of its frequency are found in the long commentary on Ex. 17:7: "The custom of the holy tongue is that when two points are mentioned one *always* begins with the second, which is nearer." A more cautious phrasing can be found in his commentary on Isa. 56:6; Joel 3:3; Ps. 74:16; and in *Sabbath,* ch. 3 (p. 75).

159. Saadiah (in his long introduction to Psalms) had noted that the psalms are not arranged in chronological order and even relied, inter alia, on these two psalms. But for him this is a sort of negative proof for the existence of other principles of arrangement—thematic on the one hand and functional on the other. See above, pp. 30–31.

160. In light of these statements it is evident that when he says, in his commentary on Deut. 22:12, "[the law of fringes] is attached to [the law of] *šaᶜaṭnez*

because the latter is permitted with fringes,'' he does not mean that the dispensation for clothing combining wool and linen with regard to the fringes is learned from the juxtaposition of the sections, but that the dispensation known from tradition can explain why the verses follow one another. Since this approach is incompatible with the discussion of the juxtaposition of biblical sections found in BT Yevamot 3a–4b, it is difficult to assume that Ibn Ezra remembered the Talmudic discussion when he wrote his commentary.

161. Even though, in opposition to Saadiah, the Karaite commentators distinguished between the individual psalmists and the editor of the entire Book of Psalms (the *mudawwin*), they made much greater efforts to discover a thematic link running throughout the book, because they believed that the editor as well was prophetically inspired (see above on both Salmon ben Yeruḥam, p. 71, and Yefet ben ʿAli, pp. 96f.). Here both Ibn Giqatilah and Ibn Ezra disagreed with them.

162. Proof that Ibn Ezra indeed assumed an original pre-editorial connection among certain psalms is found in his comments about the common theme of adjacent psalms. Five of these have to do with psalms that are part of the fifteen Songs of Degrees, which clearly constitute a defined block. On 124:1 he notes: ''[The meaning of] this poem is like the meaning of the previous one:'' (cf. his similar remarks on 126:1 and 128:1); whereas on 133:1 and 134:1 he notes that these psalms develop a certain facet of the subject discussed in their predecessors. We also find such a note with regard to Psalms 148 and 149, which belong to the Hallelujah groups of psalms (see his comm. on 149:1).

163. From the fact that the only surviving exemplars of Ibn Ezra's *diwan* and Judah Halevy's *diwan* were written in Yemen, Schirmann (''Poets,'' p. 125) deduces that Yeshuʿah was born there; from the fact that Yeshuʿah had trouble identifying anonymous poems, erroneously attributed poems to Judah Halevy, and did not know many of Ibn Ezra's poems, he infers that he lived quite a while after them (*Encyclopedia Judaica,* s.v. ''Yeshuah ben Elijah Halevi'': ''No later than the fifteen century''). On the other hand, Stern (''Ibn Ezra,'' p. 383) assumes that Yeshuʿah was a Spaniard who lived no later than the thirteenth century, since it is hard to attribute such expertise in Moorish girdle poems to a Jew so remote in time and place from the arena of their growth. See also pp. 224 and 256.

164. Something similar is to be found in MS Oxford, Neubauer Catalogue no. 1970, in which the earlier collection of Judah Halevy's poems is entitled ''Maḥaneh Yᵉhudah'' (Judah's camp) while the poems added by the later editor are grouped separately under the rubric ''Ha-maḥaneh ha-nišʾar'' (The remaining camp).

165. See H. Schirmann, ''A resurrected poet'' (Heb.), *Tarbiz* 28 (1959), pp. 330–42; S. D. Goitein, ''The history of Isaac Ibn Ḥalfon's poetry'' (Heb.), *Tarbiz* 29 (1960), pp. 357–58.

166. See H. Schirmann, ''Isaac Ibn Halfon'' (Heb.), *Tarbiz* 7 (1936), p. 307. The twenty-six poems are presented in their original order in the edition of A. Mirsky, *Poems of R. Isaac Ibn Ḥalfon* (Jerusalem, 1961), pp. 63–98. Neither is any

particular order evident in a fragment from another manuscript, with seven poems (notes 64–71 in Mirsky's edition).

167. Ibn Ezra expresses this attitude in his criticism of the liturgical poets found in his commentary on Eccles. 5:1: "Consequently it is forbidden for a man to pray and insert into his prayer liturgical poems that he does not understand; he should not rely on the original intention of the author, because there is no man who does not sin, or perhaps the copyists erred." (Monroe ("Poetry," p. 102, note 7) quotes the complaint of the Arabic author Ibn ʿAbd-Rabbihi (Cordova, 860–940) about the lordly manner of the grammarians towards poets and the supposed errors they found in their poems (see also ibid., p. 108). By contrast, Yeshuʿah went no further than to decide among the variant readings in the MSS available to him, on the basis of their relative plausibility (see his preface to Ibn Ezra's *Diwan*, p. xvi).

168. See Schirmann, "Poets," pp. 124–25; on the topic of editing in general, Y. Ratzaby, "The *diwans* and their editors" (Heb.), *Yavne* 3 (1942), pp. 136–52.

169. In his preface to Ibn Ezra's *Diwan*, he says that he himself recognizes Ibn Ezra's work as expressed especially in his individual style (Ibn Ezra, *Diwan*, pp. xvi–xvii). On the other hand, in his preface to Yehudah Halevy's *Diwan* he acknowledges that he is unable to distinguish Yehudah Halevy's poems from those of other poets with the same name—Yehudah Ibn Giath, Yehudah Ibn Balaam, Yehudah Ibn Abas, and Levi Ibn Altaban—because their excellence is on a par with his. (The preface was published on the basis of MS Luzzatto, with a German translation, by A. Geiger, *Diwan des Castiliers Abu'l-Hassan Juda Ha-Levi* [Breslau, 1851], pp. 168–75.)

170. See A. S. Tritton, "Shiʿr," *Enzyklopaedie des Islām*, vol. 4 (Leiden-Leipzig, 1934), pp. 401–404.

171. For Ibn Ezra's uncritical approach to the biblical text, see Simon, "Two Approaches."

172. As he says in the Third Inquiry: "The correct answer, given by the Sages, is that the Book of Psalms was said through the Holy Spirit" (lines 84f.).

173. Since the text here is somewhat difficult to understand, we checked all the manuscripts, but no significant textual variants were found.

174. See, for example, the preface by Yehoseph to *Ben Tehillim*, where he writes that he included in this *diwan* "his metrical discourses and poems *([wa-l-] ḳiṭʿat)* in various meters" (Samuel ha-Nagid, *Ben Tehillim*, p. 1).

175. In Ṣaḥot, (ed. Rodriguez, p. 109; ed. Lippmann, p. 43b) he says that Samuel ha-Nagid glossed "of the child that was born" *[la-naʿar ha-yullad]* (Judges 13:8) as "a prophetic past," and describes this stylistic phenomenon in much the same terms as here: "A verb in the past tense is used instead of one in the future, as is the custom of the prophets, who sometimes speak of the future in the past tense because it has already been decreed that such [an event] will occur." All the same,

this does not really help us identify the advocate of the opinion cited by Ibn Ezra as "some say," since so long as we do not have Samuel ha-Nagid's Arabic commentary on Psalms we cannot know whether he relied on the prophetic past to solve the problem of the word *mizmor.*

176. See Bacher, *Ibn Ezra,* p. 127, which provides many references from Ibn Ezra's writings on this subject. Among Ibn Ezra's endeavors antedating the first Psalms commentary noted there is his gloss on "if I am to perish, I perish" *[we-ka'ašer 'avadti 'avadti]* in the standard commentary on Esther 4:16. He says there that the first "*'avadti*" should be understood as an actual past, referring to Esther's estrangement from her people, whereas the second "*'avadti*" relates to the future: "I will be lost totally; the verb in the past tense is used instead of a future tense, since it refers to her thought; an analogous case: 'if I am to be bereaved, I shall be bereaved' (Gen. 43:14)." (Thus Ibn Ezra would have us translate these verses: "Just as I perished [i.e., was separated from my people], so too shall I perish [physically]"; "just as I was bereaved [of Joseph], so too shall I be bereaved [of Benjamin].") His commentary on that verse in Genesis also distinguishes between the temporal reference of the two verbs ostensibly in the same tense; there too he does not make the expression of future action by a past tense depend on prophecy: " 'just as I was bereaved' when Joseph died I *think* now that I shall be bereft of everything."

177. No one seems to have anticipated him in this. In the Midrash the difficulty is resolved by various homiletical means; see BT B^e^rakot 7b; *Midrash Tehillim* 3,3. True, Ibn Giqatilah neutralized the term *mizmor,* but by a most implausible derivation. On the other hand, Yefet Ben ʿAli (in the survey of terminology at the beginning of his commentary on Psalm 3) acknowledged that the word is hard to understand, since on the one hand it denotes singing and musical performance, while on the other hand it is found at the beginning of psalms "that contradict this interpretation, like 'a *mizmor* of David when he was in the wilderness of Judah' (63:1)." His solution is to assume that "even if initially this psalm was said with no melody or musical accompaniment, it is not impossible that the musicians later performed it with musical accompaniment and melody." This divorce of the poetical character of the psalm as written by its author and its musical performance by the singers in the Temple was also proposed by R. David Kimḥi (who seems to have reached the conclusion independently): "They were not called *mizmorim* when they were written but because they sang [*m^e^zamm^e^rim*] them in the Temple" (comm. on 3:1).

178. Compare with this view the remarks of the Faithful Brothers at the beginning of their *Epistle on Music*: "Some melodies stimulate the soul to carry out difficult labor and exhausting tasks and help men be energetic and decisive in carrying out difficult and back-breaking jobs that require great effort and physical sacrifice" (*Epistle,* pp. 12–13).

179. The opinion with which Ibn Ezra is here agreeing, according to which the *m^e^naṣṣeaḥ* is the supervisor of the singers, is presented as contradicting Saadiah,

who asserted that the term indicates that David "gave it to a musician to play it all the time." How, then, does Ibn Ezra, in his commentary on Ps. 31:1, adopt language very close to Saadiah's, at which he had previously demurred: "He gave it to one of the singers to perform"? The absence of the key word "always" indicates that Ibn Ezra had not changed his mind. Moreover, "to one" is a mistake that can be traced to the *editio princeps* (Venice, 1525) since in all twelve complete manuscripts that have survived the reading is: "gave it to the greatest of the singers to perform."

180. This was pointed out by Zunz, *Poetry,* p. 114 (he notes that Eliezer ha-Kallir had already used *noᶜam* and *nᵉᶜimah* alongside *niggun* and *nᵉginah*); and also by Kaufmann, *Senses,* p. 133, note 18.

181. I have not discovered an instance of Ibn Ezra's use of the plural form *noᶜamim*, but neither have I found the singular *nᵉᶜimah.*

182. For many uses of this term by his predecessors, see N. Allony, "*Nᵉᶜimah-naǵma* in the Middle Ages" (Heb.), *Yuval* 2 (1971), pp. 9–27.

183. R. David Kimḥi, in his commentary on Ps. 61:1, refutes this proof by arguing that *nᵉginaṯ* is not a construct form but an absolute form like "makkaṯ bilti sarah" (Isa. 14:6), "ḥoḵmaṯ wa-daᶜaṯ" (Isa. 33:6), and "rabbaṯ taᶜśᵉrennah" (Ps. 65:10). Ibn Ezra, on the other hand, is willing to acknowledge that the *taw* replaces a *heh* only for the adjectival (or adverbial) *rabbaṯ* (comm. *ad loc.*); whereas he views the nouns *makkaṯ* and *ḥoḵmaṯ* as elliptical constructs, for which the reader must provide the supporting absolute noun. In fact, from his commentary on Ps. 60:13 and 88:1 we can infer that the decisive sign of the construct state is not the final *taw* but the preceding *pataḥ.*

184. He is probably referring to Saadiah, who wrote in his introduction (*Psalms,* pp. 31–32) that the reference is to the two-headed drum known in Arabic as *tabl;* to Ibn Ganach, who writes in his *Dictionary,* s.v. *ḥol:* "*mᵉḥoloṯ* means drums"; and to Moses Ibn Ezra, who identified *maḥalaṯ* with the flute (in the musicological section of *ᶜArugaṯ ha-bośem*, line 36). Salmon Ben Yeruḥam, too, in his commentary on Ps. 53:1, glosses *maḥalaṯ* as a synonym for the musical instrument *maḥol;* in a poem by Samuel ha-Nagid, too, *maḥol* is the name of an instrument (*Ben Tehillim,* p. 165, line 8). Cf. also Ibn Ezra on Ps. 53:1.

185. Ibn Ezra glosses *lᵉ-ᶜannoṯ* in his commentary on Ps. 88:1 as "to perform," relying on "ḳol ᶜannoṯ" (Ex. 33:18), which he glosses, in his short commentary *ad loc.*, as "like melodies, similar to 'they shall sing [*ᶜannu*] of it: "Vineyard of Wine' " (Isa. 27:2)." Accordingly, "ᶜal maḥalaṯ lᵉᶜannoṯ" means to perform (the psalm) to the tune of *maḥalaṯ*. In order to make this truncated construct form plausible, Ibn Ezra hypothesizes that the original song whose melody was borrowed had " 'my heart' or 'my body,' on which *maḥalat* [the illness of] depended." To buttress this hypothesis he adds that "this psalm too is about the poet's illness." In this case, the proximity of content and theme was the basis for borrowing the melody!

186. In fact, there are sixteen cues left, since in the standard commentary the directions *šiggayon*, *miḵtam*, and *maśkil* are also defined as melodic cues (see comm. on 7:1; 16:1; and 32:1). Did Ibn Ezra really forget these three? His intention to review all of the cues is quite evident in the first introduction; what is more, at the beginning of the Fourth Inquiry (lines 98f.) Ibn Ezra promises to explain *miḵtam* and *maśkil*! Given the fact that Ibn Ezra precedes each cue with *we-ḵen*, it is perfectly possible that the copyist (because of homoeoarchthon) simply skipped the words "also *šiggayon lᵉ-Dawid* before "also *ʿal ha-gittiṯ*" (line 145), and the same fate could have befallen *miḵtam* and *maśkil*.

187. He uses exactly the same language in the first introduction, speaking of "ʾayyeleṯ ha-šaḥar" (22:1)—a certain melody" (line 148).

188. MS Warsaw 150 reads: "It may be like '*ʾafiloṯ hennah*' (Ex. 9:32)." In his two commentaries on Exodus Ibn Ezra explains this word as the plural of *ʾafelah* 'darkness' (meaning that the stalks were underground and therefore not visible); hence the analogy *nᵉḥiloṯ-ʾafilot* is a matter of form rather than meaning. On the other hand, perhaps this is not a parallel variant, but the original continuation of the reading of the other manuscripts, and the correct text would run: "perhaps it is from *nᵉḥiloṯ*, a plural like '*ʾafiloṯ hennah*'."

189. Additional confirmation of this is provided by Ibn Ezra on Ps. 33:2, where he comes out against Ibn Giqatilah and asserts that *ʿaśor* is not an adjective modifying *neḇel* but an instrument in its own right.

190. The words "concerning Cush" should be deleted (as proposed by Pilwarg in his supercommentary *ad loc.*), although they are missing in only two of twelve MSS (Parma 510 and Vatican 78). First, it is very difficult to assume that this is the continuation of the melodic cue, since the words do not immediately follow *šiggayon* but are separated from it by four other words. Second, while assigning them to the cue should have neutralized them with respect to the psalm, Ibn Ezra interprets the psalm as David's entreaty for God to save him from a Benjaminite enemy named Cush (commentary on verses 1, 7, and 8).

191. In his *Tafsir,* Saadiah translates paraphrastically: "From the descendants of Obed-Edom the Levite, known as the Gittite"; in his commentary he notes: "People get confused about the meaning of '*ha-gittiṯ*,' but it is as I have glossed it" (*Psalms*, p. 64): the reference is to the long introduction (ibid., pp. 30–31).

192. Ibn Ezra says that something is "empty" (*heḇel*) even when he rejects a gloss that has no fundamental or theological value (see his commentary on Gen. 38:15), just as he applies the terms "empty words" and "prater" even to sages whom he admired, like Saadiah (short comm. on Ex. 38:26) and Ibn Ganach (ibid., 19:12 and 21:8).

193. The words in parentheses are an explanatory addition by the translator into Hebrew, Judah Ibn Tibbon.

194. Ibn Ezra himself began one of his poetical riddles with the word *maśkil* (Ibn Ezra, *Diwan*, p. 129); he could have found something similar in Samuel ha-

Nagid's *Ben Mishlei (Diwan,* ed. D. Sasson [Oxford, 1934], p. 212), and in *Sefer ha-ᶜanaḳ* (H. Brody, *Moses Ibn Ezra: Secular Poetry,* vol. 1 [Berlin, 1935], p. 352).

195. A similar unequivocal assertion can also be found in his commentary on 74:1: "The word *maśkil* is the beginning of a poem, and this psalm has a similar meaning." If we read here *noᶜam,* "melody," for *ṭaᶜam,* "meaning," the second half of the statement would be comprehensible but superfluous. In fact, in the twelve MSS that I checked the text clearly reads *ṭaᶜam.* It seems evident, then, that there are two statements in this sentence, and that the second clause means that the subject of the psalm resembles that of its predecessor. In Ibn Ezra's commentary on the previous psalm (73:1), too, there is a note about its subject: "The subject of this psalm resembles that of 'Hear this, all you peoples' (Ps. 49:2)"; see also the end of his gloss on 39:1.

196. In the superscription of Psalm 77, too, the word *Yᵉduṯun* lacks the prepositional *lamed,* and Ibn Ezra notes: "To the melody of a poem that began *'Yᵉduṯun,'* " which may be viewed as supporting the unique reading of the Munich MS.

197. He was familiar with the similar phenomenon in the Spanish poetry of his time, such as a friendship poem by Solomon Ibn Gabirol ("šošan ᶜalei saᶜif kᵉmo ṣammereṯ" [*Secular Poetry* 1, p. 135]) and Judah Halevy's "šošan ḥasadim wᵉ-ḥaḇaṣeleṯ yofi" (*Diwan,* ed. H. Brody, vol. 1 [Berlin, 1894], p. 133).

198. Saadiah in his commentary does not rely on *la-yiṣhar* to prove his view that "labben" is a personal name prefixed by the prepositional *lamed* coalesced with the definite article; in our biblical texts we find only "la-yiṣhari" (1 Chron. 24:22 and 26:23 and 29).

199. This criticism cannot be applied to "hu yᵉnahagenu ᶜal-muṯ" (Ps. 48:15), not only because here Dunash quotes Saadiah's commentary on 9:1, but also because Dunash elsewhere (§139) discusses Saadiah's gloss on "ᶜalamoṯ/ᶜal-muṯ" in 48:15 (Ibn Ezra for his part deals with this in §100).

200. The wording in *Hashem,* fol. 3b, confirms the manuscript reading here: "It is impossible to say 'the Isaac,' 'the Abraham,' because a proper noun is definite in and of itself and does not require the definite article."

201. Here Ibn Ezra seems to have employed anonymous terms in order to make his comments apply also to Ibn Giqatilah, who at least partially accepted Saadiah's opinion on the matter, as can be inferred from his commentary on "ᶜal muṯ labben"—"Some say that it is reversed, that is: 'ᶜal muth naval'. But I say that *ᶜalamoṯ* is one word, and its meaning is like 'ᶜal ᶜalamoṯ šir,' that is, of this genre (*haḏā-ʾn-nawᶜ*), even though it is written with a hyphen" (cited by Poznanski, "Psalms," p. 57). Like Saadiah, Ibn Giqatilah glossed "ᶜal muṯ" as one word, even though he was aware that it is written as two, and like him understood it as designating the genre of the psalm (musical or literary), like "ᶜalamoṯ šir." Ibn Ganach (*Dictionary,* s.v. *ᶜelem*) and Judah Ibn Balaam (*Homonyms,* p. 137) both understood *ᶜalamoṯ* as a type of melody, whereas Menaḥem Ben Saruk (*Maḥbereṯ,* s.v. *gaṯ*) and Samuel ha-Nagid (*Ben Tehillim,* p. 279, line 4) glossed *ᶜalamoṯ* as a musical instrument.

202. See Defense, §§ 67, 93, and 100, and Simon, "Two Approaches," pp. 201–203.

203. Apparently his source for this is Dunash, who cited and rebutted these three identifications in his other book (*Criticism of Menaḥem,* s.v. *'labben,'* pp. 15–16; ed. Bedilius, p. 28*).

204. This misquotation from the Mishnah was discussed above, note 37.

205. *Li* 'I' has been added on the basis of six MSS, whereas *t^e ḥilat* 'beginning' has been added by conjecture, even though it is lacking in the twelve surviving MSS and in the *editio princeps.*

206. The words in parentheses—missing in two MSS—should be deleted, as argued above, note 190.

207. See N. Allony, "Spanish poetry and its language" (Heb.), *ʾOṣar Y^e hudei S^e farad* 3 (1960), pp. 18–19. See the discussion there, as well as Jarden's introduction to his edition of *Ben Tehillim,* pp. v–vi.

208. For more detail, see Stern, "Poetry," pp. 33–41. On Ibn Ezra's conception of the term *mizmor* as expressing total correspondence between the words and melody of a poem, see above, pp. 226f. On the hypothetical influence of Spanish melodies on the rhyme scheme of strophic poetry, see J. T. Monroe, *Hispano-Arabic Poetry* (Berkeley and Los Angeles, 1974), pp. 30–31 and 41.

209. S. M. Stern, "Four Famous Muwaššaḥs from Ibn Bušrā's Anthology," *Al-Andalus* 23 (1958), pp. 248–354.

210. For clarity's sake this sequence can be summarized as follows: secular girdle poem by al-ʾAbiaḍ → poem of praise by Moses Ibn Ezra → poem of praise by Yehudah Halevy and liturgical poem by Yehudah Halevy → two liturgical poems by Abraham Ibn Ezra.

211. The third poem, too, whose model (according to Stern, "Abraham Ibn Ezra," p. 385) was correctly identified by Yeshuʿah, is a liturgical poem by Abraham Ibn Ezra (*Religious Poems,* vol. 1, p. 245) that imitates a secular poem by Yehudah Halevy.

212. An example of this is the liturgical poem "hallel t^e mallel l^e-maleʾ lo ḥasar" (*Diwan,* p. 17, no. 60; *Religious Poems* 1, p. 74), whose superscription reads: "To the melody of 'yiḵru l^e-hallel Yah m^e hal^e leḵa' ". These are the opening words of an *ʾofan* by Isaac Ibn Giath (Schirmann, *Hebrew Poetry,* vol. 1, p. 306), which is also written in an indeterminate meter (based on eight or nine syllables per line, not counting semi-vowels). There is no other similarity between the two liturgical poems, neither in the rhyme scheme nor in the structure of the line and stanza. Isaac Ibn Giath preceded Ibn Ezra, it is true. All the same, it is difficult to assume that the poet himself borrowed a melody from a poem with so few features in common; it is more likely that this was done later, by those who sang the poem. Hence

Yeshuʿah's heading merely provides information about the custom of singing Ibn Ezra's *Nišmaṯ* hymn in the synagogue to the melody of Ibn Giath's *ʾofan*.

213. Ibn Ezra writes of the need for a basic correspondence between the musical phrase and the length of the poetic line in *Ṣaḥoṯ* (ed. Rodriguez, p. 31; ed. Lippmann, p. 11b): "As for poems that have a melody, each line should scan the same." He also deals with this in his survey of the various interpretations of the word *selah* (comm. on Ps. 3:3): "The one who translated the Book of Psalms for the [Christians (thus in all MSS)] said that the word *selah* has no meaning, but merely serves to fill out the melody; evidence for this is that this word is not found anywhere in Scripture except three times in the prayer of Habakkuk, which is like the Book of Psalms." He himself believed, it is true, that *selah* is a word of affirmation, meaning "it is so," but he expatiates upon the prosodic explanation of *selah* as a filler for the poetic line so that its length will match the melody. I do not know to what biblical translation he is referring, however, since in the Septuagint *selah* is rendered as "interlude" (*diapsalma*) and in the Vulgate in the sense of "always" (*semper*).

214. See H. Brody, in *Studies of the Research Institute for Hebrew Poetry,* vol. 2 (1946), p. 41 (Heb.); Ibn Ezra, *Religious Poems,* vol. 1, p. 364; Stern, "Imitations," pp. 174–76; and his article cited above (note 209), pp. 357–59.

BIBLIOGRAPHY

Abramson, "Letter" — S. Abramson, "A Letter of Rabbi Judah ha-Levi to Rabbi Moses Ibn Ezra," in: S. Abramson & A. Mirsky, eds., *Ḥayyim Schirmann Jubilee Volume*, Jerusalem 1970, pp. 397–403 (Heb.).

Adler, *Writings* — I. Adler, *Hebrew Writings Concerning Music (In MSS and Printed Books from Geonic Times up to 1800)*, Munich 1975 (= RISM, vol. B IX^2).

Al-Fasi, *Dictionary* — S. L. Skoss, ed., *The Hebrew-Arabic Dictionary of the Bible of David ben Abraham Al-Fasi*, I–II, New Haven 1936–1945.

Al-Kumissi, "Fragments" — A. Marmorstein, "Fragments of Daniel al-Kumissi's Commentaries," *Hatsofe Leḥochmat Israel* 8 (1924), pp. 44–60, 321–37; 9 (1925), pp. 129–45.

Al-Kumissi, *Minor Prophets* — Daniel Al-Kumissi, *Commentary on the Minor Prophets*, ed. I. D. Markon, Jerusalem 1958.

Allony, "Ibn Balaam" — N. Allony, "Three New Fragments of ibn Balaam's Writings," *Beth Mikra* 9 (1964), No. 20–21, pp. 87–122 (Heb.).

Allony, *Scansion* — N. Allony, *The Scansion of Medieval Hebrew Poetry: Dunash, Jehuda Halevi and Abraham Ibn Ezra*, Jerusalem 1951 (Heb.).

Anan, *Commandments* — Anan ben David, *Book of Commandments* (Fragments), ed. A. Harkavy, *Studien und Mittheilungen*, vol. 8, St. Petersburg 1903 (Heb.).

Ankori, *Karaites* — Z. Ankori, *Karaites in Byzantium*, New York/Jerusalem 1959.

Ankori, "Studies" — Z. Ankori, "Studies in the Messianic Doctrine of Yehuda Hadassi the Karaite," *Tarbiz* 30 (1961), pp. 186–208 (Heb.).

Ashtor, *Moslem Spain* — E. Ashtor, *The Jews of Moslem Spain*, I–III, Philadelphia 1973–1984.

Avenary, "Geniza" — H. Avenary, "A Geniza Find of Saadya's Psalm-Preface and its Musical Aspects," *HUCA* 39 (1968), pp. 145–62.

Bacher, *Ibn Ezra*	W. Bacher, *Abraham Ibn Ezra als Grammatiker*, Strassburg 1882.
Bachya, *Duties*	Bachya ibn Paquda, *Duties of the Heart*, tr. into English by M. Hyamson, I–II, Jerusalem 1965[2] (1925–1947); Arabic original ed. and tr. into Hebrew by J. Kafiḥ, Jerusalem 1973.
Ben-Menachem, *Ibn Ezra*	N. Ben-Menachem, *Ibn Ezra Studies*, Jerusalem 1978 (Heb.).
Ben-Shammai, *Doctrines*	H. Ben-Shammai, *The Doctrines of Religious Thought of Abu Yusuf Yaaqub al-Qirqisani and Yefet ben Eli*, I–II, Dissertation, The Hebrew University, Jerusalem 1977 (Heb.).
Ben-Shammai, "Review"	H. Ben-Shammai, Review of the Hebrew edition of *Four Approaches to the Book of Psalms* by U. Simon, *Kiryat Sefer* 58 (1983), pp. 400–406 (Heb.).
Ben-Shammai, "Yefet's Commentaries"	H. Ben-Shammai, "Edition and Versions in Yephet b. Ali's Bible Commentary," *Alei Sefer* 2 (1976), pp. 17–32 (Heb.).
Carca, *M*e*ḳor Ḥayyim*	Samuel Carca, *M*e*ḳor Ḥayyim* [Supercommentary on Ibn Ezra's Commentary on the Torah], Mantua 1559.
Driver-Neubaur, *Isaiah LIII*	S. R. Driver and A. D. Neubaur, *The Fifty-Third Chapter of Isaiah According to the Jewish Interpretations*, vol. 2, Oxford and London 1877 (repr. New York 1969).
Dukes, *Exegetes*	L. Dukes, *Literaturhistorische Mittheilungen über die altesten hebräischen Exegeten, Grammatiker und Lexicographen,* Stuttgart 1884.
Dunash, *Criticism of Saadiah*	Dunaš ben Labrat, *Sefer Tešuḇoth al Rabbi Saadiah Gaon*, ed. R. Schroeter, Breslau 1866 (repr. Israel 1971).
Farmer, *Saadiah*	H. G. Farmer, *Saadyah Gaon on the Influence of Music*, London 1943.
Finkel, "Psalms"	Y. Finkel, "R. Moshe ben Shemuel Hacohen ibn Giqatila's Commentary on Psalms 3, 4, 8," *Ḥoreḇ* 3 (1936/7), pp. 153–62 (Heb.).
Fleischer, "France"	J. L. Fleischer, "Rabbi Abraham Ibn Ezra in France," *Mizraḥ Oumaarav* 4 (1930), pp. 352–60; 5 (1930–1931), pp. 38–40, 217–24, 289–300 (Heb.).
Fleischer, "Lucca"	J. L. Fleischer, "R. Abraham Ibn Ezra and his Literary Work in the City of Lucca, Italy," *Hasoqer* 2 (1934), pp. 77–85; 4 (1936/7), pp. 186–94 (Heb.).
Fleischer, "Rome"	J. L. Fleischer, "R. Abraham Ibn Ezra and his Literary Work in Rome," *Otsar-Hachayyim* 8 (1932),

pp. 97–100; 129–31; 148–50; 169–71; 9 (1933), pp. 18–22; 85–86; 96–99; 134–36; 151–55 (Heb.).

Fleischer, *"S^{e}faṯ Yeṯer"* — J. L. Fleischer, "Ibn Ezra's *Sefer Hayesod* and *Sefath Yeter*," *Kiryat Sefer* 3 (1926), pp. 165–68 (Heb.).

Fleischer [Ezra], *Poetry* — Ezra Fleischer, *Hebrew Liturgical Poetry in the Middle Ages*, Jerusalem 1975 (Heb.).

Friedlaender, *Essays* — M. Friedlaender, *Essays on the Writings of Abraham Ibn Ezra*, London 1877.

Golb, *Rouen* — N. Golb, *History and Culture of the Jews of Rouen in the Middle Ages,* Tel-Aviv 1976 (Heb.).

Hadassi, *ʾEškol Ha-kofer* — Yehudah Hadassi, *Eskol Hakkofer* [Cluster of Henna—Encyclopedia of Karaite Law], Gozlow 1836.

Halkin, "Introduction" — A. S. Halkin, "A Fragment of Saadya's Introduction to his Commentary on the Pentateuch," in: *Louis Ginzberg Jubilee Volume* (Hebrew Section), New York 1945, pp. 129–57 (Heb.).

Ibn Balaam, *Homonyms* — S. Abramson, ed., "Rab Yehudah ben Balaam's Kitab Attagnis—Sefer Hatsimud," in: S. Lieberman, et al., eds., *Ḥanoch Yalon Jubilee Volume*, Jerusalem 1963, pp. 51–149 (Arabic and Heb.).

Ibn Daud, *Tradition* — G. D. Cohen, *A Critical Edition with a Translation and Notes of* The Book of Tradition *by A. Ibn Daud*, Philadelphia 1967.

Ibn Ezra, *Daniel* (short comm.). — Abraham Ibn Ezra's Short Commentary on Daniel. [1] ed. H. J. Mathews, *Miscellany of Hebrew Literature*, vol. II (1877), pp. 257–76; [2] ed. A. Mondshine, M.A. Thesis, Bar-Ilan University, Ramat-Gan 1977 (Heb.).

Ibn Ezra, *Defense* — Abraham Ibn Ezra, *Sefat Yeter* (Defense of Saadiah Gaon), ed. G. H. Lippmann, Frankfurt a. M. 1843.

Ibn Ezra, *Diwan* — Abraham Ibn Ezra, *Diwan*, ed. J. Egers, Berlin 1886 (Heb.).

Ibn Ezra, *Esther* (Second Recension) — Abraham Ibn Ezra, *Commentary on the Book of Esther* (Second Recension), ed. J. Zedner, London 1850 (Heb.).

Ibn Ezra, *Exodus* (short comm.) — Abraham Ibn Ezra, *The Short Commentary on Exodus*, edition and supercommentary by J. L. Fleischer, Vienna 1926 (Heb.).

Ibn Ezra, *Genesis* (fragmentary) — Abraham Ibn Ezra, *The Second Recension on Genesis*, edited by M. Friedlaender, in Friedlaender, *Essays*, Hebrew section, pp. 1–64; Weiser, *Ibn Ezra*, vol. 1, pp. 137–93.

Ibn Ezra, *Ha-Shem* — Abraham Ibn Ezra, *Sepher Haschem* (The Book on the Tetragrammaton), ed. G. H. Lippmann, Fürth 1834.

Ibn Ezra, *Minor Prophets*	Abraham Ibn Ezra, *Two Commentaries on the Minor Prophets—An Annotated Critical Edition,* ed. U. Simon, Ramat-Gan 1989.
Ibn Ezra, *Moznayim*	Abraham Ibn Ezra, *Mozne Leshon Haqqodesh* [Hebrew Grammer], ed. W. Heidenheim, Offenbach 1791.
Ibn Ezra, *Poems*	Abraham Ibn Ezra, *Reime und Gedichte*, ed. and tr. into German by D. Rosin, in *Jahres-Bericht des judisch-theologischen Seminars "Fraenckel'scher Stiftung"* 1–4 (1885–1891/4).
Ibn Ezra, *Religious Poems*	Abraham Ibn Ezra, *Religious Poems*, ed. I. Levin, I–II, Jerusalem 1975–1980 (Heb.).
Ibn Ezra, *Sabbath*	Abraham Ibn Ezra, *Letter of the Sabbath*, ed. M. Friedlaender, Appendix of "Ibn Ezra in England," *Transactions of the Jewish Historical Society of England* 2 (1894/5), pp. 61–75 (Heb.).
Ibn Ezra, *Ṣaḥoṯ*	Abraham Ibn Ezra, *Sefer Tsachoth* (Hebrew Grammar), ed. G. H. Lippmann, Fürth 1827 (repr. Jerusalem 1970); edited and translated into Spanish by C. dell Valle Rodriguez, Salamanca 1977.
Ibn Ezra, *Safah B^{e}rurah*	Abraham Ibn Ezra, *Safah Berurah* (Hebrew Grammar), ed. G. H. Lippmann, Fürth 1839; ed. M. Wilensky, *D^{e}vir* 2 (1924), pp. 274–302 (first part only).
Ibn Ezra, *Song of Songs* (first comm.)	Abraham Ibn Ezra, *Commentary on the Canticles* (First Recension), ed. H. J. Mathews, London 1874 (Heb.).
Ibn Ezra, *Y^{e}sod Diḳduḳ*	Abraham Ibn Ezra, *Y^{e}sod Diḳduḳ* (Hebrew Grammar), ed. N. Allony, Jerusalem 1985 (Heb.).
Ibn Ezra, *Y^{e}sod Mora᾽*	Abraham Ibn Ezra, *Sefer Y^{e}sod Mora᾽ Ve-Sod Torah*, Jerusalem 1931 (repr. in *The Works of R. Abraham Ibn Ezra*, II, Jerusalem 1970).
Ibn Ezra, Moses, *Discussions*	Moses Ibn Ezra, *Kitab Almuḥāḏara wal-Mudhākara (The Book of Studies and Discussions)*, ed. and tr. into Hebrew by A. S. Halkin, Jerusalem 1975.
Ibn Gabirol, *Secular Poetry*	D. Jarden, *The Secular Poetry of Rabbi Shelomo Ibn Gabirol*, I–II, Jerusalem 1975/1976 (Heb.).
Ibn Ganach, *Dictionary*	Jonah Ibn Ganaḥ, *Sefer Hashorashim*, translated into Hebrew by Jehuda Ibn Tibbon, ed. W. Bacher, Berlin 1896 (repr. Amsterdam 1969).
Ibn Ganach, *Ha-Riḳmah*	Jonah Ibn Ganaḥ, *Sefer Ha-Riḳmah* (Hebrew Grammar), translated into Hebrew by Judah Ibn Tibbon, ed. M. Wilensky, second revised edition, I–II, Jerusalem 1964.
Ibn Giath, *Ecclesiastes*	Isaac Ibn Giath, *Commentary on Ecclesiastes*, in *The Five Scrolls with Ancient Commentaries* [this

commentary is mistakenly attributed there to Saadiah], edited and translated into Hebrew by J. Kafiḥ, Jerusalem 1962, pp. 155–296.

Kaufmann, *Senses* — D. Kaufmann, *Die Sinne - Beiträge zur Geschichte der Physiologie und Psychologie im Mittelalter aus hebräischen und arabischen Quellen*, Budapest 1884.

Kimḥi, *Psalms* — David Kimḥi, *The Complete Commentary on the Book of Psalms*, ed. A. Darom, Jerusalem 1971 (Heb.).

Klar, *Inquiries* — B. Klar, *Inquiries and Studies in Language, Poetry and Literature*, Tel-Aviv 1954 (Heb.).

Levin, *Ibn Ezra* — I. Levin, *Abraham Ibn Ezra: His Life and His Poetry*, Tel-Aviv 1969 (Heb.).

Maimonides, *Epistle to Yemen* — Moses Maimonides, *Epistle to Yemen*, ed. A. S. Halkin, tr. into English by B. Cohen, New York 1952.

Maimonides, *Guide* — Moses Maimonides, *The Guide of the Perplexed*, tr. into English by S. Pines, Chicago 1963.

Malter, "Messianic Computation" — H. Malter, "Saadia Gaon's Messianic Computation," *Journal of Jewish Lore and Philosophy* 1 (1919), pp. 46–59.

Malter, *Saadiah* — H. Malter, *Saadia Gaon: His Life and Works*, New York 1926 (1969).

Mann, "Karaite Commentaries" — J. Mann, "Early Karaite Bible Commentaries," *JQR* (N.S.) 12 (1921/2), pp. 435–526.

Mann, "Tract" — J. Mann, "A Tract by an Early Karaite Settler in Jerusalem," *JQR* (N.S.) 12 (1921/2), pp. 257–98.

Marwick, "Al-Fasi" — L. Marwick, "A First Fragment from David b. Abraham al-Fasi's Commentary on Psalms," *Studies in Bibliography and Booklore* 6–7 (1962/5), pp. 53–72.

Marwick, "Yefet" — L. Marwick, "The Order of the Books in Yefet's Bible Codex," *JQR* (N.S.) 33 (1942/3), pp. 445–60.

Melammed, *Commentators* — E. Z. Melammed, *Bible Commentators*, I–II, Jerusalem 1975 (Heb.).

Menachem, *Maḥberet* — Menaḥem Ben Saruk, *Maḥberet Menaḥem*, ed. H. Filipowski, London-Edinburgh 1854; edited and translated into Spanish by A. Sáens-Badillos, Granada 1986.

Menachem's Disciples, *Polemics* — S. G. Stern (ed.), *Liber Responsionum* (Part 1: The Polemics of Menachem Ben Saruk's Disciples; Part 2: The Responses of Dunaš Ben Labrat's Disciple), Vienna 1870 (Heb.). *Tešuḇot de Yehudi Ben Šešet*, edited and translated into Spanish by M. E. Varela Moreno, Granada 1981.

Midrash Tehillim	S. Buber, ed., *Midrasch Tehillim (=Schocher Tob̲)*, Vienna 1891 (Heb.).
Monroe, "Poetry"	J. T. Monroe, "Hispano-Arabic Poetry during the Caliphate of Cordoba," *Ha-Sifrut* 6 (1975), no. 21, pp. 101–118 (Heb.).
Mottot, *M^egillat̲ S^et̲arim*	Samuel Mottot, *M^egillat̲ S^et̲arim* (Supercommentary on Ibn Ezra's Commentary on the Torah), Venice 1554.
Nemoy, *Anthology*	L. Nemoy, *Karaite Anthology*, New Haven 1952.
Neubauer, "Titles"	A. Neubauer, "The Authorship and the Titles of the Psalms According to Early Jewish Authorities," *Studia Biblica et Ecclesiastica* 2 (1890), pp. 1–58.
Ochs, "Reconstruction"	S. Ochs, "Die Wiederherstellung der Kommentare Ibn Ezras zu den Büchern Jer., Ez., Spr., Es., Neh., und Chr.," *MGWJ* 60 (1916), pp. 41–58, 118–34, 193–212, 279–94, 437–52.
Pagis, *Change and Tradition*	D. Pagis, *Change and Tradition in Hebrew Secular Poetry: Spain and Italy*, Jerusalem 1976 (Heb.).
Pagis, *Secular Poetry*	D. Pagis, *Secular Poetry and Poetic Theory: Moses Ibn Ezra and His Contemporaries*, Jerusalem 1970 (Heb.).
Perez, "Contribution"	M. Perez, "The Contribution of R. Yehuda Ibn Balaam to the Philological Exegesis of the Bible in Spain," *Bar-Ilan* 20/21 (1983), pp. 151–71 (Heb.).
Pilwarg, *Supercommentary*	J. Pilwarg, *Bene Reshef* [Supercommentary on Ibn Ezra's Commentaries], I–II, Piotrekow 1900.
Pines, "Abuʾl-Barakat"	S. Pines, "Studies in Abuʾl-Barakat al-Baghdadi's Poetics and Metaphysics," *Scripta Hierosolymitana* 6 (1960), pp. 120–98 (=*Studies in Abu ʾl-Barakat al-Baghdadi's Physics and Metaphysics*, Jerusalem and Leiden 1979, pp. 259–334).
Pinsker, *Lickute*	S. Pinsker, *Lickute Kadmoniot: Zur Geschichte des Karaismus und der Karaischen Literatur*, I–II, Vienna 1860 (repr. Jerusalem 1968) (Heb.).
Poznanski, "Anan"	S. Poznanski, "Anan et ses ecrits," *REJ* 44 (1902), pp. 161-87; 45 (1902), pp. 50–69, 176–203.
Poznanski, "Catalogue"	S. Poznanski, "Catalogue of Hebrew and Samaritan MSS in the British Museum," *REJ* 41 (1900), pp. 301–308.
Poznanski, *Giqatilah*	S. Poznanski, *Moše B. Samuel Hakkohen Ibn Chiquitilla nebst den Fragmenten seiner Schriften*, Leipzig 1895.
Poznanski, "Karaites"	S. Poznanski, "Karaite Miscellanies," *JQR* (O.S.) 8 (1896), pp. 681–704.

Poznanski, "Opponents" S. Poznanski, "The Karaite Literary Opponents of Saadiah Gaon in the Tenth Century," *JQR* (O.S.) 18 (1906), pp. 209–250; 19 (1907), pp. 59–85.

Poznanski, "Psalms" S. Poznanski, "Aus Mose Ibn Chiquitilla's arabischem Psalmenkommentar," *Zeitschrift für Assyriologie und Verwandte Gebiete* 26 (1912), pp. 38–60.

Poznanski, "Saadiah" S. Poznanski, "Miscellen über Saadja, III: Die Berechnung des Erlosungsjahres bei Saadja," *MGWJ* 44 (1900), pp. 400–416; 508–529.

Prijs, "Psalm" L. Prijs, "Abraham Ibn Ezra's Commentary on Psalm I," *Tarbiz* 28 (1959), pp. 181–89 (Heb.).

Ratzaby, *Dictionary* Y. Ratzaby, *A Dictionary of Judaeo-Arabic in R. Saadya's Tafsir*, Ramat-Gan 1985 (Heb.).

Rivlin, "Prefaces" J. J. Rivlin, "R. Saadiah Gaon's Prefaces to his Commentaries as an Introduction to the Bible," in J. L. Fishman, ed., *Rav Saadya Gaon*, Jerusalem 1943, pp. 382–427 (Heb.).

Rosen-Moked, *Girdle Poem* T. Rosen-Moked, *The Hebrew Girdle Poem in the Middle Ages*, Haifa 1985 (Heb.).

Rosin, *Philosophy* D. Rosin, *Die Religionsphilosophie Abraham Ibn Ezras*, in *MGWJ* 42 (1898), pp. 17–33, 58–73, 108–115, 154–61, 200–214, 241–52, 305–315, 345–62, 394–407, 444–57, 481–505; 43 (1899), pp. 22–31, 75–91, 125–33, 168–84, 231–40.

Saadiah, *Beliefs* Saadia Gaon, *The Book of Beliefs and Opinions*, tr. Samuel Rosenblatt, New Haven 1948; Arabic original ed. and tr. into Hebrew by J. Kafiḥ, Jerusalem 1970.

Saadiah, *Daniel* Saadiah Gaon, *The Book of Daniel: Tafsir and Arabic Commentary*, ed. and tr. into Hebrew by J. Kafiḥ, Jerusalem 1981.

Saadiah, *Genesis* Saadiah Gaon, *Commentary on Genesis*, ed. and tr. into Hebrew by M. Zucker, New York 1984.

Saadiah, *Ha-ʾEgron* Rav Saadiah Gaon, *Ha-ʾEgron: Kitab Uṣul al-Shir al-Ibrani* [Hebrew Rhyming Dictionary], ed. N. Allony, Jerusalem 1969 (Heb.).

Saadiah, *Ha-Galui* Saadiah Gaon, *Sefer Ha-Galui* (The Open Book), ed. A. Harkavi, *Zikron Larishonim* v, St. Petersburg-Berlin 1891, pp. 133–238.

Saadiah, *Job* Saadiah Gaon, *The Book of Job: Tafsir and Arabic Commentary*, ed. and tr. into Hebrew by J. Kafiḥ, Jerusalem 1973.

Saadiah, *Proverbs* Saadiah Gaon, *The Book of Proverbs: Tafsir and Arabic Commentary*, ed. and tr. into Hebrew by J. Kafiḥ, Jerusalem 1976.

Saadiah, *Psalms* — Saadiah Gaon, *The Book of Psalms: Tafsir and Arabic Commentary*, ed. and tr. into Hebrew by J. Kafiḥ, Jerusalem 1966.

Saadiah, *Siddur* — Saadja Gaon, *The Siddur*, ed. and tr. into Hebrew by I. Davidson, S. Assaf, and B. I. Joel, Jerusalem 1970.

Saadiah, *Torah Comments* — Saadiah Gaon, *Comments on the Pentateuch*, gleaned by J. Kafiḥ, Jerusalem 1963 (Heb.).

Salmon, *Psalms* — L. Marwick, ed., *The Arabic Commentary of Salmon ben Yeruḥam the Karaite on Psalms 42–72*, Philadelphia 1956.

Salmon, *Wars* — Salmon ben Yeruḥim, *Sefer Milḥemoth Hashem* [The Book of the Wars of the Lord], ed. I. L. Davidson, New York 1934.

Samuel Ha-Nagid, *Ben Tehillim* — Samuel Hannagid, *Diwan: Ben Tehillim*, ed. D. Jarden, Jerusalem 1966 (Heb.).

Schechter, *Saadyana* — S. Schechter, *Saadyana: Geniza Fragments of Writings of R. Saadya Gaon and Others*, Cambridge 1903 (repr. Tel-Aviv 1969).

Scheiber, "Siddur" — A. Scheiber, "A Rabbinic *Siddur* Quoted by Kirkisani," in *Ignace Goldziher Memorial*, vol. I, Budapest 1948, pp. 27–40 (Heb.).

Schirmann, *Hebrew Poetry* — H. Schirmann, *Hebrew Poetry in Spain and Provence*, I–II Jerusalem and Tel-Aviv 1961^2 (Heb.).

Schirmann, "Poets" — H. J. Schirmann, "Poets Contemporary with Moses Ibn Ezra and Jehuda Hallevi," *Studies of the Research Institute for Hebrew Poetry in Jerusalem*, 2 (1936), pp. 119–93 (Heb.).

Shiloaḥ, *Epistle* — A. Shiloaḥ, *The Epistle on Music of the Ikhwan al-Safa (Baghdad, 10th century)*, Tel-Aviv 1978.

Shunary, *Methods* — J. Shunary, *Saadia Gaon's Exegetical Methods as Represented in his Arabic Translation of Psalms*, Dissertation, The Hebrew University, Jerusalem 1970 (Heb.).

Shunary, "Salmon" — J. Shunary, "Salmon ben Yeruham's Commentary on the Book of Psalms," *JQR* 73 (1982), pp. 155–75.

Simon, "Exegete" — U. Simon, "Ibn Ezra: The Exegete and his Readers," *Proceedings of the Ninth World Congress of Jewish Studies—Central Sessions: Bible and Ancient Near-East*, Jerusalem 1988, pp. 23–42 (Heb.).

Simon, "Exegetic Method" — U. Simon, "The Exegetic Method of Abraham Ibn Ezra, as Revealed in Three Interpretations of a Biblical Passage," *Bar-Ilan* 3 (1965), pp. 92–138 (Heb.).

Simon, "Medievalism" — U. Simon, "Ibn Ezra Between Medievalism and Modernism: The Case of Isaiah XL—LXVI", *SVT* 36 (1985), pp. 257–71.

Simon, "Two Approaches" — U. Simon, "Ibn Ezra and Kimḥi: Two Approaches to the Masoretic Text," *Bar-Ilan* 6 (1986) pp. 191–237 (Heb.).

Ṣof^{e}nat̲ Paᶜneaḥ — Joseph Bonfils (Ṭob̲ ᶜElem), *Ṣophnath Paᶜneaḥ: Ein Beitrag zur Pentateuchexegese des Mittelalters*, ed. D. Herzog, vol. I, Cracow 1912; vol. II, Berlin 1930 (repr. Haifa 1967).

Steinschneider, *Literatur* — M. Steinschneider, *Die Arabische Literatur der Juden*, Frankfurt a.M. 1902.

Steinschneider, *Translation* — M. Steinschneider, *Die hebräischen Übersetzungen des Mittelalteres und die Juden als Dolmetscher*, Berlin 1893.

Stern "Ibn Esra" — S. M. Stern, "The Muwashshahs of Abraham Ibn Esra," in: F. Pierce, ed., *Hispanic Studies in Honour of I. Gonzalez Llubera*, Oxford 1959, pp. 367–86.

Stern, "Imitations" — S. M. Stern, "Imitations of Arab Girdle Poems in Hispano-Hebrew Poetry," *Tarbiz* 18 (1947), pp. 166–86 (Heb.).

Stern, "Poetry" — S. M. Stern, *Hispano-Arabic Strophic Poetry*, Oxford 1974.

Tadros, *Gan ha-M^{e}šalim* — Tadros Abu-L-ᶜAfiah, *Gan ha-Meshalim we-ha-Ḥidoth*, ed. D. Yellin, I–III, Jerusalem 1932–1937.

Tadros, *Girdle Poems* — Tadros Abu-L-ᶜAfiah, *The Girdle Poems*, in Tadros Abu-L-Afiah, *Gan ha-Meshalim we-ha-Ḥidoth*, vol. III, ed. D. Yellin, Jerusalem 1936, pp. 5–36.

Vajda, *Two Commentaries* — G. Vajda, *Deux Commentaires Karaïtes sur l'Ecclésiaste*, Leiden 1971.

Weiser, *Ibn Ezra* — A. Weiser, ed., *Perushe ha-Torah le-Rabbenu Abraham Ibn Ezra* (Ibn Ezra's Two Commentaries on the Pentateuch), I–III, Jerusalem 1976.

Werner-Sonne, "Music" — E. Werner and I. Sonne, "The Philosophy and Theory of Music in Judaeo-Arabic Literature," *HUCA* 16 (1941), pp. 251–319; 17 (1942/3), pp. 511–73.

Wieder, "Exegesis" — N. Wieder, "The Dead Sea Scrolls Type of Biblical Exegesis among the Karaites," in A. Altmann, ed., *Between East and West*, London 1958, pp. 75–106.

Wieder, "Qumran" — N. Wieder "The Qumran Sectaries and the Karaites," *JQR* (N.S.) 47(1956/7), pp. 97–113; 269–92.

Wieder, *Scrolls* — N. Wieder, *The Judean Scrolls and Karaism*, London 1962.

Wilensky, *Studies*	M. Wilensky, *Meḥqarim Belashon Oubesifrut* (Collected Studies in Language and Literature), Jerusalem 1978.
Yefet, *Daniel*	Jephet Ibn Ali, *An Arabic Commentary on the Book of Daniel*, ed. and tr. into English by D. S. Margoliouth, Oxford 1899.
Yefet, *Ecclesiastes*	Yefet ben ʿAli, *The Arabic Commentary on the Book of Ecclesiastes Chapter 1–6*, ed. and tr. into English by R. M. Bland, Dissertation, University of California (Ann Arbor 1966).
Yefet, *Hosea*	Yefet ben Ali, *The Arabic Commentary on the Book of Hosea*, ed. P. Birnbaum, Philadelphia 1942.
Yefet, *Nahum*	Yefet ben Ali, *The Arabic Commentary on the Book of Naḥum*, ed. H. Hirschfeld, with an abridged translation into English, London 1911.
Yefet, *Proverbs*	I. Günzig, ed., *Der Commentar des Karaers Jephet ben Ali Halevi zu den Proverbien* [Cap. I–III], Cracow 1898.
Yefet, *Psalm XXII*	T. Hofmann, *Arabische Übersetzung und Erklärung des XXII. Psalms von R. Jepheth ben Eli Ha-Bacri, nach Handschriften veröffentlicht und ins deutsche übersetzt*, Tübingen 1880.
Yefet, *Psalms*	Yefet ben Ali, *The Commentary on the Book of Psalms* [Cap. I–II], ed. and tr. into Latin by J. J. L. Bargès, Paris 1846.
Yefet, *Ruth*	N. Schorstein, ed., *Der Commentar des Karaers Jephet ben Ali zum Buch Ruth* [Cap. I–II], Berlin 1908.
Yefet, *Song of Songs*	Yappeth Abou Aly, *The Arabic Commentary on the Book of Song of Songs*, ed. and tr. into Latin by J. J. L. Bargès, Paris 1884.
Yehudah Halevi, *Diwan*	Yehudah Hallevi, *Diwan*, ed. S. D. Luzatto, Lyck 1864.
Yehudah Halevi, *Kuzari*	Judah Hallevi, *Kitab Al Khazari*, tr. into English by H. Hirschfeld, London 1905.
Yellin, "Metrical Forms"	D. Yellin, "The Metrical Forms in the Poetry of Samuel Hannagid," *Studies of the Research Institute for Hebrew Poetry in Jerusalem* 5 (1939), pp. 181–208 (Heb.).
Zucker, "Commentary"	M. Zucker, "Fragments from Rav Saadya Gaon's Commentary to the Pentateuch from Mss.," *Sura* 2 (1955/6), pp. 313–55 (Heb.).
Zucker, "Fragments"	M. Zucker, "Fragments of Saadiah's *Kitab Taḥsil Al-Sharayi Al-Samayya,*" *Tarbiz* 33 (1971/72), pp. 373–410 (Heb.).

Zucker, "Notes" — M. Zucker, "Notes on Saadya's Introduction into the Psalms," *Lešonenu* 33 (1968–1969), pp. 223–30 (Heb.).

Zucker, "Prayer" — M. Zucker, "A Fragment of R. Saadiah's *Kitab Wugub As-Sala*," *PAAJR* 43 (1976), Hebrew Section, pp. 29–36.

Zucker, *Translation* — M. Zucker, *Rav Saadya Gaon's Translation of the Torah*, New York 1959 (Heb.).

Zulay, *Saadiah's Poetry* — M. Zulay, *The Liturgical Poetry of Saadiah Gaon and his School*, Jerusalem 1964 (Heb.).

Zunz, *Poetry* — L. Zunz, *Die synagogale Poesie des Mittelalters*, Berlin 1855.

APPENDIX

Ibn Ezra's Introduction and Commentary on Psalms 1—2: The "First Recension" *

Note: The numbers in the margin refer to the lineation of the Hebrew text as printed herein.

In the name of God Who is great over all divinities
I begin a commentary on the Book of Psalms.
"Hear, O Lord, and have mercy on me; O Lord, be my help!"
(Ps. 30:11)
In the name of God Whom I call my desire to fulfill
And He is my help to commence as well as to conclude
To reveal the secrets of grammar and words
And interpret the meanings of the Book of Psalms.

[5] Thus says Abraham, the son of R. Meir (his soul rests in Paradise) Ibn Ezra the
Spaniard: Blessed be the Lord who gives power to the ear that is implanted to understand every sound, and whose power is connected with that of the higher soul—
[7] not like the power of the eye, for its virtue is lacking neither by day nor by night,
and it hears from all six directions, and is not obstructed by veil or wall. Moreover,
were it not for the ears speech would not have been created, for who would hear
[it]? The words are like bodies and the meanings like spirits. There are sounds that
[10] delight and sounds that depress; when the meaning of the speech is lofty, it may do
great things, even angering one's friend or appeasing one's enemy—all the more so
if it is said poetically; and when instrumental music is joined with the poem, then

* *Note on the text:* The introduction and commentary on Psalm 1 in the "First Recension" are here presented on the basis of the unique manuscript—Verona Municipal Library 294 (described above, pp. 154f.); the commentary on Psalm 2:1–5 is based on the direct continuation of the former in MS Leipzig University Library XL (described above, p. 155). The prefatory poem is also extant in MS Rome Angelica 72 and MS Mantua 13. A textual apparatus is provided in the notes to the Hebrew text. The English translation reflects the emendations suggested in the apparatus.

ההקדמה ופירוש מזמורים א׳–ב׳ שבשריד — ׳השיטה הראשונה׳

בשם אל גדול על כל אלהים   אחל פירוש ספר תהלים
״שמע יי וחנני, יי היה עוזר לי״ (תה׳, ל׳, 11)
בְּשֵׁם אֵל אֶקְרָאָה חֶפְצִי לְמַלְּא(ו)ת   וְהוּא עֶזְרִי לְהָחֵל גַּם לְכַלּוֹת
לְגַלּוֹת מִסְתְּרֵי* דִקְדּוּק וּמִלּוֹת   וּפֵירוּשׁ טַעֲמֵי סֵפֶר תְּהִלּוֹת

נאם אברהם בר׳ מאיר נ״ע בן עזרא הספרדי: ברוך השם השם כח באזן הנטועה / להבין כל שמועה / וכחה קשור בכח הנשמה העליונה; לא ככח העין, כי גם ביום ובלילה לא נעדר כחה, והיא שומעת משש קצוות, ולא יחשכנה מסך או קיר. ולולי האזנים לא נברא ניב שפתים, כי מי שומע? והדברים כגופות והטעמים כרוחות. והנה יש קול מענג וקול משומם, וכאשר ינשא הטעם במאמר, אז יגדיל לעשות עד שיכעיס האוהב וירצה האויב, ואף כי אם היה על דרך שיר; ואם יתחבר עם שיר נגון בכלי, אז יראה

הערה על דרך ההדרה: ההקדמה ופירוש מזמור א׳ של ׳השיטה הראשונה׳ ניתנים בזה על־פי כתב־היד היחיד — וירונה־הספריה העירונית 294, ופירוש מזמור ב, 1–5 — על־פי המשכו הישיר בכתב־יד לייפציג–הספרייה האוניברסיטאית XL (ראה תיאוריהם לעיל, פרק ד׳, § 1). לגבי חרוזי־הפתיחה יש בידינו שני עדי־נוסח נוספים: כ״י רומא־אנג׳ליקה 72 וכ״י מנטואה 13, אשר בהם הם מובאים בצדו של שיר הפתיחה של הפירוש הנדפס לתהילים. לנוכח עדיפות הנוסח שבכ״י מנטואה ניתנים בזה חרוזי־הפתיחה על־פיו. שינויי הגירסאות ירשמו בהערות בעזרת סימנים אלה: **ו** = וירונה; **מ** = מנטואה; **ר** = רומא־אנג׳ליקה. גוף ההקדמה מועתק כאן כנתינתה בכתב־יד וירונה בתוספת של סימני פיסוק ומראי־מקומות. כדי להקל על קריאתה הרהוטה, על אף השיבושים הלא־מעטים שנפלו בכתב־היד, שולבו הצעות־התיקון בתוך הטקסט. הן צויינו בצורה בולטת: השמטות — בסוגריים עגולים ( ), השלמות מחמת השמטה — בסוגריים מרובעים [ ], השלמות מחמת חֶסֶר — בסוגריים מרובעים כפולים [[ ]], ושינויים — בסוגריים זוויתיים ובתוספת של ׳צריך להיות׳ <צ״ל:>. במידה שהצעות־התיקון הללו אינן מובנות מאליהן הן נומקו בהערות.

3 **למלא(ו)ת** — **ר** למלאת (כפי שכתוב בשמ׳, ל״א, 5 וכפי שדורשת החריזה) **ו** למלות (אך בשוליים רשום [בכתיבת ידו של המעתיק] התיקון: א׳). **להחל גם** — **ו** בתחל עד (יתרון גירסת **מר** ניכר גם מן ההשוואה לטור האחרון בשיר הפתיחה לפירוש הנדפס, הכתוב גם הוא במשקל ׳המרובה׳: ״ובשמו אכתבה ספר תהלות / והוא עזרי להחל גם לכלות״).

4 **מסתרי*** — **ומר** מספרי. על אף עדותם האחידה של שלשת כתבי־היד מחייבים הענין והמשקל לגרוס: מִסְתְּרֵי ע״פ לשון הכתוב ״גליתי את מסתריו״ (יר׳, מ״ט, 10). והשווה לחרוזי־הפתיחה של ספר ׳יסוד דקדוק׳ (עמ׳ 84), שנרשמו בטעות גם בראש ספר ההגנה על רס״ג: ״ספר בשם תלמיד שמו חיים/ספר יגלה לו דבר סתר״ (ראב״ע, ׳שירים׳, עמ׳ 22), ושל ׳ספר היסוד׳ האבוד: ״קרא ספר היסוד/יגלה לך כל סוד/שפת העבריים״ (שם, עמ׳ 21). **ופירוש** — **ו** ופי׳. **תהלות** — **ר** תהילות.

6 **הנטועה...שמועה** — בעוד ששתי ההקדמות לפירושי ראב״ע לתורה כתובים בפרוזה חרוזה, הוא מסתפק כאן בחריזת מילות הפתיחה.

[12] will marvels be beheld. Consider an evil spirit (and no disease is worse than that):
when David the man of God played on the lyre before Saul he found relief. Moreover: "As the musician played, the spirit of the Lord came upon him" (2 Kings
3:15). There are many such [incidents] with profane songs, and all the more so with
[15] sacred songs—the songs of God, as the Levites said to the Babylonians: "How can
we sing *a song of the Lord* on alien soil?" (Ps. 137:4). We find that David appointed singers to stand before the Ark and before the Tabernacle of the Lord, and
established five principles, as it is written: "All these David and Samuel the Seer
[18] ordained by their faith" (1 Chron. 9:22). *The first principle*: only Levites could
perform music [in the Temple], as it is written—that the officers of the musicians
were Heman and Asaph and Ethan, from the three Levite families. *The second prin-*
[21] *ciple*: he [David] placed Asaph, who was a Gershonite, on the right of Heman, who
was a Kehathite, and Ethan, who was a Merarite, on his left, just as the Levites
were encamped around the Tabernacle. *The third principle*: there was a prescribed
[24] song for a given day, like: "A Psalm. A song of the Sabbath Day" (Ps. 92), and the
Sages, their memory for a blessing, handed down which song the Levites used to
say in the Temple on each day (Mishnah Tamid 7,4). *The fourth principle*: [the
prescription of] different musical instruments, since there were three musicians who
[27] played the cymbals, and eight the harp, and six the lyre. *The fifth principle*: [a
prescribed] melody—those who played the harp—[the tune of] *ʿal ʿalamoṯ* (1
Chron. 15:20)—and those who played the lyre—*ʿal ha-šᵉminiṯ* (verse 21).

[30] Blessed be God who sanctified his own people. For [consider] the Ishmaelites: all of
their poems are about amours and passion; while the poetry of the Edomites [i.e.,
European Christians] is about war and vengeance; the poetry of the Greeks is of
[32] wisdom and discretion; and the poetry of the Indians deals with all sorts of parables.
Only the poetry of Israel [is dedicated] to show them that He is their God alone.
The poet of the divine poetry is our master David, and this book is ascribed to him.

פלאים. כי הנה רוח רעה, שאין מחלה קשה ממנה, כנגן דוד איש האלהים בכנור לפני שאול אז רוח לו. ועוד: ״והיה כנגן המנגן ותהי עליו רוח אלהים״ (מל״ב, ג׳, 15). וכאלה רבות עם שירי חול, אף כי שירי קדש והם שירי השם, כאשר אמרו הלויים לבבליים: ״איך נשיר את שיר יי על אדמת נכר״ (תה׳, קל״ז, 4). והנה מצאנו כי דוד העמיד לפני הארון, גם לפני משכן השם, משוררים. והנה יסד חמש[ה] מוסדים, וכת׳: ״המה יסד דוד ושאול <צ״ל: ושמואל> הרואה באמונתם״ (דה״א, ט׳, 22). היסוד האחד — שלא ינגן רק מי שהוא מבני לוי, כאשר הוא כתוב כי ש(י)רי המשוררים הם הימן ואסף [ואיתן] משלש(ה) משפחות בני לוי. והיסוד השני — ששם אסף שהוא גרשוני לימין הימן שהוא קהתי ואיתן בשמאל שהוא מבני מררי, כדרך שהיו הלוים חונים סביבות המשכן. והיסוד השלישי — שהיה שיר ידוע ליום ידוע, כמו: ״מזמור שיר ליום השבת״ (צ״ב). וקדמונינו ז״ל העתיקו השיר שהיו הלוים אומרי׳ בבית המקדש בכל יום (תמיד, פרק ז׳, משנה ד׳). והיסוד הרביעי — כלי נגינות שונות <צ״ל: שונים>, כי היו השרים [אשר] ישמיעו קול במצלתים [שלשה], ושמנה בנבלים, וששה בכנורות. והיסוד החמשי — נועם בנגינות, כי המנגנים בנבלים הם ״על עלמות״ (דה״א, ט״ו, 20), ואנשי הכנור — ״על השמינית״ (שם, 21).

וברוך השם שקדש עמו בעצמו, כי הנה הישמעאלים כל שיריהם — בדרך אהבים ועגבים, ושירי האדומים — במלחמות ונקמות, ושירי היונים — בחכמות ומזמות, ושירי אנשי הודו — במיני משלים, ושירי ישראל לבדם — להורות להם שהוא אלהיהם לבדו. והנה שירי <צ״ל: שר> שיר השם הוא אדוננו דוד, וזה הספר נקרא על שמו.

18 **<צ״ל: ושמואל>** — תוקן על פי לשון הכתוב, שכן טעות גסה זו היא בעליל של אחד הסופרים. גם בפירוש הארוך לשמ׳, י״ב, 1 נידון ענין זה, וגם שם נשתבש שמו של שמואל בדפוסים ותחתיו בא ״שלמה״, אך בכ״י פריז 176 כתוב כראוי ״שמואל״.

19 **ש(י)רי המשוררים... [ואיתן]** — התיקון וההשלמה מבוססים על לשון הכתוב: ״ואמר דויד לשרי הלוים להעמיד את אחיהם המשֹררים... ויעמידו הלוים את הימן... אסף... איתן...״ (דה״א, ט״ו, 16–17). ואמנם איתן נזכר לקמן בשורה 21.

26 **[שלשה]** — הושלם על פי דה״א, ט״ו, 19, שכן בפסוק זה מנויים שלשת המשוררים שניגנו במצלתים, ואילו בשני הפסוקים שלאחריו מנויים שמונת המשוררים שניגנו בנבלים, וששת המשוררים שניגנו בכנורות.

33 **<צ״ל: שר>** — מכיון שנושא המשפט הוא ״דוד״ ברור שהנשוא צריך להיות בלשון יחיד. ׳שר׳ בשי״ן ימנית משמשת בפי הראב״ע במשמע של משורר (ראה שורה 26 לעיל, וכן הכינוי ״אברהם השר״ שבו הוא מכנה את עצמו בפתח הקדמתו לפירוש הקצר לתורה); אך מאחר שהראב״ע לא ייחס את כל המזמורים לדויד, יתכן שנשמטה כאן מילת ׳שר׳ בשי״ן שמאלית, ושצריך לשחזר את הנוסח כך: שַׂר שָׁרֵי שיר השם.

[35] We must undertake four inquiries. *The first inquiry*: Is the entire book by David?
Some say that the entire book is by David, and interpret *mizmor l^{e}-ʾAsaf* (50, 73—
83) to mean that the psalm [was written] by David, who gave it to Asaph to play;
[38] and similarly *libnei Ḳoraḥ* (42, 44—49; 84—85; 87—88). Their proof [for this] is
"la-m^{e}naṣṣeaḥ li-Y^{e}dutun mizmor l^{e}-Dawid" (39), "la-m^{e}naṣṣeaḥ ʿal Y^{e}dutun mizmor l^{e}-Dawid" (62). They explain that "a prayer of Moses, the man of God" (90)
was written by David, who gave it to the descendants of Moses [to play]. They
[41] explain that "Of Solomon. O God, endow the king with Your judgments" (72)
means that [David] prophesied about Solomon or the Messiah who is his descendant. They interpret "la-m^{e}naṣṣeaḥ. A psalm of David. May the Lord answer you in
time of trouble" (20) as referring to his son or to the Messiah. "A psalm of David.
[44] The Lord said to my lord" (110) they understand to refer to the Messiah, while
some say that it refers to our father Abraham. All of the psalms without an explicit
ascription of authorship—like the first two—are by David. But some of the Sages
said that "A prayer of Moses, the man of God" (90) was written by Moses when he
[47] erected the Tabernacle, and that all of the psalms that come after that prayer, which
do not have an explicit ascription, are by the seventy members of the Sanhedrin.

[49] R. Moses ha-Kohen (his soul rests in Paradise) said that most but not all of the
psalms bearing the ascription *l^{e}-Dawid* are by David, for example: "May the Lord
answer you in time of trouble" (20), which he said was written by one of the poets
[51] about David, and similarly "The Lord said to my lord" (110). He inferred this from
"A psalm. A song of the Sabbath Day" [*l^{e}-yom ha-šabbat*] (92), because the Sabbath Day certainly did not write the psalm! Although we find [that the Sabbath did
"compose" the psalm] in the homiletical exegeses of the rabbis (*Midrash Tehillim*
[53] on Ps. 92, §3; Saadiah, *Siddur*, p. 121), this is not meant literally. He also said that
the heading *l^{e}-ʾAsaf* (50; 73—83) does not refer to Asaph the singer who lived in the
time of David; similarly the Koraḥides (42; 44—49; 84—85; 87—88) are not the
[56] sons of Heman but their later descendants; "A Prayer of Moses the man of God"
(90) is his [Moses']; the psalm "Of Solomon. O God, endow the king with your
judgments" (72) was said by some poet about King Solomon; the attributions to
Ethan and Heman are to be taken literally, though he had doubts about the psalm "I
[59] will sing of the Lord's steadfast love forever" (89). But *li-Y^{e}dutun* (39) means [for

והנה יש לחקור ארבעה מחקרים. המחקר האחד: אם הספר כלו הוא של דוד? [יש אומרים כי כל הספר לדוד,] ויפרשו "מזמור לאסף" (נ'; ע"ג–פ"ג) שהמזמור לדוד, ונתנו ביד אסף לנגן; וכן "לבני קרח" (מ"ב; מ"ד–מ"ט; פ"ד–פ"ה; פ"ז–פ"ח) וראייתם: "למנצח לידותון מזמור לדוד" (ל"ט), "למנצח על ידותון מזמור לדוד" (ס"ב). ויפרשו "תפלה למשה איש האלהים" (צ') שהוא לדוד ונתנה לבני משה. ויפרשו כי "לשלמה אלהים משפטיך למלך תן" (ע"ב), כי התנבא על שלמה או על המשיח שהוא בן בנו. ויפרשו "למנצח מזמור לדוד יענך יי ביום צרה" (כ'), שהוא כנגד בנו או המשיח. וכן יאמרו על "מזמור לדוד נאם יי לאדני" (ק"י) שהוא כנגד המשיח, ויש אומרי' על אברהם אבינו. וכל המזמורות שאין עליהם כתו' מי חברם — כשנים הראשונים — הכל לדוד. ויש מהקדמונים שאמרו כי "תפלה למשה איש האלהים" (צ') היא למשה, כאשר הקים המשכן, וכל המזמורות שהם אחרי התפלה הנזכרת, שאין עליהם כתו' שם, הן לשבעים סנהדרין.

ויאמר ר' משה הכהן נ"ע, כי המזמורות שעליהם כתוב "לדוד" רובם לדוד ולא כלם, כמו: "יענך יי ביום צרה" (כ') אמר כי חבר זה המזמור אחד מה[מ]שוררים על דוד, וכן "נאם יי לאדני" (ק"י). ואמ' כי כן "מזמור שיר ליום השבת" (צ"ב), כי יום השבת לא חברו! ואם נמצא בדרש ('מדרש תהילים', צ"ב, ג'; רס"ג, 'סידור', עמ' קכ"א), יש לו סוד. ואמר כי הכת' "לאסף" (נ'; ע"ג–פ"ג) [איננו] אסף המשורר שהיה בימי דוד; וכן "לבני קרח" (מ"ב; מ"ד–מ"ט; פ"ד–פ"ה; פ"ז–פ"ח) אינם בני הימן רק בני בניהם; "ותפלה למשה איש האלהים" (צ') היא שלו; ומזמור "לשלמה אלהים משפטיך למלך תן" (ע"ב) — דברי אחד מהמשוררי' על שלמה המלך; ודברי איתן והימן — כמשמעם, רק הסתפק לו במזמור "חסדי יי עולם אשירה" (פ"ט). וכאשר אמר "לידותון" (ל"ט) — לנגן. והמזמורות,

35 **[יש אומרים כי כל הספר לדוד]** — מחמת דמיון הסופות ("לדוד... של דוד") נשמטה, ככל הנראה, ההגדרה של העמדה הראשונה, והשלמתיה על פי ניסוחה בפתח ההקדמה השניה (שורות 10–11).

42 **מזמור לדוד** — הציטוט אינו מדויק, וצריך להיות "לדוד מזמור" (וראה דבריו לגבי ההיפוך הזה לקמן שורות 122–123).

51 **מה[מ]שוררים** — לפי שהשם 'שורר' אינו מצוי במקרא, תיקנתי כאן (וכן לקמן בפירוש ל־ב', 1, שורה 33) בהתאם ללשון "אחד מהמשוררים" הבאה לקמן בשורה 57, וכן בפירושו הנדפס לתה', ב', 1; כ', 1 המתייחסים לאותו הענין.

54 **[איננו]** — מילת השלילה הושלמה בהתאם להמשך המשפט שבו נאמר "וכן 'לבני קרח' אינם בני הימן רק בני בניהם" (שורות 54–56). ראיה נוספת משמש הניסוח של עמדתו שלו, החלוקה על זו של אבן ג'קטילה: "וכל 'מזמור לאסף' הוא לאסף המשורר שהיה בימי דוד, וכל 'לבני קרח' הם בני הימן המשורר..." (שורות 72–73).

Jeduthun] to perform. As for the psalms without a name [in the heading], we do not know who wrote them. He also said that *liḇnei Ḳoraḥ* refers to one of the sons of Koraḥ who are the descendants of Heman the singer, but we do not know which of them wrote these psalms. He also said that "*a maśkil.* A love song" (45) is to be
[62] taken literally as said about David, as are "Daughter of Tyre" (ibid., 13 [AV 12]) and "take heed, lass, and note" (ibid., 11[10]).

[64] Many arguments can be made against him: For example, we know that "Praise the Lord; call on His name" (105) is by David, because we find this written explicitly in the Book of Chronicles (1 Chron. 16:7), while in the Book of Psalms there is no
[67] inscription *l*^{e}*-Dawid*; though he can rebut this argument weakly, claiming that only what is ascribed to David in Chronicles is by him. In my opinion, while we do not know who wrote a psalm that lacks a name, it is possible that it is attached to the one that comes before, like "Bless the Lord, O my soul" (104) to the other psalm
[69] [with the same heading] (103) and also to the one after it, "Praise the Lord; call on His name" (105). The same is true for "a prayer of Moses" (90), which is by him, and [is followed by] "O you who dwell in the shelter of the Most High" (91),
[72] which may also be by Moses—as the Sages said. Every *mizmor l*^{e}*-ʾAsaf* (50; 73—83) is by Asaph the singer who lived in the time of David. Every *liḇnei Ḳoraḥ* (42; 44—49; 84—85; 87—88) [means] the sons of Heman the singer, the grandson of the prophet Samuel, namely Heman the Ezraḥite (88) who lived in the time of
[75] David. Only Rabbi Moses ha-Kohen's claim that *li-š*^{e}*lomoh* (72) was written by one of the singers about Solomon is not farfetched—though it may be by David, because of the conclusion: "End of the prayers of David son of Jesse" (72:20). Similarly, some of the psalms ascribed to David—despite the words *mizmor l*^{e}*-Dawid*—are
[78] about David. But "la -m^{e}naṣṣeaḥ li-Y^{e}duṯun" (39) and "ʿal Y^{e}duṯun" (62) are by David.

[80] *The second inquiry*: Who edited this book? There is no need to answer this, since the Sages, their memory for a blessing, handed down to us that the men of the Great Assembly edited it, and this satisfies us.

[82] *The third inquiry*: Are these words of David and the other poets veritable songs, psalms, and prayers, or were they said through the Holy Spirit? Do some refer to incidents that have already occurred and some to those that will yet come to pass?
[84] The correct answer, given by the Sages, is that the Book of Psalms was said through the Holy Spirit. For we find written: "by the ordinance of David the man of God" (Neh. 12:24); and of the poems we read: "All these David and Samuel the Seer ordained by their faith" (1 Chron. 9:22), where "by their faith" means by the faith

שאין עליהם שם, לא ידענו למי הם. ג״כ אמר כי ״לבני קרח״ — לאחד מבני קרח שהם מזרע הימן המשורר, ולא נודע מי חברו מהם. ויאמר כי (ה)״משכיל שיר ידידות״ (מ״ה) — כמשמעו על דוד, וכן ״ובת צור״ (שם, 13), ״שמעי בת וראי״ (שם, 11).

והנה יש לטעון עליו בתשובות רבות, מהם שמצאנו ״הודו ליי קראו בשמו״ (ק״ה) שהוא לדוד, כי כן כתו׳ בספר דברי הימים (דה״א, ט״ז, 7), ואין בספר תהלות כת׳ ׳לדוד׳; אעפ״י שיוכל לדחות בקנה רצוץ, כי הכתו׳ בדברי הימים הוא לדוד. ולפי דעתי שכל מזמור שאין עליו שם, לא ידענו מי חברו; ויתכן היות סמוך עם אשר לפניו, כמו ״ברכי נפשי את יי״ (ק״ד) עם המזמור השני (ק״ג), גם אחריו — ״הודו ליי קראו בשמו״ (ק״ה). ג״כ ״תפלה למשה״ (צ׳) שהיא שלו, ויתכן היות גם ״יושב בסתר עליון״ (צ״א) דברי משה, וכן אמרו קדמוננו. וכל ״מזמור לאסף״ (נ׳; ע״ג–פ״ג) הוא לאסף המשורר, שהיה בימי דוד. וכל ״לבני קרח״ (מ״ב; מ״ד–מ״ט; פ״ד–פ״ה; פ״ז–פ״ח) הם בני הימן המשורר נכד שמואל הנביא, והוא ״הימן האזרחי״ (פ״ח) הוא (ישיהו) שהיה בימי דוד. רק מה שאמר ר׳ משה הכהן כי ״לשלמה״ (ע״ב) הוא לאחד המשוררים על שלמה איננו רחוק. ויתכן היותו לדוד, כי באחרונה — ״כלו תפלות דוד בן ישי״ (ע״ב, 20). ג״כ שלמה <צ״ל: שכמה> מזמורות על דוד — אעפ״י שהוא כתו׳ ״מזמור לדוד״ הוא על דוד. רק ״למנצח לידותון״ (ל״ט), גם ״על ידותון״ (ס״ב) הוא לדוד.

והמחקר השני: מי חבר זה הספר? — אין צורך להשיב; אחר שהחכמים ז״ל העתיקו, כי אנשי כנסת הגדולה חברוהו, די לנו.

והמחקר השלישי: אלה דברי דוד ודברי המשוררים אם הם שירות ומזמורות ותפלות ממש, אם נאמרו ברוח הקדש, ויש מהם דברים שעברו, ו[מ]הם עתידים להיות? הנכון מה שאמרו קדמוננו, כי ברוח הקדש נאמ׳ ספר תהלות. והנה מצאנו כתו׳: ״במצות [דוד] איש האלהים״ (נחמ׳, י״ב, 24), ואמ׳ על השירים: ״המה יסד דוד ושמואל הרואה באמונתם״ (דה״א, ט׳, 22), וטעם ״באמונתם״ — באמונת (ה)רוח הקדש. וכת׳ על דוד:

74 **(ישיהו)** — בכתב היד כתוב: ״יושיהו״, אך האות ו׳ מסומנת למחיקה. אין זאת כי המעתיק, או מתקנהו, הניח שהכוונה ל־יִשִּׁיָּהוּ, הנזכר בדה״א, י״ב, 6 כאחד מבני קורח שבאו אל דויד לצקלג. ברם, לא מחוור כלל מדוע זה יזוהה הימן דוקא עם איש זה; ואמנם הן בהמשך (שורות 74–75) והן בפירוש הנדפס לתה׳, פ״ח, 1 אין שום התיחסות לזיהוי מעין זה. לפיכך מוטב, אולי, להניח שתיבה זו אינה אלא פרי הכפלה דיטוגרפית של התיבה ״שהיה״ הבאה לאחריה.

77 **<צ״ל: שכמה>** — בהשפעת השם ״שלמה״, הנזכר שתי פעמים במשפט הקודם (שורה 75), חזר המעתיק וכתב כאן בטעות ״שלמה״ במקום ״שכמה״.

85 **[דוד]** — המילה הושלמה על פי לשון הכתוב, ובאשר היא חיונית לטיעון.

[88] of the Holy Spirit. Scripture says of David: "the plan of all that he had by the Holy
Spirit" (1 Chron. 28:12), and he himself said, in his last words: "The spirit of the
Lord has spoken through me" (2 Samuel 23:2). About Heman the Ezraḥite it is
written: "Heman, the seer of the king, [who uttered] prophecies of God" (1 Chron.
[91] 25:5); and about Asaph: "by Asaph who prophesied by order of the king" (1 Chron.
25:2); also: "Heman, and Jeduthun who prophesied" (1 Chron. 25:1). It was because of the holiness of these songs and psalms that in Solomon's time the Temple
[93] was filled with the glory of God, as it is written: "as the sound of the trumpets,
cymbals, and other musical instruments, and the praise of the Lord . . . grew
louder, the House was filled with a cloud" (2 Chron. 5:13). Should someone object—what is the meaning of prayer uttered under divine inspiration—we can show
[96] him: "A prayer of the Prophet Habakkuk" (Hab. 3); "O Lord, be gracious to us! It
is to You we have looked" (Isa. 33:2); "Heal me, O Lord, and let me be healed"
(Jer. 17:14).

[98] *The fourth inquiry*: what are the meanings of certain words found in the headings of
some psalms, such as *la-m^{e}naṣṣeaḥ*, *miḵtam*, *maśkil*, *ʾayyeleṯ ha-šaḥar*—and are the
psalms linked one to another? The Gaon [i.e., Saadiah], his memory for a blessing,
[101] said that they are linked one to another, and that "when he fled from his son Absalom" (3) is linked to "why do nations assemble" (2), and the meaning is that
those who plot against the Messiah should meet the same fate as did Absalom. But
this is a homiletical explanation. For this book is divided into five parts, like the
[104] Pentateuch, and "when he fled from his son Absalom" (3), which happened late in
David's life, is in the first part, whereas "while he was in the cave" (142) is in the
fifth part! Similarly, in the Torah we find "On the first day of the second month in
the second year" (Num. 1:1), and only after that "on the first new moon of the

"תבנית כי כאשר <צ"ל: כל אשר> היה ברוח הקדש עמו" (דה"א, כ"ח, 12), ובדבריו האחרונים: "רוח יי דבר בי" (שמ"ב, כ"ג, 2). וכתב על הימן האזרחי: "להימן חוזה המלך בדבר האלהים" (דה"א, כ"ה, 5), וכתב על אסף: "על יד אסף הנביא <צ"ל: הַנִּבָּא> על ידי המלך" (דה"א, כ"ה, 2), וכתב: "הימן וידותון הנביאים <קרי: הַנִּבְּאִים>" (דה"א, כ"ה, 1). ובעבור קדושת אלה השירים והמזמורות מלא הבית בימי שלמה כבוד השם כי כן כת': "וכהרים קול בחצוצרות ובמצלתים ובכלי השיר ובהלל ליי... והבית מלא עשן" (דה"ב, ה', 13). ואם טען טוען: מה טעם תפלה ברוח הקדש? הראינו לו: "תפלה לחבקוק הנביא" (פרק ג'), ובישעיה: "יי חננו לך קוינו" (ל"ג, 2), ובירמיה: "רפאני יי וארפא" (י"ז, 14).

והמחקר הרביעי: מה טעם אלה השמות הכתובים על קצות המזמורות — כמו: 'למנצח', 'מכתם', ו'משכיל', [ו]'על אילת השחר' — והם ה' מזמורים <צ"ל: ואם המזמורים> דבקים זה עם זה? והנה הגאון ז"ל אמ' כי הם דבקים, ואמ' כי טעם "בברחו מפני אבשלום בנו" (תה', ג'), דבק עם "למה רגשו גוים" (תה', ב'), והטעם: שיקרה לקושרים על המשיח כמו לאבשלום. וזה דרך דרש. כי הנה זה הספר נחלק על חמשה חלקים כחלקי התורה, והנה בחלק הראשון כתב "בברחו מפני אבשלום בנו" (תה', ג'), שהיה קרוב מאחרית ימי דוד, ובחלק החמישי כתו' "בהיותו במערה תפלה" (תה', קמ"ב)! והנה בתורה כתו' "באחד לחדש השני בשנה השנית" (במ', א', 1), [ואחר כן: בחדש הראשון בשנה השנית (ע"פ במ',

88 <**צ"ל: כל אשר**> — תוקן על פי לשון הכתוב, מפני שגירסת "כי כאשר" משובשת בעליל. לעומת זאת לא הושמטה בסיפא מילת "הקדש", אף־על־פי שהיא חסרה בכתוב, מכיון שיתכן מאד שהיא נוספה בידי הראב"ע עצמו על דרך הפראפראזה המבהירה או מכוח טעות בציטוט.

91 <**צ"ל: הַנִּבָּא**> — תוקן על־פי לשון הכתוב, שכן קשה ליחס לראב"ע החלפה כזאת של צורה נדירה בשכיחה. המעתיק חזר וטעה בזאת בפירוש ל־ב', 1, שורה 33.

100 <**צ"ל: ואם המזמורים**> — צריך לתקן את "והם" ל'ואם' משום שבהמשך אין שום זיקה בין בירור פשרו של המינוח שבכותרות לבין בירור שאלת הזיקה הענינית שבין מזמורים סמוכים, ולפיכך מסתבר שכאן תוצגנה שתי שאלות נפרדות. גם ההנחה שהשאלה השניה תוסב על חמישה מזמורים סמוכים מסוימים, אשר מונח זהה בא בכותרתם, אינה סבירה משום שהתופעה אינה נידונה כלל בהמשך. ואף טיבה של התופעה אינו מחוור, שכן 'למנצח' בא אמנם בחמשת המזמורים הסמוכים י"ח–כ"ב, אך בנוסף לכך גם בשנים עשר המזמורים נ"א–ס"ב, ובשבעת המזמורים ס"ד–ע'. ואילו המונחים 'מכתם', 'משכיל' ו'אילת השחר' אינם באים כלל ברצף של חמישה מזמורים.

107 [**ואחר כן... השנית**] — הראב"ע מסתמך על העובדה ששני הכתובים במ', א', 1 ו־ט', 1 באים בסדר כרונולוגי הפוך, גם בפתיחה לפירושו הקצר לדניאל (מהד' מאתיוס, עמ' 2; מהד' מונדשיין, עמ' 7), בפירושו לבר', י"א, 29 ובשיטה האחרת לבר', ה', 32 (מהד' וייזר, א', עמ' קע"ד). בשלושת המקומות הללו הוא מביא את שני הכתובים, ואינו סומך על הקורא שיצרף מכוח בקיאותו את הפסוק השני (ט', 1). לכן השלמתיו כאן, על סמך ההנחה שהוא נשמט מחמת שוויון הסופות ("השנית... השנית"). את המילים המוספות לקחתי כלשונן מפירושו לבר', י"א, 29.

[108] second year'' (Num. 9:1), which is why the Sages said: ''There is no chronological
order in the Torah'' (*Sifre, Bᵉ-haʿaloṯᵉḵa*, 64). The truth, thus, is that every psalm
stands by itself.

[111] The word *mizmor*, in the opinion of Rabbi Moses ha-Kohen, is related to ''you shall
not . . . prune [*tizmor*] your vineyard'' (Lev. 25:4), i.e., something that is severed
and stands by itself, as with the word for poem in Arabic. But in my opinion the
[113] correct answer is that *mizmor* means a poem [performed] in accordance with the
musical art, and adapted fully to its purpose and time, be it for joy or sadness. We
have thus: ''[*mizmor lᵉ-Dawid*] when he fled from his son Absalom'' (3), [on the
one hand, and] ''*Mizmor lᵉ-ʾAsaf*. O God, heathens have entered Your domain''
[117] (79), [on the other]. Some say that *mizmor* [*lᵉ-Dawid*] means that he saw by the
Holy Spirit that he would escape, and thus ''He answered me from His holy mountain'' (3:5)—the verb is in the past tense, as I have explained, because with any
[divine] decree—even if it applies to the future—prophets are free to speak as they
[119] wish, for example: ''heathens have entered'' (79). Or in Moses' words, ''Jᵉšurun
grew fat and kicked'' (Deut. 32:15), and in *mizmor lᵉ-ʾAsaf*: ''Pay back our neigh-
bors . . . we are Your people, the flock You shepherd'' (79:12–13). In my opinion
[122] there is no difference between *mizmor lᵉ-Dawid* and *lᵉ-Dawid mizmor*, since
''ḥayyim tifśum'' and ''tifśum ḥayyim'' (1 Kings 20:18) both mean ''take them
alive.''

[124] The word *la-mᵉnaṣṣeaḥ*—we find this word only in the writings of David, and in
[other] psalms and in the prayer of Habakkuk, which is similar to the Book of
Psalms, for ''ʿal šigyonoṯ'' (Hab. 3:1) is like ''šiggayon lᵉ-Dawid'' (Ps. 7:1); at the
[127] end [of Habakkuk's prayer] ''bi-nᵉginoṯai'' (Hab. 3:19) is like ''ʿal nᵉginaṯ lᵉ-
Dawid'' (Ps. 61:1); and the word *selah* [appears] in three places in Habakkuk (3:3,
9, 13). But the commentators disagree about the word *la-mᵉnaṣṣeaḥ*. Some say that
mᵉnaṣṣᵉḥim refers to the officers in charge of the singers, like Heman, Asaph, and
[131] Ethan. Their proof is ''three thousand and six hundred'' supervisors [*mᵉnaṣṣᵉḥim*] to
see that the people worked'' (2 Chron. 2:17), who were the officers over ''one
hundred fifty thousand'' (ibid., 16). Thus the meaning of *la-mᵉnaṣṣeaḥ* [would be]
that he gave this song to the supervisors. Some say —and I think they are correct—

ט׳, 1),] על כן אמרו המעתיקים ז״ל: ״אין מוקדם ומואחר <צ״ל: ומאוחר> בתורה״ (ספרי, ׳בהעלותך׳, ס״ד). הנה האמת שכל מזמור ומזמור עומד בפני עצמו.

מלת ׳מזמור׳, לדעת ר׳ משה הכהן, מגזרת ״לא תזמור״ (ויק׳, כ״ה, 4), כאלו הוא דבר נכרת, עומד בפני עצמו, וכן בשירי קדר כפי לשונם. והנכון בעיני שמלת ׳מזמור׳ — שיר שהוא על דרך מערכת חכמת הנגינות והוא על מתכונת שלמה, אמור כל דבר בעתו, בין שיהיה לשמחה או לאנחה, על כן: ״[מזמור לדוד] בברחו מפני אבשלום בנו״ (תה׳, ג׳), ״מזמור לאסף אלהים באו גוים בנחלתך״ (תה׳, ע״ט). ויש אומרים כי טעם ״מזמור [לדוד]״ שראה ברוח הקדש שימלט על כן כתו׳: ״ויענני מהר קדשו סלה״ (תה׳, ג׳, 5) — פעל עבר, כאשר פירשתי, כי כל גזרה שנגזרה — ואם היא לעתיד! — דרך הנביאים לדבר כרצונם, וכמהו: ״באו גוים״ (תה׳, ע״ט). ובדברי משה: ״וישמן ישורון ויבעט״ (דב׳, ל״ב, 15), וב״מזמור לאסף״: ״והשב לשכנינו... ואנחנו עמך וצאן מרעיתך״ (ע״ט, 12–13). ולפי דעתי שאין הפרש בין ״מזמור לדוד״ ובין ״לדוד מזמור״, כי ״חיים תפשום... תפשום חיים״ (מל״א, כ׳, 18) שוים הם.

מלת ׳למנצח׳ — זאת המלה לא מצאנוה כי אם בדברי דוד, ובדברי השירות ובתפלת חבקוק שהוא על דרך ספר תהלות, כי שם כתו׳ ״על שגיונות״ (חב׳, ג׳, 1) — כמו ״שגיון לדוד״ (תה׳, ז׳, 1), ובסוף ״בנגינותי״ (חב׳, ג׳, 19) — כמו ״על נגינ(ו)ת לדוד״ (תה׳, ס״א, 1), ומלת ׳סלה׳ — בשלשה מקומות (חב׳, ג׳, 3, 9, 13). והנה נחלקו המפרשים במלת ׳למנצח׳, כי יש אומרים שמלת ׳מנצחים׳ — השרים הפקודים על המשוררים, כמו הימן, ואסף ואיתן. וראייתם שאמר ״ושלשת אלפים ושש מאות מנצחים להעביד את העם״ (דה״ב, ב׳, 17), והנה שרים על ״מאה וחמשים אלף״ (שם, 16). והנה טעם ׳למנצח׳ — שנתן זה השיר המנצחים <צ״ל: למנצחים>. ויש אומ׳ — והוא הנכון בעיני — שהמלה מגזרת נצח,

115 **[מזמור לדוד]** — לנוכח הנוהג הרווח אצל המעתיקים לקצר במובאות ובדבור המתחיל השלמתי את המובאה, שכן הדיון נסב על מילת ׳מזמור׳ (ואמנם במובאה השניה היא כלולה).

117 **[לדוד]** — יש צורך בהשלמת המובאה משום שקיצורה מטשטש את העובדה שמדובר כאן באורח ספציפי על מזמור ג׳, כפי שבהמשך מאוזכר מזמור ע״ט (שורות 120–121).

124 **המלה לא** — אחרי תיבות אלה באה בכה״י הדיטוגרפיה ״המלה ל״, מסומנת למחיקה.

127 **נגינ(ו)ת** — מילת ״נגינות״ באה בלשון רבים בפסוקים רבים, ואילו הצירוף ״על נגינת לדוד״ בא רק בלשון יחיד. לכן צריך לתקן הן כאן והן בציטוט החוזר של פסוק זה (לקמן שורה 140), מקום שם אומר הראב״ע במפורש שהמילה מנוקדת בפתח.

133 **<צ״ל: למנצחים>** — בכה״י כתוב: ״למלת המנצחים״, והתיבה הראשונה מסומנת למחיקה. התוכן מחייב לגרוס ׳למנצחים׳, ושמא מעידה המילה המחוקה שהסופר אכן ראה לפניו את האותיות ״למ...״ אך נשתבש, ומשחש בטעותו לא תיקן אותה כראוי.

[134] that the word is derived from *neṣaḥ* [forever], and that *la-m^{e}naṣṣeaḥ* means "to a
musician who always plays." We read about the singers: "they were on duty day
and night" (1 Chron. 9:33). Thus the meaning of *la-m^{e}naṣṣeaḥ* is that David gave
[136] this song to a *m^{e}naṣṣeaḥ*—one who always plays. This is attested to by "to perpet-
uate [*l^{e}-naṣṣeaḥ*] the service in the House of the Lord twenty-four thousand and six
[138] thousand officers and magistrates" (1 Chron. 23:4). *La-m^{e}naṣṣeaḥ bi-n^{e}ginot̲* (Ps.
4:1 et passim)—in my opinion, the Israelites performed many melodies before the
time of David. Here he indicates the melody by quoting the first word of the song,
which is "bi-n^{e}ginot̲," and similarly: "ʿal n^{e}ginat̲ l^{e}-Dawid" (61:1); the proof being
[140] that [the word *n^{e}ginat̲*] is in the construct case and the *taw* is [preceded] by a *pataḥ*.
The same is true for "ʿal maḥalat̲ l^{e}-ʿannot̲" (Ps. 88:1)—[*maḥalat̲*] is a construct
derived from "any disease [*maḥalah*]" (1 Kings 8:37) as I will explain, although
[143] many have explained that it is derived from *maḥol* [= dance]. Similar are the cases
of "ʾel ha-n^{e}ḥilot̲" (Ps. 5:1) and "ʿal ha-š^{e}minit̲" (Ps. 6:1; 12:1), though some say
this is an instrument with eight strings, [like]: "b^{e}-nevel ʿaśor" ([= ten-stringed
lyre] Ps. 33:2; 144:9). Also similar is "ʿal ha-gittit̲" (Ps. 8:1; 81:1, 84:1), though
[146] some say this is related to *gat̲* [= winepress], as in "like one who treads a press"
(Isa. 63:2); but the Gaon said that this song was given to the Gittite family, namely
"Obed-Edom the Gittite" (2 Sam. 6:10–11; 1 Chron. 13:13). Also "ʿal ʾayyelet̲
[149] ha-šaḥar" (Ps. 22:1)—meaning a particular melody; but many say it is about the
congregation of Israel, and *ʾayyelet̲* means that they yearn through the night like a
hind [*ʾayyelet̲*], longing for daybreak, which is a symbol of redemption. Rabbi
Moses said that *ʾayyelet̲* is related to "like a man with no strength" [*ʾeyal*] (Ps.
[151] 88:5); but the correct interpretation is what I said above. Again, "l^{e}-hazkir" (Ps.
38:1; 70:1), and also "ʿal Y^{e}dut̲un" (Ps. 62:1; 77:1)—or he may have given this
psalm to Jeduthun. Or again: "ʿal šošannim" (Ps. 45:1 et passim)—[these words
were] the beginning of a certain song. Also "ʿal ʿalamot̲" (46:1); the Gaon, his
[154] memory for a blessing, said that this means a quiet [*neʿelam*] voice, but there is no
need for this. Also: "yonat̲ ʾelem r^{e}ḥoḳim" (56:1), although most commentators
[say] that this refers to the congregation of Israel, and Rabbi Moses said that he
likened himself to a dove [*yonah*] that lives inside a distant sheaf [*ʾalummah*
[157] *r^{e}ḥokah*]. Similarly: "ʾal tašḥet̲" (Ps. 57:1 et passim)—to the melody of *ʾal
tašḥet̲*—[these words were] the beginning of a song. Also "šušan ʿedut̲" (60:1), as
well as "šir la-maʿalot̲" (121:1) or "ha-maʿalot̲" (120:1 et passim). The Gaon said

והנה ׳למנצח׳ — למנגן נצח. וכת׳ על המשוררים: ״כי יומם ולילה עליהם במלאכה״ (דה״א, ט׳, 33), והנה (ה)טעם ׳למנצח׳ — שנתן דוד זה השיר אל מנצ׳ — למנגן נצח. והעד כי הוא כן: ״לנצח על מלאכת בית יי ארבעה ועשרים אלף, ושוטרים ושופטים ששת אלפים״ (דה״א, כ״ג, 4). ״למנצח בנגינות״ (תה׳, ד׳, 1; ועוד) — לפי דעתי, שהיו לישראל נגינות רבות על נעימות קודם דוד. והנה הזכיר הנועם, ואמר תחלת השיר והוא ״בנגינות״, וכן: ״על נגינ(ו)ת לדוד״ (תה׳, ס״א, 1), והעד שהוא סמוך ופתוח התי״ו. וכן: ״על מחלת לענות״ (תה׳, פ״ח, 1) — סמוך מגזרת ״כל המחלה״ (מל״א, ח׳, 37) כאשר אפרש, כי רבים פירשוהו מגזרת ׳מחול׳. וכן: ״אל הנחילות״ (תה׳, ה׳, 1) וכן: ״על השמינית״ (תה׳, ו׳, 1; י״ב, 1), ויש אומרי׳: כלי שיש לו שמנה יתרים, [כמו]: ״בנבל עשור״ (תה׳, ל״ג, 2; קמ״ד, 9). וכן: ״על הגתית״ (תה׳, ח׳, 1; פ״א, 1; פ״ד, 1), ויש אומרי׳ מגזרת ׳גת׳, כטעם ״כדורך בגת״ (יש׳, ס״ג, 2), והגאון אמר כי זה השיר נתנו למשפחה הגתית והם ״בית עובד אדום הגתי״ (שמ״ב, ו׳, 10–11; דה״א, י״ג, 13). וכן: ״על אילת השחר״ (תה׳, כ״ב, 1) — נועם כך וכך, ורבים אמרו: על כנסת ישראל, וטעם ״אילת״ שהיא עורגת בלילה כאילת, עד עלות השחר הדומה לישועה. ור׳ משה אמ׳ כי ״אילת״ מגזרת ״כגבר אין איל״ (תה׳, פ״ח, 5), והנכון — מה שהזכרתי. וכן: ״להזכיר״ (ל״ח, 1; ע׳, 1), ג״כ: ״על ידותון״ (תה׳, ס״ב, 1; ע״ז, 1), או — נתן המזמור לידותון. וכן: ״על שושנים״ (תה׳, מ״ה, 1; ועוד) תחלת השירה היתה. וכן: ״על עלמות״ (תה׳, מ״ו, 1), והגאון ז״ל אמר שהיא קול נעלם, ואין צרך. וכן: ״יונת אלם רחוקים״ (תה׳, נ״ו, 1), ורובי המפרשים [אמרו] שהיא כנסת ישראל, ור׳ משה אמר שדמה עצמו ליונה שתדור בין אלומה רחוקה. וכן: ״אל תשחת״ (תה׳, נ״ז, 1; ועוד) — על נועם ״אל תשחת״ — תח[ל]ת שיר. וכן: ״שושן עדות״ (תה׳, ס׳, 1), וכן: ״שיר למעלות״ (תה׳, קכ״א, 1), או ״המעלות״ (תה׳, ק״כ, 1; ועוד). והגאון אמר שהוא הפך ״על

135 **(ה)טעם** — האות ה׳ הושמטה למען נהירות המשפט, ומן הסתם מקורה בדיטוגרפיה.

140 **נגינ(ו)ת** — ראה ההערה לשורה 127 לעיל.

144 **[כמו]** — השלמתי למען הנהירות, אם כי הראב״ע מוותר לעתים על מילת קישור זו. **בנבל** — בכה״י המילה אינה ברורה, וביחוד קשה לפענח את האות ב׳ השניה. ואכן בשוליים חזר וכתב הסופר את האות ב׳, ככל הנראה כדי להבהיר זאת.

149 **ורבים אמרו** — בכה״י כתוב: ״אמרו ורבים״, אך המילים מסומנות להיפוך.

155 **[אמרו]** — השלמתי למען הנהירות.

158 **תח[ל]ת** — בקושי ניתן לקיים גם את גירסת כה״י ״תחת״, אך לשון ״תחלת״ נהירה יותר, והיא המשמשת תדיר בפי הראב״ע.

[160] that it is the opposite of "ʿal ʿalamot̲" (46:1), because this [psalm] is to be sung in
a loud and high voice, which is why these psalms are short. But our Sages, their
memory for a blessing, said that there were fifteen steps in the Temple, to which
these songs correspond (Mishnah Sukkah 5,4).

[Commentary on Psalm 1]

1. *ʾAšrei*. The word *ʾašrei*, though neither noun nor verb, is related to "women will
deem me *fortunate*" (Gen. 30:13), and never appears without the *yod*—the sign of
[3] the plural—to avoid confusion with the word *ʾašer*. The wicked [*r*^{e}*šaʿim*] are worse
than sinners [*ḥaṭṭaʾim*]; thus the sense is that he did not follow their counsel, nor
stand in the way where sinners stand, nor even [sit] in the company of the insolent
[*leṣim*], i.e., those who scoff, like "at *scoffers* He scoffs" (Prov. 3:34). But the
[6] Sages said that if he walked he would eventually stand, and if he stood he would
eventually sit (BT Avodah Zarah 18b), and this is also correct. The import of this
verse resembles what Moses said about the Torah, and the first fundamental of the
[8] Torah is the declaration of the unity of God "when you sit in your house and walk
on the road and lie down and rise up" (Deut. 6:7). Following the counsel of the
wicked means doing deeds like theirs; and "did not stand in the way of the sinners"—like a man who is considering what path to take; and "did not sit"—to
listen to scoffing talk.

[10] 2. *ki*. He has no interest in mundane affairs, but only in "God's Law" and in doing
whatever is written there, for this is his pleasure. "He *studies* His Law": this word
[13] [*yehgeh*] can refer both to the tongue and to the heart, as in "they can make no
sound [*lo yehgu*] in their throat" (Ps. 115:7), and "the prayer [*higgayon*] of my
heart" (Ps. 19:15), which explains the word "night".

[14] 3. *w*^{e}*-hayah*. "*Streams* of water"—related to rivulets, similar to "a river whose
streams [*p*^{e}*lagaw*]" (Ps. 46:5). He said "streams of water" because there are many
[16] of them. The meaning of "its fruit" is that he opens his heart to understand words
of truth and the secret of his soul, which is the fruit. "Whose leaves never
wither"—his name will not be blotted out. But some say that God will give him
progeny at the proper time, while "whose leaves never wither" alludes to his
wealth. "Whatever he does prospers" refers back to "happy is the man" (verse 1),
[19] and is like: "Blessed is the Lord, who did not let us be ripped apart by their teeth"
(124:6). But Rabbi Moses interpreted "whatever he does prospers" [as referring to
the tree]—any branch that may be taken from it [will flourish].

[20] 4. *lo*: Here he [the psalmist] explained that "happy is the man" means that "the
wicked," even if they flourish like grass, when disaster strikes they will perish
suddenly; and if they survive, their children, who are considered to be equivalent to
[23] them, will not. While the soul of one who cleaves to God is sated like a tree planted
by water, while the soul that is far from Him is always hungry in this world, and all
the more so in the world to come. "That wind blows away" and it no longer exists,

עלמות״ (תה׳, מ״ו, 1), כי זה ינגנוהו בקול בעלה <צ״ל: נעלה> וגבוה, על כן שירי המעלות קטנים. וחכמינו ז״ל אמרו כי חמש עשרה מעלות היו במקדש וכנגדם עשה שירים (סוכה, פרק ה׳, משנה ד׳).

[פירוש מזמור א׳]

1. אשרי. מלת אשרי אעפ״י שאיננה שם ולא פועל היא מגזרת ״אשרוני בנות״ (בר׳, ל׳, 13), ולא תמצא בלא יו״ד — סימן לשון רבים — שלא תתערב עם מלת ׳אשר׳. ורשעים פחותים מחטאים והנה הטעם שלא הלך בעצתם, ואפי׳ בדרך שיעמדו החטאים לא עמד, ואפי׳ במושב ליצים, הם הלעגנים, כמו ״אם ללצים הוא יליץ״ (משלי, ג׳, 34). וחכמים אמרו, כי אם הלך סופו לעמוד, ואם עמד סופו לשבת (עבודה זרה, י״ח, ע״ב), גם הוא נכון. וטעם זה הכתוב כדברי משה על התורה, ותחלת התורה ייחוד השם: ״בשבתך בביתך ובלכתך בדרך ובשכבך ובקומך״ (דב׳, ו׳, 7). והנה טעם הליכה בעצת רשעים — לעשות כמעשיהם, ובדרך חטאים לא עמד — כאדם שחושב אי־זה דרך ילך, ולא ישב — לשמוע דבר לעג. 2. כי. אין לו חפץ אפי׳ בדברי העולם כי אם בתורת השם לעשות ככתו׳ בה כי היא תענוגו. ובתורתו יהגה וזאת המלה תמצא על הלשון ועל הלב, כמו ״לא יהגו בגרונם״ (תה׳, קט״ו, 7), ״והגיון לבי לפניך״ (תה׳, י״ט, 15), על כן מלת לילה. 3. והיה. פלגי מים — מגזרת חלקים שיצאו מהנהר, וכן ״נהר פלגיו״ (תה׳, מ״ו, 5). ואמ׳ פלגי מים כי הם רבים. וטעם אשר פריו — שיפתח לבו להבין דברי אמת וסוד נפשו שהוא הפרי. ועלהו לא יבול — לא ימחה שמו. ויש אומרים כי השם יתן לו זרע בעתו, ועלהו לא יבול — רמז להונו. וכל אשר יעשה יצליח שב אל ״אשרי האיש״ (לעיל, פס׳ 1) וכמוהו: ״ברוך ייי שלא נתננו טרף לשניהם״ (תה׳, קכ״ד, 6). ור׳ משה [אמר] כי כל אשר יעשה — לכל סעיף שילקח ממנו. 4. לא. הנה פירש טעם ״אשרי האיש״ כי הרשעים, ואם פרחו כעשב, בבא עליהם הצרה פתאם יאבדו, ואם עמדו הם, לא יעמדו בניהם, שהם חשובים כמוהם. והנה הדבק בשם, נפשו היא שבעה כעץ השתול על המים, והנפש הרחוקה ממנו — לעולם רעבה בעולם הזה, ואף כי בעולם הבא. אשר תדפנו רוח ואיננו,

160 <צ״ל: נעלה> — גירסת כה״י ״בעלה״ חסרת כל מובן, והחילוף המשוער של האותיות הדומות ב׳–נ׳ משמש כראיה אחרונה לכך שכה״י היחיד שבידנו הגיענו באמצעות סופר אשר עשה את מלאכתו באופן מכאני מבלי לשים לבו לתוכן.

[25] but the wind cannot carry away the planted tree. The meaning [of this metaphor] is that God will rescue the righteous man from his distress.

[26] 5. *ʿal*. "Stand" [*yaḳumu*] is like: "it will be assured to him" [*we-ḳam lo*] (Lev. 27:19), i.e., they will not be able to survive the future Day of Judgment, or they will not be able to stand in the place of judgment, and in that case "nor will sinners in the assembly of the righteous" doubles the meaning as is customary in synonymous parallelism.

[28] 6. *ki yodeaʿ*. All the parts and subparts [of creation] only God who created them knows them, and no creature can truly know them; but the meaning of "For He knows" is that [only] one who knows God will survive, and his knowledge of God
[31] will preserve him forever; or, metaphorically, like a king, for the king favors those whom he recognizes, and recognizes only those who recognize him. Thus the "path of the wicked is doomed" is the opposite of "For the Lord knows."

[Commentary on Psalm 2]

[33] 1. *lamah rag^{e}šu goyim*. These are the words of one of the prophet-poets about David or about the Messiah. The word *rag^{e}šu* means "assembled," like "from a *crowd* of evildoers [*me-rig^{e}šaṯ poʿalei ʾawen*]" (Ps. 64:3). [. . .] said that the
[36] word *rag^{e}šu* is like "a tumult" [*hamon*] and "an uproar" [*ḳol šaʾon*] (Isa. 13:4), and interpreted also *me-rig^{e}šat* and "we walked in God's house *b^{e}-rageš*" (Ps. 55:15) in the same way. And this is also correct, because of "peoples utter vain
[38] things." If this [psalm] is about the Messiah the reference here is to Gog and Magog; if it is about David the reference is to the nations around Jerusalem who fought against him, like the Arameans, Edom, Philistines, and Amalek.

[39] 2. *yiṯyaṣṣ^{e}ḇu*. *Roz^{e}nim* are princes, like "a ruler [*razon*] is ruined" (Prov. 14:28).

והרוח לא תוכל לנדוף העץ השתול. והטעם — כי השם יציל הצדיק מצרותיו. 5. על. יקומו — כמו: "וקם לו" (ויק', כ"ז, 19) — לא יוכלו לעמוד ביום המשפט לעתיד לבא, או לא יעמדו במקום המשפט, ויהיה וחטאים בעדת צדיקים בטעם כפול כמשפט. 6. כי יודע. כל החלקים וחלקי החלקים השם שבראם הוא ידעם לבדו, ואין נברא יוכל לדעתם באמת, רק טעם כי יודע רמז כי היודע השם אז יעמוד, ודעת השם תעמידנו לנצח, או על דרך משל — כדרך מלך, כי המלך יעשה טוב לאשר יכיר, ולא יכיר כי אם מי שיכירנו. והנה ודרך [רשעי]ם תאבד הפך כי יודע השם.

[פירוש מזמור ב']

1. למה רגשו גוים. דברי אחד מה[מ]שוררים הנב(י)אים [[על]] דוד או על המשיח. ומלת רגשו — התחברו, כמו "מרגשת פועלי און" (תה', ס"ד, 3), [[ ]] אמר שמלת רגשו כמו "המון" (יש', י"ג, 4) ו"קול שאון" (שם), וכן פירש "מרגשת" גם "[ב]בית אלהים נהלך ברגש" (תה', נ"ה, 15), גם [[ה]]וא נכון בעבור ולאומים יהגו ריק. אם זה על המשיח, הנה הוא על גוג ומגוג, ואם על דוד [[הוא]] על הגוים שהיו סביבות ירושלם שנלחמו עמו, כמו ארמים ואדום ופלשתים ועמלק. 2. [[י]]תיצבו. ורזנים הם

32 **ודרך** — כאן נקטע כ"י וירונה ומתחיל כ"י לייפציג.

33 **מה[מ]שוררים** — ראה הערתנו לעיל, הקדמת השריד, שורה 51.

הנב(י)אים — מסתבר שהראב"ע כתב הנְבִּאִים (כלשון הקרי בדה"א, כ"ה, 1), ושאחד המעתיקים לא הבין צורה נדירה זו והוסיף יו"ד, וכך הפך את הפועל לשם עצם (הוא טעה כזאת כבר בהקדמת השריד, שורה 92).

35 **[[ ]]** — זוהי המלה היחידה המחוקה בכתב־היד (שאר החסֵרים הם מחמת הדבקה כמוסבר לעיל), ומן הצילום קשה לומר מה גרם לכך. נותר ממנה רק הקצה השמאלי של האות האחרונה, אשר יתכן שאפשר לפענחו כשריד של האות ה', מפני שהוא מחולק לחלק עליון ולחלק תחתון (ראה בתצלום, תחילת השורה השלישית). מבחינה עניינית, ובהתחשב ברוחבו של המקום הפנוי, יש שלוש אפשרויות שחזור: (1) 'והגאון' (השווה "והגאון אמר" בהקדמת השריד, שורה 146), (2) 'ויפת', (3) 'ור' משה' (השווה "ור' משה אמר" בהקדמת השריד, שורה 150). בעד ההצעה השלישית עומד השיקול הגראפי — האפשרות שלפנינו שריד של האות ה', והשיקול הסטאטיסטי — ר' משה הכהן אבן ג'קטילה הוא המפרש המצוטט ביותר בפירושו הנדפס של ראב"ע לתהילים (מאה וחמישים איזכורים לעומת אחד־עשר של רב סעדיה גאון וארבעה של יפת בן עלי). אך מצד שני, אין בידינו שום עדות ישירה או עקיפה לכך שאבן ג'קטילה אכן פירש את "רגשו גוים" בהוראה של המו ורעשו. לעומת זאת ברי לנו שרס"ג ויפת כאחד ביארו כך את שלושת האיזכורים של השורש רג"ש שבספר תהילים (ב', 1; נ"ה, 15; ס"ד, 3). מבחינה ענינית מתאימים, אם כן, רס"ג ויפת למילוי החֶסֶר, ואף על פי כן יתכן מאד שהראב"ע ציטט כאן את אבן ג'קטילה (ושמא אף מישהו אחר).

36 **[ב]בית** — השלמתי על־פי לשון הכתוב מתוך השיקול שסביר יותר להניח שהפלוגראפיה זו היא פרי טעות־העתקה של אחד הסופרים, ולא פרי טעות־זיכרון של הראב"ע.

Nos^e du—they lay a foundation [*y^e sod*] to conspire "against the Lord and against His anointed." Many say that the word is derived from *sod* [= assembly]; but the first interpretation is the correct one, because the [verb] is in the *nif^cal*.

[42] 3. *N^e natt^e ḳah* ["let us break"]. They say this to one another, or think it. "Their cords"—the laws of God and the laws of the kingdom; for the laws are like the ropes that they place around the neck of an ox so it will plow.

[45] 4. *yošeḇ*: "He . . . laughs" [*yiśḥaḳ*] is to be taken metaphorically, and means that he will make them objects of derision and laughter. The reason for [naming God] "He who is enthroned in the heavens" is "kings of the earth" (verse 2), for they are all subject to the will of Heaven.

[47] 5. *ʾaz*. Some say that *ye dabber* means "will destroy" . . .

Notes to Commentary on Psalms 1 and 2

1 He does not discuss this matter in the standard commentary *ad loc.*, but alludes to it in his commentary on 119:5; see also on Eccles. 10:17.

3 Here he is explaining that the verse ranges the nouns in descending order of wickedness, while offering the contrary opinion of the Sages; in the standard commentary, on the other hand, he agrees with the Sages (this was Saadiah's opinion as well: *Psalms*, p. 41) and disagrees with Ibn Giqatilah, whose position is the same as his own here and even phrased similarly. Ibn Ezra had not changed his opinion diametrically, since already here he is willing to acknowledge that the Sages' interpretation is plausible.

7 The comparison with the Shema is also found in the standard commentary as well as in *Y^e sod Moraʾ*, chapter 10.

11 His glosses in the two commentaries are identical: only the prooftexts differ.

14 Whereas here he explains that the tree is planted among many streams, in the standard commentary he prefers to explain the plural noun as meaning one of many, and offers three proofs for this usage.

19 This attempt by Ibn Giqatilah to explain "whatever he does prospers" as the continuation of the metaphor is also cited in the standard commentary, albeit anonymously ("some say").

20 In the psalm the righteous man is compared to a planted tree, and the wicked man to chaff, but the contrast between these two images is not clear. Ibn Ezra proposes various solutions to this problem in his two commentaries. Here he is of the opinion that the contrast between the righteous man and the wicked man is double, and each image is to be complemented by its contrary: the righteous man will endure like a tree with a guaranteed source of water, while the wicked man will wither like grass in a drought (the image of grass is borrowed from Ps. 92:8); the wicked man will be blown away like chaff, while the righteous man stands his ground like a planted tree. In the standard commentary, however, he does not oppose the image of chaff to that of the tree, and by restricting the contrast to verse 4 must also find its opposite there: the wind blows away the wicked man like chaff, while the righteous man "is like grain that stands," i.e., remains on the threshing floor.

26 In both commentaries the word *yaḳumu* is glossed in the sense of "survive." Only here,

השרים, כמו ״מחתת רזון״ (מש׳, י״ד, 28). נוסדו — ישימו יסוד למעשיהם לקשור על השם ועל משיחו. ורבים אמרו שהמלה מגזרת ׳סוד׳, והראשון הוא הנכון כי [[הו]]א מבנין נפעל. 3. ננתקה. והם אומר׳ זה אל זה, או חושבים. מוסרותימו — משפטי [[אלו]]ה ומשפטי המלוכה; והנה המשפטים דומים לעבותות שישימו בצואר השור עד [[שיחר]]וש. 4. יושב. [ישחק] — ד״מ, והטעם — שישימם ללעג ולשחוק. וטעם יושב בשמים בעבור ״מלכי ארץ״ (פס׳ 1), והם כלם ברשות שמים. 5. אז. יש אומר כי ידבר כמו יאבד [...]

43 **משפטי [[אלו]]ה** — בהתאמה לפסוק 2, שבו נאמר שהמרד הוא כפול — נגד ה׳ ונגד משיחו — מסביר כאן הראב״ע שהמלכים והרוזנים פורקים את עול משפטי ה׳ ומשפטי המלך. לכאורה אפשר היה להשלים את החֶסֶר כך — משפטי [[התור]]ה, אך לפי שהמדובר בנוכרים מסתבר שהראב״ע נקט מינוח כללי יותר. ראיה לכך יש בדבריו בפירוש הנדפס לפס׳ 2: ״וטעם על ה׳ — שיצאו מתחת יד שקול הדעת, שנטע השם בלב כל אדם״, רוצה לומר: הם מתמרדים נגד המצוות השכליות, שניתן לדעת אותן ללא התגלות (השווה להגדרתו בראש השער החמישי של ׳יסוד מורא׳: ״המצות שהן עקרים שאינן תלויות במקום או בזמן או בדבר אחר, הן הנטועות בלב — — — ואלה היו ידועות בשקול הדעת לפני תת התורה ביד משה והן רבות״).

45 **[ישחק]** — מאחר שדברי ההסבר ״שישימם ללעג ולשחוק״ אינם מתייחסים למלת ״יושב״, ומאחר שהצירוף ״יושב בשמים״ מוסבר בדיבור הבא, מסתבר שנשמט כאן הדיבור־המתחיל. על כל פנים ברי שמלת ״יושב״ אינה משמשת כאן כדיבור־מתחיל, אלא כציון ראשיתו של פסוק 4, וזאת בהתאם לנוהגו של הראב״ע לציין את התחלתו של פסוק חדש בֿאמצעות המלה הפותחת אותו (בשריד צויינו כך גם כל יתר הפסוקים). את מלת ״ישחק״ מבאר הראב״ע בדיוק כך גם בפירוש הנדפס, אך שם הוא מביא זאת בשם הגאון. ואכן רס״ג מתרגם כך בתפסיר, ומצרף לכך הסבר זה בַּפירוש: ״הסיבותי ׳ישחק׳ אשר ביושב בשמים אל הנבראים, ואמרתי ׳ישחיק בהם׳, כפי שמצאתי כל הפעולות אשר השכל שוללם ממנו יתעלה מוסבים אל ברואיו״. ואילו הראב״ע (בנדפס על אתר) מצא לנחוץ להסביר את עצם הכורח שבהתבטאות האנתרופומורפית — האדם אינו יכול להתבטא אלא בלשון בני אדם, ואין הוא מסוגל להבין לשון זולתה. מחוסר יכולתו לחרוג מעולם המושגים והחוויות שלו, הוא נאלץ להחיל אותם הן על ההוויה העל־אנושית שבשמים והן על ההוויה התת־אנושית שבטבע. ודין זה חל גם על כל דבר נבואה שנועד לאוזניים אנושיות.

47 **יש אומר** — אין ספק שהפירוש לפסוק 5 נפסק באמצע הדיבור, שכן הביאור המפתיע של ״ידבר״ במובן של ׳יאבד׳ טעון ביסוס, ולפתיחה ״יש אומר״ מתלווה בדרך כלל הסתייגות של הראב״ע. הביסוס וההסתייגות מצויים בפירוש הנדפס, וניתן לשער שגם ב׳שיטה הראשונה׳ הביא הראב״ע את הראיה מן הטקסטים המקבילים: ״ותאבד את כל זרע המלוכה״ (מל״ב, י״א, 1) || ״ותדבר את כל זרע המלוכה״ (דה״ב, כ״ב, 10), ושגם כאן הוא הסתייג מביאור ״אֵלֵימוֹ״ במשמע של ״אילי הארץ״ (יח׳, י״ז, 13), משום שההעדר של יו״ד ראשונה ב״אלימו״ מוכיח שאין זו אלא צורה פיוטית של מלת היחס ׳אליהם׳. על עצם האפשרות לייחס לשורש דב״ר משמע של הכחדה אין הוא אומר דבר בפירוש הנדפס, שכן ברי שבצירוף למלת היחס ״אלימו״ הכוונה בעליל לדיבור כמשמעו.

though, does he support this from Lev. 27:19, and even offer two alternate ways to interpret "standing" in judgment: as referring to time or to place. According to the first interpretation, the wicked will not be able to survive the day of judgment, that is, will not be acquitted; according to the second interpretation, they will not be able to stand in the place of judgment, that is, they will fail in their judicial confrontation with the righteous.

27 If we opt for the second possibility, the end of the verse repeats the same meaning in different words, as is common in poetry and prophecy: "nor will sinners [be able to stand] in the assembly of the righteous" (with his terminology here cf. his commentary on Ps. 73:2: "The meaning is doubled, as is the custom of eloquence").

28 Since God's knowledge is all-encompassing, one cannot interpret the verse to mean that He knows only the way of the righteous. According to Ibn Ezra's first explanation, the verse is a concise allusion that it is the way of the righteous to know God, and this, in contrast to the way of the wicked, guarantees their survival, since only knowlege of God can grant eternal life to the soul of the righteous man. According to the second explanation, the verse does refer to God's knowledge of the righteous, but this is not meant literally (as a matter of information) but rather metaphorically—God is compared to a mortal sovereign who recognizes only those who recognize him, and rewards them accordingly.

32 At this point MS Verona breaks off and MS Leipzig begins.

36 In the standard commentary on Ps. 55:15 he glosses *regeš* as meaning "in one group."

37 Although Ibn Ezra acknowledges that the parallelism of *ragᵉsu-yehgu* is a strong proof of the alternate interpretation, he does not consider it to be decisive, because the parallel can be complementary rather than synonymous.

37 These nations require different identification in accordance with the era to which the psalm refers.

39 In his commentary on Isa. 40:23, too, Ibn Ezra glosses *rozᵉnim* by reference to the parallelism *meleḵ-razon* in Prov. 14:28, while adding a laconic reference to the distinction between *rozen* and *razon*: "because adjectives vary." This means that because the vocalization patterns of nouns and adjectives are not fixed and limited in number, as are the verbal inflections, we should not wonder at such variations (see Bacher, *Ibn Ezra*, pp. 66–67).

40 In his *Tafsir* Saadiah translated *nosᵉdu* as "gathered together"; in his commentary on Psalm 2, incorporated into his long introduction to Psalms, he derives this sense of the word from the noun *sod*, "group" (referring to Ps. 31:14, Gen. 49:6, and Ps. 64:3). Nevertheless it is doubtful whether Ibn Ezra is referring to Saadiah, given the latter's failure to consider the morphological problem, which stems from the fact that "the grammar of the Holy Tongue was unknown until the rise of R. Judah son of R. David, the first of the grammarians" (*Defense*, section 74). This also applies, of course, to Yefet ben ʿAli, who offered a double translation in his *Tafsir*—"gathered together or came in a single group"—and explained how the two meanings derive from the root *swd*, before proceeding to mention the possibility of deriving it from the root *ysd*: "This would mean that they hold to their words and do not change them—and this interpretation too is possible." But Ibn Ezra must have Ibn Ganach in mind, who glosses *nosᵉdu* (*Shorashim*, s.v. *swd*) as derived from the root *swd* on the assumption of a metathesis of the letters *yod* and *waw*. Ibn Ganach also acknowledges that *nosᵉdu* can be derived from *ysd*, and refers the reader to that entry, where he mentions that that derivation was supported by Ibn Ḥayyuj. (In Ibn Ḥayyuj's *Book of Silent Letters*, translated from Arabic into Hebrew by Ibn Ezra, he writes that in the *nifʿal* the root *ysd* can have a different meaning—i.e., the sense of gathering together—from its normal one, and offers this verse as an example. See *Sifrei Diḳduḳ*, ed. J. L. Ducas [Frankfurt a.M., 1844], p. 48.) We do not know what Ibn Giqatilah's opinion was on the matter; Ibn Ezra himself drew back from his definitive assertion, as can be

inferred from the standard commentary on this verse and on Ps. 35:1, as well as from *Safah B^e^rurah*, p. 28a.

44 This is presented with greater clarity in the standard commentary: "Because he mentioned 'kings of the earth take their stand' (verse 1) he contrasts to them 'He who is enthroned in heaven,' which is above men." Structural notes of this sort relating the antithetical links between elements of the psalm occur frequently in Ibn Ezra's commentaries (see, for example, the standard commentary on 2:9–11).

47 The commentary on verse 5 has certainly been cut off in the middle, since the surprising gloss of *y^e^dabber* in the sense of "destroy" requires justification, and the phrase "some say" generally introduces an opinion to which Ibn Ezra demurs. The missing justification and demurral are to be found in the standard commentary, as follows: "she . . . killed off [*wa-te^c^ abbed*] all who were of royal stock" (2 Kings 11:1) is parallel to "she . . . destroyed [*wa-t^e^dabber*] all who were of the royal stock" (2 Chron. 22:10). He rejects explaining *ʾelemo* in the sense of "the nobles of the land" [*ʾeilei ha-ʾareṣ*] (Ezek. 17:13) because the absence of the first *yod* proves that the word is merely a poetical form of *ʾaleihem*, "to them." He says nothing in the standard commentary about understanding the root *dbr* in our verse in the sense of destroy, since in association with "to them" the word clearly refers to speech. Ibn Ganach (*Shorashim*, s.v. *dbr*), offers this sense based on "He subjects [*yadber*] people to us (Ps. 47:4), on the parallelism *wa-t^e^ ʾabbed* || *wa-t^e^dabber* mentioned above, on the noun *de<u>b</u>er*, "plague," and on a similar sense of the same root in Arabic. Ibn Baroun (*Kitab al-Muwarnah*, ed. Kokovtsov [St. Petersburg, 1916], p. 168, s.v. *dbr*) adopted Ibn Ganach's method *in toto*, but Ibn Ezra sought to reduce it to the bare minimum, as we see from his long commentary on Ex. 9:3: "The word *de<u>b</u>er* has a general sense ['plague' rather than some specific illness]; as a verb it occurs only on<u>c</u>e . . . [here he compares the passages in 2 Kings and 2 Chronicles]. Although the interpretation is rather improbable I don't know a better one." Accordingly he does not apply this sense of the root to Ps. 47:4 (instead, he glosses it as "He will lead them like a flock within its pasture [*do<u>b</u>^e^ro*]"), while from the context he rejects applying it not only to the verse under discussion here but also to Numbers 20:8 ("speak to the rock").

Ibn Ezra's Introduction to the Standard Commentary: The "Second Recension"

I shall magnify the Lord, for all magnitudes are as
 nought compared to one of His magnificent deeds;
His breath turns all the spheres and impels all His hosts in
 their courses;
All the angelic bands perform His will—His wondrous acts
 both hidden and revealed.
I will perpetually set forth His glory in precious words that
 cannot be weighed against pure gold.
It is my heart's delight to entreat my Creator and my entire
 desire to devise prayers to Him.
In His name let me write on the Book of Psalms, for He is my
 help both to commence as well as to conclude.

[7] Thus says Abraham, the son of Meir Ibn Ezra the Spaniard: This Book of Psalms
contains some psalms in which the name of the poet or author is found in the heading, and many others where the name of the poet is not mentioned, such as
[10] Psalm 1, and also Psalm 2, and "O you who dwell in the shelter of the Most High"
(91) and the one after it. There is a major controversy among the commentators:
some say that the entire book is by David, who was a prophet. Their evidence: "by
the ordinance of David the man of God" (Neh. 12:24), which is [a description] not
[13] found in our Scriptures except of a prophet. Also, because [David] said in his "last
words," "The spirit of the Lord has spoken through me" (2 Sam. 23:2)—which is
like "who spoke with me" (Zech. 1:9), and "His message is on my tongue" (2
Sam. 23:2). We also find the name of J^{e}duṯun linked with that of David in one
[15] psalm (62). This is because the psalm is by David, who gave it to J^{e}duṯun to perform, because he was one of the chief musicians. Similarly, "Of Solomon. O God,
endow the king with Your judgments" (72) is David's prophecy about his son Solomon; and "A prayer of Moses, the man of God" (90) is by David, who gave the
[18] psalm to Moses' descendants, Sheḇuel and his sons (1 Chron. 23:15–17) [to play].
Similarly every *l^{e}-ʾAsaf* psalm; and [the] *liḇnei Ḳoraḥ* [psalms were given] to one of
the sons of Heman the grandson of Samuel, who was a descendant of Koraḥ, as we
[21] find in Chronicles (1 Chron. 6:18); while "by the rivers of Babylon" (137) and "O
God, heathens have entered Your domain" (79) are David's prophecies about future
events, in the manner of "a son shall be born to the House of David, Josiah by
name" (1 Kings 13:2).

[23] Others say that this book contains no prophecies about future events, which is why
the Sages transcribed it with Job and the Scrolls, and this is attested by [the terms]
"psalm," "song," and "prayer." They say that "by the rivers of Babylon" (137)

הקדמת הפירוש הנדפס — 'השיטה השניה'

אֲגַדֵּל אֵל אֲשֶׁר כָּל הַגְּדוֹלוֹת   לְמוּל אַחַת גְּדוֹלוֹתָיו נְקַלּוֹת
בְּרוּחַ פִּיו יְסוֹבֵב הָעֲגָלוֹת   וְיָרִיץ כָּל צְבָאָיו עַל מְסִלּוֹת
רְצוֹנוֹ תַּעֲשֶׂנָּה כָּל הֲמוּלוֹת   עֲלִילוֹתָיו פְּלִיאוֹת גַּם מְגוּלוֹת
הֲדָרוֹ אֶעֱרוֹךְ תָּמִיד בְּמִלּוֹת   יְקָרוֹת כִּי בְּכֶתֶם לֹא מְסוּלוֹת
מְשׂוֹשׂ לִבִּי פְּנֵי צוּרִי לְחַלּוֹת   וְכָל חֶפְצִי לְכוֹנֵן לוֹ תְּפִלּוֹת
וּבִשְׁמוֹ אֶכְתְּבָה סֵפֶר תְּהִלּוֹת*   וְהוּא עֶזְרִי לְהָחֵל גַּם לְכַלּוֹת

נאם אברהם בר (נ"א: בר') מאיר אבן עזרא הספרדי: זה ספר תהלות יש בו מזמורים ושם המשורר או המחבר כתוב בראש המזמור, ויש מהם רבים בלא זכר שם המשורר — כמזמור הראשון, גם השני, ומזמור "יושב בסתר עליון" (צ"א) ואשר אחריו. ומחלוקת גדולה יש בינות המפרשים: יש אומרים כי כל הספר לדוד, והיה נביא. והעד — "כמצות דוד איש האלהים" (נחמ', י"ב, 24), וככה לא נמצא בספרינו, כי אם על נביא! ועוד שאמר בדבריו האחרוני' "רוח יי דבר בי" (שמ"ב, כ"ג, 2) — כמו: "הדובר בי" (זכ', א', 9) — ועוד: "ומלתו על לשוני" (שמ"ב, כ"ג, 2). ומצאנו שם ידותון מחובר עם דוד במזמו' (ס"ב). והיה כן כי המזמור לדוד, ונתנו לידותון לנגן, כי הוא אחד מהמנצחים. וככה "לשלמה אלהים משפטיך למלך תן" (ע"ב) — נבואת דוד על שלמה בנו; ו"תפילה למשה איש האלהים" (צ') הוא לדוד, ונתן המזמור לבני משה, לשבואל ובניו; וככה כל מזמור "לאסף"; ו"לבני קרח" — לאחד מבני הימן נכד שמואל שהיה מבני קרח, ככתו' בדברי הימים (דה"א, ו', 18); ו"על נהרות בבל" (קל"ז), גם "אלהים באו גוים בנחלתך" (ע"ט) — נבואת דוד שהתנבא לעתיד, על דרך: "הנה בן נולד לבית דוד יאשיהו שמו" (מל"א, י"ג, 2). ויש אחרים אומרים, כי אין בספר הזה נבואה לעתיד, ובעבור זה כתבוהו הקדמונים עם איוב ומגילות, והעד — "מזמור" ו"שיר" ו"תפלה". ואמרו כי "על נהרות

הערה על דרך ההדרה: מאחר שעומדת להופיע מהדורה מדעית של הפירוש הנדפס מעשה־ידי מ' סילבר, לא יובא בזה מנגנון של חילופי גירסאות להקדמה זו. היא ניתנת כאן (לצורך הציטוט והאיזכור בגוף הספר) על־פי הדפוס הראשון — ונציה רפ"ה/1525 — אשר נוסחו מצטיין במהימנותו, בתוספת של סימני פיסוק ומראי־מקומות. שני חילופי גירסאות הובאו בסוגריים בתוך הטקסט (שורות 7 ו־50) ושניים ניתנים בזה. בשורה 6: **תהלות*** — בכ"י אחד ובדפוס הראשון: "תפלות", ואילו באחד־עשר כ"י: "תהלות" וכצ"ל. בשורה 11: **כמצות** — לשון הכתוב היא "במצות", וכך הנוסח בשני כ"י.

[25] was written by one of the poets in Babylon. Similarly, they say that all the *lib̲nei*
Ḳoraḥ psalms (42; 44—49; 84—85; 87—88) are by one of the descendants of Heman who lived in Babylon, and their words are referring to the exile, and this cannot be found in David's psalms. They say that Asaph, too, is the name of a poet
[29] who lived in Babylon, and is not [the same as] Asaph the chief musician who lived
in the time of David. And thus too Ethan the Ezraḥite wrote Psalm [89] at the fall
of the House of David in the time of Zedekiah. As for those psalms that have no
explicit attribution, the editors of this Book of Psalms did not know the name of the
[31] author. Thus "the Koraḥides" [means] one of [Koraḥ's] descendants whom they did
not know by name. As for "Happy are those whose way is blameless" (119), this
[psalm] was written by some young man [of Israel] who was honored by the Babylonian kings, as witness: "How can a young man keep his way pure" (verse 9), "I
am belittled and despised" (verse 141); "though princes meet and speak against
me" (verse 23).

[35] But I tend to agree with the Sages, their memory for a blessing, that this entire
book is divinely inspired. Why are some [exegetes] surprised by the word "song,"
when the song of Moses (Deut. 32:1) proves [that this term can refer to prophecy],
[37] and also "a prayer of Habakkuk" (Hab. 3). He also prophesied [a prayer] on behalf
of the righteous: "How long, O Lord, shall I cry out" (Hab. 1:2), and [the same] in
Isaiah, "Why, Lord, do You make us stray from Your ways" (Isa. 63:17). Every
psalm that says in its heading *l^{e}-Dawid* is by David, or by one of the poets proph-
[40] esying about David, like "Of Solomon. O God, endow the king with your judgments" (72), which is also by one of the poets [and] about Solomon. "A prayer of
Moses" (90) is by Moses. "A psalm of Asaph," too, is by the Asaph who lived in
the time of David, about whom it is written, "who prophesied by order of the
[43] king" (1 Chron. 25:2). The *lib̲nei Ḳoraḥ* psalms are by the sons of Heman
the singer, who all lived in the time of David; for Heman is called "the seer of the
king" (verse 5). "Of Solomon" (127) is by someone who prophesied about
[46] Solomon, or about the Messiah his descendant, who is called [by] his name [like]
"with My servant David their prince for all time" (Ez. 37:25), which is like "have
no fear, My servant Jacob" (Jer. 30:10 and 46:27). Those psalms that have no one's
name in the heading may not be by David, or again they may be, like "Praise the
[49] Lord, call on His name," (105) which has no ascription to David but is by him,
since it is said explicitly in Chronicles (1 Chron. 16:7) that David wrote it about the
Ark, and gave it to Asaph the singer. Why do some commentators wonder that the
book does not begin [with the heading] "the prophecy of David"? For there is no
[52] doubt among the Jews that our master Moses wrote Genesis, for we have received
this tradition from our holy ancestors, their memory for a blessing, even though it
does not begin "the Lord spoke to Moses."

בבל״ (קל״ז) חברו אחד מן המשוררי׳ בבבל. וככה אמרו כי כל מזמור ״לבני קרח״ (מ״ב; מ״ד–מ״ט; פ״ד–פ״ה; פ״ז–פ״ח) הוא לאחד מן המשוררי׳ מבני בני הימן שהיו בבבל, ודבריה׳ יורו על הגלות ולא ימצא ככה בדברי דוד. ואמרו כי גם אסף — שם משורר היה בבבל, ואיננו אסף המנצח שהיה בימי דוד. וככה איתן האזרחי חבר מזמור (פ״ט) בהכרת מלכות בית דוד בימי צדקיהו. והמזמורי׳, שאין כתוב עליהם שם, לא ידעו המחברי׳ זה ספר תהילו׳ שם המחבר. וככה ״לבני קרח״ — לאחד מזרעו, ולא ידעו שמו. ו״אשרי תמימי דרך״ (קי״ט) — דברי נער מנערי ישראל, היה לו כבוד ממלכי בבל, והעד: ״במה יזכה נער״ (שם, 9); ״צעיר אנכי ונבזה״ (שם, 141); ״גם (כי) ישבו שרים בי נדברו״ (שם, 23).

ודעתי נוטה עם דברי הקדמונים ז״ל, כי זה הספר כולו נאמר ברוח הקודש. ולמה תמהו ממלת ״שיר״, והנה ״שירת האזינו״ (דב׳, ל״ב, 1) תוכיח, גם ״תפילה לחבקוק״ (חב׳, ג׳). גם התנבא על לשון הצדיקי׳ — ״עד אנה יי שועתי״ (חב׳, א׳, 2), ובספר ישעיה — ״למה תתענו יי מדרכיך״ (יש׳, ס״ג, 17). וכל מזמור כתוב בראשו ״לדוד״ הוא לדוד, או לאחד מן המשוררים המתנבאים על דוד, על דרך ״לשלמה אלהים משפטיך למלך תן״ (ע״ב), שגם הוא לאחד מהמשוררי׳ על שלמה. ו״תפילה למשה״ (צ׳) הוא למשה. ו״מזמור לאסף״ גם הוא לאסף שהיה בימי דוד, וכתוב עליו: ״הַנִּבָּא על ידי המלך״ (דה״א, כ״ה, 2). ו״לבני קרח״ — לבני הימן המשורר, וכולם היו בימי דוד, וכתו׳ על הימן ״חוזה המלך״ (שם, 5). ו״לשלמה״ (קכ״ז) — לאחד המתנבאי׳ על שלמה, או על המשיח בנו, כאשר נקרא שמו ״ודוד עבדי נשיא להם לעולם״ (יח׳, ל״ז, 25), על דרך: ״ואתה אל תירא עבדי יעקב״ (יר׳, ל׳, 10; מ״ו, 27). והמזמורים, שאין כתו׳ בראשם שם אדם, יתכן שאינן לדוד, [ו]אולי הם לדוד, כמזמור ״הודו ליי קראו בשמו״ (ק״ה), שאין שם שם ׳דוד׳, והוא לדוד. וזה מפורש בדברי הימים (דה״א, ט״ז, 7), כי דוד חיברו על הארון, ונתנו לאסף המשורר (בכה״י: לשורר). ולמה תמהו מפרשים, בעבור שאין בתחילת הספר ׳נבואת דוד׳, כי אין ספק בין הישראלים, כי ספר בראשית משה אדונינו כתבו, כי ככה קבלו אבותינו הקדושים ז״ל, אע״פ שאין כתו׳ בתחילה ׳וידבר השם אל משה׳.

Index of Citations

Exodus *(continued)*

7:7	48n.36, 192, 147	20:2	281n.122
7:11	109n.76	20:3	109n.76
7:29	261n.23	20:8	147
8:22	109n.77	21:1–2	218
9:3	329	21:8	292n.192
9:32	292n.188	22:15	147
11:5	267n.51	23:2	265n.42
12:1	48n.36, 192, 268n.55, 277n.105	23:20	267n.50, 267n.53, 281n.126
13:9	275n.95	24:12	286n.152
13:18	275n.96	25:3	273n.87
14:3	53n.71, 273n.84	25:4	261n.23
14:14	262n.24	25:17	261n.23
14:20	147	25:31	246
15:1	105n.52, 269n.60	25:40	226
15:2	148, 262n.24	27:7	265n.42
15:20	68	28:4	262n.24
15:22	275n.99	29:39	262n.24
15:27	273n.87	30:31–33	52n.64
16:15	217	30:32	226
17:7	287n.158	30:37–38	52n.64
18:1	217	31:18	48n.36, 211
19:1	217	32:4	260n.17
19:8	261n.23	32:9	267n.51
19:12	292n.192	32:11f	70
19:17	267n.50	32:11	217, 235
20	229	33:4	147
20:1	48n.36, 142n.40, 267n.50, 267n.51, 285n.141	33:11	14
		33:13	210
		33:18	291n.185
		34:11	147, 273n.87
		36:5	147
		38:8	68
		38:26	292n.192

Leviticus

1:1	47n.36	11:13	56n.94
9:24	48n.37	11:24	69, 100n.19
10:8	48n.36	16:29	275n.95
11:1–2	71	16:31	8
11:1	13	18:4–5	281n.124

19:10 269n.60
19:26 202, 204, 205
23:3 57n.96
23:40 205
24:6 226
25:1 217
25:4 225, 318
25:45 159
27:8 226
27:19 324, 328

Numbers
1:1 217, 316
1:19 268n.56
3:10 48n.41
3:23 164
3:29 164
3:35 164
4:18–19 48n.41
4:47 170
4:49 16
5:7 159
5:20 280n.115
6:24 228
8:25–26 170
8:26 217
9:1 217, 316
10:9 34
10:10 106n.64
11:6–7 108n.75
11:25 103n.40
12:1–8 14
12:1 147
12:7 80
12:8 138n.12
12:13 70
13:24 109n.75
14:13ff 70
16:15 95
16:22 70
17:28 7
18:3 48n.41
20:8 138n.3, 329
20:12 80
21:14 272n.76
22:5–6 92
22:7 92
22:9 128
22:13 218, 262n.24
22:16–17 92
22:17 115
23:7 279n.112
24:17 115
31:21 69
31:23 159
33:1 13

Deuteronomy
1:2 153, 280n.118
1:3 81
1:41 147
3:24 212
4:1 281n.122
4:2 215
4:5 281n.122
4:7 281n.122
4:39 210
5:5 267n.51
5:16 285n.141
5:26 226
5:28 287n.152
5:30 285n.141
6:7 322
8:13 262n.24
8:15 228
9:26f 70
10:1–3 159
10:21 46n.27
16:18 218
18:18 81–82
21:7–8 108n.75
22:1–42 29

21:17 135
23:2 80, 187, 188, 316, 330
23:23 118
24:9 47n.33

1 Kings
3:5 277n.104
5:12 171, 192, 270n.62, 272n.76
6 202
7:19 18
7:22 18
7:26 18
8:1 133
8:37–40 199
8:37 233, 320
8:38 10
8:41–43 199
9:2 277n.104
13:2 278n.110, 330
14:19 272n.76
20:18 228, 229, 318

2 Kings
3:15 19, 66, 310
11:1 329
11:12 239
14:5–6 202

Isaiah
2:14 148
5:1 172
5:11–12 169
5:12 100, 268n.57
8:18 278n.110
11 114
11:3 161
11:6 114
11:10–15a 117
11:14 118
12:2 148
13:4 324
14:6 291n.183
19:4 260n.17
22:24 269n.58
23:16 102n.32
25:1 8
26:4 148
27:2 291n.185
28:29 260n.17
30:10 95
33:1–6 29, 189
33:2 189, 316
33:6 291n.183
36:1 267n.51
38:10 260n.17
38:20 23, 163
40:12 208, 226
40:23 328
40:28 260n.17
40:28 260n.17
41:2 277n.103
42:11 173
43:21 10
45:1 277n.103
49:1 271n.71
50:4 40
51:4b–6 117
52:13f 107n.66
53:4–5 114–115
54:5 260n.17
55:1 210
56:6 287n.158
57:19 277n.107
58:1 143n.54
60:14 97

Index